Web Technologies

Uttam K. Roy
Department of Information Technology
Jadavpur University
Kolkata

OXFORD
UNIVERSITY PRESS

Oxford University Press is a department of the University of Oxford. It furthers the University's objective of excellence in research, scholarship, and education by publishing worldwide. Oxford is a registered trademark of Oxford University Press in the UK and in certain other countries

Published in India by
Oxford University Press
22 Workspace, 2nd Floor, 1/22 Asaf Ali Road, New Delhi 110 002

First Edition published in 2010
17th impression 2022

ISBN-13: 978-0-19-806622-4
ISBN-10: 0-19-806622-8

Typeset in Times New Roman
By Shubham Composers, New Delhi
Printed in India by Rakmo Press, New Delhi 110 020

For product information and current price, please visit www.india.oup.com

Preface

The World Wide Web (commonly known as 'WWW', or 'Web', or 'W3') was first commercially introduced in 1993. Within less than two decades, it has become the most widely used and the fastest growing medium for communication on the globe. One of the primary reasons for this growth is the drastic increase in the number of professionals and proportionate increase in the number and types of users. The Internet has become such an integral part of our lives, with such powerful capabilities, that it is easy to forget that this technological marvel was created by the long, hard, dedicated efforts of human beings.

With the growth of the Internet, new services are being added everyday and new technologies being introduced. Moreover, specifications of these technologies are changing continuously. Every user in this community is trying to develop their own web applications. Developing web applications is not an issue nowadays, but developing them using suitable technologies effectively and efficiently by applying them at the right time and right place is a challenge. In addition, web applications are no longer developed but engineered. Therefore, it is not surprising that a need has arisen to review the technologies of the Internet in order to address its current problems and make it viable for the future. As a consequence, a thorough understanding of these technologies is essential.

About the Book

Web technologies collectively cover various technologies used on the web such as JavaScript, JSP, XML, HTML, Servlet, etc. Each of these technologies is an important discipline in its own right and there is ample literature available on them. However, at the undergraduate level these technologies are taught as one course. Therefore, having a single comprehensive book on the subject is not only logical but also desirable for both faculty and students of this domain. Moreover, this book not only includes all the technologies defining Web 2.0 but also explains critical issues such as how to use these technologies effectively along with the logic behind using these technologies at the right place.

The book covers prime technical issues that every web developer should understand such as HTTP, HTML, CSS, X-Technologies (XML, XML-DTD, XML-Schema, XPath, XSLT, XLink, XPointer, XQuery), JavaScript including AJAX, Applet, Server-Side Programming (CGI, Servlet, JSP with database connectivity), and J2EE in an in-depth manner supported with extensive examples and references. Each chapter provides detailed working examples illustrating how these technologies function and can be used to build robust, browser-independent, efficient web designs.

Real-world examples are supported with ample number of screenshots so that students can grasp and apply them easily to web applications that they may develop in near future.

Although this book is intended as a textbook for undergraduate and postgraduate level courses on web technologies it can very well be used as a supplementary textbook for undergraduate courses on network programming, XML technologies, server-side programming, client-side programming, Internet technologies, etc. The book is also a useful resource for students and researchers to learn about commonly used technologies used on the WWW. In addition, it will provide useful background and reference information for professionals working in the area of Internet and web technologies.

Content and Structure

The book is organized into twenty-two chapters which are grouped into four parts:

- Part I—Web Fundamentals
- Part II—XML Technologies
- Part III—Client-side Programming
- Part IV—Server-side Programming

In Part I (Chapters 1 to 5), some fundamental web-related concepts are discussed such as HTTP, HTML, CSS, etc. Part II (Chapters 6 to 12) includes XML-related concepts such as XML-DTD, XML-Schema, XPath, XSLT, XQuery, XLink, and XPointer. Part III (Chapters 13 to 18) covers technologies used at the client side of WWW such as JavaScript including regular expression, HTML DOM, Forms and Frames, AJAX, and Java Applets. The technologies that are used at the server-side of WWW, such as CGI, Java Servlet, JSP, and J2EE are covered in Part IV (Chapters 19 to 22).

Chapter 1 primarily focuses on key concepts of the WWW. A brief history and evolution of the web along with major issues in developing web applications are discussed. The concepts of web browsers and web servers are explained in detail. The chapter also discusses the layering architecture of TCP/IP which is the foundation of the Internet specifying major functionality of each of these layers. It also provides an overview of the two key concepts: IP addressing and MIME.

Chapter 2 covers HTTP which is a primary protocol of the WWW. It highlights the functions of web servers and web clients. The anatomy of HTTP URL is described. An overview of the communication structure using HTTP is given. It describes the structure and purpose of HTTP request and response messages. The concept and importance of web caching and HTTP proxies are also discussed.

Chapter 3 discusses three fundamental networking concepts in Java: Socket, Mail, and RMI. It deals with two types of sockets with their relative merits and demerits. It shows how to send e-mails using basic SMTP and Java socket technology as well as Java mail API. It also shows how to retrieve mails using POP3 and socket. The Java RMI, which is an object-oriented RPC mechanism, is also discussed with a generic example.

Chapter 4 starts with a brief history of HTML and its available flavors. The structure of an HTML document is described. It describes basic HTML tags together with their attributes specifying their functions. It also covers various advanced tags to create tables, frames, inline frames, forms and form elements, and gives an idea about how to plan and design good websites.

Chapter 5 describes different ways of adding style information to HTML documents with their relative advantages and disadvantages. The syntax of CSS files containing style rules is discussed. Most of the selectors and pseudo classes and elements are presented with extensive examples.

Chapter 6 starts with an overview of the importance and role of XML documents in the area of document representation. The chapter then explains the notion of well-formed and valid XML documents. It also discusses the concept of namespace which provides a straightforward and an elegant way to avoid name clashes.

Chapter 7 covers document type definition (DTD) which is one of the most powerful XML languages used to describe the structure of an XML document. The different ways in which a DTD can be used in an XML file are discussed. The chapter then describes how to write constraints in a DTD file for conforming XML documents. It also provides some sample programs written in various languages that can be used to validate XML documents against DTDs.

Chapter 8 outlines another powerful XML Schema language called W3C XML schema (WXS). The limitations of DTD are identified. It discusses different components of an XML schema. It then describes how to write constraints in a schema file for conforming XML documents. The chapter also explains different unique features of schema such as referencing, grouping, derivation, restriction, substitution group, uniqueness constraint, and referential integrity.

Chapter 9 covers the document object model (DOM). The structure of DOM tree corresponding to an XML document is highlighted. It discusses interfaces provided by the Java language to work with DOM. The chapter also provides a thorough description of validating XML documents against a DTD or schema.

Chapter 10 introduces XPath which is a popular query language for XML documents. It describes the representation of XML document in XPath. The notions of important concepts such as location step and location path are discussed with extensive examples. It also outlines the set of operators and functions available in XPath.

Chapter 11 deals with XSLT which is a transformation language for XML documents. The structure of XSLT documents is described. Then it outlines commonly used XSLT elements and their functions. It also explains some key concepts such as recursive template, functions, variables, and dynamic XSLT documents.

Chapter 12 highlights four XML technologies XLink, XPointer, XQuery, and XSL-FO giving emphasis to XQuery. Basic syntax and semantics of XQuery language are discussed. It shows how to write basic queries using XQuery to retrieve information from XML documents. It also shows how to display XML documents using CSS and XSL-FO.

Chapter 13 outlines the well-known scripting language for the web, JavaScript. It explains execution philosophy of a JavaScript program from within a web page. It highlights basically those features that are usually not present in other languages. The various unique features of JavaScript such as dynamic arrays, nested functions, anonymous functions, and associative arrays are discussed.

Chapter 14 focuses on the interaction of JavaScript with HTML documents. It discusses how to navigate and manipulate HTML DOM through JavaScript programming language. It also gives an overview of the JavaScript event handling mechanism as well as the W3C event propagation model.

Chapter 15 discusses some advanced features of JavaScript and HTML. These features include conditional compilation, tabular data control (TDC), dynamic script loading, dynamic table and form generation, form validation, etc.

Chapter 16 discusses regular expression which is JavaScript's most powerful feature used for pattern matching and searching. The chapter then covers how regular expressions can be used to validate data before sending them to the server.

Chapter 17 outlines the emerging technology AJAX. The primary benefits and basic steps to use this technology are discussed. Numerous practical examples are given to show the power of AJAX.

Chapter 18 introduces applet which is a Java-based client-side technology. The execution philosophy and life cycle of applets are explained. It also describes how to pass and retrieve parameters and communication with other applets. It lists a set of limitations of this technology.

Chapter 19 focuses on a general purpose server-side technology. The execution philosophy of CGI programs is mentioned. Different CGI programs written using different languages are shown. It also shows how to pass and retrieve parameters to CGI programs using environmental variables. The chapter also identifies some limitations of CGI technology.

Chapter 20 discusses another powerful Java-based server technology namely servlet. Alternative technologies to servlets with relative merits and demerits are highlighted. The strengths of servlet technology are also mentioned. The servlet architecture and life cycle of a servlet are also described. Moreover, the chapter describes some problems of servlets and their related security issues.

Chapter 21 outlines JSP which is an extension of Java servlet technology. The relation between JSP and servlet is explained. The chapter then discusses the structure, syntax, and semantics of JSP pages. Some features such as tag extension, beans are also discussed. The Java DataBase Connectivity (JDBC) is discussed in detail with numerous examples.

Chapter 22 outlines J2EE technology. It primarily focuses on JavaBeans, EJB, and Struts framework. Different types of beans together with their features are discussed with numerous examples. Their relative merits, demerits, and application areas are identified. The chapter then gives an overview of EJB technology and the struts framework.

Answers to multiple-choice questions are also given as an Appendix at the end of the book.

Acknowledgements

This whole project was a mixed experience. The task was not easy at all, as I had initially thought. During the course of developing this manuscript I realized that writing a book on a subject is far more difficult than teaching it. The task was even harder due to the large volume of the manuscript. I would like to acknowledge the following persons who have contributed in successful completion of this project.

Only three persons were aware of this project. One is none other than my beloved wife Banhishikha Roy. Whatever I mention about her contribution is insufficient. I heartily acknowledge her extreme patience. She used to always help me finding some time to develop the manuscript. This project would not have been successfully completed without her understanding and cooperation.

Another person, who knew about the book, is my best friend Gitashri Mahapatra. She finally succeeded to extract this information from me and since then she has been continuously encouraging me to write this book. I wish to express my thanks to her.

I am also thankful to Mr. Tapas K Tunga for his assistance in the preparation of this book.

I am extremely grateful to the reviewers as their feedback helped me improve the technical accuracy and presentation of the chapters.

I have taken utmost care in eliminating any technical or typographical errors in the book and would like to urge the readers to send their valuable comments, constructive criticism, and suggestions preferably through e-mail at u_roy@it.jusl.ac.in or royuttam@gmail.com. I will appreciate your feedback and hope that you enjoy reading this book.

Uttam K. Roy

Brief Contents

Detailed Contents

Part II—XML Technologies

Part III—Client-side Programming

Part IV—Server-side Programming

Part I

Web Fundamentals

- Introduction to the Web
- HyperText Transfer Protocol (HTTP)
- Java Network Programming
- HyperText Markup Language (HTML)
- Cascading Style Sheet (CCS)

INTRODUCTION TO THE WEB

Key Objectives

After completing this chapter readers will be able to—

- **get an idea about key terms in WWW**
- **identify basic steps that are followed to develop web applications**
- **appreciate the functionality of web browsers and web servers**
- **understand the layering architecture of TCP/IP**
- **get an overview about the IP address**

1.1 UNDERSTANDING THE INTERNET AND WORLD WIDE WEB

The Internet is a global system that consists of millions of public, private, academic, business, and government networks of local to global scope. It allows all the computers connected to it to exchange information with one another. To make communication possible, computers on the Internet use a common set of rules, called protocols. The standard TCP/IP (Transmission Control Protocol/Internet Protocol) suite is used by the Internet to serve millions of users worldwide.

A large number of government, corporate, profit and non-profit organizational, and educational networks are interconnected to form the Internet. The information contained within the Internet can be accessed through a number of standardized interfaces. It is believed that approximately 30 million people worldwide are somehow connected to the WWW. The primary way to query this giant database is the WWW. Although there are many other ways to retrieve information from the Internet, WWW is mainly responsible for tremendous growth of the Internet and the people who access it. The information is typically accessed as 'web pages' or HTML (HyperText Markup Language) documents. Web pages contain links (called hyperlinks), which allow us to access other web pages by simply clicking on them.

Web pages are viewed using a software called 'browser'. The first successful browser was 'Mosaic'. Commonly used browsers are Microsoft's Internet Explorer, Netscape's Navigator, Mozilla's Firefox, etc.

Many people often use the terms Internet and World Wide Web interchangeably. However, the Internet and the World Wide Web are not one and the same. In fact, the Internet is a global data communication system. The WWW, on the other hand, is a repository of information (called resources) that can be accessed via the Internet.

1.2 HISTORY OF THE WEB

The World Wide Web was started at the **E**uropean **O**rganization for **N**uclear **R**esearch (CERN), Laboratory, Switzerland, as a networked information project by an Englishman Tim Berners-Lee [Figure 1.1] in the late 1980s. In March 1989, he wrote his first proposal entitled "A large hypertext database with typed links". In this proposal, he showed how information could be transferred easily over the Internet by using hypertext. However, the proposal generated little interest. Tim's boss, Mike Sendall encouraged him to implement his system with a workstation NeXTcube, which later became the world's first web server [Figure 1.2]. Tim considered several names such as Information Mesh, The Information Mine or Mine of Information but finally settled on World Wide Web.

Figure 1.1 Tim Berners-Lee: Founder of WWW

The proposal was rewritten and published on November 12, 1990 by Robert Cailliau—one of his collaborators. Lee and Cailliau presented this proposal at the European Conference on Hypertext Technology in September 1990, but there ideas were not appreciated much.

In December 1990, Lee developed all the tools for the WWW: the **H**yper**T**ext **T**ransfer **P**rotocol (HTTP) 0.9, the HyperText Markup Language (HTML), the first web browser (which was also a web editor), the first HTTP server, the first website http://info.cern.ch, and a few web pages. The history of the WWW can also be found at this first site.

The first web page address was http://info.cern.ch/hypertext/WWW/TheProject.html, which primarily focused on the WWW project itself.

The first practical web browser 'Mosaic' was introduced in 1993 by Marc Andreessen and it was the turning point of WWW. Till then, within less than two decades, web technologies have become the most widely used and fastest growing technologies on the Globe.

In September 1994, Berners-Lee founded the **W**orld **W**ide **W**eb **C**onsortium (W3C), which is the well-known standard making body for royalty-free softwares all over the world.

Figure 1.2 NeXTcube computer used by Berners-Lee at CERN

The WWW became commercially viable during 1996–98 when a large number of dot-com companies used it for placing their services on the web.

The Internet has become such an integral part of our lives, with such powerful capabilities, that it is easy to forget that this technological marvel was created by the long, hard, dedicated efforts of human beings.

1.3 PROTOCOLS GOVERNING THE WEB

In computing, a *protocol* is a set of rules that define the syntax and semantics of the connection, communication, and data transfer between two computing endpoints. The WWW has a body of such protocols. The TCP/IP suite of protocols is actually the set of protocols which is used to govern the web and to communicate across the Internet. TCP/IP has a set of layers each of which implements a specific set of protocols. The commonly used protocols are HTTP (HyperText Transfer Protocol), SMTP (Simple Mail Transfer Protocol), and DNS (Domain Name System). We shall discuss other protocols in Section 1.17.

1.4 CREATING WEBSITES FOR INDIVIDUALS AND THE CORPORATE WORLD

A *website* is a set of related web pages that are addressed with a common domain name or IP address (see Section 1.18). A website is hosted on a machine called *web server*, which should be accessible via a network.

The web pages of a website are accessed using URLs (Uniform Resource Locator). The web pages are organized into a hierarchy. They contain hyperlinks that guide the visitors navigating the website.

Each website could be developed on behalf of an individual, a business or other organization and is usually designed for a specific purpose. Websites are organized depending on their function into two groups:

- Personal websites
- Corporate websites

Personal websites contain web pages that are created by an individual. Each personal website contains information about a person or about something the person is interested in. An individual can host his or her website under a separate domain or can place it under a larger domain.

Personal web pages may be as simple as a single page or may be large number of complex pages having huge data. Many Internet Service Providers (ISPs) provide a few megabytes of space to their subscribers for hosting their own personal web pages.

A corporate website is developed and maintained by a company or other private enterprises such as charities or non-profit organizations.

Any website can contain a hyperlink to any other website, so the distinction between individual sites, as perceived by the user, may sometimes be blurred.

1.5 WEB APPLICATIONS

Web applications (or simply webapps) are applications that are accessed via web browsers usually through networks. Web applications run on a server called web server. Each web application is identified by a Uniform Resource Locator (see Chapter 2). There are two types of web applications: *Service oriented* and *Presentation oriented.*

- Service-oriented web applications
  These applications implement web services and are typically coded using server-side technologies [Figure 1.3] such as CGI, JSP, ASP, etc.
- Presentation-oriented web applications
  These applications are usually clients of service-oriented applications. They are coded in browser supported languages such as HTML, XML, JavaScript, etc. Presentation-oriented applications generate interactive web pages.

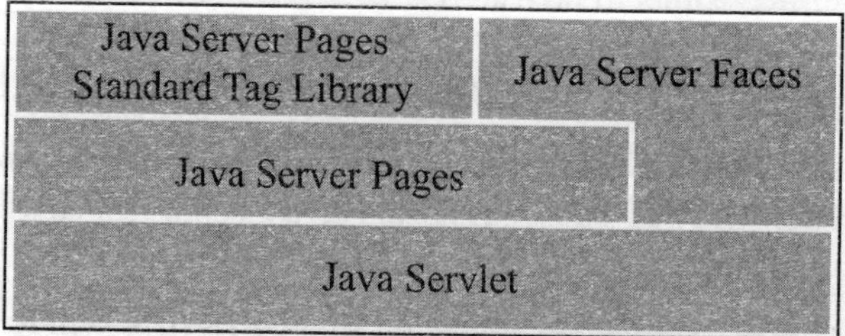

Figure 1.3 Java web applications technologies

1.6 WRITING WEB PROJECTS

To become a successful web programmer one must have some ideas about concepts related to distributed applications and services. They should know the fundamentals of HyperText Transfer Protocol, HTML, and a scripting language such as JavaScript. They should also know user authorization and authentication, session management, data exchange, etc. Throughout this book, we shall discuss each of these concepts in detail.

In addition to these technical aspects, it is also important to create a visual model of various aspects before beginning to write a code. The visual model approach helps us to eliminate problems and ensures that proper set of functionalities are incorporated in the web applications. Model-View-Controller (MVC) is one such pattern commonly used in web applications. We shall discuss how to apply the MVC model in Chapter 22.

Even before applying the MVC model, we should identify the objectives and target users of the web applications that we shall be using. Capturing requirements is one of the most important tasks to be performed while writing web projects. The following sections highlight some of these requirements.

1.7 IDENTIFICATION OF OBJECTS

The first step is to determine the objectives of your website. To identify them, it is a good idea to dissect the entire idea into more manageable tasks. Then ask a question to yourself; why are you going to develop this website? Some typical reasons are as follows:

- Improve quality of the existing website. In such cases, a set of objectives are already identified.
- Sell goods or services online
- Educate people or disseminate information
- Build customer relationship
- Provide an interface to book airline tickets
- Help travelers plan a trip
- Make available product information and price lists to distributors
- Offer customer service, technical support, or other online services
- Encourage site visitors to take action on some issues or programs

1.8 TARGET USERS

Identify the potential visitors of your website. It helps you to structure the website design to fulfill their expectations and needs. The users' knowledge, interests, and needs vary widely. Users may range from novices to experts. A well-designed website should satisfy a range of users' interests and skills. For example, your website should accommodate users that visit your site many times in a day as well as visitors who refer to this site occasionally.

1.9 WEB TEAM

A typical web application consists of a large number of components. Usually, a number of people are involved in developing an entire application. They form a group called the web team. The roles and responsibilities are divided among the team members. The title and job description vary widely but a good web team has a structure and covers a full range of distinct competencies. A good web team should make use of the following strategies:

- User Research—Identify users' needs, how they think and how they react/behave and incorporate the understanding into every aspect of the process.
- Technology Strategy—Identify the relevant technologies needed for this site—platforms, technologies, standards, and how they all can interoperate as websites are becoming more complex day by day.
- Content Strategy—Before producing the site content, you should be able to answer the following questions: Will the content meet users expectations? Is the content appropriate? What form should it take? What tone or style should it have?
- Abstract Strategy—Have a conceptual framework from information architecture and interaction design for the final user experience. These are the emerging discipline in the web development process.
- Technology Implementation—Implementing the idea requires specialized knowledge about languages, protocols, coding, debugging, testing, and maintenance.
- Concrete Design—Identify the details of interfaces, navigation, information, and visual design.
- Project Management—Integrate all the above steps as well as control and drive the entire team towards the completion of the project.

1.10 PLANNING AND PROCESS DEVELOPMENT

Websites are developed by a group of experts called a web team to fulfill requirements of other groups of people. Members are key to successful web projects. To develop a moderate site, you need various experts such as content experts, information architects, technical experts, graphic designer, writers, and finally a supervisor. Your site is said to be successful if it meets the expectations and needs of a target audience. Note that the people who will evaluate your site are not involved in the website design. So, you should plan the entire set of tasks carefully.

There are numerous steps to be followed in the website design and development process starting from information gathering to the creation of a website and finally maintaining the website. Though the exact task may vary, following are the basic tasks that you should follow:

Information Gathering

This is the first step of any web project. The following things should be taken into consideration:

- Purpose
- Goals
- Target audience
- Content

Planning

In this phase, the information gathered in phase 1 is put together to develop a site map. A site map is a list of main topics of the website and sub-topics (if any). It helps you to develop the rest of the system easily. The site map is essential to develop a consistent and easy to understand navigation system.

Design

In this phase, we determine the look and feel of the website. Target audience and type of the website are major factors to decide the look and feel. For example, a site meant for young people should have a different look and feel from a site meant for banking applications.

Development

In this phase, the website is actually created with the help of relevant technologies. Web designers may use prototypes before developing the actual content. Typically, the development starts from the home page followed by a 'skeleton' for interior pages. The skeleton serves as the template for the entire website. Once the skeleton is developed, developers can develop other pages.

Testing and Delivery

Before the website is delivered, it is tested extensively. It includes testing of complete functionality of scripts and forms and other elements. You should also deal with compatibility issues, optimization, etc.

Maintenance

Website development is a continuous process. You can provide newer and newer content, update information or use different look and feel from time to time to attract your visitors.

1.11 WEB ARCHITECTURE

The WWW is a two-tier architecture consisting of web servers, which produce and deliver information, and web clients, which retrieve and display information. Three primary concepts are involved in this process: HyperText Markup Language (HTML), Uniform Resource Locator (URL), and HyperText Transfer Protocol (HTTP).

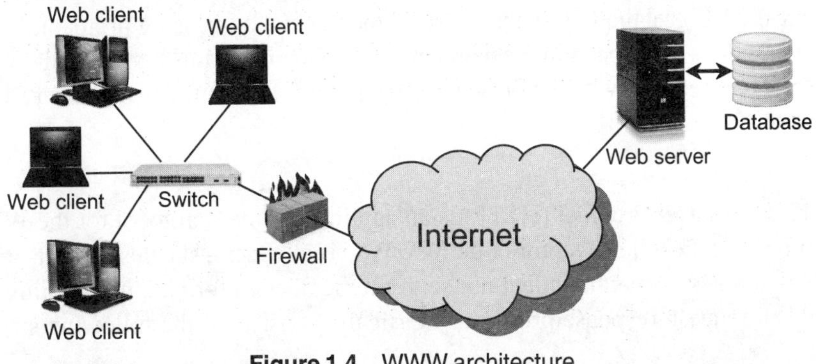

Figure 1.4 WWW architecture

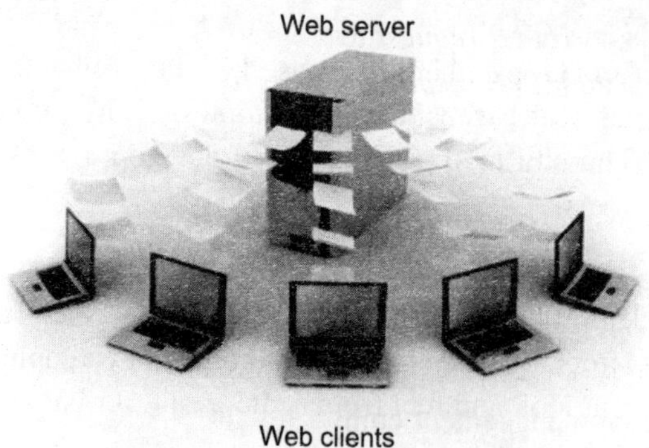

Figure 1.5 WWW: conceptual view

HTML

HTML is the primary language used to encode documents containing hyperlinks. Its first public version was released in 1991 by Tim Berners-Lee, the inventor of the WWW. After several modifications, HTML got its final shape in May 2001, known as HTML 4.01. This current version is supported by most of the web browsers.

HTML is an application of Standard Generalized Markup Language (SGML), a standard that specifies a formal meta-language for markup documents [Figures 1.4 and 1.5]. HTML documents consist of case-insensitive tags organized in hierarchical structure. Document contents are embedded in starting and ending tags. Each tag has its own functionality. The starting tag may have optional attributes that control the behavior of the tag. In addition, documents are linked by special tags called anchor tags. These anchor tags are also called hyperlinks. HTML allows us to embed virtually all kinds of data such as text, images, audio, video, etc.

HTML documents are viewed by a software called 'browser'. Note that anchor tags are used to link other HTML documents. When a user selects a hyperlink, the web browser retrieves the document and displays it on the screen. A detailed description of HTML can be found in Chapter 4.

URL

The WWW is a repository of information called resources. URLs are used to address these resources. URL is actually a special case of the general addressing protocol, Uniform Resource Identifier. URLs are a location independent addressing mechanism used on the WWW. It consists of several parts each of which represents a specific information. The format of a URL is described in Chapter 2.

HTTP

HyperText Transfer Protocol (HTTP) is an application layer protocol for the WWW. According to Tim Berners-Lee, the inventor of the WWW, it is a 'generic stateless object-oriented protocol'. HTTP is stateless as neither client nor server remembers information according to this protocol. HTTP is a request–response protocol. It basically consists of the following steps:

- HTTP client establishes a TCP connection to the HTTP server.
- Client sends an *HTTP request* to the server specifying the resource it wants to access.
- Server sends an *HTTP response* containing the desired information.

A detailed description of HTTP can be found in Chapter 2.

1.12 MAJOR ISSUES IN WEB SOLUTION DEVELOPMENT

A web application typically consists of lot of components running around such as HTML client, HTTP server, HTTP network, middle-tier components, server-side components, database components, resource-management components, etc. Performance tuning can be tricky in such internet related projects. It depends on a large number of parameters. Sometimes, a single parameter can increase the performance drastically while at other times several parameters need to be changed.

HTML Performance

- Avoid using too many images on web pages as they can slow down the page load process; use image maps whenever possible.
- Use nested tables but do not use too many levels of nesting.
- Frames are another source of bottlenecks; use tables as far as possible.
- Avoid redundant tags.
- Avoid using too many comments. It reduces the page size and consequently reduces loading time.
- Use relative path names (if possible).
- HTTP compression may be used to compress HTML documents. It is now widely supported by web servers and browsers.
- Avoid AJAX (see Chapter 17) technology as far as possible. It increases the server load. If possible use the callback mechanism (see Chapter 15) instead.

Database Issues

Many web applications use backend database servers. A good database design can increase the performance significantly. The following points should be considered while working with databases:

- Avoid dynamic queries. Use stored procedures or database views. Analyze the SQL query and optimize it before firing it to the database.
- Inspect the join type used in the SQL query. A join may increase or decrease the performance of the query.
- Replicate the database if load on the server is high.

Network bandwidth issues

In many cases, network performance may degrade overall performance. It is advisable to run the web server and the database server on different machines.

1.13 WEB SERVERS (APACHE WEB SERVER)

In this section, we shall take a look at the web server provided by Apache. Let us first discuss what a web server is and how communication between a web client and a web server takes place.

Web communication takes place between a client process (typically a browser) and a web server. The server process (web server) creates a socket (typically on port 80) and the client process accesses the server through the socket mechanism.

What happens when a user types a URL at the address bar of some browser and presses 'Enter'? The browser creates a socket connection with the server process running in a computer specified by the URL. The browser then retrieves the desired information using HTTP. For the entire mechanism to function, we need a web server first.

The web server provided by Apache is one of the most popular (since 1996) and commonly used open-source HTTP servers. It is a secure, efficient, powerful, extensible, and fully featured web server which is available for both Windows and Unix/Linux environments. It is used to host almost anything from small personal websites to complex corporate websites. The Apache web server also supports sever plug-ins to integrate other software. Though the Apache HTTP Server project was started as one project, it has continued to add newer and newer features over the last 15 years. Recently, Apache celebrated its 10th anniversary through ApacheCon US 2009 during 2–6 November, 2009 held in Oakland, CA. The latest version 2.2.14 is claimed to be a security and bugfix release.

The installation and configuration procedure for Apache web server is described in Chapter 20.

1.14 WEB BROWSERS (MICROSOFT INTERNET EXPLORER AND NETSCAPE NAVIGATOR)

A web browser is a software typically used to display HTML documents. The 'Mosaic' was the first web browser introduced in 1993 by Marc Andreessen. Today, many different browsers are available varying in functionalities. Among these browsers, Microsoft's Internet Explorer, Netscape's Navigator, and Mozilla's Firefox are the most popular. The competition between Microsoft and Netscape to dominate the web market led to continual improvement in their respective browsers.

The Internet Explorer web browser is a proprietary software from Microsoft Corporation. Microsoft distributes this software as a freeware over the Internet. It is sometimes abbreviated as MSIE or simply IE. Its current version is 8.0.

The Navigator web browser was created by Marc Andreessen and his team from Netscape Communications Corporation where Marc was a co-founder. Navigator is also a freeware and can be downloaded. Netscape Navigator was later acquired by AOL.

1.15 INTERNET STANDARDS

An internet standard is a specification of technologies and methodologies related to the Internet. Internet standards are created and published by a body called the Internet Engineering Task

Force (IETF). An Internet standard is basically a Request For Comment (RFC) or a set of RFCs. An RFC, after going through several revisions, is accepted by an RFC editor. Finally, the Internet Engineering Steering Group (IESG) approves the RFC. Each RFC is identified by a unique integer. They can be found at http://www.ietf.org/rfc.html and are extremely helpful for all Internet users. For example, specifications for HTTP/1.0 and HTTP/1.1 can be found in RFC 1945 and 2616, respectively. More information can be found at http://www.ietf.org/.

1.16 TCP/IP PROTOCOL SUITE

The TCP/IP protocol suite is a set of protocols used in the Internet and other communication networks. It creates the technical foundation of the Internet. The name was given after the two primary protocols Transmission Control Protocol (TCP) and Internet Protocol (IP), but it consists of many other protocols [Table 1.1].

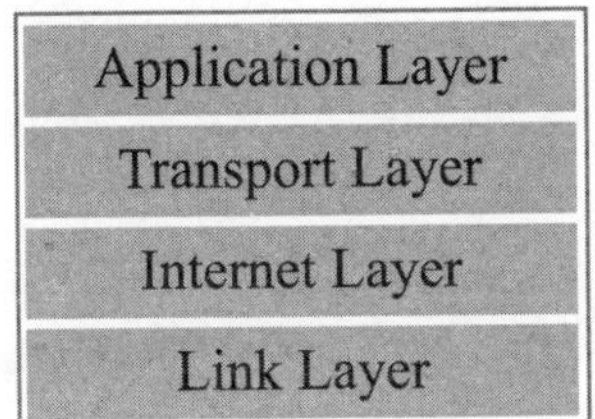

Figure 1.6 TCP/IP protocol suite

The TCP/IP protocol suite consists of several layers each of which deals with a set of issues that arise while designing a communication network. According to RFC 1122, there are four layers [Figure 1.6] in a TCP/IP protocol suite: Link Layer, Internet Layer, Transport Layer, and Application Layer. Each layer provides a well-defined set of services to its upper layer. Similarly, each layer uses services provided by its lower layer.

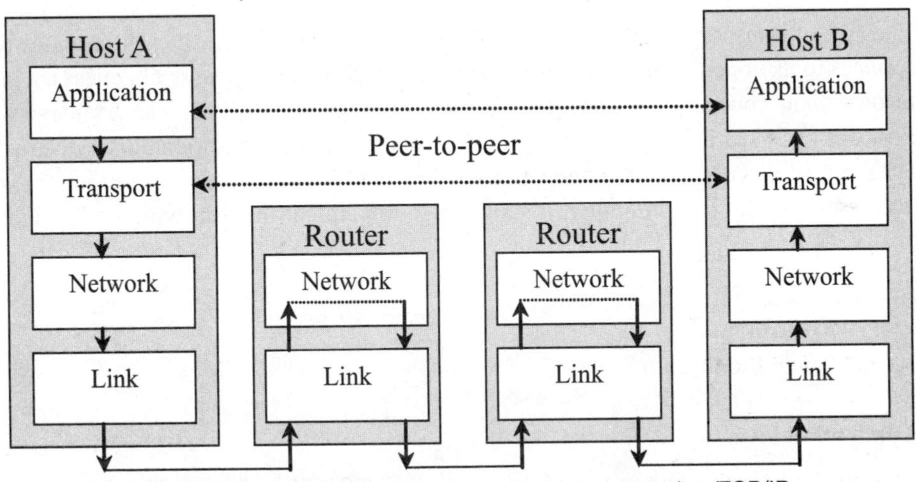

Figure 1.7 Communication between two hosts using TCP/IP

Table 1.1 TCP/IP suite of protocols

Layer	Protocols
Application	HTTP, SMTP, SSH, Telnet, SIP, Gopher, IMAP, SNMP, Rlogin, POP3, DNS, SSL, FTP
Transport	TCP, UDP
Internet	IP, ICMP, IGMP, OSPF, BGP, RIP, ARP, RARP
Link	HDLC

Following is a brief description of each layer according to the TCP/IP network model:

Link layer

This is the lowermost layer in the TCP/IP protocol suite. Link layer deals with Local Area Network (LAN). It is responsible for transferring data from one machine to another within the same local network. Following are the primary functions of the Link layer:

- Framing
- Error Detection
- Error Correction
- Flow Control
- Error Control
- Medium Access Control

Internet Layer

The link layer cannot deliver packets across different Local Area Networks (LANs). The primary task of the Internet Layer is to deliver packets from one network to another. It determines a suitable route from the source computer to the target and delivers packets through this route. This process is called *routing*. For this purpose, it introduces an addressing mechanism called IP addressing. We shall discuss the format of an IP address in Section 1.17.

Transport Layer

The task of transport layer is end-to-end message transfer [Figure 1.7]. It provides two types of services to its upper layer; *connection-oriented*—where the segments of a message are delivered in order and *connection-less*—where no such guarantee is given. The Transmission Control Protocol (TCP) in a TCP/IP protocol suite provides connection-oriented service, whereas User Datagram Protocol provides connection-less service. It also introduces port numbers to identify processes that run in a computer. It should also implement the following optional tasks:

- Segmentation
- Flow Control
- Error Control
- Congestion Control

Application layer

Application Layer is the top-most layer in the TCP/IP protocol suite. This is the layer that users actually interact with. It provides interfaces to users for network communication. For example, it provides an interface using which users can transfer files from one computer to another computer. Following is a list of some other protocols it implements [Table 1.1]:

HTTP, SMTP, Telnet, SSH, DNS, POP3, rlogin, SSL.

1.17 IP ADDRESSES

Internet Protocol in the TCP/IP protocol suite assigns a unique address called *IP Address* to each device participating in a computer network. An IP address serves basically two purposes: identifying a host/network interface and location addressing. According to Internet Protocol version 4, an IP address is a 32-bit binary number. Although the total number of possible addresses is 2^{32}(=4,294,967,296), we can use much less number of addresses in practice. Due to the tremendous growth of the Internet, a new system (IPv6) was introduced that uses 128-bit address. In this section we shall only discuss IPv4.

IP addresses are usually written using 4 decimal numbers, each representing 8 bits, in the range 0–255, separated by three dots (.). This notation is known as *dotted decimal notation.* Following is an example of an IP address:

```
203.197.107.107
```

It can be viewed in binary form as follows:

```
        203.       197.       107.       107
11001011.11000101.01101011.01101011
```

Every IP address has two parts: the network part and the host part. The network part identifies the network the host belongs to. The network part is same for all hosts belonging to the same network. The host part identifies the host within the network uniquely. The number of bits in the host part determines the number of possible hosts within the network.

IP addresses are categorized into five classes as follows [Table 1.2]:

- Class A—Address starts with 0. Possible values of first octet are 1 to 126. The values 0 and 127 are reserved for other purposes.
- Class B—Address starts with 10. Possible values of first octet are 128 to 191.
- Class C—Address starts with 110. Possible values of first octet are 192 to 223.
- Class D—Address starts with 1110. Possible values of first octet are 224 to 239.
- Class E—Address starts with 1111. Possible values of first octet are 240 to 255.

Class D and E are reserved for research purpose and are not used.

Table 1.2 Historical classful network architecture

Class	First octet in binary	Range of first octet	Network ID	Host ID	Number of class A networks	Number of possible hosts per class A network
A	0XXXXXXX	0 – 127	w	x.y.z	$2^7 - 2 = 126$	$2^{24} - 2 = 16{,}777{,}214$
B	10XXXXXX	128 – 191	w.x	y.z	$2^{14} = 16{,}384$	$2^{16} - 2 = 65{,}534$
C	110XXXXX	192 – 223	w.x.y	z	$2^{21} = 2{,}097{,}152$	$2^8 - 2 = 254$

1.17.1 Classless Inter-Domain Routing

With the rapid expansion of the Internet, classful network design limits scalability under use of available IP addresses. Consequently, a new idea called Classless Inter-Domain Routing (CIDR) was created for the allocation of IP address blocks and new rules of routing protocol using IPv4 addresses were implemented. It introduced the idea of variable-length network ID and resulted in moderate utilization of IP addresses. In CIDR, a network consisting of consecutive IP addresses is very often represented as X/Y where X is the first IP address in the series (called subnet ID) and Y is the number of bits in the network ID field. For example, 203.197.107.96/28 is a network having 28 bits in the network ID. It means host ID field has 4 (32–28) bits. So, the number of possible IP addresses in this subnet is 16 (=2^4). They are 203.197.107.96–203.197.107.111. Out of these 16 addresses, only 14 (16–2) can be assigned to hosts. The first (203.197.107.96) and the last (203.197.107.111) are used as subnet's IP address and broadcast IP address, respectively.

Note that the concept of classful IP address is not used in practice. It is only used in the technical jargon in network administrators' discussions.

1.17.2 IPv4 Private Addresses

In early network design, IP addresses assigned to particular computers or network devices were intended to be unique for global end-to-end communication. Consequently, IP addresses exhausted quickly. So, there was a tremendous demand to find a way out from this IPv4 address exhaustion. Fortunately, a novel idea was developed. It was released that IP addresses used by the computers in private networks need not be unique. Computers not connected to the Internet, such as factory machines that communicate only with each other via TCP/IP, need not have globally unique IP addresses.

Table 1.3 Private IPv4 network ranges

Network	First address	Last address	No. of addresses
10.0.0.0/8 (1 class A network)	10.0.0.0	10.255.255.255	16,777,216
172.16.0.0/12 (16 class B networks)	172.16.0.0	172.31.255.255	1,048,576
192.168.0.0/16 (256 class C networks)	192.168.0.0	192.168.255.255	65,536

Three ranges of IPv4 addresses [Table 1.3] for private networks, one range for each class (*A*, *B*, *C*), were reserved in RFC 1918. These addresses are not routed on the Internet and thus their use need not be coordinated with an IP address registry.

Today, when needed, such private networks typically connect to the Internet through Network Address Translation (NAT).

1.18 MIME

The Simple Mail Transfer Protocol (SMTP) is an important and frequently used protocol in the TCP/IP protocol suite. It is used to deliver Electronic mails (E-mail). SMTP was designed to transfer only text messages. Multipurpose Internet Mail Extension (MIME) extends the format of e-mail to support the following:

- Text in character sets other than ASCII
- Non-text attachments
- Message bodies with multiple parts
- Header information in non-ASCII character sets

Virtually all human written e-mails can be transmitted through this SMTP in MIME format. This format is specified as a part of HTTP/1.1. See RFC 2045 for details. MIME's use, however, has grown beyond describing the content of e-mail to describing content type in general. For example, it has an important role in communication protocols like HTTP for the World Wide Web. HTTP requires that data be transmitted in the context of e-mail-like messages, although the data most often are not actually text.

MIME defines mechanisms to use character encodings other than ASCII, and 8-bit binary content. Mapping messages into and out of MIME format is typically done automatically by an e-mail client or by mail servers when sending or receiving e-mail (SMTP/MIME) via the Internet.

1.19 CYBER LAWS

The WWW evolved in a completely unplanned and unregulated manner. Even the inventor of the WWW, Tim Berners-Lee, could not possibly anticipate the scopes and consequences of cyberspace.

The Internet is growing drastically with the number of users doubling roughly every 100 days. New and sensitive issues related to various legal aspects of cyberspace began cropping up. Consequently, a new and highly specialized branch of law came into existence called the Cyber law—the Law of Internet and World Wide Web.

In this law, cyber crime is unlawful act where a computer is either a tool or a target or both. Cyber crimes involve traditional criminal activities such as theft, fraud, forgery, defamation, and mischief. Cyber laws regulates these crimes.

Cyber crimes can be categorized into two types:

- Using computers as a tool
  In this type of crime, computers are used to attack other computers. It includes hacking/hijacking, virus/worm attacks, DOS attacks, denial of service attacks, Trojan attacks, etc.
- Using computers as a weapon
  In this type of crime, computers are used as a weapon. Examples include credit card frauds, email spoofing, email spamming, email bombing, Cyber terrorism, EFT frauds, pornography, IPR violations, etc.

KEYWORDS

Cyber Laws: The Law of Internet and World Wide Web to control cyber crime and unlawful activities.

HTML: HTML is the primary language used to encode documents containing hyperlinks.

HTTP: A protocol used in WWW to access resources.

IP addresses: A 32-bit address used to identify a device participating in a computer network.

MIME: Multipurpose Internet Mail Extension (MIME) extends the format of SMTP messages to allow non-ASCII, non-textual messages.

Protocol: A protocol is a set of rules that define the syntax and semantics of the connection, communication, and data transfer between two computing endpoints.

TCP/IP protocol suite: The TCP/IP protocol suite is a set of protocols used in the Internet and other communication networks.

URL: URLs are used to address resources in the WWW.

W3C: A well-known standard making body for royalty-free software all over the world.

Web browser: A web browser is a software typically used to display HTML documents.

Web server: A web server is a process typically run on port 80 that is responsible for providing resources.

Web Team: A web team is a group of people responsible for developing a website.

Website: A website is a set of related web pages that are addressed with a common domain name or IP address.

WWW: The World Wide Web (WWW), a repository of information (called resources) distributed all over the world, is defined as a world-wide network of networks.

SUMMARY

The Internet is a global system that consists of millions of public, private, academic, business, and government networks of local to global scope. The World Wide Web was started at European Organization for Nuclear Research (CERN), Laboratory, in late 1980s. The Internet has now become an integral part of our lives.

The WWW uses a set of protocols, called the TCP/IP protocol suite, which governs the web to communicate across the Internet. The WWW is actually a distributed repository of resources such as web pages that are accessed through URLs. A website is a set of related web pages. Web pages contain hyperlinks that guide the visitors navigating the website. Web pages are developed using HTML and JavaScript accompanied by other related tools such as CSS. A website is hosted on a machine called a web server.

Depending upon the function, websites are categorized as personal and corporate websites. Identifying key requirements such as objectives and target users is one of the most important tasks to be performed while writing web projects. A typical web application consists of a large number of components. Usually, a number of people are involved in developing an entire application. They form a group called a web team.

A web browser is a software typically used to display HTML documents (web pages). Common browsers are Microsoft's Internet Explorer, Netscape's Navigator, Mozilla's Firefox, Google's Chrome, Apple's Safari, Opera, etc.

The TCP/IP protocol suite consists of several layers each of which deals with a set of issues that arise while designing a communication network.

An IP address is a 32-bit binary address assigned by the Internet layer of the TCP/IP protocol suite used to identify a device taking part in the computer network. IP addresses are written in dotted decimal notation.

Multipurpose Internet Mail Extension (MIME) extends the format of e-mail to support text in character sets other than ASCII, non-text attachments, message bodies with multiple parts, and header information in non-ASCII character sets.

The Internet is growing drastically with the number of users doubling roughly every 100 days. New and sensitive issues related to various legal aspects of cyberspace began cropping up. Consequently, a new and highly specialized branch of law came into existence called the Cyber law—the Law of Internet and World Wide Web.

WEB RESOURCES

`http://www.ietf.org/rfc/rfc2616.txt`
Hypertext Transfer Protocol -- HTTP/1.1

`http://en.wikipedia.org/wiki/History_of_the_World_Wide_Web`
History of the World Wide Web

`http://en.wikipedia.org/wiki/Internet_Protocol_Suite`
Internet Protocol Suite

`http://tools.ietf.org/html/rfc1180`
A TCP/IP Tutorial

http://en.wikipedia.org/wiki/Cyberlaw
Cyberlaw

http://www.w3.org/MarkUp/
XHTML2 Working Group Home Page

http://www.w3.org/MarkUp/draft-ietf-iiir-html-01.txt
Hypertext Markup Language (HTML)

http://www.ietf.org/rfc/rfc2045.txt
Multipurpose Internet Mail Extensions (MIME)

EXERCISES

Multiple Choice Questions

1. A protocol is a
   (a) software that facilitates connection to the Internet
   (b) list of rules for transferring data over a network
   (c) gateway calling program for internet bridging
   (d) software that allows file copying

2. What is the full form of WWW?
   (a) Wide Web & Wet (b) World Wide Wait
   (c) World Wide Web (d) World Working Web

3. What is the full form of Email?
   (a) Elective Mail (b) Easy Mail
   (c) Empty Mail (d) Electronic Mail

4. What is the full form of FTP?
   (a) File Transfer Protocol
   (b) File Transfer Process
   (c) File Translation Process
   (d) File Transfer Program

5. Telnet is a
   (a) dialup program
   (b) teller network
   (c) standard Internet protocol for remote login
   (d) telephone network

6. What is the full form of LAN?
   (a) Local Area Network
   (b) Least Accessed Nodes
   (c) Link And Node
   (d) Large Area Network

7. ISP is an acronym of
   (a) Internet System Provider
   (b) Internet Service Provider
   (c) Internal System Provider
   (d) Internet Service Procedure

8. Which of the following layers of the TCP/IP reference model routes packets?
   (a) Application (b) Transport
   (c) Internet (d) Link

9. Networks of computers connected over greater distances are called
   (a) LAN (b) WAN
   (c) Subnet (d) None of the above

10. Which of the following is not a layer in the TCP/IP reference model?
    (a) Application (b) Session
    (c) Transport (d) Internet

11. How many bits are their in an IP address?
    (a) 30 (b) 31
    (c) 32 (d) 33

12. Rules contained in programs on router computers that determine the best path on which to send packets are called:
    (a) Switches (b) Routing Algorithm
    (c) Gateways (d) Proxies

13. What is the top-level domain in www.yahoo.com/sports
    (a) /sports (b) .com
    (c) www. (d) yahoo.com

14. Which of the following protocols is used to send and receive emails?
    (a) SMTP (b) POP3
    (c) HTTP (d) FTP

15. Which of the following protocols is used to transfer files over a network?

(a) HTTP (b) FTP
(c) Both (a) and (b) (d) None of the above

16. What is the full form of URL?

(a) Uniform Resource Location
(b) Universal Resource Locator
(c) Universal Resource Location
(d) Uniform Resource Locator

17. Which of the following is a transport layer protocol in the TCP/IP protocol suite?

(a) HTTP (b) UDP
(c) SMTP (d) FTP

18. Which of the following is used to retrieve mails from remote mail server?

(a) SMTP (b) POP3
(c) HTTP (d) DNS

19. Which of the following application layer protocols uses UDP as its underlying transport protocol?

(a) DNS (b) FTP
(c) SMTP (d) HTTP

20. A web server is a

(a) Software
(b) Hardware
(c) Combination of both
(d) None of the above

Review Questions

1. What does DNS stand for? What is its main purpose?
2. Suppose the IP address of a device is 172.16.4.1. Write the IP address in binary.
3. What are the various types of websites? Discuss briefly.
4. Discuss the need for Cyber laws.
5. Discuss the steps a web designer should follow to develop a website.
6. What are governing protocols in the web?
7. What is a web server? Name two web servers.
8. What is a web browser? Name two web browsers.
9. What is the difference between a web browser and a web server?
10. Discuss the task of different layers of the TCP/IP reference model of network.
11. Write the format of an IP address.
12. How many IP address classes are there? How do you identify them?
13. Write the purpose of MIME in the Internet.

2 HYPERTEXT TRANSFER PROTOCOL (HTTP)

KEY OBJECTIVES

After completing this chapter readers will be able to—

- **understand the need for HTTP**
- **get an idea about how web servers and web clients function**
- **learn the anatomy of HTTP URL**
- **understand the structure of HTTP communication**
- **learn the format of request and response messages**
- **learn about web caching and HTTP proxies**

2.1 INTRODUCTION

HTTP is an acronym for **H**yper**T**ext **T**ransfer **P**rotocol. It is an application layer protocol in the TCP/IP protocol suite. HTTP was originally developed to transfer files and data (collectively known as *resources*) in distributed, collaborative, hypermedia information systems.

The well-known World Wide Web (see Chapter 1) is basically based on HTTP. Note that the WWW is a repository of resources (web pages) stored in different computers all over the world. The primary purpose of HTTP is to transfer web pages from one computer (web server) to another computer (web client). It is useful to transfer web pages containing links (hypertexts) in an environment where there are rapid jumps among such hyperlinked web pages. HTTP can be used to access virtually all types of resources on the web. It allows us to transfer a wide variety of data such as text, image, audio, video, and even the result of a query.

HTTP was standardized by the World Wide Web Consortium (W3C) and the Internet Engineering Task Force (IETF). The first version, HTTP/1.0, was released in February, 1996. The specification of the current version HTTP/1.1 [RFC 2616] was published in June 1999 and is in constant use since then.

In this chapter, we shall discuss different aspects of HTTP and how we can transfer resources using the set of rules specified by HTTP.

2.2 WEB SERVERS AND CLIENTS

HTTP protocol is basically a request–response protocol between clients and a server. It is simple as well as powerful. To learn this protocol, you need to first understand what web servers and web clients are.

According to this protocol, a process is run which creates and stores *resources* such as HTML files, images, etc. This process provides the resources on request and is called a *web server* or *HTTP server*. A web server is designed to wait for incoming requests. Once a request for a resource comes to it, it processes the request, identifies the correct resource to be provided, and finally responds with the desired resource.

Now, the question is who will send the requests? Obviously, those who want to access some resources available on this web server. To access resources stored on the web server, a process is designed to communicate with the server. This process is called a *web client* or *user agent*. Web clients communicate with the web server using a set of rules. This set of rules is actually specified by the HTTP protocol. Web browsers are nothing but those web clients. They use HTTP protocol to communicate with the web server to access resources specified by the URL at the address bar of the web browsers.

Web servers typically run on port 80 though any available port number may be used. In the TCP/IP protocol suite, a process in a machine is assigned a locally unique positive integer called *port* number. This port number can be used to identify a process within a machine uniquely. We also know that a device connected to the Internet is assigned a unique 32-bit address called IP address. So, IP address together with the port number uniquely identifies a process all over the world. This (IP address, port) pair is called a *socket address* of the process. To communicate with a web server, web clients need to specify the socket address of the web server.

2.3 RESOURCES

The idea of *resource* is fundamental to the WWW (see Chapter 1). It is used to represent basic elements in the web. The term *resource* was first introduced in 1990–94, during the early specification of the web. The definition of resource is extended further to refer to any element that can be identified, named, addressed, and handled in any form in the large web or in a smaller networked system. In this section we shall consider only those resources that are elements of the WWW.

The early web was a network of objects (typically static), primarily files. Each of these objects is called a *resource*. A resource in the web is now defined any *entity* that can be identified. The most common kind of resource is a file such as a text file, an image file, an audio file, or a video file. It may even be a dynamically generated query result, the output of a CGI program, or something else. Identification of a resource consists of two phases: *naming* and *addressing*. The addressing part is protocol dependent. HTTP has its own scheme to address web resources. These addresses are called URLs. In the next section, we shall describe the format of a URL.

2.4 URL AND ITS ANATOMY

A resource on the web is identified by an address called **U**niform **R**esource **L**ocator (URL). [See RFC 1738 for details]. The URL was first introduced in 1994 as a part of the **U**niform **R**esource **I**dentifier (URI). It is a general addressing scheme used to identify any resource (such as a book) all over the world. In practice, URLs are subset of URIs and are used to address basically electronic resources.

A URL is used to identify resources in many protocols such as `ftp`, `http`, `gopher`, `mailto`, `news`, `nntp`, `telnet`, `wais`, `file`, and `prospero`. Before describing the actual protocol, let us discuss the syntax and semantics of URLs that are used to access web resources via HTTP.

The syntax of a URL is pretty simple. It is similar to a mailing address. It consists of several parts each of which contains a specific information to identify a resource. Every time you view or get a file on the web, you need to specify its URL.

An HTTP URL has the following form:

```
protocol://host:[port]/[path[?params][#anchor]]
```

It encapsulates a lot of information such as the protocol to be used for this URL, host address (either a domain name or an IP address), port number, etc. The items in the square bracket are optional. Let us now discuss the meaning of each item in detail.

`protocol`

It indicates the protocol to be used for this URL. For HTTP URL, the protocol is `http`. Other possible protocols are `ftp`, `gopher`, `mailto`, `news`, `nntp`, `telnet`, `wais`, `file`, and `prospero`. The syntax of a URL is different for different protocols. Here we shall only describe the syntax of HTTP URL.

`host`

This is the ***F****ully* ***Q****ualified* ***D****omain* ***N****ame* (FQDN) or the *IP address* of the computer where the web server runs. The *Domain Name* is a hierarchical name assigned to a host according to the **D**omain **N**ame **S**ystem (DNS). A Fully Qualified Domain Name consists of a series of domain levels separated by dots (.). For example, the Fully Qualified Domain Names of the popular Google and Yahoo web servers are `www.google.com` and `www.yahoo.com`, respectively. Domain Names are case-insensitive. So, `www.google.com` and `WWW.GOOGLE.COM` refer to the same host.

The IP address, which also identifies a computer uniquely all over the world, may also be specified in the host part. It is a 32-bit address of the computer used by the **I**nternet **P**rotocol (IP) of the TCP/IP protocol suite. An IP address is divided into four parts each having 8 bits. These four parts are written usually in decimal numbers separated by three dots (.). This notation is called *dotted decimal notation*. For example, the IP addresses of `www.google.com` and `www.yahoo.com` are `64.233.169.147` and `69.147.76.15`, respectively.

`port`

This indicates the optional port number of the process to connect to. The port number of a process is a locally (within the computer) unique positive integer assigned to it. If many processes run in a computer, the port number uniquely identifies a particular process within it. Web servers typically run on port 80; though any unused positive integer may be used. In the URL, if no port is specified, port 80 is assumed.

`path`

This is the location of a file or a program (CGI, Perl, PHP, JSP, etc.) on the server relative to a *document root* specified by the web server. The document root is a directory where resources are stored. The path of a resource is calculated relative to this document root. The document root varies from one web server to another. In the Apache web server, the document root is usually set to `/var/www/html` whereas Microsoft's IIS (Internet Information Server) uses `C:\Inetpub\www` as the default document root. However, it can be configured. A document root is case-insensitive, in principle, but may be case-sensitive for servers that typically run on the Windows environment.

`params`

This portion of the URL contains the parameters to be passed to web applications such as CGI, Perl, PHP, or JSP. The path and params are separated by ? character. The `params` consists of a (`name=value`) pair separated by an ampersand (&). For example, `login=ukr&sid=145321& page=inbox` specifies three parameters, `login`, `sid`, and `page` whose values are "ukr", "145321", and "inbox", respectively. The server-side program typically extracts this information from the URL for processing.

`anchor`

This part indicates a specific location in the web page. For example, `#appendix` specifies the appendix section of the web page. This location is created using `<a>` tag as follows:

```
<a name="appendix">Appendix</a>
```

The named section can then be referred to as

```
http://www.it.jusl.ac.in/httphelp.html#appendix
```

2.4.1 URL Examples

Some sample URLs with their components are shown in Figure 2.1.

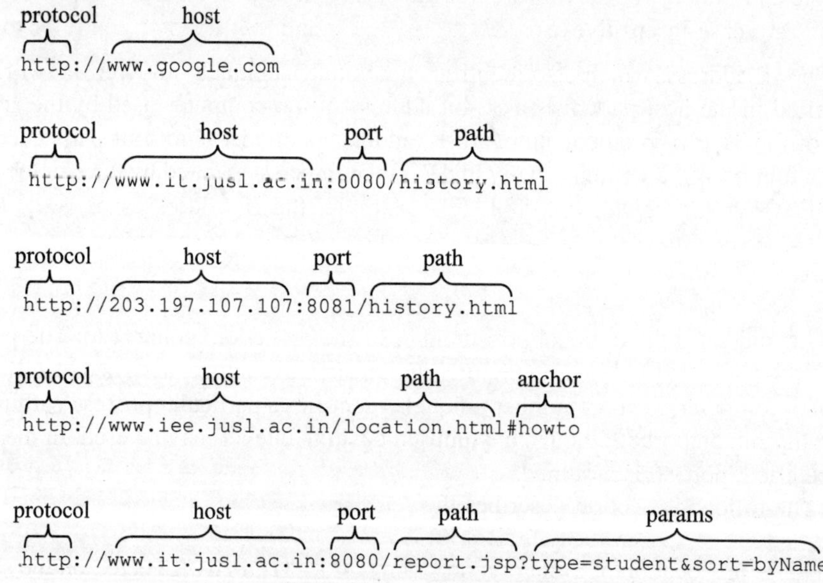

Figure 2.1 URL examples

2.5 MESSAGE FORMAT

As mentioned earlier, HTTP is a request–response protocol [Figure 2.2]. It specifies a set of rules that clients and servers use to communicate:

- An HTTP server process is created on a port (usually 80), which waits for clients to establish a TCP connection.
- An HTTP client initiates a TCP connection with the HTTP server (process) at the designated port.
- The HTTP server accepts this connection.
- The HTTP client then sends a *request* for a resource to the server.
- Upon receiving the *request*, the server processes the request, performs the desired task, and sends a *response* back to the client.
- The HTTP server closes the TCP connection.
- The HTTP client receives the *response* containing information and processes it.

Note that every time the HTTP client wants to get resource from the server, it has to follow these steps. This makes the HTTP *stateless*. This means that web server treats every request as a new request. There is no way to specify that some requests are related.

The advantage of this mechanism is that the client/server need not retain information between successive requests. However, keeping the information about successive related requests is sometimes necessary. As HTTP protocol is inherently stateless, designer of the web pages must use alternative methods such as Cookies, URL rewriting, etc. to remember the previous request(s).

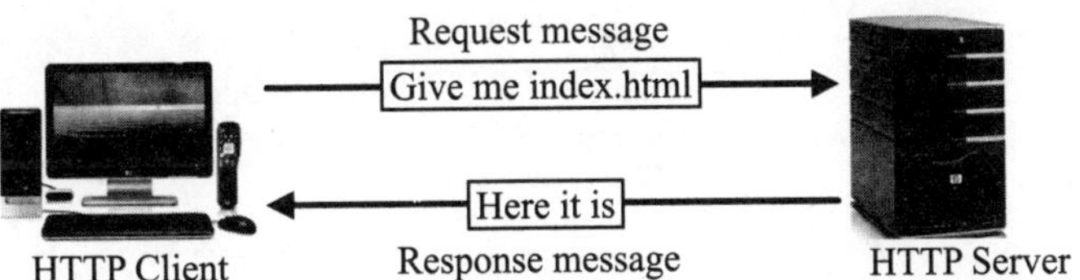

Figure 2.2 HTTP request and response

These requests and responses are encapsulated via HTTP messages [Figure 2.3]. There are two types of messages: *request message* and *response message*.

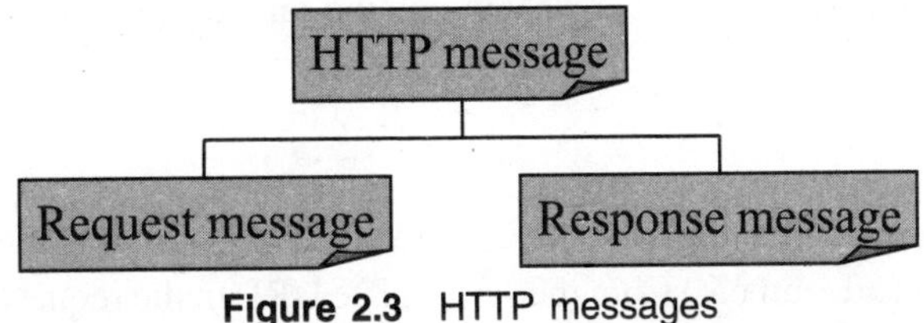

Figure 2.3 HTTP messages

The following section describes the format of each of these two messages.

2.5.1 Request Message

A *request message* is sent by a web client to the web server. It consists of the following parts [Figure 2.4]:

- A request line
- A header
- An empty line
- An optional body

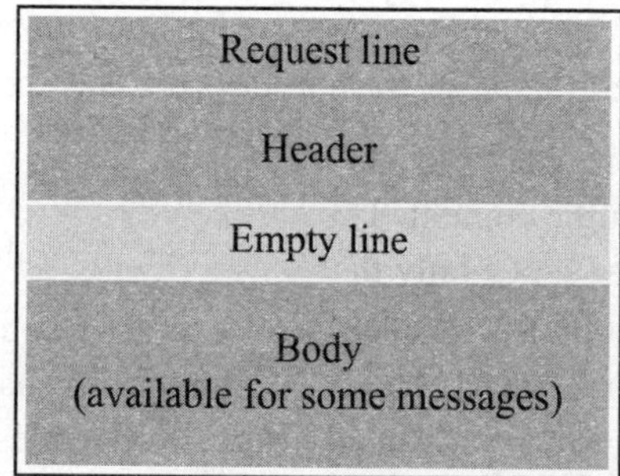

Figure 2.4 HTTP request message format

2.5.1.1 Request line

A request line consists of three parts: *request type*, *URL*, and *HTTP version* [Figure 2.5]. Two consecutive parts are separated by a space.

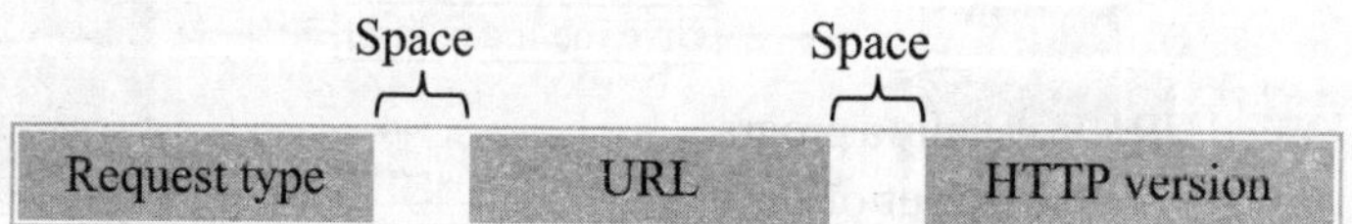

Figure 2.5 HTTP request line

2.5.1.2 Request type (method)

It indicates the type of the request, a client wants to send. They are also called *methods*. A method makes a message either a request or a command to the server. Request messages are used to retrieve data from the server whereas a command tells the server to do a specific task. Some of the HTTP methods are discussed here:

GET

This is the most frequently used method in the WWW. It is specified when a client wants to retrieve (GET) a resource (document) from the server. The URL in the request line identifies the resource. If the URL specified is a valid one, the server reads the content of the resource and sends the content back to the client; otherwise an error message is sent back to the client. If the resource being requested is a server-side program such as a CGI script, or ASP or JSP, the result generated by that program is returned instead of the content of the resource. The message body is empty for the GET method.

The GET method may be a "conditional GET" method. In such a case, the request message includes an "If-Modified-Since" [see Section 2.5.3] header that specifies a date. This header specifies that the identified resource has to be transferred only if it is modified after the specified date. So, users can avoid downloading resources that were downloaded on some earlier date and have not been modified since. The conditional GET method effectively reduces network bandwidth and helps increasing network performance.

This method may also be used to send information (possibly small) to the server for processing without using an HTML form. The information is sent by appending it to the URL using name–value pair [see Section 2.4 for details].

HEAD

It is used when the client wants to know the header information (meta-information) about a resource but not the resource content. The address of the document is defined by the URL. If the URL is correct, the server sends only the meta-information about the resource. The response of the HEAD request contains only headers and a status line but no document content.

It is useful to inspect the characteristics of the resource (possibly large) without actually downloading it. This effectively saves the bandwidth.

POST

It is used when a client wants to send (POST) some information (possibly large) to the server. The actual information is included in the body part of the request message instead of appending it to the URL as done in the GET method. The headers describe the message body such as content type and content length. The commonest form of the POST method is to submit an HTML form to the server.

The specified URL is usually a program that processes the information. The response is generally a dynamically generated output of the program, instead of the static resource. The result of the POST method may be updates of an existing resource or creation of a new resource or both.

Since the information is included in the body, large chunks of data such as an entire file can be sent to the server. Consequently, the length of the request can be unlimited. It is more versatile but slower than using the GET method.

PUT

It is used to upload a new resource or replace an existing document. The actual document is specified in the body part. As the PUT method can modify or replace an existing document, it is vulnerable and is not permitted by most of the web servers. However, developers can customize their web servers to accept this method. However, it is not recommended to configure web servers in such a way without any valid reason.

HTTP is used not only for downloading files from a web server to the client but may also be used to upload a file to the server. In addition, tasks like copying, moving, and deleting files can also be performed using HTTP. The following methods describe these tasks:

PATCH

This is similar to the PUT method except that it specifies a list of differences that must be applied on the existing file.

COPY

The HTTP protocol may be used to copy a file from one location to another. The method COPY is used for this purpose. The URL specified in the request line specifies the location of the source file. The location of the target file is specified in the entity header (discussed in Section 2.5.3). Note that the target web server must be configured properly to accept the COPY method. This method is also vulnerable.

MOVE

It is similar to the COPY method except that it deletes the source file. The location of the source file is specified by the URL in the request line. The entity header (discussed in Section 2.5.3) specifies the location of the target file. Note that the target web server must be configured properly to accept the MOVE method. This method is also vulnerable.

DELETE

This method is used to remove a document from the server. The location of the document to be deleted is specified by the URL in the request line. This method is vulnerable.

LINK

This is used to create a link or links from one document to another. The URL in the request line specifies the location of the source file and the entity header specifies the location of the target document.

UNLINK

It is used to remove a link or links created by the LINK method.

OPTIONS

It is used to retrieve the set of methods supported by the server. It is usually used to check whether a server is functioning properly before performing other tasks. It is also used to check whether the web server really supports a method before actually using that method.

CONNECT

It is used to convert a request connection into the transparent TCP/IP tunnel. It is usually done to facilitate Secured Socket Layer (SSL) encrypted communication (e.g. HTTPS) through an unencrypted HTTP proxy server.

TRACE

It is used to instruct the web server to echo the request back to the client. The client can then see what additions or changes are done by the immediate servers.

Safe and unsafe methods

Among the methods discussed, some methods such as GET, HEAD, OPTIONS, and TRACE are used only to retrieve information from the server. Such methods are called safe. They cannot change the state of the server. This means, they do not have any harmful side effects except certain harmless effects such as caching, logging, etc.

On the other hand, methods such as DELETE, MOVE, UNLINK take actions that may change the state of the server. These methods have harmful side effects and hence are vulnerable. Sensitive web servers are usually not configured to accept these methods.

URL

This is the URL of the resource as described in Section 2.4.

HTTP Version

This field specifies the version of the HTTP protocol being used. It can have the following values: `HTTP/1.0` and `HTTP/1.1`. The current version is `HTTP/1.1`

Before discussing HTTP request headers and body, let us take a look at the response message.

2.5.2 Response Message

In response to the request message, a *response message* is sent by a server to the client. It consists of the following parts [Figure 2.6]:

- A status line
- A header
- An empty line
- An optional body

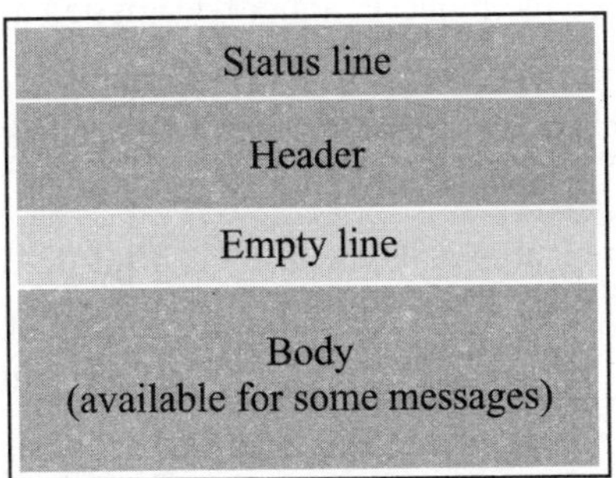

Figure 2.6 HTTP response message format

Status Line

Status line consists of three parts: *HTTP version*, *Status code*, and *Status phrase* [Figure 2.7]. Two consecutive parts are separated by a space.

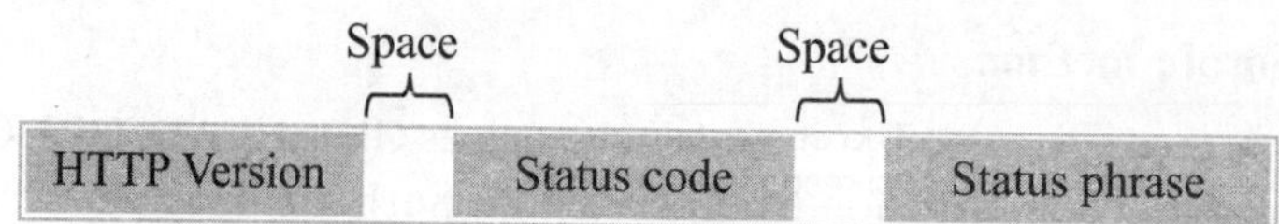

Figure 2.7 HTTP response line

HTTP Version

This field specifies the version of the HTTP protocol being used by the server. The current version is `HTTP/1.1`

2.5.2.1 *Status code*

It is a three-digit code that indicates the status of the response. The status codes are classified with respect to their functionality into five groups as follows:

- 1xx series (Informational)—This class of status codes represents provisional responses.
- 2xx series (Success)—This class of status codes indicates that the client's request are received, understood, and accepted successfully.
- 3xx (Redirectional)—These status codes indicate that additional actions must be taken by the client to complete the request. The user agent may take further actions in order to fulfill the request automatically, provided that it uses either the HEAD or the GET method.
- 4xx (Client error)—These status codes are used to indicate that the client request had an error and therefore it cannot be fulfilled. Except for the HEAD method, the body of the response message contains the explanation that caused the error. The user agent should display the error message to inform the user.
- 5xx (Server Error)—This set of status codes indicates that the server encountered some problem and hence the request cannot be satisfied at this time. The reason of the failure is embedded in the message body. It is also indicated whether the failure is temporary or permanent. The user agent should accordingly display a message on the screen to make the user aware of the server failure.

Table 2.1 shows some status codes with their brief description.

Table 2.1 HTTP status code

Status code	Status phrase	Description
1xx series—Informational		
100	Continue	The server has received the initial part (request headers) of the request and the client may proceed further. For example, a client can proceed to send the request body for the POST method. This way, the client can avoid sending a large message body if the request is already rejected.
101	Switching	The server switches the protocol on receiving a request from the client to do the same.

(Contd.)

(Contd.)

102	Processing	The server has received the request which is currently under process and no response is available yet.
2xx series—Success		
200	OK	Indicates that the request was valid. Actual response depends upon the request method used.
201	Created	The request was successful and a desired resource was created.
202	Accepted	The request is accepted for further processing. When processing will take place, it may or may not act as specified in the request.
203	Non-Authoritative Information	The server is not authoritative for information being sent back. It is possibly from another source.
204	No Content	The request is processed successfully but the body of the response has no content.
205	Reset Content	Same as 204 except that the client needs to reset the document view.
206	Partial Content	The server is sending partial content in response to the range header specified by the client. It is useful to enable interrupted downloads or to divide a download into many simultaneous streams.
207	Multi-Status	The body of the message is an XML file that contains a number of response codes. The number of response codes depends on the number of sub-requests made.
3xx series—Redirection		
300	Multiple Choices	The client may follow multiple options for resources. For example, the server may provide videos with different format or files with different extensions.
301	Moved Permanently	The resource request no longer exists. The client should redirect this and all future requests to the given URI.
302	Found	The request is not available currently. Clients should temporarily redirect requests to the given URI.
303	See Other	The method is possibly wrong. The response may be obtained using another URI and a GET method.
304	Not Modified	The request resource is not modified since the last request. This code is typically sent in response to the 'If-Modified-Since' request header issued by the client. This way bandwidth may be saved as only request header and response header are necessary to check whether a document has been modified or not before sending the actual document content.
4xx series—Client Error		
400	Bad Request	The request contains syntax error and cannot be fulfilled.
401	Unauthorized	The request has failed to be authorized.
403	Forbidden	The request was valid but server is refusing to respond to it.
404	Not Found	The requested resource was not found on the server but may be available in the future.
405	Method Not Allowed	The method specified in the request message is not supported by the resource.
406	Not Acceptable	The requested resource cannot generate the content in the format mentioned in the request message using Accept header.
408	Request Timeout	The server timed out waiting for the request.

(Contd.)

(Contd.)

409	Conflict	The request could not be processed due to conflict. This may happen if a resource is edited by more than one user at a time and a request has come for this resource.
410	Gone	The requested resource is no longer available or will not be available also due to the fact that the resource has been moved intentionally. So, the client should not request the same resource further.
411	Length Required	The length of the content, which is required by the requested resource, was not specified in the request message.
412	Precondition Failed	The server has failed to follow the preconditions mentioned in the request message.
413	Request Entity Too Large	The request is too large for this server to process.
414	Request-URI Too Long	The URI specified was too long for this server to process.
415	Unsupported Media Type	The server does not support the media type specified.
416	Requested Range Not Satisfiable	The server was unable to send the portion of a file requested. The requested portion is possibly beyond the end of the file.
417	Expectation Failed	The server cannot meet with the value specified by the Expect request-header field.
422	Unprocessable Entity	The request contains semantic errors and cannot be fulfilled.
423	Locked	The requested resource is locked.
424	Failed Dependency	This request has failed due to the failure of the previous request
5xx series—Server Error		
500	Internal Server Error	An error message indicating that a problem has occurred in the server.
501	Not Implemented	The server is unable to recognize the method specified and unable to fulfill the request.
502	Bad Gateway	The server is a gateway or proxy and has received an invalid response from the downstream server.
503	Service Unavailable	The service is currently unavailable possibly due to maintenance, shutting down, or overload.
504	Gateway Timeout	The server is a gateway or proxy and has received a timeout response from the downstream server.
505	HTTP Version Not Supported	The server does not support the HTTP version specified.

2.5.3 Headers

HTTP headers are very important part of both *request message* and *response message*. They collectively specify the characteristics of the resource requested and the data that are provided. For example, a client may want to accept image files only in some specified format. Similarly, the server may provide additional information about the resource being sent such as the length of the message content or the last modification date of the resource, etc. The headers are separated by an empty line from the request and response body [Figure 2.4].

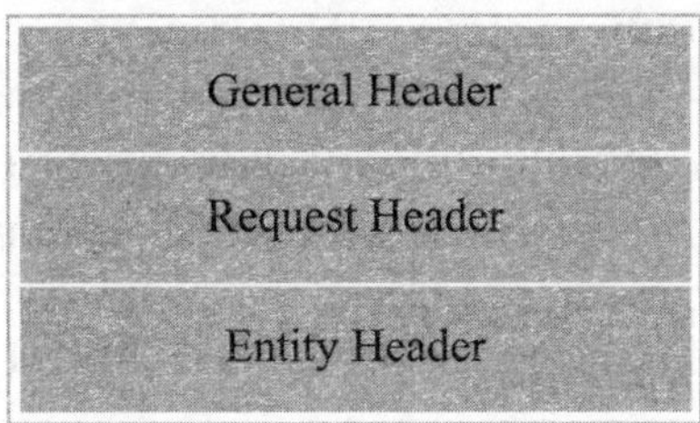

Figure 2.8 HTTP Request Header format

The request header consists of three parts [Figure 2.8]: *General Header, Request Header,* and *Entity Header*.

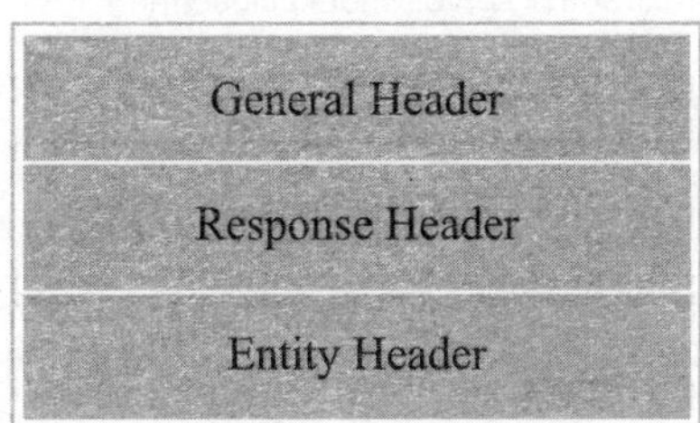

Figure 2.9 HTTP Response Header format

Similarly, the response header also consists of three parts [Figure 2.9]: *General Header, Response Header,* and *Entity Header*.

A header consists of a single line or multiple lines. Each line is a single header of the following form:

```
Header-name: Header-value
```

Each header line consists of a header name followed by a colon, one or more spaces, and the header value [Figure 2.10].

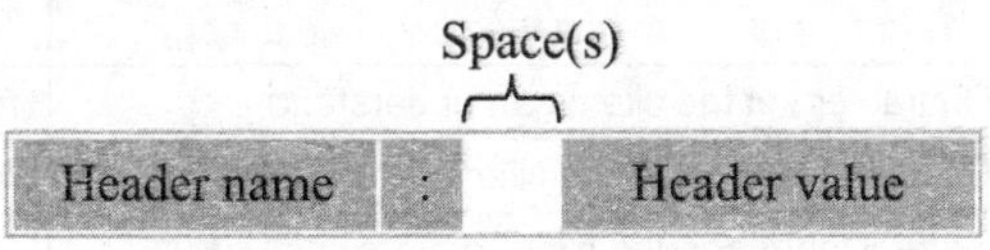

Figure 2.10 HTTP Header Format

The header name is not case-sensitive; but the header value may be. If a header line starts with a space, it is considered to be a part of the previous header line. This happens if a long header value is broken into multiple lines for easy reading. So, the following headers are equivalent.

```
Date: Fri, 18 Sep 2009 11:13:03 GMT

Date: Fri, 18 Sep 2009
      11:13:03 GMT
```

2.5.3.1 General header

HTTP *General Headers* provide information about the messages themselves instead of what content they carry. They are primarily used to specify how messages should be processed and handled. Some *General Headers* are present in both *request message* and *response message* but have somewhat different meaning in each. Some are present in either of the two messages. Table 2.2 shows some of the *General Headers* with their brief description.

Table 2.2 HTTP General header

Header name	Description	Example
Cache-control	Shows whether the caching should be used	Cache-Control: no-cache Cache-Control: max-age=10
Connection	Specifies whether the server should close the connection or not	Connection: close Connection: keep-alive
Date	Shows the date and time of the message originated	Date: Wed, 14 Oct 2009 08:12:31 GMT
MIME-version	Shows version of the MIME used	MIME-Version: 1.0
Upgrade	Specifies the preferred communication protocol	Upgrade: HTTP/2.0
Transfer-Encoding	Shows the type of transformation that has been used in the message body to safely transfer it between the sender and the recipient.	Transfer-Encoding: chunked
Warning	A message specifying the status of message transfer	Warning: 199 Galaxy warning
Via	Specifies the intermediate hosts the message passed through	Via: 1.0 fred, 1.1 source.com (Apache/1.1)

2.5.3.2 Request header

Request header is present only in the request message. It contains information about the client sending the request as well as the data format that the client expects. Table 2.3 shows some of the request headers with their brief description.

Table 2.3 HTTP Request header

Header name	Description	Example
Accept	The format of the media the client can accept	Accept: text/plain
Accept-Charset	Character set the client can understand	Accept-Charset: iso-8859-5
Accept-Encoding	Encoding technique the client can understand	Accept-Encoding: compress, gzip
Accept-Language	Natural language the client prefers	Accept-Language: en
Authorization	The authorization information the client has, to access the resource being requested	Authorization: Basic Wexij6Rpb67FghGVulHNlc2F3Gf
From	Email address of the user sending request	u_roy@it.jusl.ac.in
Host	Domain name of the server	mail1.jusl.ac.in
If-Modified-Since	Only return the resource if it is modified after the specified date	If-Modified-Since: Wed, 14 Oct 2009 19:43:31 GMT
If-Match	Only perform action if the entity supplied by the client matches the same entity on the server	If-Match: "678060c98se84d83dd34e02d9"

(Contd.)

(Contd.)

If-None-Match	If the content is unchanged, it allows the server to send a 304 Not Modified status.	If-None-Match: "678060c98se84d83dd34e02d9"
If-Range	Send the part(s) that is missing if the entity is unchanged, otherwise, send the entire entity	If-Range: "678060c98se84d83dd34e02d9"
If-Unmodified-Since	Only return the resource if it is not modified after the specified date	If-Unmodified-Since: Sat, 10 Oct 2009 15:34:41 GMT
Referrer	The URL of the resource from which this request was made	Referer: http://mail.jusl.ac.in/index.html
User-Agent	The name of the user agent (browser)	Mozilla/4.0
Range	Specifies the sequence of bytes in the entity-body	Range: bytes=50-99,100-120
Max-Forwards	Specifies the maximum number of proxies or gateways that can forward the message	Max-Forwards: 8

2.5.3.3 Response header

The response header is present only in a response message. It contains the information about the server and the data being sent. Table 2.4 shows some response headers with their brief description.

Table 2.4 HTTP Response header

Header name	Description	Example
Accept-Ranges	The partial range type the server supports	Accept-Ranges: bytes
Age	The age of the resource in the proxy cache in seconds	Age: 18
Public	List of supported methods	Public: HEAD, GET, POST
Retry-After	Specifies a date after which the requested resource will be available	Retry-After: 60
Server	The name and version number of the server	Apache/2.0.40 (Red Hat Linux)
Location	The actual location (URL) of the resource requested, created, or modified	Location: http://it.jusl.ac.in/doc/result.html
Vary	Determines whether a cache is allowed to use the response to reply to a subsequent request without revalidation	Vary: *
WWW-Authenticate	Specifies the authentication scheme which should be used to access the requested entity.	WWW-Authenticate: Basic

2.5.3.4 Entity header

It is present in both request and response messages. It contains the information about the message body. Table 2.5 shows some of the entity headers with their description.

Table 2.5 HTTP Entity header

Header name	Description	Example
Allow	List of valid methods that can be applied on a URL	Allow: GET, HEAD, POST
Content-Encoding	The type of encoding used on the data	Content-Encoding: x-gzip

(Contd.)

(Contd.)

Content-Language	The language of the content	Content-Language: en
Content-Length	The length of the response body in bytes	Content-Length: 2453
Content-Range	The location of this partial message in the full body message	Content-Range: bytes 10-15/25-35
Content-Type	The MIME type of the content	Content-Type: text/html
Etag	An identifier for a specific version of the resource	ETag: "678060c98se84d83dd34e02d9"
Expires	The date and time the content will be modified	Expires: Thu, 15 Oct 2009 16:00:00 GMT
Last-Modified	The last date of modification of the request resource	Last-Modified: Tue, 13 Oct 2009 12:45:26 GMT

2.6 EXAMPLE

Suppose the following URL is entered in the address bar of a browser window.

`http://mail.jusl.ac.in/src/login.php`

The browser application first creates a TCP connection with the server `mail.jusl.ac.in` on port 80 (as no port is specified). It then creates a request message as shown in Figure 2.11 and sends it through the TCP connection. On receiving the request, server responds with the data as shown in Figure 2.11.

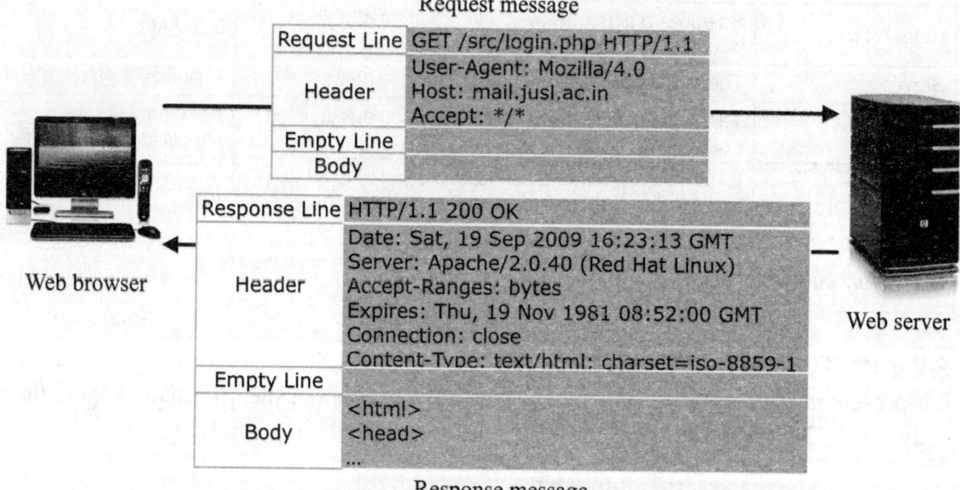

Figure 2.11 HTTP HEAD method example

Figure 2.12 shows the request and response messages if the HEAD method is used for URL `http://www.google.com/index.html`.

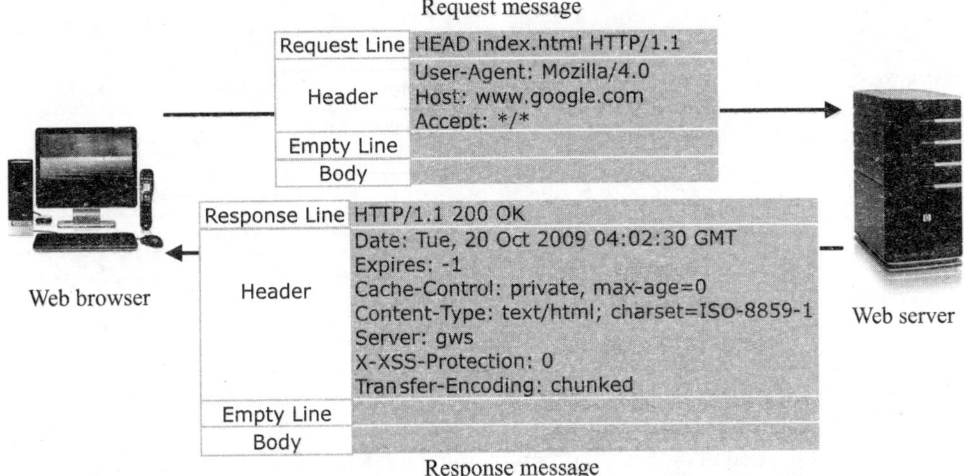

Figure 2.12 HTTP GET method example

2.6.1 Testing HTTP using Telnet

The well-known `telnet` application can be used to establish a TCP connection to a server on a specified port. It also allows us to send and receive messages through this TCP connection. So, it can be used to study and troubleshoot HTTP. You can also view messages including headers and collect other information about the server.

Suppose, we want to get the HTML file `index.html` from the server `www.google.com`. First open a terminal. Then, open a TCP connection to the server on port `80` using the following command:

```
#telnet www.google.com 80
Trying 64.233.169.104...
Connected to www.google.com.
Escape character is '^]'.
```

A sample response to the command is shown in the preceding lines. At this point, a TCP connection to the server `www.google.com` on port `80` is established. The server is now waiting to receive a ***request message***. For the URL `http://www.google.com/index.html`, our request message looks like this:

```
GET index.html HTTP/1.1
```

The request message consists of a request line followed by an empty line. To send the request, type the above line and press enter twice. The telnet application will then send the request message to the server through the existing TCP connection. The server will then respond with the following message:

```
HTTP/1.1 200 OK
Date: Thu, 15 Oct 2009 05:10:22 GMT
Expires: -1
Cache-Control: private, max-age=0
Content-Type: text/html; charset=ISO-8859-1
```

```
Server: gws
X-XSS-Protection: 0
Transfer-Encoding: chunked

fef
<!doctype html>
<html><head>
<meta http-equiv="content-type" content="text/html; charset=ISO-8859-1">
<title>Google</title>
...
</html>
Connection closed by foreign host.
```

The first line is the *Status line*. The next 7 (seven) lines are headers. The next line is a blank line which is a separator between the header and the message body. The message body consists of a series of chunks as specified by the `Transfer-Encoding` header. Note that the body section is nothing but the code that we obtain by typing the URL at the address bar of the web browser.

Here is another example.

```
#telnet mail.jusl.ac.in 80
Trying 203.197.107.102...
Connected to mail.jusl.ac.in.
Escape character is '^]'.
HEAD /src/login.php HTTP/1.0

HTTP/1.1 200 OK
Date: Tue, 20 Oct 2009 04:14:21 GMT
Server: Apache/2.2.3 (Red Hat)
X-Powered-By: PHP/5.1.6
Set-Cookie: SQMSESSID=u6d67n70c8298p8kji1jiba5p3; path=/
Expires: Thu, 19 Nov 1981 08:52:00 GMT
Cache-Control: no-store, no-cache, must-revalidate, post-check=0, pre-check=0
Pragma: no-cache
Set-Cookie: SQMSESSID=u6d67n70c8298p8kji1jiba5p3; path=/; HttpOnly
Set-Cookie: SQMSESSID=2c6fcmb8jg2e16gkqb9272vv90; path=/
Set-Cookie: SQMSESSID=2c6fcmb8jg2e16gkqb9272vv90; path=/; HttpOnly
Connection: close
Content-Type: text/html; charset=iso-8859-1
```

2.7 PERSISTENT AND NON-PERSISTENT CONNECTIONS

Remember, HTTP is an application layer protocol of the TCP/IP protocol suite. It provides an interface to the user to transfer resources in terms of request–response messages using the underlying TCP protocol. Before the actual message exchange, TCP establishes a logical connection between the client and the server. This requires a three-way handshaking. Once the connection is established, the client can send a request to the server. The web server receives the request and responds with a response message. According to HTTP/0.9 and HTTP/1.0 specifications, the server terminates the connection immediately after the response is sent. The connection termination again requires four-way handshaking. If the client wants to send another request, it must follow the same set of steps that we have just discussed. It means every request is considered as a new request. These types of connections are called *non-persistent* connections. This means the connection does not exist (persist) after a response is sent.

The major problem of this mechanism is that it consumes significant bandwidth due to connection establishment and connect release procedure every time the client wants to send a request to the server.

To avoid this problem, a mechanism, called *persistent* connection, is introduced in HTTP/1.1. In this mechanism, the TCP connection is established once and remains open (persists) even after the response is sent. The client can send a number of related requests using this existing TCP connection. Finally, the connection is released only once whenever a session is over. This improves the performance of HTTP significantly.

Another improvement that was done in HTTP/1.1 is *byte serving*, i.e., a server may send just the requested portion of the document instead of sending the entire content.

2.8 WEB CACHING

The caching of web pages is an important technique to improve the Quality of Service (QoS) of the web servers. Caching can reduce network latency experienced by clients. For example, web pages can be loaded more quickly in the browser. Caching can also conserve bandwidth on the network, thus increasing scalability of the network with the help of an HTTP proxy cache. Caching also increases the availability of web pages. Web resources that are cached remain accessible even if the source of the resources or an intermediate network link goes down.

2.9 PROXY

In computer network terminology, a *proxy* is an application program or a computer system that behaves like an intermediary between servers and clients looking for services from those servers. There are many kinds of proxies. Each one is designed to perform some specific task. In this section, we shall describe *web proxy*.

Web proxy is one that sits between web clients and web servers and provides web services on behalf of web servers. Proxy servers are especially important on relatively large networks such as institutional networks, corporate intranets, and ISP networks. In these cases, the need for data privacy is critical and as a consequence greater is the need for a proxy server. Proxies are application layer applications and provide more granularity in controlling traffic. A proxy server may provide the following functionalities:

- Connection sharing
- Traffic filtering and fire walling
- Caching

The most common use of web proxy is to provide *caching* service. To access a resource, a client sends the request to the proxy instead of the original web server. The proxy, in turn, searches for the resource in its cache. If the resource is found, it is delivered to the client. Otherwise, it contacts the specified server and gets the resource, puts that resource in its local cache, and finally returns the resource to the client. The subsequent requests for the same resource are served by the copy in its local cache thereby avoiding remote web server access. This way, proxy speeds up the access to the resource.

In addition to speeding up, a proxy can be configured to filter traffic by IP address as well as a protocol that makes content filtering possible. Content filtering is used in crucial commercial and non-commercial sectors such as corporate, education, or digital library environment, etc. If the requesting client is validated by the filter, it is allowed to get the service. Following are some commonly used content filtering techniques: URL or DNS blacklist, MIME filtering, content keyword filtering, URL regexp filtering, etc.

It may also ensure that the bandwidth usage by different computers conforms to some predefined usage policy. For example, it can divide the available bandwidth equitably to all computers.

2.9.1 Architecture

A web proxy may be placed in user's local computer or at various other points between clients and target web servers. One such arrangement is shown in Figure 2.13.

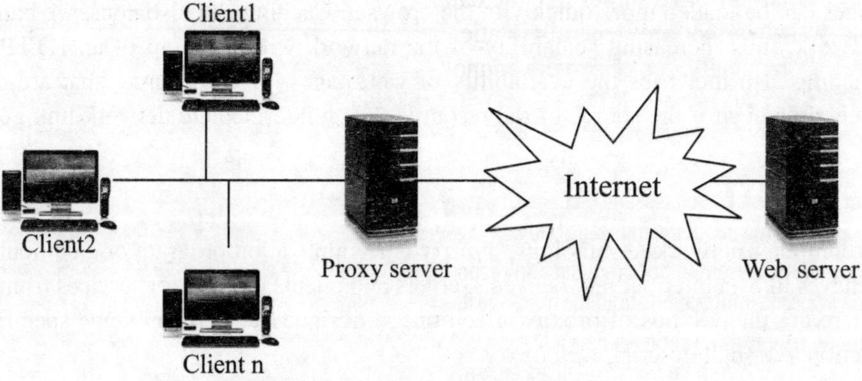

Figure 2.13 HTTP Proxy Architecture

2.9.2 Cache Consistency

Cache consistency mechanisms ensure that cached copies of web pages are eventually updated to reflect changes in the original web pages. There are basically, two cache consistency mechanisms currently in use for HTTP proxies: *pull method* and *push method*.

2.9.2.1 Pull method

In this mechanism, each web page cached is assigned a *time-to-store* field, which indicates the time of storing the web page in the cache. An expiry time of one or two days is also maintained. Expiry time determines how long a web page should remain valid in the cache. Whenever the page is referred, and the page is found in the cache, the web server checks whether the web page has expired or not. If so, a fresh copy is obtained (pulled) from the original server and forwarded to the client.

2.9.2.2 Push method

In this case the web server is assigned the responsibility of making all cached copies consistent with the server copy. Whenever a web page is modified, the web server sends an update request to every web proxy that cached this web page.

The advantage of this mechanism is that the cached pages are modified only when the original copies are modified.

The disadvantage is that the web server has to update all cached copies that are stored in different client's caches. This increases the load on the web server.

2.9.3 Drawbacks

Proxy servers are not useful in the case of *refreshed pages*. Web pages, on some sites, use HTML META tags to expire quickly. In such cases, proxy servers must reload these expired pages in the cache. Similarly, caching exhibits poor performance for the pages whose contents are changed very frequently such as news sites, web blogs, etc.

Moreover, web pages that are generated by server-side scripting such as Perl, PHP, ASP, JSP cannot be cached. This is because the contents of the web pages depend on the user input as well as information from a server like the database server. Proxy servers can only cache home pages from websites that are generally static. Since most websites generate contents of subsequent pages dynamically, proxy servers cannot help much in this regard.

KEYWORDS

Entity Header: Present in both request and response messages and specifies information about the message body.

General Header: It is present in both request and response messages and provides information about the message itself.

Host: A computer where a web server runs.

Method: The type of the request such as GET, HEAD, or POST issued by the web client.

Non-persistent Connection: In this method, the web server closes the TCP connection immediately after sending the response message.

Persistent Connection: In this method, the connection remains open even after the response is sent by the server.

Port: An integer used to identify a process uniquely within the computer.

Proxy Server: Computers that cache web pages and data to improve the performance of HTTP.

Request Header: It is present only in the request message and specifies the client's configuration and the data format the client can understand.

Request Line: The first line of the request message consisting of a method, a URL, and the HTTP version being used.

Response Header: It is present only in the response message and specifies the server's configuration and provides information about the response message.

Status Code: It represents general information, success information, redirection information, or error information.

Status Line: The first line of the response message consisting of the HTTP version, a three-digit status code, and a status phrase.

Uniform Resource Locator (URL): An address used to identify resources on the World Wide Web (WWW) uniquely.

Web Caching: To improve the performance of HTTP, web pages and data are cached in the intermediate computers.

Web Client: A process that accesses resources on the WWW through HTTP.

Web Server: A process that creates, stores, and provides resources through HTTP.

SUMMARY

Hyper**T**ext **T**ransfer **P**rotocol (HTTP) is an application layer protocol in the TCP/IP protocol suite. It is primarily used to access resources on the **W**orld **W**ide **W**eb (WWW). The resource is identified by **U**niform **R**esource **L**ocator (URL). The URL consists of a method, a domain name or an IP address of the web server, an optional port number, pathname and optional parameters, and anchors. HTTP is a request–response protocol between the web server and web clients. The requests and responses are sent and received in terms of HTTP messages. There are two types of messages: *request message* and *response message.*

The request message is sent by web clients to the web server. The response message is sent by the web server to the web clients. A request message consists of a request line, header, a blank line, and an optional body. The request line consists of a method, a URL, and an HTTP version being used. A method indicates the type of the request/command issued by the client.

The structure of the response message is similar to the request message except that it uses a status line instead of the request line. A status line consists of the HTTP version number, a three-digit status code, and a status phrase. The status code represents general information, success information, redirection information, or error information. The status phrase describes the status code.

Headers represent additional information needed by the client and the server for successful communication. There are four types of headers: *General Header*, *Request Header*, *Response Header,* and *Entity Header.* General Headers represent general information about the message itself. Request Headers represent information about the client's configuration and format of the data the client can accept. Response Headers specify server's configurations and the information about the response message. The Entity Header specifies the information about the message body.

HTTP version 1.1 uses persistent connection where several HTTP messages can be exchanged using a single TCP connection. Proxy servers are introduced to cache web pages and result in improved performance.

Byte serving is another concept introduced in HTTP 1.1 to improve the performance of HTTP. In this case only the requested portion of a resource is sent instead of the entire (possibly large) content.

WEB RESOURCES

`http://tools.ietf.org/html/rfc1738`
Uniform Resource Locators

`http://www.w3.org/Protocols/HTTP/1.0/spec.html`
Hypertext Transfer Protocol -- HTTP/1.0

`http://tools.ietf.org/html/rfc2616`
Hypertext Transfer Protocol -- HTTP/1.1

`http://www.w3.org/Protocols/rfc2616/rfc2616-sec14.html`
Header Field Definitions

`http://www.ietf.org/rfc/rfc1521.txt?number =1521`
MIME (Multipurpose Internet Mail Extensions) Part One

`http://www.web-caching.com/`
Web Caching Overview

`ftp://ftp.rfc-editor.org/in-notes/rfc3143.txt`
Known HTTP Proxy/Caching Problems (RFC 3143)

`http://www.squid-cache.org/`
SQUID Web Proxy Cache

`http://www.jmarshall.com/easy/http/`
HTTP Made Really Easy, James Marshall.

EXERCISES

Multiple Choice Questions

1. The term HTTP stands for

(a) HyperText Transfer Program
(b) HyperText Transfer Process
(c) HyperText Transfer Protocol
(d) HyperText Tracing Protocol

2. A proxy server is a computer that

(a) acts as a backup server
(b) resolves name to IP address
(c) gives user permissions
(d) is used to access external resources

3. The full form of URL is
 (a) Universal Resource Locator
 (b) Uniform Resource Locator
 (c) Unique Routing Link
 (d) Universal Resource Location

4. A web server is a software for
 (a) analyzing web traffic
 (b) sending emails
 (c) serving a web page upon user's request
 (d) packet filtering

5. A web browser runs on
 (a) Linux only (b) Web-client computers
 (c) Windows only (d) Web-server computers

6. Which of the following protocols is used to send and receive HTML files?
 (a) HTTP (b) FTP
 (c) POP3 (d) SMTP

7. An entity header is present in
 (a) Request message only
 (b) Response message only
 (c) Both Request message and Response message
 (d) None of the above

8. In a non-persistent connection
 (a) the connection is closed after sending the response
 (b) the connection is closed after receiving the response
 (c) the connection is never closed
 (d) the connection remains open after sending the response

9. A web server by default runs on port
 (a) 23 (b) 25
 (c) 80 (d) 22

10. Which of the following methods is used to get meta-information of a resource?
 (a) TOP (b) HEAD
 (c) GET (d) META

11. HTTP status code is
 (a) two-digit code (b) three-digit code
 (c) four-digit code (d) five-digit code

12. A general header is present in
 (a) Request message only
 (b) Response message only
 (c) Both Request message and Response message
 (d) None of the above

13. A header name and header value is separated by
 (a) a single colon
 (b) a single colon and one or more space
 (c) a single space
 (d) a semicolon

14. HTTP 1.1 uses
 (a) Persistent connection
 (b) Non-persistent connection
 (c) Both (a) and (b)
 (d) None of the above

15. Which one of the following statements is correct regarding HTTP URL?
 (a) Port number is mandatory
 (b) IP address of the web server cannot be specified
 (c) The resource name is mandatory
 (d) The protocol is mandatory

16. Which one of the following statements is correct?
 (a) Client sends a response message
 (b) Server sends a request message
 (c) Client sends a request message
 (d) Server receives a response message

17. The header and body of a message is separated by a
 (a) a colon (b) a semicolon
 (c) a space (d) new line

18. How may parts are there in a request line?
 (a) 1 (b) 2 (c) 3 (d) 4

19. HTTP version is present in
 (a) Only request line (b) Only response line
 (c) Both (a) and (b) (d) None of the above

20. 4xx series status codes are for
 (a) providing information
 (b) Success request
 (c) Server error
 (d) Client error

Review Questions

1. What is a *web browser*?
2. Is it possible to transfer a resource from the client computer to the web server? If yes, how?
3. Compare and contrast FTP and HTTP.
4. What are web browsers and what are they used for? Which web browsers do you know?
5. Why is HTTP known as a *stateless* protocol? Write advantages and disadvantages of the stateless protocol.
6. Suppose a web server is running in a computer having IP address 203.197.107.107 on port 8080. The path of the resource relative to the document root is "index.jsp". What will be the URL of this resource?
7. Consider the above question. Suppose, we have to pass two parameter "login" and "page" with values "uroy" and "inbox", respectively. What will be the URL now? What will this URL be if it runs on port 80?
8. Identify the different parts of the following URL.
   `http://www.it.jusl.ac.in:8765/result.jsp?name=student&sort=byMarks`
9. Discuss differences between GET and POST methods of the HTTP protocol.
10. What are *safe* and *unsafe* methods? Name two methods of each category.
11. For HTTP URL, the protocol is "http". Mention the name of two other possible protocols.
12. Suppose a resource that was requested by the client is not found by the server. Write a sample response message for it.
13. Suppose you downloaded a JPEG file whose URL is "http://www.myserver.com/campus.jpg". When you downloaded it, its modification time was "Wed, 14 Oct 2008 19:43:31 GMT". You want to download it again if it is modified after this date and time. Write a sample request message for this.
14. Show how the performance of the HTTP protocol is improved.
15. Why is a *Proxy Server* used? What are its functions? Name two proxy servers. Mention some limitations of proxy servers.
16. Mention some other tasks of a proxy server except caching web pages. How web pages in the proxy's cache are made consistent with web pages stored on the original web server?
17. Write a sample request message for a persistent connection.

3 JAVA NETWORK PROGRAMMING

KEY OBJECTIVES

After completing this chapter readers will be able to—

- **get an overview about the Java network classes and interfaces**
- **write Java socket programs**
- **access web pages using HTTP and Java network APIs**
- **send emails using Java mail API and SMTP**
- **retrieve emails using Java mail API and POP3**
- **understand how to invoke methods on a remote object using Java RMI technology**

3.1 JAVA AND THE NET

Java has some distinct advantages over other programming languages as far as network applications are concerned. One of the important features of Java is that it supports 16-bit Unicode for International character sets, which is still difficult to implement in other languages. In addition, Java can excellently handle network security issues. These features together with other features such as platform independence and garbage collection allow us to develop efficient and elegant network applications without worrying about the system crashes, spread of viruses, or stealing of sensitive data.

This chapter demonstrates how to use Java network APIs to write network programs easily and quickly.

3.2 JAVA NETWORKING CLASSES AND INTERFACES

Java, like other programming languages, provides well-designed classes and interfaces (APIs) to most network features. Table 3.1 shows some of the commonly used network classes and interfaces. The network classes and interfaces are provided basically as three packages `java.net`, `java.rmi`, and `javax.mail`. The first two are parts of the JVM (Java Virtual Machine) and the last one can be downloaded from Sun's website. With this rich set of interfaces, writing network programs is quite simple. Programmers having experience in network programming in other languages can readily discover how easy it is to develop the same programs in Java.

Table 3.1 Java networking classes and interfaces

NetworkInterface	InetAddress	ServerSocket	Socket
DatagramSocket	DatagramPacket	URL	URLConnection
HttpURLConnection	InetSocketAddress	SocketAddress	Authenticator
PasswordAuthentication	MulticastSocket	URLEncoder	URLDecoder
Remote	Naming	Registry	LocateRegistry
UnicastRemoteObject	RMISecurityManager	RMISocketFactory	RMIClassLoader
RemoteServer	RemoteObject	Session	MimeMessage
Transport	Store	Folder	Message
URLName	Header	ContentType	InternetAddress
MimeBodyPart	MimeMultipart	InternetHeaders	MimeUtility

3.3 LOOKING UP INTERNET ADDRESS

Before developing actual network applications, let us first work with the network interfaces available on a host. Each network interface is represented by the Java class `NetworkInterface`. It has several useful methods to gather information about available network interfaces. The following program (`NetworkInterfaceDemo.java`) displays information about available network interfaces.

```
import java.net.*;
import java.util.*;
class NetworkInterfaceDemo {
   public static void main(String args[]) throws Exception {
      try {
         Enumeration intfs = NetworkInterface.getNetworkInterfaces();
         while(intfs.hasMoreElements()) {
            NetworkInterface intf = (NetworkInterface)intfs.nextElement();
            System.out.println("\nInterface: "+intf.getName());
            System.out.println("Display name: "+intf.getDisplayName());
            Enumeration addresses = intf.getInetAddresses();
            while(addresses.hasMoreElements()) {
               InetAddress addr = (InetAddress)addresses.nextElement();
               System.out.println("Address: "+addr);
            }
         }
      }catch(Exception e) {e.printStackTrace();}
   }
}
```

Compile the program using the following command:

```
javac NetworkInterfaceDemo.java
```

Now, run the program as follows:

```
java NetworkInterfaceDemo
```

A sample output of this program is shown in Figure 3.1.

```
C:\WINDOWS\system32\cmd.exe
E:\Net>java NetworkInterfaceDemo

Interface: lo
Display name: MS TCP Loopback interface
Address: /127.0.0.1

Interface: eth0
Display name: Broadcom NetXtreme Gigabit Ethernet - Packet Scheduler M
iniport

Interface: eth1
Display name: Intel(R) PRO/Wireless 2200BG Network Connection - Packet
 Scheduler Miniport
Address: /192.168.1.2

E:\Net>_
```

Figure 3.1 Getting information about network interfaces

3.4 CLIENT/SERVER PROGRAMS

One of the central ideas of network computing is the *client–server* model. Many networking applications including Internet's primary protocols such as HTTP, SMTP, DNS, etc. use this model. It has some distinct advantages over its counterpart, the peer-to-peer model.

In this programming paradigm, there are two basic components: service providers, known as *servers* and service requesters, known as *clients*. This client–server model is sometimes called the *two-tier* model. Server programs are usually run in high-performance computers and share resources with its clients. Clients make use of these resources to perform its designated task.

Each client sends one or more service requests to one or more servers. The servers, in turn, accept these requests, process them, and provide the requested service. This simple but powerful idea can be used in a variety of network applications, though the fundamental concept remains the same.

A server may provide a variety of services such as web service, remote login service, mail service, database service, file service, name service, print service, and many more. One server may provide multiple services. Similarly, one client may get many services from the same or different servers. A program may act as a server or as a client. Popular clients include web browsers, chat clients, email clients, etc.

In the next section, we shall discuss how to develop client–server applications using three Java technologies, namely, Socket, RMI, and mail API.

3.5 SOCKET PROGRAMMING

TCP allows serialized, reliable data communication between two parties using a logical point-to-point channel. A *socket* is one end point of this channel between two programs.

The TCP/IP protocol suite allows us to identify a machine uniquely all over the world using a 32-bit IP address. Many processes may run on a single computer. Each of these processes is assigned a locally unique positive integer called the *port* number. Any process can now be identified uniquely all over the world by using this port number together with the IP address of the machine in which it is running. This IP address and port number combination can be thought of as an address called the *socket address*. The socket address makes the communication between two processes possible.

3.5.1 Overview

In the client–server programming paradigm using socket, a server program creates a server socket and listens for connection requests from clients.

The client is another process that usually runs on a different computer. It must know the socket address of the server process to communicate. In the TCP socket, it first sends a request for connection establishment to the server. During the connection establishment, the client should provide its own socket address to the server, so that the server can communicate back to the client. The client's port number is generally assigned by the system.

On receiving a request from a client, the server establishes a socket connection. Once this socket connection is established, both processes can now communicate in both ways simultaneously [Figure 3.2].

Java provides a rich set of classes and interfaces to make this socket communication possible. It provides two types of sockets: TCP and UDP. TCP socket provides a serialized, reliable data communication whereas UDP socket provides unreliable, connection-less service.

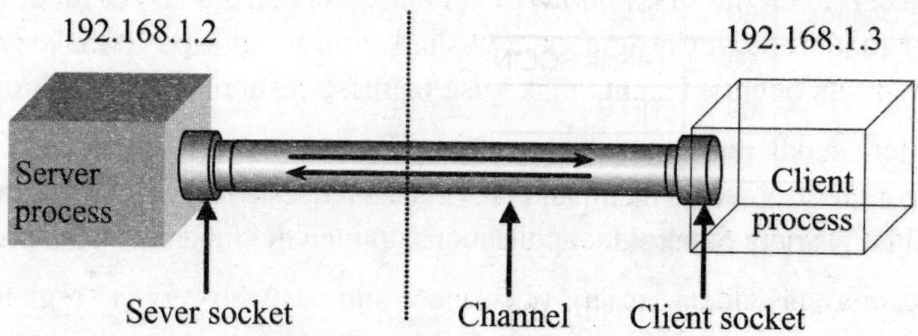

Figure 3.2 Socket communication

Communication using TCP sockets consists of the following steps:

- The server creates a `ServerSocket` object, specifying the port number it listens on.
- The server invokes the `accept()` method on this object. This method makes the server waiting until a request comes from the client.
- The client creates a `Socket` object, specifying the server address and port number to connect to.
- The constructor of the `Socket` class attempts to establish a connection to the specified server and port number. If the connection is established, it returns a `Socket` object that represents the logical connection to the client. The client uses this `Socket` object to communicate with the server.
- The `accept()` method on the `ServerSocket` object also returns a `Socket` object to the server that is connected to the client's socket.

Each socket has both an `InputStream` and an `OutputStream`. The client's `InputStream` is connected to the server's `OutputStream`, and the client's `OutputStream` is connected to the server's `InputStream`. Now, both the client and the server can communicate using I/O streams.

3.5.2 Reserved Sockets

It was mentioned earlier that each process is assigned a locally unique integer. Ideally, any available (not assigned yet) integer can be used. However, remember that the client must know this port number to make communication possible. If port numbers are assigned arbitrarily, the client process will not have any idea about them. That is why standard server processes are assigned some fixed port numbers agreed upon at design time. These port numbers are reserved for those well-known processes. According to Internet Assigned Numbers Authority (IANA), port numbers from 0 to 1023 are reserved. You should not use these port numbers in your network programs. Some reserved port numbers and their corresponding processes are mentioned in Table 3.2.

Table 3.2 Reserved ports

Port	Server	Port	Server	Port	Server	Port	Server
7	Echo	37	Time	110	POP3	434	MobileIP-Agent
18	MSP	43	WhoIs	111	Sun RPC	443	HTTPS
20	FTP Data	80	HTTP	115	SFTP	458	Apple QuickTime
21	FTP Control	53	DNS	118	SQL Services	531	Chat
22	SSH	66	Oracle SQL*NET	161	SNMP	541	rlogin
23	Telnet	69	TFTP	179	BGP	547	DHCP Server
25	SMTP	70	Gopher	197	DLS	563	SNEWS

3.5.3 TCP/IP Server Sockets

A TCP server socket is created using the `ServerSocket` class. It has four overloaded constructors. The most frequently used one creates a server socket at the specified port.

```
ServerSocket(int port)
```

The port *must* be an unused one otherwise it throws an exception `BindException`. The following statement creates a server socket at port 6789:

```
ServerSocket serverSocket = new ServerSocket(6789);
```

Suppose the IP address of the machine running this server process is `192.168.1.2`. Then the socket address of the process is `192.168.1.2, 6789`. This information can be used by clients to establish connections. To accept incoming connections, the server must listen to a specified port. This is done by calling the `accept()` method on the server socket.

```
Socket clientSocket = serverSocket.accept();
```

This results the server waiting to accept incoming connections. The method `accept()` is a *blocking* one. It sends the calling process to a suspended state. The process wakes up when a connection request is received. If everything goes well, a socket connection is established and a `Socket` object is returned which represents the connection and is used subsequently to communicate with the client.

To send data to or receive data from the client, stream objects are created. The `Socket` object provides two methods, `getInputStream()` and `getOutputStream()`, which can be used to obtain `InputStream` and `OutputStream` objects, respectively. The `InputStream` object is used to receive data from the client whereas the `OutputStream` object is used to send data to the client. They are usually wrapped by other stream classes to send and receive data conveniently. The following example creates a `BufferedReader` object and a `PrintWriter` object to read from and write to the socket:

```
BufferedReader fromClient = new BufferedReader(new
InputStreamReader(socket.getInputStream()));
PrintWriter toClient = new PrintWriter(socket.getOutputStream(), true);
```

3.5.4 TCP/IP Client Sockets

The TCP client socket is created using the `Socket` class. It has several overloaded constructors which can be used depending upon the requirement. The commonly used one creates a socket connection with the specified host and the port.

```
Socket(String host, int port)
```

The host can be an IP address or a Fully Qualified Domain Name (FQDN). It can be any loop-back address (e.g. 127.0.0.1) or the name "localhost" if the server process is running on the same machine. The following statement makes a socket connection to the process running locally on port `6789`:

```
Socket socket = new Socket("localhost", 6789);
```

The object `socket` represents the socket connection to the server and is used to communicate with the server process. The client process, like the server process, can obtain `InputStream` and `OutputStream` objects to send data to or receive data from the server.

```
BufferedReader fromServer = new BufferedReader(new
   InputStreamReader(socket.getInputStream()));>
PrintWriter toServer = new PrintWriter(socket.getOutputStream(), true);
```

This code creates a `BufferedReader` object and a `PrintWriter` object to read from and write to the socket. At this point both the client and the server are ready to communicate with each other. Now the question is, what will they send and receive?

3.5.5 Sending and Receiving Data

In this section, we shall develop a simple but elegant application using the TCP socket. In this application, a client `TCPFactClient` connects to the server `TCPFactServer` and gives an integer obtained from the user. The server, in turn, calculates the factorial of the integer and sends the result back. The client finally displays the result.

The server and client programs for this application are straightforward and simple as they implement a simple protocol. They are only for demonstration purposes. In practice, clients and servers perform complicated tasks. However, they use the same basic steps as follows:

- Server creates a server socket.
- Client connects to this socket.
- Both obtain input and output streams on the socket.
- They send and receive data using these streams.
- They close streams.
- They close socket.

To accept an integer from the user and send it to the server, a client program uses the following piece of code:

```
BufferedReader fromUser = new BufferedReader(new InputStreamReader(System.in));
String n = fromUser.readLine();
toServer.println(n);
```

The server must be ready to accept data sent by the client. The following piece of code does this.

```
int n = Integer.parseInt(fromClient.readLine());
```

The server then calculates the factorial of that number and sends the result back to the client.

```
int fact = 1;
for(int i=2;i<=n;i++)
   fact*=i;
toClient.println(fact);
```

Finally, the client reads the result from the socket and prints it using the following code:

```
fact = fromServer.readLine();
System.out.println("Received from server: " + fact);
```

3.5.6 Complete Example

Here is the complete source code of the client stored in the file `TCPFactClient.java`.

```
//TCPFactClient.java
import java.io.*;
import java.net.*;
public class TCPFactClient {
   public static void main(String argv[]) throws Exception {
      String fact;
      //create a socket to the server
      Socket socket = new Socket("localhost", 6789);
      System.out.println("Connected to localhost at port 6789");
      //get streams
      PrintWriter toServer = new PrintWriter(socket.getOutputStream(), true);
      BufferedReader fromServer = new BufferedReader(new
InputStreamReader(socket.getInputStream()));
      BufferedReader fromUser = new BufferedReader(new
InputStreamReader(System.in));
```

```
            //get an integer from user
            System.out.print("Enter an integer: ");
            String n = fromUser.readLine();
            //send it to server
            toServer.println(n);
            System.out.println("Sent to server: " + n);
            //retrieve result
            fact = fromServer.readLine();
            System.out.println("Received from server: " + fact);
            //close the socket
            socket.close();
        }
    }
```

Here is the complete source code of the server stored in the file `TCPFactServer.java`.

```
//TCPFactServer.java
import java.io.*;
import java.net.*;
public class TCPFactServer {
    public static void main(String argv[]) throws Exception {
        //create a server socket at port 6789
        ServerSocket serverSocket = new ServerSocket(6789);
        //wait for incoming connection
        System.out.println("Server is listening on port 6789");
        Socket socket = serverSocket.accept();
        System.out.println("Request accepted");
        //get streams
        BufferedReader fromClient = new BufferedReader(new
InputStreamReader(socket.getInputStream()));
        PrintWriter toClient = new PrintWriter(socket.getOutputStream(), true);
        //receive data from client
        int n = Integer.parseInt(fromClient.readLine());
        System.out.println("Received from client: " + n);
        int fact = 1;
        for (int i = 2; i <= n; i++) {
            fact *= i;
        //send result to the client
        }
        toClient.println(fact);
        System.out.println("Sent to client: " + fact);
    }
}
```

In this application, we have assumed that both the client and the server programs run on the same computer. If they run on different computers, the client program must specify the address of the computer where the server process is running. For example, if the server program runs on port `8765` on a computer having IP address `192.168.1.2`, the following line of code is used by the client to establish a socket connection with the server.

```
Socket socket = new Socket("192.168.1.2", 8765);
```

Now, open a terminal and go to the directory containing the source file `TCPFactServer.java`. To compile the server program use the following command:

```
javac TCPFactServer.java
```

Similarly, compile the client program using the following command:

```
javac TCPFactClient.java
```

Start the server as follows:

```
java TCPFactServer
```

Now, start the client as follows:

```
java TCPFactClient
```

A sample output is shown in Figure 3.3.

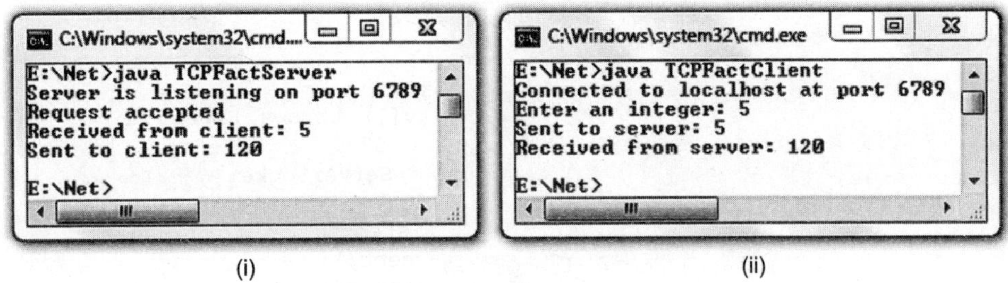

Figure 3.3 (i) TCPFactServer (ii) TCPFactClient

3.5.7 Accepting Simultaneous Connections

The server, we have designed so far, can handle only one request. It terminates after serving one client request. Ideally, a server process should run continuously and should serve multiple requests simultaneously. The following arrangements can be made in the server to implement this:

- Accept a new connection.
- Create a new thread. Handover, the connection to this thread. Go to the listening mode again to accept further connections immediately.
- The thread handles the client request independently and finally terminates.

Create a class `Handler` whose objects can handle client requests. It has a constructor that takes a `Socket` object as argument. This `Socket` object is used to receive an integer from the client and send the factorial of that integer. The constructor creates a new thread with itself. So, each `Handler` object runs concurrently and communicate with one client independently.

The server simply waits for the incoming request from clients. Upon receiving a request, it establishes a socket connection, creates a `Handler` object and handovers this connection to the object. The `Handler` object runs in parallel and serves the client through the socket connection. Following is the source code for our modified server stored in the file `TCPMTFactServer.java`:

```
//TCPMTFactServer.java
import java.io.*;
import java.net.*;
class TCPMTFactServer {
```

```
    public static void main(String argv[]) throws Exception {
        int n, fact = 1;
        //create a server socket at port 6789
        ServerSocket welcomeSocket = new ServerSocket(6789);
        System.out.println("Server ready");
        while (true) {
            //wait for incoming connection
            Socket socket = welcomeSocket.accept();
            System.out.println("Request accepted");
            //hand over this connection request to Handler
            new Handler(socket);
        }
    }
}
class Handler implements Runnable {
    Socket socket;
    Handler(Socket s) {
        this.socket = s;
        new Thread(this).start();
        System.out.println("A thread created");
    }
    public void run() {
        try {
            while (true) {
                //get streams
                BufferedReader fromClient =
                new BufferedReader(new InputStreamReader(socket.getInputStream()));
                PrintWriter toClient = new PrintWriter(socket.getOutputStream(),
                true);
                int fact = 1;
                //receive data from client
                int n = Integer.parseInt(fromClient.readLine());
                System.out.println("Received " + n);
                if (n == -1) {
                    socket.close();
                    break;
                }
                for (int i = 2; i <= n; i++)
                    fact *= i;
                //send result to the client
                toClient.println(fact);
                System.out.println("Sent: " + fact);
            }
        } catch (IOException e) { }
    }
}
```

Now, modify the client program slightly so that it can send many integers one by one. To terminate, it sends a –1. The source code for the client stored in `TCPMTFactClient.java` is as follows:

```
import java.io.*;
import java.net.*;
public class TCPMTFactClient {
    public static void main(String argv[]) throws Exception {
        String sentence, modifiedSentence, fact;
```

```
        //create a socket to the server
        Socket socket = new Socket("localhost", 6789);
        System.out.println("connected to localhost at port 6789");
        //get streams
        PrintWriter toServer = new PrintWriter(socket.getOutputStream(), true);
        BufferedReader fromServer = new BufferedReader(new
InputStreamReader(socket.getInputStream()));
        BufferedReader fromUser = new BufferedReader(new
InputStreamReader(System.in));
        while (true) {
           //get an integer from user
           System.out.print("Enter an integer: ");
           String n = fromUser.readLine();
           //send it to server
           toServer.println(n);
           System.out.println("Sent to server: " + n);
           if (n.equals("-1"))
              break;
           //retrieve result
           fact = fromServer.readLine();
           System.out.println("Received from server: " + fact);
        }
        //close the socket
        socket.close();
     }
  }
```

Compile and start the server program as described. You can now start as many clients as you wish. The server can serve them simultaneously. A sample output using two clients is shown in Figure 3.4.

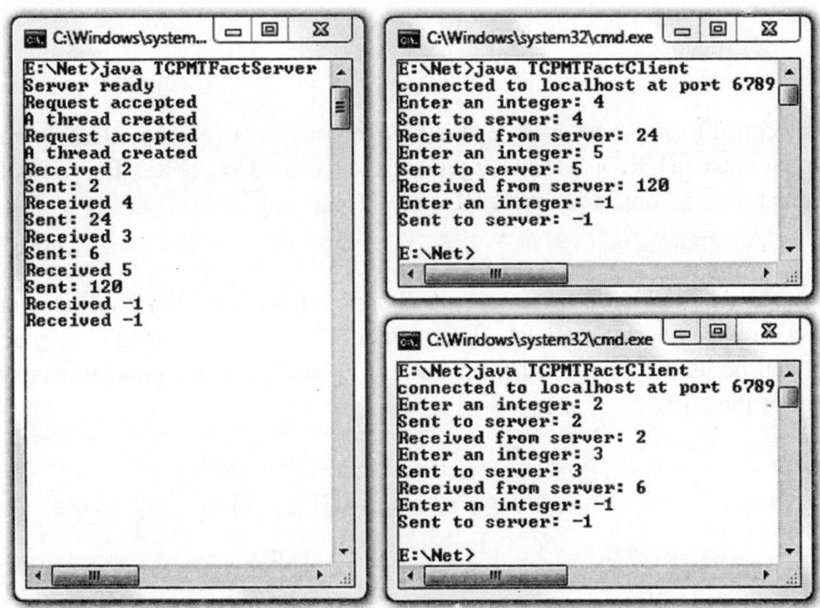

Figure 3.4 TCP Multi-threaded server and clients

If the computer where the server program runs is situated in a different network, client's network must be configured properly. In particular, the IP address of the gateway must be specified. If the client's network is connected to the server's network through a proxy that supports sockets, use the following lines of code:

```
System.setProperty("socksProxyHost", "192.168.1.1");
System.setProperty("socksProxyPort", "1080");
```

Here, `1080` is the port number of the proxy process and `192.168.1.1` is the IP address of the host where the proxy runs. Alternatively, you can pass this information to the Java Runtime Environment during execution as follows:

```
java -DsocksProxyHost=192.168.1.1 -DsocksProxyPort=1080 TCPMTFactClient
```

3.5.8 Web Page Retrieval

Making a connection to a web server in the Internet using socket is sometimes problematic especially when the client computer is connected to the Internet through a proxy computer that does not support this socket. The Java classes `URL` and `URLConnection` allow client applications to connect to a HTTP server very easily. This mechanism will work even if the clients are behind the firewall and use HTTP proxy. These classes are special-purpose classes, used for accessing HTTP servers only.

3.5.9 Using URL

The class `URL` encapsulates the **U**niform **R**esource **L**ocator (URL), which identifies a resource in the WWW uniquely. It provides mechanisms to download web resources to the client computer. The class `URL` has several overloaded constructors some of which are mentioned as follows:

```
URL(String url)
URL(String protocol, String host, String file)
URL(String protocol, String host, int port, String file)
```

Any constructor can be used depending upon one's convenience. The most commonly used constructor takes a URL as a string argument and creates a `URL` object. For example, the following code creates a `URL` object for the URL `http://www.yahoo.com`.

```
java.net.URL yahoo = new java.net.URL("http://www.yahoo.com");
```

You can then call its `openStream()` method to establish an HTTP socket connection with the web server specified by the URL. The method `openStream()` returns an `InputStream` object which can be used to read data from this HTTP socket. The following example displays the content of the URL `www.yahoo.com`.

```
//YahooURL.java
public class YahooURL {
   public static void main(String args[]) throws Exception {
      int c;
      java.net.URL yahoo = new java.net.URL("http://www.yahoo.com");
      java.io.InputStream in = yahoo.openStream();
      while (((c = in.read()) != -1))
         System.out.print((char) c);
```

```
        in.close();
    }
}
```

A sample output is shown in Figure 3.5.

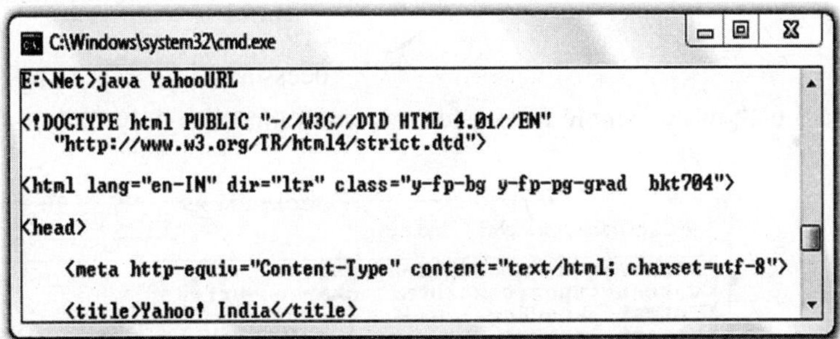

Figure 3.5 Web page retrieval using URL

The class `URL` allows us to only read the content of the URL. It does not allow us to apply other parts of the HTTP protocol, e.g. accessing the header. The class `URLConnection` provides mechanisms to access content as well as to inspect properties of the resource. These properties are HTTP specific and do not make any sense for protocols other than HTTP.

The class `URLConnection` represents an HTTP connection. The `openConnection()` method on a URL object establishes an HTTP socket connection to the web server and returns a `URLConnection` object that represents the connection. The method `getInputStream()` on this `URLConnection` object returns an `InputStream` object which can be used to read data from this HTTP socket. The following example does the same as the previous example:

```
//YahooURLConnection.java
public class YahooURLConnection {
    public static void main(String args[]) throws Exception {
        int c;
        java.net.URL yahoo = new java.net.URL("http://www.yahoo.com");
        java.net.URLConnection con = yahoo.openConnection();
        java.io.InputStream in = con.getInputStream();
        while (((c = in.read()) != -1))
            System.out.print((char) c);
        in.close();
    }
}
```

As mentioned earlier, `URLConnection` class also provides methods to retrieve information about the resource. The following example illustrates this:

```
//YahooURLProperties.java
import java.util.*;
public class YahooURLProperties {
    public static void main(String args[]) throws Exception {
        int c;
        java.net.URL yahoo = new java.net.URL("http://www.yahoo.com");
        java.net.URLConnection con = yahoo.openConnection();
```

```
            System.out.println("Content-type: " + con.getContentType());
            System.out.println("Content Encoding: " + con.getContentEncoding());
            System.out.println("Content-length: " + con.getContentLength());
            System.out.println("Last-Modified: " + new Date(con.getLastModified()));
            System.out.println("Date: " + new Date(con.getDate()));
            System.out.println("Expires: " + con.getExpiration());
            System.out.println("Connection Timeout: " + con.getConnectTimeout());
        }
    }
```

Figure 3.6 shows a sample output for this program.

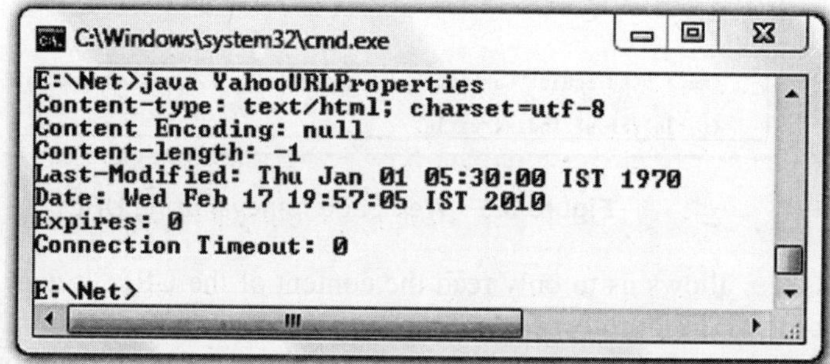

Figure 3.6 www.yahoo.com properties

If your client computer is connected to the Internet through an HTTP proxy, pass the information about the proxy server to the Java Runtime Environment. For example, if the proxy process runs at port `8080` in the machine having IP address `192.168.1.1`, use the following command:

```
java -DproxySet=true -DproxyHost=192.168.1.1 -DproxyPort=8080 YahooURLProperties
```

Alternatively, the same information can be specified in the client programs as follows:

```
System.setProperty("http.proxyHost", "192.168.1.1");
System.setProperty("http.proxyPort", "8080");
```

3.5.10 UDP Sockets

Communication with a server using TCP socket basically consists of two steps. First, create a channel with the server at the desired port. Then, send and receive data through this channel. This way, TCP sockets provide reliable communication of ordered stream of bytes. TCP provides this reliability and data ordering using complicated algorithms. Moreover, the performance of TCP in case of data loss or network congestion is not satisfactory.

UDP socket allows data communication using a different mechanism. In this case, no connection with the server socket is established prior to the communication. In the UDP style of data communication, data are send and received using containers called datagrams. The server program first creates a datagram socket and waits for the incoming datagrams.

A client, on the other hand, creates a datagram packet, specifies the IP address and the port number of the server, and puts it on the network. The datagram packet is then forwarded by possibly many intermediate hosts and eventually reaches at the server. However, UDP does not guarantee that the datagram will arrive at the server. It does not also assure that a process will really be there to accept the datagram. This style of communication is desired in some situations such as real-time applications.

3.5.10.1 Datagram packets

A datagram is represented in Java by `DatagramPacket` class and can be created using one of the following constructors:

```
DatagramPacket(byte[] data, int size);
DatagramPacket(byte[] data, int size, int offset);
DatagramPacket(byte[] data, int size, int offset, InetAddress address, int
port);
DatagramPacket(byte[] data, int size, int offset, SocketAddress socket)
DatagramPacket(byte[] data, int size, InetAddress address, int port);
DatagramPacket(byte[] data, int size, SocketAddress socket);
```

In our application, to receive the data, we shall use the first constructor. It takes an array of bytes where the data bytes are stored and the size of the packet. To send data, we shall use the third constructor. It takes four arguments. The first two argument are same as before. The rest two specify the address and port number of the target host, respectively. There are many methods available on the `DatagramPacket` object to get and set the internal properties of the packet.

3.5.10.2 Datagram server and client

Let us now develop our factorial application using UDP socket. The server first creates a `DatagramSocket` at port 5000 as follows:

```
DatagramSocket socket = new DatagramSocket(5000);
```

It then creates a `DatagramPacket` object where the incoming data will be stored.

```
byte[] rbuf = new byte[10];
DatagramPacket rpkt = new DatagramPacket(rbuf, rbuf.length);
```

To receive a `DatagramPacket`, it uses the `receive()` method on this socket.

```
socket.receive(rpkt);
```

The method `receive()` is a blocking one. The server comes up when a `DatagramPacket` arrives. It then extracts the data from this packet.

```
String data = new String(rpkt.getData(), 0, 0, rpkt.getLength());
```

The server extracts the address and port of number of the client, calculates the factorial of this data, and creates another packet with these information and sends this packet. Here is the complete source code for our UDP server `UDPFactServer.java`.

```
//UDPFactServer.java
import java.net.*;
import java.io.*;
public class UDPFactServer {
   public static void main(String args[]) throws Exception {
      byte[] rbuf = new byte[10], sbuf = new byte[10];
      //create a server socket at port 5000
      DatagramSocket socket = new DatagramSocket(5000);
      System.out.println("Server ready");
      DatagramPacket rpkt = new DatagramPacket(rbuf, rbuf.length);
```

```
            //receive a packet from client
            socket.receive(rpkt);
            //extract data and client information from this packet
            String data = new String(rpkt.getData(), 0, 0, rpkt.getLength());
            InetAddress addr = rpkt.getAddress();
            int port = rpkt.getPort();
            int fact = 1, n = Integer.parseInt(data);
            System.out.println("Received: " + n + " from " + addr + ":" + port);
            for (int i = 2; i <= n; i++)
               fact *= i;
            sbuf = String.valueOf(fact).getBytes();
            DatagramPacket spkt = new DatagramPacket(sbuf, sbuf.length, addr, port);
            //send result to the client
            socket.send(spkt);
            System.out.println("Sent: " + fact);

      }
   }
```

Our client first creates a `DatagramSocket` object.

```
DatagramSocket socket = new DatagramSocket();
```

Note that no port number or IP address of the server is specified here. This line of code does not create a channel to the server, it simply creates a socket that will be used to send and receive packets.

It then accepts an integer from the user and creates a `DatagramPacket` with this data. It also specifies the address and port number of the server. The client then sends the packet using the `send()` method on the `Socket` object. Whenever a reply comes, it extracts and prints the result. Here is the complete source code for the UDP client `UDPFactClient.java`.

```
//UDPFactClient.java
import java.net.*;
import java.io.*;
public class UDPFactClient {
   public static void main(String args[]) throws Exception {
      byte[] rbuf = new byte[1024], sbuf = new byte[1024];
      BufferedReader fromUser =
        new BufferedReader(new InputStreamReader(System.in));
      DatagramSocket socket = new DatagramSocket();
      InetAddress addr = InetAddress.getByName(args[0]);
      //get an integer from user
      System.out.print("Enter an integer: ");
      String data = fromUser.readLine();
      sbuf = data.getBytes();
      DatagramPacket spkt = new DatagramPacket(sbuf, sbuf.length, addr, 5000);
      //send it to server
      socket.send(spkt);
      System.out.println("Sent to server: " + data);
      DatagramPacket rpkt = new DatagramPacket(rbuf, rbuf.length);
      //retrieve result
      socket.receive(rpkt);
      data = new String(rpkt.getData(), 0, 0, rpkt.getLength());
      System.out.println("Received from server: " + data);
```

```
        //close the socket
        socket.close();
    }
}
```

Compile and run the programs as before. A sample output is shown in Figure 3.7.

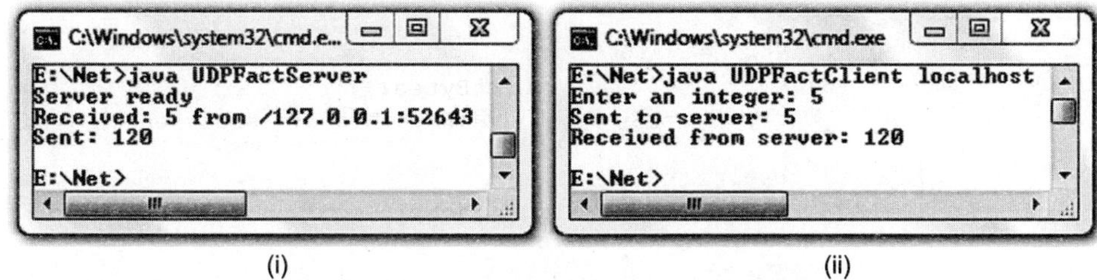

(i) (ii)

Figure 3.7 (i) UDPFactServer (ii) UDPFactClient

We can extend our UDP server so that it can handle multiple requests simultaneously. Here is the complete source code for our multithread UDP server stored in the file `UDPMTFactServer.java`.

```
import java.net.*;
import java.io.*;
public class UDPMTFactServer {
    public static void main(String args[]) throws Exception {
        //create a server socket at port 5000
        DatagramSocket socket = new DatagramSocket(5000);
        System.out.println("Server ready");
        while (true) {
            byte[] rbuf = new byte[10];
            DatagramPacket rpkt = new DatagramPacket(rbuf, rbuf.length);
            //receive a packet from client
            socket.receive(rpkt);
            System.out.println("Receiver a packet");
            //hand over this packet to Handler
            new Handler(rpkt, socket);
        }
    }
}

class Handler implements Runnable {
    DatagramSocket socket;
    DatagramPacket pkt;
    Handler(DatagramPacket pkt, DatagramSocket socket) {
        this.pkt = pkt;
        this.socket = socket;
        new Thread(this).start();
        System.out.println("A thread created");
    }
    public void run() {
        try {
            byte[] sbuf = new byte[10];
            //extract data and client information from this packet
```

```
            String data = new String(pkt.getData(), 0, 0, pkt.getLength());
            InetAddress addr = pkt.getAddress();
            int port = pkt.getPort();

            int fact = 1, n = Integer.parseInt(data);
            System.out.println("Received: " + n + " from " + addr + ":" + port);

            for (int i = 2; i <= n; i++)
               fact *= i;
            sbuf = String.valueOf(fact).getBytes();

            DatagramPacket spkt = new DatagramPacket(sbuf, sbuf.length, addr,
port);
            //send result to the client
            socket.send(spkt);
            System.out.println("Sent: " + fact);
         } catch (IOException e) { }
      }
}
```

To test our multithreaded server, we can write a UDP client as follows:

```
import java.net.*;
import java.io.*;
public class UDPMTFactClient {
   public static void main(String args[]) throws Exception {
      byte[] rbuf = new byte[1024], sbuf = new byte[1024];
      BufferedReader fromUser =
         new BufferedReader(new InputStreamReader(System.in));
      DatagramSocket socket = new DatagramSocket();
      InetAddress addr = InetAddress.getByName(args[0]);
      while(true) {
         //get an integer from user
         System.out.print("Enter an integer: ");
         String data = fromUser.readLine();
         sbuf = data.getBytes();
         DatagramPacket spkt = new DatagramPacket(sbuf, sbuf.length, addr,
5000);
         //send it to server
         socket.send(spkt);
         System.out.println("Sent to server: " + data);
         if(data.equals("-1")) break;
         DatagramPacket rpkt = new DatagramPacket(rbuf, rbuf.length);
         //retrieve result
         socket.receive(rpkt);
         data = new String(rpkt.getData(), 0, 0, rpkt.getLength());
         System.out.println("Received from server: " + data);
      }
      //close the socket
      socket.close();
      }
}
```

A sample output with two clients is shown in Figure 3.8.

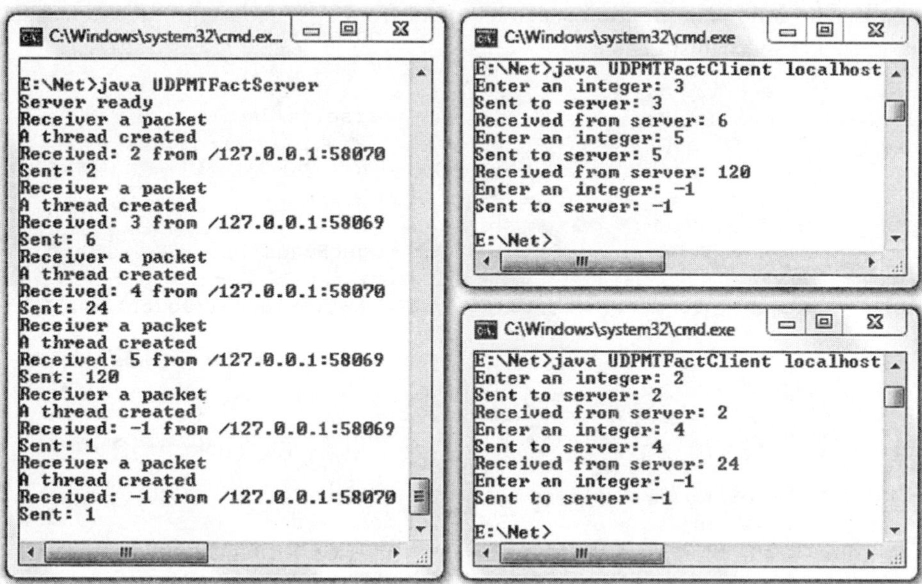

Figure 3.8 UDP multi-threaded server and clients

3.6 E-MAIL CLIENT

The **S**imple **M**ail **T**ransfer **P**rotocol (SMTP) is an application layer protocol in the TCP/IP protocol suite, which is used to send electronic mails (email). It uses TCP as its underlying transport layer protocol. The SMTP protocol specifies a set of commands and responses to send emails. A sample set of SMTP commands and responses to send an email is shown in Figure 3.9.

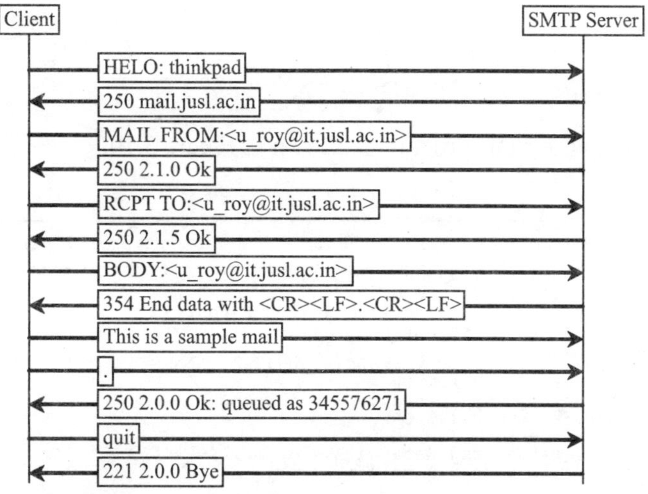

Figure 3.9 A typical SMTP message exchange

SMTP does not specify any user authorization procedure. This suggests us to establish a simple TCP socket to the server that implements the basic SMTP and gives commands to send emails. The following program sends an email from `u_roy@it.jusl.ac.in` to itself using the basic socket mechanism.

```
import java.io.*;
import java.net.*;
class MailClient {
   public static void main(String argv[]) throws Exception {
      int port = Integer.parseInt(argv[1]);
      BufferedReader inFromUser =
         new BufferedReader(new InputStreamReader(System.in));
      Socket clientSocket = new Socket(argv[0], port);
      if(clientSocket == null) System.out.println("error");
      else {
            System.out.println("connected to the server " + argv[0] + " at port
" + port);
         DataOutputStream outToServer =
         new DataOutputStream(clientSocket.getOutputStream());
         BufferedReader inFromServer =
      new BufferedReader(new InputStreamReader(clientSocket.getInputStream()));
         String[] out = { "HELO : thinkpad\n",
               "mail from: <u_roy@it.jusl.ac.in>\n",
               "rcpt to: <royuttam@gmail.com>\n",
               "data\n",
               "This is a sample mail\n.\n",
               "quit\n"
               };
         try {
            System.out.println("From server: " + inFromServer.readLine());
            for(int i = 0; i < out.length; i++) {
               outToServer.writeBytes(out[i]);
               System.out.print("To server: " + out[i]);
               System.out.println("From server: " + inFromServer.readLine());
            }
         }catch(Exception e) {clientSocket.close();}
      }
   }
}
```

A sample output for this program is shown in Figure 3.10.

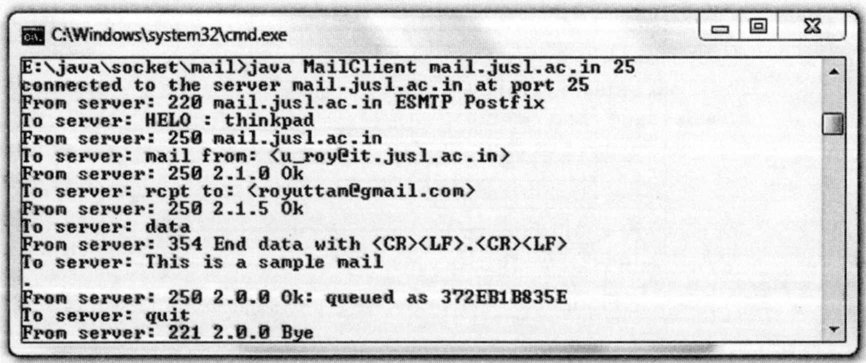

Figure 3.10 Sending email using Java TCP socket

Since the basic SMTP protocol does not provide any user authorization mechanism, a user who has an account in the mail server can send an email to any other user without any password verification. This makes the system vulnerable and must be avoided. So, an SMTP server runs an authorization protocol (typically Secure Socket Layer (SSL)) over the SMTP protocol. In this case, users are not allowed to connect to the SMTP port directly. A user typically connects to the SSL first and provides authorization information. The SSL starts the authorization procedure and if the user passes this authorization procedure, SSL forwards the request to the actual SMTP server. The entire procedure is tedious and sending emails using the basic socket mechanism is difficult.

Fortunately, Java provides API for different mail-related protocols such as SMTP, POP3, and IMAP. The necessary class files for Java mail API are provided as a separate jar file `mail.jar`, which can be downloaded from the following URL:

`http://java.sun.com/products/javamail/downloads/index.html.`

In this section, we shall discuss how to send mails using Java mail API. The following program sends a mail from the user `usr.some@gmail.com` to itself.

```
import java.util.Properties;
import javax.mail.*;
import javax.mail.internet.*;
public class EmailDemo {
   public static void main(String[] args) {
      String host = "smtp.gmail.com", port = "465";
      String userName = "usr.some@gmail.com", passWord = "some.usr";
      String subject = "test mail", text = "This is a test mail";
      String[] to = { "usr.some@gmail.com" };

      Properties props = new Properties();
      props.put("mail.smtp.host", host);
      props.put("mail.smtp.port", port);
      props.put("mail.from", userName);
      props.put("mail.smtp.starttls.enable", true);
      props.put("mail.smtp.auth", true);

   props.put("mail.smtp.socketFactory.class","javax.net.ssl.SSLSocketFactory");
      props.put("mail.smtp.socketFactory.port", port);
      props.put("mail.smtp.socketFactory.fallback", "false");

      try {
         Session session = Session.getDefaultInstance(props, null);
         session.setDebug(true);
         MimeMessage msg = new MimeMessage(session);
         msg.setSubject(subject);
         msg.setText(text);
         msg.setFrom();
         for(int i = 0; i < to.length; i++)
            msg.addRecipient(Message.RecipientType.TO, new
InternetAddress(to[i]));
         msg.saveChanges();
         Transport transport = session.getTransport("smtp");
```

```
                transport.connect(host, userName, passWord);
                transport.sendMessage(msg, msg.getAllRecipients());
                transport.close();
            }
            catch (Exception e) {
                e.printStackTrace();
            }
        }
    }
```

A sample output of this program is shown in Figure 3.11.

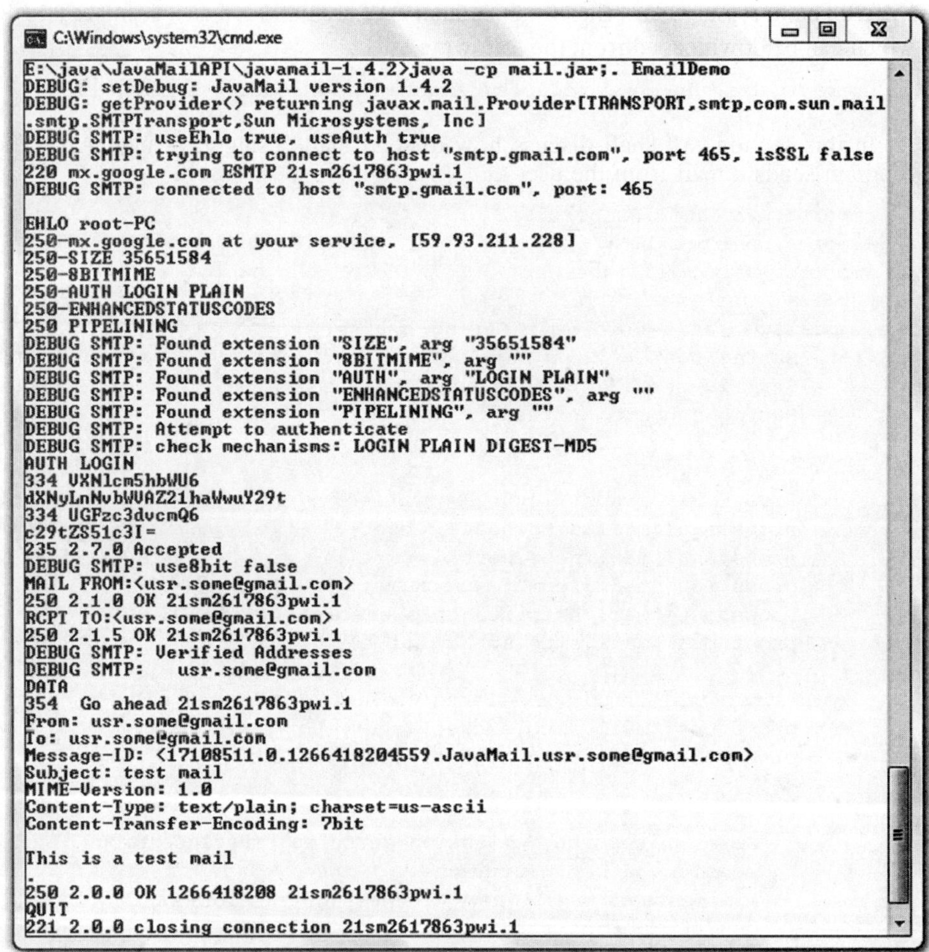

Figure 3.11 Sending email using Java mail API

3.7 POP3 PROGRAMS

POP is an acronym for **P**ost **O**ffice **P**rotocol. Its current version is 3.0 and is known as POP3. It is a standard protocol used to retrieve emails from remote mail servers. It allows us to download emails in local machine and read them offline. The POP3 is a simple request–response protocol. The following program shows how to retrieve the second mail from the inbox of the user `u_roy` in the mail server `mail.jusl.ac.in`.

```
import java.io.*;
import java.net.*;
class POP3Client {
   public static void main(String argv[]) throws Exception {
      int port = Integer.parseInt(argv[1]);
      BufferedReader inFromUser =
         new BufferedReader(new InputStreamReader(System.in));
      Socket clientSocket = new Socket(argv[0], port);
      if(clientSocket == null) System.out.println("error");
      else {
      System.out.println("connected to the server " + argv[0] + " at port
" + port);
         DataOutputStream outToServer =
         new DataOutputStream(clientSocket.getOutputStream());
         BufferedReader inFromServer =
          new BufferedReader(new
InputStreamReader(clientSocket.getInputStream()));
         String[] out = { "USER u_roy@it.jusl.ac.in\n",
                  "PASS 12345678\n",
                  "retr "+argv[2]+"\n",
                  "quit\n"
                  };
         try {
            System.out.println("From server: " + inFromServer.readLine());
            for(int i = 0; i < out.length; i++) {
               outToServer.writeBytes(out[i]);
               System.out.print("To server: " + out[i]);
               String result = inFromServer.readLine();
               System.out.println("From server: " + result);
               int sum = 0;
               int noc = 0;
               try {
                  noc = Integer.parseInt(result.substring(4,
result.indexOf('o')).trim());
                  do {
                     result = inFromServer.readLine();
                     System.out.println("From server: " + result);
                     sum += result.length()+2;
                  }while(sum <= noc);
               }catch(Exception e) {}
            }
         }catch(Exception e) {clientSocket.close();}
      }
   }
}
```

A sample output of this program is shown in Figure 3.12.

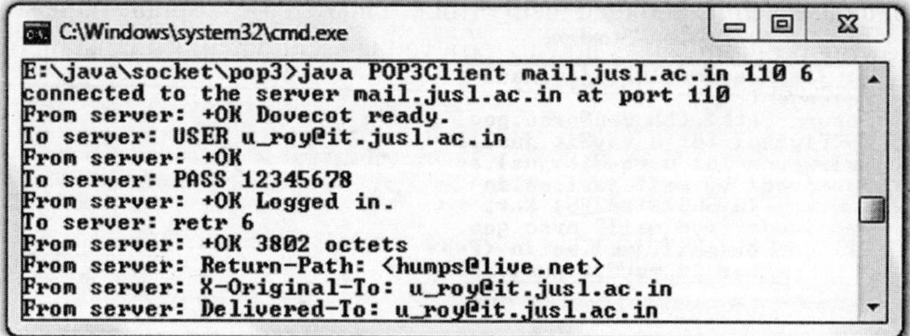

C:\Windows\system32\cmd.exe
E:\java\socket\pop3>java POP3Client mail.jusl.ac.in 110 6
connected to the server mail.jusl.ac.in at port 110
From server: +OK Dovecot ready.
To server: USER u_roy@it.jusl.ac.in
From server: +OK
To server: PASS 12345678
From server: +OK Logged in.
To server: retr 6
From server: +OK 3802 octets
From server: Return-Path: <humps@live.net>
From server: X-Original-To: u_roy@it.jusl.ac.in
From server: Delivered-To: u_roy@it.jusl.ac.in

Figure 3.12 Retrieving email using Java socket

The program uses the basic socket mechanism to retrieve email. Java mail API provides a rich set of classes and interfaces that can be used to retrieve emails very conveniently. The following program shows how to retrieve all emails of the user `u_roy` from the mail server `mail.jusl.ac.in` using Java mail API and POP3.

```
import java.util.Properties;
import javax.mail.*;
public class POP3Demo {
  public static void main(String[] args) throws Exception {
    Properties props = new Properties();
    String host = "mail.jusl.ac.in", provider = "pop3";
    String username = "u_roy@it.jusl.ac.in";
    String password = "12345678";
    Session session = Session.getDefaultInstance(props, null);
    Store store = session.getStore(provider);
    store.connect(host, username, password);
    Folder inbox = store.getFolder("Inbox");
    if (inbox != null) {
      inbox.open(Folder.READ_ONLY);
      Message[] emails = inbox.getMessages();
      for (int i = 0; i < emails.length; i++) {
        System.out.println("Message " + (i + 1));
        emails[i].writeTo(System.out);
      }
      inbox.close(false);
    }
    else
      System.out.println("Inbox not available");
    store.close();
  }
}
```

A sample output of this program is shown in Figure 3.13.

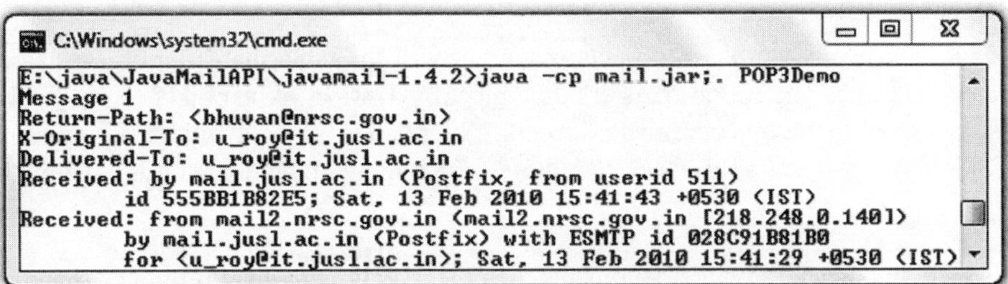

Figure 3.13 Retrieving email using Java mail API and POP3

3.8 REMOTE METHOD INVOCATION

Java **R**emote **M**ethod **I**nvocation (RMI) is an object-oriented **R**emote **P**rocedure **C**all (RPC) technique. It allows us to invoke methods on an object that exists in a different address space. This address space may exist on the same computer or even on a different computer connected to the source computer by a network. So, it enables objects, distributed in different computers, to communicate with one another. Figure 3.14 shows how methods on a remote object are invoked.

One of the important features of Java RMI is that it allows us to dynamically download the definition of object's class if the same is not available in the receiver's JVM. Figure 3.14 illustrates how classes are downloaded from a client to a server and from a server to a client using the URL protocol.

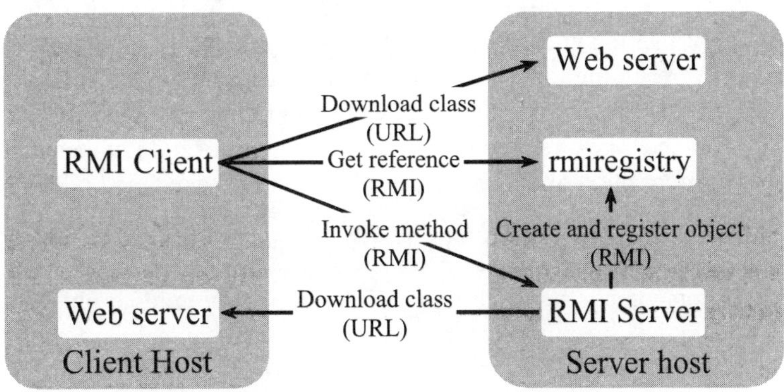

Figure 3.14 Dynamic class loading using RMI

3.8.1 Basic Idea

Three entities are basically involved in Java RMI: *server*, *client*, and *object registry*.

Server

This is a process that typically creates a remote object to be used for method invocation. This object is an ordinary object except that its class implements a Java RMI interface.

Object Registry

It is basically a table of objects. Each entry of the table maps the object name to its proxy known as stub. The server registers the object by a name to the object registry. Once the object is registered to the object registry successfully, it is said to be available for other programs use. Clients can now get a reference (handle) to the remote object and can invoke methods on it.

Client

A client program typically consults the object registry to get a reference (handle) to a remote object with a specified name. It can then invoke methods on the remote object using this reference (handle) as if the object is stored in the client's own address space. The RMI handles the details of communication between the client and the server.

3.8.2 Limitations

In Java RMI, we can only use two types of objects: Remote objects and Serializable objects.

A remote object is the one that implements remote interface. A remote interface has the following characteristics:

- It extends the interface `java.rmi.Remote`.
- Each method of the interface throws `java.rmi.RemoteException`.

There are other ways also to define a remote object. However, this form is the simplest and commonly used.

It is necessary to know how RMI handles remote and non-remote objects when transferring them from one JVM to another. For remote objects, the RMI system passes a representative of that object to the receiving JVM instead of passing the actual implementation. This representative acts like a proxy for the remote object in the client host and is known as *stub*. To invoke methods on the remote object, the client gets a reference to this stub and invokes methods on it. The stub has complete information about the actual object and invokes methods on the actual object on behalf of the client and returns the result (if any).

The class definition of stub for a remote object is created from the remote object's class definition. It implements the same remote interface as the remote object's class. The methods that are added to the object implementation later for its own tasks are not added to the stub. So, methods that are defined in the remote interface can only be called.

Not all the data can be copied from one JVM to another. Java RMI allows entities to be passed to and returned from a remote method if they are *serializable*. All instances of primitive data type, remote objects, and objects whose classes implement the `java.io.Serializable` interface are serializable. Most of the Java core classes implement the `java.io.Serializable` interface and hence object of these classes are serializable. Logically, an object is said to be serializable if it can be transformed into a byte stream and can be reconstructed successfully in another address space.

Some objects such as thread objects, file descriptors, database connection, and socket connection created in one address space do not make any sense in another address space. So, ideally they should not be allowed to pass to or return from a remote method. Indeed, these objects do not implement the `java.io.Serializable` interface and hence are not serializable.

Developing and running RMI applications consists of the following steps:

- Design and implement components
- Compile them
- Generate stub and skeleton
- Start the application

3.8.3 Design and Implement Components

This phase consists of the following steps:

Define a remote interface

First, we define an interface that contains methods that the server wishes to publish. This interface is made public so that clients come to know what methods (services) are available on this object. They can also identify the exact signature of the methods to be invoked.

Implement the remote interface

We then write a concrete class implementing one or more such remote interfaces. These classes may implement other interfaces or other methods may be added that can only be invoked locally. All classes that are used by these methods as parameters or return type must also be implemented.

Implement the server

Implementing a server application that creates an instance of the remote object and registers it to the RMI registry with a name is called *object deployment*. There are many ways to register an object to the RMI registry. We shall describe them separately later in this chapter.

Implement the client

A client application gets a handle to this remote object and invokes methods on it.

Compile them

Use Java compiler to compile all source files including interfaces and other subsidiary classes.

Generate stub and skeleton

To make the RMI technology work successfully, we need to generate the stub and the skeleton. The interface files and class file for stub must be kept in a network accessible place so that rmiregistry and clients can download the necessary files at runtime.

Start the application

First, start an object registry. In Java, the object registry is started using the application rmiregistry. Though it can also be created dynamically. Then start the server program. Finally, start the client program.

3.9 EXAMPLE

In this section, we shall develop a simple but elegant distributed application using RMI technology. In this application (Figure 3.15), the server creates a remote object called *scheduler,* which accepts jobs from the clients, executes these jobs locally, calculates the execution time, and finally returns the output as well as completion time. This way, clients can execute their jobs remotely on a powerful computer, or a computer having specialized hardware or one that has special permissions.

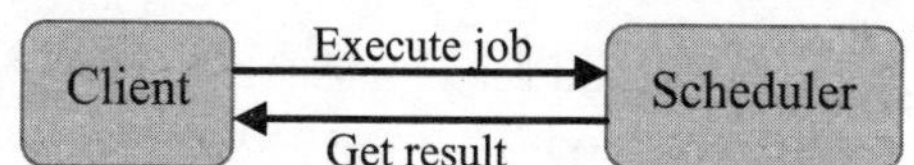

Figure 3.15 Remote job execution scenario

The interesting part of the application is that the scheduler does not have to define the jobs that it executes. Clients can create their custom jobs as and when required and submit them to the scheduler for execution. The only restriction imposed on a job is that its class must implement an interface defined by the scheduler. The class definition of a job can be downloaded at runtime from the client that submits the job using RMI technology. Once the class file is available, the scheduler can execute the job locally using its own resource.

How can a scheduler return the result to the client? If the result's class is a built-in class, the client already has the class definition and can use it easily. However, if the result's class is a scheduler-defined custom class, how can the client get it? Again there is no problem, since the client can download it from the server side and get the result. The only requirement of a result object is that its class implements an interface known to the client.

This way, the scheduler can execute arbitrary jobs without any prior knowledge of the job's class definition. Clients can also get the result without any prior knowledge of result's class definition. The Java RMI runtime environment will download the necessary class files from the specified location as and when required. This way, Java RMI allows us to change the behavior of an object and install it in a remote machine dynamically.

3.9.1 Writing an RMI Server

The server has three parts: scheduler interface, an implementation of that interface, and code that creates the scheduler object.

3.9.1.1 Write an interface

In this section, we shall describe the interface `Scheduler` that defines the client's view of the remote object. It provides a description of what methods are available on the remote object and how to invoke them. The server creates an object whose class implements and publishes this interface. The client makes use of this interface to know the details of services that the object provides. This way, the `Scheduler` interface makes a connection between the server and the client. Here is the source code (`Scheduler.java`) for the `Scheduler` interface.

```
package intf;

import java.rmi.Remote;
import java.rmi.RemoteException;

public interface Scheduler extends Remote {
    Result run(Job aJob) throws RemoteException;
}
```

This interface extends the interface `java.rmi.Remote` and hence becomes a remote interface. Any object, whose class implements this interface, is a remote object whose methods can be invoked from another JVM.

The interface has a single method `run()` that throws an exception `java.rmi.RemoteException` and hence becomes a remote method. This is the method that clients will use to submit their jobs.

It throws the exception `java.rmi.RemoteException` when a protocol error or communication error occurs. The exception `java.rmi.RemoteException` is a checked exception. So, the code that calls this method must handle this exception by either catching it explicitly or re-throwing it.

This interface uses two other interfaces `Job` and `Result`. The interface `Job` defines the structure of a job to be submitted by the client. Here is the source code (`Job.java`) for the `Job` interface.

```
package intf;
public interface Job {
  String run();
}
```

The `Job` interface defines a single method `run()` that actually executes the job and returns the result as a `String`. The class of every job submitted by clients must implement this interface and must define the `run()` method. The scheduler must download this class definition to execute the job locally.

The `Result` interface describes the structure of the result returned by the scheduler. Here is the source code (`Result.java`) for the `Result` interface.

```
package intf;
public interface Result {
  String output();
  double completionTime();
}
```

It defines two methods, `output()` and `completionTime()`. The methods `output()` and `completionTime()` return output and execution time of the job, respectively. The `Result` object's class must implement this interface. The client must download this `Result` object's class definition to get the result.

Java's *object serialization* procedure is used by RMI to transfer objects. Consequently, objects that are transferred across different JVM must be *serializable*. An object is said to be *serializable* if its class implements the `java.io.Serializable` interface. The interface `java.io.Serializable` does not define anything, it just specifies that the object of the class is serializable. So, classes that implement `Job` and `Result` must implement the `java.io.Serializable` interface.

3.9.1.2 Implement the interface

In this section, we describe how to write a class implementing a remote interface. Writing a remote class consists of the following steps:

- Define the class by implementing the remote interface.
- Define a constructor for the remote class.
- Implement all methods declared in the remote interface.

The server defines two classes: `SchedulerImpl` and `ResultImpl`, which implements remote interfaces `Scheduler` and `Result`, respectively. Here is the source code (`ResultImpl.java.`) for the `ResultImpl` class.

```
package impl;
import java.io.Serializable;
import intf.Result;
public class ResultImpl implements Result, Serializable {
   String output;
   double completionTime;
   public ResultImpl(String o, double c) {
      output = o;
      completionTime = c;
   }
   public String output() { return output; }
   public double completionTime() { return completionTime; }
}
```

An object of this class represents the result of a job in terms of its output and completion time. This result object, generated by the scheduler, will be transferred to the client side and hence must be serializable. This object is indeed serializable as its class implements the `Serializable` interface. The definition of `ResultImpl` must be downloaded to the client side to reconstruct the result object.

Here is the source code (`SchedulerImpl.java.`) for the `SchedulerImpl` class.

```
package impl;
import java.rmi.RemoteException;
import intf.*;
public class SchedulerImpl implements Scheduler {
   public SchedulerImpl() {
      super();
   }
   public Result run(Job aJob) throws RemoteException {
      double startTime = System.nanoTime();
      String output = aJob.run();
      double endTime = System.nanoTime();
      return new ResultImpl(output, endTime-startTime);
   }
}
```

In the `run()` method of the scheduler object, the job is executed. Note that the class for job object is defined by the client. As a result, the scheduler does not have any idea about the job. So, it simply calls the `run()` method on the job object. The server must download the class definition of the job object from the client side before calling the `run()` method. It calculates the execution time, creates a result object, and returns it.

3.9.1.3 Implement the server

A server first creates an instance of the `SchedulerImpl` class using the usual syntax as follows:

```
SchedulerImpl scheduler = new SchedulerImpl();
```

This object is then exported to the RMI runtime so that it can accept the incoming remote method call. This is done using the static `exportObject()` method on the `UnicastRemoteObject` class as follows:

```
Scheduler stub = (Scheduler) UnicastRemoteObject.exportObject(scheduler, 0);
```

The `exportObject()` method essentially creates and installs a proxy for the `scheduler` object at the server end. This proxy is known as *skeleton*. The task of the skeleton is to listen for the incoming remote method call on behalf of this `scheduler` object on the TCP port specified by the second argument. Usually, the port is specified as 0 which indicates the anonymous port. In this case, the actual port number is chosen by RMI or an underlying operating system at runtime.

Whenever a request for method call comes to this skeleton, it unpacks the request to obtain the method name and arguments to be used for this method. This procedure is called *un-marshalling*. Note that the object and its skeleton belong to the same JVM and skeleton has also reference to this local object. So, skeleton can invoke the desired method on the actual object and get the result. It then packs (called *marshalling*) the result and sends it back to the sender.

The method `exportObject()` creates and returns another proxy for this object to be uploaded to the object registry. This proxy is called *stub*. The stub knows the port the skeleton listens on as well as IP address of the computer. The object registry essentially provides this stub object on request. The type of this stub must be `Scheduler`, not the `SchedulerImpl`. This is because stub for a remote object (`SchedulerImpl` in this case) implements the interface (`Scheduler`) which is implemented by the exported object.

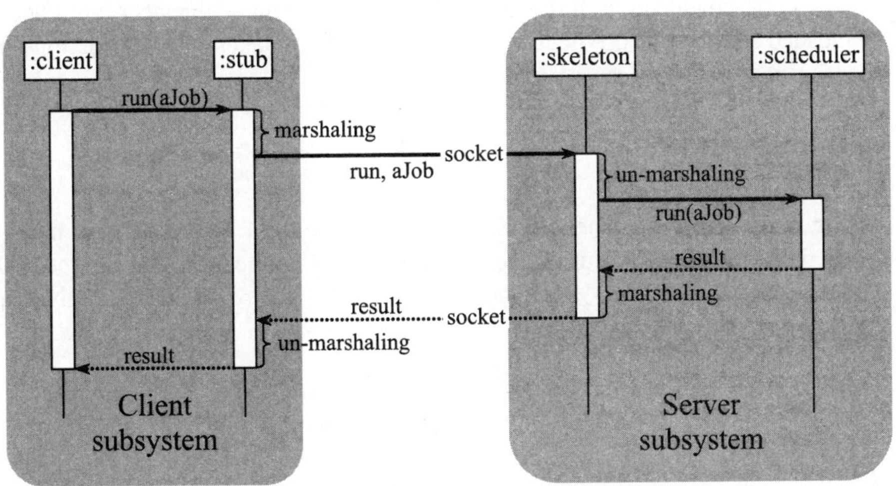

Figure 3.16 Java RMI framework

To register this stub with the object registry, we need to have a reference to object registry. A new object registry may be created or an existing one may be used. The class `java.rmi.registry.LocateRegistry` provides many static methods for this purpose. In our example, we shall use an existing object registry which can be started using the `rmiregistry` application provided by JVM. Java RMI only allows us to run rmiregistry and server in the same computer currently. The following code is used to get a reference to an existing object registry which is running on the same computer on default port (1099). Specify the port number to the `getRegistry()` method, if object registry runs on a port other than 1099.

```
Registry registry = LocateRegistry.getRegistry();
```

The stub is then registered with object registry as follows:

```
String name = "Scheduler";
registry.rebind(name, stub);
```

The stub hereafter known by its name 'Scheduler' is used by the clients. When a client requests the object registry to have a reference to the remote object, the stub for the remote object is passed. The client-side application that contacted the object registry creates and installs an instance of this stub in the client's computer and returns a reference to the client. Client basically invokes methods on this local stub object. As mentioned earlier, this stub has complete information about the skeleton, which is object's server side proxy. The stub creates a socket to the skeleton. It packs the information such as the method name to be invoked, parameters, etc. This is called *marshalling*. The stub then sends the packed data to the skeleton through the socket. The skeleton then un-marshals the data and follows the steps as mentioned previously. The entire execution sequence is shown in Figure 3.16.

The entire piece of code is embedded in a try–catch block.

Since class files of the Job will be downloaded to the Scheduler, it is always safe to install a security manager that will protect access to the system resources by this downloaded code. If the code upon download performs any operation, the security manager will check whether the downloaded code has the privilege to do that operation and takes necessary actions. The following code is used to install a security manager:

```
if (System.getSecurityManager() == null) {
  System.setSecurityManager(new SecurityManager());
}
```

A security policy must be specified which will be used by the security manager. We shall specify the security policy during the execution of the application. The source code for `Server` is stored in the file `Server.java`. The source code for the `Server` class is given as follows:

```
package impl;
import java.rmi.registry.LocateRegistry;
import java.rmi.registry.Registry;
import java.rmi.server.UnicastRemoteObject;
import intf.*;
import impl.*;
public class Server {
   public static void main(String[] args) {
      if (System.getSecurityManager() == null) {
         System.setSecurityManager(new SecurityManager());
      }
      try {
         SchedulerImpl scheduler = new SchedulerImpl();
         Scheduler stub = (Scheduler)
UnicastRemoteObject.exportObject(scheduler, 0);
```

```
            Registry registry = LocateRegistry.getRegistry();
            String name = "Scheduler";
            registry.rebind(name, stub);
            System.out.println("SchedulerImpl bound");
        } catch (Exception e) {
            System.err.println("SchedulerImpl exception:");
            e.printStackTrace();
        }
    }
}
```

3.9.2 Writing a Client

A client gets a reference to the scheduler and submits jobs. However, the client must define the job to be executed by the scheduler. Here we shall define a simple job that calculates the factorial of a number. In practice, clients submit computationally intensive jobs to the server for execution. The class definition of `Factorial` is shown as follows:

```
package impl;
import intf.*;
import java.io.Serializable;
public class Factorial implements Job, Serializable {
    int n;
    public Factorial(int v) {
        n = v;
    }
    public String run() {
        int result = 1;
        for(int i = 2; i <= n; i++)
            result *= i;
        return String.valueOf(result);
    }
}
```

The `Factorial` class implements the `Job` interface. Its `run()` method calculates and returns the factorial of a specified integer. When a client submits such a `Factorial` job object to the remote scheduler, the object is transferred to the scheduler using Java's serialization procedure. So, `Factorial` job object must be serializable. Since the `Factorial` class implements the `Serializable` interface, objects of the `Factorial` class are indeed serializable.

To reconstruct the `Factorial` job object in the `Scheduler` object's JVM, job object's class definition is needed. The RMI system downloads the class definition of `Factorial` on behalf of the `Scheduler` object. The client must specify the location where the RMI system can find the object's class definition. Now, `Scheduler` object's `run()` method is invoked which, in turn, invokes `Factorial` object's `run()` method where the job is executed.

Clients may also submit other jobs to the remote `Scheduler` object. The `Scheduler` executes these jobs using the same procedure described. It need not know each job's implementation procedure. It only knows that each job it receives implements the `Job` interface and has the method `run()`.

Let us now write the code for the client. The client will first get a reference to the remote registry using the `LocateRegistry.getRegistry()` method as follows:

```
Registry registry = LocateRegistry.getRegistry(args[0]);
```

The argument to the `getRegistry()` method is the first command line argument `args[0]` which is the name or IP address of the computer where the registry runs on the default port (`1099`). If the registry runs on a port other than `1099`, you specify the port as the second argument to the `getRegistry()` method.

The client then uses the `lookup()` method on this registry to get a reference to the remote `Scheduler` object as follows:

```
String name = "Scheduler";
Scheduler scheduler = (Scheduler) registry.lookup(name);
```

Note that the client uses the same name that the server uses to export the object. The lookup method consults the remote registry, downloads the stub for the `Scheduler` object having the name "Scheduler" specified as argument. It then creates and installs an instance of the stub and returns a reference to the client. The reference `scheduler` is actually a local reference to the stub. This stub sits behind the scene and behaves as a proxy of the remote `Scheduler` object. When client invokes a method using the `scheduler` reference, a similar method invocation on stub occurs. The stub then creates a TCP socket connection with the skeleton and sends the request. When the result comes back from the skeleton, the stub returns the result to the client. The underlying procedure is transparent to the client.

To submit a task, the client has to create an instance of the `Factorial` object.

```
Factorial aJob = new Factorial(Integer.parseInt(args[1]));
```

The second command line argument, after converting it to an integer, is passed to the `Factorial` constructor. This argument indicates the integer whose factorial has to be calculated. The client can now submit the job to the remote object for execution.

```
Result r = scheduler.run(aJob);
```

The result of job execution is stored in the `Result` object. Remember that the `Result` interface was implemented by the server. So, the client does not have the definition of `Result` object's class. The RMI system will download the necessary class definition from the location as specified by the server. So, the client can invoke methods on this `Result` object to get the desired result and other information such as completion time.

```
System.out.println("Execution time = " + r.completionTime() + " micro sec(s)");
```

The entire piece of code is embedded in a try–catch block to handle the error that may occur at runtime. A security manager should also be installed to protect the system as `Result` object's class definition is downloaded in the client's JVM.

Here is the complete source code for the client which is stored in `Client.java`.

```
package impl;
import java.rmi.registry.LocateRegistry;
import java.rmi.registry.Registry;
import intf.*;
import impl.*;
public class Client {
```

```
    public static void main(String args[]) {
        if (System.getSecurityManager() == null) {
            System.setSecurityManager(new SecurityManager());
        }
        try {
            Registry registry = LocateRegistry.getRegistry(args[0]);
            String name = "Scheduler";
            Scheduler scheduler = (Scheduler) registry.lookup(name);
            Factorial aJob = new Factorial(Integer.parseInt(args[1]));
            Result r = scheduler.run(aJob);
            System.out.println(args[1] + "! = " + r.output());
            System.out.println("Execution time = " + r.completionTime() + "
micro sec(s)");
        } catch (Exception e) {
            e.printStackTrace();
        }
    }
}
```

3.9.3 Compiling the Program

In practice, the server should deploy the necessary files for a client program to use. In our case the client must have a `Scheduler`, `Job`, and `Result` interface. The client also needs the `Result` object's class (`ResultImpl` in this case) definition which will be downloaded by the RMI system from the location specified by the server at runtime. So, server must deploy these four classes.

The server will then write the implementation of `Scheduler` and `Result` interfaces and deploy an object in a computer accessible by the clients. The client programmers can then download the necessary class files and develop their applications which will use the `Scheduler` object.

All the files are packaged as follows:

Server machine

intf: `Scheduler, Job, Result`

impl: `SchedulerImpl, ResultImpl, Server`

Client machine

impl: `Factorial, Client`

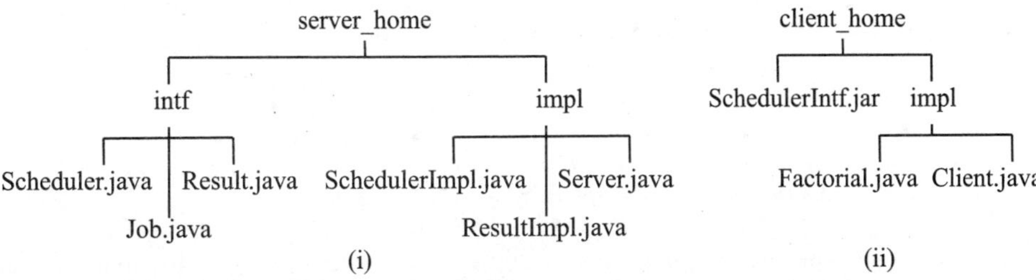

Figure 3.17 Directory configuration for scheduler (i) server (ii) client

Suppose developer of the server is developing an application in the directory "E:\Net\rmi\scheduler\server" of a computer having IP address 192.168.1.2. Hereafter, we shall refer to this directory as server_home. Create the directory structure and put server-side files as shown in Figure 3.17(i).

3.9.3.1 Creating interface classes

Go to the directory server_home. Give the following command to compile the interface source files and generate a jar file (SchedulerIntf.jar) containing the generated interface class files.

```
javac intf\*.java
jar cvf schedulerIntf.jar intf\*.class
```

Make sure that the directory containing the java compiler is included in your PATH environment variable. The jar command will generate the following output:

```
added manifest
adding: intf/Job.class(in = 129) (out= 112)(deflated 13%)
adding: intf/Result.class(in = 167) (out= 143)(deflated 14%)
adding: intf/Scheduler.class(in = 222) (out= 169)(deflated 23%)
```

This SchedulerIntf.jar file is needed by the client to develop its own application. This file must be put in a network accessible place so that the client can access it. For example, it can be put on a web server accessible by the client.

3.9.3.2 Compiling server

The impl package contains three source files: SchedulerImpl.java, ResultImpl.java, and Server.java. SchedulerImpl.java is the implementation of the Scheduler interface, ResultImpl.java is the implementation of the Result interface, and Server.java creates and exports the Scheduler object. Use the following command to compile these source files.

```
javac impl\*.java
```

The stub and skeleton for SchedulerImpl implements the Scheduler interface which refers to the Job and Result interfaces. So, Java's object registry needs the definition for these interfaces. Remember, the class definition of the Result interface is needed by the client. So, create a jar file containing these four classes and put it in a network accessible place. Give the following command to create the jar file scheduler.jar:

```
jar cvf scheduler.jar intf\*.class impl\ResultImpl.class
```

This generates the following sample output:

```
added manifest
adding: intf/Job.class(in = 129) (out= 112)(deflated 13%)
adding: intf/Result.class(in = 167) (out= 143)(deflated 14%)
adding: intf/Scheduler.class(in = 222) (out= 169)(deflated 23%)
adding: impl/ResultImpl.class(in = 688) (out= 417)(deflated 39%)
```

To deploy this jar file, we shall use Apache's tomcat web server running in the server computer (IP address is 192.168.1.2) on a port 8080. Put this jar file in the web server's document root. So, the URL of this jar file will be http://192.168.1.2:8080/scheduler.jar. We shall specify this URL while running the server application.

3.9.3.3 Compiling client

Suppose client application is developed in another computer having IP address 192.168.1.3 in the directory `E:\Net\rmi\scheduler\client` which we shall refer to as `client_home`. Create the directory structure and put client-side files as shown in Figure 3.17(ii).

First download the `SchedulerIntf.jar` file from a location specified by the server and put it in the directory `client_home`. In the client computer, there are two files in the impl package `Factorial.java` and `Client.java`. `Factorial.java` is the implementation of the `Job` interface. The `Client.java` gets a reference of the `Scheduler` object and invokes the `run()` method using this reference. Give the following command to compile source files:

```
javac -cp schedulerIntf.jar;. impl/*.java
```

Note that the server needs the implementation of the `Job` interface, i.e., `Factorial` class in our case which will be downloaded by the Java RMI system. However, the client must specify the location of this class file. In the client application, we shall again use Apache's tomcat server to deploy the `Factorial` class. Configure the tomcat web server and put the `Factorial.class` in the document root so that the RMI system can download this file whenever necessary. The base URL of this class file is `http://192.168.1.3:8080/`. We shall specify this URL while running the client application.

3.9.4 Running the Application

Remember, we had installed a security manager in the `Server.java` and `Client.java` applications. When we run these applications, we must specify a security policy for them. In this case we shall specify the policy as a file in the command line argument. Create a file `server.policy` in the `server_home` directory. The content of the file looks like this:

```
grant codeBase "file:/E:/Net/rmi/scheduler/server" {
    permission java.security.AllPermission;
};
```

Similarly, create another file `client.policy` in the directory `client_home` with the following content:

```
grant codeBase "file:/E:/Net/rmi/scheduler/client" {
    permission java.security.AllPermission;
};
```

Before starting the server application, we need to start an object registry. In Java RMI, it is started using the `rmiregistry` command. So, open a terminal and type the following command:

```
rmiregistry
```

The command does not generate any output; it starts the object registry application on the default port 1099. Give the following command to start the server:

```
java -Djava.rmi.server.codebase=http://192.168.1.2:8080/scheduler.jar
    -Djava.security.policy=server.policy
     impl.Server
```

It produces a sample output as shown in Figure 3.18.

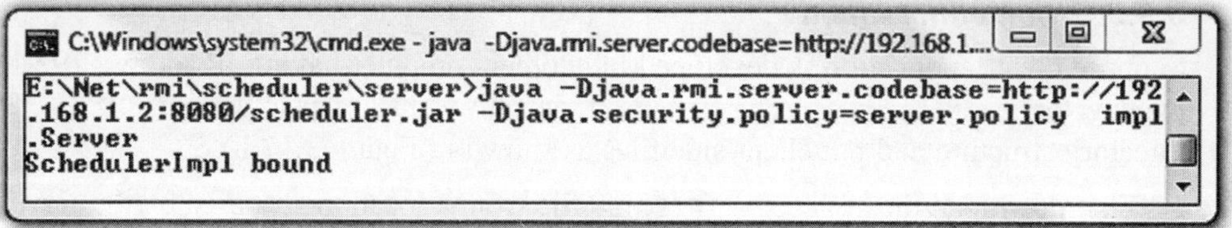
C:\Windows\system32\cmd.exe - java -Djava.rmi.server.codebase=http://192.168.1....

```
E:\Net\rmi\scheduler\server>java -Djava.rmi.server.codebase=http://192
.168.1.2:8080/scheduler.jar -Djava.security.policy=server.policy impl
.Server
SchedulerImpl bound
```

Figure 3.18 RMI server

3.9.5 Start Client

Give the following command to start the client:

```
java -cp ./schedulerIntf.jar;.
     -Djava.rmi.server.codebase=http://192.168.1.3:8080/
     -Djava.security.policy=client.policy
      impl.Client 192.168.1.2 5
```

It produces a sample output as shown in Figure 3.19.

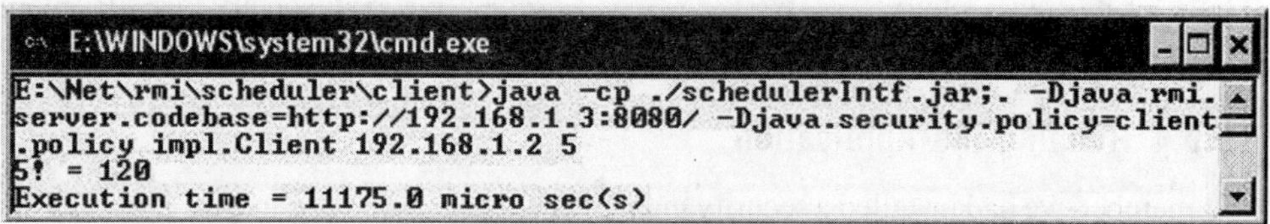
E:\WINDOWS\system32\cmd.exe

```
E:\Net\rmi\scheduler\client>java -cp ./schedulerIntf.jar;. -Djava.rmi.
server.codebase=http://192.168.1.3:8080/ -Djava.security.policy=client
.policy impl.Client 192.168.1.2 5
5! = 120
Execution time = 11175.0 micro sec(s)
```

Figure 3.19 RMI client

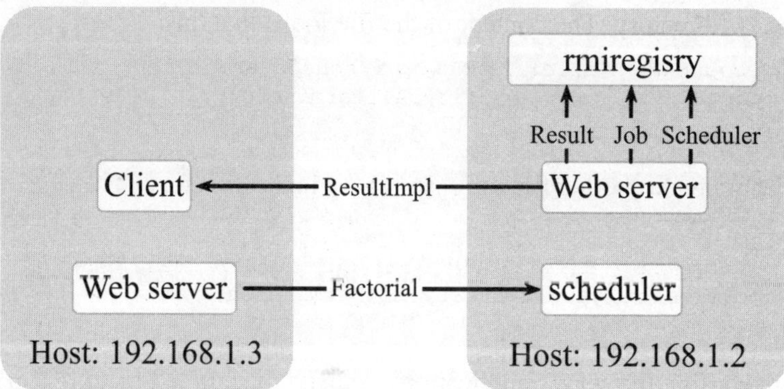

Figure 3.20 Scheduler runtime environment

Figure 3.20 illustrates where Client, rmiregistry, and scheduler find necessary classes at runtime.

3.9.6 Using RMI URL

In our scheduler example, server exports and registers a remote object using a tedious procedure. The client also gets a reference to the remote object using a long method. Java RMI provides a simple addressing mechanism, known as RMI URL, that may be used by the server as well as the client for the same purpose.

The server application creates an object and registers it to the RMI registry using the static `rebind()` method of the `java.rmi.Naming` class. The server must specify the port number of RMI registry application and the IP address or name of the computer where it runs. The server must also specify a logical name by which the object will be known to clients. Clients use this name to get a reference to this object.

The entire information may be encapsulated using RMI URL. It is similar to the HTTP URL (see Chapter 2) except that it uses "rmi" as the protocol name. It takes the following form:

```
rmi://host:[port]/objectName
```

The `host` is the IP address or Fully Qualified Domain Name (FQDN) of the computer where the RMI registry runs. The optional `port` is the port number of the RMI registry. The default port number is `1099`. The `objectName` is a logical name of the object. For example, if RMI registry runs in a computer having IP address `192.168.1.2` on port `2000`, and object name is `myObject`, the RMI URL for this object will be as follows:

```
protocol    host        port   name
rmi://192.168.1.2:2000/Scheduler
```

If RMI registry runs on default port (1099), this URL reduces to

```
rmi://192.168.1.2/Scheduler
```

If RMI registry and server run on the same computer, this URL further reduces to

```
Scheduler
```

Since, Java RMI only supports to run RMI registry and server on the same computer, the URL of our remote object is simply `Scheduler`.

Now, create an object and register it using the `Naming.rebind()` method as follows:

```
String url = "Scheduler";
SchedulerImpl scheduler = new SchedulerImpl();
java.rmi.Naming.rebind(url, scheduler);
```

The class definition of `SchedulerImpl` needs to be modified slightly in this case as follows:

```
package impl;
import java.rmi.RemoteException;
import intf.*;
import java.rmi.server.UnicastRemoteObject;
public class SchedulerImpl extends UnicastRemoteObject implements Scheduler {
   public SchedulerImpl() throws RemoteException {
      super();
   }
   public Result run(Job aJob) throws RemoteException {
      double startTime = System.nanoTime();
      String output = aJob.run();
      double endTime = System.nanoTime();
      return new ResultImpl(output, endTime-startTime);
   }
}
```

Here is the modified source code of `Server.Java`.

```
package impl;
import intf.*;
import impl.*;
public class Server {
   public static void main(String[] args) {
      if (System.getSecurityManager() == null) {
         System.setSecurityManager(new SecurityManager());
      }
      try {
         SchedulerImpl scheduler = new SchedulerImpl();
         String url = "Scheduler";
         java.rmi.Naming.rebind(url, scheduler);
         System.out.println("SchedulerImpl bound");
      } catch (Exception e) {
         System.err.println("SchedulerImpl exception:");
         e.printStackTrace();
      }
   }
}
```

The `Naming.rebind()` method registers the scheduler object with the name "Scheduler" to the registry running on the same machine on the default port. Note that the `Naming.rebind()` method does not create a stub and a skeleton. In this case, we have to create the stub and the skeleton of the Scheduler implementation explicitly using `rmic` compiler as follows:

```
rmic impl.SchedulerImpl
```

In Java 2, it generates the single file `SchedulerImpl_Stub.class` that acts as a stub as well as a skeleton. You should include this file in the `scheduler.jar` file

```
jar cvf scheduler.jar intf\*.class impl\ResultImpl.class
impl\SchedulerImpl_Stub.class
```

You can now start the rmiregistry and server as before.

The client application can also make use of RMI URL to get a reference. We are assuming that the RMI registry will run on the default port. So, the URL of the remote object for the client looks like this:

```
String url = "rmi://" + args[0] + "/Scheduler";
```

The name of the object is "Scheduler". The first command line argument args[0] is the IP address or Fully Qualified Domain Name (FQDN) of the server.

```
Scheduler scheduler = (Scheduler) java.rmi.Naming.lookup(url);
```

The rest of the client code is the same. Compile the code and start the client application as before.

KEYWORDS

Client Socket: Client-side end point of the socket.

Datagram Packet: Data container used to send and receive information by UDP.

IP address: A 32-bit address used by the IP layer of the TCP/IP protocol suite to identify a host uniquely.

Object registry: A database that keeps the information about objects and provides a reference to the remote object on request.

POP3: The Post Office Protocol version 3, used to retrieve emails from a mail server.

Port address: A locally unique positive integer assigned to a process to identify it within the computer uniquely.

Remote Interface: The interface of a remote object used to publish the prototypes of methods on a remote object.

Remote Method: Methods on a remote object that can be called by remote clients.

Remote Object: An object created and exported by a server in such a way that remote clients can invoke methods on it.

Reserved ports: Some predefined port numbers allocated to some processed.

RMI: A Java mechanism of Remote Procedure Call (RPC) used to invoke methods on a remote object.

Serialization: The procedure to converting an object to byte stream used by the Java RMI mechanism.

Server Socket: Server-side end point of the socket.

Skeleton: An object that resides at the server computer and acts as a proxy of the remote server object.

SMTP: A standard protocol used to send emails from a mail server.

Socket address: A socket address of a process consists of the port number of the process and the computer where it is running. It can be thought of as a channel connecting two entities.

Stub: An object that resides at the client computer and acts as a proxy of the remote server object.

TCP socket: A channel is established between the client and the server prior to the communication.

UDP socket: In this type of socket, no dedicated channel is established prior to the communication.

URL Connection: It represents an HTTP connection established with a web server.

URL: An address used to identity a resource typically on the web.

SUMMARY

Java, like other programming languages, provides well-designed classes and interfaces (APIs) for network programming. The class NetworkInterface is used to retrieve most of the information about the installed network devices.

One of the central ideas of network computing is the client–server model. Many networking applications including Internet's primary protocols such as HTTP, SMTP, DNS, etc. use this model. In this programming paradigm, there are two basic components: service providers, known as servers and service requesters, known as clients. Java allows us to write such client–server programs using TCP as well as UDP sockets.

In the TCP socket, a client establishes a connection to the server socket and sends and receives data through this connection. In the UDP socket data are sent and received in terms of datagrams. Datagrams are containers of data. The client creates a datagram and mentions the socket address of the target host and sends the datagram. The datagram is then forwarded typically by many intermediate routers and eventually reaches its destination host. A UDP socket does not guarantee that the packets will be delivered to the target host, while TCP does. The UDP socket allows us to send packets to the server even if the server is not available at that time but will be up soon.

A server is typically a multithreaded program. For every request that the server process receives, a new thread is created where the new request is handed over while the server goes to the listening state again.

The concept of socket can be used to send emails programmatically using the SMTP protocol. Note that the basic SMTP does not provide user authentication. So, traditional socket programming fails to work if SMTP server does not support the basic SMTP.

Post Office Protocol version 3 is a standard protocol to retrieve emails from a SMTP server. Java's mail API also supports POP3. POP3 is a simple protocol that consists of a set of commands and responses.

Java Remote Method Invocation (RMI) is an object-oriented Remote Procedure Call (RPC) technique. It allows us to invoke methods on a remote object. One of the important features of Java RMI is that it allows us to dynamically download the definition of object's class if the same is not available in the receiver's JVM. Similarly, it also allows the client to upload an object's implementation to the server dynamically if it is not available on the server. Primarily four components are involved in a Java RMI application: an interface, its implementation, a server programs that creates and exports a remote object, and a client which gets a reference on a remote object and invokes method on it. Java RMI uses a mechanism very much similar to the URL to access remote objects.

WEB RESOURCES

http://www.ietf.org/rfc/rfc1939.txt
Post Office Protocol - Version 3

http://www.ietf.org/rfc/rfc2821.txt
Simple Mail Transfer Protocol

http://java.sun.com/javase/technologies/core/basic/rmi/index.jsp
Remote Method Invocation

http://java.sun.com/docs/books/tutorial/networking/sockets/
Lesson: All About Sockets

EXERCISES

Multiple Choice Questions

1. Which of the following statements is used by the server to listen for a connection request from a client?
   (a) Socket s = serverSocket.listen();
   (b) Socket s = serverSocket.wait();
   (c) Socket s = serverSocket.getSocket();
   (d) Socket s = serverSocket.accept();

2. Which of the following is used by a client to establish a socket connection with the server?
   (a) Socket s = serverSocket.getSocket();
   (b) Socket s = serverSocket.accept();
   (c) Socket s = new Socket(ServerName, port);
   (d) Socket s = serverSocket.connect();

3. What happens when a server uses a port to bind an object, but the port is not available?
   (a) the object is bound successfully.
   (b) the server is blocked until the port is available.
   (c) the server encounters a fatal error and must be terminated.
   (d) the exception java.net.BindException occurs.

4. What happens when a client requests connection to a server that has not yet started?
   (a) the exception java.net.ConnectionException occurs.
   (b) the client gets blocked until the server is started.
   (c) the exception java.net.BindException occurs.
   (d) the client encounters a fatal error and must be terminated.

5. Which of the following is used to get an InetAddress object on a socket object skt.
   (a) skt.obtainInetAddress();
   (b) skt.retrieveInetAddress();
   (c) skt.InetAddress();
   (d) skt.getInetAddress();

6. Which of the following can be used for the host name to establish a socket connection with the server running on the same machine with the client?
   (a) "127.0.0.1"
   (b) InetAddress.getLocalHost()
   (c) "localhost"
   (d) All of the above.

7. To obtain an InputStream on a socket skt, we use ___________.
   (a) InputStream in = skt.obtainInputStream();
   (b) InputStream in = skt.getInputStream();
   (c) InputStream in = skt.getStream();
   (d) InputStream in = new InputStream(skt);

8. To create an InputStream to read data sent by a web server, we use the method __________ in the URL class.
   (a) connectStream();
   (b) obtainInputStream();
   (c) openStream();
   (d) getInputStream();

9. What is the port number of RMI?
(a) 1099 (b) 23
(c) 25 (d) 110

10. A remote object must be an instance of
(a) java.rmi.RemoteObject
(b) java.io.Serializable
(c) java.lang.Cloneable
(d) java.rmi.Remote

11. Which of the following is a utility that registers remote objects and provides naming services for locating objects?
(a) rmiregistry (b) rmic
(c) java (d) javac

12. Which of the following is an object that resides on the client host and serves as a proxy for the remote server object?
(a) Stub
(b) RMI Registry
(c) Server implementation
(d) Skeleton

13. ________ is an object that resides on the server host and communicates with the stub and the actual server object.
(a) Server object interface
(b) RMI Registry
(c) Skeleton
(d) Stub

14. Which of the following command is used in Java RMI to start the object registry on port 1080?
(a) rmiregistry 1080
(b) rmiregistry
(c) objectregistry 1080
(d) objectregistry

15. Which of the following is used to register a remote object o with the name "obj" at the port 1080 on the host it.jusl.ac.in?
(a) Naming.bind("rmi://it.jusl.ac.in/obj", o);
(b) Name.rebind("rmi://it.jusl.ac.in:1080/obj", o);
(c) Naming.rebind("rmi://it.jusl.ac.in:1080/obj", o);
(d) Name.bind("rmi://it.jusl.ac.in:1080/obj", o);

16. Which of the following is used to retrieve emails from a mail server?
(a) SMTP (b) POP3
(c) HTTP (d) FTP

17. Which of the following is used to send emails from a mail server?
(a) SMTP (b) POP3
(c) HTTP (d) FTP

18. __________ is a sub interface of java.rmi. Remote that defines the methods for the server object.
(a) Skeleton
(b) Server object interface
(c) Server implementation
(d) RMI Registry

19. When retrieving mail, which of the following is the proper order of working with classes?
(a) Store, Folder, Message, Transport
(b) Session, Store, Folder, Message
(c) Session, Store, Folder, Transport, Message
(d) Session, Folder, Message, Transport

20. To locate a remote object with the name obj at port 1080 on host it.jusl.ac.in, we use
(a) Remote remoteRef = Name.lookup("rmi://it.jusl.ac.in:1080/obj");
(b) Remote remoteRef = Name.lookup("//it.jusl.ac.in:1080/obj");
(c) Remote remoteRef = Name.lookup("http://it.jusl.ac.in:1080/obj");
(d) Remote remoteRef = Naming.lookup ("rmi://it.jusl.ac.in:1080/obj");

Review Questions

1. What is a *socket?*
2. What is a *ServerSocket* and how is it used?
3. Mention some advantages and disadvantages of Java Sockets?
4. How do you get the IP address of a machine from its hostname?
5. What are the differences between a TCP socket and a UDP socket? How are they created in Java?

6. Write a Java socket program to get the resource http://www.google.com/index.html using HTTP protocol.
7. What is the difference between URL and URL Connection?
8. Mention some limitations of POP3.
9. What is the difference between RMI and Socket?
10. What is RMI Registry?
11. What are the exceptions thrown by RMI?
12. What is the difference between a stub and a skeleton?
13. Why does RMI require an interface?
14. What is a serializable object? Give some examples of non-serializable objects in java.

4 HYPERTEXT MARKUP LANGUAGE (HTML)

KEY OBJECTIVES

After completing this chapter readers will be able to—

- **get an idea about commonly used HTML tags**
- **learn the functions of different HTML tags and how to use them**
- **understand what attributes are and how they can change the appearance of tags**
- **handle tables, frames, and images in a web page**
- **design and develop basic web pages using HTML**

4.1 HISTORY OF HTML AND W3C

The primary scripting language for developing web pages is **H**yper**T**ext **M**arkup **L**anguage (HTML). It is used to describe how a web page will appear in a browser's window. HTML allows us to write formatting instructions for web pages. Web browsers interpret the formatting instructions specified for the web page and render the web page on the screen.

HTML provides simple mechanisms for formatting text, creating links and lists, inserting images, embedding audio and video, etc. It can also include **C**ascading **S**tyle **S**heets (CSS) to specify the style and layout of text and other components. Scripts written in various languages such as JavaScript and VBScript may also be used to change the appearance of web pages and make them interactive.

HTML documents are written using HTML "tags" embedded in angular brackets. Even an average user can make use of these tags to create HTML documents. The set of tags that we can use to write HTML documents is defined by the **W**orld **W**ide **W**eb **C**onsortium (W3C). W3C has published many standards for HTML. Its current version is 4.01.

4.2 HTML AND ITS FLAVORS

The first public version of HTML specification, called *HTML tags*, was introduced in late 1991 by Berners-Lee. In this version, only 20 tags were incorporated to develop simple websites. Thirteen out of twenty still exist in the current version.

In November 1995, HTML version 2.0 was introduced by **I**nternet **E**ngineering **T**ask **F**orce (IETF). In this version, several features such as forms, tables, and image maps were added. However, this version became obsolete in 2000.

The World Wide Web Consortium (W3C) published its first recommendation, HTML 3.2, in 1997. The math formulae were dropped entirely.

In the same year, W3C published HTML version 4.0, which consists of three flavors: Strict, Transitional, and Frameset. In the Strict model, deprecated elements are forbidden whereas they are allowed in the Transitional model. In the Frameset model, frames and related elements are allowed. In the next year, minor improvements were added without changing the version number.

In 1999, W3C published an enhanced version, HTML 4.01, which was modified in May 12, 2001. This current version is supported by most of the web browsers and is widely used.

4.3 HTML BASICS

An HTML document itself is a text file that contains text and markups called *tags*. So, any simple text editor such as Notepad in Windows or SimpleText in Macintosh can be used to create and edit HTML files. If you use any word processor, save your HTML files in plain ASCII text format. The only requirement is that the documents must have the extension .html or .htm.

Several HTML editors are also available in the market. Most of these editors provide a GUI, which the users use to design their web pages. These editors automatically generate HTML codes for the web pages and help us focus on the visual result instead of codes. Two popular HTML editors are Microsoft's FrontPage and Adobe's Dreamweaver.

If you are new to HTML or if you want to be above average in web page design, you should concentrate solely on learning the structure of an HTML page, tags and their functionality, etc. This enables you to use tags the editor does not support. You can also understand others' code and use important portions to create interesting effects in your own pages. Basic knowledge about HTML is also necessary for debugging purposes. At some later point of time, when you become comfortable enough to write your own web pages, you may use any suitable HTML editor to accelerate your design.

An HTML page is all about tags. Tags are similar to instructions or codes. Web browsers know their meaning and interpret them to render text, images, and other elements on the screen properly. The set of HTML tags is fixed and is standardized by W3C. Invalid tags are displayed on the screen as they are.

4.4 ELEMENTS, ATTRIBUTES, AND TAGS

An HTML document is a simple text document that basically consists of HTML elements which, in turn, consist of tags and attributes.

4.4.1 HTML Elements

HTML elements are the fundamental building blocks of a web page. An element consists of a tag, its attributes, and content. The content of a tag may be simple text, or may be one or more tags, or both. These elements are organized in a tree-like structure. The root element of an HTML document is `<html>`, which contains all other elements.

4.4.2 HTML Tags

Tags are codes each of which marks up a certain region in an HTML document. These marked-up regions are displayed on the screen using the style as mentioned by the marking tag. A tag is written within angular brackets (< and >). The general format of a tag is as follows:

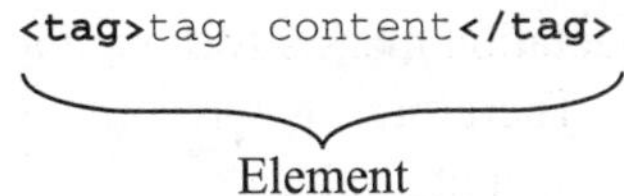

Here, `<tag>` is the opening tag and `</tag>` is the closing tag. The closing tag looks exactly like the opening tag except that it contains an extra forward slash "/" character after "<" character. Everything within these opening and closing tags is the tag's content. The content can be any simple text, or other tags or even be empty. The opening tag, its corresponding closing tag, and its content together is called an *element*. The browser starts tagging the text when an opening tag is encountered and stops when its corresponding closing tag is found. Following is an example:

```
This is an example of <i>italic</i> text.
```

The tag pair `<i>` and `</i>` instructs the browser to display its content in italic style as follows:

This is an example of *italic* text.

This tag is called an *embedded* tag. Each embedded tag has both opening and closing tags. There are some tags that do not have their corresponding closing tags. These tags are called *standalone* tags. In this case, only starting tags are sufficient to describe the meaning of the tags. For this reason, the closing tag is omitted. Following is an example of the standalone tag:

```
<hr>
```

This tag inserts a horizontal rule on the screen.

According to XHTML (e**X**tensible **H**yper**T**ext **M**arkup **L**anguage) specification, every tag must have a closing tag. So, in XHTML, this tag is written as `<hr></hr>` which can also be written in shorthand notation as `<hr/>`. Most of the browsers support XHTML syntax. XHTML is going to substitute HTML as the former has several distinct advantages over the latter. The following points should be noted:

- HTML tags are case-insensitive. So, browsers do not distinguish between `<i>` and `<I>`.
- Tags that are not known to the browser are ignored altogether.
- Tags must be properly nested.

4.4.3 Attributes

Tags may have properties that can optionally be assigned values to change the default behavior of these tags. These properties are called *attributes*. Attributes are placed within the starting tag. So, even standalone tags may have attributes. Following is an example:

```
<hr width="400">
```

This tag represents horizontal rule whose length is specified by the attribute `width` as 400 pixels. Multiple attributes can be specified separated by white space(s).

```
<hr width="400" color="red">
```

Note that this tag indicates the same attributes as the previous tag except that the line is in `red` color. Now, consider the following tag:

```
<hr width=400 color=red>
```

The values of the attributes are specified without any quotation marks. Although it works in almost all browsers, it might not work in some browsers. Therefore, it is recommended that double quotation marks should always be used to specify attribute values so as to avoid any unexpected appearance. XHTML specification also recommends the same.

Each tag has its own set of predefined attributes. If an attribute is not specified, its value is given by the browser itself and then the tag is processed. The value specified for a specific attribute for a specific tag is browser-specific.

4.4.4 Basic Structure

Every HTML document starts with the `<html>` tag. This tells browsers that it is the beginning of an HTML document. This may appear anywhere in the document. This tag is an embedded tag. So, it must have the corresponding `</html>` tag, which informs browsers that the end of the HTML document has been reached. The `<html>` tag does not have any properties. Everything within opening `<html>` and closing `</html>` tags is parsed by the browser. Every other tag and all text must be contained within this `<html>` tag pair. Some common HTML tags along with their functionalities are mentioned in Tables 4.1 and 4.2.

An HTML page has basically two distinct logical sections: *head* section specified by `<head>` and `</head>` tags and *body* section specified by `<body>` and `</body>` tags. The skeleton of an HTML page looks like this:

```
<html>
   <head>
      ...
   </head>
   <body>
      ...
   </body>
</html>
```

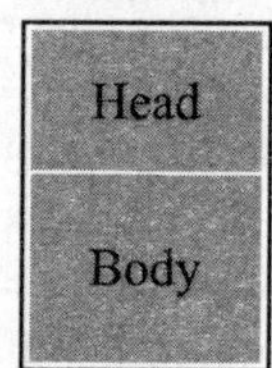

The head section contains meta-information about the HTML page. This section is processed but not rendered to display on the screen. Typically, the head section contains `<title>` tag that is used to assign a title to the web page, which appears on the title bar of the browser's window. This section, quite often, contains JavaScript (a scripting language for web pages) code, Cascading Style Sheet (see the following chapter) codes, etc.

The body section contains text and other tags, which are rendered on the screen as specified there. The following sections describe the different important tags and their functionality in detail.

Table 4.1 Common HTML tags and their functionality

Tag	Meaning
<html>...</html>	Root tag of any web page
<body>...</body>	Represents the body of an HTML document. Must be contained within the <html> and </html> tag pairs.
<head>...</head>	Represents the header of a web page and contains information about the page header. Must be contained within the <html> and </html> tag pairs.
<p>...</p>	Starts a new paragraph
 	Inserts a line break
<b>...</b>	Makes the enclosed text bold
<i>...</i>	Makes the enclosed text italic
<tt>...</tt>	Makes the enclosed text teletype face
<u>...</u>	Makes the enclosed text underlined
<center></center>	Aligns the enclosed text in center
<hr>	Inserts a horizontal rule
<hn>...</hn>	Inserts a heading varying in size designated by n where n varies from 1 to 6. h1 is the largest and h6 is the smallest heading
<strong>...</strong>	Makes the enclosed text bold. Similar to the <b> tag
<table>...</table>	Inserts a table. Each row is created by <tr>...</tr> and each column within a row is created by <td>...</td>
<img src="...">	Inserts an image whose source is specified by the src attribute

Table 4.2 Common HTML tags placed in head tag

Tag	Meaning
<title>...</title>	Makes the enclosed text the title of the web page. The title appears in the title bar of the web page. Must be contained within the <head> and </head> tag pairs.
<style>...</style>	Links or inserts a style sheet
<link>	Makes a link between an external source and this html file
<script>...</script>	Contains scripts such as JavaScript and VBScript
<meta>	Used to specify document properties
<base>	Specifies base URL of the document

Table 4.3 Common attributes of body tag

Tag	Meaning	Tag	Meaning
bgcolor	Specifies background color of the document	alink	Represents the color of an active link
background	Specifies background image of the document	vlink	Represents the color of a visited link
link	Specifies the color of a not yet visited link	text	Specifies the color of the enclosed text

4.5 BASIC TAGS

These tags have simple functionality and are used to create simple HTML documents. In the next section, we shall discuss commonly used tags.

4.5.1 HTML Comments

An HTML comment is not really a tag. It starts with <!-- and ends with -->. Everything within these character sequences will be ignored by the browsers and will not be parsed. Comments are used to explain the purpose of critical tags in an HTML document. Comments can be placed anywhere in the document. Following is the general syntax:

```
<!--comment text-->
```

4.5.2 Adding a Title

The `<title>` and `</title>` tags represent page titles. Their content is displayed on the top of the browser window. For example, the following example adds the title "My Home Page" to your page.

```
<title>My Home Page</title>
```

The result is shown in Figure 4.1

Figure 4.1 Adding a title to your web page

4.5.3 First HTML Page

Let us now write our first simple but complete HTML document that displays a simple text "Hello World" on the screen. The result of this web page is shown in Figure 4.2.

```
<html>
   <head>
      <title>My First html page</title>
   </head>
   <body>
      Hello World!
   </body>
</html>
```

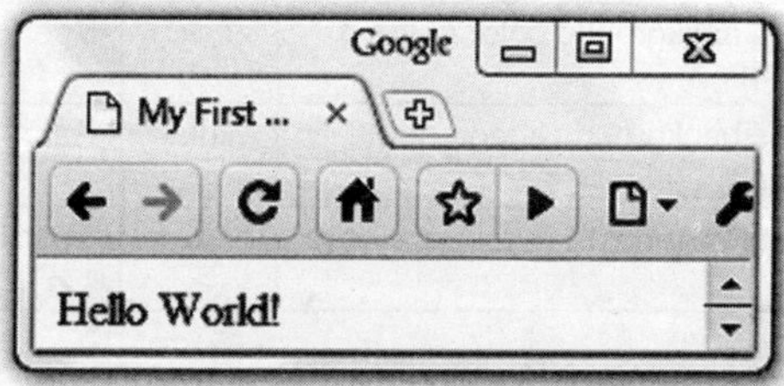

Figure 4.2 First HTML page

4.5.4 HTML Background

The background of an HTML page is specified in the <body> tag. You may use plain color or an image as background. If an image is used, loading the page takes more time than when plain color is used. However, a good background image may give your web page a better look. Ultimately, it is designer's own choice. The designer should choose the background in such a way that it does not affect the clarity and readability very much.

Using plain color

To set a plain color as the background use the `bgcolor` attribute of the <body> tag. The following example makes the page background yellow.

```
<body bgcolor="yellow">
```

Hexadecimal color codes may also be used to specify a color. A color code starts with a '#' sign followed by six hexadecimal digits in the following form:

```
#RRGGBB
```

Here `RR`, `GG`, and `BB` represent hexadecimal gray levels of red, green, and blue colors, respectively. The actual color is obtained by mixing them with the specified gray levels. For example, yellow color is obtained by mixing equal amounts of red and green colors and its color code is `#RRGG00`. So, the code may be written as

```
<body bgcolor="#RRGG00">
```

Typically, color codes are used to specify any custom color.

Using Image

To use an image as background, we use the `background` attribute of the <body> tag. The following example sets the jpg image "Windows XP.jpg" as background.

```
<body background="Windows XP.jpg">
```

Since the image takes some time to load, it is a good idea to specify a matching background color. This background color is displayed until the image is loaded. The following example illustrates this.

```
<body background="Windows XP.jpg" bgcolor="#004FAF">
```

4.5.5 Paragraph

Web browsers ignore any carriage return or new line character encountered in the HTML document. HTML provides a paragraph tag <p>, which is used to start a fresh paragraph. The tag <p> inserts a blank line immediately before the new paragraph.

```
<p>This is a one sentence paragraph.</p>
<p>Every paragraph starts on its own line, with a little extra line space.</p>
```

This code segment will look as shown in Figure 4.3.

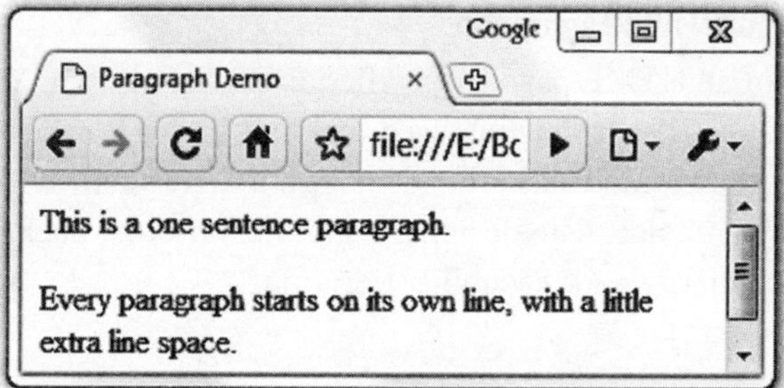

Figure 4.3 Inserting paragraphs

4.5.6 Inserting Line Breaks

Browsers ignore the new line characters inserted in the HTML source file and text is displayed continuously. The tag `<br>` is used to insert a line break. It is similar to the `<p>` tag, but it does not insert any blank line. The following example illustrates this and its effect is shown in Figure 4.4.

```
This is first line.<br>This is second line.
```

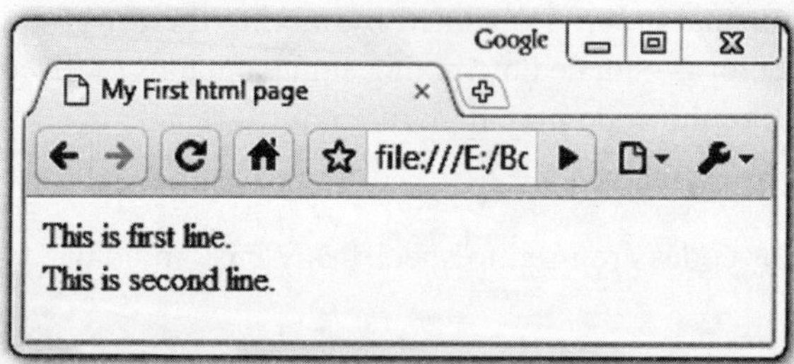

Figure 4.4 Inserting a line break

4.5.7 Text Styles

HTML provides several tags to add styles to the text.

4.5.7.1 Changing base font

To set the default font style, color, etc., we use the `<basefont>` tag. The `face`, `size`, and `color` attributes are used to specify font style, font size, and font color, respectively. The following code sets the font style "arial", font size "2", and font color "red".

```
<basefont face="arial" size="2" color="red">
```

4.5.7.2 Changing style of a specific text

The `<basefont>` tag changes the style of the entire text of the page. If you want to change the style of a specific text, use the `<font>` tag.

```
This is a line<br>
<font face="verdana" size="4" color="black">This is another line</font><br>
This is another line
```

The result is shown in Figure 4.5.

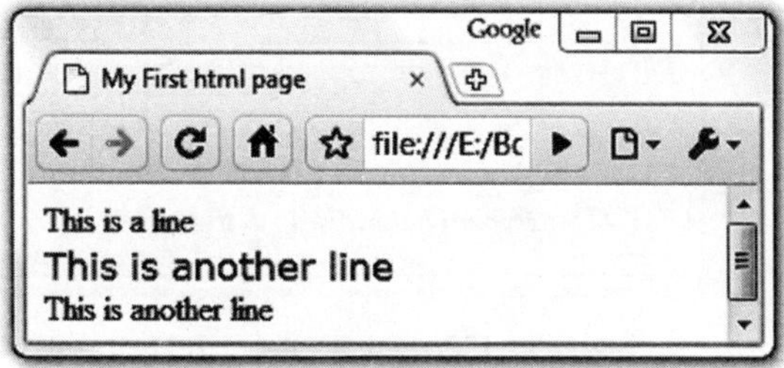

Figure 4.5 Changing font

4.5.7.3 Bold text

The tag <b> makes the enclosed text bold. Following is an example.

```
HTML = <b>H</b>yper<b>T</b>ext <b>M</b>arkup <b>L</b>anguage
```

The result is shown in Figure 4.6.

Figure 4.6 Bold text

4.5.7.4 Underlined text

Similarly, the <u> tag makes the enclosed text underlined. Following is an example.

```
HTML = <u>H</u>yper<u>T</u>ext <u>M</u>arkup <u>L</u>anguage
```

The result is shown in Figure 4.7.

Figure 4.7 Underlined text

4.5.7.5 Italicized text

The tag <i> is used to make the enclosed text italic. Following is an example.

```
HTML = <i>HyperText Markup Language</i>
```

The result is shown in Figure 4.8.

Figure 4.8 Italicized text

4.5.7.6 Combining styles

The style tags can be combined. For example, to get a bold and underlined text, `<b>` tag and `<u>` tag can be combined in any order as long as they are nested correctly. Consider the following HTML code segment:

```
HTML = <b><u>HyperText Markup Language</u></b>
```

The result is shown in Figure 4.9.

Figure 4.9 Bold and underlined text

The following code illustrates how to combine different text formatting tags to get the desired effect. The effect is shown in Figure 4.10. Figure 4.11 summarizes common text formatting tags.

```
<b>Bold</b> |
<i>Italic</i> |
<b><i>Bold and Italic</i></b> |
<i><b>Italic and Bold</b></i> |
<tt>Teletype</tt>
```

Figure 4.10 Combining styles

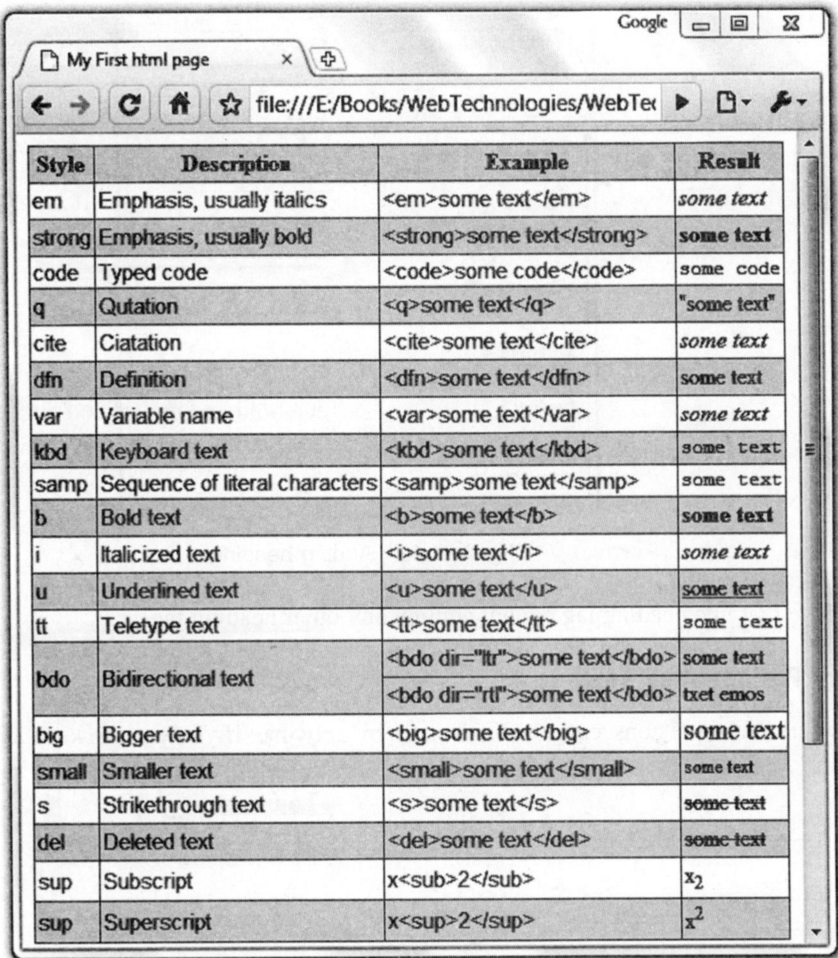

Style	Description	Example	Result
em	Emphasis, usually italics	<em>some text</em>	*some text*
strong	Emphasis, usually bold	<strong>some text</strong>	**some text**
code	Typed code	<code>some code</code>	some code
q	Qutation	<q>some text</q>	"some text"
cite	Ciatation	<cite>some text</cite>	*some text*
dfn	Definition	<dfn>some text</dfn>	some text
var	Variable name	<var>some text</var>	*some text*
kbd	Keyboard text	<kbd>some text</kbd>	some text
samp	Sequence of literal characters	<samp>some text</samp>	some text
b	Bold text	<b>some text</b>	**some text**
i	Italicized text	<i>some text</i>	*some text*
u	Underlined text	<u>some text</u>	some text
tt	Teletype text	<tt>some text</tt>	some text
bdo	Bidirectional text	<bdo dir="ltr">some text</bdo>	some text
		<bdo dir="rtl">some text</bdo>	txet emos
big	Bigger text	<big>some text</big>	some text
small	Smaller text	<small>some text</small>	some text
s	Strikethrough text	<s>some text</s>	~~some text~~
del	Deleted text	<del>some text</del>	~~some text~~
sup	Subscript	x₂	x_2
sup	Superscript	x²	x^2

Figure 4.11 Common HTML text styles

4.5.8 Heading

You may have noticed that many web pages contain different section headings with different sizes and perhaps different colors and fonts. HTML provides tags for such section headings. There are total six levels of headings h1 through h6. The h1 heading has the largest and h6 has the smallest font size. The exact size is determined by the browser used. Consider the following HTML code:

```
<h1>Heading 1</h1>
<h2>Heading 2</h2>
<h3>Heading 3</h3>
<h4>Heading 4</h4>
<h5>Heading 5</h5>
<h6>Heading 6</h6>
```

The result is shown in Figure 4.12.

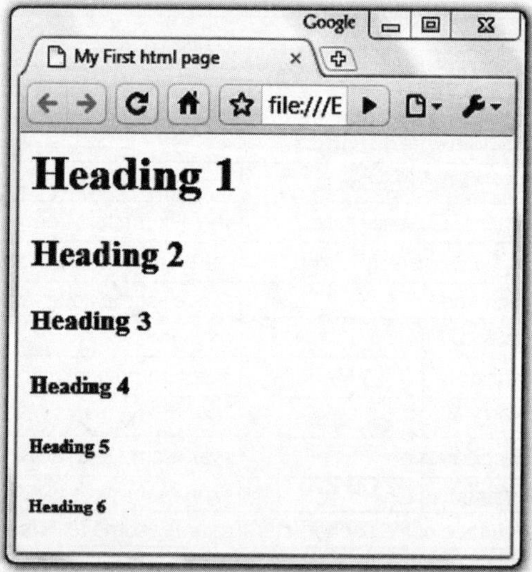

Figure 4.12 Adding headings

Note that one heading tag cannot contain any other heading tag.

4.5.9 Preformatted Text

Browsers substitute consecutive white spaces by only one. If you want to keep them as they are, use the `<pre>` tag. It essentially creates a table-like layout. Consider the following HTML code:

```
<pre>
   <b>item            Specification           Manufacturer</b>
   <hr>
      CPU            Pentium-III             Intel
      Disk           40 GB                   Seagate
      Monitor        SVGA                    Samsung
      Printer        LaserJet                HP
</pre>
```

This code is displayed as shown in Figure 4.13.

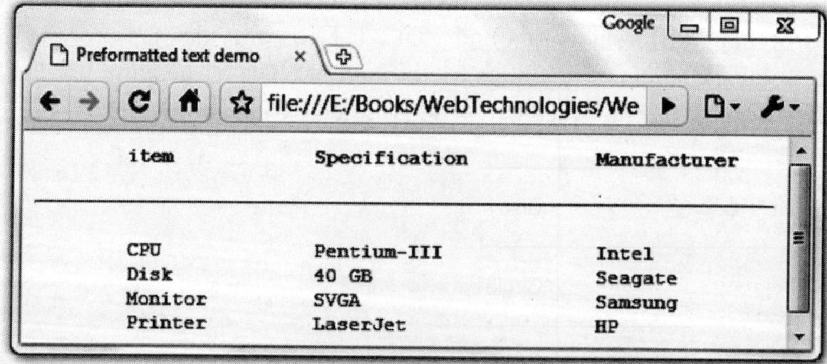

Figure 4.13 Preformatted text

Note that the tag `<pre>` works only for text and not for images.

4.5.10 Strikethrough Text

The strikethrough text is created using the `<del>` tag as follows:

```
2 GB RAM is now Rs.<del>2000</del> 1500.
```

The result is shown in Figure 4.14.

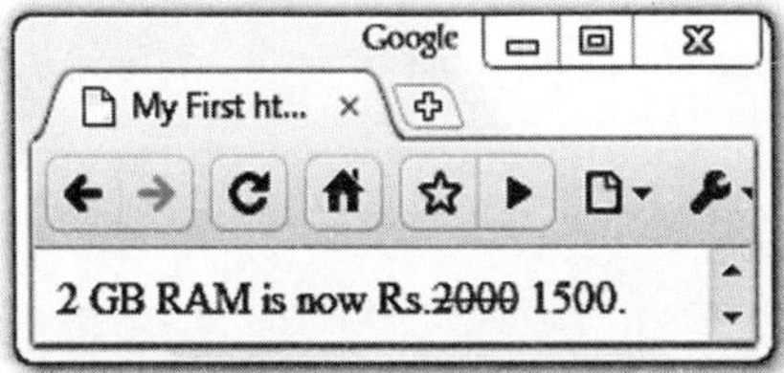

Figure 4.14 Strikethrough text

4.5.11 Lists

A list is a collection of one or more items. HTML supports effectively three types of lists for formatting text: unordered (bulleted), ordered (numbered), and definition lists. The lists can also be nested. For example, you can use an unordered list in an ordered list and vice versa.

Unordered Lists

An unordered list is created using the `<ul>` tag. Items in the list are created using the `<li>` tag and are displayed using bullets. Note that an item itself may be a separate ordered or unordered list.

```
<ul>
<li>Unordered Lists</li>
<li>Ordered Lists</li>
<li>Definition Lists</li>
</ul>
```

- Unordered Lists
- Ordered Lists
- Definition Lists

This code creates an unordered list of three items. The type attribute of the `<ul>` tag specifies the bullet options. Table 4.4 illustrates this.

Table 4.4 Bullet options

Bullet options	Meaning	Result
<ul>	Default bullet shape is disc.	• One • Two
<ul type="disc">	Disc shaped bullets are used.	• One • Two
<ul type="circle">	Circle shaped bullets are used.	o One o Two
<ul type="square">	Square shaped bullets are used.	▪ One ▪ Two

Ordered Lists

In this type of list, items are displayed using numbers. The list is created using the `<ol>` tag and items are created using the `<li>` tag. Note that an item itself may be a separate ordered or unordered list.

```
<ol>
<li>Unordered Lists</li>
<li>Ordered Lists</li>
<li>Definition Lists</li>
</ol>
```

1. Unordered Lists
2. Ordered Lists
3. Definition Lists

This HTML code creates the same list of ordered items. The different numbering options for ordered lists are shown in Table 4.5.

Table 4.5 Number options

Numbering options	Meaning	Result	Numbering options	Meaning	Result
<ol>	Use default number type	1. One 2. Two	<ol type="a">	Use Small letters for numbering	a. One b. Two
<ol type="1">	Use default number type	1. One 2. Two	<ol type="a" start="4">	Use Small letters starting from d	d. One e. Two
<ol type="A">	Use Capital letters for numbering	A. One B. Two	<ol type="i">	Use small roman numbers	i. One ii. Two
<ol start="3">	Use default number starting from 3	3. One 4. Two	<ol type="i" start="2">	Use small roman numbers starting from ii	ii. One iii. Two
<ol type="A" start="4">	Use Capital letters starting from D	D. One E. Two	<ol type="I">	Use Capital roman numbers	I. One II. Two

Definition Lists

A definition list is one where list items consist of two parts: a term and its description. It is created using the `<dl>` tag. The term part and the definition part of each item are created using `<dt>` (definition term) and `<dd>` (definition description) tags, respectively.

```
<dl>
   <dt>dl tag</dt>
   <dd>It is the outermost tag of definition list</dd>
   <dt>dt tag</dt>
   <dd>Contains item to be described</dd>
   <dt>dd tag</dt>
   <dd>Contains description of the item</dd>
   <dd>Each term may have multiple descriptions</dd>
</dl>
```

The result is shown in Figure 4.15.

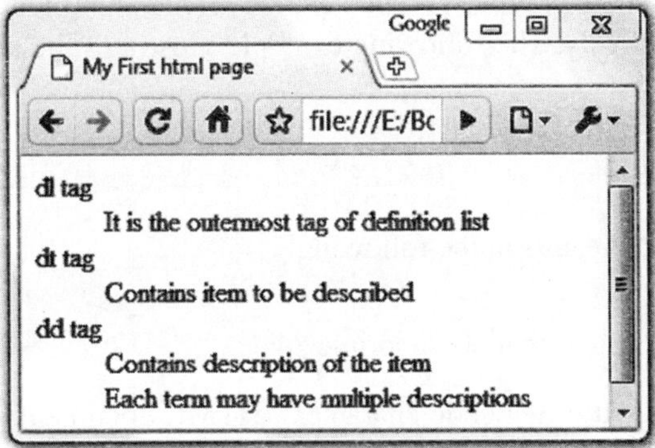

Figure 4.15 Definition list

Nested Lists

Nested lists may be used to display sub-elements of an item. Any of the three types of lists may be nested in another. Arbitrary levels of nesting is possible. In the following example, an ordered list is nested in an unordered list.

```
<ul>
  <li>First Item of unordered list</li>
  <li>
    Second item itself is an ordered list
    <ol>
      <li>First item of ordered list</li>
      <li>Second item of ordered list</li>
    </ol>
  </li>
  <li>Last Item of unordered list</li>
</ul>
```

Figure 4.16 shows the result of this list.

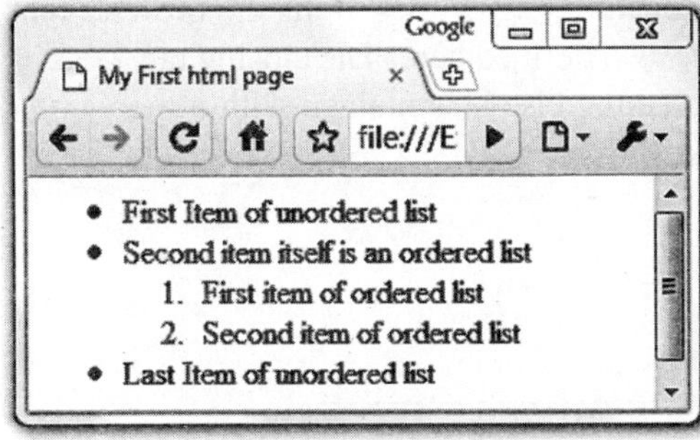

Figure 4.16 Nested list

4.5.12 HTML Symbols

HTML allows document authors to insert symbols and characters that cannot be typed in the form of *character entities* or simply *entities*. Entities are case-sensitive and take the form `&name;`

For example, α and © represent the Greek small letter alpha (α) and the copyright symbol (©), respectively. The following example illustrates the use of symbols:

```
&radic;2=1.414
<br>
&forall; i &exist; s[i] &isin; N such that s[i] is prime
```

This HTML code results in the following:

√2=1.414
∀ i ∃ s[i] ∈ N such that s[i] is prime

Entities are limited to Unicode characters. HTML document authors may also use *numeric character entities* to specify any character, including English characters. Numeric character entities may be specified as decimal or hexadecimal numbers. Decimal reference are of the form `&#number;` while hexadecimal references take the form `&#xnumber;`. Hexadecimal entities are case-insensitive. Numeric entities include `α` or `α` for the Greek small letter alpha and `©` or `©` for the copyright symbol. The details of character entities and numeric entities may be found in Appendix at the end of this chapter.

4.6 ADVANCED TAGS

The HTML consists of a rich set of tags some of which provide advanced features. In the following sections, we shall discuss some of these advanced tags.

4.6.1 Table

Tabular structure was first introduced in HTML 3.2. It is sometimes useful to display data in a two-dimensional tabular format. Tables are also powerful tools for formatting your web pages. You may have seen web pages with a navigation panel at the left. Perhaps these web pages use tables. Table 4.6 describes the set of tags used to create tables along with their meaning.

A table is created using three basic tags: `table`, `tr`, and `td`. The tag `table` is the container of the whole table. The opening tag `<table>` tells the browser that a table is to be created. Table-specific properties are also defined here. The closing tag `</table>` tells the browser that it is the end of the table. Everything else is contained within the `<table>` and `</table>` tag pair. So, a table always looks like this:

```
<table>
...
</table>
```

Table 4.6 HTML table tags

Tag	Meaning
table	Represents the whole table
tr	Represents a row
td	Represents a cell in a row
th	Column header
caption	Title of the table

A table consists of a number of rows each of which is made up of a number of cells. The tag <tr> creates a row. The total number of rows in a table is equal to the number of <tr> elements. The opening tag <tr> and closing tag </tr> indicate the beginning and ending of a table row, respectively.

```
<table>
  <tr>…</tr>
  <tr>…</tr>
  …
  <tr>…</tr>
</table>
```

A table or a row cannot contain data. To add data, cells are created within a row. Each cell in a row is defined by the tag <td>. The number of columns in a row is equal to the number of <td> elements. The content of a cell is written within the <td> and </td> tag pair. Textual as well as graphical content can be used in a cell. Usual tags such as <p>, <br>, <i>, <b>, and <u> may be used within a cell.

```
<table>
  <tr><td>…</td><td>…</td>…<td>…</td></tr>
  <tr><td>…</td><td>…</td>…<td>…</td></tr>
  …
  <tr><td>…</td><td>…</td>…<td>…</td></tr>
</table>
```

Two other tags are defined: <th> and <caption>. To add a column header, the <th> tag is used. The title of a table is added using the <caption> tag. The details of these two tags will be discussed later in this chapter.

Let us first create a simple 2x2 table to display the marks of two students in two different subjects. We shall then add more and more features subsequently as and when necessary. The following code creates one such table:

```
<table>
  <tr><td>82</td><td>80</td></tr>
  <tr><td>80</td><td>75</td></tr>
</table>
```

This gives us a table as shown in Figure 4.17(i). Each row of this table contains the marks of one student. This table is very simple but makes use of all three primary tags that all tables must have. We shall now first add a border to the table.

4.6.1.1 Border

Adding a table border is very simple. The attribute border specifies that a border has to be used. Its value indicates the thickness of the outermost table boundary in pixels. A value 0 (zero) indicates no border.

```
<table border="1">
  <tr><td>82</td><td>80</td></tr>
  <tr><td>80</td><td>75</td></tr>
</table>
```

This code segment creates a table with a border which is 1 pixel wide [Figure 4.17(ii)]. Adding a table border also adds boundaries of 1 pixel thick to all cells in the table. The thickness of individual cell boundaries cannot be changed. The color of cell boundaries can be changed using `border` attribute to cells, however.

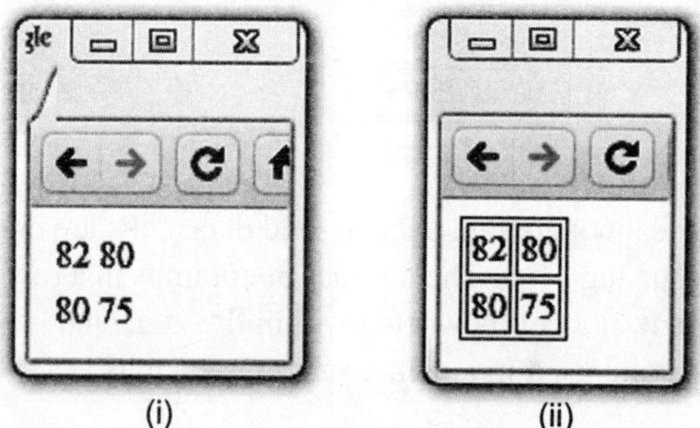

Figure 4.17 (i) Simple table (ii) Table with border

It is recommended that a border should always be added during development time even if it is removed from the final design. A border will help us identify the boundaries of individual cells visually. Accordingly, we can modify cell's properties easily.

4.6.1.2 Row and column header

Sometimes, you might want to add a title to a row/column. It helps to understand the meaning of data in a row/column. The tag `<th>` is used to add row/column headers. They are also added using cells. All column headers form a separate row that precedes all other rows. Similarly, all row headers form another column that precedes all other columns. Row/column headers are center-aligned and in bold font, which distinguishes them from other cells.

```
<table border="1">
<tr><th>Name</th><th>OS</th><th>OOP</th></tr>
<tr><td>Sujay</td><td>82</td><td>80</td></tr>
<tr><td>Tuhina</td><td>80</td><td>75</td></tr>
</table>
```

This code segment adds column headers as shown in Figure 4.18 (i).

The tag `<th>` is also used to add a row header. The following example creates the same table with student names as row headers.

```
<table border="1">
<tr><td> </td><th>OS</th><th>OOP</th></tr>
<tr><th>Sujay</th><td>82</td><td>80</td></tr>
<tr><th>Tuhina</th><td>80</td><td>75</td></tr>
</table>
```

The effect is shown in Figure 4.18 (ii).

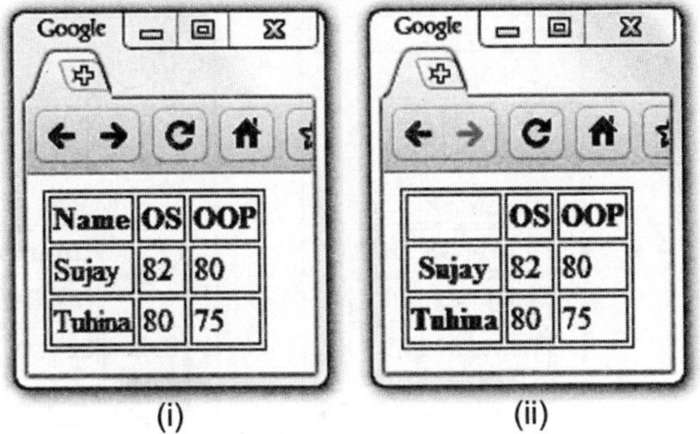

Figure 4.18 Headers (i) Column header (ii) Row header

4.6.1.3 Caption

It is a good idea to add a title/caption to a table that describes the table data. To add a caption to the table, the `<caption>` tag is used. For example, the following code creates a table with the caption "Marks".

```
<table border="1">
<caption>Marks</caption>
<tr><th>Name</th><th>OS</th><th>OOP</th></tr>
<tr><td>Sujay</td><td>82</td><td>80</td></tr>
<tr><td>Tuhina</td><td>80</td><td>75</td></tr>
</table>
```

The result is shown in Figure 4.19 (i). The `<caption>` tag must appear only once and must appear immediately after the `<table>` tag and before the first `<tr>` tag.

The caption is centered with respect to the table itself. It may appear below or above the table. This can be specified by the `align` attribute. If nothing is mentioned, the caption is placed on the top of the table.

4.6.1.4 Rowspan and colspan

To make a cell span multiple rows and columns, the tags `<rowspan>` and `<colspan>` are used, respectively. The tag `<rowspan>` indicates the number of rows a cell spans while `<colspan>` indicates the number of columns a cell spans.

```
<table border="1">
<caption>Marks</caption>
<tr>
<th rowspan=2>Name</th>
<th colspan=2>Marks</th>
</tr>
<tr><th>OS</th><th>OOP</th></tr>
<tr><td>Sujay</td><td>82</td><td>80</td></tr>
<tr><td>Tuhina</td><td>80</td><td>75</td></tr>
</table>
```

The table is displayed as shown in Figure 4.19 (ii).

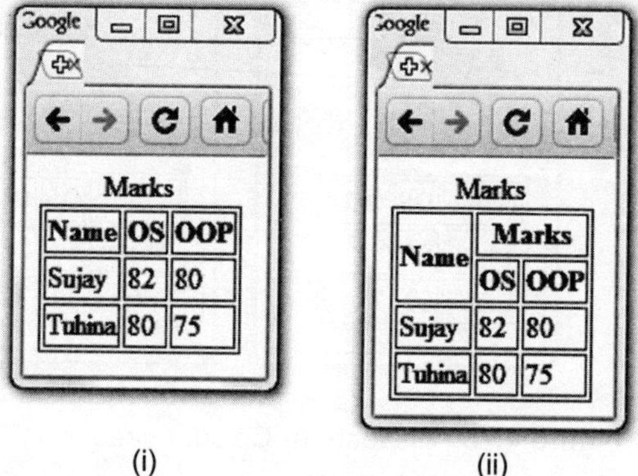

(i) (ii)

Figure 4.19 (i) Adding a table caption (ii) Rowspan and colspan

4.6.2 Cellspacing and cellpadding

These attributes are used to adjust white spaces in your table. The attribute `cellspacing` specifies the amount of spaces, in pixels, between adjacent cells. Similarly, `cellpadding` specifies the amount of spaces in pixels between the cell border and its content.

```
<table border cellspacing="6" cellpadding="3" width=300>
<caption>Marks table</caption>
<tr><th rowspan=2>Name</th><th colspan=2>Marks</th></tr>
<tr><th>OS</th><th>OOP</th></tr>
<tr><td>Sujay</td><td>82</td><td>80</td></tr>
<tr><td>Tuhina</td><td>80</td><td>75</td></tr>
</table>
```

The result is shown in Figure 4.20.

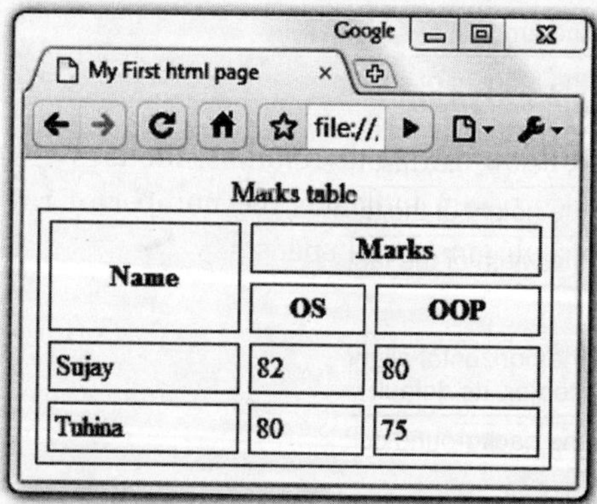

Figure 4.20 Cellspacing and cellpadding

4.6.3 Nested Tables

What happens if you want to place two tables side-by-side? It does not work; the table tag automatically inserts a line break at the end. So, they will be placed vertically. One good idea is to place them in another table shown as follows:

```
<table border="1">
<tr><td>
      <table border="1">
      <tr><td>In the left nested table.</td></tr>
      </table>
</td>
<td >
       <table border="1">
       <tr><td>In the right nested table.</td></tr>
       </table>
</td></tr>
</table>
```

It creates the table as shown in Figure 4.21:

Figure 4.21 Nested table

Table 4.7 lists the attributes of the table tag.

Table 4.7 Attributes of the table tag

Attributes of the table tag	
Attribute	**Meaning**
align	Specifies table alignment. Can have values: left, right, and center.
background	Specifies the URL of the background image
bgcolor	Specifies the background color. Color names or hexadecimal color codes are allowed.
border	Specifies the thickness of the table border in number of pixels
bordercolor	Specifies the color of the table border. Color names and hexadecimal color codes are allowed.
cellpadding	Specifies the amount of space in number of pixels between the cell border and its content
cellspacing	Specifies the amount of space in number of pixels between table cells
frame	Specifies whether a frame around the table should be used or not. It can have values border, box, above, below, lhs, rhs, hsides, and rsides.
height	Specifies the height of the table in pixels
width	Specifies the width of the table in pixels
Attributes of tr tag	
align	Specifies the horizontal alignment of the content of all cells in this row. Can have values: left, right, and center. Its default value is left.
bgcolor	Specifies the background color of all cells in this row. Color names or hexadecimal color codes are allowed.
bordercolor	Specifies the border color of all cells in this row. Color names or hexadecimal color codes are allowed.
height	Specifies height, in pixels, of all cells in this row
width	Specifies width, in pixels, of all cells in this row
valign	Specifies the vertical alignment of the content of all cells in this row. Can have values: top, bottom, and middle. Its default value is middle.

(Condt.)

(Condt.)

Attributes of td tag	
align	Specifies the horizontal alignment of the content of this cell. Overrides the align attribute of the `<tr>` tag. Its default value is left.
bgcolor	Specifies the background color of this cell. Overrides the bgcolor attribute of the `<tr>` tag. Color names or hexadecimal color codes are allowed.
bordercolor	Specifies the border color of this cell. Overrides the bordercolor attribute of the `<tr>` tag. Color names or hexadecimal color codes are allowed.
colspan	Specifies the number of columns this cell must span
rowspan	Specifies the number of rows this cell must span
height	Specifies the height of a cell in pixels
width	Specifies the width of a cell in pixels
valign	Specifies the vertical alignment of the content of this cell. Overrides the valign attribute of the `<tr>` tag. Its default value is middle.

4.6.4 Forms

The HTML `<form>` tag is a very important tag, which creates a section in your HTML document. It is used to collect information from visitors. In addition to usual contents and markups, it contains special elements called *controls*. HTML provides several control elements such as buttons, text boxes, password fields, check boxes, radio buttons, selection boxes, hidden fields, etc. Visitors enter data using these control elements. These data are then usually sent (submitted) to a program at the server side. The server program, in turn, processes data and takes necessary actions. In this way interactivity in the web pages is introduced. The tag `<form>` is a container tag and is created as follows:

```
<form>
  <!--Form elements, markups and other contents go here -->
</form>
```

Form elements are written within opening and closing tags.

The `<form>` tag has an optional attribute `action` that specifies the target URL, which handles the data. If none is mentioned, URL of the current web page is assumed. Usually this is a server-side script such as JSP, ASP, CGI, etc. These scripts process data and in many cases consult database server and typically generate an HTML/XML output.

```
<form action="handler.jsp">
  <!--Input elements go here -->
</form>
```

This code interprets that the data contained within this form are to be sent to the URL `handler.jsp` for processing. The URL mentioned is relative to the URL of the current web page. It may be an absolute URL as well. We have not yet specified any form element. The time at which the data will be sent for processing is also not mentioned yet. These issues will be discussed later in this chapter.

The tag `<form>` has another optional attribute `method` which specifies the HTTP method to be used. It can have values GET or POST. If GET (the default) is used, the data are appended to the URL. So, information being passed will be visible in the address bar of the browser. This is vulnerable for sensitive data and is not used usually. However, it is useful during the development as it helps us verify if the data are really being sent or not.

If the POST method is used, data are sent as a part of the HTTP request message and are not appended to the URL. Data sent using this method are not visible and is useful for sensitive data.

```
<form action="handler.jsp" method="post">
  <!--Input elements go here -->
</form>
```

The method GET allows only ASCII data to be sent. However, the POST method supports non-ASCII character sets.

A form has, typically, a `name` attribute that may be used to refer to this form from scripts or style sheets.

```
<form action="handler.jsp" method="post" name="loginForm">
  <!--Input elements go here -->
</form>
```

Following is a simple form to send login information to the server.

```
<form action="handler.jsp" method="post" name="loginForm">
Login: <input type="text" name="login"><br>
Password: <input type="password" name="password"><br>
<input type="submit" name="submit" value="Login">
</form>
```

This form uses several control elements. Let us now discuss them.

4.6.5 Form Elements

As mentioned in the previous section, data are collected using different types of control elements. Each control element should have a name which is specified by the attribute `name`. Each element has an *initial value* which is typically specified by the `value` attribute. Users may, however, change this value. Whenever a form is submitted, the name–value pair of *some* controls is sent. These control elements are called *successful control elements*. The following rules are used to determine successful controls:

- A successful control must have a name.
- Disabled controls are not successful.
- All checkboxes that are on are successful.
- All radio buttons that are on are successful.
- Activated submit button is successful.
- For select element, the value of selected option is successful.
- Hidden controls are successful.

Most of the control elements are created using the `<input>` tag. It has an attribute `type` that specifies the type of the input. Table 4.8 shows the attributes of the input tag. There are ten input types: `text`, `password`, `checkbox`, `radio`, `button`, `submit`, `reset`, `hidden`, `file`, and `image`. Let us now discuss each of these input elements one by one in detail.

Table 4.8 Attributes of the input tag

Attribute	Meaning
type	Specifies the type of a control element. Can have values text, password, checkbox, radio, submit, reset, file, hidden, image, button. Its default value is text.
name	Specifies the name of a control element. Submitted as a part of form.
value	Specifies the initial value of the control element, e.g., text for the text control, caption for submit, reset and button elements, etc. Optional except for check box and radio button.
size	Specifies the maximum number of characters that can be viewed in case of a text or password field. Otherwise, it specifies the width of the control in pixels.
maxlength	Specifies the maximum number of characters a user can enter in a text or password field
checked	Used for check boxes and radio buttons. Indicates that the control is on. The browser ignores for all other controls.
readonly	Used for text, password, and file controls. If set, prevents changes to the controls.
disabled	If set, disables controls from the user input.

4.6.5.1 Text field

The most commonly used input element is text field. It is used to get single-line textual data. Its common usage include name, date of birth, address, email address, login name, etc.

```
Name: <input type="text" name="name">
```

It results in the following output:

Name: U.K. Roy

4.6.5.2 Password field

Password fields are similar to text fields except that characters entered are displayed as dots or asterisks. This allows us to hide information from others. It is commonly used to accept sensitive information such as password, credit card number, bank account number, etc. Note that characters entered are not encrypted, they are only shown as asterisks or dots, and hence are unsafe. All the attributes of a text field are also valid for a password field.

```
Password: <input type="password" name="pass">
```

This code creates a password field with the name “pass”. It will be displayed on the screen as follows:

Password: ••••••••

4.6.5.3 Hidden field

Hidden fields are not displayed by the browser and users can never interact with them. However, users can see the field by viewing the source code. Scripts, like other fields, can access them. One of the important applications of a hidden field is session tracking where information is sent back and forth between the server and the browser.

Like other form fields, a hidden field is created using the `<input>` tag and specifying the `type` attribute value as “hidden”:

```
<input type="hidden" name="userid" value="u_roy">
```

The values of `name` and `value` attributes are passed to the server like other fields when the enclosing form is submitted.

4.6.5.4 Label

The content of the `<label>` tag is a piece of ordinary text. It is used to add a label to a form field. It describes the meaning of the associated form field. This way, web page designers can provide hints about the associated control.

To make the association, `for` attribute is required. The value of `for` attribute must be the same as the `id` of the control to bind them. The following code adds a label to the checkbox:

```
<label for="married">
Married
<input type="checkbox" id="married">
</label>
```

The result is as follows:

Married ☐

Note that a label does not do much for a user. Some browsers allow to check and uncheck a check box by clicking on its label. The association between a label and a form field, which is not within the content of label, is also possible.

4.6.5.5 Check box

A checkbox is like a toggle switch, i.e., it can be in either of the two states *checked* or *unchecked*. Checkboxes allow visitors to select one (or more) options from a set of related alternatives. A checkbox is created using the `<input>` tag and specifying the `type="checkbox"`.

```
Which of the following items do you have?<br>
<input type="checkbox" name="Carc value="yes">Car<br>
<input type="checkbox" name="Computer" value="yes">Computer<br>
<input type="checkbox" name="Camera" value="yes">Camera
```

The `value` attribute stores the value to be returned when the checkbox is checked. If the attribute `value` is not present and the checkbox is checked, the value "on" is returned. However, if it is not checked, no value is returned. A checkbox, by default, is off. If you want to turn it on, use the `checked` attribute. This code creates the result as shown in Figure 4.22.

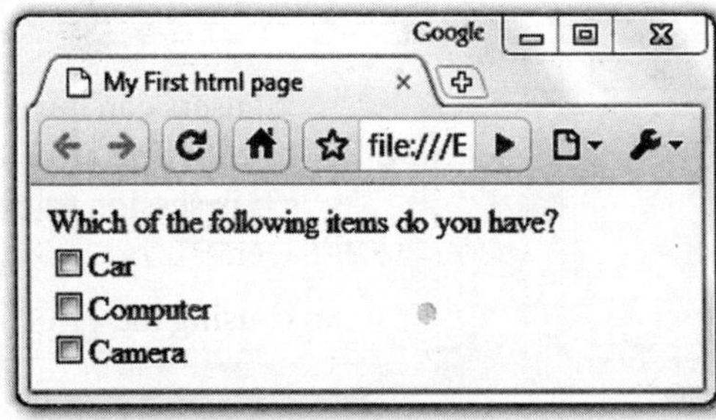

Figure 4.22 Adding check box

4.6.5.6 Radio button

Radio buttons allow visitors to select any one among a set of related alternatives. A radio button, like a checkbox, can be in either of the two states: on (checked) or off (unchecked). A group of radio buttons is created by giving the same name to each button in the group. This way, we can create several groups of radio buttons. When one radio button in a group is selected, the previously selected radio button (if any) is unselected. Radio buttons are unchecked by default. You can make a radio button checked initially, but only one in a group may be in the checked state.

A checkbox is created using the `<input>` tag and by specifying `type="radio"`. The following code allows you to choose any one browser among the four options.

```
Gender:<br>
<input type="radio" name="gender" value="Male">Male<br>
<input type="radio" name="gender" value="Female">Female<br>
```

In the browser it looks as shown in Figure 4.23(i).

4.6.5.7 Selection list

A selection list (also called the drop-down list), like a group of radio buttons or checkboxes, allows visitors to choose one (or more) options among a set of options. The advantage of selection list is that, it takes less space than check boxes or radio buttons. The disadvantage is that users cannot see all the options until they click on it. However, designer may also choose the number of options to be displayed.

A selection list is created using the `<select>` tag. Items of a selection list are created using the `<option>` tag. By default, the first option is displayed, although any item can be displayed using the selected attribute for it. The size attribute specifies how many items are to be displayed. If the attribute multiple is given the value "yes", users may select multiple items. If no size attribute is provided, all items are displayed.

```
Gender:
<select>
<option>Male
<option selected>Female
</select>
```

The result is shown in Figure 4.23(ii).

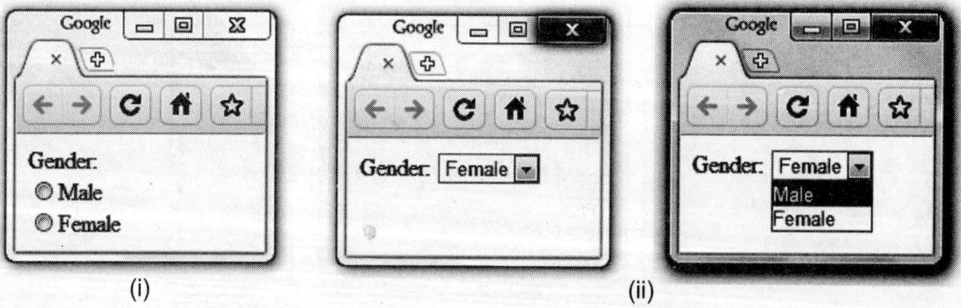

Figure 4.23 (i) Adding radio button (ii) Selection list

4.6.5.8 Text area

A text area is an extension of a text field, where the text can span multiple lines. It is used when visitors want to enter a large amount of text.

Unlike other form fields, a text area is created using the `<textarea>` and `</textarea>` tags. Everything within the tag pair is displayed in the text area box. The number of rows and columns may be set using the attributes `rows` and `cols`, respectively.

```
Comment:<br>
<textarea rows="4", cols="20">
Enter your comment here
</textarea>
```

The result is shown in Figure 4.24(i).

4.6.5.9 File upload

The file form field allows users to select one or more files to be sent to the server side. The files could be a text, image, or other files. When the form is submitted, the content of the file is sent to the server.

```
<form action="upload.jsp" method="post">
Select a question file(.xml)<br>
<input type="file" name="question"><br>
<input type="submit" value="Upload">
</form>
```

The result of this code is shown in Figure 4.24 (ii). The difficult part of file control is to write server-side script that processes the file data. Such processing must be robust and controlled so that no one can fill server disk space intentionally or unintentionally. The Java Server Page `upload.jsp` processes the file data. We shall discuss how to write such processing codes in JSP in Chapter 21.

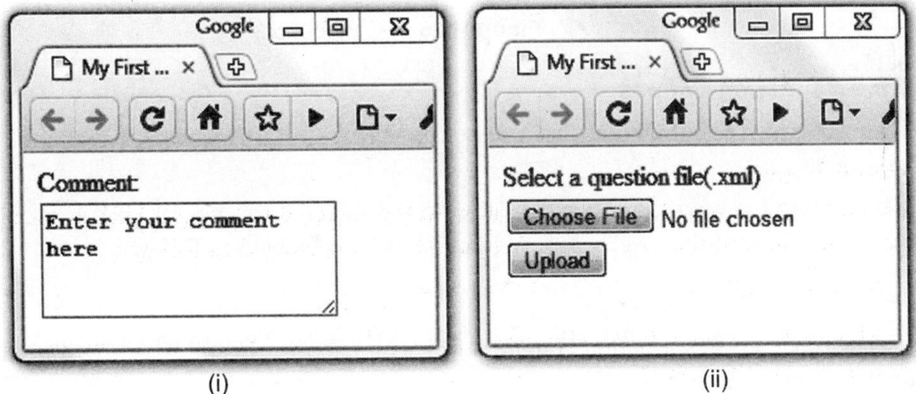

Figure 4.24 (i) Adding text area (ii) Adding file upload

4.6.5.10 Button

Push buttons can be created using the `<input>` tag, with the `type` attribute set to "button". The caption is the value of the `value` attribute of the input tag. The following code creates a button with caption "Logout".

```
<input type="button" value="Logout">
```

Buttons, created using the `<input>` tag, can only have text caption. Buttons can also be created using the `<button>` tag. The following code creates the same button as already discussed.

```
<button>Logout</button>
```

Buttons, created this way, can have fancy text as well as image as their caption. Figure 4.25 shows how to create different types of buttons using the `<input>` and `<button>` tags.

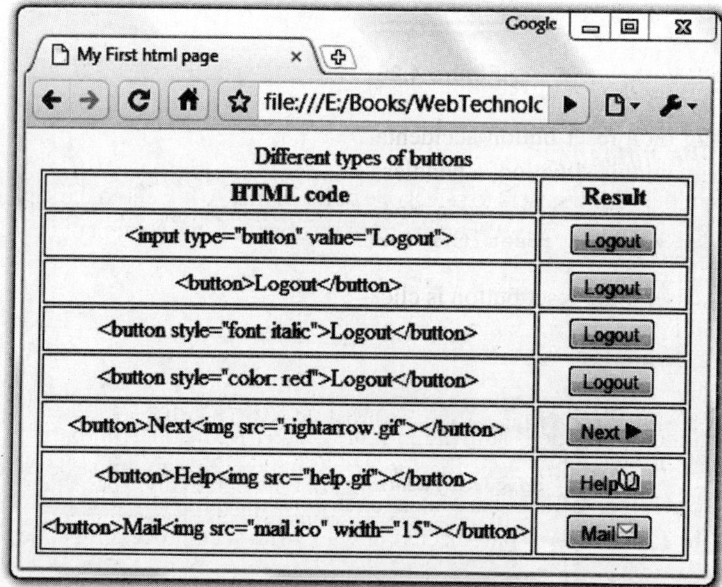

Different types of buttons

HTML code	Result
<input type="button" value="Logout">	Logout
<button>Logout</button>	Logout
<button style="font: italic">Logout</button>	Logout
<button style="color: red">Logout</button>	Logout
<button>Next<img src="rightarrow.gif"></button>	Next
<button>Help<img src="help.gif"></button>	Help
<button>Mail<img src="mail.ico" width="15"></button>	Mail

Figure 4.25 HTML buttons

4.6.5.11 Action buttons

There are two types of buttons that we use for almost all forms: *submit* button and *reset* button.

Submit button

Submit button is used to send information to the server script whose URL is specified by the `action` attribute of the `<form>` tag. A submit button is created as follows:

```
<input type="submit" value="Send">
```

This code creates a button [Figure 4.26] with caption "Send" which when clicked, sends form's data to the server.

Reset button

When a reset button is clicked, form fields are assigned their default initial values. It is created as follows:

```
<input type="reset" value="Restore Defaults">
```

The attribute type specifies that it is a reset button [Figure 4.26] and value specifies the text to be displayed on the reset button.

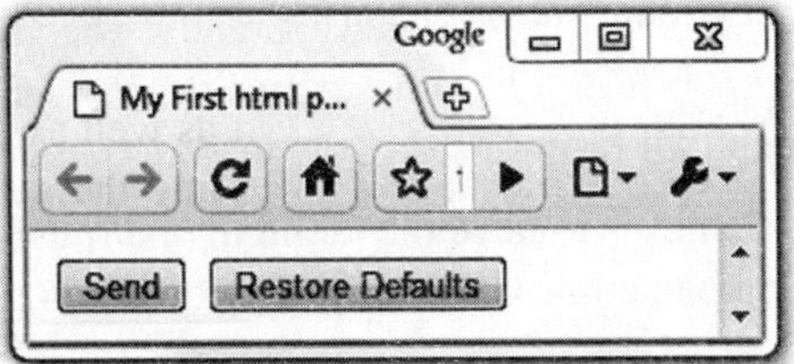

Figure 4.26 Submit and reset buttons

Clicking on a reset button accidentally erases the values supplied by the users to the form fields. To avoid this situation, a handler may be added as follows:

```
<input type="reset" value="Restore Defaults" onclick="return confirm('Do you really want to reset the form?')">
```

In this case, if the reset button is clicked, a dialog box [Figure 4.27] appears for confirmation as follows:

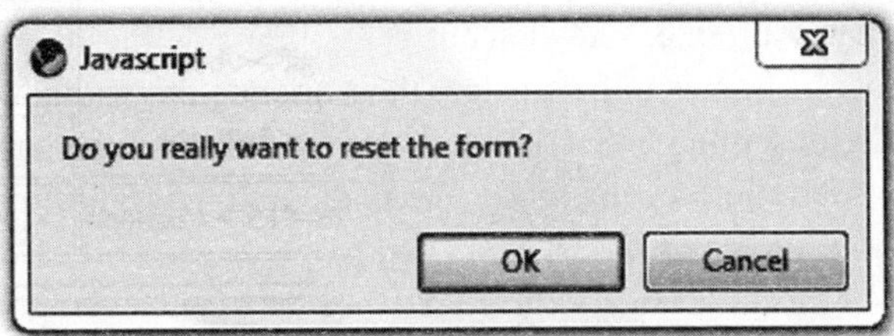

Figure 4.27 Confirm dialog box

So, even if the reset button is clicked accidentally, the user has a chance to cancel it.

4.6.5.12 Image button

The submit button in a form has a gray colored simple appearance, unless you use styles for it. A simple way to create a good looking graphic submit button is to use the `<input>` tag with `type` attribute set to "image".

```
<input type="image" src="rightarrow.gif">
```

It creates a button as follows:

Clicking on image buttons has the same effect as clicking on submit buttons. When an image button is clicked, form data are sent to the server script as specified in the `action` attribute of the `<form>` tag. The `<button>` tag could be used to create a stylist button. But, in practice, many browsers do not support the `<button>` tag.

4.7 FRAMES

HTML allows us to divide a web page into several blocks called *frames*. Each frame may display a separate web page. So, frames allow us to display multiple HTML document in one browser window simultaneously. They are refreshed separately. They maintain their own content without having any relation to others. Certain frames may display some information while others scroll or even replace the content. All browsers do not support frames, but most of them do.

The typical use of frames is to have the menu in one frame and the content in another frame. When users click on some menu in one frame, the corresponding content is displayed in another frame.

For example, the following code creates two frames separated vertically.

```
<frameset cols="40%,60%">
  <frame name="left" src="left.htm">
  <frame name="right" src="right.htm">
</frameset>
```

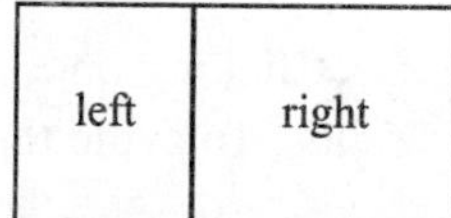

4.7.1 Frameset Element

The layout of a document is specified using the `<frameset>` element. The structure of an HTML document having frames is different from that of a document without frames. The `<frameset>` element is put in the parent HTML document without any `<body>` tag. It contains `<frame>` elements each of which creates a frame. The element `<frameset>` defines the characteristics of the frames such as the number of frames to be created, their orientation, width, height, etc. For example, the `frameset` element (described in Section 4.7)vertically divides the page into two blocks (frames). The left frame is set to 40% of the total page width and the right frame is set to 60% of the total page width.

4.7.2 Frame Element

The element `<frame>` specifies the HTML document to be loaded in each frame. It has several attributes discussed as follows:

- `name`—refers to the (unique) name of the frame.
- `src`—specifies the location of the initial web page to be loaded.
- `noresize`—if present, indicates that the frame is not resizable.
- `scrolling`—specifies the scroll information about the frame. It can have the following values:
  - `auto`—specifies that the scrollbar will be added as and when necessary.
  - `yes`—specifies that scrollbars are to be added always.
  - `no`—specifies that no scrollbars will be provided.
- `frameborder`—specifies the border information about the frame. It can have the following values:
  - `1`—indicates that a border will be drawn.
  - `0`—indicates that the frame will not have any border. Borders are drawn if the next frame has the frameborder attribute set to 1.

- `marginwidth`— specifies the amount of space in pixels to be added between the frame's contents in its left and right margins.
- `marginheight`— specifies the amount of space in pixels to be added between the frame's contents in its top and bottom margins.

The frame named `left` is created to contain the web page `left.htm` whereas the `right` frame is created to contain the web page `right.html`. The value of the `src` attribute may be a local file name or a URL.

4.7.3 Layout

Each frameset creates a set of rows or columns.

```
<frameset rows="30%,70%">
  <frame name="top" src="top.htm">
  <frame name="bottom" src="bottom.htm">
</frameset>
```

top
bottom

This `frameset` element divides the page horizontally into two frames. The top frame is set to 30% of the total page height and the bottom frame is set to 70% of the total page height. The orientation and relative size of frames may be specified using the `cols` and `rows` attributes of the frameset element.

- `cols`—This attribute is used to create frames vertically. Its value is a comma-separated list of percentages, pixels, and relative lengths that indicate the width of frames. The default value is 100%. This indicates one column.
- `rows`—This attribute is used to create frames horizontally. Its value is a comma-separated list of percentages, pixels, and relative lengths that indicate the height of frames. The default value is 100%. This indicates one row.

For the `cols` attribute, frames are created left-to-right vertically, and for the `rows` attribute frames are created top-to-bottom horizontally. If both are specified, frames are created left-to-right in the top row, then left-to-right in the second row, and so on.

The following specifications are valid:

`cols="10%,*"`	Two frames are created vertically. The left frame has the width 10% of the total page width and the right frame will use the rest (90%).
`cols="10%,60%,30%"`	There are three frames created vertically whose width will be 10%, 60%, and 30%, respectively.
`cols="20%,50%,*%"`	There are three frames created vertically. The left and middle frames will have widths of 20% and 50%, respectively. The right one will use the rest (30%) of the page width.
`rows="20%,*"`	Two frames are created horizontally. The first row has the width 20% of the total page width and second row will use the rest (80%).
`rows="30%,40%,30%"`	There are three frames created horizontally whose width will be 30%, 40%, and 30%, respectively.

`cols="10%,60%,*%"` There are three frames created horizontally. The top and middle frames will have widths of 10% and 60%, respectively. The bottom one will use the rest (30%) of the page width.

Note that the value of `rows` and `cols` attributes may be specified as pixels. For example, `cols="200,*%"` specifies that the first column has the fixed width of 200 pixels and the second column will use the rest of the browser window.

Nested frames are also possible.

```
<frameset rows="20%,80%">
  <frame name="top" src="top.htm">
  <frameset cols="40%,60%">
    <frame name="bottom-left" src="bottom-left.htm">
    <frame name="bottom-right" src="bottom-right.htm">
  </frameset>
</frameset>
```

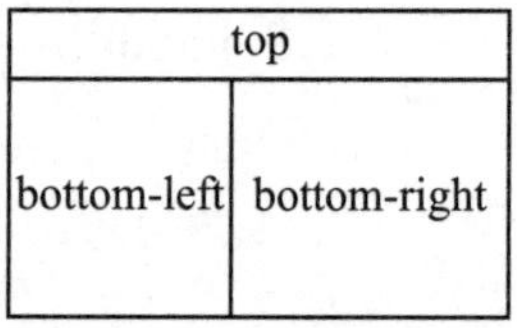

top	
bottom-left	bottom-right

This HTML code first divides the window into two rows. The first row is given a name `top` and is set to 20% of the height of the browser window and the second row is set to 80% of the height of the browser window. In the first row, the HTML document `top.htm` is loaded. The second (bottom) row is further divided into two frames vertically. The first column of the bottom row is given a name `bottom-left` and is set to 40% of the width of the bottom frame and the second column is given a name `bottom-right` and is set to 60% of the width of the bottom frame. The HTML documents `bottom-left.htm` and `bottom-right.htm` are loaded in the `bottom-left` and `bottom-right`, respectively.

```
<frameset cols="40%,60%">
  <frame name="left" src="left.htm">
  <frameset rows="40%,60%">
    <frame name="right-top" src="right-top.htm">
    <frame name="right-bottom" src="right-bottom.htm">
  </frameset>
</frameset>
```

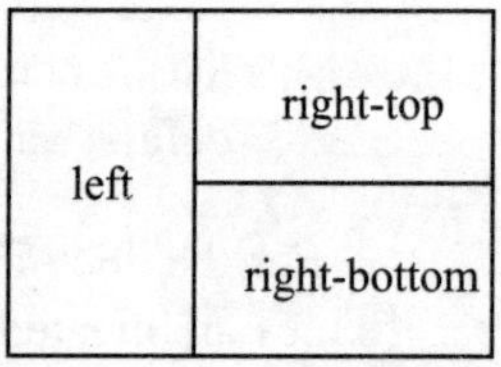

left	right-top
	right-bottom

The HTML code creates three frames as shown on the right-hand side.

```
<frameset rows="20%,80%">
  <frameset cols="40%,60%">
    <frame name="top-left" src="top-left.htm">
    <frame name="top-right" src="top-right.htm">
  </frameset>
  <frameset cols="40%,60%">
    <frame name="bottom-left" src="bottom-left.htm">
    <frame name="bottom-right" src="bottom-right.htm">
  </frameset>
</frameset>
```

top-left	top-right
bottom-left	bottom-right

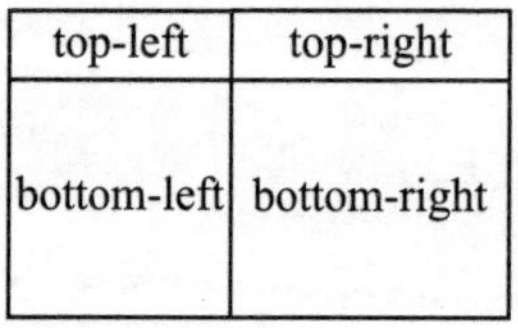

The HTML code creates four frames as shown on the right-hand side. Any level of nesting is possible. This code may also be written as

```
<frameset rows="20%,80%" cols="40%,60%">
  <frame name="top-left" src="top-left.htm">
  <frame name="top-right" src="top-right.htm">
```

```
    <frame name="bottom-left" src="bottom-left.htm">
    <frame name="bottom-right" src="bottom-right.htm">
  </frameset>
```

4.7.4 Specifying Target

The `target` attribute may be set for elements that create links such as `<a>`, `<link>`, `<area>`, `<form>`, etc. The value of `target` attribute refers to the frame where the document is to be loaded. The value of the `target` attribute must be an existing frame name. The following example demonstrates how to specify the target attribute.

First we define a frameset document `main.htm` as follows:

```
<html>
  <frameset cols="20%,80%">
    <frame name="left" src="left.htm">
    <frame name="right" src="right.htm">
  </frameset>
</html>
```

This divides the window into two frames vertically. In the left frame, HTML document `left.htm` is loaded. It looks like this.

```
<html>
  <head>
    <title>Target demo</title>
  </head>
  <body>
    <a href="http://www.google.com" target="right">Google</a><br>
    <a href="http://www.yahoo.com" target="right">Yahoo</a><br>
  </body>
</html>
```

It contains two links `Google` and `Yahoo` each of which when clicked, the respective link is opened in the frame named `right`. Figure 4.28 shows the result when the link 'Yahoo' is clicked.

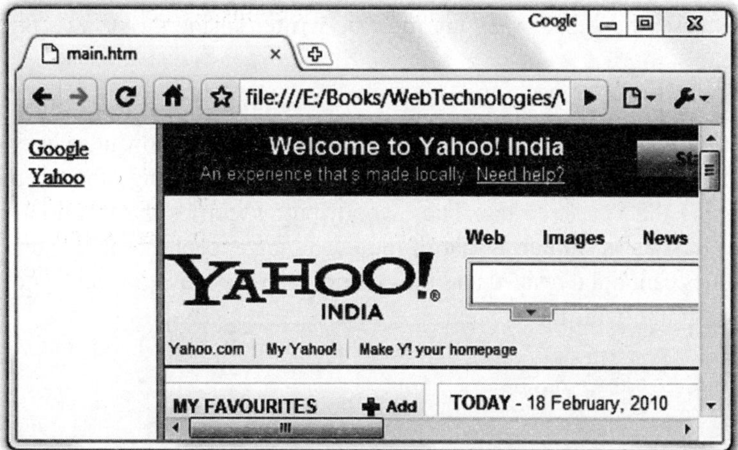

Figure 4.28 Multiple frames and target attribute

If a document has multiple links with a same target, it is a good idea to specify the target once globally and omitting the `target` attribute for an individual link. So, `left.htm` may be written as

```
<html>
  <head>
    <title>Target demo</title>
    <BASE href="http://www.gmail.com" target="right">
  </head>
  <body>
    <a href="http://www.google.com">Google</a><br>
    <a href="http://www.yahoo.com">Yahoo</a><br>
  </body>
</html>
```

4.7.4.1 *Target rules*

The following rules are used by the browser when determining the target frame of a link:

- If a link has the `target` attribute set, the designated resource is loaded in the frame specified by the `target` attribute.
- If the `target` attribute is not set but the base element is defined, its `target` attribute specifies the target frame.
- If none is specified, the resource is loaded in the frame in which the contained document is loaded.

4.7.5 Alternate Message

Every browser does not support frames. The authors of the web pages must handle it explicitly. To display some message in case a browser does not support frames, place it in the `<noframes>` and `</noframes>` tag pair as follows:

```
<body>
<noframes>The page that you have loaded uses frames and your browser does not
support frames. Please upgrade your browser to see it correctly.</noframes>
</body>
```

In this case, the `<noframes>` tag must be written inside the `<body>` tag.

4.7.6 Inline Frames

HTML *inline frames* (also called *iframes* or *floating frames*) allow us to insert a frame even within a block of text. Iframes may contain external objects including other web pages. An iframe is created using the `<iframe>` tag. The `src` attribute specifies the location of the frame content. The `<iframe>` tag is similar to that of the `<img>` tag except that its content is a web page. The inline frames cannot be resized and thus do not take the `noresize` attribute. The following code creates an iframe with the content `http://www.yahoo.com`.

```
<iframe src="http://www.yahoo.com">
  You browser does not support iframe
</iframe>
```

This results in the inline frame as shown in Figure 4.29.

Figure 4.29 Inline frame

All major browsers support the `<iframe>` tag. If you want to display a text in the iframe in a browser that does not support iframes, place the text between the `<iframe>` and `</iframe>` tag pair.

An iframe may be specified as the target of hyperlinks as follows:

```
<a href="http://www.google.com" target="canvas">Google</a><br>
<a href="http://www.yahoo.com" target="canvas">Yahoo</a><br>

<iframe name="canvas">
  You browser does not support iframe
</iframe>
```

4.8 IMAGES

An image is placed in an HTML document using the standalone `<img>` tag. The attribute `src` (stands for source) indicates the URL of the image file. If the image file is located in the same directory of the HTML document, only the name of the image file may be specified. The browser inserts the image [Figure 4.30] where `<img>` tags occur in the document.

```
<img src="Autumn.jpg" width="150">
<img src="azul.jpg" width="150">
```

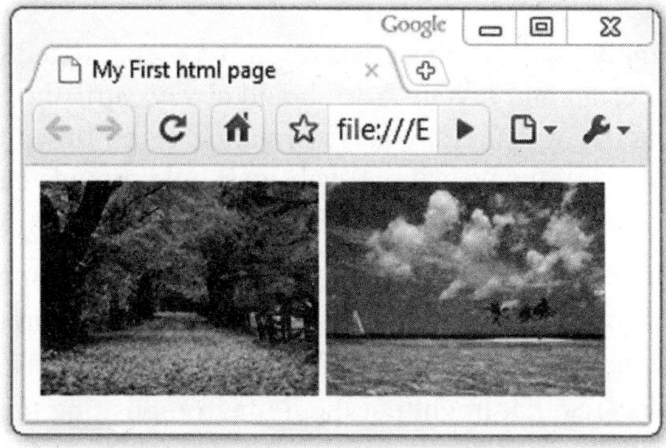

Figure 4.30 Inserting images

The height and width of images are controlled by the `height` and `width` attributes, respectively.

4.9 META TAG

The <head> element often includes <meta> elements which are used to provided meta-information about the document. They are not rendered on the screen. Very often the <meta> element is used to provide information that is relevant to search engines such as describing the content of web pages. It is also used to redirect the current page to another page after a specified number of seconds. For example, the following <meta> tag redirects the current page as soon as it is loaded to another page "old.html".

```
<meta http-equiv="refresh" content="0;URL=old.html" >
```

It is useful if original web page is moved to somewhere else and the author of the page does not want to affect the users.

Some search engines use the `name` and `content` attributes of the <meta> tag to index your pages. So, they can be used to describe the content of your web pages so that search engines can find them. For example, the following <meta> element defines a description of a page:

```
<meta name="description" content="Tutorial on XML technologies " >
```

The following <meta> element defines keywords for a page:

```
<meta name="keywords" content=" XML, DTD, Schema, XPath, XQuery" >
```

Note that <meta> tags were introduced to tell search engines what your page was about. Consequently, various tactics were discovered to get higher ranking for certain keywords, and an entire industry sprang up to optimize search engine positioning. This was, in effect, cheating, and "keyword spamming" became a serious problem for search engines, which vainly attempted to add filters that would notice when a webmaster was loading wrong keywords. So, most of the search engines (including Google) do not rely on the information provided by the <meta> tag. Consequently, the actual purpose of the <meta> tag cannot be achieved.

4.10 PLANNING OF WEB PAGE

A website is not simply a collection web pages; it is a set of related web pages. Planning of pages is as important as design and layout. You should always structure your web pages so that they are easy to navigate. A website allows information to be flown between the provider of the website and the visitors of the website. A website should provide basic needs of website visitors. To plan a website you should consider the following points:

- Identify the people and groups who will view your website.
- For each of these people and groups, identify their requirements.
- Identify the information that is needed to fulfill their requirements.
- Identify concerns that might put them off from visiting this site.
- Also identify the information that you should include their to motivate them to visit your website.

If you consider these points, you will have an idea about a list of web pages with their basic contents. You can then start analyzing each page in detail and go to the designing phase.

Requirements of all users are not the same. Some users want to have more information than others. Some users may have little awareness about the concept of websites. So, you should always provide alternative options so that they can use your site conveniently.

Identify what you want to provide

Look at as many websites as you can. You will have an idea about the common features used in the website. Try to make a list of content, features, and your preferred design components. Also make a list of element that you do not want to use. Think about the placement of different elements, preferred color combinations, use of animations, etc.

Identify target users

Identify the class of users who will view your website. Think about their performance, computer literacy, frequency of internet access, etc.

4.11 MODEL AND STRUCTURE FOR A WEBSITE

Many website designing tools provide readymade structures. A sample structure of an educational department is shown in Figure 4.31.

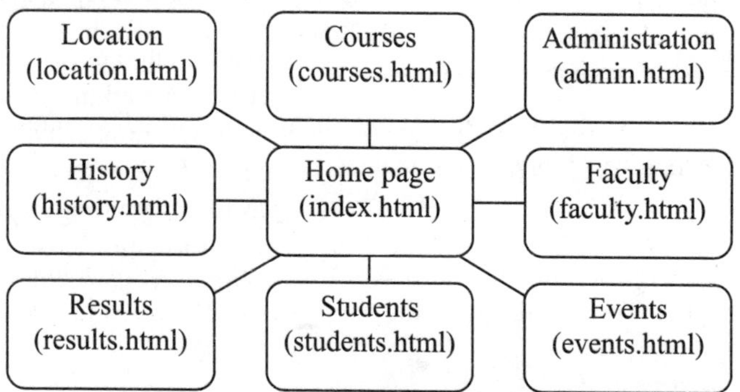

Figure 4.31 Sample structure of a departmental web page

Individual sections may be stored in separate directories as shown in Figure 4.32:

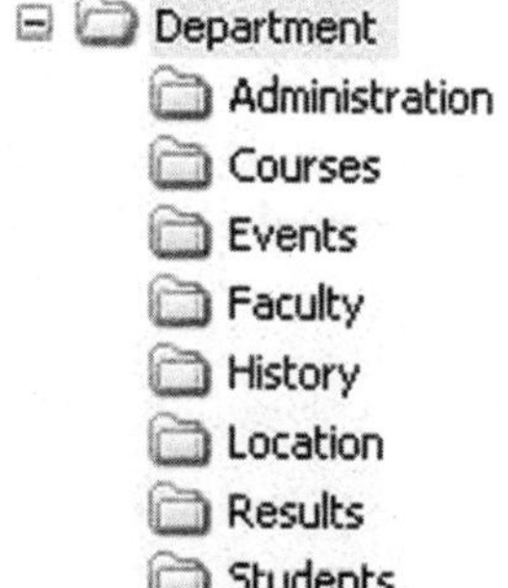

Figure 4.32 Sample directory structure for a departmental website

4.12 DESIGNING WEB PAGES

Web pages of a website should be designed in such a way that visitors of the website can find their desired information quickly and conveniently. This is the fundamental principle of any usable website design. A typical website should provide an outline of the path that the visitors will traverse to get the desired information. The path should start addressing visitors' fundamental concern and should provide more detailed information as they navigate the website.

4.13 MULTIMEDIA CONTENT (AUDIO AND VIDEO) FRAMES

The most important factor behind the growth of WWW is the ability to integrate multimedia content in web pages. Early versions of HTML allows only to reference images. The current version allows including not only static images, but also audio, video and even VRML files. With these facilities, navigating internet is a charming experience. So, web designers must always keep this fact into consideration while developing a website. Web designers must remember that not all browsers support (most do) multimedia, and should not include multimedia content extensively. Alternative methods for the inclusion of multimedia content are also available for the browsers that do not support them. For example, the <img> tag allows us to insert a text string when image cannot be loaded. The `<object>` tag displays a text representation on an image map when image map cannot be used. Web designer should always use those options so that some visible content is delivered to the user.

There are many ways in which you can include multimedia content in your web pages for browsers that support it. Some of the tags are described briefly as follows:

img

This is the primitive multimedia tag. It was first introduced to include multimedia elements in HTML documents. The details about the `<img>` tag is described in Section 4.8.

area, map

This method allows us to handle transit decisions related to image maps, i.e., links for geometric regions of an image. Multiple image files were used to handled this previously. However, this requires extra download time. Using `<area>`, information is included in the HTML document itself and relatively faster.

BGSound, Sound

The `<BGSound>` tag allows us to add a background sound which plays when the page is viewed. Browsers may have their own tag to do the same.

Object

The `<object>` tag may be used on behalf of all other multimedia tags. It has made most of the multimedia elements such as `<img>`, `<area>`, `<map>`, `<BGSound>`, `<sound>` `<embed>`, and `<applet>` obsolete.

KEYWORDS

Attribute: Tags may have properties that can optionally be assigned values to change the default behavior of the tags. These properties are called *attributes*.

Background: Canvas of an HTML document where other components are displayed.

Element: HTML elements are fundamental building blocks of a web page. An element consists of a tag, its attributes, and the content.

Form: Used to send data to the server-side scripts.

Frames: An HTML page may be divided into parts, called frames.

HTML Comment: Everything within <!-- and --> will be ignored by the browsers and will not be parsed.

HTML Symbols: Special Characters that can appear in an HTML document.

Inline Frames: These are frames that can be inserted even within a text.

Lists: An ordered or unordered collection of related items.

Table: Used to present data in a tabular format.

Tag: Marked-up regions are displayed on the screen using the style as mentioned by the marking tag.

Text Formatting: Tags used to change the style of text.

Title: A title is a piece of text that is displayed on the top of your browser window.

SUMMARY

We started this chapter with a brief history of HTML and its available flavors. An HTML document consists of elements. An element consists of a tag, its attributes, and contents. A tag is written in angular brackets. A tag may be embedded or standalone. An embedded tag has its corresponding closing tag. Standalone tags do have any closing tag. Attributes are used to change the default behavior of a tag. Attributes are written within the starting tag. Each tag has its own set of valid attributes. If the value of an attribute for a tag is not specified, browser supply a value and renders the tag accordingly. The default value supplied is browser-specific.

An HTML document has basically two sections: head and body. The head section contains meta-information about the document, script, or style information. The head section is processed but not displayed on the screen.

The body section is rendered to display on the screen. It contains different tags to be displayed on the screen.

We discussed various text formatting tags. We also mentioned how to set the background of an HTML document using plain color or an image. HTML allows us to insert characters that cannot be typed using entities.

We then discussed various advanced tags to create tables, frames, inline frames, forms, and form elements. We ended with giving an idea about how to plan and design good websites.

WEB RESOURCES

`http://www.w3.org/TR/html401/`
HTML 4.01 Specification

`http://www.w3.org/TR/html4/sgml/entities.html`
Character entity references in HTML 4

`http://tools.ietf.org/html/rfc1867`
Form-based File Upload in HTML

`http://tools.ietf.org/html/rfc1942`
HTML Tables

`http://tools.ietf.org/html/rfc1980`
A Proposed Extension to HTML : Client-Side Image Maps

`http://tools.ietf.org/html/rfc2070`
Internationalization of the Hypertext Markup Language

EXERCISES

Multiple Choice Questions

1. HTML is an acronym of
   (a) Hyper Terminal Making Language
   (b) How To Markup Library
   (c) Hyper Text Markup Language
   (d) Hyper Text Machine Language

2. Which of the following HTML codes displays the content in bold face?
   (a) <b>This text is big<b>
   (b) <b>This text is big</b>
   (c) <b/>This text is bold</b>
   (d) <b>This text is bold<\b>

3. Which of the following forms is a valid attribute specification?
   (a) name="value" (b) name=value
   (c) name=(value) (d) name='value'

4. Which of the following is the correct syntax for creating an anchor tag?
   (a) <ref="http://mail.jusl.ac.in/">JUSL web mail</ref>
   (b) <a href="http://mail.jusl.ac.in/">JUSL web mail</a>
   (c) <a ref="http://mail.jusl.ac.in/">JUSL web mail</a>
   (d) <href="http://mail.jusl.ac.in/">JUSL web mail>

5. Which of the following tag sequence is correct?
   (a) <html><head></head><body><title> </<title></body></html>
   (b) <html><head><title></<title><body> </body></head></html>
   (c) <html><title></<title><head></head><body></body></html>
   (d) <html><head><title></<title></head><body></body></html>

6. Which of the following attributes of the font tag is used to choose the type of font in HTML?
   (a) type (b) text-type
   (c) face (d) font-type

7. Which of the following tags is not written in the <head> section?
   (a) title (b) table
   (c) meta (d) script

8. Which of the following tags is used to add a row to a table?
   (a) <td> and </td>
   (b) <row> and <row>
   (c) <tablerow> and </tablerow>
   (d) <tr> and </tr>

9. Which of the following is not a valid HTML tag declaration?
   (a) <frameset columns="30%, 70%">
   (b) <frameset rows="20%, 80%">
   (c) <frameset cols="10%, *">
   (d) <frameset rows="40%, *">

10. To insert images, we use the ________ tag.
    (a) picture (b) pic
    (c) img (d) image

11. Which of the following form attributes specifies the URL to be used to submit form data?
    (a) action (b) method
    (c) id (d) name

12. Which of the following represents the value attribute of a text field?
    (a) The number of characters the text field can contain
    (b) The possible value that the text field can have
    (c) Whether the text field is editable or not
    (d) The text that appears in the field as the default value

13. Which of the following is true regarding password field?
    (a) It is similar to text area except that text is shown as "." (dot)
    (b) It is similar to text field except that text is shown as "." (dot)
    (c) It is similar to hidden field except that text is shown as "." (dot)
    (d) It is similar to selection list.

14. Which of the following fields can hold information that is not displayed?

(a) Text field (b) Text Area field

(c) Hidden field (d) Table

15. Which of the following tags is used to set the background color of your web page?

(a) <html> (b) <body>

(c) <head> (d) <font>

16. Which of the following properties of the body tag prevents scrolling of a background image?

(a) background="still"

(b) background="fixed"

(c) bgproperties="stationary"

(d) bgproperties="fixed"

17. Which colors consist of equal amounts of all basic colors?

(a) black, blue, and gray

(b) olive, green, and red

(c) white, black, and gray

(d) yellow, magenta, and red

18. Which of the following adds a plain color to the background of a web page?

(a) <body color="#FF0000">

(b) <body color="3,454">

(c) <body bgcolor="#FF0000">

(d) <body bgcolor="36,24,35">

19. Which of the following tags make the text content bold?

(a) strong (b) thick

(c) fat (d) large

20. What is the purpose of REFRESH meta tag?

(a) To refresh the page at periodic intervals

(b) To redirect to a different web page

(c) To refresh your keywords

(d) To allow search engines to retrieve information about your page

Review Questions

1. Why should you specify a background color if you are using an image for the actual background of your page ?
2. What is the purpose of the meta tag in HTML?
3. How may basic sections are there in an HTML page?
4. Create an ordered list of items: Asia, Africa, Australia. Use capital roman numbers to order them.
5. What are the different types of bullets available for an unordered list? How are they created?
6. How do you add an alternative text to images? Why are they used?
7. How do you create a web page having a fixed background image?
8. What is the difference between width="100" and width="100%"?
9. Write an HTML page to display the following:

   $\sqrt{2}=1.414$

   $\forall$ i $\exists$ s[i] $\in$ N such that s[i] is prime
10. Write an HTML page to display the following.

    First Name:

    Middle Initial:

    Last name:
11. Write an HTML page to create the following lists:
    - Pentium I
    - Pentium II
      1. 1.6 GHz
      2. 2.4 GHz
      3. 3.2 GHz
    - Pentium III
12. Create an HTML page containing a text area as follows:

    Tell us about your interests (maximum of 100 words)

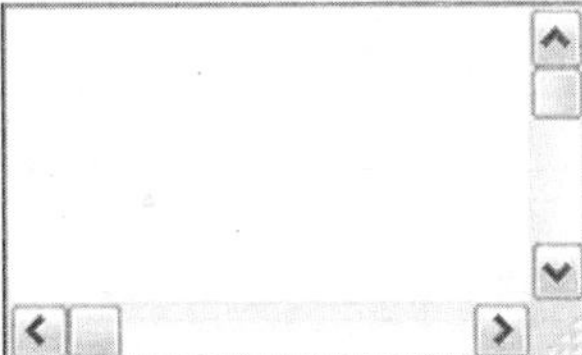

Appendix—HTML symbols

Table 4.9 HTML symbols

Special Characters			
Entity Name	**Entity Number**	**Description**	**Result**
"	"	Double quotes	"
&	&	Ampersand sign	&
<	<	Less than sign	<
>	=	Greater than sign	>
Mathematical Symbols			
Entity Name	**Entity Number**	**Description**	**Result**
∀	∀	for all	∀
∂	∂	partial differential	∂
∃	∃	Exist	∃
∅	∅	Empty	ø
∇	∇	nabla = backward difference	∇
∈	∈	Belongs to	∈
∉	∉	Does not belong to	∉
∋	∋	Ni	∋
∏	∏	Prod	Π
∑	∑	Sum	Σ
√	√	square root	√
∝	∝	proportional to	∝
∞	∞	Infinity	∞
∠	∠	Angle sign	∠
∧	∧	logical and	∧
∨	∨	logical or	∨
∩	∩	Intersection	∩
∪	∪	Union	∪
∫	∫	Integral	∫
∴	∴	Therefore	∴
≈	≈	almost equal to = asymptotic to	≈
≠	≠	not equal to	≠
≡	≡	identical to	≡
≤	≤	Less or equal	≤
≥	≥	Greater or equal	≥
⊂	⊂	subset of	⊂
⊃	⊃	superset of	⊃
⊄	⊄	not a subset of	⊄
⊆	⊆	subset of or equal to	⊆

(Contd.)

(Contd.)

⊇	⊇	superset of or equal to	⊇
⊕	⊕	circled plus = direct sum	⊕
⊗	⊗	circled times = vector product	⊗
⊥	⊥	up tack = orthogonal to = perpendicular	⊥
⋅	⋅	dot operator	·
⌈	⌈	left ceiling = APL upstile	⌈
⌉	⌉	right ceiling	⌉
⌊	⌊	left floor = APL downstile	⌊
⌋	⌋	right floor	⌋
⟨	〈	left-pointing angle bracket	〈
⟩	〉	right-pointing angle bracket	〉

Greek Symbols						
Description	Capital Letter			Small Letter		
	Entity Name	Entity Number	Symbol	Entity Name	Entity Number	Symbol
alpha	Α	Α	Α	α	α	α
beta	Β	Β	Β	β	β	β
gamma	Γ	Γ	Γ	γ	γ	γ
delta	Δ	Δ	Δ	δ	δ	δ
epsilon	Ε	Ε	Ε	ε	ε	ε
zeta	Ζ	Ζ	Ζ	ζ	ζ	ζ
Eta	Η	Η	Η	η	η	η
theta	Θ	Θ	Θ	θ	θ	θ
Iota	Ι	Ι	Ι	ι	ι	ι
kappa	Κ	Κ	Κ	κ	κ	κ
lambda	Λ	Λ	Λ	λ	λ	λ
Mu	Μ	Μ	Μ	μ	μ	μ
Nu	Ν	Ν	Ν	ν	ν	ν
Xi	Ξ	Ξ	Ξ	ξ	ξ	ξ
omicron	Ο	Ο	Ο	ο	ο	ο
Pi	Π	Π	Π	π	π	π
Rho	Ρ	Ρ	Ρ	ρ	ρ	ρ
sigma	Σ	Σ	Σ	σ	σ	σ
Tau	Τ	Τ	Τ	τ	τ	τ
upsilon	Υ	Υ	Υ	υ	υ	υ
Phi	Φ	Φ	Φ	φ	φ	φ
Chi	Χ	Χ	Χ	χ	χ	χ
Psi	Ψ	Ψ	Ψ	ψ	ψ	ψ
omega	Ω	Ω	Ω	ω	ω	ω

Entity Name	Entity Number	Description	Result
		Non-breaking space	
¡	¡	Inverted exclamation mark	¡
¢	¢	Cent sign	¢
£	£	Pound sign	£
¤	¤	Currency sign	¤
¥	¥	Yen sign	¥
¦	¦	Broken vertical bar	¦
§	§	Section sign	§
¨	¨	Spacing diaeresis – umlaut	¨
©	©	Copyright sign	©
ª	ª	Feminine ordinal indicator	a
«	«	Left double angle quotes	«
¬	¬	Not sign	¬
		Soft hyphen	
®	®	Registered trade mark sign	®
¯	¯	Spacing macron – overline	–
°	°	Degree sign	°
±	±	Plus-or-minus sign	±
²	²	Superscript two – squared	2
³	³	Superscript three – cubed	3
´	´	Acute accent - spacing acute	´
µ	µ	Micro sign	µ
¶	¶	Pilcrow sign - paragraph sign	¶
·	·	Middle dot - Georgian comma	·
¸	¸	Spacing cedilla	¸
¹	¹	Superscript one	1
º	º	Masculine ordinal indicator	o
»	»	Right double angle quotes	»
¼	¼	Fraction one quarter	¼
½	½	Fraction one half	½
¾	¾	Fraction three quarters	¾
¿	¿	Inverted question mark	¿
À	À	Latin capital letter A with grave	À
Á	Á	Latin capital letter A with acute	Á
Â	Â	Latin capital letter A with circumflex	Â
Ã	Ã	Latin capital letter A with tilde	Ã
Ä	Ä	Latin capital letter A with diaeresis	Ä
Å	Å	Latin capital letter A with ring above	Å
Æ	Æ	Latin capital letter AE	Æ

(Contd.)

(Contd.)

Ç	Ç	Latin capital letter C with cedilla	Ç
È	È	Latin capital letter E with grave	È
É	É	Latin capital letter E with acute	É
Ê	Ê	Latin capital letter E with circumflex	Ê
Ë	Ë	Latin capital letter E with diaeresis	Ë
Ì	Ì	Latin capital letter I with grave	Ì
Í	Í	Latin capital letter I with acute	Í
Î	Î	Latin capital letter I with circumflex	Î
Ï	Ï	Latin capital letter I with diaeresis	Ï
Ð	Ð	Latin capital letter ETH	Ð
Ñ	Ñ	Latin capital letter N with tilde	Ñ
Ò	Ò	Latin capital letter O with grave	Ò
Ó	Ó	Latin capital letter O with acute	Ó
Ô	Ô	Latin capital letter O with circumflex	Ô
Õ	Õ	Latin capital letter O with tilde	Õ
Ö	Ö	Latin capital letter O with diaeresis	Ö
×	×	Multiplication sign	×
Ø	Ø	Latin capital letter O with slash	Ø
Ù	Ù	Latin capital letter U with grave	Ù
Ú	Ú	Latin capital letter U with acute	Ú
Û	Û	Latin capital letter U with circumflex	Û
Ü	Ü	Latin capital letter U with diaeresis	Ü
Ý	Ý	Latin capital letter Y with acute	Ý
Þ	Þ	Latin capital letter THORN	Þ
ß	ß	Latin small letter sharp s - ess-zed	ß
à	à	Latin small letter a with grave	à
á	á	Latin small letter a with acute	á
â	â	Latin small letter a with circumflex	â
ã	ã	Latin small letter a with tilde	ã
ä	ä	Latin small letter a with diaeresis	ä
å	å	Latin small letter a with ring above	å
æ	æ	Latin small letter ae	æ
ç	ç	Latin small letter c with cedilla	ç
è	è	Latin small letter e with grave	è
é	é	Latin small letter e with acute	é
ê	ê	Latin small letter e with circumflex	ê
ë	ë	Latin small letter e with diaeresis	ë
ì	ì	Latin small letter i with grave	ì

(Contd.)

(Contd.)

í	í	Latin small letter i with acute	í
î	î	Latin small letter i with circumflex	î
ï	ï	Latin small letter i with diaeresis	ï
ð	ð	Latin small letter eth	ð
ñ	ñ	Latin small letter n with tilde	ñ
ò	ò	Latin small letter o with grave	ò
ó	ó	Latin small letter o with acute	ó
ô	ô	Latin small letter o with circumflex	ô
õ	õ	Latin small letter o with tilde	õ
ö	ö	Latin small letter o with diaeresis	ö
÷	÷	Division sign	÷
ø	ø	Latin small letter o with slash	ø
ù	ù	Latin small letter u with grave	ù
ú	ú	Latin small letter u with acute	ú
û	û	Latin small letter u with circumflex	û
ü	ü	Latin small letter u with diaeresis	ü
ý	ý	Latin small letter y with acute	ý
þ	þ	Latin small letter thorn	þ
ÿ	ÿ	Latin small letter y with diaeresis	ÿ

5 CASCADING STYLE SHEET (CSS)

KEY OBJECTIVES

After completing this chapter readers will be able to—

- **learn how to include style sheets in an HTML document**
- **learn the basic syntax of the CSS style rule**
- **get an idea about different CSS selectors**
- **know about the different styles of elements**
- **use style rules to apply styles to different elements**

5.1 INTRODUCTION

In web page designing, style sheets introduce a major breakthrough. They allow web page designers to improve and change the appearance of their web pages very efficiently. In earlier days, web page designers used to write presentation information within the web pages. This mechanism increased the complexity of web pages significantly. Moreover, changing the presentation on demand required considerable overhead. Style sheets solve these problems easily.

A style sheet is a document that contains style information about one or more documents written in markup languages. It enables us to control rendering of styles such as fonts, color, typeface, size, spacing, margins, and other aspects of document style. A style sheet is composed of a set of style rules written in a specified format. This set of style rules instructs browsers on how to present a document on the screen.

Cascading Style Sheet (CSS) is a style sheet language that specifies how to incorporate style information in a style sheet. The term "cascading" indicates that several style sheets can be blended to present a document on the browser's screen. The later style sheets have greater precedence than earlier ones. Not all style sheet languages support cascading.

5.2 ADVANTAGES

The primary intention of CSS is to separate document presentation from document content written in markup languages. So, document writers can concentrate on developing the document content using markup languages such as HTML (or XHTML), and XML without bothering about the visual presentation of these documents. On the other hand, style sheet writers can think about the visual presentation of these documents without bothering about the document content. This mechanism allows us to give a different look to the same document, without significant effort. The only thing we have to do is to use a separate style sheet for different presentations. The same style sheet can also be applied on different documents. This way, CSS reduces development time significantly [Figure 5.1].

Figure 5.1 Separation of style from content

Most of the browsers cache external style sheets. So, once a style sheet is cached, there is no delay in document presentation. The size of a document using external style sheet is comparatively smaller and hence, download time is also smaller. This speeds up overall response time.

CSS provides many more style attributes for defining the look and feel of web pages, than plain HTML.

5.3 ADDING CSS

There are four ways to specify style information in a document:

- External
- Embedded
- Imported
- Inline

Each one has its own set of advantages and disadvantages. Following is a brief description of each of them.

5.3.1 External Style Sheets

In this case, style information is written in a separate file and is referenced from an HTML document. An external style sheet is useful when the same style is applied on different documents. For example, the designer of a website may keep one style sheet file for entire website. This helps to update and maintain the look and feel of the entire website from a single file, without significant effort. It was mentioned that external style sheets are cached by most of the browsers. So, browsers have to download only documents. This implies faster response.

If the document is an HTML document, the external style sheet is specified using the HTML `<link>` tag. Following is an example:

```
<link rel="stylesheet" type="text/css" href="mystyle.css" />
```

This tag specifies that the style information to be used to display this document is stored in a file named `mystyle.css`. It is inserted in the head section of an HTML document.

According to W3C specification, external style sheets can be of three types: *persistent*, *alternate*, and *preferred*. A persistent style sheet is one that is always applied. Document authors may also specify a set of *alternate* style sheets, one of which is selected by the user depending on their choice. Authors may also specify one of the alternate style sheets as the *preferred* style sheet which is applied when no style sheet is selected. Several alternate style sheets may be grouped under a single *title*. All styles in a group must be applied when a user selects an alternate style sheet by its title. Note that current browsers do not support alternate style sheets.

The attribute `rel` specifies the type of style sheet used. Its value is `"stylesheet"` for persistent and preferred style sheets and `"alternate stylesheet"` for alternate style sheets. The optional attribute `title` is used to name a style sheet. Persistent style sheet is specified by the absence of the `title` attribute whereas preferred and alternate style sheets are specified by the presence of the `title` attribute. Following is an example of the preferred style sheet.

```
<link rel="stylesheet" type="text/css" href="mystyle.css" title="large"/>
```

The following example shows an alternate style sheet:

```
<link rel="alternate stylesheet" type="text/css" href="mystyle.css"
title="large"/>
```

Table 5.1 lists the attributes of the `<link>` tag along with their meaning.

Table 5.1 Attributes of the `link` tag and their meaning

Attribute	Meaning
`href`	Target file of a link.
`charset`	Character set of the target of a link.
`hreflang`	Language (in the form of a language code) of the target of a link. It should only be used when `href` is also used.
`type`	The type of the target of a link.
`rel`	Relationship of the target of the link to the current page.
`rev`	Relationship of the current page to the target of the link.
`media`	Refers to media the link is associated with. A value such as `screen`, `print`, `projection`, `braille`, `speech` or `all` or a combination of these can be used in a comma-separated list.

Any number of external style sheets can be specified for a document. If the same style information is specified in different style sheets, it is resolved using the rules described later in this chapter.

5.3.2 Embedded Style Sheets

In this method, style information is placed under the style tag in the head section of an HTML page.

```
<style>
   p {
      color: green;
   }
</style>
```

This makes all paragraphs green.

5.3.3 Imported Style Sheets

Another way of importing a style sheet is to use `@import` statement. It works in much the same way linking. It allows importing a style sheet from another style sheet. The import statement is used within the style tag in an HTML document as follows:

```
<style>
   @import url("style1.css");
</style>
```

This code segment imports all style rules written in the CSS file `style1.css`. The style element may include other internal style rules, but the `import` statement *must* be the first rule within a style tag. Even a comment before the `import` statement can cause it to fail. The style sheet may be mentioned as a string as follows:

```
<style>
   @import "style1.css";
</style>
```

This import statement will be interpreted as if it had `url(...)` around it.

Internal rules override the conflicting rules in the imported style sheets. For example, the following style rule makes all paragraphs green even if a `style1.css` file contains a rule `p{color: red;}`

```
<style>
   @import url("style1.css");
   p{color: green;}
</style>
```

A `<style>` tag may contain an arbitrary number of `import` statements, but the order in which the style sheets are imported is important in determining cascading rules. The later style sheets get preference if there is any conflicting rule in the imported style sheets.

```
<style>
   @import url("style1.css");
   @import url("style2.css");
</style>
```

If `style1.css` contains the style rule `p{color: red;}` and `style2.css` contains the style rule `p{color: blue;}`, the color of the paragraphs will be `blue` as the value corresponding to the color `blue` is described last. Similarly, the following code makes all paragraphs `green`.

```
<style>
   @import url("style1.css");
   @import url("style2.css");
   p {color: green;}
</style>
```

A CSS file may also import another style sheet. For example, `style3.css` imports another style sheet `style4.css` as follows:

```
@import url("style4.css");
p{color: red;}
```

Consider the content of `style4.css` as follows:

```
p{font-weight: bold;}
```

The following style rule makes all paragraph `red` and `bold`.

```
<style>
   @import url("style3.css");
</style>
```

The style sheet that imports other style sheets itself may contain style rules. Conflicting rules are resolved using the rules described so far.

We can also import style sheets for specific media. A list of valid media type is shown in Table 5.2.

Table 5.2 Recognized media types

Media type	Meaning
`all`	Apply rules for all devices.
`braille`	Targets are Braille tactile feedback devices.
`embossed`	Specified for paged braille printers.
`eandheld`	Used for handheld devices (e.g., small screen, limited bandwidth).
`print`	Used for documents viewed on screen in print preview mode and for paged material.
`projection`	Intended for projected presentations, such as projectors.
`screen`	Intended primarily for color computer screens.
`speech`	Intended for speech synthesizers.
`tty`	Intended for media using a fixed-pitch character grid (such as terminals, teletypes, or portable devices with limited display capabilities).
`tv`	Intended for television-type devices (color, low resolution, limited-scrollability screens with sound).

Note that not all browsers support the importing of style sheets. For example, IE 3.x and Netscape Navigator 4.x do not support the import rule. Similarly, some browsers such as IE 6 and below do not support media designation.

5.3.4 Inline Style Sheets

In this case, style information is incorporated directly into the HTML tags.

```
<p style="color: red">Hello World!</p>
```

This is the least flexible styling method. If you want to modify the style of an element, you have to work through the document and modify it.

5.3.5 Cascading Rule

There are several ways to specify style rules. If more than one rule is specified, conflicting rules are resolved according to the following rules:

Specificity rules

More specific rules get preference over less specific rules. Consider the following rules:

```
p b {color: green;}
b{color: red;}
```

The former makes text under the tag <b>, which is a descendant of the tag <p>, green. The latter makes text under the <b> tag red. Every <b> tag that matches the former rule also matches the latter, but the reverse is not true. So, former is a more specific one. For example, for the following code segment, the word "Hello" will be in `red` color whereas the word "World!" will be in `green` color.

```
<b>Hello</b><p><b>World!</b></p>
```

Order rules

For conflicting rules, latter rules get preference over the earlier rules. Figure 5.2 shows the rules for resolving conflicting styles.

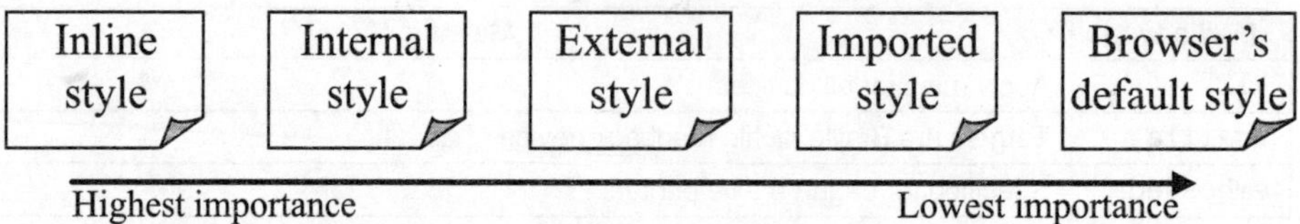

Figure 5.2 Rules resolving conflicting styles

5.4 BROWSER COMPATIBILITY

Not all browsers support the full CSS specification. The following list mentions commonly used browsers that support CSS2:

- Microsoft Internet Explorer version 8 supports CSS level 2 and some internationalization features from level 3.
- Google has a browser called chrome (beta version), which is available freely and supports CSS2.
- The Safari (version 3) web browser from Apple support CSS2 specification. It is based on the open source HTML/CSS library "WebKit".
- Mozilla has released version 3 of the Firefox web browser, which supports CSS level 2 and parts of level 3.
- Opera has released version 9.50 of its browser for multiple platforms, including cell phones. It is free on most platforms. It supports CSS level 2 and parts of level 3.
- The Lobo browser (current version is 0.98) also supports CSS2.
- The iCab is a browser for the Mac OS. It supports CSS2 and can help you fix errors in CSS or HTML files.
- Oregan Networks has released a browser for various embedded platforms, called Oregan TV Browser. It supports CSS2, XHTML, XML, etc.
- The KDE (K Desktop Environment) has released version 3.5, which supports CSS 2.

5.5 CSS AND PAGE LAYOUT

We have discussed how to incorporate style sheets in an HTML document. Let us now discuss how to specify styles.

A CSS file contains a set of one or more style rules that apply to an HTML document. Each rule specifies the stylistic aspect of one or more HTML elements.

5.5.1 Anatomy of a Style Rule

A style rule has basically two parts: `selector` and `declaration`.

```
body { background-color: gray; }
```

Selector Declaration

A `selector` specifies which HTML elements are affected by this style rule. This rule has the selector `body`. It is only applied on the `<body>` tag in an HTML document. The selector used here is a name of an HTML tag. These types of selectors are called *type selectors*. A type selector may select a single element or a set of HTML elements.

The `declaration` specifies what the effect will be. The declaration is a semicolon-separated (;) list of `property:value` pairs. Here, `property` is a specific style that some elements possess and `value` is the specific information that property holds. This example makes `background-color` of the `body` element `gray`. The general syntax of every rule looks like this:

```
selector {
   property1:  value1;
   property2:  value2;
   ...
   propertyN:  valueN;
}
```

5.6 SELECTORS

The basic building blocks of style rules are *selectors*. Selectors determine elements on which rules are to be applied. The elements selected by selectors are called *subjects* of the selectors. A selector may simply be the name of an element called *simple selector* or may consist of a rich contextual pattern called *complex selector*. A complex selector consists of one or more simple selectors separated by *combinators* such as a white space, ">", and "+".

5.6.1 Grouping

Selectors having common declarations are grouped into a comma-separated (,) list. Consider the following selectors having identical declaration sections:

```
h1 { color: red; }
h2 { color: red; }
h3 { color: red; }
```

This is equivalent to:

```
h1, h2, h3 { color: red; }
```

5.6.2 Type Selectors

A type selector is a simple selector, which is the name of a document element and it matches every single element of the document. For example, the selector `p` selects every <p> element in the document. Similarly, the selector `b` selects every <b> element.

5.6.3 Universal Selectors

CSS has a special selector *, which matches with every single element in the document. For example,

```
* { color: red; }
```

It makes all the text in the document red. If the universal selector has an additional component, * may be omitted. So, the following pairs are equivalent:

- `*.note` and `.note`
- `*[class="left"]` and `[class="left"]`
- `*#example` and `#example`

The universal selector is useful when element names are not known in advance during the development of a style sheet.

5.6.4 Descendant Selectors

Descendant selectors, also called *contextual selectors*, allow us to determine the elements depending upon their hierarchical relationship. A descendant selector selects only those elements that are descendants of a specified element. They provide an elegant way to apply styles to very particular elements. In many cases, they also eliminate the need to create many class names. Descendant selectors consist of one or more simple selectors separated by white spaces. Consider the following HTML code segment:

```
<div><b>C</b>ascading <b>S</b>tyle <b>S</b>heet</div>
<p>Descendant <b>selectors</b></p>
<p>This<b>is</b>a<i><b>paragraph</b></i><p>
```

How can one select all <b> elements, which are highlighted in this code segment? Note that all highlighted <b> elements are descendants of the <p> element. The type selector `b` will not work in this case as it selects all <b> elements. The correct method is to use the descendant selector as follows:

```
p b
```

It selects only those <b> elements that are descendants of <p> elements, i.e., every <b> element that has a <p> element as its ancestor. The other <b> elements will not be affected.

A descendant selector of any depth can be created. The following selector selects all <b> elements that are descendants of <i> elements that are, in turn, descendants of <p> elements.

```
p i b
```

The following selector selects all <b> grandchildren elements of <p> elements.

```
p * b
```

The combinator that we can use in a descendant selector is a white space character. A white space character includes a space, a horizontal tab, a carriage return, a line feed, or a form feed. More than one white space characters may also be used.

5.6.5 Child Selectors

Child selectors select elements that are *immediate* children of a specified element. The combinator used for child selector is ">". Consider the following HTML code segment:

```
<p>This<b>is</b>a<i><b>paragraph</b></i><p>
```

The selector `p > b` selects only highlighted <b> elements. It does not match with the other <b> element because its parent is an <i> element. Remember the descendant selector `p b` matches with both <b> elements.

Like descendant selectors, child selectors of any depth can be created.

The following selector selects the <b> element whose parent is the <i> element whose parent is, in turn, the <p> element.

```
p > i > b
```

Child selectors can be combined with other selectors to get interesting results as follows:

`body > *` select all children of the <body> element

`body > * > *` select all grandchildren of the <body> element

`body > * > p` select all <p> grandchildren of the <body> element

CSS provides a way to format ordered lists in almost any style. Consider the following HTML document fragment:

```
Title: Web Technology<br>
Table of Content
<ol>
   <li>HTML</li>
   <li>CSS</li>
   <ol>
      <li>Introduction</li>
      <li>Adding style sheets</li>
      <ol>
         <li>External</li>
         <ol>
            <li>External style sheets are useful...</li>
         </ol>
         <li>Inline
      </ol>
      <li>Browser incompatibility </li>
   </ol>
   <li>XML</li>
</ol>
```

Now, consider the following CSS style rules:

```
OL { list-style-type: decimal; }
OL > OL { list-style-type: upper-roman; }
OL > OL > OL { list-style-type: lower-alpha; }
OL > OL > OL > OL { list-style-type: lower-roman; }
```

If this style is applied to the ordered list, it will look as shown in Figure 5.3.

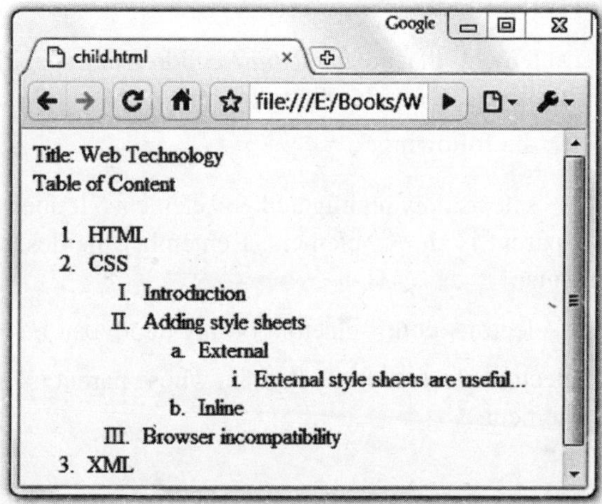

Figure 5.3 Automatic creation of ordered list using CSS

Child selectors are more specific selectors as they allow the selection of only child elements of another element and not any more deeply-nested elements.

5.6.6 Pseudo Classes and Elements

Traditional publishing, very often, uses a different first letter of a paragraph than rest of the letters. Traditional selectors cannot address such special cases. Pseudo classes and elements are used to add style to those elements not accessible by traditional selectors. These special classes are useful when information about an element is not available from the document tree. For example, no selector refers to the first line of a paragraph or the first letter of a line. Pseudo classes match elements using the information other than their name, content, or attribute such as states of an anchor element. Pseudo elements, on the other hand, address sub-parts of an element such as the first letter of a paragraph. Pseudo elements and pseudo classes are always preceded by a colon.

The general forms of pseudo class and pseudo element look like this:

```
selector:pseudo-class {declaration}
```

or

```
selector:pseudo-element {declaration}
```

These classes and elements cannot be used with the class attribute. Normal classes and elements may be used with pseudo classes and elements, however.

```
selector.class:pseudo-class {declaration}
```

or

```
selector.class:pseudo-element {declaration}
```

5.6.6.1 The :first-child, :last-child, and :only-child pseudo classes

The first-child selector selects an element if it is the first child of its parent regardless of what this parent element is. For example, `p:first-child` selects all p elements that are the first children of any element. The following example selects any `<p>` element that is the first child of the `<span>` element.

```
span > p:first-child
```

So, it matches with the following:

```
<p>This is not a child of span</p>
<span>
   <p>This is first child of span</p>
   <p>This is last child of span</p>
</span>
```

Similarly, `ul > li:first-child` selects the first `<li>` child element of the `<ul>` element.

```
<ul>
<li>One</li>
<li>Two</li>
</ul>
```

`* > li:first-child` and `li:first-child` are identical each of which selects the first `<li>` element of all (`<ol>` and `<ul>`) elements.

The `last-child` pseudo class selects the last child element of another element. For example, `span > p:first-child` matches the following:

```
<p>This is not a child of span</p>
<span>
   <p>This is first child of span</p>
   <p>This is last child of span</p>
</span>
```

Similarly, the `only-child` pseudo class selects an element if it is the only child of another element. For example, `span > p:only-child` selects the following:

```
<span>
   <p>This is only child of span</p>
</span>
```

Table 5.3 summarizes CSS selectors.

Table 5.3 CSS selector summary

Selector	Meaning
`E`	Selects all E elements
`*`	Selects all * elements
`P D`	Selects all descendants D of parent P

(Contd.)

(Contd.)

`P > C`	Selects all children C of parent P
`E:first-child`	Selects all E elements which are the first child elements of its parent
`E + S`	Selects all following sibling S elements of E
`E[A]`	Selects all E elements having attribute "A"
`[A]`	Selects all elements having attribute "A"(equivalent to *[A])
`E[A="V"]`	Select all E elements having "A" attribute value "V"
`[A="V"]`	Select all elements having "A" attribute value "V" (equivalent to *[A=V])

5.6.6.2 The anchor pseudo classes: :link and :visited

These pseudo classes are used to apply style rules on anchor tags otherwise known as hyperlinks. Before CSS, the only way to add effects on anchor tags was to use JavaScript code. A hyperlink may go through different states: normal (unvisited) or visited. CSS provides two pseudo classes to display respectively unvisited and visited hyperlinks differently. These two states are mutually exclusive. The `:link` pseudo class applies to those hyperlinks that have not yet been visited. The `:visited` pseudo class applies to hyperlinks that have already been visited at least once.

```
a:link    { color: blue; }      /* regular links    */
a:visited { color: red; }       /* visited links    */
```

5.6.6.3 The dynamic pseudo classes: :hover, :active, :focus

CSS provides three more pseudo classes that allow us to change rendering of anchor tags in response to user actions such as mouse over and mouse click on anchor tags. These pseudo classes are `:hover`, `:active`, and `:focus`.

The `:hover` pseudo class selects elements that are being designated by the user with a pointing device (e.g., moving mouse pointer over the element). Consider a web page having underlined text and hyperlinks (hyperlinks are underlined). In such a case users may not distinguish between hyperlinks and normal text quickly. A CSS author may make an arrangement such that whenever the mouse pointer moves over a link, it loses the underline. This way users may easily distinguish between normal texts and hyperlinks. Following is an example.

```
a:hover    { text-decoration: none;}
```

You can add other rendering rules depending on your choice.

The `:active` pseudo class applies to an element that is currently being activated by the user. Activation includes pressing a mouse button, releasing a mouse button, etc.

The `:focus` pseudo class applies to an element that has currently got the focus by keyboard events or other means. Following is an example of dynamic pseudo classes:

```
a:focus   { color: green; }     /* focused links    */
a:hover   { color: yellow;}     /* hover links      */
a:active  { color: pink; }      /* active links     */
```

Pseudo classes that are not mutually exclusive can be combined to form a complex class. For example, `a:link:hover`, `a:visited:hover`, and `a:focus:hover` are valid selectors. However, `a:link:visited` is not a valid selector as `:link` and `:visited` are mutually exclusive.

```
a:link:hover     { color: red; }
a:visited:hover { color: green; }
a:focus:hover { color: yellow; }
```

The order in which the selectors are defined is important. For example, `:hover` must be placed after `:link` and `:visited`. The correct order is `:link`, `:visited`, `:focus`, `:hover`, and `:active`. Otherwise, the cascading rule may override the properties and the selectors may not work correctly as desired.

```
a:link     { color: blue; }       /* regular links    */
a:visited  { color: red; }        /* visited links    */
a:focus    { color: green; }      /* focused links    */
a:hover    { color: yellow;}      /* hover links      */
a:active   { color: pink; }       /* active links     */
```

5.6.6.4 The lang() pseudo class

Different languages have different conventions. For example, the English language uses quote marks (“ and ”) for quoting purposes whereas, the French language uses angle brackets (< and >) for the same. The pseudo class `:lang` provides a way to specify the language to be used for a specific element. Consider the following example:

```
q:lang(fr) { quotes: "<<" ">>" "<" ">"; }
q:lang(en) { quotes: '"' '"' "'"  "'"; }
```

The first rule specifies that the quotation marks to be used in French are <<, >> <, and >. The second rule specifies the regular quotation marks used in English.

Consider the following HTML code segment:

```
<q lang="en">An English quotation</q><br>
<q lang="fr">A French quotation</q>
```

The result is shown in Figure 5.4:

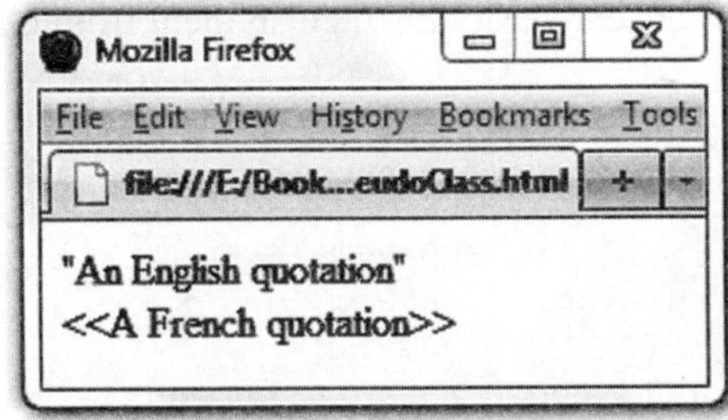

Figure 5.4 The lang pseudo class

Table 5.4 shows a summary of CSS pseudo classes.

Table 5.4 CSS pseudo classes summary

Pseudo class	Meaning	Applies to
`:first-child`	Matches an element that is the first child of another element	All
`:link`	Applies to links that have not yet been visited	Anchors
`:visited`	Applies to links that have already been visited	Anchors
`:hover`	Applies to an element when the cursor is held over it	All
`:active`	Applies to an element when it is active (e.g., the mouse is held down over)	All
`:focus`	Applies to an element while it has the user focus.	All
`:lang()`	Applies to an element when it is in the designated language.	All

5.6.7 Pseudo Elements

In the last section, we discussed pseudo classes. In this section, let us discuss about pseudo elements.

5.6.7.1 The :first-line pseudo element

The `:first-line` pseudo element allows us to add styles to the first line of an element. This element actually exists in the document tree. This hypothetical element is addressed depending on factors such as block width, page width, font size, etc. The following properties apply to this pseudo element:

- `color`
- `font`
- `background`
- `vertical-align`
- `line-height`
- `text-decoration`
- `text-transform`
- `word-spacing`
- `letter-spacing`
- `clear`

The `:first-line` pseudo element is used mostly with the `<p>` element to give a different look and feel so that users can easily distinguish them from others.

```
p:first-line { text-decoration: underline; }

<p>The :first-line pseudo element allows us to add styles to the first line
of an element. This element actually exists in the document tree. This
hypothetical element is addressed depending on the factors such as block
width, page width, font size etc.</p>
```

The result is shown in Figure 5.5.

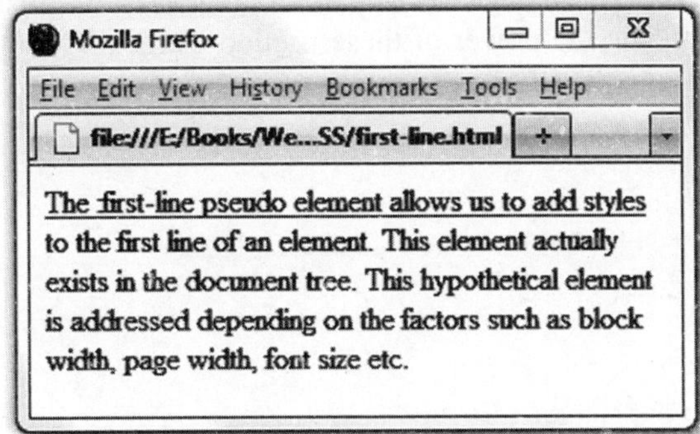

Figure 5.5 The first-line pseudo element

5.6.7.2 The :first-letter pseudo element

The `:first-letter` pseudo element is used to add styles to the first letter of the first line of block elements. It is also mostly used with `<p>`, `<div>`, and `<span>` elements.

The following example demonstrates how to use the `:first-letter` pseudo element to add special effects to the first letter:

```
p:first-letter { font-size: 300%; float: left; }

<p>The :first-letter pseudo element is used to add styles to the first letter
of the first line of block elements. It is also mostly used with p, div and
span elements.</p>
```

The result is shown in Figure 5.6.

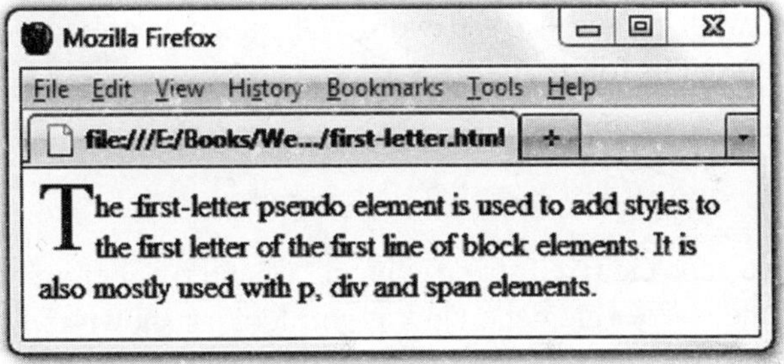

Figure 5.6 The first-letter pseudo element

5.6.7.3 The :before and :after pseudo elements

Usually, CSS allows us to add styles to the existing elements in an HTML file. However, it can also be used to insert some new content into the HTML file. The pseudo elements `:before` and `:after` are used for this purpose. The pseudo element `:before` inserts some new content before an existing element whereas `:after` inserts some new content after an existing element. The content may be anything such as text, images, audio, or even video. The inserted content will be treated as a part of the element after insertion and the usual style rules are applied to them. Internet Explorer does not support these pseudo elements.

The `content` property is used to define the content to be inserted before and after the selected elements. To appreciate the power of these pseudo elements let us consider a simple example. We shall be modifying this example continuously to get progressively better appearances.

```
<html>
   <head>
      <style type="text/css">
         ol { list-style-type: none; }
      </style>
   </head>
   <body>
      <ol>
         <li>Introduction to Web</li>
         <li>HTTP</li>
      </ol>
   </body>
</html>
```

If it is opened in a browser, it will look as shown in Figure 5.7.

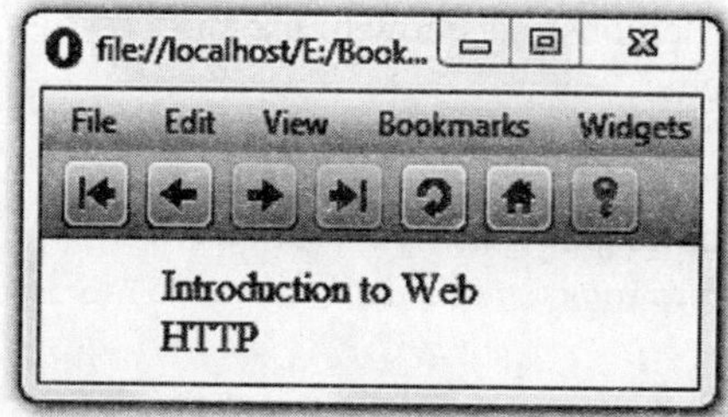

Figure 5.7 List without numbering

Suppose we want to add a fixed word "Chapter: " before every line. The pseudo class `:before` may be used as follows:

```
body > ol > li:before {
   content: "Chapter : ";
}
```

This style rule adds the fixed string content "Chapter : " before every `<li>` element which is a grandchild of the `<body>` element. Now it will look as shown in Figure 5.8.

Figure 5.8 CSS to add content

Is it not more promising? It will be even more promising if we add chapter numbers automatically.

```
Chapter 1: Introduction to Web
Chapter 2: HTTP
```

This can be achieved using the function `counter` in conjunction with the `content` property. The function `counter` takes an `identifier` whose value you want to insert and an optional `list-style` that specifies the style of the counter. It has the following form:

```
counter(identifier, list-style)
```

When a `counter` function is encountered, the browser determines the value of the identifier at that point of the document and inserts this value at the designated position. What is the value of this identifier? When is it created? And who will increment it to get the correct chapter number? Nobody will do it. We have to do it explicitly. This is done by the `counter-increment` property. The property `counter-increment` takes an identifier and an optional increment as arguments. The value of the increment is a positive or a negative integer. The value of the identifier is incremented by the value of the increment every time the enclosing element is encountered. The increment is assumed to be 1 if nothing is specified. The identifier is created with the initial value 0 the first time it is used. To reset a counter, the `counter-reset` property is used. It has the same syntax as `counter-increment`. It resets a given counter to a specified value. If no reset value is specified, 0 is assumed. The property `counter-reset` is not required for our example, but it may be required for a complex scenario. The property `counter-reset` affects only descendants and siblings.

```
body> ol > li:before {
   content: "Chapter " counter(chap) ": ";
   counter-increment: chap 1;
}
```

This style rule increments the value of the identified `chap` and then adds its value between "Chapter " and ": " the result of which is shown in Figure 5.9.

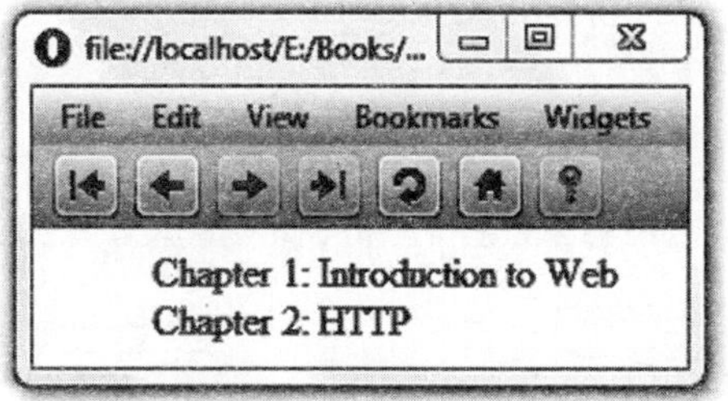

Figure 5.9 Adding content and numbering using CSS

Note that the numbering style is simple and may also be done with the help of a traditional ordered list. However, a complex numbering style may not be achieved with the help of ordered lists. Following is a complete example for more advanced numbering style:

```
<html>
   <head>
      <style type="text/css">
         ol { list-style-type: none; }
         body > ol > ol{ counter-reset: sec1 0}
         body > ol > ol > ol{ counter-reset: sec2 0}
         body > ol > ol > ol > ol{ counter-reset: sec3 0}
         body> ol > li:before {
            content: "Chapter " counter(chap) ". ";
            counter-increment: chap 1
         }
         body > ol> ol >li:before {
            content: counter(chap) "." counter(sec1) " ";
            counter-increment: sec1 1
         }
         body > ol> ol > ol > li:before {
            content: counter(chap) "." counter(sec1) "." counter(sec2) " ";
            counter-increment: sec2 1
         }
         body > ol> ol > ol> ol > li:before {
            content: counter(chap) "." counter(sec1) "." counter(sec2) "."
            counter(sec3) " ";
            counter-increment: sec3 1
         }
      </style>
   </head>
   <body>
      Title: Web Technology<br>
      Table of Content
      <ol>
         <li>Introduction to Web</li>
         <li>HTTP</li>
         <li>Java Network Programming</li>
         <li>HTML</li>
         <li>CSS</li>
         <ol>
            <li>Introduction</li>
            <li>Advantages</li>
            <li>Adding style sheets</li>
            <ol>
               <li>External</li>
               <ol>
                  <li>External style sheets are useful...</li>
               </ol>
               <li>Inline
            </ol>
            <li>Browser incompatibility </li>
         </ol>
         <li>XML</li>
      </ol>
   </body>
</html>
```

The result of this code is shown in Figure 5.10.

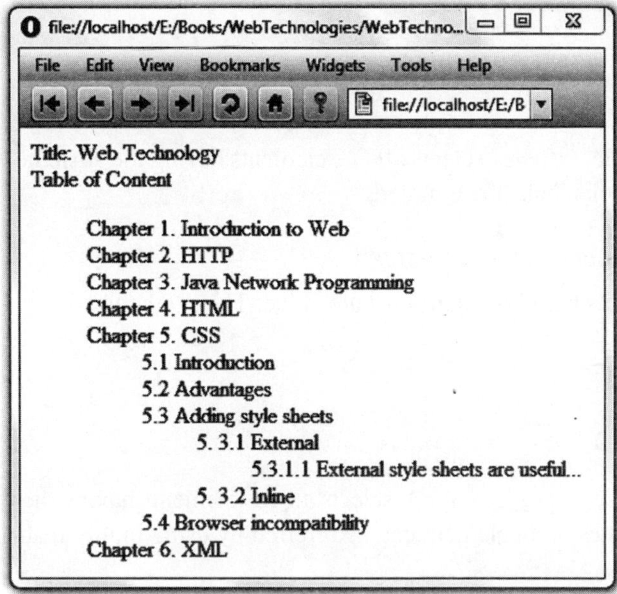

Figure 5.10 Automatic nested numbering using CSS

The `counter-reset` property resets a named counter to a specified value.

Note that CSS already supports generated content to some extent. In ordered and unordered lists numbers and bullets are automatically generated. The `:before` and `:after` pseudo elements provide an elegant and powerful way to add new content.

Table 5.5 gives a summary of CSS pseudo elements.

Table 5.5 CSS pseudo elements summary

Pseudo element	Meaning	Applies to
`:first-line`	Applies to the first formatted line of a paragraph	Block level elements
`:first-letter`	Applies to the first letter of a paragraph	Block level elements
`:before`	Inserts some new content before an existing element	Any element
`:after`	Inserts some new content after an existing element	Any element

5.6.8 Attribute Selectors

Attribute selectors provide a way of selecting elements depending on the presence of an attribute or the presence of certain attribute values. Attribute selectors are not supported by IE but are supported by Firefox and Opera. CSS2 specified four attribute selectors. CSS3 added three more. They are discussed as follows:

5.6.8.1 Simple attribute selector

It selects elements having a specified attribute. The general syntax of a simple attribute selector is as follows:

```
element[attribute_name]
```

or

```
[attribute_name]
```

For example, `a[href]` selects all `<a>` elements having the attribute `href`. If the element name is omitted, all elements are assumed.

5.6.8.2 Attribute value selector

Selects elements based on their attribute value. The syntax is:

```
element[attribute_name="attribute_value"]
```

or

```
[attribute_name="attribute_value"]
```

For example, `p[type="note"]` selects all `<p>` elements having the type attribute value "note". Several attributes of an element can be referred by using multiple attribute selectors as follows:

```
p[type="note"][align="left"]
```

5.6.8.3 One of many attribute value selector

It allows us to select elements having an attribute with a value equal to any one of the values separated by white spaces. It is used as:

```
element[attribute_name~="value"]
```

or

```
[attribute_name~="value"]
```

The following example

```
p[class~="bold"]
```

matches with the following:

```
<p class="bold italic">...</p>
<p class="underlined bold">...</p>
```

5.6.8.4 Hyphen attribute value selector

This selector selects an element having attribute value exactly equal to the specified value or beginning with the specified value immediately followed by "-". The basic purpose of this selector is to match language sub-code. Here is an example:

```
p[lang|="en"]
```

that matches `<p lang="en">…</p>` and `<p lang="en-UK">…</p>`.

5.6.8.5 Starts-with attribute value selector

This selector selects elements having an attribute value that starts with the value specified. The general syntax is

```
element[attribute_name^="attribute_value"]
```

or

```
[attribute_name^="attribute_value"]
```

For example, the selector `p[type^= "copy"]` matches `<p type="copyright">Copyright…</p>` as well as `<p type="copyleft">Copyleft…</p>`

5.6.8.6 Ends-with attribute value selector

This attribute selects elements having attribute value that ends with the value specified. The general syntax is

```
element[attribute_name$="attribute_value"]
```

or

```
[attribute_name$="attribute_value"]
```

For example, `a[href$=".com"]` selects those anchor tags that point to `.com` websites. So, it matches

```
<a href="http://www.yahoo.com">Yahoo</a>
<a href="http://www.rediffmail.com">Rediff Mail</a>
```

but not

```
<a href="http://www.jadavpur.edu">Jadavpur University</a>
```

5.6.8.7 Substring match attribute value selector

This selector selects those elements having an attribute value containing at least one occurrence of the value specified. The general syntax is

```
element[attribute_name*="attribute_value"]
```

or

```
[attribute_name*="attribute_value"]
```

For example, `a[href*="image"]` selects those anchor tags that have `image` in the `href` attribute.

5.6.9 Class Selectors

These selectors provide a flexible way to apply styles to elements. Class selectors deal with the elements having the attribute `class`. The `class` attribute adds an element to a group whose name is the attribute's value. This way a set of related elements can be grouped and a common style can be applied to every element in the group. An element may belong to more than one group.

This selector is a specific case of one of many attribute value selectors with the attribute name class and "~=" substituted by ".". So, p[class~="bold"] and p.bold are identical in meaning. It matches <p class="bold">...</p> as well as <p class="italic bold">...</p> but not <p class="left">...</p>.

Similarly, the following selectors are equivalent:

- p[class~="bold"][class=~="italic"]
- p[class~="italic"][class=~="bold"]
- p.italic.bold
- p.bold.italic

Each of these selectors selects those p elements that belong to both bold and italic groups. They match <p class="italic bold">...</p> as well as <p class="bold italic">...</p> but not <p class="bold">...</p>.

Class selectors are useful to control elements that belong to a group as well as to remove limitations of the selector. Class selectors are normally used to group top level elements in a document. If done so, they reduce the flexibility of design and make customization difficult without significant effort. Therefore, before doing so make sure that class selectors are really needed and cannot be implemented using other selectors. The excessive use of class selectors makes style files and documents complicated.

Note that class names are case-sensitive. So, class1 and CLASS1 are two different class names.

5.6.10 ID Selectors

The attribute id of an element is a unique identifier in a web page. This means that no two id attributes can have the same value within the document. The id differs from class in that id identifies a single element uniquely whereas class identifies a set of related elements. However, they work in a very similar way and also have similar syntax. This property is used by the id selector. An id selector selects a single element based on its unique id attribute value regardless of its position in the document tree.

An id selector is defined by placing a # symbol before the selector name.

The selector p#para1 selects the p element having id attribute value para1. So, it matches the following:

```
<p id="para1">...</p>
```

but not

```
<div id="para1">...</div>
```

The selector #para1 matches both. However, before using it make sure that id attribute values are unique. Although some browsers accept duplicate id attribute value in such a case the behavior is not standardized.

ID selectors and other selectors can be combined. That way you can eliminate the need to use an id for each element. Following is an example:

```
<div id="book1">
  <h1>Web Technology</h1>
  <p>HTML</p>
<div>
```

The elements `h1` and `p` can be accessed as follows:

```
#book1 h1 { color: red; }
#book1 p { color: blue; }
```

The id selector can be written as an attribute value selector but the id selector has higher cascading precedence. For example, `#chapter1` is more specific than `[id="chapter1"]`.

An id can have only alphanumeric characters and hyphens (-). It cannot contain underscore or white spaces. The first character of an id cannot be a numeric character. Id names are case-sensitive. So, `id1` and `ID1` are two different names. Table 5.6 details CSS selector compatibility.

Table 5.6 CSS selector compatibility

<table>
<tr><th>Selector</th><th colspan="4">IE</th><th colspan="3">Firefox</th><th colspan="3">Safari</th><th colspan="2">Chrome</th><th colspan="2">Opera</th><th>Konquer</th></tr>
<tr><td></td><td>5.5</td><td>6</td><td>7</td><td>8</td><td>2</td><td>3.0</td><td>3.1</td><td>3.0</td><td>3.1</td><td>4.0</td><td>1</td><td>2</td><td>9.6</td><td>10</td><td>3.5.7</td></tr>
<tr><td>*</td><td colspan="4">Yes</td><td colspan="3">yes</td><td colspan="3">yes</td><td colspan="2">yes</td><td colspan="2">yes</td><td>yes</td></tr>
<tr><td>></td><td colspan="2">No</td><td colspan="2">Yes</td><td colspan="3">yes</td><td colspan="3">yes</td><td colspan="2">yes</td><td colspan="2">yes</td><td>yes</td></tr>
<tr><td>+</td><td colspan="2">No</td><td>fixed</td><td>almost</td><td>fixed</td><td colspan="2">yes</td><td colspan="2">fixed</td><td>yes</td><td>fixed</td><td>yes</td><td colspan="2">yes</td><td>yes</td></tr>
<tr><td>[attr]</td><td colspan="2">No</td><td colspan="2">Yes</td><td colspan="3">yes</td><td colspan="3">yes</td><td colspan="2">yes</td><td colspan="2">yes</td><td>yes</td></tr>
<tr><td>class</td><td colspan="2">buggy</td><td colspan="2">Yes</td><td colspan="3">yes</td><td colspan="3">yes</td><td colspan="2">yes</td><td colspan="2">yes</td><td>yes</td></tr>
<tr><td>:before/
:after</td><td colspan="3">No</td><td>Yes</td><td colspan="3">yes</td><td colspan="3">yes</td><td colspan="2">yes</td><td colspan="2">yes</td><td>yes</td></tr>
<tr><td>:hover/
:active</td><td colspan="2">minimal</td><td>incomplete</td><td>Yes</td><td colspan="3">yes</td><td colspan="3">yes</td><td colspan="2">yes</td><td colspan="2"></td><td>Almost</td></tr>
</table>

KEY WORDS

Attribute Selectors: Attribute selectors provide a way of selecting elements depending on the presence of an attribute or the presence of certain attribute values.

Child Selectors: Selectors select elements that are immediate children of a specified element.

Class Selectors: Class selectors deal with the elements having an attribute class.

Combinators: Set of symbols used to form a complex selector from one or more simple selectors.

Declaration: The declaration portion of a style rule tells what the effect will be.

Descendant Selectors: Descendant selectors select elements depending upon their hierarchical relationship.

Embedded Style Sheets: In this method, style information is placed under the style tag in the head section of an HTML page.

External Style Sheets: In this case, style information is written in a separate file and is referenced from an HTML document.

ID Selectors: An id selector selects a single element based on its unique id attribute value regardless of its position in the document tree.

Imported Style Sheets: It allows importing a style sheet from another style sheet.

Inline Style Sheets: In this case, style information is incorporated directly into the HTML tags.

Pseudo Classes: Pseudo classes match elements using the information other than their name, content, or attribute such as states of an anchor element.

Pseudo Elements: Pseudo elements, on the other hand, address sub-parts of an element such as the first letter of a paragraph.

Selector: A selector portion of a style rule specifies what HTML elements are affected by style rule.

Type Selector: A type selector is a simple selector, which is a name of a document element and matches every element of the document.

Universal Selector: Selector that matches any single element in the document

SUMMARY

A style sheet is a document that contains style information about one or more documents written in markup languages. It enables us to control rendering of styles such as fonts, color, typeface, size, spacing, margins, and other aspects of document style. A style sheet is composed of a set of style rules written in a specified format. This set of style rules instructs browsers on how to present a document on the screen.

Cascading Style Sheet (CSS) is a style sheet language that specifies how to incorporate style information in a style sheet. The primary advantage of CSS is to separate document presentation from document content written in markup languages. So, document writers can concentrate on developing the document content using markup languages such as HTML, XHTML, and XML without bothering about the visual presentation of those documents. It also allows us to give a different look to the same document without significant effort.

There are four ways in which you can incorporate style information in your web page: External, Embedded, Imported, and Inline. If conflicting style rules are specified, they are resolved using their preference. The inline style has the highest importance while browser's default settings has the lowest importance.

A CSS file consists of a set of style rules to be applied on elements. Each rule has basically two parts: selector and declaration. The basic building blocks of style rules are selectors. Selectors determine elements on which rules are to be applied. The declaration tells what the effect will be. There are many kinds of selectors using which a style sheet writer can select the desired element and can specify style information for that element. Some of them are descendant selector, child selector, type selector, universal selector, etc.

Pseudo classes match elements using information other than their name, content, or attribute such as states of an anchor element. Examples include first-child, last-child, only-child, link, visited, lang, hover, active, focus, etc. Pseudo elements, on the other hand, address sub-parts of an element such as the first letter of a paragraph. Examples include first-line, first-letter, before, after, etc.

WEB RESOURCES

`http://web5.w3.org/TR/REC-CSS1`
Cascading Style Sheets, level 1

`http://www.w3.org/TR/CSS2`
Cascading Style Sheets Level 2 Revision 1 (CSS 2.1) Specification

`http://www.w3.org/Style/Examples/011/firstcss`
CSS tutorial starting with HTML + CSS

`http://www.w3.org/TR/css3-selectors/`
Selectors Level 3 W3C Working Draft 10 March 2009

`http://www.w3.org/Style/CSS/current-work`
Cascading Style Sheets Current Work

EXERCISES

Multiple Choice Questions

1. Which one of the following is the correct syntax for importing a stylesheet in CSS?
   (a) @import url("example.css");
   (b) @import-css url("example.css");
   (c) @import-style url("example.css");
   (d) @import-stylesheet url ("example.css");

2. What is the full form of CSS?
   (a) Cascade Style Streams
   (b) Color Sensitive Style
   (c) Colorful Style Systems
   (d) Cascading Style Sheets

3. A declaration is terminated by a
   (a) } — end curly bracket
   (b) . — period
   (c) ; — Semi colon
   (d) ! — exclamation sign

4. Which of the following HTML tags is used to refer to an external style sheet?
   (a) <link url="stylesheet" type="text/css" href="mystyle.css">
   (b) <style src="mystyle.css">
   (c) <link rel="stylesheet" type="text/css" href="mystyle.css">
   (d) <stylesheet>mystyle.css</stylesheet>

5. Which of the following CSS declarations is correct?
   (a) body:color=black
   (b) {body;color:black}
   (c) {body:color=black(body}
   (d) body {color: black}

6. Which of the following properties is used to change the background color?
   (a) bgcolor: (b) background-color:
   (c) color: (d) background:

7. How do you convert the first letter of each word in text to a capital letter?
   (a) text-transform: uppercase
   (b) text-transform: capitalize
   (c) text-translate: uppercase
   (d) You cannot do that with CSS

8. How do you remove underline from hyperlinks?
   (a) a {text-decoration: no underline;}
   (b) a {decoration: no underline;}
   (c) a {underline: none;}
   (d) a {text-decoration: none;}

9. How do you set background color for all <h1> tags?
   (a) all.h1 {background-color: #FFFFFF;}
   (b) h1 {background-color: #FFFFFF;}
   (c) h1.all {background-color: #FFFFFF;}
   (d) * > h1 {background-color: #FFFFFF;}

10. Which of the following is a valid syntax to insert comments in a CSS file?
   (a) /* this is a comment */
   (b) // this is a comment //
   (c) // this is a comment
   (d) ' this is a comment

11. In CSS, a:link defines the style for which of the following?
   (a) visited links (b) virtual links
   (c) active links (d) normal unvisited links

12. Which of the following properties is used to change the left margin of an element?
   (a) margin: (b) indent:
   (c) margin-left: (d) text-indent:

13. Which of the following options is available for changing the text color in CSS?
   (a) Hex color only
   (b) Common name and Hex color only
   (c) Common name, RBG value, Hex color
   (d) RBG value, Hex color

14. Which of the following properties is used to set the maximum height for an element?
   (a) maximum-height (b) max-height
   (c) m-height (d) maxi-height

15. How do you display a border like this?
   top border = 10 pixels, bottom border = 5 pixels, left border = 20 pixels, right border = 1pixel
   (a) border-width:10px 1px 5px 20px
   (b) border-width:10px 5px 20px 1px
   (c) border-width:5px 20px 10px 1px
   (d) border-width:10px 20px 5px 1px

16. Which of the following is an invalid CSS selector?
   (a) Title selectors (b) HEAD selectors
   (c) TAG selectors (d) ID selectors

17. Which of the following styles is the most flexible styling?
    (a) Multiple styles (b) Embedded styles
    (c) In-Line styles (d) External styles

18. In what form are style rules presented?
    (a) selector { property: value; }
    (b) selector (property= value;)
    (c) selector (property: value;)
    (d) selector { property= value; }

19. What is the correct CSS syntax for making all the <p> elements bold?
    (a) p {text-size: bold;}
    (b) <p style="text-size: bold";>
    (c) p {font-weight: bold;}
    (d) <p style="font-size: bold";>

20. Which CSS property controls the text size?
    (a) text-size (b) font-style
    (c) text-style (d) font-size

Review Questions

1. What are the advantages of CSS?
2. What does the term "Cascading" in CSS indicate?
3. Specify cascading order rules.
4. How do you define grouping in CSS?
5. What are block elements in CSS?
6. What are inline elements in CSS?
7. In how many ways can you select HTML tags?
8. What is the purpose of a class selector?
9. Describe with examples how to use pseudo classes of the <a> element.
10. Write the purpose of syntax of id selector?
11. How do you insert comments in a CSS file?
12. Discuss, with examples, different methods of incorporating style information in an HTML document.
13. How is the conflict among multiple style sheets resolved?
14. Write style information to set background color of <body>, <h1>, <h2>, and <p> elements.
15. Describe the method of changing font using CSS.
16. Demonstrate, with an example, how inner elements inherit style information from outer elements in CSS.

Part II

XML Technologies

- eXtensible Markup Language (XML)
- XML DTD
- W3C XML Schema
- Parsing XML
- XPath
- XML Transformation
- Other XML Technologies

6 EXTENSIBLE MARKUP LANGUAGE (XML)

KEY OBJECTIVES

After completing this chapter readers will be able to—

- **understand the importance of XML**
- **learn the basic building blocks of XML documents**
- **get an idea about well-formed and valid XML documents**
- **get an idea about how to display XML documents**
- **understand how name clashes are avoided using namespaces**

6.1 COMMON USAGE

XML is the acronym of e**X**tensible **M**arkup **L**anguage. The XML standard was developed by the **W**orld **W**ide **W**eb **C**onsortium (W3C) in the late 1990's and since then, it has received a great hype. XML is an application profile or restricted form of the **S**tandard **G**eneralized **M**arkup **L**anguage (SGML). The primary purpose of this standard was to provide a way to store self-describing data easily. Self-describing data are those that describe both their structure and their content.

XML is used to describe structured data or information. The data are intended to be used by machines or people. HTML documents describe how data should appear on the browser's screen; they carry no information about the data. XML documents, on the other hand, describe the meaning of data. XML documents may also refer to presentation information.

XML is used as a primary means to manipulate and transfer structured data over the web. The content and structure of XML documents are accessed by a software module, called *XML processor*.

Similar to HTML documents, data are marked up by tags in XML documents. HTML supports a predefined fixed set of tags. Authors of HTML documents can use only those tags. XML allows us to define new tags and use them in XML documents to satisfy application requirement. Since more such new tags may be defined, XML is said to be extensible.

6.2 ROLE OF XML

One of the major difficulties in developing documents such as word processor documents, spreadsheets, and HTML documents is that they mix document content with structure and formatting. This makes managing content and designing difficult.

An XML document separates the contents from their presentation. It does not specify how the contents should be displayed. It only specifies the contents with their logical structure. The formatting task is imposed on an external style sheet. This helps authors of the XML documents to develop contents and find a logical relation among them without bothering about the formatting information. Since formatting is done on an external style sheet, the look and feel may be changed very easily by choosing different style sheets.

XML also promotes easy data sharing among applications. Since applications hold data in different structures, mapping data from one to another is a difficult task. XML can help us in this regard. Each data structure is mapped to an agreed-upon XML structure. This XML structure may then be used by other applications. So, each application has to deal with only two structures: its own and the XML structure. This way, applications can share data with others even if they are stored in a different format.

Each XML file, if written with a little care, can describe itself. So, far we have not given any example of XML documents. In spite of this, you can understand the meaning of the following XML document:

```
<?xml version="1.0"?>
<email>
  <to>parama@it.jusl.ac.in</to>
  <from>u_roy@it.jusl.ac.in</from>
  <subject>Reminder</subject>
  <body>Next BoS meeting will held on 10 June at 3:00 P.M.</body>
</email>
```

It is not difficult to understand that this XML document describes an email message. The message here is from `u_roy@it.jusl.ac.in` to `parama@it.jusl.ac.in` to remind the latter regarding the BoS meeting.

An XML document consists of the following parts:

- Prolog
- Body

6.3 PROLOG

This part of the XML document may contain the following parts:

- XML declaration
- Optional processing instruction
- Comments
- Document Type Declaration

6.3.1 XML Declaration

Every XML document should start with a one-line XML declaration. It is not mandatory, but W3C recommends it. The declaration describes the document itself. Here is a sample XML declaration:

```
<?xml version="1.0"?>
```

The XML declaration is a processing instruction that tells the processing agent that the document is an XML document. The mandatory `version` attribute indicates the version used in this document. The current version is 1.0. The declaration may use two optional attributes: `encoding` and `standalone`.

`encoding`
It specifies the type of encoding scheme used in the document.

```
<?xml version="1.0" encoding="UTF-8"?>
```

In this example, "UTF-8" (UTF stands for Unicode Transformation Format) is used which has the same character set as ASCII. XML parsers must support 8-bit and 16-bit Unicode encoding.

`standalone`
This optional attribute indicates whether the document can be processed as a standalone document or is dependent on other documents. If "yes" is specified, the XML document must not contain any external **D**ocument **T**ype **D**eclaration (DTD). The value "no" leaves the issue open, i.e., the XML document may or may not refer to external DTDs. If nothing is specified "no" is assumed.

```
<?xml version="1.0" encoding="UTF-8" standalone="no"?>
```

Note that the attribute `standalone` is required if a DTD is used. Most often, XML documents use schema instead of DTD and hence the attribute `standalone` is not required.

6.3.2 Processing Instruction

Processing instructions start with `<?` and end with `?>`. They allow XML documents to contain special instructions that are used to pass parameters to the application. These parameters instruct the application about how to interpret the XML document. XML parsers do not take care of processing instructions, instead, they pass parameters to the underlying application. Processing instructions are not a textual part of the XML document. The XML declaration discussed in Section 6.3.1 is a processing instruction. Consider the following processing instruction:

```
<?xml-stylesheet href="simple.xsl" type="text/xsl"?>
```

This processing instruction states that the XML document should be transformed using the style sheet `simple.xsl`.

6.3.3 Comments

Like HTML, comments may appear anywhere in the XML documents. An XML comment starts with <!-- and ends with -->. Everything within these character sequences will be ignored by the parsers and will not be parsed. They are not part of the document's textual portion. Comments are used to explain the purpose of critical tags in an XML document. They take the following form:

```
<!--comment text-->
```

The following points should be remembered while using comments:

- Do not use the double hyphen '--' within comments as it might confuse the XML processor.
- Never place a comment inside an entity declaration.
- Never place a comment within a tag. This would result in poorly-formed XML.
- Never place a comment before the XML declaration. An XML declaration must always be the first line in any XML document.

6.3.4 Document Type Declaration

Although XML allows us to create new tags, it is probably not meaningful to use completely new tags that too in a completely arbitrary order. XML documents, to have a meaning, must have a logical structure created using a set of related tags.

The Document Type Declaration (or DOCTYPE declaration) is used to specify the logical structure of the XML document. The structure is specified by imposing constraint on what tags can be used and where. A parser reads this section and checks whether the XML document has been written according to the rules specified.

A Document Type Declaration may contain the following:

- Name of the root element
- Reference to an external DTD
- Element declaration
- Entity declaration

Detailed information about DTD may be found in Chapter 7.

6.4 BODY

This portion of the XML document contains textual data marked up by tags. It must have one element, called the *document element* or *root element*, which defines the content in the XML document. In an HTML document, the root element is <html>. Consider the following XML document:

```
<?xml version="1.0" encoding="UTF-8"?>
<greeting>Hello World!</greeting>
```

In this document, the name of the root element is <greeting>, which contains the text "Hello World".

The root element must be the top-level element in the document hierarchy and there can be one and only one root element. The following XML document is not valid as it has two top-level elements, <greeting> and <message>:

```
<?xml version="1.0" encoding="UTF-8"?>
<greeting>Hello World!</greeting>
<message>World is beautiful!</message>
```

The root element contains other elements which, in turn, contain other elements and so on.

```
<?xml version="1.0" encoding="UTF-8"?>
<contact>
   <person>
      <name>B. S. Roy</name>
      <number>9674141547</number>
   </person>
   <person>
      <name>G. Mahapatra</name>
      <number>919441804070</number>
   </person>
</contact>
```

This XML document has the root element `<contact>` which has two `<person>` elements. Each `<person>` element has two elements, `<name>` and `<number>`.

6.5 ELEMENTS

An XML element consists of a starting tag, an ending tag, and its contents and attributes. The content may be simple text, or other elements, or both. Each element contains different types of data that are stored in the XML document.

The XML tags are very much similar to that of HTML tags. A tag begins with the less than character ('<') and ends with the greater than ('>') character. It takes the form <tag-name>. Every tag must have its corresponding ending tag. The ending tag looks exactly like the starting tag except that it includes a slash ('/') character before the tag name. All information in this element must be contained in the starting and ending tags. Following is an example of an XML element:

```
<greeting>Hello World!</greeting>
```

Here, `<greeting>` is the starting tag and `</greeting>` is the ending tag. The starting tag, the ending tag and everything between these two form an element. This element has only text content "Hello World!".

6.5.1 Anatomy of an Element

An element consists of an opening tag, a closing tag, and contents.

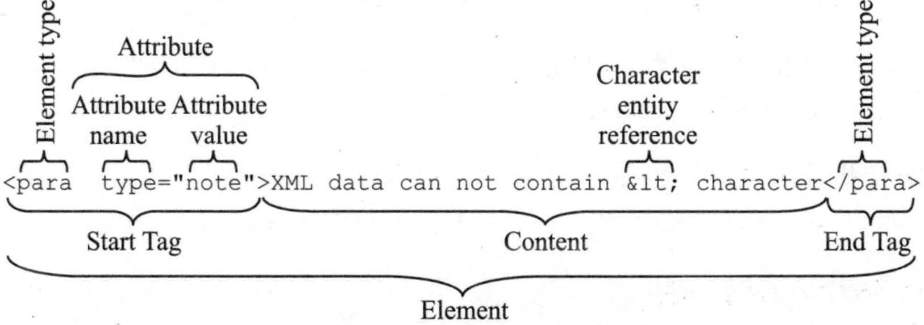

Figure 6.1 Structure of an element

Figure 6.1 shows the structure of an element. The name of the element is `para`. The opening tag is written within angular brackets. The closing tag is written exactly the same way, except that a slash (/) is added before the element name. Attributes are declared within the opening tag. For example, the para element has only one attribute `type` whose value is `note`. The attribute value must be quoted. An element can have an arbitrary number of attributes. The element content can be simply text, content, another element, or both. For the para element, the content is text. The text content may contain entities that refer to some piece of text to be substituted while processing. An entity starts with '&' and ends with ';' characters. XML specification defines five entities as shown in Table 6.1. XML document writers can also define their own entities in the DTD or XML declaration. Such declaration is discussed in Chapters 7 and 8.

6.5.2 Naming Rules

The following rules must be obeyed while selecting an element name:

- Names can only contain letters, digits, and some other special characters.
- Names cannot start with a number or punctuation marks.
- Names must not contain the string "xml", "XML", or "Xml".
- Names cannot contain white space(s).

6.5.3 Empty Elements

Empty elements are those that do not have any content. However, they can have attributes. According to the well-formedness constraint, every XML element must have a closing tag. So, a closing tag must be specified even for an empty element. Following is an example of an empty element:

```
<line width="100"></line>
```

XML specification provides a shorthand notation for empty elements as follows:

```
<line width="100"/>
```

6.6 ATTRIBUTES

Attributes are used to describe elements or to provide more information about elements. They appear in the starting tag of the element. The syntax for specifying an attribute in an element is:

```
<element-name attribute-name="attribute-value">…</element-name>
```

For example, the following example shows an attribute gender of the employee element.

```
<employee gender="male">…</employee>
```

An element can also have multiple attributes:

```
<employee gender="male" id="12345">…</employee>
```

6.6.1 Well-formed XML

An XML document is said to be well-formed if it contains text and tags that conform with the basic XML well-formedness constraints. Well-formed XML documents are not created by a rigid structural definition but by their use. It frees authors from the fixed nature of XML and allows their imagination to prevail over restraint. Authors can extend existing documents by creating new elements that fit their applications. The only thing they have to remember is the well-formedness constraint.

The following rules must be followed by the XML documents to be well-formed:

An XML document must have one and exactly one root element.

Consider the following well-formed XML document. It has one root element <contact>, which contains one <person> element which, in turn, contains two elements, <name> and <number>.

```
<contact>
   <person>
      <name>B. S. Roy</name>
      <number>9674141547</person>
   </person>
</contact>
```

The following document is not well-formed as it has two top-level elements, <contact> and <phonebook>.

```
<contact>
   <person>
      <name>B. S. Roy</name>
      <number>9674141547</person>
   </person>
</contact>
<phonebook>
      <name>G. Mahapatra</name>
      <number>919441804070</number>
</phonebook>
```

All tags must be closed.

Every element must have a closing tag corresponding to its opening tag. The following document fragment is not well-formed as there is no closing tag for the opening tag <name>:

```
<!--Incorrect-->
<name>B. S. Roy
```

However, the following code is well-formed because the opening tag <name> has its corresponding closing tag </name>.

```
<!--Correct-->
<name>Mozart</name>
```

A tag must be closed even if it does not have any content (empty element). In HTML, some tags such as <img>, <br>, <hr> do not require any closing tag. However, in XML closing tags are always needed. So, the following syntax is incorrect in XML:

```
<br>
```

Its correct representation is

```
<br></br>
```

Alternatively, XML has an abbreviated version for it as follows:

```
<br/>
```

All tags must be properly nested.

Elements must not overlap. An ending tag must have the same name as the most recent unmatched tag. The following code is not well-formed as `</b>` appears when the most recent (closest) starting tag is `<i>`.

```
<b><i>This is incorrect nesting</b></i>
```

The following code shows the correct nesting:

```
<b><i>This is correct nesting</i></b>
```

XML tags are case-sensitive

Unlike HTML, XML element names are case-sensitive. So, `Message` and `message` refer to two different names. So, the following code is not well-formed as there is no ending tag corresponding to the starting tag `<Message>`.

```
<Message>This is incorrect</message>
```

The following two elements are well-formed:

```
<Message>This is correct</Message>
<message>This is also correct</message>
```

Attributes must always be quoted

The value of an attribute must be quoted by double inverted comma. In HTML, for most of the cases it works even if no quotation is used. But, it is mandatory for an XML document to be well-formed.

```
<speed unit="rpm">7200</speed>
```

The following syntax is incorrect because the value `rpm` is specified without any quotation marks:

```
<speed unit=rpm>7200</speed>
```

Certain characters are reserved for processing

Certain characters cannot be used in the XML document directly. For example, '<', '>', and '"' cannot be used. So, the following syntax is incorrect as it confuses the XML parsers:

```
<!--Incorrect-->
<condition>if salary < 1000 then</condition>
```

XML provides entities for these special characters and may be used. XML parsers will substitute each entity by its actual value. An entity starts with an '&' character and ends with a ';'. The following code is correct.

```
<!--Correct-->
<condition>if salary &lt; 1000 then</condition>
```

6.6.2 Predefined Entities

In the W3C XML specification, five entities are defined, each of which represents a special character that cannot be used in the XML document directly. All XML processors must recognize those entities, whether they are declared or not. XML also allows us to define entities of arbitrary size in the DTD or schema.

Table 6.1 shows the predefined entities.

Table 6.1 Predefined entities

Entity Name	Entity number	Description	Character
<	<	less than	<
>	>	greater than	>
&	&	ampersand	&
"	"	quotation mark	"
'	'	apostrophe	'

6.6.3 Valid XML

Well-formed XML documents obey only basic well-formedness constraints. So, valid XML documents are those that

- are well-formed
- comply with rules specified in the DTD or schema.

The basic difference between a well-formed and a valid XML document is that the former is defined without any DTD or schema and the latter requires a DTD or schema. A DTD or schema specifies a set of rules, which the valid XML documents must follow. The rules usually specify the name and content of the element that can occur in the valid documents. XML parsers check whether the XML documents are developed using these rules.

Authoring, processing, storing, and displaying valid XML documents are easier as they follow a predefined structure. Data stored in the XML documents can be verified against the underlying DTD or schema. Use of style sheets is easy as they can be created using DTD or schema as opposed to a relatively unknown set of markups used in well-formed documents. Valid XML documents may be shared among a set of DTD or schema-aware applications.

6.7 VALIDATION

It is a method of checking whether an XML document is well-formed and conforms to the rules specified by a DTD or schema. Many tools are available to validate XML documents against DTD or schema. UNIX/Linux provides one such application called xmllint for this purpose. The following example shows how to validate the XML document sample.xml using this command:

```
xmllint --valid sample.xml
```

Java, JavaScript, and C/C++ also provide interfaces to validate XML documents. A detailed description about XML validation can be found in Chapter 9.

6.7.1 Elements or Attributes

Attributes are usually used to provide information that is not an integral part of the XML document. Attributes may always be converted to embedded elements to provide the same information. For example, the example depicted in Section 6.6 could be written as

```
<employee>
  <gender>male</gender>
  <id>12345</id>
  ...
</employee>
```

There is no rigid rule that decides when to use elements and when to use attributes. However, it is recommended not to use attributes as far as possible due to the following reasons:

- Too many attributes reduce the readability of an XML document.
- Attributes cannot contain multiple values, but elements can.
- Attributes are not easily extendable for future changes.
- Attributes cannot represent logical structure, but elements together with their child elements can.
- Attributes are difficult to access by the parsers.
- Attribute values are not easy to check against DTD.

6.8 DISPLAYING XML

XML documents do not carry information about how to display the data. New tags can be added in the XML document. Web browsers do not have any idea about the tags used in the XML file. So, if you open an XML file in a browser, the entire content (data and tags) is displayed in a tree-like structure.

There are many ways to display data stored in an XML document. The two common methods are

- CSS (Cascading Style Sheets)
- XSL (eXtensible Stylesheet Language)

The use of CSS is exactly the same as HTML and was discussed in Chapter 5. XSL was specially designed for XML. Consider the following XML document:

```
<?xml version="1.0" encoding="ISO-8859-1"?>
<?xml-stylesheet type="text/xsl" href="books.xsl"?>
<bookstore>
   <book category="literature">
      <title lang="beng">Sanchoita</title>
      <author>Rabindranath Tagore</author>
      <year>2009</year>
```

```
      <price>200.00</price>
   </book>
   <book category="literature">
      <title lang="en">Gitanjali</title>
      <author>Rabindranath Tagore</author>
      <year>2008</year>
      <price>29.00</price>
   </book>
   <book category="WEB">
      <title lang="en">Essential XML</title>
      <author>Don Box</author>
      <year>2000</year>
      <price>150</price>
   </book>
</bookstore>
```

To link an XML document to an XSL style sheet, the following processing instruction is added:

```
<?xml-stylesheet type="text/xsl" href="books.xsl"?>
```

The style sheet `books.xml` looks like this.

```
<?xml version="1.0" encoding="ISO-8859-1"?>
<xsl:stylesheet version="1.0"
xmlns:xsl="http://www.w3.org/1999/XSL/Transform">
   <xsl:output method='html' version='1.0' encoding='UTF-8' indent='yes'/>
   <xsl:template match="/">
      <html>
         <body>
            My Book Collection:
            <table border="1">
               <tr bgcolor="#9acd32">
                  <th>Title</th><th>Author</th><th>Year</th><th>Price</th>
               </tr>
               <xsl:for-each select="bookstore/book">
               <tr>
                  <xsl:for-each select="./*">
                     <td><xsl:value-of select="."/></td>
                  </xsl:for-each>
               </tr>
               </xsl:for-each>
            </table>
         </body>
      </html>
   </xsl:template>
</xsl:stylesheet>
```

The syntax of XSL is discussed in Chapter 11. This time you simply write such a style and link it with the XML document. Now, if you open this document in Google Chrome, it looks as shown in Figure 6.2.

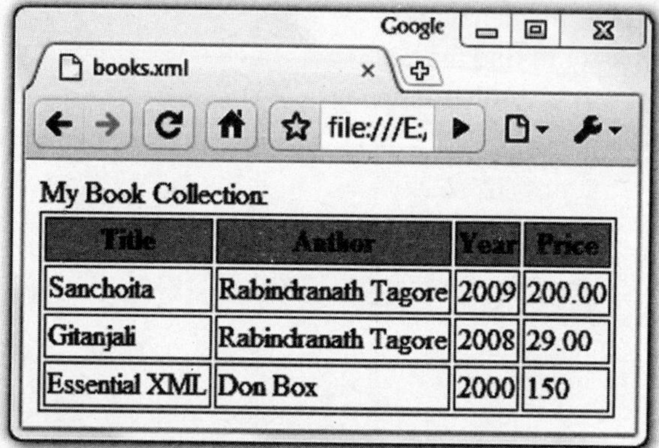

Figure 6.2 Displaying XML document using CSS

6.9 NAMESPACE

XML was developed to be used by many applications. If many applications want to communicate using XML documents, a potential problem may occur.

6.9.1 The Problem

In an XML document, element names and attribute names are selected by developers. According to the XML 1.0 specification, element and attribute names are unstructured flat strings. So, name conflicts may occur when merging XML documents from different developers to get a final XML document. Consider the following XML document (client.xml) which represents an HTML table of client-side technologies:

```
<table>
   <tr><td>JavaScript</td><td>VBScript</td></tr>
</table>
```

This XML document has the root element `table`. The following XML document (server.xml) carries information about a table of server-side technologies.

```
<table>
   <row><col>JSP</col><col>ASP</col></row>
</table>
```

This XML document also contains the root element `table`. Let us now merge these two XML documents to obtain a single XML document as follows:

```
<technology>
   <table>
      <tr><td>JavaScript</td><td>VBScript</td></tr>
   </table>
   <table>
      <row><col>JSP</col><col>ASP</col></row>
   </table>
</technology>
```

This new XML document has two <table> elements which have different content and meaning. So, if we query a parser to find the table containing server-side technologies, it fails. One simple, but not-too-flexible way to resolve this problem is to embed them in two different elements as follows:

```
<technology>
   <client>
      <table>
         <tr><td>JavaScript</td><td>VBScript</td></tr>
      </table>
   </client>
   <server>
      <table>
         <row><col>JSP</col><col>ASP</col></row>
      </table>
   </server>
</technology>
```

Now, the first and second table elements can be uniquely referred by referring to their parent element names, which are unique. Needless to say, this mechanism needs not only extra elements to be inserted, but also knowledge about the XML documents to be merged.

6.9.2 Solution

XML namespace provides a simple, straightforward, but elegant way to distinguish between element names in the XML document, no matter where they come from. XML namespace suggests that we use a prefix with every element. So, client.xml can now be written like this:

```
<c:table>
   <c:tr><c:td>JavaScript</c:td><c:td>VBScript</c:td></c:tr>
</c:table>
```

Similarly, we can write server.xml.

```
<s:table>
   <s:row><s:col>JSP</s:col><s:col>ASP</s:col></s:row>
</s:table>
```

Who guarantees that the prefixes used by different developer will be unique? One good idea is to use Uniform Resource Identifier (URI). URIs are unique all over the world. Usually we use Uniform Resource Locator (URL) to choose a unique name. The developers will then use their own unique URL as the prefix to every element they use. But, what happens if we use a long URL repeatedly in our XML documents? Will it not create a mess? XML namespace has the answer: instead of using an entire URL as the prefix for all elements, use a small prefix and make an association between this prefix and the URL. It means prefixes are just shorthand placeholders of URLs.

6.9.3 Binding

How to make this association between a prefix and a URL? This association is done in the starting tag using the reserved XML attribute `xmlns`. It takes the following form:

```
xmlns:prefix="URI"
```

Let us now rewrite the file client.xml.

```
<c:table xmlns:c="http://it.site.jusl.ac/client">
   <c:tr><c:td>JavaScript</c:td><c:td>VBScript</c:td></c:tr>
</c:table>
```

This declaration states that the prefix `c` is associated with a namespace whose value is `http://it.site.jusl.ac/client`. The prefix does not have any meaning, its only purpose is to point to the namespace name. The namespace declaration does not suggest nor require that the URL be used to access the associated resource. For example, the URL `http://it.site.jusl.ac/client` does not really represent any resource. The URLs are used only to make element names unique. Using a URL instead of a flat, simple string reduces the chance of different developers using duplicate names.

The actual name (W3C calls it expanded name or qualified name) is then obtained by using this prefix and a local name separated by ":". So, the name of the table element has the expanded name `c:table`. Essentially, it maps to

```
<{http://it.site.jusl.ac/client}table>
```

Note that the `xmlns:c` attribute is removed during this mapping. Not only the table element but also all the descendant elements are mapped as follows:

```
<{http://it.site.jusl.ac/client}table>
   <{http://it.site.jusl.ac/client}tr>
   <{http://it.site.jusl.ac/client}td>JavaScript</{http://it.site.jusl.ac/
client}td>
      <{http://it.site.jusl.ac/client}td>VBScript</{http://it.site.jusl.ac/
client}td>
   </{http://it.site.jusl.ac/client}tr>
</{http://it.site.jusl.ac/client}table>
```

Now, every element has a unique name. A prefix is needed in both starting tag as well as ending tag. The prefix simply indicates which namespace the elements belong to. The same prefix may be used to all of its descendants to indicate that they belong to the same namespace. This way, name clashes can be avoided using a combination of universally managed URI namespace with the vocabulary's local name.

The file client.xml can use a separate namespace as follows:

```
<s:table xmlns:s="http://it.site.jusl.ac/server">
   <s:row><s:col>JSP</s:col><s:col>ASP</s:col></s:row>
</s:table>
```

The two files can then be safely merged as follows:

```
<technology>
   <c:table xmlns:c="http://it.site.jusl.ac/client">
      <c:tr><c:td>JavaScript</c:td><c:td>VBScript</c:td></c:tr>
   </c:table>
   <s:table xmlns:s="http://it.site.jusl.ac/server">
```

```
        <s:row><s:col>JSP</s:col><s:col>ASP</s:col></s:row>
    </s:table>
</technology>
```

A namespace, in practice, is identified by a URL.

When defining a namespace for an element, all descendant elements inherit the same namespace and the associated prefix may be used. So, it is a common practice to define all namespaces within the root element.

```
<technology xmlns:c="http://it.site.jusl.ac/client" xmlns:s="http://
it.site.jusl.ac/server">
    <c:table>
        <c:tr><c:td>JavaScript</c:td><c:td>VBScript</c:td></c:tr>
    </c:table>
    <s:table>
        <s:row><s:col>JSP</s:col><s:col>ASP</s:col></s:row>
    </s:table>
</technology>
```

However, namespaces declared explicitly in an element overrides the namespace obtained from its parent.

6.9.4 Namespace Rules

The `xmlns` attribute identifies the namespace and makes association between a prefix and the created namespace. Many prefixes may be associated with one namespace. The following example illustrates this:

```
<small:root xmlns:small="http://it.site.jusl.ac" xmlns:capital="http://
it.site.jusl.ac">
    <small:a>
        <small:b/>
    </small:a>
    <capital:A>
        <capital:B/>
    </capital:A>
</small:root>
```

In this example, elements are from the same namespace but use different prefixes. Similarly, elements may use the same prefix, but belong to different namespaces.

```
<root>
    <it:a xmlns:it="http://it.site.jusl.ac/small" >
        <it:b/>
    </it:a>
    <it:A xmlns:it="http://it.site.jusl.ac/capital">
        <it:B/>
    </it:A>
</root>
```

The elements `<it:a>` and `<it:b>` belong to the namespace `http://it.site.jusl.ac/small`, but `<it:A>` and `<it:B>` belong to the namespace `http://it.site.jusl.ac/capital`. Note that namespace defined in an element is only valid within the element and its descendant elements.

6.9.5 Default Namespace

Namespaces may not have their associated prefixes. These are called default namespaces. In such cases, a blank prefix is assumed for the element and all of its descendants.

```
<root xmlns="http://it.site.jusl.ac">
   <a>
      <b/>
   </a>
   <A>
      <B/>
   </A>
</root>
```

In this example, all the elements belong to the default namespace `http://it.site.jusl.ac.` Even if a default namespace is used for an element, its children can still define their own namespaces.

```
<root xmlns="http://it.site.jusl.ac">
   <small:a xmlns:small="http://it.site.jusl.ac/small">
      <small:b/>
   </small:a>
   <capital:A xmlns:capital="http://it.site.jusl.ac/capital">
      <capital:B/>
   </capital:A>
</root>
```

Even for the default namespace, a value of the attribute `xmlns` must be specified. Otherwise, the namespace remains undeclared.

```
<root xmlns="http://it.site.jusl.ac">
   <a xmlns="">
      <b/>
   </a>
   <A xmlns="http://it.site.jusl.ac/capital">
      <B/>
   </A>
</root>
```

In this example, the default namespace for the element `<a>` remains undeclared. However, the default namespace for the element `<A>` is declared correctly.

Attributes may be assigned to namespaces also.

```
<small:root xmlns:small="http://it.site.jusl.ac/small" xmlns:capital="http:/
/it.site.jusl.ac/capital">
   <small:a small:id="aaa">
      <small:b/>
   </small:a>
   <capital:A capital:ID="AAA">
      <capital:B/>
   </capital:A>
</small:root>
```

Attributes may belong to a namespace different from that of their embedding element.

```
<small:root xmlns:small="http://it.site.jusl.ac/small" xmlns:capital="http:/
/it.site.jusl.ac/capital">
   <small:a capital:ID="aaa">
      <small:b/>
   </small:a>
   <capital:A small:id="AAA">
      <capital:B/>
   </capital:A>
</small:root>
```

In this example, the `ID` attribute belongs to a namespace different from that of its embedding element. Similarly, the `id` attribute belongs to a namespace different from that of its embedding element.

Attributes without any prefix do not belong to any namespace.

```
<small:root xmlns:small="http://it.site.jusl.ac/small" xmlns:capital="http:/
/it.site.jusl.ac/capital">
   <small:a ID="aaa">
      <small:b/>
   </small:a>
   <capital:A id="AAA">
      <capital:B/>
   </capital:A>
</small:root>
```

In this example, attributes `ID` and `id` do not belong to any namespace. The attributes do not belong to the default namespace even if a default namespace is defined in the embedded element.

```
<small:root xmlns:small="http://it.site.jusl.ac/small" xmlns:capital="http:/
/it.site.jusl.ac/capital">
   <small:a>
      <b xmlns:capital="http://it.site.jusl.ac" id="bbb"/>
   </small:a>
   <capital:A>
      <capital:B/>
   </capital:A>
</small:root>
```

In this example, the `id` attribute of the `<b>` element does not belong to the default namespace even if the default namespace is defined for `<b>`.

KEY WORDS

Attributes: Attributes are used to describe elements or to provide more information about elements.

Document Type Declaration: The Document Type Declaration is used to specify the logical structure of the XML document.

Element: An XML element consists of a starting tag, an ending tag, and its contents and attributes.

Entities: Entities are character sequence used to insert reserved characters or the characters that cannot be typed.

Processing Instruction: Processing instructions start with <? and end with ?> and allow XML documents to contain special instructions that are used to pass parameters to the application.

Root Element: Every XML document must have one top-level element called root element.

Valid XML: An XML document is said to be valid against a DTD or a schema if it conforms to the rules specified there.

Validation: It is a procedure for validating an XML document against a set of rules usually specified by a DTD or a schema.

Well-Formed XML: An XML document is said to be well-formed if it contains text and tags that conform with the XML syntax.

XML Declaration: Every XML document should start with a one-line XML declaration that describes the document.

SUMMARY

The XML standard was developed by the World Wide Web Consortium (W3C). The primary purpose of this standard was to provide a way to store self-describing data easily.

XML is used to describe structured data or information. It is also used as a primary means to manipulate and transfer structured data over the web. The content and structure of XML documents are accessed by a software module, called XML processor.

An XML document separates the contents from their presentation. It does not specify how the content should be displayed. It only specifies the contents with their logical structure. The formatting task is imposed on an external style sheet. This helps authors of the XML documents to develop contents and finding the logical relation among them without bothering about the formatting information. Since formatting is done on an external style sheet, the look and feel may be changed very easily by choosing different style sheets.

Every XML document has basically two parts: a prolog and a body. The prolog section contains an XML declaration, optional zero or more processing instructions, comments, and Document Type Declaration. The XML declaration describes the version and encoding used in the document. It can also specify whether the document can be processed independently.

Processing instructions are used to pass information to the underlying application for further processing. Comments are used to describe critical XML elements and can be inserted anywhere in the document. The DTD section contains the set of rules the XML document must conform with.

The body of an XML document contains textual data marked up by tags. It must have one element, called the document element or root element, which defines the content in the XML document.

An XML element consists of a starting tag, an ending tag, and its contents and attributes. The content may be simple text, other elements, or both. Each element contains different types of data that are stored in the XML document.

XML documents are categorized as well-formed or valid. An XML document is said to be well-formed if it conforms to the basic XML syntax. The XML document is valid if it follows the set of rules specified in the DTD or schema.

The procedure for checking whether an XML document obeys the rules of a DTD or a schema is known as validation. There are many validators freely available in the market. Programming languages such as Java, JavaScript, and C/++ also provide validation interfaces.

There are many ways to display data stored in an XML document. The two common methods are: CSS and XSL.

WEB RESOURCES

`http://www.w3.org/TR/REC-xml/`
Extensible Markup Language (XML) 1.0 (Fifth Edition)

`http://www.w3.org/TR/REC-xml/#sec-origin-goals`
XML 1.0 Origin and Goals

`http://www.sgmlsource.com/history/AnnexA.htm`
Introduction to Generalized Markup

`http://www.w3.org/2008/02/xml10-pressrelease`
W3C XML is Ten!

`http://www.w3.org/TR/REC-xml-names/`
Namespaces in XML 1.0 (Second Edition), W3C Recommendation 16 August 2006

`http://www.w3.org/TR/2006/REC-xml-names11-20060816/`
Namespaces in XML 1.1 (Second Edition), W3C Recommendation 16 August 2006

`http://www.w3.org/1999/xhtml/`
XHTML namespace

EXERCISES

Multiple Choice Questions

1. Regarding XML, which of the following is true?
   (a) XML was designed to carry data.
   (b) XML is free and extensible.
   (c) XML is not a replacement for HTML.
   (d) All of the above

2. What is the full form of XML?
   (a) eXtra Markup Language
   (b) eXtensible Markup Language
   (c) X-Markup Language
   (d) eXpandable Markup Language

3. Which of the following is a correct XML declaration?
   (a) <xml version="1.0"/>
   (b) <?xml version="1.0"/>
   (c) <?xml version="1.0"?>
   (d) <?xml version=1.0?>

4. Which of the following statements is true?
   (a) All XML elements must be properly closed.
   (b) All XML documents must have a DTD.
   (c) All XML elements must be in lower case.
   (d) All the statements are true.

5. Which of the following statements regarding XML is true?
   (a) XML documents must have a root tag.
   (b) XML tags are case-sensitive.
   (c) XML elements must be properly nested.
   (d) All the statements are true.

6. Which one of the following is the correct syntax to refer to the style sheet "simple.xsl"?
   (a) <?xml-stylesheet type="text/xsl" href= "simple.xsl"?>
   (b) <stylesheet href="simple.xsl" type="text/xsl"/>
   (c) <link type="text/xsl" href="simple.xsl"/>
   (d) <!xml-stylesheet href="simple.xsl" type= "text/xsl"!>

7. What is the correct syntax of the CDATA section in an XML document?
   (a) <CDATA> Text to be ignored </CDATA>
   (b) <PCDATA> Text to be ignored </PCDATA>
   (c) <xml:CDATA[Text to be ignored]>
   (d) <![CDATA[Text to be ignored]]>

8. How is an empty XML element defined?
   (a) <sample></sample>
   (b) <sample/>
   (c) All of the above
   (d) None of the above

9. Which of the following is the correct syntax to insert comments into an XML document?
   (a) <comment>This is a comment</comment>
   (b) <?-This is a comment->
   (c) <!--This is a comment-->
   (d) </This is a comment>

10. Which of the following recommended XML?
    (a) W3C (b) Microsoft
    (c) Sun (d) IEEE

11. Which of the following XML documents are well-formed?
    (a) <one><two></two></one>
    (b) <one></one><two> </two>
    (c) <one><two> </one></two>
    (d) </one></two><two><one>

12. Which one of the following is a correct attribute declaration?
    (a) <element-name attribute-name=attribute-value/>
    (b) <element-name attribute-name="attribute-value"/>
    (c) <element-name attribute-name='attribute-value'>
    (d) <element-name attribute-name="attribute-value"/>

13. Which of the following technologies is used to display XML data?
    (a) CSS (b) XPath
    (c) XQuery (d) XHTML

14. Which of the following is not a correct name for an XML document?
    (a) <para>
    (b) <line>

(c) <1st>
(d) All three names are incorrect

15. What is the full form of DTD?
(a) Document Type Declaration
(b) Dynamic Type Definition
(c) Direct Type Definition
(d) Dynamic Type Declaration

16. Which of the following namespace declaration is correct?
(a) <root ns:p="<http://it.jusl.ac.in>">
(b) <root xmlns:p="<http://it.jusl.ac.in>">
(c) <root p:xmlns="<http://it.jusl.ac.in>">
(d) <root namespace:p="<http://it.jusl. ac.in>">

17. Which of the following statements is incorrect?
(a) Namespace is used to avoid name clashes.
(b) Namespace is used to group a set of related elements.
(c) Namespace is used to structure XML elements.
(d) A default namespace is one that has no prefix.

18. Which of the following is not provided by a namespace?
(a) Generates a unique name
(b) Help in avoiding name collisions
(c) Access control
(d) Displays name in boldface

19. Which of the following is the correct syntax of a qualified name?
(a) localname:prefix (b) localname-prefix
(c) prefix-localname (d) prefix:localname

20. Which of the following attributes is used to define a namespace?
(a) ns (b) name-space
(c) xml-ns (d) xmlns

Review Questions

1. Write the differences between HTML and XML.
2. Describe the role that XSL can play to generate HTML pages from a relational database dynamically.
3. Provide some examples of applications that can benefit from using XML.
4. Which parts of an XML document are case-sensitive?
5. How does XML handle white space in your documents?
6. What modifications should you make for your HTML files to work in XML?
7. What is the purpose of XML namespaces?
8. What do you understand about XML Namespaces?
9. Describe different techniques that are used to process XML files.

7 XML DTD

KEY OBJECTIVES

After completing this chapter readers will be able to—

- **understand the importance of XML schema languages**
- **understand the concept of DTD and its purpose**
- **know how to use a DTD in an XML document**
- **learn how to declare elements, attributes, and entities in XML documents**
- **write complete DTDs for simple XML documents**
- **learn the procedure for validating an XML document against a DTD**

7.1 XML SCHEMA LANGUAGES

In computer science, a *schema* is an abstract representation of an object's characteristics and its relationship to other objects. An *XML schema* represents the interrelationship between the elements and attributes in an XML document. In addition to the basic syntactical constraints (well-formedness) imposed by XML itself, an XML schema is a description, typically expressed in terms of constraints on the structure and content of XML documents. It defines the structure of XML documents by specifying a list of valid elements and attributes. The content description includes the order and quantity of elements that can be contained within the element being declared.

An *XML schema language* is a formal language to express XML schemas. Several such XML schema languages (Table 7.1) have been proposed. The **D**ocument **T**ype **D**efinition (DTD) is one such XML schema language that is native to the XML standardized by the **W**orld **W**ide **W**eb Consortium (W3C). Two other very popular, expressive XML schema languages are **W**3C **X**ML **S**chema (WXS) and RELAX NG. A DTD, apart from the expression of schemas, has other uses in XML and is widely used.

Two primary XML schema languages, namely, DTD, which is very popular and is widely used and W3C XML Schema, which is known to be an extremely powerful schema language are discussed in this book. The features that have made W3C XML Schema powerful are discussed in Chapter 8. Discussing other XML schema languages is out of the scope of this book.

The notion of DTD is discussed in this chapter while W3C XML Schema is dealt in Chapter 8.

Table 7.1 Major XML schema languages

DTD family	
Name	Description
Document **T**ype **D**efinition (DTD)	Introduced as a part of XML 1.0 Recommendation. Even though a DTD is not mandatory for an application to read and understand an XML document, many developers recomm-end writing DTDs for your XML applications.
W3C XML Schema	
Name	Description
XML-Data	Introduced in January, 1998 by Microsoft, DataChannel, Arbortext, Inso Corporation, and University of Edinburgh and included most of the basic concepts developed by W3C XML Schema.
XML-**D**ata-**R**educed (XDR)	Submitted in July 1998 by Microsoft and University of Edinburgh. It was presented to refine and subset the XML-Data down to a more manageable size in order to allow faster progress toward adopting a new schema language for XML (mappings were left out). XDR has been implemented by Microsoft and used by the BizTalk framework.
Document **C**ontent **D**escription for XML (DCD)	Also submitted in July 1998 by Textuality, Microsoft, and IBM. It was a "subset of the XML-Data and expressed it in a way which was consistent with W3C's RDF (Resource Descrip-tion Framework) effort". Mapping considerations were left out, but the language took care to be consistent with RDF through features such as "Interchangeability of Elements and Attributes".
Schema for **O**bject-Oriented **X**ML (SOX)	Developed by Veo Systems/Commerce One and submitted final version in July 1999 as "informed by the XML 1.0 specification as well as XML-Data, DCD, and the EXPRESS language reference manual (ISO-10303-11)". SOX was very influenced by OOP language design and included concepts of interface and implementation, but it was also influenced by DTDs and also included a support for "parameters". SOX has been widely used by Commerce One.
Document **D**efinition **M**arkup **L**anguage or XSchema (DDML)	Submitted as a note in January 1999. Its purpose was to "encode the logical (as opposed to physical) content of DTDs in an XML document". Great attention had been paid to the definition of the back and forward conversions between DTDs and DDML. DDML made a clear distinction between structures and data and left data types out.
W3C XML Schema	Published as a Recommendation in May 2001. It acknowledges the influence of DCD, DDML, SOX, XML-Data, and XDR in its list of references and appears to have picked pieces from each of these proposals but is also a compromise between them. The main sponsors of the two languages still actively used and developed (Microsoft for XDR and Commerce One for SOX) have both announced that they would support W3C XML Schema for their new developments, and that W3C XML Schema should become the only surviving member of this family.
RELAX NG Family	
Name	Description
RELAX	First published in March 2000 as a Japanese ISO Standard Technical Report written by Murata Makoto. RELAX is both simple ("Tired of complicated specifications? You just RELAX!"), and built on a solid mathematical foundation (the adaptation of the hedge auto-mata theory to XML trees). It was approved as an ISO/IEC Technical Report in May 2001.
XDuce	First announced in March 2000: "XDuce ('transduce') is a typed programming language that is specifically designed for processing XML data. One can read an XML document as an XDuce value, extract information from it or convert it into another format, and write out the result value as an XML document". Although its purpose is not to be a schema language, its typing system has influenced the schema languages.

(Contd.)

(Contd.)

Tree **R**egular **E**xpressions for **XML** (TREX)	Published by James Clark in January 2001. It is "basically the type system of XDuce with XML syntax and with a bunch of additional features". The names and content model of the elements used to define the tree patterns of a TREX schema have been carefully chosen, and TREX schemas are usually as easy to read as a plain text description. The simplicity of the structure of the language also allows the resurrection of a consistent treatment between elements and attributes, a feature lost since DCD.
RELAX New Generation (RELAX NG)	Announced in May 2001. It is a result of a merger of RELAX and TREX, developed by an OASIS TC and co-edited by James Clark and Murata Makoto: "The key features of RELAX NG are that it is simple, easy to learn, uses XML syntax, does not change the information set of an XML document, supports XML namespaces, treats attributes uniformly with elements as far as possible, has unrestricted support for unordered content, has unrestricted support for mixed content, has a solid theoretical basis, and can partner with a separate data typing language (such as W3C XML Schema Data types)".

7.2 VALIDATION

XML *validation* [Figure 7.1] is a procedure used to verify whether an XML document conforms to the rules specified by a given XML schema. This task is accomplished by a special program called XML parser (also called XML processor). This parser typically takes two arguments: an XML document to be verified and an XML schema (e.g., W3C XML Schema or a DTD) where the rules to be followed by an XML instance document are specified. If the XML document follows the rules specified in the XML schema, it is said to be *valid*. Otherwise, the XML processor reports a set of diagnostic error messages. These messages are used to filter the errors out from the XML document.

Moreover, an XML processor may optimize the XML document. Optimization includes removal of white space, insertion of default elements and attributes, and so on.

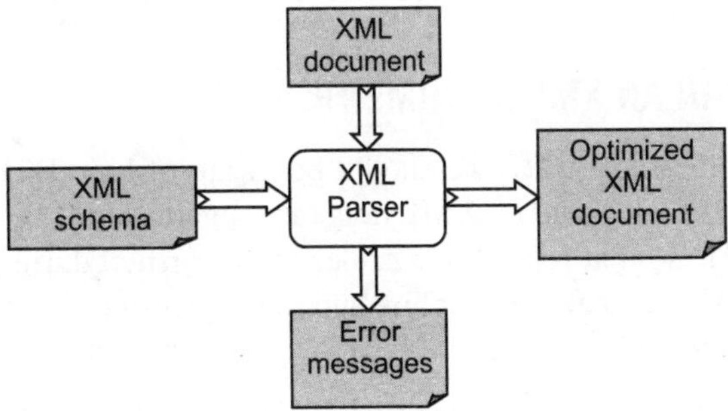

Figure 7.1 Schema processing

Validating an XML instance document against a schema is language-specific. This chapter discusses, with sample programs written in Java and JavaScript, the exact procedure of validation with respect to DTD in detail in Section 7.9.

7.3 INTRODUCTION TO DTD

Document **T**ype **D**efinition (DTD) is one of several XML schema languages[§] and was introduced as a part of the XML 1.0 Recommendation. Even though a DTD is not mandatory for an application to read and understand an XML document, many developers recommend writing DTDs for your XML applications because it is considered easy to read and write.

7.4 PURPOSE OF DTD

In Chapter 6, we have seen that XML lets applications share data easily. XML lets it happen by allowing you to make up your own set of tags. The purpose of a DTD[§], like other schema languages, is to define the legal building blocks of an XML document. It specifies the document structure with a list of legal elements. It is also used to specify a content model for each element and attribute used in an XML document. The content description is a part of the element declaration in the DTD and specifies the order and quantity of elements that can be contained within the element being declared. A DTD cannot specify all the constraints that may arise in an XML document. A greater subset of constraints can be specified using W3C XML Schema (or simply XML Schema), which will be discussed in Chapter 8.

It was mentioned in Chapter 6 that there are two types of XML documents: (i) *well-formed* and (ii) *valid*.

An XML document is said to be *valid* with respect to a DTD, if it conforms with the rules specified by a given XML DTD. Independent developers can agree to use a common DTD for exchanging XML documents. They can use this agreed-upon DTD to validate the XML documents they receive. The DTD may also be used to verify our own XML documents.

DTD standards are defined by the World Wide Web Consortium (W3C). The W3C site [http://www.w3c.org] provides a comprehensive reference of DTDs.

7.5 USING A DTD IN AN XML DOCUMENT

Before we start developing a DTD, we should be aware of how DTDs and conforming XML documents are linked. To validate an XML document against a DTD, we must tell the validator where to find the DTD so that it knows the rules to be verified during validation. A Document Type Declaration is used to make such a link and the keyword `DOCTYPE` is used for this purpose. There are three ways to make this link.

- The DTD can be embedded directly in the XML document as a part of it—called *internal* DTD.
- From an XML document, a reference to an external file containing the DTD can be made—called *external* DTD.
- Both *internal* and *external* DTD can be used.

[§] The Document Type Definition (DTD) is basically a method used to define markup languages. These languages are based on the Standardized General Markup Language (SGML), which is the mother of all markup languages. There are DTDs for each version of HTML and for other markup languages. In fact, we can write our own DTDs and define our own markup languages.

7.5.1 Internal DTD

When we embed a DTD in an XML document, the DTD information is included within the XML document itself. Specifically, the DTD information is placed between the square brackets in a DOCTYPE declaration. The general syntax for an internal Document Type Declaration is

```
<!DOCTYPE root-element [
   <!-- doctype-declaration -->
]>
```

The keyword DOCTYPE specifies that a DTD is to be used by the document. It states that, we are going to define the structure of the element root-element. Since every XML document must have one and exactly one *root* element, this is also a structure definition of the entire XML document.

The following rules must be followed:

- The keyword DOCTYPE must be in uppercase (well-formedness constraint).
- The document type declaration must appear before the first element in the document (well-formedness constraint).
- The name following the word DOCTYPE (root-element in this case) must match with the name of the root element (top-level element) in the XML document (validity constraint).

The following example shows a DTD embedded in an XML document:

```
<?xml version='1.0'?>
<!DOCTYPE greeting [
   <!ELEMENT greeting (#PCDATA)>
]>
<greeting>Hello World!</greeting>
```

This DTD says that an XML document can contain the root element greeting, which can contain some text. The exact meaning and syntax of the element and attribute declaration will be discussed throughout this chapter.

The advantage of an internal DTD is that you only have to handle a single XML document instead of many. It is useful particularly when you are debugging and editing both DTD and XML documents, while you are experimenting. In addition, it is a good idea, if your DTDs are smaller in size or one that you will use for smaller documents.

The problem of an internal DTD is that it makes XML documents difficult to read as your document potentially becomes packed with markups. Every time you want to view or modify XML content, rather than view only DTD information or XML document content, as you would with an external DTD, you are forced to walk through the DTD information.

So, if your DTDs are complex or if you want to use one repeatedly, you should use an external DTD.

7.5.2 External DTD

Another way of connecting a DTD to the XML document is to reference it within the XML document, i.e., create a separate document, put DTD information there, and point to it from the XML document. The general syntax for an external Document Type Declaration is

```
<!DOCTYPE root-element [SYSTEM OR PUBLIC FPI] 'URI'>
```

It states that DTD information can be found in the resource identified by `URI`. A **U**niform **R**esource **I**dentifier (URI) is a string of characters used to identify or name a resource on the Internet. A URI can be classified as a locator, a name, or both. The term "**U**niform **R**esource **L**ocator" (URL) refers to the subset of URIs that identifies resources via a representation of their primary access mechanism (e.g., their network "location"), rather than identifying them by name or by some other attribute(s) of that resource. The term "**U**niform **R**esource **N**ame" (URN) refers to the subset of URIs that is required to remain globally unique and persistent even when the resource ceases to exist or becomes unavailable. A URN is like a person's name, while a URL resembles that person's address. The URN defines an item's identity, while the URL provides a method for finding it. An example of a URL is "http://www.site.jusl.ac.in/hello.dtd" whereas the string "urn:isbn:0-486-27557-4" represents a URN.

URNs are an acceptable part of the URI specification, but XML processors may have no way to resolve them into actual resources. Therefore, the only possible URI for DTD declarations is URL.

The keywords `SYSTEM` and `PUBLIC` suggest the type of DTD used. The keyword `SYSTEM` indicates that the DTD is a system resource such as a local file or a URL and is used in one's private application. The keyword `PUBLIC` indicates that the DTD is a publicly accessible object that may span more than one application and may be used by anybody. In the latter case the DTD is represented by a formatted string, to be universally unique, called **F**ormal **P**ublic **I**dentifier (FPI). HTML/XHTML DTDs are specified by `PUBLIC` identifiers. If the `SYSTEM` keyword is chosen, the URI of the DTD may follow; if the `PUBLIC` keyword is chosen, the declaration must have an FPI following it and then the URI of the DTD.

The following example depicts DTD declaration using external reference and the `SYSTEM` keyword:

```
<?xml version='1.0'?>
<!DOCTYPE greeting SYSTEM 'hello.dtd'>
<greeting>Hello World!</greeting>
```

This declaration states that we are going to define the structure of an element `greeting`, which is the root element of the XML document, and that the actual definition can be found in the file `hello.dtd`. It also says that the DTD contained in `hello.dtd` is written only for this XML document and will not be used by any other application.

The file `hello.dtd` and the XML document should be kept in the same directory. The external DTD file `hello.dtd` referenced in the example contains information about the XML document's structure, as follows:

```
<!ELEMENT greeting (#PCDATA)>
```

Remember that the location of DTD need not always be a local file; it can be any valid URL. Following is a declaration for the same using a URL:

```
<?xml version='1.0'?>
<!DOCTYPE greeting SYSTEM 'http://www.site.jusl.in/hello.dtd'>
<greeting>Hello World!</greeting>
```

Following is a DOCTYPE declaration for XHTML using a PUBLIC DTD:

```
<?xml version='1.0' standalone='no' ?>
<!DOCTYPE HTML PUBLIC '-//W3C//DTD HTML 4.0 Transitional//EN'
   'http://www.w3.org/TR/REC-html40/loose.dtd'>
<HTML>
   <HEAD>
      <TITLE>A typical HTML file</TITLE>
   </HEAD>
   <BODY>
   This is the typical structure of an HTML file. It follows
   the notation of the HTML 4.0 specification, including tags
   that have been deprecated (hence the "transitional" label).
   </BODY>
</HTML>
```

If any elements, attributes, or entities that are referenced or defined in an external DTD are used in the XML document, the `standalone` attribute of the `xml` element must be set to `'no'` as follows:

```
<?xml version='1.0' standalone='no'?>
```

External DTDs are useful for creating a common DTD that can be shared among multiple documents. You can create a DTD once and reference it as many times as you need. Any changes that are made to the external DTD automatically reflect in all the documents that reference it. Additionally, you can access and modify DTD markups more easily if it is in a separate file as compared to when it is embedded in an XML document.

The disadvantage of using a separate DTD is that you have to deal with two documents. It may not be a problem in many cases. However, for small and simple DTDs, experimental DTDs, or ones under development, embedding a DTD may be a better option.

7.5.3 Combining Internal and External DTDs

External DTDs are useful for common rules for a set of XML documents, whereas internal DTDs are beneficial for defining customized rules for a specific document. Document authors can take advantage of both these approaches. XML specification allows document authors to combine both *internal* and *external* DTD subsets for a complete collection of rules for a given document. The general form of such a DTD declaration is

```
<!DOCTYPE root-element [SYSTEM OR PUBLIC FPI] 'URL' [DTD]>
```

The internal DTD subset is specified between the square brackets of the DOCTYPE declaration. The declaration for the external DTD subset is placed before the square brackets immediately after the SYSTEM keyword.

```
<?xml version='1.0'?>
<!DOCTYPE greeting SYSTEM 'hello.dtd' [
   <!ENTITY excl '&#x21;'>
]>
<greeting>Hello World &excl;</greeting>
```

This is an example for combining external and internal DTDs. In this case, part of the DTD is defined in `hello.dtd`, the other part (ENTITY declaration) is defined within the XML document.

Note:

- If both the external and internal subsets are used, the internal subset *must* be considered to occur before the external subset. This has the effect that entity and attribute-list declarations in the internal subset take precedence over those in the external subset.
- Declaring an element with the same name in both the internal and external DTDs is invalid.

7.6 ELEMENT TYPE DECLARATION

Elements are primary building blocks in an XML document. Element type declarations set the rules for the type and number of elements that may appear in an XML document, how these elements may be nested, and what order they must appear in. The general syntax for an element declaration is

```
<!ELEMENT element-name type>
```

or

```
<!ELEMENT element-name (content)>
```

Here, `element_name` is the name of the element we are defining. Here, the value of `type` can be either `EMPTY` or `ANY`. The `content` could indicate a specific rule, data, or another element.

The following rules must be followed:

- The keyword `ELEMENT` must be in upper case.
- Element names are case-sensitive.
- All element types used in an XML document must be declared in the Document Type Definition (DTD) using an element type declaration.
- The same name cannot be used in multiple element type declarations.
- The name in the element type's end tag must match the name in the element type's start tag.

In DTD, elements are classified depending upon their content:

Standalone elements: These elements are also called *singleton* elements. They cannot contain anything and as a consequence they are also called *empty* elements.

Simple elements: These are elements that contain text or "Parsed Character DATA" (represented as #PCDATA in your DTD).

Compound elements: These elements contain text, other (children) elements, or both text and other (children) elements.

7.6.1 Standalone/empty Elements

A standalone or empty element, as the name implies, cannot have any content. However, it may have attributes. The procedure for declaring an attribute will be discussed in Section 7.7. Empty elements are declared using the type keyword `EMPTY` (in uppercase) as follows:

```
<!ELEMENT element-name EMPTY>
```

The keyword EMPTY indicates that the content of the element element-name will be empty. Consider the element br used in HTML. It does not contain anything; it merely gives the hint that a line has to be inserted at the designated place. The following example shows how to declare this element in our DTD.

```
<!ELEMENT br EMPTY>
```

This element can then be used in an XML document as

```
<br />
```

or

```
<br></br>
```

Empty-element tags may be used for any element that has no content, whether or not it is declared using the keyword EMPTY. The keyword EMPTY only restricts the element from having any content. XML processors may (and should) treat `<br />` and `<br></br>` as equivalent, but document authors may want to make the distinction. It is recommended to use the former one to indicate that the elements are really empty.

Declarations of some other common empty elements are as follows:

```
<!ELEMENT hr EMPTY>
<!ELEMENT bool EMPTY>
<!ELEMENT logo EMPTY>
<!ELEMENT homePage EMPTY>
<!ELEMENT redirect EMPTY>
<!ELEMENT photo EMPTY>
```

These elements should have some attributes to be meaningful. For example, the element bool might have an attribute value, which can have the values either true or false. Similarly, the element photo will probably have an attribute src, which will refer to the image file of this photo.

7.6.2 Unrestricted Elements

If it does not matter what your element contains, you can create such an element using the content model of ANY (in uppercase). These elements are declared as follows:

```
<!ELEMENT element_name ANY>
```

The keyword ANY indicates that the content of the element element-name can be anything including text and other elements (provided that they are declared) in any order and any number of times, as long as the XML well-formedness rule is followed. The keyword ANY is useful when you have yet to decide the allowable contents of the element or when you are experimenting. For example,

```
<!ELEMENT container ANY>
<!ELEMENT tutorials ANY>
```

Note: Declaring an element using ANY removes all validity checking for this element and is a potential source of problem. So, you should avoid using this, if possible. It would be better to define a specific content model.

7.6.3 Simple Elements

Simple elements cannot contain other elements. They can contain only text, which may have references to entities. These elements, in general, are declared as follows:

```
<!ELEMENT element_name (#PCDATA)>
```

This interprets that the element `element-name` can have only text content. The type of text is specified as PCDATA (Parsed Character DATA), and in this case, the text *will* be parsed by a parser and will be examined for entities and markups, and expanded as and when necessary. **Note that PCDATA is the only available text type for simple element declaration.**

Sometimes, it is wrongly specified that CDATA can also be used. It is also mentioned that text specified as CDATA will *not* be parsed and tags/entities will *not* be treated as markups and entities will *not* be expanded. This statement is not true as most modern XML parsers (SAX parser in Java, XML parser used in IE 6) do not support them. Such parsers always parse text, examine for entities and markups, and expand only entities (if any). Text containing markups is supposed to be invalid.

To avoid expansion, the desired segment of text may be embedded by the sequence of characters "<![CDATA[" and "]]>". Everything within "<![CDATA[" and "]]>" will *not* be examined and hence, not expanded. The usage of `CDATA` for element will be discussed in detail in Section 7.6.4.

Following is a declaration of the simple element `greeting`:

```
<!ELEMENT greeting (#PCDATA)>
```

This line in your DTD allows the `greeting` element to contain non-markup (it can contain entities however) data in your XML document. So, following is a valid usage:

```
<greeting>Hello World!</greeting>
```

Text containing entity references will be expanded by its actual value provided that the entity is either a built-in entity or has been declared elsewhere. Consider the following instance document fragment:

```
<note>'&lt;' and '&gt;' can not occur inside text</note>
```

The text between <note> and </note> will be expanded as

```
'<' and '>' can not occur inside text
```

This is because < and > are built-in entities and they represent the characters '<' and '>', respectively. Table 7.2 gives a list of built-in entities:

Table 7.2 Built-in entities

Entity	Meaning	Entity	Meaning
&	&	'	'
<	<	"	"
>	>		

7.6.4 CDATA—(Unparsed) Character DATA

It was mentioned earlier that text between "<![CDATA[" and "]]>" is treated as a *single* item and will not be parsed by XML parsers. Consequently, if the text contains entities, they will not be replaced with their actual value and any markup will not be treated as a markup. So, if you want to use some text that probably contains illegal characters such as ‘<’, ‘>’, and ‘&’, then it can be embedded within "<![CDATA[" and "]]>". JavaScript code contains such illegal characters. So, it is a good idea to use the CDATA section to use JavaScript code in your XML document and to avoid using entities every time those illegal characters occur. Here is an example

```
<code>
  <![CDATA[
    <script language="JavaScript">
      function less(x, y) {
        return x < y;
      }
      a = less(2, 3);
    </script>
  ]]>
</code>
```

In this example, everything inside the CDATA section is ignored by the parser.

The following rules must be followed while using the CDATA section.

- A CDATA section cannot contain the string "]]>".
- The "<![CDATA[" and "]]>", which marks the beginning and end of the CDATA section, respectively, cannot contain spaces or line breaks.
- Nested CDATA sections are neither allowed nor needed.

Some other examples of text-only elements are

```
<!ELEMENT message (#PCDATA)>
<!ELEMENT title (#PCDATA)>
<!ELEMENT firstName (#PCDATA)>
<!ELEMENT surname (#PCDATA)>
<!ELEMENT dob (#PCDATA)>
```

Note that DTD does not support data types. Hence, the value of a dob (**d**ate **o**f **b**irth) is represented as text.

7.6.5 Compound Elements

Compound elements can contain other elements. In the simplest case, an element contains one child element. It is specified by providing the name of the child element. Here's how we can do that:

```
<!ELEMENT element_name (child_element_name)>
```

Example:

```
<!ELEMENT employee (name)>
```

This indicates that the element employee can contain another child element name exactly once. The child element name must also be declared separately. Here is a complete declaration:

```
<?xml version="1.0"?>
<!DOCTYPE employee [
  <!--'employee' must have one child element 'name'-->
  <!ELEMENT employee (name)>
  <!--'name' may only contain text -->
  <!ELEMENT name (#PCDATA)>
]>
<employee>
  <name>U. K. Roy</name>
</employee>
```

7.6.5.1 Occurrence indicators

Sometimes, it is necessary to specify how many times an element may occur in a document. This is done by the *occurrence indicator*. When no occurrence indicator is specified, the child element must occur exactly once in an XML document. Table 7.3 gives a list of occurrence indicators (with their meaning) we can use when defining child elements.

Table 7.3 Occurrence indicators in DTD

Operator	Syntax	Description
None	*a*	Exactly one occurrence of *a*
* (Asterisk)	a*	Zero or more occurrences of *a* (any number of times)
+ (Plus sign)	*a*+	One or more occurrences of *a* (at least once)
? (Question mark)	*a*?	Zero or one occurrence of *a* (at most once)

Zero or more occurrences [*]

This indicator specifies that a child element may appear an arbitrary number of times within its enclosing element. Following is an example:

```
<!ELEMENT employee (contact*)>
```

This example indicates that the element `employee` can have the child element `contact` any number of times. Indeed, an employee may have any number of contact numbers.

One or more occurrences [+]

In this case the child element may also appear an arbitrary number of times, but it must occur at least once within its enclosing element. The following example illustrates this:

```
<!ELEMENT company (employee+)>
```

This example indicates that the `company` can contain `employee` one or more times. Indeed, a company cannot exist without any employee. Consider another element `book` which resembles a book. Since a `book` must have at least one `author`, `book` element can be declared as

```
<!ELEMENT book (author+)>
```

Zero or One occurrence [?]

This indicator makes an element optional.

```
<!ELEMENT employee (PAN?)>
```

This example indicates that the element `employee` can have an optional `PAN` (Permanent Account Number) child element. Indeed, an employee may have exactly one PAN or none.

7.6.5.2 Declaring multiple children

Elements with multiple children are declared with the names of the child elements inside parenthesis. The child elements must also be declared. Several operators can be specified when declaring elements with multiple children. These indicators impose constraints on child elements. Table 7.4 gives a list of DTD operators.

Table 7.4 DTD operators

Operator	Syntax	Description
, [sequence]	a, b	a followed by b
I [choice]	a I b	a or b
() [singleton]	(expression)	An expression surrounded by parentheses is treated as a unit and could have any one of the following suffixes: ?, *, or +.

Sequence Operator [,]

The sequence operator (,) is used to enforce the ordering of child elements. The general syntax of using a sequence operator is

```
<!ELEMENT parent (expr1, expr2, expr3, …) >
```

This enforces that the expressions `expr1`, `expr2`, `expr3` ... must occur in an instance document in the order as specified. An expression is either a single element or a set of elements combined using different DTD operators. Here is an example.

```
<!ELEMENT employee (firstName, middleName, lastName)>
<!ELEMENT firstName (#PCDATA)>
<!ELEMENT middleName (#PCDATA)>
<!ELEMENT lastName (#PCDATA)>
```

This declaration requires `firstName` followed by `middleName` and `lastName`. So, the following XML document fragment is valid.

```
<employee>
   <firstName>Uttam</firstName>
   <middleName>Kumar</middleName>
   <lastName>Roy</lastName>
</employee>
```

However, the following is not valid.

```
<employee>
   <firstName>Uttam</firstName>
   <lastName>Roy</lastName>
   <middleName>Kumar</middleName>
</employee>
```

In this DTD declaration, elements `firstName`, `middleName`, and `lastName` contained by the `employee` element are simple. In general, an element can contain a combination of simple and compound child elements. Here is an example.

```
<!ELEMENT employee (name, contact)>
<!ELEMENT name (firstName, middleName, lastName)>
<!ELEMENT firstName (#PCDATA)>
<!ELEMENT middleName (#PCDATA)>
<!ELEMENT lastName (#PCDATA)>
<!ELEMENT contact (#PCDATA)>
```

For this DTD declaration, a valid XML document fragment is as follows:

```
<employee>
   <name>
      <firstName>Uttam</firstName>
      <middleName>Kumar</middleName>
      <lastName>Roy</lastName>
   </name>
   <contact>9433880334</contact>
</employee>
```

Choice Operator [|]

The choice operator (|) is used to select one from among choices separated by the '|' symbol. The general syntax of using the choice operator is

```
<!ELEMENT parent (expr1 | expr2 | expr3 | …) >
```

This enforces the fact that one of many expressions `expr1`, `expr2`, `expr3` … can occur as the child of the element `parent`.

```
<!ELEMENT product (price | discountprice)>
```

This declaration requires that the element `product` can have either `price` or `discountprice` as child. Following is another example:

```
<!ELEMENT tutorial (name | title | subject)>
```

This means that `tutorial` can have either a `name`, or a `title`, or a `subject`, but not all.

Composite Operator [()]

An expression surrounded by parentheses is treated as a single unit and could have any one of the following occurrence indicators: `?`, `*`, or `+`. Consider the following example:

```
<!ELEMENT biodata (dob, (company, title)*, contact+)>
<!ELEMENT dob (#PCDATA)>
<!ELEMENT company (#PCDATA)>
<!ELEMENT title (#PCDATA)>
<!ELEMENT contact (#PCDATA)>
```

In this example, `company` and `title` form a singly ordered unit. The `biodata` element can contain zero or more such units, together with a single `dob` and one or more `contact` elements.

Combining Operators

The choice and sequence operators can be combined with the occurrence indicators to specify more sophisticated structure for the XML document.

```
<!ELEMENT employee (firstName, middleName?, lastName) >
```

This element declaration says that the element `employee` may contain `firstName` and `lastName` exactly once and an optional `middleName`. Consider another example.

```
<!ELEMENT book (title, author+, chapter+) >
```

This specifies that `book` has exactly one `title`, at least one `author`, and at least one `chapter`.

Sometimes, it is difficult to write a DTD with elements having arbitrary constraint. Consider the following requirement:

```
Element E must have zero or exactly one F, G and H elements.
```

The DTD declaration of the element E, keeping this constraint in mind, is not impossible. Following is one possible declaration:

```
<!ELEMENT E
((F) | (G) | (H) | (F,G) | (F,H) | (G,F) | (G,H) | (H,F) | (H,G) | (F,G,H) | (F,H,G) | (G,F,H) | (G,H,F) | (H,F,G) | (H,G,F)) >
```

The declaration exhaustively uses all possible permutation of F, G, and H. Think about the same situation with 10 elements. The declaration will be so long and tedious that the errors are almost impossible to avoid. This is a limitation of DTD. These types of constraints can easily be handled by W3C XML Schema.

7.6.6 Element Containing Both Text and Other Elements

We have seen so far that an element may contain either text or child elements. Sometimes, it is necessary to use both text and elements simultaneously. Such elements are said to be mixed content elements. Here is an example.

```
<!ELEMENT order (item+)>
<!ELEMENT item (#PCDATA | description)*>
<!ELEMENT description (#PCDATA)>
```

This declaration specifies that the element `order` can contain one or more `item` elements. The element `item` can contain mixed content, i.e., both text and the element `description`. The following example shows how an actual XML document might look.

```
<order>
   <item>
      XBee
      <description>WPAN development kit</description>
   </item>
</order>
```

The mixed content model is less flexible. For example, only names of child elements can be specified in case of the mixed content model. The order of child elements and their occurrence cannot be specified. Due to these reasons, it is recommended not to use the mixed content model as far as possible. Instead, a new element with the content model PCDATA may be used.

7.7 ATTRIBUTE DECLARATION

Attributes are used to associate (name, value) pairs with elements. They are useful when you want to provide some additional information about the element's content. They are intended for interpretation by an application. The declaration starts with `ATTLIST` followed by the name of the element the attributes are associated with, and the declaration of the individual attributes.

An attribute declaration has the following syntax:

```
<!ATTLIST element-name attribute-name attribute-type default-value>
```

where `element_name` is the name of the element to which the attribute `attribute-name` applies. Following is an example of the attribute declaration:

```
<!ELEMENT line EMPTY>
<!ATTLIST line width CDATA '100'>
```

This specifies that element `line` has an optional attribute `width`, which will assume the value '100' if the attribute is not mentioned.

The following rules must be followed while declaring an attribute:

- The keyword `ATTLIST` must be in upper case.
- All attributes used in an XML document must be declared in the DTD.
- Attributes may only appear in start or empty tags.
- An element can have any number of attributes.

7.7.1 Default Value of Attribute

The `default-value` can be one of the following, as shown in Table 7.5:

Table 7.5 Default value of an attribute

Default Value	Explanation
`Default`	The default value of the attribute
`#REQUIRED`	The attribute is required
`#IMPLIED`	The attribute is not required
`#FIXED value`	The attribute value is fixed

7.7.1.1 Default

In this case, the attribute is optional. This means that the XML document author may or may not provide this attribute. When an attribute is declared with a default value, the value of the attribute is whatever value appears as the attribute's content in the instance document. If the attribute does not appear, the XML processor provides the attribute with a value equal to the `default-value`.

The following example illustrates this:

```
<!ATTLIST line width CDATA '100'>
```

This declaration interprets that the attribute `width` is optional. So, if it occurs, the value of this attribute will be the value specified there. If it does not occur, a width attribute with the value 100 will be supplied by the XML processor.

```
<line width='200'/>
```

In this declaration, the `width` attribute is specified with a value 200.

```
<line/>
```

In this example, no `width` attribute is specified. So, the XML processor will provide a width attribute with a value 100. So, this example is equivalent to the following:

```
<line width='100'/>
```

7.7.1.2 #REQUIRED

This means that the attribute must be specified with a value every time the enclosing element is listed. Consider the following schema fragment:

```
<!ATTLIST price currency CDATA #REQUIRED>
```

It interprets that the attribute `currency` *must* appear for element `price`. So, following is a valid example:

```
<price currency='INR'>100</price>
```

However, following is not:

```
<price>100</price>
```

7.7.1.3 #FIXED

In this case also, the attribute is optional. It is used to ensure that the attributes are set to particular values. It interprets that if the attribute does appear, its value must be a fixed value specified after it, and if the attribute does not appear, the schema processor will provide the attribute with the value specified after the `#FIXED` keyword. Consider the following element declaration:

```
<!ATTLIST speed unit CDATA #FIXED 'rpm'>
```

This declaration means that the attribute `unit` is optional. If it appears, its content must be `rpm`, and if the attribute does not appear, the XML processor will provide a `unit` attribute with the value `rpm`. So, the following example is valid:

```
<speed unit='rpm'>7200</speed>
```

so is

```
<speed>7200</speed>.
```

However, the following is not

```
<speed unit='rps'>120</speed>
```

7.7.1.4 #IMPLIED

It is similar to that of the default attribute except that no default value is provided by the XML processor if an attribute of this type does not appear in the instance document. The processor ignores this attribute unless it is used as part of the element. Unless otherwise specified, attributes are implied. Consider the following attribute declaration:

```
<!ATTLIST speed unit CDATA #IMPLIED>
```

Following example is valid

```
<speed unit='rpm'>7200</speed>
```

so as

```
<speed>7200</speed>
```

In this example, the attribute `unit` is not provided. However, the XML processor will not supply any value to this attribute. So, it is the responsibility of the processing application to assume some value for this attribute and proceed further.

7.7.2 Attribute Types

The `attribute-type` can be one among *string type*, *tokenized type,* and *enumerated type*. They are further classified as follows:

7.7.3 String Type

The string type may take any literal string as a value. Attributes of string type are declared using the keyword CDATA. The attribute type CDATA and CDATA sections are absolutely different.

7.7.3.1 CDATA

CDATA stands for Character DATA. An attribute of CDATA type can contain any character if it conforms to the well-formedness constraints. So, it cannot contain escape characters such as <, >, &, ', and ", and hence cannot contain markup. However, it can contain (only internal) entities. The value of this type of attribute is always parsed and internal entities (if any) are replaced by their actual values. The concept of internal and external entities are described later.

7.7.4 Tokenized Type

The following tokenized types are available:

7.7.4.1 ID

ID is a globally unique identifier of the attribute. This means that the value of an ID attribute must not appear more than once throughout an XML document. ID resembles the *primary key* concept used in databases. For example, attribute `no` (question number) of the element `question` should always have a unique value so that it can be used to identify a `question` uniquely. The following examples clearly illustrate this.

```
<!ATTLIST question no ID #REQUIRED>
<!ATTLIST employee id ID #REQUIRED>
<!ATTLIST car serial ID #REQUIRED>
```

It is assumed that the elements `question`, `employee`, and `car` are already defined somewhere else.

The `ID` attribute has a variety of restrictions on its use.

- An element may only have one `ID` attribute.
- An `ID` attribute can only have `#IMPLIED` or `#REQUIRED` default value.
- The first character of an ID value must be a letter, '_', or ':'.

7.7.4.2 IDREF

It is similar to that of the *foreign key* concept in databases. `IDREF` is used to establish connections between elements. The `IDREF` value of the attribute must refer to an `ID` value declared elsewhere in the document. For example, the attribute `qno` of the element `answer` must refer to the attribute `no` of the `question` element. This way, we can find a question for which the answer is given. After all, an `answer` can never exist without any `question`. The following example shows this connection:

```
<!ATTLIST question no ID #REQUIRED>
<!ATTLIST answer qno IDREF #REQUIRED>
```

Here, the `qno` attribute of `answer` refers to a `question` for which it is the answer. So, the following XML document segment is valid:

```
<question no='Q1'>
  What is the full form of DTD?
</question>
<question no='Q2'>
  What is the full form of XML?
</question>
<answer qno='Q1'>
  Document Type Definition
</answer>
```

An `IDREF` attribute can only have `#IMPLIED` or `#REQUIRED` default values. The first character of an `IDREF` value, like `ID`, must be a letter, '_', or ':'

7.7.4.3 IDREFS

It allows a list of ID values separated by white spaces (one or more blank, tab, carriage return, line feed, etc.). Here is an example.

```
<!ATTLIST student roll ID #REQUIRED>
<!ATTLIST subject sid ID #REQUIRED>
<!ATTLIST marks ref IDREFS #REQUIRED>
```

Following is an example of how to use it:

```
<student roll='r01'>Samir Roy</student>
<subject sid='s1'>Web Technology</subject>
<marks ref='r01 s1'>82</marks>
```

Here, the attribute `ref` of the element `marks` indicates that this is marks of the student having `roll` = 'r01' in subject having `sid` = 's1'. In this way, connections among a set of related elements can be established. The following example also shows valid usage:

```
<marks ref='s1 r01'>82</marks>
```

This indicates that each `ID` value in an `IDREFS` refers to some `ID` value, but there is no way to specify the particular `ID` value it refers to.

Here is another example.

```
<!ATTLIST employee id ID #REQUIRED>
<!ATTLIST managers emp IDREFS #REQUIRED>
```

And here is a valid usage.

```
<employee id='e01'>Rahul Saha</employee>
<employee id='e02'>S. K. Mitra</employee>
<employee id='e03'>Pritam Biswas</employee>
<managers emp='e01 e03' />
```

This indicates that only 'Rahul Saha' and 'Pritam Biswas', whose employee ids are e01 and e03, respectively are managers.

7.7.4.4 NMTOKEN

The attribute type of `NMTOKEN` restricts the attribute's value to one that is a valid XML name. Remember that in an XML name, alphanumeric characters and the punctuation marks _, -, ., and : are allowed. Unlike an XML name (which can only start with a letter, '_' or ':'), `NMTOKEN` can have a number or all previously mentioned punctuation marks as the first character. Note that they cannot contain spaces. For example, the `serialno` attribute of the `item` element is always a single word and does not, in general, contain special characters. In this case, it is a good idea to declare the `serialno` attribute as `NMTOKEN`. The following example illustrates this clearly:

```
<!ATTLIST item serialno NMTOKEN #REQUIRED>
```

So, "A8GD-SX34" is a valid `serialno`, but "A8GD SX34" is not (because of the white space).

7.7.4.5 NMTOKENS

`NMTOKENS` can contain the same characters and white spaces as `NMTOKEN`. White space includes one or more space characters, carriage returns, line feeds, and tabs. Here is an example:

```
<!ATTLIST employee profile NMTOKENS #REQUIRED>
```

The following is an example of valid usage with this declaration:

```
<employee profile='male married'>Mark</employee>
<employee profile='female single'>Anni</employee>
```

7.7.4.6 ENTITY

Use this attribute type to refer to external non-parsed entities. Following is an example of `ENTITY` type attribute declaration:

```
<!ATTLIST photo src ENTITY #REQUIRED>
```

This declaration indicates that the value of the attribute `src` of the photo element is an external unparsed entity. The following example shows the usage of this attribute:

```
<photo src='logo'/>
```

Remember, `logo` is an external non-parsed entity, which is declared as follows:

```
<!NOTATION jpg SYSTEM 'image/gif'>
<!ENTITY logo SYSTEM 'ju.jpg' NDATA jpg >
```

You do not refer to this entity as `&logo;`. This syntax is used to refer to only parsed entities. The declaration of entities as well as notations will be discussed later in this chapter.

7.7.4.7 ENTITIES

The value of an `ENTITIES` attribute may contain multiple entity names separated by one or more white spaces.

```
<!ATTLIST sponsorsPhoto src ENTITIES #REQUIRED>
```

This declaration states that the `src` attribute of the `sponsorsPhoto` element refers to one or more external unparsed entities. Following is an example:

```
<sponsorsPhoto src='ju_logo cu_logo'/>
```

The external non-parsed entities `ju_logo` and `cu_logo` must be declared elsewhere.

7.7.5 Enumerated Type

Enumerated attribute values are used when we want the attribute value to be one of a fixed set of values. There are two kinds of enumerated types: *enumeration* and *notation.*

7.7.5.1 Enumeration

In this case, attributes are defined by a list of acceptable values from which the document author must choose a value. The values are explicitly specified (enumerated) in the declaration, delimited by pipes (|). For example, the `gender` attribute of an `employee` element can have either of the two values `male` and `female`.

```
<!ATTLIST employee gender (male|female) #REQUIRED>
```

So, the only valid usage is

```
<employee gender='male'>...</employee>
```

or

```
<employee gender='female'>...</employee>
```

Following is another example of enumerated attribute declaration.

```
<!ATTLIST payment mode (cash|cheque) #REQUIRED>
```

This indicates that a `payment` can be made either by `cash` or by `cheque`. For this attribute declaration, the only valid usage of mode attribute is

```
<payment mode='cash'>1000</payment>
```

or

```
<payment gender='cheque'>...</payment>
```

Table 7.6 lists two enumerated attributes.

Table 7.6 Enumerated attribute

Enumerated Type	Description
(en1|en2|..)	The value must be one from an enumerated list.
NOTATION	The value is a name of a notation.

7.7.5.2 NOTATION

The attribute type of `NOTATION` allows you to use a value that has been declared as a `NOTATION` in the DTD. A notation is used to specify the format of non-XML data. A common use of notations is to describe MIME types such as image/gif, image/jpeg, etc.

A `NOTATION` type attribute must contain the name of the notation declared in the DTD.

```
<!NOTATION jpg SYSTEM 'image/gif'>
<!ENTITY logo SYSTEM 'ju.jpg' NDATA jpg>

<!ELEMENT photo (#PCDATA)>
<!ATTLIST photo format NOTATION (jpg) #IMPLIED>
<!ATTLIST photo src ENTITY #REQUIRED>
```

This declaration says that the value of the attribute `format` of the `photo` element must be a notation defined somewhere else. Indeed, the notation `jpg` is defined which represents the MIME type `image/jpg` format. So, the photo element can be used as

```
<photo src='logo' format='jpg'/>
```

The following rules must be followed while declaring notation type attributes:

- All notations used must first be declared.
- An attribute of type NOTATION *must not* be declared in an element declared `EMPTY`.
- The notation names *must* all be distinct.
- There may only be one `NOTATION` attribute per element.

The last one is courtesy of a new erratum, which says in effect that NOTATION attributes suggest classes, not types, for the elements with which they are associated.

7.7.5.3 Declaring multiple attributes

So far, we have declared one attribute at a time. Multiple attributes can be declared using a single `ATTLIST` element as follows:

```
<!ATTLIST employee
   homepage CDATA #IMPLIED
   gender (male|female) #REQUIRED
>
```

This declaration means, the element `employee` has two possible attributes: `homepage`, which is optional and may contain any valid XML text, and `gender`, which is mandatory and can have any of the two values `male` and `female`.

Note:

- No attribute name may appear more than once in the same start-tag or empty-element tag.
- The attribute must have been declared; the value must be of the type declared for it.
- No external entity references can be made.
- Attribute values cannot contain direct or indirect entity references to external entities.
- The replacement text for any entity referred to directly or indirectly in an attribute value (other than "<") must not contain a <.

7.7.6 Notation Declaration

In XML, you may come across non-XML data such as sound or image that you would like to refer to in your XML documents. NOTATION allows you to refer that data in your documents by describing the format and allowing your application to recognize and handle it.

The format for a `NOTATON` declaration is

```
<!NOTATION name SYSTEM 'external_ID'>
```

where `name` is the name you are giving to the notation and `external_id` is something (typically MIME types) that can describe your data. For example, a notation `jpeg` can be declared that represents MIME media type image/jpeg as follows:

```
<!NOTATION jpeg SYSTEM 'image/jpeg'>
```

You can also use the `PUBLIC` identifier, instead of `SYSTEM`. To do this you need to include both a public ID and a URI. The following example shows the usage of the `PUBLIC` identifier.

```
<!NOTATION gif PUBLIC
 '-//IETF/NOSGML Media Type image/gif//EN'
 'http://www.isi.edu/in-notes/iana/assignments/media-types/image/gif'>
```

There is absolutely no standard or even a suggestion for exactly what this identifier should be. Individual applications must define their own requirements for the contents and meaning of notations.

The `NOTATION` declaration is used in conjunction with the attribute declaration and external parsed entity declaration.

7.8 ENTITY DECLARATION

Remember, entities are *variables* that represent other values. If a text contains entities, the value of the entity is substituted by its actual value whenever the text is parsed. To use our own entity in an XML document, the entity must be defined in the DTD declaration. Note that built-in entities and character entities need not be declared as they are recognized by XML processors. There are two types of entity declarations: *general entity* declarations and *parameter entity* declarations. Each type can be again *parsed* or *unparsed.*

7.8.1 General and Parameter Entities

General entities (or simply entities) are entities for use within the document content. Parameter entities are parsed entities for use within the DTD. These two types of entities use different forms of reference and are recognized in different contexts. Furthermore, they occupy different namespaces; a parameter entity and a general entity with the same name are two distinct entities.

The name identifies the entity in an entity reference or, in the case of an unparsed entity, in the value of an ENTITY or ENTITIES attribute. If the same entity is declared more than once, the first declaration encountered is bound; at user option, an XML processor may issue a warning if entities are declared multiple times.

7.8.2 Parsed and Unparsed Entities

Entities may be either parsed or unparsed. A *parsed* entity is an entity whose content (referred to as replacement text) is parsed and checked for well-formedness constraint during the parsing procedure, i.e., the content of a parsed entity is treated as an integral part of the document and must conform to the well-formedness constraint.

An *unparsed* entity, on the other hand, is a resource whose contents may or may not be text, and if text, may not be XML. It means there are no constraints on the contents of unparsed entities. Each unparsed entity has an associated notation, identified by name. For each entity and notation available in the XML document, the XML parser makes an identifier. Parsed entities are invoked by name using entity references whereas unparsed entities are invoked by the names, given in the value of the ENTITY or ENTITIES attributes.

7.8.3 General Entity Declaration

There are three kinds of general entity declarations: *internal parsed*, *external parsed,* and *external unparsed* entity declarations.

7.8.3.1 Internal (parsed) entity declaration

An internal entity declaration has the following form:

```
<!ENTITY entity-name 'entity-value'>
```

Here `entity-name` is the name of the entity and `entity-value` is the replacement text. An internal general entity is always parsed and must conform to well-formedness constraints. So, `entity-value` can be a string comprising any character that is not an &, %, ' or ", a parameter entity reference ('%Name;'), an entity reference ('&Name;'), or a Unicode character reference ('&#Unicode;'). Once an entity is declared, it can be referenced by writing entity-name surrounded by an ampersand (&) and a semicolon (;). Following is an example:

```
<!ENTITY UKR 'Uttam Kumar Roy'>
```

The entity `UKR` can then be referenced in an XML document as follows:

```
<author>&UKR;</author>.
```

This will be interpreted as

```
<author>Uttam Kumar Roy</author>
```

Entity reference can also occur in the attribute value. For example:

```
<book author='&UKR;'>Web Technology</book>
```

The value of an entity can have references to other entities. If the value of an entity e1 contains another entity reference e2, then the value of e2 is substituted while calculating the value of e1 and this procedure is repeated until the value does not contain any further entity reference.

```
<!ENTITY UKR 'Uttam Kumar Roy'>
<!ENTITY copyright '&#169; &UKR;'>
```

A usage of such an entity reference is as follows:

```
<book>Web Technology &copyright;</book>
```

The content of the book element will be represented as follows:

```
Web Technology © Uttam Kumar Roy
```

7.8.3.2 External parsed entity declaration

External entities allow an XML document to refer to an external resource. Parsed external entities refer to data that an XML parser has to parse. External entity references are generally used for long replacement text which is kept in another file. They are useful for creating a common reference that can be shared among multiple documents. Any changes that are made to external entities are automatically updated in the documents they are referenced.

There are two types of external parsed entities: *private* and *public*. Private external entities are identified by the keyword `SYSTEM`, and are intended for use by a single author or a group of authors. Public external entities are identified by the keyword `PUBLIC` and are intended for general use. The general form of private entity declaration is

```
<!ENTITY entity-name SYSTEM 'URI'>
```

Here URI, in practice, is a URL where the value of external parsed entity can be found. Remember, value contained in URL will be parsed by the XML processor and hence must conform to the well-formedness constraint.

The general form of private entity declaration is

```
<!ENTITY entity-name PUBLIC 'FPI' 'URI'>
```

Here, FPI (Formal Public Identifier) may be used by an XML processor to generate a URI where the value of an external parsed entity can be found. If the XML processor is unable to generate such a URI, it must use the normal URI.

An example of private parsed external declaration is

```
<!ENTITY author SYSTEM 'author.xml'>
```

Consider the file `author.xml` that contains the following information:

```
<firstName>Uttam</firstName>
<middleName>Kumar</middleName>
<lastName>Roy</lastName>
```

Then, `<book><author>&author;</author></book>` will produce the following:

```
<book>
  <author>
    <firstName>Uttam</firstName>
    <middleName>Kumar</middleName>
    <lastName>Roy</lastName>
  </author>
</book>
```

The external entity reference need not be a local file; it can be any valid URL where the value of the entity can be found. One such example is as follows:

```
<!ENTITY author SYSTEM 'http://www.site.jusl.ac.in/author.xml'>
```

Following is an example of public parsed external declaration:

```
<!ENTITY author PUBLIC 'NONE' 'http://www.site.jusl.ac.in/author.xml'>
```

7.8.3.3 External unparsed entity declaration

External unparsed entities refer to data that an XML processor does not have to parse. For example, there are numerous ASCII text files in the world. There are probably even more JPEG photographs, GIF line art, QuickTime movies, MIDI sound files, and so on. None of these are well-formed XML. Yet, all of them are necessary components of many documents.

The mechanism that XML suggests for embedding these files in your documents is the *external unparsed entity*. There are two types of external unparsed entities: *private* and *public*. The general form of private entity declaration is

```
<!ENTITY entity-name SYSTEM 'URI' NDATA notation-name>
```

This declaration specifies `entity-name` and a `URI` for the entity containing the non-XML data.

```
<!ENTITY logo SYSTEM 'ju.jpg' NDATA jpeg>
```

For example, this `ENTITY` declaration associates the name `logo` with the JPEG image at `ju.jpg`. Since the data is not in XML format, the `NDATA` declaration specifies the type of the data. Here, the name `jpeg` is used. XML does not recognize this as an image in a format defined by the Joint Photographs Experts Group. Rather this is the name of a *notation* declared elsewhere in the DTD using a `NOTATION` declaration.

NOTATION allows you to refer to non-XML data by describing the format and allowing your applications to recognize and handle it. The format for a `NOTATON` declaration is

```
<!NOTATION name SYSTEM 'external_ID'>
```

where `name` is the `name` you are giving to the notation and `external_id` is something that can describe your data. For example, the notation `jpeg` used in this external unparsed entity declaration may be declared as follows:

```
<!NOTATION jpeg SYSTEM 'image/jpeg'>
```

Here we have used the MIME media type image/jpeg as the external identifier for the notation. So, `logo` is an entity that refers to the external non-XML data file `ju.jpg` whose format is `jpeg`, i.e., MIME type `image/jpeg`.

7.8.4 Parameter Entity Declaration

In addition to general entities, DTD supports another kind of entity called parameter entity. A parameter entity is used within a DTD. It allows us to assign a collection of elements, attributes, and attribute values to a name and refer them using the name instead of explicitly listing them every time they are used. For example, a parameter entity may be used to store a set of commonly used attributes that are shared among multiple elements. Like general entities, a parameter entity must be declared before using it in a DTD. There are two kinds of parameter entity declarations: *internal parsed* and *external parsed* entity declarations.

7.8.4.1 Internal parsed entity declaration

Internal parsed parameter entity declarations have the following form:

```
<!ENTITY % EntityName EntityDef>
```

Parameter entity declarations are very similar to general entity declarations, with the only difference being the presence of the percent sign (%) and the space on either side of it. The unique name of the parameter entity is specified in `EntityName`, whereas the entity content is specified in `EntityDef`. Following is an example of a parameter entity declaration:

```
<!ENTITY % name "firstName, middleName, lastName">
<!ENTITY % info "year, make, model">
```

This parameter entity describes a portion of a content model that can be referenced within elements in a DTD. Keep in mind that parameter entities apply only to DTDs. Parameter entities are referenced using the entity name sandwiched between a percent sign (%) and a semicolon (;), as the following form shows:

```
%EntityName;
```

Following is an example of referencing the `info` parameter entity in a hypothetical automotive DTD:

```
<!ELEMENT car (%info;)>
<!ELEMENT truck (%info;)>
<!ELEMENT bus (%info;)>
```

This code is equivalent to the following:

```
<!ELEMENT car (year, make, model)>
<!ELEMENT truck (year, make, model)>
<!ELEMENT bus (year, make, model)>
```

It is important to note that parameter entities really come into play only when you have a large DTD with repeating declarations. Even then you should be careful how you modularize a DTD with parameter entities because it is possible to create unnecessary complexity if you layer too many parameter entities within one another.

7.8.4.2 External parsed entity declaration

These entities are used to link external DTDs. An external parsed parameter entity may be *private* or *public* and is identified by the keywords `SYSTEM` and `PUBLIC`, respectively. Private entities are intended for use by a single author whereas public entities can be used by anyone. Following are the general syntax of the private and public entity declarations:

```
<!ENTITY %entity_name SYSTEM 'URI'>
%entity_name;

<!ENTITY %entity_name PUBLIC 'public_id' 'URI'>
%entity_name;
```

URI is the location where the external entity can be found. The XML processor may use the unique id `public_id` to generate an alternate URI where the external entity may be found.

7.9 DTD VALIDATION

Like any other schema processor, DTD has its own processor. Many such schema processors are readily available in the market.

The simplest way is to use the `xmllint` program that comes with the Unix/Linux OS. The `--valid` option turns on validation of the XML files given as input. For example, the following validates an XML document named `test.xml`.

```
xmllint --valid --noout test.xml
```

The `--noout` option is used to disable the output of the resulting tree. The `--dtdvalid dtd` option allows validation of the document(s) against a given DTD.

The Java implementation of such a processor is given as follows:

```
import org.w3c.dom.*;
import javax.xml.parsers.*;
public class DTDValidator {
   public static void main(String args[]) {
      try {
         DocumentBuilderFactory factory = DocumentBuilderFactory.newInstance();
         factory.setValidating(true);
         Document doc = factory.newDocumentBuilder().parse(args[0]);
      }catch(Exception e) {System.out.println(e);}
   }
}
```

Compile the source file `DTDValidator.java` using the following syntax:

```
javac DTDValidator.java
```

This will generate the class file `DTDValidator.class`. To validate the XML document `text.xml` having a DTD declaration (internal, external or both) use the following command:

```
java DTDValidator.java text.xml
```

The command terminates silently if the XML document `test.xml` conforms to the DTD mentioned there. Otherwise, it generates useful diagnostic error messages.

JavaScript also provides a DTD validation interface. A sample .html file is given as follows:

```
<html>
   <head>
      <title>DTDValidator</title>
      <script language='JavaScript'>
         function validate(xmlFile) {
            var xmlDoc = new ActiveXObject('Microsoft.XMLDOM');
            xmlDoc.async = 'false';
            xmlDoc.validateOnParse='true';
            xmlDoc.load(xmlFile);
            mesg='\nError Code:'+xmlDoc.parseError.errorCode;
            mesg+='\nError Reason: '+xmlDoc.parseError.reason;
            mesg+='\nError Line: '+xmlDoc.parseError.line;
            alert(mesg);
         }
      </script>
   </head>
   <body>
      <input type='file' name='uploadfile' size='40'> <br>
      <input type='submit' name='Submit' value='Validate'
onclick='validate(uploadfile.value)'>
   </body>
</html>
```

KEYWORDS

Attribute: Attributes are used to associate (name, value) pairs with elements. They are useful when you want to provide some additional information about the element's content.

Character DATA (CDATA): Text of this type is parsed and tags/entities are not treated as markup and entities are not expanded.

Choice Operator [|]: The choice operator (|) is used to select one from among choices separated by '|' symbol.

Composite Operator [()]: An expression surrounded by parentheses is treated as a single unit.

Compound elements: Compound elements are those that contain text, other (children) elements, or both text and other (children) elements.

Entity: Entities are *variables* that represent other values.

External DTD: DTD that is stored in a separate file and is referenced from an XML document.

Formal Public Identifier (FPI): A universally unique formatted string used to identify a public resource.

General Entities: General entities (or simply entities) are entities for use within the document content.

Internal DTD: When we embed DTD in an XML document, DTD information is included within the XML document itself.

Occurrence Indicators: Specify how many times an element may occur in a document.

Parameter Entities: Parameter entities are parsed entities for use within the DTD.

Parsed Character DATA (PCDATA): Text of this type is parsed by a parser and is examined for entities and markups and expanded as and when necessary.

Parsed Entity: A *parsed entity* is an entity whose content is parsed and checked for well-formedness constraint during the parsing procedure.

Sequence Operator [,]: The sequence operator (,) is used to enforce the ordering of child elements.

Simple elements: Simple elements are those that contain text or Parsed Character DATA (PCDATA).

Standalone elements: Standalone elements are those that cannot contain anything. They are also called *singleton* or *empty* elements.

Uniform Resource Identifier (URI): A string of characters used to identify or name a resource all over the world.

Uniform Resource Locator (URL): A string of characters used to identify or name a resource on the Internet.

Unparsed Entity: An *unparsed entity* is a resource whose contents may or may not be text, and if text, may not be XML.

Validation: XML *validation* is a procedure used to verify whether an XML document conforms to the rules specified by a given XML schema.

SUMMARY

The **D**ocument **T**ype **D**efinition (DTD) is an XML schema language that is native to the XML standardized by the **W**orld **W**ide **W**eb Consortium (W3C).

The purpose of a DTD, like other schema languages, is to define the legal building blocks of an XML document. It specifies the document structure with a list of legal elements. It is also used to specify a content model for each element and attribute used in an XML document. The content description is a part of the element declaration in the DTD and specifies the order and quantity of elements that can be contained within the element being declared.

An XML document is said to be *valid* with respect to a DTD, if it conforms with the rules specified by a given XML DTD. Independent developers can agree to use a common DTD for exchanging XML documents. They can use this agreed-upon DTD to validate the XML documents they receive. The DTD may also be used to verify our own XML documents.

To validate an XML document against a DTD, we must tell the validator where to find the DTD so that it knows the rules to be verified during validation. A Document Type Declaration is used to make such a link and the keyword DOCTYPE is used for this purpose. There are three ways to make this link. A DTD can be used in an XML file internally, externally or both.

In case of Internal DTD, DTD information is included within the XML document itself. Another way of connecting DTD to the XML document is to reference it within the XML document, i.e., create a separate document, put DTD information there and point to it from XML document called external DTD. External DTDs are useful for common rules for a set of XML documents whereas internal DTDs are beneficial for defining customized rules for a specific document.

There are three primary building blocks for an XML document: elements, attributes, and entities. Elements are categorized with respect to their content into three types: standalone elements, simple elements, and compound elements.

A standalone or empty element, as the name implies, cannot have any content. Simple elements cannot contain other elements. Compound elements can contain other elements.

Occurrence indicators are used to specify how many times an element may occur in a document. Common occurrence indicators include zero or more occurrences (*), one or more occurrence (+), and zero or one occurrence (?). One of the limitations of DTD is that it cannot specify a specific number of occurrences.

Operators are useful if an element has multiple children elements. They are used to indicate the order of the children elements within the contained element.

Attributes are declared with the keyword ATTLIST. Different types of attributes can be declared in a DTD.

Entities are declared using the keyword ENTITY. There are two types of entity declarations: *general entity* declarations and *parameter entity* declarations. Each type can be again *parsed* or *unparsed.*

WEB RESOURCES

`http://www.w3.org/TR/2004/REC-xml11-20040204/#NT-doctypedecl`
Extensible Markup Language (XML) 1.1. W3C.

`http://www.w3.org/TR/REC-xml/#dt-doctype`
Document Type Definition

`http://www.w3.org/QA/2002/04/valid-dtd-list.html`
Recommended list of DTDs

EXERCISES

Multiple Choice Questions

1. The full form of DTD is
   (a) Data Type Definition
   (b) Document Type Declaration
   (c) Document Type Definition
   (d) Dynamic Type Declaration

2. DTD defines the document structure with a list of
   (a) elements (b) bad elements
   (c) legal elements (d) None of these

3. A DTD for an XML document can be declared
   (a) Internally (b) Externally
   (c) Both (a) and (b) (d) None of the above

4. Which of the following syntax is used to include DTD in your XML document?
   (a) <DOCTYPE root-element [element-declarations]>
   (b) <DOCTYPE root-element (element-declarations)>
   (c) <!DOCTYPE root-element [element-declarations]>
   (d) <!DOCTYPE [element-declarations]>

5. Which of the following DOCTYPE declarations is valid?
   (a) <!DOCTYPE SYSTEM PUBLIC "sample.dtd">
   (b) <!DOCTYPE SYSTEM SYSTEM "sample.dtd">
   (c) <DOCTYPE PUBLIC SYSTEM "sample.dtd">
   (d) <!DOCTYPE PUBLIC PUBLIC "sample.dtd">

6. Which of the following XML declarations for DTD is valid?
   (a) <?xml version="1.0" standalone="true"?>
   (b) <?xml version="1.0" standalone="false"?>
   (c) <xml version = "1.0" standalone="yes">
   (d) <?xml version="1.0" standalone="yes"?>

7. Which of the following syntax is used to reference an external DTD?
   (a) <!DOCTYPE root-element SYSTEM "filename">
   (b) <DOCTYPE root-element SYSTEM "filename">
   (c) <!DOCTYPE root-element SYSTEM 'filename'>
   (d) <!DOCTYPE SYSTEM "filename">

8. Which of the following element declarations is valid?
   (a) <!ELEMENT root (#CDATA)>
   (b) <!ELEMENT root (#PCDATA)>
   (c) <!ELEMENT root (#ANY)>
   (d) <ELEMENT root (#PCDATA)

9. Which of the following DTDs is valid?
   (a) <!ENTITY abc "(#PCDATA)" > <!ELEMENT elm1 &abc;>
   (b) <!ENTITY sample elm "file1">
   (c) <!ENTITY sample SYSTEM "file1">
   (d) <!ENTITY %test "(#PCDATA)"> <!ELEMENT elm1 %test;>

10. Which of the following is a predefined attribute?
    (a) xml:lang (b) xml:space
    (c) both (d) none

11. Which of the following can be verified with DTD?
    (a) control (b) data
    (c) description (d) None of these

12. Parameter entities can appear in
    (a) xml file (b) xsl file
    (c) dtd file (d) Both (a) and (b)

13. Which one of the following is the main building block of an XML file?
    (a) Attributes (b) Entities
    (c) Elements (d) Text

14. Which of the following best describes attributes?
    (a) Provide information
    (b) Provide more data
    (c) Provide extra information about data
    (d) None of these

15. Entities are variables
    (a) used to control data
    (b) used to create databases
    (c) used to define document structure
    (d) used to define common text

16. Which of the following expands entities?
    (a) compiler (b) debugger
    (c) linker (d) parser

17. Which of these characters cannot be used as an entity reference in XML?
    (a) < (b) $ (c) " (d) &

18. What is the full form of PCDATA?
    (a) Public Character DATA
    (b) Private Character DATA
    (c) Parsed Character DATA
    (d) Parsed and Compiled DATA

19. Given the following declarations in the same DTD, which one is actually used?
    (a) <!ENTITY make "Sun" >
    <!ENTITY make "Micro Systems">
    (b) <!ENTITY make "Sun">
    <!ENTITY make "Micro Systems">
    (c) <!ENTITY make "Sun Micro Systems">
    (d) None of the above. This is an error.

20. What is the full form of CDATA?
    (a) Computer DATA (b) Character DATA
    (c) Common DATA (d) Compiled DATA

21. Which of the following syntax is used to declare an element in DTD?
    (a) <ELEMENT element-name category>
    (b) <!ELEMENT element-name category>
    (c) <!element-name ELEMENT category>
    (d) <!ELE element-name category>

22. Which of the following is used to declare an element having only character data?
    (a) #CHAR (b) #PCDATA
    (c) #TEXT (d) #CDATA

23. Which of the following is used to declare attributes?
    (a) ATTRIBUTELIST (b) ATTRIBUTE
    (c) ATTLIST (d) ALIST

24. Which of the following describes a DTD element that contains both text and other child elements?
    (a) Complex Declaration
    (b) Mixed content
    (c) Empty elements
    (d) Simple elements

25. Which of the following declarations must every XML document that uses a DTD have?
    (a) A <!DTD> declaration
    (b) A <STANDALONE> declaration
    (c) A <DOCTYPE> declaration
    (d) A <!DOCTYPE> declaration

26. Which of the following declarations must be used for an external DTD?
    (a) <?xml version="1.0" standalone="no"?>
    (b) <!DOCTYPE standalone="no">
    (c) <?xml version="1.0" standalone="yes"?>
    (d) <! DOCTYPE standalone="yes"!>

Review Questions

1. When is an XML document called valid against a DTD?
2. What are the different steps of validating an XML document against a DTD?
3. What is a well-formed XML document?
4. Show with an example how to use a DTD in an XML document internally.
5. What are the advantages and disadvantages of internal DTDs?
6. Show with an example how to use a DTD in an XML document externally.
7. What are the advantages and disadvantages of external DTDs?
8. How can both internal and external DTDs be used in an XML file? Show with an example.
9. What are empty elements?
10. How can an empty element be declared in a DTD?
11. When elements are called simple?
12. Show with examples how to declare simple elements.
13. Suppose you want to declare an element whose structure is not yet known. How will you declare it?
14. Describe the procedure for preventing parsing of a piece of code by XML parsers.
15. Consider the following scenario: An employee may have zero or more credit cards, one or more bank accounts, and exactly one PAN number. Write an element declaration for this element employee.
16. A book has exactly one title, one or more chapters, one or more authors, a price, and an ISBN number. An author has a first name, an optional middle name, and a last name. A chapter consists of one or more paragraphs. Write a DTD for this scenario.
17. Show with examples how to declare mixed content elements.
18. Why are attributes used?

19. Suppose the default value for an attribute is mentioned as "#FIXED". What does it mean?
20. What is the importance of the attribute type ID? Explain with examples.
21. What are the restrictions imposed on the ID attribute?
22. How will you declare an entity?
23. Show with examples how to declare multiple attributes of an element using a single declaration.
24. What are the different kinds on entities? Discuss their properties.
25. What is the importance of parameter entities?
26. Write a Java Program to validate an XML document against a DTD.
27. Consider the following XML document fragment. A company has a number of employees. The element `employee` contains information about an employee. The middle name of an employee is optional. Write a DTD for it.

```
<company>
    <employee>
        <firstname>Bibhas</firstname>
        <middlename>Chandra</middlename>
        <lastname>Dhara</lastname>
    </employee>
    <employee>
        <firstname>Parama</firstname>
        <lastname>Bhaumik</lastname>
    </employee>
</company>
```

28. Suppose an XML document contains one or more objective type questions. Each question has four alternatives, one of which is correct. Each question has also a number and an answer. A question can be identified uniquely by its number. Write a sample XML file and write a DTD for it. Clearly mention the assumptions you made.
29. Consider the following DTD.

```
<!ELEMENT course (name, curriculum,
teacher+, student+)>
<!ELEMENT name (#PCDATA)>
<!ELEMENT curriculum (#PCDATA)>
<!ELEMENT teacher (#PCDATA)>
<!ELEMENT students (#PCDATA)>
```

Write a sample XML document that is valid according to this DTD.

30. Consider the genealogical tree of the descendants of a person as an XML document with the following DTD:

```
<!ELEMENT person (name, (son |
daughter)*, alive?)>
<!ELEMENT son (name, (son | daughter)*,
alive?)>
<!ELEMENT daughter (name, (son |
daughter)* alive?)>
<!ELEMENT name (#PCDATA)>
<!ELEMENT alive (#PCDATA)>
```

Write a sample XML File that is valid according to this DTD.

8 W3C XML SCHEMA

KEY OBJECTIVES

After completing this chapter readers will be able to—

- **understand the importance of W3C XML Schema**
- **use a schema in an XML document**
- **declare elements, attributes, and entities in XML documents**
- **write complete schema for simple XML documents**
- **learn the procedure for validating an XML document against a schema**
- **get an idea about when to use elements and when to use attributes**

8.1 INTRODUCTION

In Chapter 7, we discussed DTD, which is a specific XML schema language. In this chapter, we shall discuss another powerful XML schema language, **W**3C **X**ML **S**chema (WXS), recommended by the World Wide Web Consortium (W3C) in May 2001. Unlike DTD, which is written in a strange syntax, W3C XML Schema (hereafter referred to as simply XML Schema) is an XML-based schema language. It is a language used to create XML-based languages and data models. Like other XML schema languages, an XML schema document defines elements and attribute names for a class of XML documents. It describes the coarse shape of XML documents, what fields an element can contain, which sub-elements it can contain, what type of content each element and attribute may hold, etc. So, basically, the XML schema document specifies the structure that those XML documents must adhere to in order to be considered 'valid' according to that schema.

8.1.1 XML Schema Definition (XSD)

XML **S**chema **D**efinition (XSD) is a specific XML schema document written using an XML schema and typically has the filename extension ".xsd". So, XSD and XML Schema are two completely different things. XML Schema refers to a schema language whereas XSD represents a schema document written using the rules specified by that XML Schema language. However, sometimes XSD is referred to informally as XML Schema.

8.1.2 XML Schema Instance

The XML documents that try to follow the rules specified by the XML schema document are said to be *instances* of that schema. If they strictly conform to the schema, they are valid instances. Verifying an XML instance against a schema is known as *validating* the document. To validate an XML instance against an XSD, validators are required. A large number of free XML schema validators are available on the web. Java also provides interfaces for XML schema validation and validators may be written. Different validation tools will be dealt with later in this chapter.

8.2 LIMITATIONS OF DTD

In Chapter 7, we have already had some experience with DTDs. DTDs were created long before the creation of XML. The basic purpose of DTDs was to define languages based on SGML, which is considered to be the parent of XML. Although DTDs are well accepted and used very frequently, they have several limitations, some of which are as follows:

- There is no built-in data type in DTDs.
- No new data types can be created in DTDs.
- The use of cardinality (the number of occurrences of an element within its enclosing element) in DTDs is limited.
- Namespaces are not supported.
- DTDs provide very limited support for modularity and reuse.
- We cannot put any restrictions on text content.
- Defaults for elements cannot be specified.
- We have very little control over mixed content (text plus elements).
- DTDs are written in a strange (non-XML) format and are difficult to validate.

8.3 STRENGTHS OF SCHEMA

Schemas are XML-based alternatives to DTDs in that they are used to create classes of XML documents that conform to the schema. XML Schema is a much more powerful language than DTD. Here are some reasons.

- XML Schemas provide much greater specificity than DTDs.
- They support large number of built-in data types.
- They are namespace-aware.
- They are extensible to future additions.
- They support the uniqueness and referential integrity constraints in a much better way.
- It is easier to define data facets (restrictions on data).

Another great strength of XML Schema is that XSDs are written in XML. There is even an XSD to describe the XSD standard. So, the same XML parsers can be used to parse and verify

XSD files. Moreover, many simple XML editors are readily available to create and edit XSD files easily.

XML Schemas are extensible as they can be reused to verify other XML documents. An XML document can also refer to multiple schemas. Users can also create their own data types, derived from the standard types.

8.4 SCHEMA STRUCTURE

An XSD is an XML document and must follow all the syntax rules like any other XML document. It must be well-formed. XSDs also have to be valid against the rules defined in the "Schema of schemas", which defines, among other things, the structure, elements, and attributes of XSD.

Since every XSD is itself an XML document, it starts with an XML declaration with `version` and optional `encoding` and `standalone` attributes. In addition, an XML Schema Definition has the following components:

- The schema element
- Element definitions
- Attribute definitions
- Annotations
- Type definitions

8.5 SCHEMA ELEMENT

An XML Schema is composed of the top-level `schema` element. The `schema` element definition must include the following namespace:

```
http://www.w3.org/2001/XMLSchema
```

Here is a sample XML schema document.

```
<?xml version='1.0'?>
<xs:schema xmlns:xs='http://www.w3.org/2001/XMLSchema'>
  …rules for conforming XML document
</xs:schema>
```

It indicates that the elements and data types used in the schema come from the `"http://www.w3.org/2001/XMLSchema"` namespace. It also specifies that the elements and data types that come from the `"http://www.w3.org/2001/XMLSchema"` namespace should be prefixed with `"xs"`.

It can also hold several default attributes.

targetNamespace

It specifies the namespace that must be used by the XML instance document for this schema. A prefix for the namespace can also be assigned. If no prefix is assigned, the schema components of the namespace can be used with unqualified references.

elementFormDefault

This attribute specifies how elements declared in the target namespace of this schema should look like. The value must be one of the following strings: `qualified` or `unqualified`. The default is `unqualified` and in this case, elements from the target namespace are not required to be qualified with the namespace prefix.

If the value is `qualified`, elements used by the XML instance document that were declared in this schema must be namespace-qualified.

This value is the global default for all elements declared in the target namespace. Individual elements can override this setting for their local scope using the `form` attribute.

version

This is the version of the schema.

xml:lang

This is the indicator of the language used in the contents.

The schema element contains type definitions (*simpleType* and *complexType* elements) and *attribute* and *element* declarations. In addition to its built-in data types (such as integer, string, and so on), XML Schema also allows for the definition of new data types using the `<simpleType>` and `<complexType>` elements.

Table 8.1 shows the list of essential XML schema elements.

Table 8.1 XML schema elements

<all>	<annotation>	<anyAttribute>	<appinfo>
<attribute>	<attributeGroup>	<choice>	<complexType>
<documentation>	<element>	<facet>	<group>
<list>	<restriction>	<schema>	<sequence>
<simpleType>	<union>		

8.6 ELEMENT DEFINITIONS

The primary building blocks of any XML document are elements. They determine the structure of the document and contain the data and/or other elements. In a schema, elements are declared by the `element` tag. Following is a general example of element declaration:

```
<xs:element name='element-name' type='element-type'>
```

Each element declaration within the XSD has the mandatory attribute `name`. The value of this name attribute is the element name that will appear in the XML document. Element definition may also have the optional `type` attribute, which provides the description of what can be contained within the element when it appears in the XML document. If no type is specified, the built-in data type `anyType` will be assumed. In that case, the element will be treated as a generic one and can have an arbitrary number of attributes as well as body contents, including child elements.

W3C XML Schema supports a number of built-in types, such as `string`, `integer`, `boolean`, and `date` (see Appendix for complete list). Users may also create their own custom types using the `simpleType` and `complexType` tags.

8.6.1 Global and Local Declaration

The attribute `type` in the element definition specifies the content model of the element being defined. If the type of an element is not a built-in type (i.e., it is a user-defined type), there are two ways to specify it: Global method and Local method.

8.6.1.1 Global declaration

This is a two-step procedure. In the first step, a named type (either simple or complex) is defined inside the top-level `schema` element. XML type definition is exactly like a class definition in any Object-Oriented Programming (OOP) language except that it uses a different syntax. It just specifies the skeleton of an element that will be declared later. Once a type is defined, this type name can be used in an element declaration. Unlike class definition, an element type definition can occur even after its use in an element declaration. XML parsers can take care of this.

Types defined in this fashion at the "top-level" of the `schema` element are available throughout the entire schema document. The advantage of this method is that the same type can be used again and again for different element declaration. This allows further scalability, extensibility, and portability.

8.6.1.2 Local declaration

In this method, the type of element is defined inline during the element declaration. A type defined in this way has no name (anonymous) and is valid only within the element declaration. This means that only the container element can use the specified type. There is no existence of this type outside the element declaration and hence can never be used for other element declaration.

Global type definition makes XSD cleaner and easily extendable. Intuitively, global definition is always recommended but it is a matter of personal taste. The exact procedure for defining a type will be discussed later in this Chapter.

8.6.2 Declaring Root Element

Every XML document must have a root element. This root element must be declared first in a schema for the conforming XML documents. This is done by an XML element named as `element` in the XML schema document.

Here is a simple schema example represented as the XML document, `greeting.xsd`

```
<?xml version='1.0'?>
<xsd:schema xmlns:xsd='http://www.w3.org/2001/XMLSchema'>
  <xs:element name='greeting' type='xs:string'/>
</xsd:schema>
```

This is a very simple, but complete XML schema document, which contains the declaration of the *simple* element `greeting`. It indicates that the conforming XML document must have the root element `greeting`. The element `greeting` cannot have any attribute or child elements but can contain a string value and is thus considered to be `simpleType`.

Here is an example XML document, `greeting.xml` that conforms to the schema represented in `greeting.xsd`:

```
<?xml version="1.0"?>
<greeting>Hello World!</greeting>
```

Of course, the schema `greeting.xsd` is too simple to be useful. A typical XSD contains declaration of many elements and attributes, and many type definitions. We shall discuss each of them in due course.

8.7 SCHEMA VALIDATION

An XML document can be verified against a schema using XML validators. Typically, a validator takes an XML document and an XML Schema and checks whether the XML document is written following the rules specified in the schema. Many readymade XML schema validators are available on the web. Following are some websites where you can find such validators:

```
http://www.w3.org/2001/03/webdata/xsv http://tools.decisionsoft.com/
schemaValidate/
http://www.validome.org/grammar/
http://validate.openlaboratory.net/
```

One such parser `xmllint` is bundled with the Unix/Linux operating system. The `xmllint` is a command-line application that parses one or more XML files, specified on the command line as *xmlfile*. `xmllint` has a large number of options. It prints various types of output, depending upon the options selected. It is useful for detecting errors both in the XML document and in the XML Schema itself. The following command is used to validate an XML document against a schema:

```
xmllint --schema xmlSchema.xsd xmlFile.xml
```

The exact set of options can be obtained from the `xmllint` manual.

Java also provides an XML schema validation interface. A Java implementation of the schema validator is given as follows:

```
//. SchemaValidator.java
import java.io.File;
import javax.xml.parsers.DocumentBuilder;
import javax.xml.parsers.DocumentBuilderFactory;
import javax.xml.transform.dom.DOMSource;
import javax.xml.validation.Schema;
import javax.xml.validation.SchemaFactory;
import javax.xml.validation.Validator;
import javax.xml.XMLConstants;
import org.w3c.dom.Document;
public class SchemaValidator {
   public static void main(String args[]) {
      try {
         SchemaFactory schemaFactory = SchemaFactory.newInstance(
XMLConstants.W3C_XML_SCHEMA_NS_URI);
```

```
            Schema schema=schemaFactory.newSchema(new File(args[1]));
            Validator validator=schema.newValidator();
            DocumentBuilder parser =
DocumentBuilderFactory.newInstance().newDocumentBuilder();
            Document document = parser.parse(new File(args[0]));
            validator.validate(new DOMSource(document));
        }catch (Exception e) {
        System.out.println(e);
        }
    }
}
```

This program is a Java application program. Compile the source file `SchemaValidator.java` using the following command:

```
javac SchemaValidator.java
```

This will generate the class file `SchemaValidator.class`. Once this class file is available, the following command is used to validate the XML document `xmlFile.xml` against the schema document `schemaFile.xsd`.

```
java SchemaValidator xmlFile.xml schemaFile.xsd
```

If the XML document conforms to the XSD, it silently terminates, otherwise it provides useful diagnostic errors messages.

JavaScript also provides a schema validation interface. A sample .html file is given as follows:

```
<html>
   <head>
      <title>DTDValidator</title>
      <script language='JavaScript'>
         function validate(xmlFile, schemaFile) {
            var schema = new ActiveXObject('Msxml2.DOMDocument.4.0');
            schema.async = false;
            schema.load(schemaFile);
            var schemaCache = new ActiveXObject('Msxml2.XMLSchemaCache.4.0');
            schemaCache.add('', schema);
            var xmlDocument = new ActiveXObject('Msxml2.DOMDocument.4.0');
            xmlDocument.async = false;
            xmlDocument.validateOnParse = true;
            xmlDocument.schemas = schemaCache
            if (xmlDocument.load(xmlFile)) {
               alert('valid');
            }
            else {
               alert('invalid'+xmlDocument.parseError.reason);
            }
         }
      </script>
   </head>
   <body>
      XML instance<input type='file' name='instance' size='40'> <br>
      XML schema<input type='file' name='schema' size='40'> <br>
```

```
      <input type='submit' name='Submit' value='Validate'
onclick='validate(instance.value, schema.value)'>
   </body>
</html>
```

8.8 BUILT-IN DATA TYPES

XML Schema 1.0 specification provides about 46 built-in data types [Figure 8.1]. All built-in data types except `anyType` are considered as simple types.

An element is limited by its type. Schema authors can use their own defined types or use the built-in types. Depending upon the content model, elements are categorized as *simple* type or *complex* type.

A simple type can further be divided into three types: *atomic types*, *list types,* and *union types*. The value of an atomic type is indivisible from XML Schema's perspective. For example, the `NMTOKEN` value "INDIA" is indivisible in the sense that no part of "INDIA", such as the character "I", has any meaning by itself. In contrast, list types are comprised of sequences of atomic types and consequently the parts of a sequence (the "atoms") themselves are meaningful. For example, `NMTOKENS` is a list type, and an element of this type would be a white-space-delimited list of `NMTOKEN`s's, such as "INDIA US UK". XML Schema has three built-in list types: `NMTOKENS`, `IDREFS`, and `ENTITIES`. In contrast, a union type enables an element or attribute value to be one or more instances of one type drawn from the union of multiple atomic and list types.

8.9 DECLARING SIMPLE ELEMENTS

Simple type elements can contain only text and/or data. They cannot have child elements or attributes, and cannot be empty. Empty elements are considered to be complex for historical reasons. Simple elements are defined as follows:

```
<xs:element name='element-name' type='someSimpleType'>
```

The value of the `type` attribute specifies an element's content type and can be any simple type (i.e., built-in simple types such as `string`, `integer`, `decimal`, `boolean`, `date`, etc. or any user-defined simple type). The `type` attribute can never be any complex type. If it is, the element being declared will itself be a complex type.

Some examples of the simple element definition are given as follows:

```
<xs:element name='name' type='xs:string'/>
<xs:element name='age' type='xs:integer'/>
<xs:element name='height' type='xs:decimal' />
<xs:element name='dob' type='xs:date' />
```

Here are the corresponding XML elements:

```
<name>Uttam Kumar Roy</name>
<age>32</age>
<height>170</height>
<dob>1977-01-09</dob>
```

The built-in data types are shown in Figure 8.1.

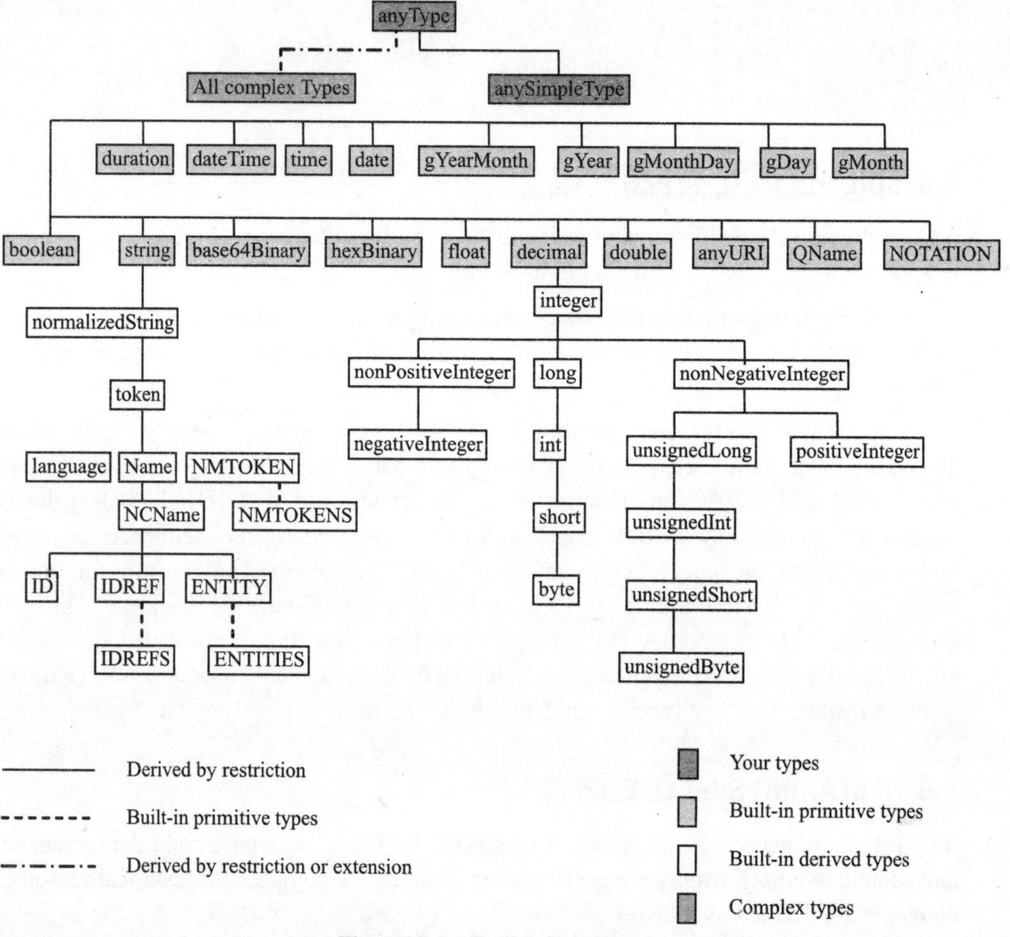

Figure 8.1 Built-in data types

8.9.1 Default and Fixed Values

A simple element may have the optional attribute `default` that specifies the default content to be used when no content is supplied.

When an element is declared with a default value, the value of the element is whatever value appears as the element's content in the instance document. If the element appears without any content, the schema processor provides the element with a value equal to that of the `default` attribute. However, if the element does not appear in the instance document, the schema processor does not provide the element at all.

The following example illustrates this:

```
<xs:element name='married' type='xs:boolean' default='false' />
```

This declaration says that the element `married` can contain either `true` or `false` and if nothing is specified, `false` will be assumed.

A simple element may also have the optional attribute `fixed`. The `fixed` attribute is used to ensure that the element's content is always set to a particular value. Consider the following element declaration with the `fixed` attribute:

```
<xs:element name='institution' type='xs:string' fixed='JU'/>
```

This declaration implies that if the element `institution` does appear, its content must be "JU", and if the element does not appear, the schema processor will *not* provide any content.

Note that the concepts of a fixed value and a default value are mutually exclusive, and so it is an error for a declaration to contain both `fixed` and `default` attributes.

8.9.2 Occurrence Indicators

An element may have two *optional* attributes (also called *occurrence indicators*), `minOccurs` and `maxOccurs`. They are used to specify the number of times an element can occur in an XML document. The default value of `minOccurs` and `maxOccurs` attribute is 1 (one). This implies that the element must appear exactly once in the XML document.

8.9.2.1 minOccurs indicator

This attribute specifies the minimum number of times an element can occur. The following is an example of the usage of the `minOccurs` attribute in a schema.

```
<xs:element name='middleName' type='xs:string' minOccurs='0'/>
```

This definition says that the element `middleName` can occur optionally. This is because the minimum number of occurrence (`minOccurs`) is 0 (zero) and the maximum number of occurrence (`maxOccurs`), which is not specified and hence is 1 (one) by default. This is indeed true and required, as any person may optionally have a middle name.

8.9.2.2 maxOccurs indicator

This attribute specifies the maximum number of times an element can occur. For example, for an objective type question, you may allow maximum of 6 and at least 1 option. The declaration of such an element will be as follows:

```
<xs:element name='option' type='xs:string' maxOccurs='6'/>
```

This violates the idea of an alternative type question, which should have more than one option. So, if you allow a minimum of 4 and a maximum of 6 options, the correct declaration is:

```
<xs:element name='option' type='xs:string' minOccurs='4' maxOccurs='6'/>
```

In this way, schema occurrence indicator can specify the range of number of times an element can occur in an XML document. Remember, a DTD cannot specify such a restriction.

The `maxOccurs` indicator can have the value `unbounded`, which is used to indicate an indefinite number of occurrences. One such case happens while defining the element `emailAddress` for a person. Since, theoretically, a person can have any number of email addresses, the definition of such an element would be as follows:

```
<xs:element name='option' type='xs:string' minOccurs='0' maxOccurs='unbounded'/>
```

The examples `minOccurs='0'` and `maxOccurs='unbounded'` basically indicate zero or more occurrences (equivalent to * in DTD).

Table 8.2 shows the equivalence of occurrence indicators used in DTD and Schema.

Table 8.2 Occurrence Indicators

Indicators used		Meaning
Schema	DTD	
minOccurs='0' maxOccurs='unbounded'	*	Zero or more
minOccurs='1' maxOccurs='unbounded'	+	One or more
minOccurs='0'	?	Optional
None	None	Exactly once

8.10 DECLARING COMPLEX ELEMENTS

Simple elements are useful. However, they are not so expressive because such elements can contain only textual data. Fortunately, XML Schema allows another class of elements, called complex elements, which can contain child elements, text, or both and can also have attributes.

Complex types, like simple types, can be named or can be anonymous. They are associated with complex elements in the same manner, typically using a type definition and an element declaration.

By default, complex-type elements have *complex content*, i.e., they have child elements. Complex-type elements can be limited to having *simple content*, i.e, they contain only text. They are different from simple-type elements in that they have attributes. Complex types can be limited to having no content, meaning they are empty, but they may have attributes.

This section illustrates complex types that are not derived from other specified types (they are by default derived from `anyType`). Derived complex types will be discussed in Section 8.15.2.

As mentioned earlier, the general form of an element declaration is

```
<xs:element name='element-name' type='element-type'>
```

For complex elements, `element-type` is a complex type (user-defined type). It was mentioned that a type can be defined in two ways: *global* and *local*. It is recommended that the global type definition be used. In this method a type is defined first and then used in an element declaration. A complex type is defined using the `complexType` schema element. The general form of a complex-type definition is

```
<xs:complexType>
   skeleton of the complex type
</xs:complexType>
```

Here is an example.

```
<xs:complexType name='personType'>
   <xs:sequence>
```

```
    <xs:element name='firstName' type='xs:string' />
    <xs:element name='lastName' type='xs:string' />
  </xs:sequence>
</xs:complexType>
```

This example is a definition for the type `personType`. It specifies that, any element of this type (specified by the `type` attribute) must have exactly two child elements: `firstName` and `lastName` in the order specified. The elements `firstName` and `lastName` are themselves declared as simple elements. This type name `personType` can now be used during element declaration. The declaration of an element of such a type will then look like this:

```
<xs:element name='employee' type='personType' />
```

As `personType` is defined globally, it can be used by other elements such as `student`. Following is a declaration of the `student` element.

```
<xs:element name='student' type='personType' />
```

The valid usage of this `employee` element is as follows:

```
<employee>
  <firstName>Uttam</firstName>
  <lastName>Roy</lastName>
</employee>
```

8.10.1 Defining Attributes

Attributes themselves are always declared as simple types as follows:

```
<xs:attribute name='attribute-name' type='attribute-type'>
```

The value of the `type` attribute, like simple elements, specifies content type of this attribute. It can be any simple type (i.e., built-in simple types or any user-defined simple type). Following is an example:

```
<xs:attribute name='id' type='xs:string' />
```

Simple types cannot have attributes. Element that have attributes are complex types. So, attribute declaration always occurs as a part of complex type declaration, immediately after its content model. Here is an attribute declaration for the `employee` element.

```
<xs:complexType name='employeeType'>
  <xs:sequence>
    <xs:element name='firstName' type='xs:string' />
    <xs:element name='lastName' type='xs:string' />
  </xs:sequence>
  <xs:attribute name='id' type='xs:string' />
</xs:complexType>
<xs:element name='employee' type='employeeType' />
```

With this attribute declaration the following XML document is valid.

```
<employee id='1234'>
  <firstName>Uttam</firstName>
  <lastName>Roy</lastName>
```

```
</employee>
```

Attributes are optional by default. So, following is also a valid XML document fragment:

```
<employee>
   <firstName>Uttam</firstName>
   <lastName>Roy</lastName>
</employee>
```

Apart from this simple definition, there can be additional specifications for attributes.

Table 8.3 Attribute element properties

Name	Description
`use`	Possible values are `optional`, `required`, and `prohibited`. `optional` (default value) specifies that the attribute is not mandatory and `required` specifies that the attribute is mandatory. Both the cases, the attribute can have any value compatible with the type specified. `prohibited` indicates that the attribute is never allowed. Normally used to prevent the use of this attribute temporarily for a specific purpose.
`default`	This specifies the value to be used if the attribute is not specified (i.e., the `use` attribute is not either used or set to `optional`).
`fixed`	It specifies that the attribute, if it appears, must always have a fixed value specified. If the attribute does not appear, the schema processor will provide an attribute with the value specified there.

Attributes may appear once or not at all, but no other number of times, and so the syntax for specifying occurrences of attributes is different from the syntax for elements. In particular, attributes can be declared with the `use` attribute. It can have values (see Table 8.3) `required`, `optional` (default value), or `prohibited` to indicate whether the attribute is required, optional, or even prohibited, respectively. Consider the following schema fragment:

```
<xs:attribute name='id' type='xs:string' use='required'/>
```

It shows that the attribute `id` *must* appear in the instance document.

Default values of attributes, like default values of elements, are also declared using the `default` attribute, although this attribute has a slightly different consequence. When an attribute is declared with a default value, the value of the attribute is whatever value appears as the attribute's value in the instance document. If the attribute does not appear in the instance document, the schema processor provides the attribute with a value equal to that of the `default` attribute. The following example illustrates this:

```
<xs:attribute name='married' type='xs:boolean' default='false' />
```

This declaration says that the attribute `married` can contain either `true` or `false` and if the attribute `married` is not specified, the schema processor will provide this attribute with the value `false`.

> *Note: Default values for attributes only make sense if the attributes themselves are optional, and so it is an error to specify both a default value and anything other than a value of* `optional` *for* `use`.

An attribute declaration may also have the optional attribute `fixed`. It is used to ensure that the attributes are always set to particular values. It suggests that if the attribute does appear (the `use` attribute is not used or set to `optional` or `required`), its value must be a fixed value specified by the `fixed` attribute, and if the attribute does not appear (the `use` attribute is not used or set to `optional`), the schema processor will provide the attribute with the value specified by the `fixed` attribute. Consider the following element declaration with the `fixed` attribute:

```
<xs:attribute name='unit' type='xs:string' fixed='rpm'/>
```

This declaration means that, if the attribute `unit` appears, its content must be "rpm", and if the attribute does not appear, the schema processor will provide the `unit` attribute with the value "rpm".

Note: The concepts of a fixed value and a default value, like elements, are mutually exclusive, and so it is an error for a declaration to contain both `fixed` and `default` attributes.

8.10.2 Occurrence Indicators

Occurrence indicators (`minOccurs` and `maxOccurs`) can also be used, with a syntax similar to that used for simple element definition. For example, a company may have one or more number of employees. So the definition of the employee element will look like this:

```
<xs:element name='employee' type='personType' maxOccurs='unbounded'/>
```

8.10.3 Order Indicators

Order indicators are used to specify which order elements should occur in the container element. The following table shows all the order indicators that are available: `sequence`, `all`, and `choice`.

Table 8.4 XML schema order indicators

Indicator	Description
sequence	The child elements in the XML document *must* appear in the order they are declared in the XSD schema.
all	The child elements described in the XSD schema can appear in the XML document in any order.
choice	Only one of the child elements described in the XSD schema can appear in the XML document.

8.10.3.1 `sequence` indicator

This indicator specifies that the elements within an enclosing element must occur in the order specified there. Elements may appear a number of times as indicated by the `minOccurs` and `maxOccurs` occurrence indicators. Consider the following example:

```
<xs:complexType name='personType'>
   <xs:sequence>
      <xs:element name='firstName' type='xs:string' />
      <xs:element name='lastName' type='xs:string' />
   </xs:sequence>
</xs:complexType>
```

The element `sequence` in the `personType` declaration says that the elements `firstName` and `lastName` must occur in this specific order.

Occurrence indicators can also be applied on the `sequence` indicator. For example, `<xs:sequence minOccurs='0'>` indicates that the minimum number of times that the particular sequence can occur is 0 (zero).

8.10.3.2 `all` indicator

This indicator indicates elements in a group to appear in *any* order in the enclosing element. Consider the following schema fragment:

```
<xs:complexType name='personType'>
   <xs:all>
      <xs:element name='firstName' type='xs:string' />
      <xs:element name='lastName' type='xs:string' />
   </xs:all>
</xs:complexType>
<xs:element name='employee' type='personType' />
```

This type definition specifies that the elements `firstName` and `lastName` must occur only once but they can occur in any order within the `employee` element.

The `all` indicator has a variety of restrictions in its use. When using the `all` indicator, you can set the `minOccurs` indicator of contained elements to 0 or 1. The `maxOccurs` indicator of contained elements can only be set to 1 (which is the default value).

```
<xs:complexType name='personType'>
   <xs:all>
      <xs:element name='firstName' type='xs:string' />
      <xs:element name='middleName' type='xs:string' minOccurs='0'/>
      <xs:element name='lastName' type='xs:string' />
   </xs:all>
</xs:complexType>
<xs:element name='employee' type='personType' />
```

It specifies that `middleName` is optional and may not occur within the `employee` element.

The `all` indicator can neither contain nor be contained in other indicators. The `all` indicator's `maxOccurs` can only have the value 1 (`minOccurs` indicator may be 0).

```
<xs:complexType name='personType'>
   <xs:all maxOccurs='0'>
      <xs:element name='firstName' type='xs:string' />
      <xs:element name='middleName' type='xs:string' minOccurs='0'/>
      <xs:element name='lastName' type='xs:string' />
   </xs:all>
</xs:complexType>
<xs:element name='employee' type='personType' />
```

This example says that the unit (having elements `firstName`, `middleName`, and `lastName`) may not occur within the `employee` element. If it occurs, `middleName` is optional.

8.10.3.3 `choice` indicator

It allows an XML element to contain any one of a set of elements. We can define as many elements as possible (with the `choice` indicator), but finally only one has to be chosen.

```
<xs:complexType name='personType'>
  ...
  <xs:choice>
  <xs:element name='dob' type='xs:date' />
  <xs:element name='age' type='xs:integer' />
  </xs:choice>
  ...
</xs:complexType>
<xs:element name='employee' type='personType' />
```

This example specifies that the `employee` element can contain either `dob` or `age` elements but not both. Actually, the age of an employee can be obtained either if it is directly given by the `age` element, or if current date is known and date of birth is specified by the `dob` element.

Occurrence indicators `minOccurs` and `maxOccurs` can also be applied on the `choice` indicator as well as the elements contained in it. If used on `choice`, they indicate the minimum and maximum number of times the choice group can iterate. If used on contained elements, they specify the minimum and maximum number of times elements can occur per iteration.

Remember that we could not write constraint using DTD that allows unbounded elements to be freely mixed with one another. This problem can be easily solved by applying `minOccurs` and `maxOccurs` indicators on the `choice` indicator. Consider the following example:

```
<xs:complexType name='documentType'>
  <xs:choice maxOccurs='unbounded'>
    <xs:element name='paragraph' type='xs:string' />
    <xs:element name='image' type='xs:string'/>
  </xs:choice>
</xs:complexType>

<xs:element name='document' type='documentType'/>
```

It specifies that the `document` element can contain an arbitrary number (>1) of `paragraph` and `image` elements in an arbitrary order.

Another such case occurs if a person has an arbitrary number of telephone and fax numbers. The definition for such an element is as follows:

```
<xs:complexType name='contactType'>
  <xs:choice minOccurs='0' maxOccurs='unbounded'>
    <xs:element name='phone' type='xs:string' />
    <xs:element name='fax' type='xs:string'/>
  </xs:choice>
</xs:complexType>

<xs:element name='contact' type='contactType'/>
```

8.10.3.4 Composite indicators

The indicators `choice` and `sequence` can be freely nested inside other indicators, and can be given their own `minOccurs` and `maxOccurs` properties. This allows quite complex combinations to be formed. However, the `all` indicator, as mentioned earlier, cannot be mixed up with either the `choice` or the `sequence` indicator. Consider the following schema fragment:

```
<xs:complexType name='personType'>
   <xs:sequence>
      <xs:element name='firstName' type='xs:string' />
      <xs:element name='lastName' type='xs:string' />
      <xs:choice>
         <xs:element name='dob' type='xs:date' />
         <xs:element name='age' type='xs:integer' />
      </xs:choice>
   </xs:sequence>
</xs:complexType>
<xs:element name='employee' type='personType' />
```

This declaration specifies that the element `employee` contains the elements `firstName` and `lastName` in that order and either the `dob` or the `age` element. So, following is a valid instance fragment:

```
<employee>
   <firstName>Uttam</firstName>
   <lastName>Roy</lastName>
   <age>32</age>
</employee>
```

So is

```
<employee>
   <firstName>Banhishikha</firstName>
   <lastName>Roy</lastName>
   <dob>1978-01-18</dob>
</employee>
```

Consider another schema fragment:

```
<xs:complexType name='employeeType'>
   ...
   <xs:choice>
      <xs:element name='salary' type='xs:integer' />
      <xs:sequence>
         <xs:element name='basic' type='xs:integer' />
         <xs:element name='DA' type='xs:integer' />
      </xs:sequence>
   </xs:choice>
   ...
</xs:complexType>
<xs:element name='employee' type='employeeType' />
```

In this case, the element `employee` can contain either `salary` or `basic` and `DA`. In both the cases, the salary of an employee can be calculated. Following is a valid instance fragment:

```
<employee>
   ...
   <salary>15000</salary>
   ...
</employee>
```

So is

```
<employee>
   ...
```

```
    <basic>12000</basic>
    <DA>3000</DA>
    ...
</employee>
```

8.11 REFERENCING

So far, we have declared elements using two steps. First, we have defined an element with a unique name. In the second step, we have declared elements with this element definition. Instead an existing element can be used. For example,

```
<xsd:element ref='dob' maxOccurs='1'/>
```

This declaration references an existing element, `dob`, which was declared elsewhere in the schema. This specifies that an element called `dob` may appear in an instance document, and its content must conform with the element's type. Consider a more concrete example.

```
<xs:element name='name' type='xs:string' />
<xs:element name='roll' type='xs:integer' />
<xs:element name='salary' type='xs:integer' />

<xs:complexType name='studentType'>
   <xs:sequence>
      <xs:element ref='name' />
      <xs:element ref='roll' />
   </xs:sequence>
</xs:complexType>

<xs:complexType name='employeeType'>
   <xs:sequence>
      <xs:element ref='name' />
      <xs:element ref='salary' />
   </xs:sequence>
</xs:complexType>
```

In this example, the type `studentType` uses two elements `name` and `roll` that are already declared, whereas `employeeType` uses the same two elements `name` and `salary`.

In general, the value of the `ref` attribute must reference a global element, i.e., one that has been declared under the schema rather than as part of a complex-type definition. There can be more than one reference to a single global element (and ideally should be, which is why one would create a global element in the first place).

8.12 GROUP INDICATORS

Group indicators are used to define reusable sets of related items. A named group can be created and can then be referenced from other content models. There are two types of group indicators: `group` and `attributeGroup`. They are used to create the element group and attribute group, respectively. Groups must have a unique name and be defined as children of the `schema` element. When a group is referred, it is as if its contents have been copied into the location it is referenced from.

8.12.1 Element Group Indicator

A set of related elements can be created using the `group` indicator. The general form for creating an element group is as follows:

```
<xs:group name='groupname'>
...
</xs:group>
```

For example, a group (call it `personInfo`) can be created by the element `firstName` and `lastName` elements as follows:

```
<xs:group name='personInfo'>
   <xs:sequence>
      <xs:element name='firstName' type='xs:string' />
      <xs:element name='lastName' type='xs:string' />
   </xs:sequence>
</xs:group>
```

One can now create two types `teacherType` and `studentType`, which can refer to the same member elements of `personInfo` together with additional elements as follows:

```
<xs:complexType name='teacherType'>
   <xs:sequence>
      <xs:group ref='personInfo' />
      <xs:element name='salary' type='xs:integer' />
   </xs:sequence>
</xs:complexType>

<xs:complexType name='studentType'>
   <xs:sequence>
      <xs:group ref='personInfo' />
      <xs:element name='roll' type='xs:integer' />
   </xs:sequence>
</xs:complexType>
```

Finally, the definition of `teacher` and `student` elements will look like this:

```
<xs:element name='teacher' type='teacherType' />
<xs:element name='student' type='studentType' />
```

For this element declaration, the following instance fragment is valid:

```
<teacher>
   <firstName>Uttam</firstName>
   <lastName>Roy</lastName>
   <salary>15000</salary>
</teacher>

<student>
   <firstName>Banhishikha</firstName>
   <lastName>Roy</lastName>
   <roll>15</roll>
</student>
```

Note that both teacher and student have the same children firstName and lastName. This way the same piece of information may be reused among different elements.

8.12.2 Attribute Group Indicator

XML schema provides the element attributeGroup, which is used to group a set of attribute declarations so that they can be incorporated into complex-type definitions. Consider the following attributeGroup definition:

```
<xs:attributeGroup name='DateAttributes'>
   <xs:attribute name='issueDate' type='xs:date' use='required' />
   <xs:attribute name='expiryDate' type='xs:date' use='required' />
</xs:attributeGroup>
```

This attribute group DateAttributes can then be referenced in various complex-type definitions. For example, DateAttributes is used in two complex-type definitions: ATMCardType and DrivingLicenseType.

```
<xs:complexType name='ATMCardType'>
   ...
   <xs:attributeGroup ref='DateAttributes' />
</xs:complexType>
<xs:complexType name='DrivingLicenseType'>
   ...
   <xs:attributeGroup ref='DateAttributes' />
</xs:complexType>
<xs:element name='ATMCard' type='ATMCardType' />
<xs:element name='DrivingLicense' type='DrivingLicenseType' />
```

Any element of type ATMCardType or LicenceType now has two mandatory attributes, issueDate and expiryDate. Following are two valid usages:

```
<ATMCard issueDate='2009-01-01' expiryDate='2009-12-31'></ATMCard>
<License issueDate='2006-03-05' expiryDate='2010-03-04'></License>
```

Note: Element group and attribute groups are not data types. They are containers holding a set of elements or attributes, which can be used to describe complex types. Moreover, group and attributeGroup cannot be extended or restricted. They are used merely to group a number of items of data that are always used together. Practically, this scenario happens occasionally. For this reason, they are not the first choice of constructs for building reusable maintainable schemas, but they can have their uses.

8.13 MIXED CONTENT

Sometimes, complex elements contain both child elements and text. For example, the biodata element might contain mostly plain character text, but it could also have other elements (e.g, company and title) littered throughout the character text. As an example, let us take a look at the following XML instance document:

```
<biodata>
   Worked for <company>TCS</company> as a <title>programmer</title>
```

```
   Worked for <company>CTS</company> as a <title>manager</title>
</biodata>
```

The types of such elements are defined using the `mixed` attribute, with value set to `true`. The general form for defining the types of complex elements having mixed content is as follows:

```
<xs:complexType name='mixedType' mixed='true'>
   ...
</xs:complexType>
```

It shows that an element of type `mixedType` can contain both text and elements where text can appear anywhere inside the mixed element. The schema fragment for the `biodata` element is as follows:

```
<xs:complexType name='biodataType' mixed='true'>
   <xs:sequence maxOccurs='unbounded'>
      <xs:element name='company' type='xs:string' />
      <xs:element name='title' type='xs:string' />
   </xs:sequence>
</xs:complexType>
<xs:element name='biodata' type='biodataType' />
```

Consider another element having mixed content.

```
<paragraph>
   This is an <bold>example</bold> of <italic>mixed</italic> content. Note there are
<italic>interleaved</italic> elements and text.
</paragraph>
```

The corresponding schema with the `choice` indicator is as follows:

```
<xs:complexType name='paragraphType' mixed='true'>
   <xs:choice maxOccurs='unbounded'>
      <xs:element name='bold' type='xs:string' />
      <xs:element name='italic' type='xs:string' />
   </xs:choice>
</xs:complexType>
<xs:element name='paragraph' type='paragraphType' />
```

8.14 ANNOTATIONS

W3C XML Schema provides three annotation elements for documentation purposes in an XML schema instance. They provide a way to write realistic and structured comments for the benefit of applications as well as human readers.

An annotation is represented by the `annotation` element which typically appears at the beginning of most schemas. However, it can appear inside any complex element definition. It can contain only two elements `appinfo` and `documentation` any number of times. The element `documentation` typically has the attribute `xml:lang`, which specifies the language of the information. The elements `appinfo` and `documentation` may contain arbitrary elements to represent relevant documentation information. Following is an example:

```
<xs:annotation>
   <xs:documentation xml:lang = 'en'>
      <author>U. K. Roy</author>
   </xs:documentation>
   <xs:appinfo>
      <version>1.2.3</version>
   </xs:appinfo>
</xs:annotation>
```

8.15 DERIVING NEW TYPES

Deriving a type in XML schemas is a very powerful concept, which provides type extensibility. It is often the case that a new context requires a somewhat modified version of an existing type. Fortunately, XML schemas support several extensibility models, which allow a type to be further redefined or enhanced, without modifying its original definition. Specifically, it allows users to create new named types (simple or complex) and to use these types to declare elements or attributes.

8.15.1 Deriving Simple Types

It is possible to define a new simple type from an existing simple type, called the *base* type, by imposing *restrictions* (also called facets) on the base type. Actually, every simple type is a restriction of another simple type. The specific restrictions might include narrowed ranges or reduced alternatives. Members of type A, whose definition is a restriction of the definition of another type B are always members of type B as well.

Note that no attributes can be added to this new simple type during derivation, which results in a complex type. The syntax for deriving a simple type is as follows:

```
<xs:simpleType name='derivedSimpleType'>
   <xs:restriction base='baseSimpleType'>
      Deriving Rule
   </xs:restriction>
</xs:simpleType>
```

This schema fragment creates a simple type `derivedSimpleType` from `baseSimpleType`. This `derivedSimpleType` will look exactly like `baseSimpleType` with some constraints mentioned within the `restriction` element. Let us take a concrete example:

```
<xs:simpleType name='temperatureType'>
   <xs:restriction base='xs:integer'>
      <xs:minInclusive value='-273' />
   </xs:restriction>
</xs:simpleType>
<xs:element name='temperature' type='temperatureType' />
```

It states that `temperatureType` is derived from the built-in `integer` type with a restriction that an element (such as `temperature`) of this type can never contain a value less than –273. Indeed, the smallest possible value of temperature is –273° Celsius.

Different restrictions can be applied on different data types. Table 8.5 lists all the restrictions on numbers.

Table 8.5 Restrictions on numbers

Facets	Meaning
`minInclusive`	number must be ≥ the given value
`minExclusive`	number must be > the given value
`maxInclusive`	number must be ≤ the given value
`maxExclusive`	number must be < the given value
`totalDigits`	number must have maximum value digits
`fractionDigits`	number must have maximum value digits after the decimal point

Table 8.6 lists all the restrictions on strings.

Table 8.6 Restrictions on strings

<table>
<tr><th>Facets</th><th colspan="2">Meaning</th></tr>
<tr><td>length</td><td colspan="2">the string must contain exactly value characters</td></tr>
<tr><td>minLength</td><td colspan="2">the string must contain at least value characters</td></tr>
<tr><td>maxLength</td><td colspan="2">the string must contain no more than value characters</td></tr>
<tr><td>pattern</td><td colspan="2">the value is a regular expression that the string must match</td></tr>
<tr><td rowspan="4">whiteSpace</td><td colspan="2">not really a “restriction”–tells us what to do with whitespace</td></tr>
<tr><td>value='preserve'</td><td>Keep all white spaces</td></tr>
<tr><td>value='replace'</td><td>Change all white space characters to spaces</td></tr>
<tr><td>value='collapse'</td><td>Remove leading and trailing white spaces, and replace all sequences of white spaces with a single space</td></tr>
<tr><td>enumeration</td><td colspan="2">Elements can have predefined values</td></tr>
</table>

Multiple restrictions can be imposed during derivation. Following is such an example:

```
<xs:simpleType name='binaryType'>
   <xs:restriction  base='xs:integer'>
      <xs:minInclusive value='0'/>
      <xs:maxInclusive value='1'/>
   </xs:restriction>
</xs:simpleType>
<xs:element name='carry' type='binaryType'/>
```

This type definition states that the element `carry` can have value either 0 or 1 (i.e., binary). So, following are schema-valid:

```
<carry>0</carry>
<carry>1</carry>
```

However, following is not

```
<carry>4</carry>
```

Another powerful facet is the `pattern`, which defines a regular expression that must be matched by elements' content. The following example defines the type called `letter`. The values for `letter` must have exactly one alphabetic character.

```
<xs:simpleType name='letter'>
   <xs:restriction base='xs:string'>
         <xs:pattern value='[a-zA-Z]'/>
   </xs:restriction>
</xs:simpleType>
<xs:element name='middleInitial' type='letter' />
```

For this declaration, the following instance fragment is valid:

```
<middleInitial>K</middleInitial>
```

However, the following fragment is not

```
<middleInitial>Kumar</middleInitial>
```

Consider the following example with a more complex pattern:

```
<xs:simpleType name='emailType'>
   <xs:restriction base='xs:string'>
         <xs:pattern value='\w+@\w+(\.\w+)+'/>
   </xs:restriction>
</xs:simpleType>
<xs:element name='email' type='emailType' />
```

For this declaration, the following instance fragment is valid:

```
<email>uroy@it.jusl.ac.in</email>
```

However, the following fragment is not

```
<email>uroy@.in</email>
```

Restrictions on other facets can be imposed as and when necessary using similar syntax.

Note: Restrictions potentially reduce the amount of complexity in your schemas, making them easier to maintain and understand. Restrictions impose constraints on data values. If a given value does not satisfy the constraint, the XML validator can figure out this mismatch during parsing. This way, we can create and use XML documents safely in applications that expect only valid data.

8.15.1.1 Derivation by union

Union types are groupings of types. They essentially allow the value of an element to be of more than one type. In the following example, two atomic simple types are derived: `HexColor` and `NameColor`.

```
<xs:simpleType name='HexColor'>
   <xs:restriction base='xs:string'>
      <xs:pattern value='[0-9A-F]{6}' />
   </xs:restriction>
</xs:simpleType>

<xs:simpleType name='NameColor'>
   <xs:restriction base='xs:string'>
      <xs:enumeration value='red' />
      <xs:enumeration value='green' />
```

```
      <xs:enumeration value='blue' />
    </xs:restriction>
  </xs:simpleType>
```

A third simple type, ColorType, is then derived as a union of the previous two.

```
  <xs:simpleType name='ColorType' >
    <xs:union memberTypes='HexColor NameColor' />
  </xs:simpleType>
  <xs:element name='color' type='ColorType' />
```

Then, any element of type ColorType such as color can be of either the HexColor or the NameColor type. So, the following usage is valid:

```
  <color>blue</color>
  <color>FF0000</color>
```

The order in which the memberTypes are specified in the definition is significant. During the validation procedure, an element or attribute's value is validated against the member types in the order in which they appear in the definition until a match is found.

8.15.1.2 Derivation by list

In addition to the built-in list types, you can create new list types by derivation from existing atomic types. Note that it is not possible to create list types from existing list types or complex types. List types are sequences of atomic types separated by white space; you can have a list of integers or a list of dates. The following example shows the creation of the list DateList:

```
  <xs:simpleType name='DateList'>
    <xs:list itemType='xs:date' />
  </xs:simpleType>
  <xs:element name='holidays' type='DateList' />
```

An element in an instance document whose content conforms to DateList is

```
  <holidays>2009-01-01 2009-08-14 2009-12-25 </holidays>
```

Several facets can be applied to list types: length, minLength, maxLength, pattern, and enumeration.

It is possible to derive a list type from the atomic type string. However, a string may contain white space, and white space delimits the items in a list type. So, you should be careful using list types whose base type is string. For example, suppose we have defined a list type with a length facet equal to 2, and base type string.

```
  <xs:simpleType name='StringList'>
    <xs:list itemType='xs:string' />
  </xs:simpleType>
  <xs:simpleType name='TwoStringList'>
    <xs:restriction base='StringList' >
      <xs:length value='2' />
    </xs:restriction>
  </xs:simpleType>
  <xs:element name='neighbor' type='TwoStringList' />
```

For this declaration, the following two-item list is legal:

```
<neighbor>India Nepal</neighbor>
```

However, the following two-item list is illegal:

```
<neighbor>India Nationalist China</neighbor>
```

Even though "Nationalist China" may exist as a single string outside of the list, when it is included in the list, the whitespace between "Nationalist" and "China" effectively creates a third item, and so the latter example will not conform to the two-item list type.

8.15.2 Deriving Complex Types

Complex type extensions are quite similar to the inherit function of Java, C++, and other object-oriented languages. New complex types can be derived by restricting or extending existing simple or complex types. Extension means taking an existing type as the base and creating a new type by adding attributes, elements, or both. Restriction means, imposing constraints on the content obtained from base type. No new content, in this case, can be added to the derived type (however, attributes can be added).

During the derivation of complex types, two content models `simpleContent` and `complexContent` are introduced. The `simpleContent` model specifies that the content of the new element type must be text or an emptiable element. However, the element can have attributes. The `complexContent` model, on the other hand, does not impose any such restriction on element content. Consider the following schema fragment:

```
<xs:complexType name='populationType'>
   <xs:simpleContent>
      <xs:extension base='xs:nonNegativeInteger'>
         <xs:attribute name='year' use='required' />
      </xs:extension>
   </xs:simpleContent>
</xs:complexType>
```

This schema fragment creates a complex type from existing simple base type `nonNegativeInteger` by adding (extending) the mandatory attribute `year`. The type of derivation in this case is extension because an attribute is added, and the `simpleContent` model is used because element's content type remains integer, and hence simple. One can now create an element of this derived type.

```
<xs:element name='population' type='populationType' />
```

With this element declaration, following is schema-valid:

```
<population year='2009'>100</population>
```

However, the following is not.

```
<population>100</population>
```

In general, when `simpleContent` is used, the base type must be a `complexType` whose content type is simple, or a complex type with mixed content and emptiable element if restriction is specified, or a simple type if extension is specified.

Consider the following schema fragment.

```
<xs:complexType name='complexInteger'>
   <xs:simpleContent>
      <xs:extension base='xs:integer'/>
   </xs:simpleContent>
</xs:complexType>
```

It simply creates a complex type from the integer type. This type is similar to integer type, except that it is complex. Then, why have we created this type? We have created this type because we want to further impose restrictions on it and restrictions expect a complex type. Following is a schema fragment that imposes a restriction on `complexType`.

```
<xs:complexType name='cellNumberType'>
   <xs:simpleContent>
      <xs:restriction base='complexInteger'>
         <xs:pattern value='9\d{9}' />
      </xs:restriction>
   </xs:simpleContent>
</xs:complexType>
```

The content of `cellNumberType` is an integer, provided that it starts with the digit '9' and has exactly 10 (ten) digits, including the start digit. Now, add an attribute that specifies the ISD code of a cell number.

```
<xs:complexType name='intlCellNumberType'>
   <xs:simpleContent>
      <xs:extension base='cellNumberType'>
         <xs:attribute name='ISDCode' type='xs:integer' />
      </xs:extension>
   </xs:simpleContent>
</xs:complexType>
```

Finally, declare an element of this type.

```
<xs:element name='cellNumber' type='intlCellNumberType' />
```

Here is a valid instance document for this type definition.

```
<cellNumber ISDCode='91'>9433880334</cellNumber>
```

Note that a derived complex type's content model is a subset of its base type's content model. This means that not all restrictions are acceptable. Examples of acceptable restrictions to declarations in the content model include

- Changing the type of an element or attribute to a subtype (e.g., going from `xs:integer` in the base type to `xs:positiveInteger` in the derived type)
- Changing an optional attribute to required
- Changing the occurrence range of an element so it is a subset of the original occurrence range (e.g., from `minOccurs="1"` & `maxOccurs="unbounded"` to `minOccurs="2"` & `maxOccurs="4"`)
- Changing the nillability of an element from `true` to `false`
- Changing an element or attribute to have a fixed value

8.15.3 Substitution Group

Substitution group construct allows elements to be substituted for other elements. A set of elements are added to a group. Elements from this group may be substituted by a particular named element called *head* element. Consider the following example.

```
<xs:simpleType name='letterType'>
   <xs:restriction base='xs:string'>
      <xs:pattern value='[a-zA-Z]'/>
   </xs:restriction>
</xs:simpleType>

<xs:element name='middleName' type='xs:string' />
<xs:element name='middleInitial' type='letterType' substitutionGroup='middleName' />
```

We declare the element `middleInitial` and assign it to a substitution group whose head element is `middleName`, and so `middleInitial` can be used any place where `middleName` is expected.

```
<xs:complexType name='personType'>
   <xs:sequence>
      <xs:element name='firstName' type='xs:string'/>
      <xs:element ref='middleName' />
      <xs:element name='lastName' type='xs:string' />
   </xs:sequence>
</xs:complexType>

<xs:element name='employee' type='personType' />
```

In this example, the `employee` element expects `middleName` to be a child element. So, `middleInitial`, instead of `middleName` can be used. The element `middlename` can also be used as before. The following instance document fragment is valid.

```
<employee>
   <firstName>Uttam</firstName>
   <middleInitial>K</middleInitial>
   <lastName>Roy</lastName>
</employee>
```

So is

```
<employee>
   <firstName>Uttam</firstName>
   <middleName>Kumar</middleName>
   <lastName>Roy</lastName>
</employee>
```

Note that the *head* element as well as the substitutable elements must be declared as *global* elements. All the elements within a substitution group need to have a type that is either the same type as the head element or a type that has been derived from the head element's type.

8.16 CONTROLLING DERIVATION

Type derivation is a powerful tool and with the help of this tool, we have been able to derive new types and use them in instance documents without any restraints. In reality, schema authors will sometimes want to control derivations of particular types, and the use of derived types in instances. Just as some object-oriented programming languages allow the creator of an object to dictate the limits on how an object can be created, XML Schema provides mechanisms that control the derivation of types. Three properties of complex types control their derivation:

- The `abstract` property forces the definition of derived types.
- The `final` property limits the definition of derived types in schemas.
- The `block` property limits the substitution of derived types in instances.

8.16.1 Abstract Elements and Types

The `abstract` attribute applies to both type and element declarations. If an element is declared as abstract (`abstract` attribute set to `true`), the element cannot appear in an instance document. However, members of a substitution group based on that element may appear in the instance document.

```
<xs:element name='contact' type='xs:integer' abstract='true'/>
<xs:element name='phone' type='xs:nonNegativeInteger' substitutionGroup='contact' />
```

This example shows that the element `contact` is abstract and that it can never appear in an instance document. However, the element `phone`, which is substitutable for `contact`, may appear wherever the element `contact` is expected.

If a type is declared as abstract (called *abstract type*), no element declared of that type may appear in an instance document. Following is an example of abstract type definition.

```
<xs:complexType name='Phone' abstract='true'>
   <xs:simpleContent>
      <xs:extension base='xs:nonNegativeInteger'>
      </xs:extension>
   </xs:simpleContent>
</xs:complexType>
```

The complex type `Phone` is declared as abstract. So, no element of this type can appear in an instance document. However, elements having type derived from abstract type `Phone` may appear. Consider the following derived type definition:

```
<xs:complexType name='STDPhone' >
   <xs:simpleContent>
      <xs:extension base='Phone'>
         <xs:attribute name='STD' type='xs:integer' use='required'/>
      </xs:extension>
   </xs:simpleContent>
</xs:complexType>
<xs:element name='contact' type='STDPhone' />
```

In this declaration, the type `STDPhone` derived from `Phone` is not abstract. So, any element of this type such as `contact` may appear in an instance document as follows:

```
<contact STD='33'>25735621</contact>
```

8.16.2 Preventing Derivation

XML schema provides another mechanism that allows schema authors to specify that for a particular complex type, new types cannot be derived from it, either (a) by restriction, (b) by extension, or (c) at all. This is accomplished by using the `final` attribute, which may have one of the following values:

- `"extension"` prevents any other types from extending your type.
- `"restriction"` prevents any other types from restricting your type.
- `"#all"` prevents any other types from extending or restricting your type.
- `"extension restriction"` and `"restriction extension"` are the values that have the same effect as `#all`.

When a type is derived from another type, which has the `final` attribute set, the schema processor verifies if the desired derivation is legal. The following example illustrates this.

```
<xs:complexType name='complexInteger'>
   <xs:simpleContent>
      <xs:extension base='xs:integer'/>
   </xs:simpleContent>
</xs:complexType>

<xs:complexType name='cellNumberType' final='restriction' >
   <xs:simpleContent>
      <xs:restriction base='complexInteger'>
         <xs:pattern value='9\d{9}' />
      </xs:restriction>
   </xs:simpleContent>
</xs:complexType>
```

For the type `cellNumberType`, no further derivation by restriction is possible. So the following derivation is invalid.

```
<xs:complexType name='BSNLCellNumberType' >
   <xs:simpleContent>
      <xs:restriction base='cellNumberType'>
         <xs:pattern value='94\d{8}' />
      </xs:restriction>
   </xs:simpleContent>
</xs:complexType>
```

However, derivation by extension is possible. The following derivation is valid.

```
<xs:complexType name='intlCellNumberType'>
   <xs:simpleContent>
      <xs:extension base='cellNumberType'>
         <xs:attribute name='ISDCode' type='xs:integer' />
      </xs:extension>
   </xs:simpleContent>
</xs:complexType>
```

Preventing derivation by extension is also possible by setting the `final` attribute to the value `extension`. If neither is allowed, set the final attribute to `#all`.

Moreover, there exists an optional `finalDefault` attribute in the `schema` element whose value can be one of the values allowed for the `final` attribute. The effect of specifying the `finalDefault` attribute is equivalent to specifying the `final` attribute on every type definition and element declaration in the schema. The restriction given on derivation by `finalDefault` can be overridden by specifying "" (an empty string) to the `final` attribute.

If no `final` attribute is specified, it takes its value from the `finalDefault` attribute of the `schema` element. If neither `final` nor `finalDefault` are specified, there are no restrictions on the derivation of that complex type.

On a simple type, final attribute can be set to `#all`, or to a list containing any combination of the values `list`, `union`, and/or `restriction`, in any order.

8.16.3 Preventing Substitution

We have seen that XML Schema provides a mechanism, called substitution groups, that allows elements to be substituted for other elements. Sometimes schema authors want to prevent this substitution of elements. This is accomplished by the attribute `block`.

The `block` attribute applies to type and element declarations. When a type is defined, the `block` attribute prevents a type that has the specified type of derivation from being used in place of this base type. In this case, the `block` attribute can have the value `#all` or a list of the values `extension`, `restriction`, `list`, or `union`. Table 8.7 illustrates this clearly.

Table 8.7 `block` attribute values for type definition

Value	Description
`extension`	Prevents complex types derived by extension from being used in place of this complex type.
`restriction`	Prevents simple/complex types derived by restriction from being used in place of this simple/complex types.
`#all`	Prevents all derived types from being used in place of this type.
`union`	Prevents simple types derived by union from being used in place of this simple type.
`list`	Prevents simple types derived by list from being used in place of this simple type.

When a type is defined, the `block` attribute can have the value `#all` or a list of the values `extension`, `restriction`, `substitution`, `list`, or `union`. Table 8.8 illustrates this clearly.

Table 8.8 `block` attribute values for element declaration

Value	Description
`extension`	Prevents substitutable elements (derived by extension from this element's type) from being used in place of this element.
`restriction`	Prevents substitutable elements (derived by restriction from this element's type) from being used in place of this element.
`substitution`	Prevents any substitutable elements from being used in place of this element.
`#all`	Prevents all derived substitutable elements from being used in place of this element.
`union`	Prevents substitutable elements (derived by union from this element's type) from being used in place of this element.
`list`	Prevents substitutable elements (derived by list from this element's type) from being used in place of this element.

8.16.4 Uniqueness and Referential Integrity Constraints

`ID` and `IDREF` in DTD provide a simple mechanism for uniquely identifying elements in an instance document and enforcing referential integrity for attributes that refer to those elements. However, it has several shortcomings some of which are mentioned as follows:

- `ID` and `IDREF` values can never be integers (the first character of an `ID` and `IDREF` value must be a letter, '_', or ':').
- The scope of a constraint is always global. For example, the value of the `ID` attribute must be unique throughout the entire instance document.
- It is not possible to specify the target element of `IDREF`.
- Constraints apply to individual, and not to a set of attributes, or element contents.

Fortunately, XML Schema outlines a powerful mechanism to specify uniqueness and referential integrity constraints based on the modified XPath expression. It provides three constructs for describing uniqueness and referential integrity constraints: `unique`, `key`, and `keyref`.

To describe a constraint, we first *select* a set of elements, and then identify the attribute and/or element *field*, relative to each previously selected element, on which to apply constraint. Selecting a set of elements is done by using the `selector` element. It has an attribute `xpath`, which contains an XPath expression that selects a set of elements. Identification of target attributes and/or elements is done by using one or more `field` elements. Each `field` element also has the attribute `xpath`, which represents attributes and/or elements on which to apply the constraint.

Uniqueness and referential integrity constraints must appear at the end of an element declaration and are local to the enclosing element. The selector XPath expression is interpreted relative to the element being declared, and can only constrain child elements relative to the element in which they are declared.

8.16.5 Uniqueness Constraint

Uniqueness constraint is described by the `unique` construct in XML Schema. It is more or less equivalent to the *primary key* constraint in DBMS. It implies that one or more field values (each indicated by a `field` sub-element and called key sequence) across a set of instance elements (specified by the `selector` sub-element) must be unique within the scope of the selected elements. When using the `unique` element, the selected node is skipped if a field is not present in the instance document. Following is an example:

```
<xs:complexType name='studentType'>
  <xs:attribute name='roll' type='xs:integer' />
  <xs:attribute name='name' type='xs:string' />
  <xs:attribute name='friend' type='xs:integer' />
</xs:complexType>

<xs:complexType name='departmentType'>
  <xs:sequence maxOccurs='unbounded'>
    <xs:element name='student' type='studentType' />
  </xs:sequence>
</xs:complexType>
```

```
<xs:element name='department' type='departmentType' >
   <xs:unique name='stdroll'>
      <xs:selector xpath='student' />
      <xs:field xpath='@roll' />
   </xs:unique>
</xs:element>
```

This uniqueness constraint states that the `roll` attribute must have a unique value across all instances of the `student` element that appear as children of the `department` element. In other words, the roll uniquely identifies each student. This means that the following is not a valid instance.

```
<department>
   <student name='Anusha' roll='1' />
   <student name='Rimisha' roll='1' />
</department>
```

This is because two instances of the `student` element have the same `roll` (=1) attribute value.

It is possible to ensure uniqueness constraint on more than one value. Consider the following instance document fragment.

```
<department>
   <marks stdRoll='1' subId='1'>80</marks>
   <marks stdRoll='1' subId='2'>84</marks>
</department>
```

In this case, `stdRoll` and `subId` should together form a unique key. To represent this constraint multiple `field` elements are used. If multiple `field` elements are used, they form an ordered list which must be unique across all selected elements. Following is an example for such a uniqueness constraint.

```
<xs:element name='department' type='departmentType' >
   <xs:unique name='stdMarks'>
      <xs:selector xpath='marks' />
      <xs:field xpath='@stdRoll' />
      <xs:field xpath='@subId' />
   </xs:unique>
</xs:element>
```

So, the following instance segment is not schema-valid as two marks elements have the same (`stdRoll, subId`) value.

```
<department>

   <marks stdRoll='1' subId='1'>80</marks>
   <marks stdRoll='1' subId='1'>84</marks>
</department>
```

8.16.6 Referential Integrity Constraint

Referential integrity constraint is very much similar to that of the *foreign key* concept in database. The `keyref` construct allows a referential integrity constraint to be expressed in terms of the `unique` or `key` constraints. The following schema fragment ensures that the `friend` attribute always refers to a valid `student` element through the `roll` attribute.

```
<xs:complexType name='studentType'>
   <xs:attribute name='roll' type='xs:integer' />
   <xs:attribute name='name' type='xs:string' />
   <xs:attribute name='friend' type='xs:integer' />
</xs:complexType>

<xs:complexType name='classType'>
   <xs:sequence maxOccurs='unbounded'>
      <xs:element name='student' type='studentType' />
   </xs:sequence>
</xs:complexType>

<xs:element name='class' type='classType' >
   <xs:unique name='stdRoll'>
      <xs:selector xpath='student' />
      <xs:field xpath='@roll' />
   </xs:unique>
   <xs:keyref name='stdRollRef' refer='stdRoll'>
      <xs:selector xpath='student' />
      <xs:field xpath='@friend' />
   </xs:keyref>
</xs:element>
```

The `keyref` construct must refer to a valid `unique` or `key` named constraint (called *target* constraint) using the `refer` attribute. The `keyref` construct selects a set of instance nodes through its `selector` attribute. This set of nodes need not be the same set of nodes evaluated by the target constraint. Each element in the set evaluated by `keyref` must match with an element in the target set field by field. Otherwise, the instance document is not a valid instance. So, for the schema fragment discussed, following is a valid instance document fragment.

```
<student name='Anusha' roll='1' />
<student name='Rimisha' roll='2' friend='1'/>
```

This is because the value of the `friend` attribute is 1 and there exists a student (Anusha) whose `roll` attribute is 1. However, the following is not a valid instance document, since the `friend` attribute does not match a `roll` value anywhere in the scope of the referential integrity constraint.

```
<student name='Anusha' roll='1' />
<student name='Rimisha' roll='2' friend='3'/>
```

The previous example used the `unique` constraint as a target of referential integrity. Non-unique values can also be used as a target of referential integrity by using the `key` constraint. However, if `key` is used, unlike `unique`, the designated field must be present. The following example illustrates this.

```
<xs:complexType name='petType'>
   <xs:attribute name='type' type='xs:string' />
</xs:complexType>

<xs:complexType name='habitType'>
   <xs:attribute name='name' type='xs:string' />
   <xs:attribute name='type' type='xs:string' />
```

```
</xs:complexType>

<xs:complexType name='listType'>
   <xs:choice maxOccurs='unbounded'>
      <xs:element name='pet' type='petType' />
      <xs:element name='habit' type='habitType' />
   </xs:choice>
</xs:complexType>

<xs:element name='list' type='listType' >
   <xs:key name='petType'>
      <xs:selector xpath='pet' />
      <xs:field xpath='@type' />
   </xs:key>
   <xs:keyref name='petTypeRef' refer='petType'>
      <xs:selector xpath='habit' />
      <xs:field xpath='@type' />
   </xs:keyref>
</xs:element>
```

The `key` constraint states that the `type` attribute must be present, but may not have a unique value across all instances of the `pet` element. Following is a valid instance fragment:

```
<pet type='dog'/>
<pet type='cat'/>
<habit name='dig' type='dog' />
```

However, following is not, as the pet type `rabbit` does not exist.

```
<pet type='dog'/>
<pet type='cat'/>
<habit name='dig' type='rabbit' />
```

It is possible to ensure referential constraint on more than one value. Consider a more complex scenario. We shall first represent this scenario from DBMS perspective and then represent the same using XML Schema.

In a department, a number of subjects are taught. Each subject has a name and can be identified by a subject number (subId) and semester number (semId). Each student has a name (name) and a unique roll number (roll). Marks obtained by a student in a particular semester in a particular subject can be identified by the student's roll number (roll), subject number (subId), and semester number (semId). These constraints can be described in DBMS as follows:

```
subject(name, subId, semId)
student(name, roll)
marks(roll, subId, semId)
```

The `roll` attribute of `marks` refers to the `roll` attribute of `student`. The `(subId, semId)` of `marks` refers to `(subId, semId)` of `subject`. To represent this scenario, database tables are created as follows:

```
CREATE TABLE subject (
   name varchar(100),
   subId integer,
```

```
   semId integer,
   PRIMARY KEY(subId, semId)
);

CREATE TABLE student (
   name varchar(100),
   roll integer,
   PRIMARY KEY(roll)
);

CREATE TABLE marks (
   roll integer,
   subId integer,
   semId integer,
   PRIMARY KEY(roll, subId, semId),
   FOREIGN KEY(roll) REFERENCES student(roll),
   FOREIGN KEY(subId, semId) REFERENCES subject(subId, semId)
);
```

The equivalent XML schema can be described as follows:

```
<xs:complexType name='studentType'>
   <xs:attribute name='roll' type='xs:integer' use='required'/>
   <xs:attribute name='name' type='xs:string' />
</xs:complexType>

<xs:complexType name='subjectType'>
   <xs:simpleContent>
      <xs:extension base='xs:string'>
         <xs:attribute name='subId' type='xs:string' use='required'/>
         <xs:attribute name='semId' type='xs:string' use='required'/>
      </xs:extension>
   </xs:simpleContent>
</xs:complexType>

<xs:complexType name='marksType'>
   <xs:simpleContent>
      <xs:extension base='xs:integer'>
         <xs:attribute name='stdRoll' type='xs:integer' use='required'/>
         <xs:attribute name='subId' type='xs:string' use='required'/>
         <xs:attribute name='semId' type='xs:string' use='required'/>
      </xs:extension>
   </xs:simpleContent>
</xs:complexType>

<xs:complexType name='departmentType'>
   <xs:choice maxOccurs='unbounded'>
      <xs:element name='student' type='studentType' />
      <xs:element name='subject' type='subjectType' />
      <xs:element name='marks' type='marksType' />
   </xs:choice>
</xs:complexType>

<xs:element name='department' type='departmentType' >
   <xs:unique name='studentKey'>
```

```
        <xs:selector xpath='student' />
        <xs:field xpath='@roll' />
    </xs:unique>

    <xs:unique name='subjectKey'>
        <xs:selector xpath='subject' />
        <xs:field xpath='@subId' />
        <xs:field xpath='@semId' />
    </xs:unique>
        <xs:unique name='marksKey'>
        <xs:selector xpath='marks' />
        <xs:field xpath='@stdRoll' />
        <xs:field xpath='@subId' />
        <xs:field xpath='@semId' />
    </xs:unique>

    <xs:keyref name='studentKeyRef1' refer='studentKey'>
        <xs:selector xpath='marks' />
        <xs:field xpath='@stdRoll' />
    </xs:keyref>

    <xs:keyref name='subjectKeyRef' refer='subjectKey'>
        <xs:selector xpath='marks' />
        <xs:field xpath='@subId' />
        <xs:field xpath='@semId' />
    </xs:keyref>

</xs:element>
```

For this schema, the following instance fragment is valid:

```
<subject subId='1' semId='5'>Web Technology</subject>
<subject subId='2' semId='5'>Web Technology</subject>

<student name='Anusha' roll='1' />
<student name='Rimisha' roll='2' friend='1'/>

<marks stdRoll='1' subId='1' semId='5'>80</marks>
<marks stdRoll='1' subId='2' semId='5'>84</marks>
```

8.17 WHICH SHOULD WE USE, ELEMENTS OR ATTRIBUTES?

We have seen that information may be stored using either attributes or elements. Now the question is whether to use an element or an attribute? A careful look at the attribute and element definitions suggests that elements describe data and attributes describe meta data. In addition, attributes are used for small pieces of data such as employee's id. Generally, it is best to use elements to store data and attribute to store properties about the data stored in elements. There are some problems in the usage of attributes:

- An attribute contains only single-valued data, but child elements can store multiple values.
- In case of any future changes to the schema, attributes are not easily extendable.
- Attributes cannot represent relationships/structures (child elements can).

If attributes are used as containers of data, the resulting documents become difficult to read and maintain. As far as possible, use elements to describe data and attributes to describe metadata (i.e., data about data). However, it is ultimately a personal choice that dictates when to use elements and when to use attributes.

8.18 MIXED ELEMENT CONTENT

As mentioned, it is always recommended not to use mixed content elements. They have several limitations. Mixed content elements are difficult to parse and may lead to unforeseen complexity in the resulting XML document. They also impose limitations on XML data binding which makes it difficult to manipulate documents containing such elements.

8.19 APPENDIX

Table 8.9 XML data types

Data Type	Description
xs:boolean	A Boolean value
xs:string	A string; typically Unicode
xs:byte	A signed 8-bit number
xs:short	A signed 16-bit number
xs:int	A signed 32-bit number
xs:long	A signed 64-bit number
xs:unsignedByte	An unsigned 8-bit number
xs:unsignedShort	An unsigned 16-bit number
xs:unsignedInt	An unsigned 32-bit number
xs:unsignedLong	An unsigned 64-bit number
xs:integer, xs:nonPositiveInteger, xs:negativeInteger, xs:nonNegativeInteger, xs:positiveInteger	Unbounded or partially bounded integers. It is recommended that these types be avoided in schemas that are intended to be used with binding tools
xs:decimal	A decimal number that includes a fractional part but is not specified using an exponent; for example, 123.45.
xs:float, xs:double	Single and double precision floating point numbers.
xs:hexBinary, xs:base64Binary	Binary data
xs:duration	For specifying elapsed time, particularly in terms of days, months, years, etc.
xs:dateTime, xs:time, xs:date, xs:gYearMonth, xs:gYear, xs:gMonthDay, xs:gDay, xs:gMonth	Date and time related types
xs:anyURI, xs:QName, xs:NOTATION, xs:normalizedString, xs:token, xs:language, xs:ID, xs:IDREF, xs:IDREFS, xs:ENTITY, xs:ENTITIES, xs:NMTOKEN, xs:NMTOKENS, xs:Name, xs:NCName	Other schema defined types

KEYWORDS

Abstract Element: If an element is declared as abstract (abstract attribute set to true), the element cannot appear in an instance document. However, members of a substitution group based on that element may appear in an instance document.

Abstract Types: If a type is declared as abstract (called *abstract type*), no element declared of that type may appear in an instance document.

all Indicator: This indicator indicates that elements in a group may appear in any order in the enclosing element.

Annotations: W3C XML Schema provides three annotation elements for documentation purposes in an XML schema instance.

Attribute Group Indicator: A set of related attributes can be created using the `attributeGroup` indicator, which is called attribute group indicator.

choice Indicator: It allows an XML element to contain any one of a set of elements.

Complex Element: Complex elements are those elements that can contain child elements, text, or both and can also have attributes.

Composite Indicator: The indicators `choice` and `sequence` can be freely nested inside other indicator.

Element Group Indicator: A set of related elements can be created using the `group` indicator, which is called element group indicator.

Facets: Restrictions that are imposed on new types created from a base type by derivation.

List: List types are sequences of atomic types separated by white spaces.

Mixed Content: Complex elements contain both child elements and text. In such cases, the content is called mixed content.

Occurrence Indicator: Specifies the number of times an element can appear in an XML document.

Referencing: An existing element may be referenced while declaring an element. This is called referencing.

Referential Integrity Constraint: Referential integrity constraint is very much similar to that of the *foreign key* concept in database.

Sequence Indicator: This indicator specifies that the elements within an enclosing element must occur in the order specified there.

Simple Element: Simple elements are those elements that can only contain text and/or data.

Substitution Group: The substitution group construct allows elements to be substituted for other elements.

Type Derivation: W3C XML Schema allows users to create new named types (simple or complex) and to use these types to declare elements or attributes.

Union: Union types are groupings of types. It essentially allows the value of an element to be of more than one type.

Uniqueness Constraint: It indicates that one or more field values across a set of instance elements must be unique within the scope of selected elements.

XML Schema Definition (XSD): XML Schema Definition (XSD) is a specific XML schema document written using XML Schema.

XML Schema Instance: The XML documents that tries to follow the rules specified by an XML schema document.

XML Schema Validation: The procedure for verifying whether an XML document follows the rules specified in a schema is called XML Schema Validation.

SUMMARY

W3C XML Schema (WXS) is a powerful XML Schema language. It has many advantages over DTD. They provide much greater specificity than DTDs could and support large number of built-in data types. They are namespace-aware. XML Schemas are extensible to future additions. They also support uniqueness and referential integrity constraints in a much better way. It is easier to define data facets (restrictions on data).

XML **S**chema **D**efinition (XSD) or simple XML Schema is a specific XML schema document written using XML Schema and typically has the filename extension ".xsd". An XML Schema is written in XML. An XML document that conforms to the schema is called an instance of the schema.

An XML document can be verified against a schema using XML validators. Typically, a validator takes an XML document and an XML schema and checks whether the XML document is written following the rules specified in the schema. Many readymade XML schema validators are available on the web.

An XML schema consists of five components: the schema element, element definitions, attribute definitions, annotations, and type definitions.

An XML Schema is composed of the top-level `schema` element. The schema element contains other elements that defined the structure of conforming XML documents.

XML Schema 1.0 specification provides about 46 built-in data types. An element is limited by its type. Schema authors can use their own defined types or use the built-in types. Depending upon the content model, elements are categorized as *simple* type or *complex* type.

Simple type elements can contain only text and/or data. They cannot have child elements or attributes or even cannot be empty. It can further be divided into three types: *atomic types, list types,* and *union types.*

An element is declared using the element tag. An element can be declared globally and locally within another element. Global elements allow scalability, extensibility, and portability.

Occurrence indicators in schema are much more powerful than the same used in DTD. Examples include `minOccurs`, `maxOccurs`, etc.

Order indicators are used to specify the order in which elements should occur in the container element. The following order indicators are available: `sequence`, `all`, and `choice`. The indicators `choice` and `sequence` can be freely nested inside other indicators, and can be given their own `minOccurs` and `maxOccurs` properties. This allows complex combinations to be formed. However, the `all` indicator, as mentioned earlier, cannot be mixed-up with either the `choice` or the `sequence` indicators.

W3C XML Schema provides some powerful constructs. XML Schema allows us to refer to an existing element declared earlier. This is called referencing. Group indicators are used to define reusable sets of related items.

W3C XML Schema also allows us to create new types using different mechanisms such as restriction, derivation, etc. Another new concept introduced in schema is 'substitution group'.

They are almost as powerful as the primary key and foreign key concepts in database.

WEB RESOURCES

`<http://www.w3.org/TR/2004/REC-xmlschema-0-20041028/>`
XML Schema Part 0: Primer Second Edition

`<http://www.w3.org/TR/2004/REC-xmlschema-1-20041028>`
XML Schema Part 1: Structures Second Edition

`http://www.w3.org/TR/2004/REC-xmlschema-2-20041028/`
XML Schema Part 2: Datatypes Second Edition

`<http://xerces.apache.org/xerces2-j/>`
Xerces2 Java Parser

EXERCISES

Multiple Choice Questions

1. W3C Schema is written in

(a) XSL (b) XSLT (c) XML (d) XHTML

2. Which of the following statements about XML schemas is incorrect?

(a) Schemas support data types.
(b) Schemas provide data-oriented data types.
(c) All XML documents must have a schema.
(d) They offer more flexibility than DTDs.

3. An XSD document describes the structure of

(a) a file (b) an XML document
(c) a page (d) a database

4. What is the full form of XSD?

(a) XSL Schema Definition
(b) XSLT Schema Definition
(c) XHTML Schema Definition
(d) XML Schema Definition

5. Which of the following is not true regarding an XML Schema?

(a) It specifies what attributes an element can have.
(b) It specifies elements that can appear in a document.
(c) It specifies which files a directory can contain.
(d) It specifies which elements are children of which elements.

6. Which of the following is the correct representation of date and time in XML Schema?
   (a) gDayMonth (b) gMonthDay
   (c) timeDate (d) gMonthYear

7. Which of the following matches best with XML Schema?
   (a) DTD (b) XSLT (c) XSL (d) XML

8. Which of the following is the greatest strength of XML Schema?
   (a) It supports graphics.
   (b) It supports images.
   (c) It supports data types.
   (d) It supports functions.

9. Which of the following is true regarding Schema?
   (a) You cannot create your own data types derived from the standard types.
   (b) You cannot reference multiple schemas in the same document.
   (c) You cannot reuse your Schema in other Schemas.
   (d) You can verify an XML document against a Schema.

10. A simple element is an XML element that can contain
    (a) Only images
    (b) Only text
    (c) Only elements
    (d) Both text and other child elements

11. Which of the following is not a kind of complex element?
    (a) Element that contains only other elements
    (b) Empty element
    (c) Element that contains only text
    (d) Element that contains both text and other child elements

12. Which of the following is false regarding a complex element?
    (a) It can contain other elements.
    (b) It cannot have any attribute.
    (c) It may be empty.
    (d) It may contain text.

13. The syntax for defining an attribute is
    (a) <xs:attribute name=aName type=aType/>
    (b) <xs:attribute name="aName" type="aType"/>
    (c) <attribute name="aName" type="aType"/>
    (d) <xs:attribute type="aType" />

14. Attributes are by default
    (a) optional (b) required
    (c) default (d) fixed

15. Restrictions that are incorporated on XML elements are called
    (a) rules (b) facts (c) facets (d) faces

16. Which of the following is false regarding an empty element?
    (a) It cannot have any attributes.
    (b) It cannot contain text.
    (c) It cannot contain other elements.
    (d) It is a simple element.

17. In XML schemas, the default model for complex type is
    (a) Text only (b) Element only
    (c) both (a) and (b) (d) no default type

18. Which of the following represents the correct format of the built-in simple type 'date'?
    (a) MM-DD-YY (b) DD-MM-YY
    (c) YY-MM-DD (d) YYYY-MM-DD

19. In XML Schema, a Boolean type can hold
    (a) 1, 0
    (b) True, False
    (c) both (a) and (b)
    (d) True/False and any number except 0

20. Which of the following is used to create a choice?
    (a) <xsd:multi> element
    (b) <xsd:choice> element
    (c) <xsd:select> element
    (d) <xsd:single> element

Review Questions

1. What are the major strengths of schema over DTD?
2. How do you define optional and required attributes?
3. How do you set default and fixed values for attributes?
4. How do you define attributes in XML Schema?
5. How do you set default and fixed values for simple Elements?
6. Which data types do we use in XML Schema?
7. What is XML Schema?
8. How we can say that XML Schemas are the successors of DTDs?
9. Why do we use XML Schemas?
10. Explain why XML Schemas are extensible.
11. How do you define the elements of an XML document in an XML Schema?
12. Write the relative advantages and disadvantages of local and global declarations.
13. When is an element called simple? How does it differ from a complex element?
14. Show with an example how to create new data types in schema.
15. Write a Java program to validate an XML document against a schema.
16. Write a JavaScript program to validate an XML document against a schema.
17. Explain with example the notion of default and fixed values for simple elements.
18. Suppose you want an element to occur zero or more number of times. How do you declare this element?
19. How do you make an element optional?
20. A complex element can have simple or complex content. What does this mean?
21. Explain with an example the notion of default and fixed values for attributes.
22. What is the advantage of referencing? How do you reference an element?
23. Explain with examples the importance of group indicators.

9 PARSING XML

KEY OBJECTIVES

After completing this chapter readers will be able to—

- **get an idea about Document Object Model (DOM)**
- **understand how DOM represents an XML document as a tree structure**
- **get an idea about DOM objects and interfaces defined by the W3C**
- **create and navigate a DOM tree for an XML document using Java**
- **manipulate a DOM tree using Java**
- **validate an XML document against DTD and schema using Java**

9.1 XML DOM

Document **O**bject **M**odel (DOM) is a language-neutral and platform-independent object model used to represent XML documents. DOM helps scripts and programs to access, add, delete, and edit content, structure, and style of XML documents dynamically.

DOM is standardized by the **W**orld **W**ide **W**eb **C**onsortium (W3C). The primary objective of this standard was to model an HTML document in an object-oriented way so that it could be exposed to scripts, and scripts could access and manipulate HTML documents through this object model dynamically. In this regard, the World Wide Web Consortium (W3C) received several proposals from its member companies. Consequently, the W3C tried to develop an interoperable and language-neutral object model to represent HTML as well as XML documents and the result was DOM. In order to provide a precise specification of the DOM interfaces independent of languages, the W3C chose to use **I**nterface **D**efinition **L**anguage (IDL), defined by **O**bject **M**anagement **G**roup (OMG) in the CORBA 2.2 specification. OMG IDL is widely used to specify interfaces in a language-independent and implementation-neutral way.

The W3C DOM specification is divided into three major parts:

- DOM Core—This portion defines the basic set of interfaces and objects for any structured documents.

- XML DOM—This part specifies the standard set of objects and interfaces for XML documents only.
- HTML DOM—This part defines the interfaces and objects for HTML documents only.

In this chapter, we shall highlight only XML DOM. The W3C added some more features to the HTML DOM for better handling.

DOM models a document as a hierarchical structure consisting of different kinds of nodes. Each of these nodes represents a specific portion of the document. This simple idea has made the entire framework elegant. Some kind of nodes may have children of different types. Some nodes cannot have anything below it in the hierarchical structure and are leaf nodes. It also provides standard and specialized set of interfaces and objects to navigate and manipulate (add, modify, delete) DOM tree. DOM is an object-oriented model that encompasses not only the document structure, but the behavior of the document also. It means, each node of the document tree is not a data structure, but an object which has identity (properties) and activity (methods). The primary objective of DOM is to identify

- interfaces and objects to be used to represent, access, and manipulate documents;
- semantics of these objects and interfaces including both attributes and behavior;
- collaboration and relationship among these objects and interfaces.

DOM was standardized to be used with any programming language. In this chapter, we shall use Java as the programming language to discuss how to navigate and manipulate the DOM tree. In Chapter 14, we shall show how to do the same using JavaScript.

Let us explain the XML DOM tree with an example. Consider the following simple XML document that contains the specification of a hard disk.

```
<?xml version='1.0'?>
<store>
   <HDD type='SATA'>
      <make>Samsung</make>
      <capacity unit='GB'>80</capacity>
      <speed unit='rpm'>7200</speed>
      <price currency='INR'>1600</price>
   </HDD>
</store>
```

The corresponding XML DOM tree is shown in Figure 9.1.

As mentioned earlier, the DOM tree consists of many types of nodes. Each of these nodes represents a particular component of the XML document. In fact, the hierarchical structure is not a single tree, but a *forest* that consists of many trees. The `Attr`, `Comment`, `CDATASection`, etc. type nodes are not considered as children of any other node. The exact representation of these nodes is implementation-dependent.

Nodes in a DOM tree have structural relationships among them. The topmost node is the *root* node. In Figure 9.2, `<store>` is the root node. Every DOM tree has exactly one root node. Except the root node, all other nodes have exactly one *parent* node. Nodes except leaf nodes, may have

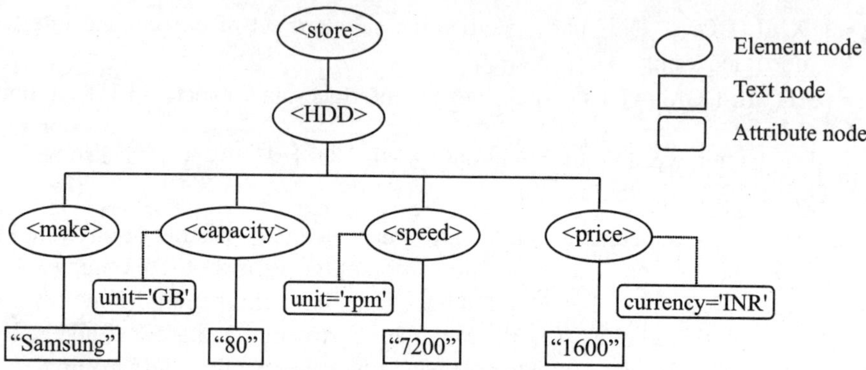

Figure 9.1 XML DOM tree

any number of *children*. Nodes having common parent are called *siblings*. For example, the elements `<make>` and `<capacity>`, and `<speed>` and `<price>` are siblings of one another as they have the common parent element `<HDD>`. The elements `<price>` and `<capacity>` are `nextSibling` and `previousSibling`, respectively, of `<speed>`.

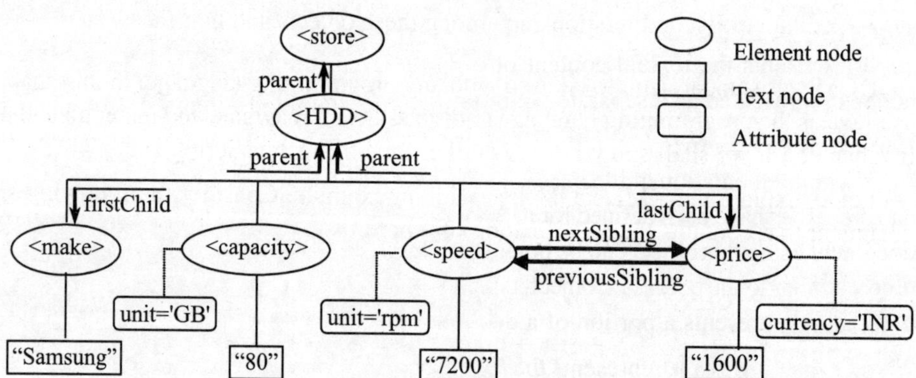

Figure 9.2 Structural relationships among nodes in DOM tree

The fundamental data type in the entire Document Object Model (DOM) is the `Node` interface. All other kinds of nodes implement this interface and hence inherit all the properties and methods of the `Node` interface. However, not all the methods and properties are available on each node type. A specific set of methods and properties are available on each node type. For example, `Text` and `Attr` nodes inherit methods dealing with children from `Node`, but these methods are not valid on `Text` and `Attr` type nodes.

9.2 DOM NODES

All components of an XML document are represented by different kinds of nodes. W3C specified 12 (twelve) types of nodes: `Document`, `DocumentFragment`, `DocumentType`, `EntityReference`, `Element`, `Attr`, `ProcessingInstruction`, `Comment`, `Text`, `CDATASection`, `Entity`, and `Notation`. In this section we shall describe each of these nodes one by one.

`Document`

The W3C `Document` type node represents an entire XML document. Only one `Document` type node exists for each XML document. It is essentially a container of all components of an XML document such as XML declaration (processing instruction), elements, attributes, comments, entities, and so on. Each of these components is represented by a specific type of node.

`Element`

This interface represents an element in the XML document. Elements may have attributes. Those attributes may be obtained from the property `attributes` inherited from the `Node` interface. It also has several useful methods to get an `Attr` node or the value of an attribute by its name.

`Attr`

An `Attr` type node represents an attribute of an `Element` node. An `Attr` node is associated with an element but is not considered as a child of the element. Therefore, though `Attr` objects inherit all the properties and methods of the `Node` interface, some are not valid (i.e., have the value `null`). For example, the properties `parentNode`, `previousSibling`, `nextSibling`, `firstChild`, and `lastChild` are not valid on an `Attr` object. However, `Attr` objects have methods to access the name and value of the attributes.

`Text`

It represents the textual content of an `Element` type node. The text content of an `Element` node is represented as a separate `Text` type node, which is a child node of the element.

`DocumentFragment`

The implementation of the `Document` object can be heavyweight as a large number of methods and properties have been defined for it. So, to cut and/or move a document fragment around the entire document using this object can be potentially costly. For this reason, we need to have a lightweight object similar to the `Document` object. `DocumentFragment` is a "lightweight" or "minimal" `Document` object that represents a portion of a document and is really useful for the purpose mentioned.

`DocumentFragment` represents the root of any sub-tree in the document structure. It essentially behaves like a context-free container of zero or more DOM nodes. So, if a `DocumentFragment` node is inserted or appended to a DOM tree, the `DocumentFragment` object itself disappears and its content is inserted or appended to the context position. The `DocumentFragment` node is not necessary if the content is rooted at an element node. It is only necessary if one or both ends of the content is a text node. In this case, the `DocumentFragment` node holds the nodes temporarily until they are dropped in the document.

The W3C provides the `createDocumentFragment()` method on the `Document` object to create an empty `DocumentFragment` container. The `DocumentFragment` object inherits all the methods and properties of the `Node` object that may be used to append or insert other nodes to this container.

`DocumentType`

It provides interfaces to get information about the document, including the list of entities defined for this document. All the properties on this node are read-only.

EntityReference

A node of this type represents an entity reference in the document. However, an XML processor may completely expand references to entities while building the document tree, instead of providing `EntityReference` nodes. The sub-tree rooted at the node of type `EntityReference` is an exact copy of the sub-tree rooted at a node of type `Entity`.

ProcessingInstruction

The `ProcessingInstruction` interface represents a "processing instruction", which is used in XML to provide specific information about the document to the processor.

Comment

It represents a comment in an XML document. Note that all the characters between the starting '<!--' and ending '-->' delimiters are not processed and are called comment.

CDATASection

This type of node represents a CDATA section in the XML document. Note that no lexical check is done on the content of the CDATA section. It is, therefore, useful to include arbitrary text containing characters, which will otherwise be interpreted as XML.

Entity

It represents a known, either unparsed or parsed entity. An XML processor may completely expand entities while building the document tree and in such a case there will be no `EntityReference` nodes in the document tree. An `Entity` node, if present, does not have any parent. W3C DOM Level 3 does not allow the editing of `Entity` nodes. If users want to change the contents of an `Entity` node, the desired changes have to be made to the related `EntityReference` node.

9.3 THE NODE INTERFACE

As mentioned earlier, it is the primary data type for the entire DOM. Every other kind of node inherits all the properties and methods of the `Node` interface. In the next two sections, we shall discuss frequently used properties and methods available on the `Node` interface.

9.3.1 Node Properties

Some properties of the `Node` interface are read-only. This means that the values of those properties can only be read but they can never be changed. The other properties are read–write. The values of these properties can be read as well as modified. Java provides a read method for each of these properties. For example, the property name is `xxx` on some object `o`, Java provides a method `getXxx()` on `o`. The following important properties are available on the `Node` interface. We shall first discuss the properties without referring to any language. We shall then discuss how to work with them using Java.

`nodeType`

This *read-only* property holds a positive integer that indicates the type of the context node. Table 9.1 shows the value of `nodeType` for different kind of nodes as well as constants defined in the W3C DOM specification.

Table 9.1 The values of nodeType property of the Node interface

Node	Value of nodeType	Constant defined
Element	1	ELEMENT_NODE
Attr	2	ATTRIBUTE_NODE
Text	3	TEXT_NODE
CDATASection	4	CDATA_SECTION_NODE
EntityReference	5	ENTITY_REFERENCE_NODE
Entity	6	ENTITY_NODE
ProcessingInstruction	7	PROCESSING_INSTRUCTION_NODE
Comment	8	COMMENT_NODE
Document	9	DOCUMENT_NODE
DocumentType	10	DOCUMENT_TYPE_NODE
DocumentFragment	11	DOCUMENT_FRAGMENT_NODE
Notation	12	NOTATION_NODE

Java provides the `getNodeType()` method on the `Node` object to inspect this property.

This property is typically inspected before obtaining other properties. Note that only `Element` type node can have children. So, if `nodeType` has the value 1, `childNodes` property (discussed later in this section) on this node is valid. However, if the node is a `Text` node (`nodeType` has the value 3), `childNodes` property is not valid. So, it is always safe to inspect this property before using other node specific properties.

The Java interface `Node` defines the following properties, which help us to determine the type of node we are dealing with.

Table 9.2 lists properties of the `Node` interface.

Table 9.2 The Node interface properties

Property	Meaning
ATTRIBUTE_NODE	It is an Attr type node.
CDATA_SECTION_NODE	It is a CDATASection type node.
COMMENT_NODE	It is a Comment type node.
DOCUMENT_FRAGMENT_NODE	It is a DocumentFragment type node.
DOCUMENT_NODE	It is a Document type node.
DOCUMENT_TYPE_NODE	It is a DocumentType type node.
ELEMENT_NODE	It is an Element type node.
ENTITY_NODE	It is an Entity type node.
ENTITY_REFERENCE_NODE	It is an EntityReference type node.
NOTATION_NODE	It is a Notation type node.
PROCESSING_INSTRUCTION_NODE	It is a ProcessingInstruction type node.
TEXT_NODE	It is a Text node type node.

nodeName

This *read-only* property holds the name of a node. The interpretation of this node is different for different types of nodes. Table 9.3 shows the value of this property for different kinds of nodes.

Table 9.3 The values of nodeName property of the Node interface

Node	Value of nodeName	Node	Value of nodeName
Element	Name of the element	ProcessingInstruction	Target of the PI
Attr	Name of the attribute	Comment	"#comment"
Text	"#text"	Document	"#document"
CDATASection	"#cdata-section"	DocumentType	Name of DTD
EntityReference	Name of the entity referenced	DocumentFragment	"#document-fragment"
Entity	Name of the entity	Notation	Name of the notation

The Java `Node` interface provides the `getNodeName()` method to inspect this property.

nodeValue

This read–write property holds the value of the node. Again, the interpretation of this node is different for different types of nodes. Table 9.4 shows the value of this property for different types of nodes.

Table 9.4 The values of nodeValue property of the Node interface

Node	Value of nodeValue	Node	Value of nodeValue
Element	null	ProcessingInstruction	Content of the PI
Attr	Value of the attribute	Comment	Content of the comment
Text	Content of the text node	Document	Null
CDATASection	Content of the CDATA section	DocumentType	Null
EntityReference	null	DocumentFragment	Null
Entity	null	Notation	Null

The Java `Node` interface provides the `getNodeValue()` method to inspect this property.

Consider the following XML document:

```
<?xml version='1.0'?>
<store>
   <HDD type='SATA'>
      <make>Samsung</make>
      <capacity unit='GB'>80</capacity>
      <speed unit='rpm'>7200</speed>
      <price currency='INR'>1600</price>
   </HDD>
</store>
```

For this code segment, suppose `hdd` refers to the `<HDD>` element. This can be done as follows:

```
var hdd = doc.documentElement.firstChild;
```

Then, `hdd.attributes["type"].nodeValue` has the value `"SATA"` and `para.firstChild.nodeValue` has the value `"This is a paragraph"`.

childNodes

This property of a node contains all child nodes of the context node. It is valid only on element type nodes. It has a property `length` that indicates number of child nodes. Individual child nodes may be referenced as `childNodes[0]`, `childNodes[1]`, etc. Consider the following code segment:

```
<html>
      <head>
         <title></title>
      </head>
      <body>
         <p>This is a paragraph</p>
      </body>
<html>
```

The `<html>` element is referenced as `document.documentElement` and `document.documentElement.childNodes` is an array of child nodes of the `<html>` element. The `<html>` element has two children: `<head>` and `<body>`. So, `document.documentElement.childNodes[0]` and `document.documentElement.childNodes[1]` refer to `<head>` and `<body>` elements, respectively. Since `<head>` has only one child, the `<title>` element `document.documentElement.childNodes[0].childNodes[0]` refers to the `<title>` element. Similarly, `document.body.childNodes[0]` refers to the `<p>` element.

Accessing elements using `childNodes` may not work correctly in some browsers as they treat blank space between tags as a child text node. This means, for a particular document, `childNodes` property may have different lengths in different browsers. Moreover, if an element changes its location (for example, another element is inserted before it), its index in the `childNodes` property will also change, which may affect some existing JavaScript code that uses `childNodes` and index to access this element. For example, if the `<div>` element is inserted before the `<p>` element, the index of `<p>` in the `childNodes` will be 1, which was 0 before inserting the `<div>` element. The only reliable way to access an element is to use the id of an element. This is described later in this chapter.

firstChild

This property refers to the first child of the context node. Its value is `null` if there is no such node. Note that `document.documentElement` refers to the `<html>` element. So, `document.documentElement.firstChild` refers to the `<head>` element. Similarly, `document.documentElement.firstChild.firstChild` refers to the `<title>` element.

lastChild

This property refers to the last child of the context node. Its value is `null` if no such node exists. The node `document.documentElement.lastChild` refers to the `<body>` element.

nextSibling

It returns the node immediately following this node. If no such node exists, it returns `null`. For example, `document.documentElement.firstChild.nextSibling` refers to the `<body>` element.

`previousSibling`

It returns the node immediately preceding this node. If no such node exists, it returns `null`. For example, `document.body.previousSibling` refers to the `<head>` element.

`attributes`

This is an unordered collection containing all attributes specified for the context node or `null` otherwise. Individual attributes may be accessed by name. Consider the following HTML document:

```
<html>
   <head>
      <title>attributes  demo</title>
   </head>
   <body  bgColor="purple">
   </body>
</html>
```

The following object refers to a list of all the attributes of the `<body>` element.

```
document.body.attributes
```

In JavaScript, it is just an array. JavaScript arrays are associative arrays. So, a specific attribute can be obtained by specifying the name of the attribute as the array index. So, the following object refers to the attribute of the <body> element having the name `bgColor`.

```
document.body.attributes["bgColor"]
```

The value of the `bgColor` attribute of the `<body>` element can then be obtained using the following code:

```
document.body.attributes["bgColor"].nodeValue
```

They may also be accessed using an usual ordinal number but DOM does not maintain any specific order for these attribute nodes.

`parentNode`

Returns the parent node of the context node. Note that `Document`, `DocumentFragment`, `Attr`, `Notation`, and `Entity` nodes do not have a parent and value of this property is `null`. Nodes that have just been created but not added to the tree or nodes that have been deleted have the value `null` for this property.

9.4 DOCUMENT NODE

It provides several useful properties that can be used to get the information about the XML document.

9.4.1 `Document` Node Properties

`documentElement`

This property of the `Document` node refers to the root node (document element) of the document tree. To navigate the document tree, we generally start from this `documentElement` node.

`docType`

It represents the Document Type Declaration for this document. Its value is `null` if there is no Document Type Declaration.

`documentURI`

It represents the location of the document. Its value is `null` if it is undefined or the document is created dynamically.

`domConfig`

Represents document configuration and maintains a table of recognized parameters. With the help of this property, one can create a new document with the specified configuration. The configuration includes removing the Comment and CDATASection nodes, normalizing the schema, canonicalizing the document, etc.

`inputEncoding`

Returns a string indicating the encoding scheme that was used during the parsing of this document.

`staticErrorChecking`

Indicates whether error checking was enabled or not.

`xmlEncoding`

The encoding (specified in the XML declaration) used in the XML document.

`xmlStandalone`

Indicates whether the document can exist independently or requires other resources.

`xmlVersion`

The version (specified in the XML declaration) used to write this XML document.

9.4.2 `Document` Node Methods

Since all kinds of nodes can only exist in the context of a document, the `Document` interface provides useful factory methods to create those objects. Each node has the attribute `ownerDocument`, which refers to the context document within which it was created.

`createAttribute`

This method creates and returns the `Attr` type node with the name specified. This attribute can then be set to an element using the `setAttribute` method available on the `Element` type node.

`createAttributeNS`

This method creates and returns the `Attr` type node with the name and namespace URI specified. This attribute can then be set to an element using the `setAttributeNS` method available on the `Element` type node.

`createCDATASection`

Creates and returns a `CDATASection` type node with the specified contained string.

`createComment`

Creates and returns a `Comment` type node with the specified comment string.

`createDocumentFragment`

Creates and returns an empty `DocumentFragment` node.

`createElement`

Creates and returns an `Element` type node with the specified element name.

`createElementNS`

Creates and returns an `Element` type node with the specified element name and namespace URI.

`createEntityReference`

Creates an `EntityReference` node with the specified node.

`createProcessingInstruction`

Creates a `ProcessingInstruction` node with the specified name and data string.

`createTextNode`

Creates and returns a `Text` type node with the specified text content.

`getElementById`

Returns the `Element` node having the specified id attribute.

`getElementsByTagName`

Returns a list of `Element` nodes with the specified element name.

`getElementsByTagNameNS`

Returns a list of `Element` nodes with the specified element name and namespace URI.

`importNode`

It imports a node from another document to this document. The node of the original document remains unchanged, instead a new copy is created and returned. Some nodes such as `Document`, `DocumentType`, cannot be imported. It takes a Boolean argument that specifies whether to perform deep copy or shallow copy.

`renameNode`

It renames an existing `Element` or `Attr` node. It takes three arguments: original name, new namespace URI, and a new qualified name.

9.5 ELEMENT NODE

It provides several useful properties and methods that can be used to get the information about the elements of the XML document.

9.5.1 `Element` Node Properties

`tagName`

It is a read-only property and is valid only for element type nodes. Its value is the tag name of the element. For example, for the `<p>` tag, its value is `P` and for `<body>`, its value is `BODY`

9.5.2 `Element` Node Methods

`getAttribute`

Returns the value of the attribute with the specified attribute name.

`getAttributeNS`

Returns the value of the attribute with the specified attribute name and namespace URI.

`getAttributeNode`

Returns the attribute node with the specified attribute name.

`getAttributeNodeNS`

Returns the attribute node with the specified attribute name and namespace URI.

`getElementsByTagName`

Returns a list of all descendant elements with a specified tag name.

`getElementsByTagNameNS`

Returns a list of all descendant elements with a specified tag name and namespace URI.

`hasAttribute`

Returns a Boolean value that specifies whether the context element has any attribute with the given attribute name.

`hasAttributeNS`

Returns a Boolean value that specifies whether the context element has any attribute with the given attribute name and namespace URI.

`removeAttribute`

Removes the attribute with the specified name.

`removeAttributeNS`

Removes the attribute with the specified name and namespace URI.

`removeAttributeNode`

Removes the specified attribute node.

`setAttribute`

Adds an attribute with the specified name and value. If the attribute is already present, its value is set by the new value.

`setAttributeNS`

Adds an attribute with the specified name and value and namespace URI. If the attribute is already present, its value is set by the new value and its prefix is changed to the new prefix.

`setAttributeNode`

Adds the specified attribute node to the content element. If an attribute with that name is already present, it is replaced by the new one.

`setAttributeNodeNS`

Adds the specified attribute node to the content element. If an attribute with that name and namespace URI is already present, it is replaced by the new one.

`setIdAttribute`

It takes two arguments, the name of an attribute and a Boolean value. If the value of the Boolean argument is `true`, this method declares the specified attribute as a user-determined ID attribute. Otherwise, it makes the specified attribute as a non-ID attribute.

`setIdAttributeNS`

It is same as `setIdAttribute`, except that it takes the namespace URI of the attribute as an argument.

`setIdAttributeNode`

It is same as `setIdAttribute`, except that it takes an attribute node instead of its name.

9.6 `TEXT` NODE

It provides several useful properties and methods that can be used to get information about the `Text` type nodes in an XML document.

9.6.1 `Text` Node Properties

`isElementContentWhiteSpace`

Returns a Boolean value indicating whether the text contains a character that is white space appearing within element content.

`wholeText`

It returns the text of this node and the text of all other logically-adjacent text nodes concatenated to it in document order.

9.6.2 `Text` Node Methods

`replaceWholeText`

It replaces the text of this node and text of all logically-adjacent text nodes with the specified text. Before replacement, it first removes current text node as well as all logically-adjacent text nodes unless they are recipient of the specified text.

`splitText`

Splits the node into two nodes. The original node contains text up to a specified offset. The new node contains the rest and is inserted as a next sibling of the original node. The new node is returned.

9.7 `ATTR` NODE

It provides several useful properties that can be used to get the information about the attributes of an element.

9.7.1 `Attr` Node Properties

`isId`

Indicates whether the attribute is an ID attribute.

`name`

Returns the name of the attribute.

`ownerElement`

The element node to which this attribute is attached.

`schemaTypeInfo`

The type information for this attribute.

`specified`

Indicates whether a value for this attribute was specified explicitly.

`value`

Returns the value of the attribute. If value contains any entity references, they are first substituted with their values.

9.8 JAVA AND DOM

In this section, we shall discuss how to access and manipulate an XML DOM tree using Java.

Java implements the W3C DOM specification as a separate package `org.w3c.dom`. Java provides interfaces and objects together with methods and properties according to the DOM specification that can be used to navigate and manipulate the DOM tree. Since Java supports data hiding, properties of an object as specified by the W3C are not exposed directly. Instead a `get` method for each property is provided. For the property `abc`, the name of the method is `getAbc()`. For example, for the property `firstChild`, it provides the method `getFirstChild()`.

Consider the following XML document "`greeting.xml`".

```
<?xml version="1.0"?>
<greeting>Hello World!</greeting>
```

The corresponding DOM tree is shown in Figure 9.3.

Figure 9.3 DOM tree for "greeting.xml"

9.8.1 Creating Document

To access the DOM tree for this XML document, you have to first create a `Document` object to put your XML into. To do this you have to first create an instance of the parser. The parser parses an XML document, checks well-formedness and creates and returns the `Document` object that represents the entire XML document. The following Java code creates an instance of the parser.

```
DocumentBuilderFactory factory = DocumentBuilderFactory.newInstance();
DocumentBuilder parser = factory.newDocumentBuilder();
```

The following packages must be imported.

```
import javax.xml.parsers.*;
import org.w3c.dom.*;
```

The parser is now ready to parse an XML document. The following overloaded methods are available that can be used to parse an XML document and to create a `Document` object.

```
Document parse(InputStream in)
Document parse(InputStream in, String base)
Document parse(String uri)
Document parse(File xmlFile)
```

The method that is commonly used takes the filename of an XML document. The following line of code parses and creates a `Document` object for the XML file `"greeting.xml"`.

```
Document doc = parser.parse("greeting.xml");
```

9.8.2 Navigating DOM Tree

A node in the DOM may be referenced in several ways. Broadly, we can categorize them as follows:

- Start from the `root` node and use structural relationships to reach other nodes.
- Use the `getElementById()` method of the `Document` object to access a particular node directly.
- Use the `getElementsByTagName()` method on the `Document` object to access all element nodes with a common tag name specified.

9.8.2.1 Using root node

Remember that W3C defined the property `documentElement` on the `Document` object that refers to the root element of the XML document. Java provides a method `getDocumentElement()` for the same.

```
Element root = doc.getDocumentElement();
```

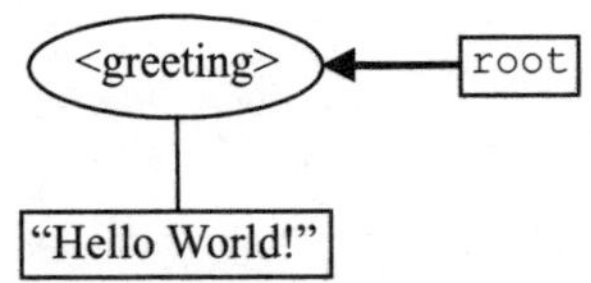

Figure 9.4 Document root

For this XML document, `root` refers [Figure 9.4] to the `<greeting>` element. You can also verify it by writing the following piece of code:

```
String name = root.getNodeName();
System.out.println(name);                //prints "greeting"
```

Now, suppose we want to get the text content of this element `<greeting>`. The text content of an element is stored in a separate node, which is a child node of this element node. Since, the `root` node has exactly one child, which is the first child of `root`, the `getFirstChild()` method may be used to get a reference to the text node as follows.

```
Node node = root.getFirstChild();
```

Since this node is a Text type node, this line of code could have been written like this:

```
Text node = (Text)root.getFirstChild();
```

The actual text content may be obtained as follows:

```
String txt = node.getNodeValue();
System.out.println(txt);                 //prints "Hello World!"
```

9.8.2.2 Getting all child nodes

So far we have considered a very simple XML document. Let us now take a more complex XML document `"questions.xml"` as follows.

```
<?xml version="1.0"?>
<question-paper>
   <question id="q1">What is DOM?</question>
   <question id="q2">What are leaves?</question>
</question-paper>
```

This XML document contains some questions. Suppose, we want to extract all questions from this XML file. To do this, get a reference to the root element `<question-paper>` using the procedure described in the previous section.

```
DocumentBuilderFactory factory = DocumentBuilderFactory.newInstance();
DocumentBuilder parser = factory.newDocumentBuilder();
Document doc = parser.parse("questions.xml");
Element root = doc.getDocumentElement();
//root refers to the <question-paper> element
```

The DOM tree corresponding to the XML document is shown in Figure 9.5.

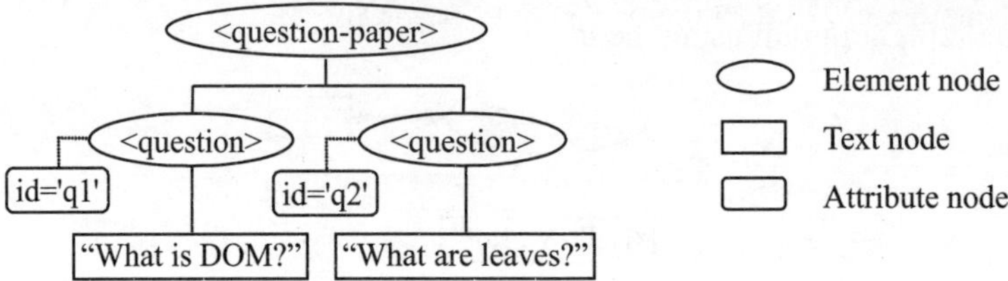

Figure 9.5 DOM tree for "questions.xml"

Let us have a list of all child nodes of this `<question-paper>` element as follows:

```
NodeList children = root.getChildNodes();    //get all child nodes of root
```

The object `children` now contains a list of child nodes of the `root` element, i.e., the `<question-paper>` element. Note that Java represents *new line* character as a `Text` type node also. So, the object `children` contains 3(three) `Element` nodes one for each `<question>` as well as 4 (four) `Text` nodes, one for each new line character in the `<question-paper>` element. You can verify by printing the length of the `children` list.

```
System.out.println(children.getLength());    //prints 7
```

Individual children can be obtained using the `item()` method on `children` and an index.

```
for(int i = 0; i < children.getLength(); i++) {
   Node node = children.item(i);
   if(node.getNodeType() == Node.ELEMENT_NODE) //if node is an Element node
      System.out.println(node.getFirstChild().getNodeValue());
}
```

Before applying the `getFirstChild()` method on a node, make sure that the node is an `Element` node and not a `Text` node.

```
if(node.getNodeType() == Node.ELEMENT_NODE)   //if node is an Element node
      System.out.println(node.getFirstChild().getNodeValue());
```

Here is the complete example.

```
import javax.xml.parsers.*;
import org.w3c.dom.*;
class GetQuestions {
   public static void main(String args[]) {
      try {
         DocumentBuilderFactory factory = DocumentBuilderFactory.newInstance();
         DocumentBuilder parser = factory.newDocumentBuilder();
         Document doc = parser.parse("questions.xml");
         Element root = doc.getDocumentElement();
         NodeList children = root.getChildNodes(); //get all children of root
         for(int i = 0; i < children.getLength(); i++) {
            Node node = children.item(i);
            if(node.getNodeType() == Node.ELEMENT_NODE)
               System.out.println(node.getFirstChild().getNodeValue());
         }
      }catch(Exception e) { e.printStackTrace(); }
   }
}
```

Compile the program using the usual procedure, i.e., using javac compiler as follows:

```
javac GetQuestions.java
```

If everything goes fine, this command generates a class file named `GetQuestions.class`. If you run this program on `"questions.xml"`, the output will look as shown in Figure 9.6.

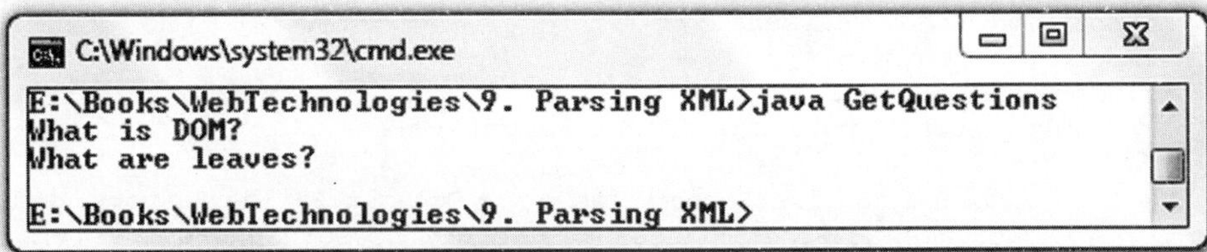

Figure 9.6 Displaying XML document using Java

9.8.2.3 Using getElementsByTagName

A list of elements having a tag name may be obtained using the `getElementsByTagName()` method on the `Document` object. So, a list of `<question>` elements may be obtained in a similar way as follows:

```
NodeList children = doc.getElementsByTagName("question");
```

Since the `<question>` elements are children of the `<question-paper>` element, the `getElementsByTagName()` method may also be invoked on the `root` element as follows:

```
NodeList children = root.getElementsByTagName("question");
```

Questions can now be obtained using a similar procedure.

```
for(int i = 0; i < children.getLength(); i++) {
   Node node = children.item(i);
   System.out.println(node.getFirstChild().getNodeValue());
}
```

However, since the nodes that we have obtained are all element (`<question>`) nodes, there is no need to check whether a node is an `Element` type node or not.

9.8.2.4 Using getElementById

To get a particular element using its unique id attribute, you need to declare a DTD or schema for it. Here is an example. We shall discuss DTD and schema in Chapters 8 and 9, respectively.

```
<?xml version="1.0"?>
<!DOCTYPE question-paper [
   <!ELEMENT question-paper (question+)>
   <!ELEMENT question (#PCDATA)>
   <!ATTLIST question id ID #REQUIRED>
]>
<question-paper>
   <question id="q1">What is DOM?</question>
   <question id="q2">What are leaves?</question>
</question-paper>
```

The method `getElementsById()` on the `Document` object is used to get an element with the specified id. So, a particular `<question>` element may be obtained as follows:

```
Element e = doc.getElementById("q1");
```

This line of code retrieves the element having the `id` attribute value "q1". Here is a complete example.

```
import javax.xml.parsers.*;
import org.w3c.dom.*;
class GetElementById {
   public static void main(String args[]) {
      try {
         DocumentBuilderFactory factory = DocumentBuilderFactory.newInstance();
         DocumentBuilder parser = factory.newDocumentBuilder();
         Document doc = parser.parse("questions.xml");
         Element e = doc.getElementById("q1");
         String value = e.getAttribute("id");
         System.out.print(value + ". "); //print question number
         System.out.println(e.getFirstChild().getNodeValue()); //print question
      }catch(Exception e) { e.printStackTrace(); }
   }
}
```

If you run this program on `"questions.xml"`, the output will look as shown in Figure 9.7.

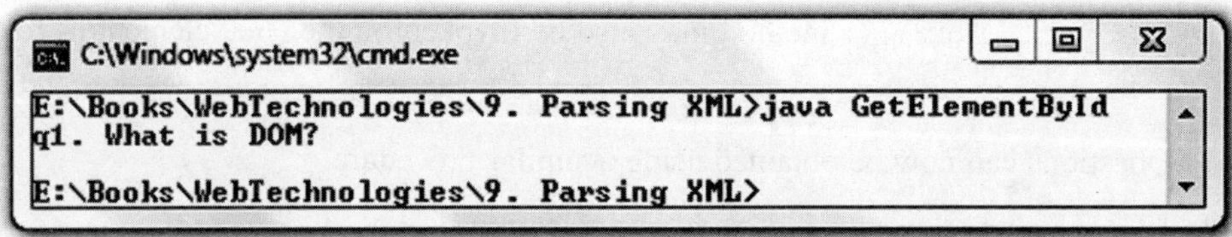

Figure 9.7 Finding an element using the getElementById() method

9.8.2.5 Getting attributes of an element

Attributes of an element are obtained using the following method:

```
NamedNodeMap getAttributes()
```

The object returned by the `getAttributes()` method contains all attributes for the context element. Individual attributes may be obtained using the `item()` method and an index. The name and value of an attribute may be obtained using the `getNodeName()` and `getNodeValue()` methods, respectively. The following example prints all attributes (and their values) of an element node.

```
NamedNodeMap attributes = node.getAttributes(); //get all attributes of node
for(int j = 0; j < attributes.getLength(); j++) { //for each attribute
   Node attribute = attributes.item(j);          //get attribute node
   String attName = attribute.getNodeName();     //get attribute name
   String attValue = attribute.getNodeValue();   //get attribute value
   System.out.println(attName + " = " + attValue); //print them
}
```

Getting a particular attribute using this procedure is not useful as Java does not maintain any specific order of attributes in the list. Moreover, it is not efficient as you need to iterate through the entire list to get the value of a particular attribute. For example, if you want to get the value of the attribute "no", the corresponding code will look like this.

```
NamedNodeMap attributes = node.getAttributes(); //get all attributes of node
String attValue = "";
for(int j = 0; j < attributes.getLength(); j++) { //for each attribute
   Node attribute = attributes.item(j);          //get attribute node
   String attName = attribute.getNodeName();     //get attribute name
   if(attName.equals("no"))
      attValue = attribute.getNodeValue();       //get attribute value
}
System.out.println(attName + " = " + attValue); //print it
```

Java provides a straightforward solution to achieve this. The value of a specific attribute may be obtained using the following method on the element node.

```
String getAttribute(String attributeName);
```

The following line of code returns the value of the attribute `no` on the element node. Note that the `getAttribute()` method is defined on the `Element` object. So, you need to typecast the `Node` object to the `Element` object first and then apply the `getAttribute()` method. Make sure that the node is really an `Element` type node. Otherwise, a `ClassCastException` will be thrown.

```
String value = ((Element)node).getAttribute("no");
```

If the node is really an `Element` type node, this method can be invoked directly without typecasting.

```
String value = e.getAttribute("no");
```

Here is the complete example.

```
import javax.xml.parsers.*;
import org.w3c.dom.*;
class GetAttributes {
   public static void main(String args[]) {
      try {
         DocumentBuilderFactory factory = DocumentBuilderFactory.newInstance();
         DocumentBuilder parser = factory.newDocumentBuilder();
         Document doc = parser.parse("questions.xml");
         Element root = doc.getDocumentElement();
         NodeList children = root.getElementsByTagName("question");
         for (int i = 0; i < children.getLength(); i++) {
            Node node = children.item(i);
            String value = ((Element)node).getAttribute("no");
            System.out.print(value + ". "); //print question number
            System.out.println(node.getFirstChild().getNodeValue());
         }
      }catch(Exception e) { e.printStackTrace(); }
   }
}
```

If you run this program on `"questions.xml"`, the output will look as shown in Figure 9.8.

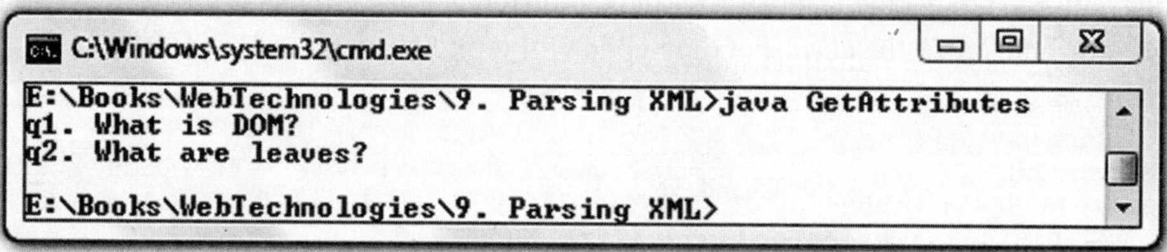

Figure 9.8 Getting attributes of an element

9.8.2.6 Viewing DOM

A DOM tree may be transformed back to an XML document which can then be displayed on the screen or stored in a file. This helps us to visualize and verify the DOM tree after adding or deleting nodes.

```
TransformerFactory tFactory = TransformerFactory.newInstance();
Transformer transformer = tFactory.newTransformer();
DOMSource source = new DOMSource(root);
StreamResult result = new StreamResult(System.out);
transformer.transform(source, result);
```

Here, we first create a `Transformer` object and a `DOMSource` object. The task of the `Transformer` object, as the name implies, is to transform the specified XML document to the specified stream. We want to display the result after transformation to the standard output. So, `System.out` is used to create the result object.

The following packages must be imported.

```
import javax.xml.transform.*;
import javax.xml.transform.dom.DOMSource;
import javax.xml.transform.stream.StreamResult;
```

Here is a program that displays the content of the `questions.xml` file on the terminal window.

```
import javax.xml.parsers.*;
import org.w3c.dom.*;
import javax.xml.transform.*;
import javax.xml.transform.dom.DOMSource;
import javax.xml.transform.stream.StreamResult;
class View {
   public static void main(String args[]) {
      try {
         DocumentBuilderFactory factory = DocumentBuilderFactory.newInstance();
         DocumentBuilder parser = factory.newDocumentBuilder();
         Document doc = parser.parse("questions.xml");
         Element root = doc.getDocumentElement();
         TransformerFactory tFactory = TransformerFactory.newInstance();
         Transformer transformer = tFactory.newTransformer();
         DOMSource source = new DOMSource(root);
         StreamResult result = new StreamResult(System.out);
         transformer.transform(source, result);
```

```
        }catch(Exception e) {e.printStackTrace();}
    }
}
```

It generates the output as shown in Figure 9.9.

```
C:\Windows\system32\cmd.exe
E:\Books\WebTechnologies\9. Parsing XML>java View
<?xml version="1.0" encoding="UTF-8"?><question-paper>
        <question id="q1">What is DOM?</question>
        <question id="q2">What are leaves?</question>
</question-paper>
E:\Books\WebTechnologies\9. Parsing XML>
```

Figure 9.9 Viewing DOM

To write the DOM tree to a file, simply create the `result` object from a file as follows:

```
FileOutputStream out = new FileOutputStream(new File("out.xml"));
StreamResult result = new StreamResult(out);
```

Figure 9.10 shows the transformation from a DOM tree to an XML document.

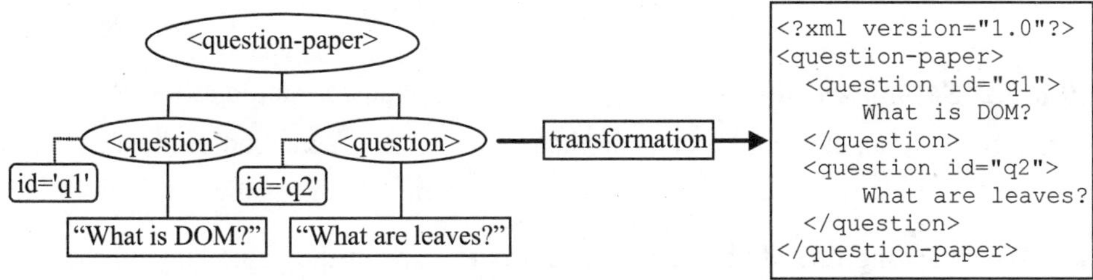

Figure 9.10 DOM tree to XML document transformation

To create a string from a DOM tree use the following code.

```
StringWriter sw = new StringWriter();
StreamResult result = new StreamResult(sw);
DOMSource source = new DOMSource(root);
transformer.transform(source, result);
String xmlString = sw.toString();
```

The variable `xmlString` now contains the XML document as a string which can be processed further.

9.8.3 Manipulating DOM Tree

So far we have navigated the DOM tree. Let us now discuss how to add, delete, or modify nodes in the DOM tree. We shall use the notation shown in Figure 9.11 to describe the result of different codes that will be used in this section.

Element node Text node Attribute node Association Parent–child relation

Figure 9.11 Notations used

9.8.3.1 Creating a node

A `Text` type node is created using the `createTextNode()` method on the `Document` node.

```
Text createTextNode(String text)
```

It takes the content of the `Text` node as a string argument. The following line of code creates a `Text` type node with the text "What is DTD?". Pictorially, the result of this code is shown on the right-hand side.

```
Text txt = doc.createTextNode("What is DTD?");
```

"What is DTD?"

The node `txt` just created does not have any meaning unless it is attached to an `Element` node. Before attaching this `Text` node to an `Element` node, let us create an `Element` node first. An `Element` node is created using the `createElement()` method.

```
Element createElement(String elementName)
```

It takes the name of the element to be created as an argument. The following line of code creates a `<question>` element. The result is shown on the right-hand side pictorially.

```
Element e = doc.createElement("question");
```

<question>

9.8.3.2 Setting an attribute

An attribute of an element is set using the `setAttribute()` method of the element node.

```
setAttribute(String attributeName, String attributeValue)
```

The following line of code adds the attribute `id` with the value "q3" to the newly created element `e`.

```
e.setAttribute("id", "q3");
```

<question>
id='q3'

The result after attaching an attribute to the nodes now become as shown on the right-hand side.

9.8.3.3 Adding a node

The `Text` node `txt` can now be attached to the `Element` node `e` using the `appendChild()` method.

```
e.appendChild(txt);
```

Finally, the `Element` node e (together with txt) is attached to the root element at the end.

```
root.appendChild(e);
```

The `appendChild()` method adds a node to the context node at the end of the child list. The element `e` does not have any child so far. So, the node `txt` will become the first child of `e`. The resultant DOM tree is shown in Figure 9.12.

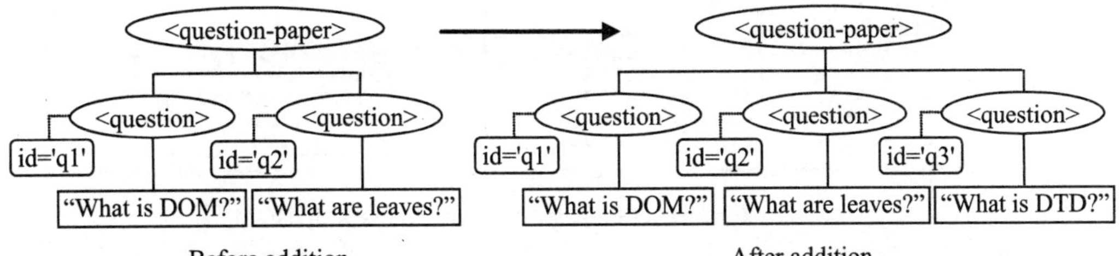

Figure 9.12 DOM tree after adding a <question> element at the end

The complete program is as follows:

```
import javax.xml.parsers.*;
import org.w3c.dom.*;
import javax.xml.transform.*;
import javax.xml.transform.dom.DOMSource;
import javax.xml.transform.stream.StreamResult;
class AppendQuestion {
   public static void main(String args[]) {
      try {
         DocumentBuilderFactory factory = DocumentBuilderFactory.newInstance();
         DocumentBuilder parser = factory.newDocumentBuilder();
         Document doc = parser.parse("questions.xml");
         Element root = doc.getDocumentElement();
         TransformerFactory tFactory = TransformerFactory.newInstance();
         Transformer transformer = tFactory.newTransformer();
         DOMSource source = new DOMSource(root);
         StreamResult result = new StreamResult(System.out);
         System.out.println("Before addition");
         transformer.transform(source, result);
         Text txt = doc.createTextNode("What is DTD?");
         Element e = doc.createElement("question");
         e.appendChild(txt);
         e.setAttribute("id", "q3");
         root.appendChild(e);
         System.out.println("\nAfter addition");
         transformer.transform(source, result);
      }catch(Exception e) {e.printStackTrace();}
   }
}
```

The program first displays the XML document before adding a `<question>` element. It then adds a `<question>` element at the end and displays the modified XML document. If you run this program on `"questions.xml"`, the output will look as shown in Figure 9.13.

```
C:\Windows\system32\cmd.exe
Before addition
<?xml version="1.0" encoding="UTF-8"?><question-paper>
        <question id="q1">What is DOM?</question>
        <question id="q2">What are leaves?</question>
</question-paper>
After addition
<?xml version="1.0" encoding="UTF-8"?><question-paper>
        <question id="q1">What is DOM?</question>
        <question id="q2">What are leaves?</question>
<question id="q3">What is DTD?</question></question-paper>
E:\Books\WebTechnologies\9. Parsing XML>
```

Figure 9.13 Adding a node to the XML DOM

9.8.3.4 Inserting a node

The method `appendChild()` appends a node at the end of the list of child nodes. If you want to insert a node at any other position, use the following method.

```
insertBefore(Node newNode, Node referenceNode)
```

This method inserts a node before a reference node. So, with the help of `appendChild()` and `insertBefore()`, we can effectively place a node at any position in the child node list. The following code inserts the new `<question>` node after the first `<question>`. The resultant DOM tree is shown in Figure 9.14.

```
NodeList questions = doc.getElementsByTagName("question"); //get all questions
Node firstQuestion = questions.item(0);                     //get first question
root.insertBefore(e, firstQuestion);                 //insert before first question
```

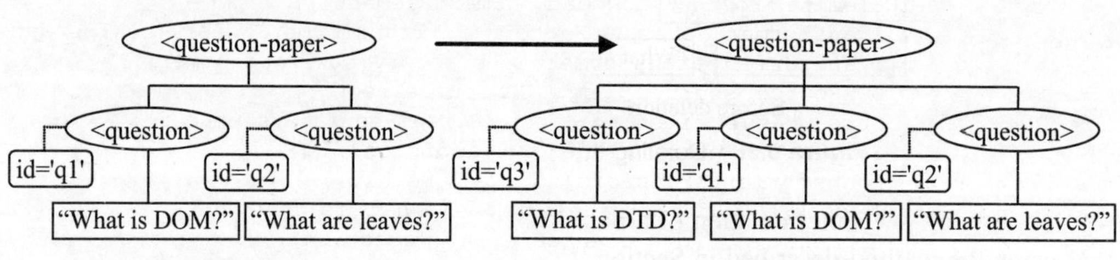

Figure 9.14 DOM tree after inserting a <question> element at the beginning

Let us now insert a `<question>` element after the first `<question>` element. Note that inserting after the first `<question>` element also implies inserting it before the second `<question>` element. The following piece of code inserts a `<question>` element after the first question using this concept.

```
NodeList questions = doc.getElementsByTagName("question"); //get all questions
Node firstQuestion = questions.item(0).getNextSibling();  //get first question
Node secondQuestion = firstQuestion.getNextSibling();  //get second question
root.insertBefore(e, secondQuestion);               //insert before second question
```

The resultant DOM tree is shown in Figure 9.15.

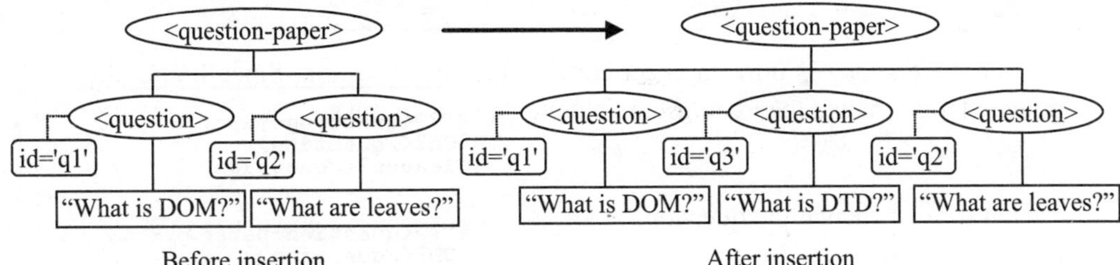

Figure 9.15 DOM tree after inserting a <question> element after the first question

9.8.3.5 Deleting a node

To delete a node from the DOM tree, we use the following method on its parent node.

```
Node removeChild(Node node)
```

If a node is deleted, the entire sub-tree rooted at this node is also deleted. It returns the root of the sub-tree deleted. The following line of code removes the first `<question>` element from the DOM tree. The effect of deleting the node is shown in Figure 9.16.

```
NodeList questions = doc.getElementsByTagName("question");  //get all questions
Node firstQuestion = questions.item(0);                     //get first question
root.removeChild(firstQuestion);                            //remove it
```

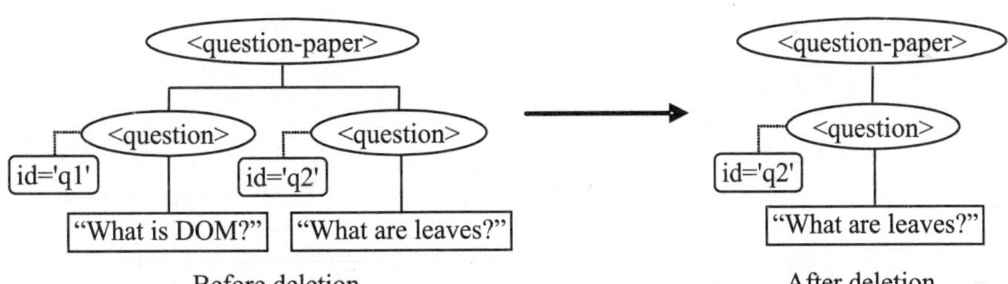

Figure 9.16 Deleting the first <question> element from DOM tree

To verify whether deletion of a node works or not, the modified DOM tree can be viewed using the method described in Section 9.8.2.6.

9.8.3.6 Cloning a node

An exact copy of a node is created using the `cloneNode()` method on the `Node` interface.

```
cloneNode(boolean deepCopy)
```

It takes a single argument, which indicates whether to perform deep copy or shallow copy. If `true` is specified, the entire sub-tree rooted at the context node is copied recursively. Let us first obtain a reference of the first question.

```
NodeList questions = doc.getElementsByTagName("question");
```

We now clone the node.

```
Node aCopy = questions.item(0).cloneNode(true);
```

The node `aCopy` is now an exact copy of the first question. Since the id attribute must be unique, let us change the id attribute value to "q3" as follows.

```
((Element)aCopy).setAttribute("id", "q3");
```

Let us also change the question.

```
((Text)aCopy.getFirstChild()).replaceWholeText("What is XML?");
```

Finally, let us append the questions at the end.

```
root.appendChild(aCopy);
```

Here is the complete example.

```
import javax.xml.parsers.*;
import org.w3c.dom.*;
import javax.xml.transform.*;
import javax.xml.transform.dom.DOMSource;
import javax.xml.transform.stream.StreamResult;
class CopyQuestion {
   public static void main(String args[]) {
      try {
         DocumentBuilderFactory factory = DocumentBuilderFactory.newInstance();
         DocumentBuilder parser = factory.newDocumentBuilder();
         Document doc = parser.parse("questions.xml");
         Element root = doc.getDocumentElement();

         TransformerFactory tFactory = TransformerFactory.newInstance();
         Transformer transformer = tFactory.newTransformer();
         DOMSource source = new DOMSource(root);
         StreamResult result = new StreamResult(System.out);

         System.out.println("Before addition");
         transformer.transform(source, result);

         NodeList questions = doc.getElementsByTagName("question");
         Node aCopy = questions.item(0).cloneNode(true);
         ((Element)aCopy).setAttribute("id", "q3");
         ((Text)aCopy.getFirstChild()).replaceWholeText("What is XML?");
         root.appendChild(aCopy);

         System.out.println("\nAfter addition");
         transformer.transform(source, result);
      }catch(Exception e) {e.printStackTrace();}
   }
}
```

The resultant DOM tree is shown in Figure 9.17.

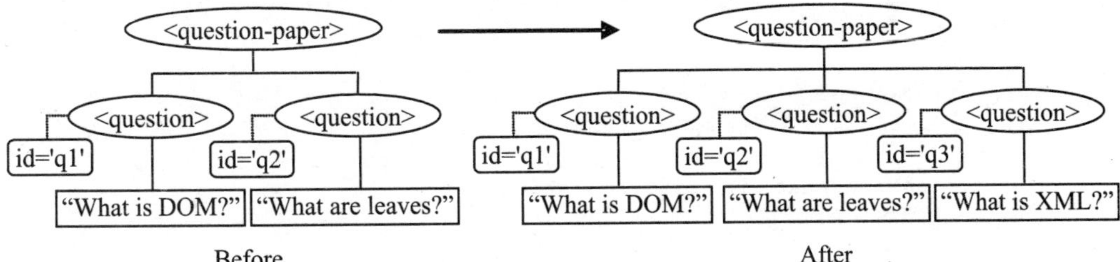

Figure 9.17 Cloning and appending a question

If you run this program on `"questions.xml"`, the output will look as shown in Figure 9.18.

```
C:\Windows\system32\cmd.exe
E:\Books\WebTechnologies\9. Parsing XML>java CopyQuestion
Before addition
<?xml version="1.0" encoding="UTF-8"?><question-paper>
        <question id="q1">What is DOM?</question>
        <question id="q2">What are leaves?</question>
</question-paper>
After addition
<?xml version="1.0" encoding="UTF-8"?><question-paper>
        <question id="q1">What is DOM?</question>
        <question id="q2">What are leaves?</question>
<question id="q3">What is XML?</question></question-paper>
E:\Books\WebTechnologies\9. Parsing XML>
```

Figure 9.18 Cloning a node in the DOM tree

9.8.4 Java DTD validation

Java also provides interfaces to validate an internal DTD. The following program takes an XML file containing DTD as the command line argument and checks whether the document has been written according to the DTD specification. It displays a diagnostic message if an error occurs.

```
import org.w3c.dom.*;
import javax.xml.parsers.*;
public class DTDValidator {
   public static void main(String args[]) {
      try {
         DocumentBuilderFactory factory = DocumentBuilderFactory.newInstance();
         factory.setValidating(true);
         DocumentBuilder parser = factory.newDocumentBuilder();
         Document doc = parser.parse(args[0]);
      }catch(Exception e) {System.out.println(e);}
   }
}
```

Consider the following xml file "ques.xml":

```
<?xml version="1.0"?>
<!DOCTYPE question-paper [
   <!ELEMENT question-paper (question+)>
   <!ELEMENT question (#PCDATA)>
```

```
    <!ATTLIST question id ID #REQUIRED>

]>
<question-paper>
    <question id="q1">What is DOM?</question>
    <question id="q2">What are leaves?</question>
    <question>What is DTD?</question>
</question-paper>
```

This XML document does not satisfy the DTD specification. DTD tells that every `<question>` element must have an attribute "id", but no "id" attribute is specified for the last question.

If this XML document is fed to our DTD validator, it will display error messages as shown in Figure 9.19.

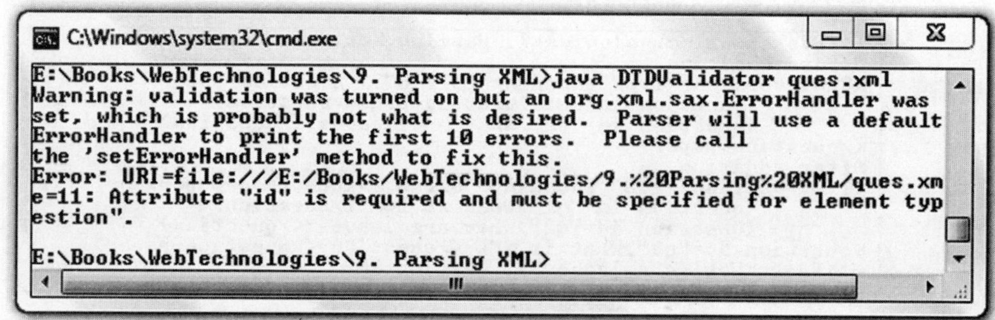

Figure 9.19 XML document validation against DTD

Java also provides interfaces to validate an XML document against an XML schema. The following program takes two arguments: an XML document and an XML schema and performs validation.

```
import java.io.File;
import javax.xml.parsers.*;
import javax.xml.transform.dom.DOMSource;
import javax.xml.validation.Schema;
import javax.xml.validation.SchemaFactory;
import javax.xml.validation.Validator;
import javax.xml.XMLConstants;
import org.w3c.dom.Document;
public class SchemaValidator {
    public static void main(String args[]) {
        try {
            String xmlFile = args[0], schemaFile = args[1];
            // build an XSD-aware SchemaFactory
            SchemaFactory schemaFactory = SchemaFactory.newInstance
            ( XMLConstants.W3C_XML_SCHEMA_NS_URI );

            // get the xsd schema specifying the required format for the XML files.
            Schema schemaXSD = schemaFactory.newSchema( new File ( schemaFile ) );

            // Get a Validator that can validate XML files according to the schema.
```

```
            Validator validator = schemaXSD.newValidator();

            DocumentBuilderFactory factory = DocumentBuilderFactory.newInstance();
            // Get a parser capable of parsing XML into a DOM tree
            DocumentBuilder parser = factory.newDocumentBuilder();

            // parse the XML purely as XML and get a DOM tree represenation.
            Document document = parser.parse( new File( xmlFile ) );

            // parse the XML DOM tree againts the XSD schema
            validator.validate( new DOMSource( document ) );
        } catch (Exception e) {
            e.printStackTrace();
        }
    }
}
```

KEY WORDS

Attr: An `Attr` type node represents an attribute of an `Element` node.

CDATASection: This type of node represents a CDATA section in the XML document.

Cloning: Creating an exact copy of an existing node in the DOM tree.

Comment: It represents a comment in an XML document.

Document: The W3C Document type node represents an entire XML document. Only one Document type node exists for each XML document.

DocumentFragment: `DocumentFragment` is a "lightweight" or "minimal" `Document` object that represents a portion of a document.

DocumentType: It provides interfaces to get the information about the document including the list of entities defined for the document.

DOM Core: This portion defines the basic set of interfaces and objects for any structured documents.

DOM tree: DOM models a document as a hierarchical structure consisting of different kinds of nodes, which constitute the DOM tree.

DOM: Document Object Model (DOM) is a language-neutral and platform-independent object model used to represent XML documents.

Element: This interface represents an element in the XML document.

Entity: It represents a known, either unparsed or parsed entity.

HTML DOM: This part defines interfaces and objects for HTML documents only.

Node: It represents a component of an XML document.

Parsing: A procedure for creating a DOM tree from an XML document.

Text: It represents the textual content of an `Element` type node.

XML DOM: This part specifies the standard set of objects and interfaces for XML documents only.

XML Validation: A procedure to verify whether an XML document is written according to the constraints specified in a DTD or a schema.

SUMMARY

Document Object Model (DOM) is a language-neutral and platform-independent object model used to represent XML documents. DOM is standardized by the World Wide Web Consortium (W3C). The W3C DOM specification is divided into three major parts: DOM Core, XML DOM, and HTML DOM.

DOM models a document as a hierarchical structure consisting of different kinds of nodes. Each of these nodes represents a specific portion of the document.

The primary objective of DOM is to identify

- interfaces and objects to be used to represent, access, and manipulate documents.
- semantics of those objects and interfaces including both attributes and behavior.
- collaboration and relationship among these objects and interfaces.

Nodes in a DOM tree have structural relationships among them. The topmost node is the root node. DOM tree consists of many types of nodes. The primary node types are `Node`, `Element`, `Document`, `Text`, `Attr`, and `Entity`.

The primary data type for the entire DOM is the Node interface. Every other kind of node inherits all the properties and methods of the Node interface. Some properties of the Node interface are read-only. Others are read–write. Notable properties are `childNodes`, `nodeType`, `nodeName`, `nodeValue`, `firstChild`, `lastChild`, `nextSibling`, `previousSibling`, etc. Java provides a read method for each of these properties.

The `Document` node is another important type node, which represents an entire XML document. It provides several useful properties and methods that can be used to navigate the DOM tree.

The `Element` type represents an element of an XML document. DOM provides a set of useful properties and methods on this type of nodes.

Java implements the W3C DOM specification as a separate package, org.w3c.dom. Java provides interfaces and objects together with methods and properties according to the DOM specification that can be used to navigate and manipulate the DOM tree.

A node in the DOM may be referenced in several ways. Broadly, we can categorize them as follows:

- Start from the root node and use structural relationships to reach other nodes.
- Use the `getElementById()` method of the `Document` object to access a particular node directly.
- Use the `getElementsByTagName()` method on the `Document` object to access all element nodes with the common tag name specified.

A DOM tree may be transformed back to an XML document, which can then be displayed on the screen or can be stored in a file. This helps us to visualize and verify the DOM tree after adding or deleting nodes.

Java also provides interfaces to validate an XML document against an internal DTD or an XML schema.

WEB RESOURCES

`http://java.sun.com/j2se/1.4.2/docs/api/org/w3c/dom/package-summary.html`
Package org.w3c.dom

`http://java.sun.com/j2ee/1.4/docs/tutorial/doc/JAXPDOM.html`
Document Object Model

`http://java.sun.com/j2se/1.4.2/docs/guide/plugin/dom/index.html`
Common DOM API

`http://developers.sun.com/sw/building/codesamples/dom/index.html`
Java API for XML Processing API (JAXP) Using DOM

`http://www.ibm.com/developerworks/xml/library/x-domjava/`
Effective XML processing with DOM and XPath in Java

`http://www.java2s.com/Code/Java/XML/DOM-Edit.htm`
Java and DOM

EXERCISES

Multiple Choice Questions

1. What is the full form of DOM?
   (a) Dynamic Object Model
   (b) Distributed Object Model
   (c) Document Object Model
   (d) Dense Object Model

2. How many parts are there in the W3C DOM specification?
   (a) 2 (b) 3 (c) 4 (d) 5

3. What is the number of parent nodes that a node in the DOM tree can have?
   (a) 1 (b) 2 (c) 3 (d) 4

4. How many `Document` nodes does a DOM tree have?
   (a) 1 (b) 2 (c) 3 (d) 4

5. Which of the following is used to inspect the type of a node?
   (a) type (b) typeOfNode
   (c) nodeType (d) getNodeType

6. What is the value of the `nodeName` attribute for a `Text` node?
   (a) $text (b) text# (c) #text# (d) #text

7. What is the value of `nodeType` attribute for a `Text` node?
   (a) 1 (b) 2 (c) 3 (d) 4

8. Which of the following has a valid `nodeValue` attribute?
   (a) Element (b) Attr
   (c) Entity (d) Document

9. Which of the following has `childNodes` attributes?
   (a) Attr (b) Text
   (c) Entity (d) Element

10. Nodes having a common parent are called
    (a) Child (b) Parent
    (c) Sibling (d) Descendant

11. Which of the following refers to the root element of an XML document?
    (a) Document (b) documentElement
    (c) Root (d) rootElement

12. Which of the following methods is used to create an `Element` type node?
    (a) newElement() (b) getElement()
    (c) createElement() (d) element()

13. Which of the following methods is used to create a `Text` type node?
    (a) createText() (b) newTextNode()
    (c) newText() (d) createTextNode()

14. Which of the following methods is used to create an `Attr` type node?
    (a) createAttribute() (b) createAttr()
    (c) newAttribute() (d) newAttr()

15. Which of the following is used to add an attribute to an `Element` node?
    (a) setAttr() (b) setAttribute()
    (c) addAttribute() (d) addAttr()

16. Which of the following methods is used to get a particular element?
    (a) getElementsByTagName()
    (b) returnElementById()
    (c) getElementById()
    (d) getElement()

17. Which of the following attributes returns the name of an element?
    (a) elementName (b) name
    (c) tagName (d) getName

18. Which of the following methods is used to instruct the parser to validate an XML document against a DTD?
    (a) setValidating() (b) validate()
    (c) doValidate() (d) getValidating()

19. Which of the following methods is used to parse an XML document?
    (a) doParse() (b) parse()
    (c) parseXML() (d) parseXMLDoc()

20. Which of the following methods is used to clone a node?
    (a) doClone() (b) cloneNode()
    (c) clone() (d) doCloneNode()

Review Questions

1. How do you add a node at the beginning of a list of child nodes?
2. Discuss how to obtain all attributes of an `element` node.
3. How do you add a node at the end of a list of child nodes?
4. Describe how to save a DOM tree in a file.
5. Write a program to display the content of a DOM tree.
6. What is the difference between shallow clone and deep clone?

7. Describe the procedure for validating XML documents against a DTD.
8. Describe the procedure for validating XML documents against a schema.
9. Discuss with examples the difference between the `nextSibling` and `previousSibling` properties.
10. Discuss with examples the difference between the `firstChild` and `lastChild` properties.

10 XPATH

Key Objectives

After completing this chapter readers will be able to—

- understand the importance of XPath
- know the structure of an XPath expression
- learn absolute and relative XPath expressions
- learn the structure of location path and location step
- write XPath expressions to retrieve information from XML documents
- know different XPath operators used to form complex XPath expressions
- get an idea about the built-in functions provided by XPath

10.1 INTRODUCTION

DOM allows application programs to navigate XML documents. However, it seems to be difficult to retrieve information from an XML document. It is not easy for an application program working in a portion of a document to refer to attributes or elements in another portion of the same document. For example, if an application, currently working on a `student` node, wants to list the `marks` of that student, it has to traverse probably the entire document tree.

Moreover, DOM does not also allow using semantic relationships to address nodes or node sets. For example, to find out all `subject` elements whose `deptId` attribute is "Information Technology", an application programmer has to write a complex and long tree traversal code. So, the way DOM allows application programs to traverse a document tree is not a general technique. Instead, a simple, straightforward technique is needed to traverse and access nodes in an XML document tree. The use of such a technique can simplify and shorten application code significantly. Programmers can write their potential solutions using smaller, compact, and convenient expressions, instead of writing tedious and long traversal and access codes.

XPath is a simple text-based and language-neutral technique, standardized by the W3C and used to navigate XML documents. XPath is a query language for XML documents, as opposed to

SQL for relational databases. XPath is the most common of many XML Path languages. Its primary purpose is to select elements, attributes, and other information from XML documents using implementation-independent XPath expressions. The real power of XML is not in storing the data, but in the ability to use XPath expressions to retrieve complex subsets of data. In addition to this, it also provides rich sets of interfaces to manipulate numbers, strings, and Booleans. XPath is used in various technologies such as XSLT, XQuery, and XPointer, etc.

10.2 XPATH FLAVORS

The first version, 1.0, of XPath was released by the W3C on November 16, 1999. Most languages and platforms support XPath 1.0. After great success and popularity, the W3C introduced a modified version, XPath 2.0, in 2007. This was necessary as XPath 1.0 supports only four expression types: node-set (unordered), Boolean, number (floating-point), and string. The second version was fairly simple in usage, however, limited in case of type values such as dates.

XPath 2.0 was an effort to provide more functionality especially for XSLT and XQuery. It supports all W3C XML schema primitive types. XPath 2.0 is backward-compatible with XPath 1.0. In this version, a number of new operators, functions, and a number of new facilities including looping, set manipulation, conditional expression, and aggregate functions were introduced.

An exhaustive search reveals that XPath 1.0 and XPath 2.0 have the same basic definition with a notable difference. Everything that can be written in XPath 2.0 is an *expression*. The result of an expression is an ordered sequence of items instead of the unordered node sets in XPath 1.0. In this book, we shall discuss facilities and constructs provided by XPath 2.0.

10.2.1 XPath 2.0 and XQuery 1.0

XPath is not an independent query language. It was designed to work with other XML languages, particularly with XSLT 1.0. There are other query languages for XML documents. XQuery 1.0 is one such query language used frequently. XPath 2.0 is a subset of XQuery 1.0. However, XPath covers almost everything in XQuery 1.0. You will realize after you have gone through XPath 2.0 that you have almost completed learning XQuery 1.0.

10.3 XPATH DOCUMENT REPRESENTATION

In XPath, an XML document is represented by a tree of nodes instead of a surface syntax. The tree consists of seven kinds of nodes: *element*, *attribute*, *text*, *namespace*, *processing-instruction*, *comment*, and *document* node. Each node in the tree represents a component of the XML document. For example, an element in the XML document is represented by an *element* node. Similarly, other components are represented by the corresponding nodes. Following is a brief description of the XPath document tree:

- The topmost node is the *root* node, which, represents the entire XML document.
- Only element nodes and the root node can have zero or more *child* nodes.
- Every node except the root node has exactly one *parent* node.

- Nodes that have common parent are called *siblings*.
- *Ancestors* of a context node are nodes that include the node's parent, parent's parent, and so on.
- *Descendants* of a context node are nodes that are children of the context node, children's children, and so on.

10.4 XPATH AXES

Each node in an XPath tree has structural relationships with others. For example, an element node (except root) has one parent and has a parent–child relationship. Similarly, two element nodes may have a common parent, which indicates a sibling relationship. XPath uses these structural relationships to navigate information from an XML document. XPath represents each of these relationships as a component called *axis*. This axis basically determines the direction of node selection with respect to the current node, called *context node*.

There are two types of axes: *forward* axis and *reverse* axis. An axis that represents nodes after the context node is called forward axis. Otherwise, the axis is called reverse axis. The axis `following` is an example of the forward axis, whereas the axis `ancestor` is a reverse axis.

Nodes are processed in document order. More explicitly, the document tree is processed using a left-to-right preorder traversal, which is the same as the order in the textual representation of the XML document. If the children and siblings of a node are included in an axis (i.e., descendant, descendant-or-self), children nodes are processed before its following siblings. This is because children nodes precede the following sibling nodes. For reverse axes, this order is a little bit tricky.

The list of axes with their meaning as provided by XPath is given in Table 10.1.

Table 10.1 XPath axes

Axis	Meaning
parent	Parent of the context node (abbreviated as '..')
child	All children of element context node (the default axis)
ancestor	Context node's parent, grand parent, and so on
ancestor-or-self	Context node as well as its ancestors
descendant	Element context node's children, grand children, and so on
descendant-or-self	Context node as well as its descendants (abbreviated as '//')
following	Everything after context node
preceding	Everything before context node
following-sibling	All siblings that occur after context node
preceding-sibling	All siblings that occur before context node
self	Context node (abbreviated as '.')
attribute	All attributes of the context node (abbreviated as '@')
namespace	Namespace nodes of context node

To understand XPath and to write different expressions, we shall use the following XML document. This XML document contains information about hard disks and monitors from different manufacturers.

```
<?xml version='1.0'?>
<store xmlns:xsi='http://www.w3.org/2001/XMLSchema-instance'>
   <HDD type='ATA'>
      <make>Samsung</make>
      <capacity>80</capacity>
      <speed>7200</speed>
      <price>1600</price>
   </HDD>
   <HDD type='SATA'>
      <make>Samsung</make>
      <capacity>160</capacity>
      <speed>7200</speed>
      <price>2200</price>
   </HDD>
   <HDD type='SATA'>
      <make>Seagate</make>
      <capacity>80</capacity>
      <speed>7200</speed>
      <price>1600</price>
   </HDD>
   <monitor type='LCD' color='yes'>
      <make>LG</make>
      <price>7500</price>
      <size>15</size>
      <resolution>1280x800</resolution>
   </monitor>
   <monitor type='LCD' color='yes'>
      <make>Samsung</make>
      <price>8000</price>
      <size>17</size>
      <resolution>1280x800</resolution>
   </monitor>
   <monitor type='CRT' color='yes'>
      <make>LG</make>
      <price>4000</price>
      <size>15</size>
      <resolution>1024x768</resolution>
   </monitor>
   <monitor type='CRT' color='no'>
      <make>LG</make>
      <price>3500</price>
      <size>15</size>
      <resolution>1024x768</resolution>
   </monitor>
</store>
```

The meaning of different XPath axes is shown in Figure 10.1.

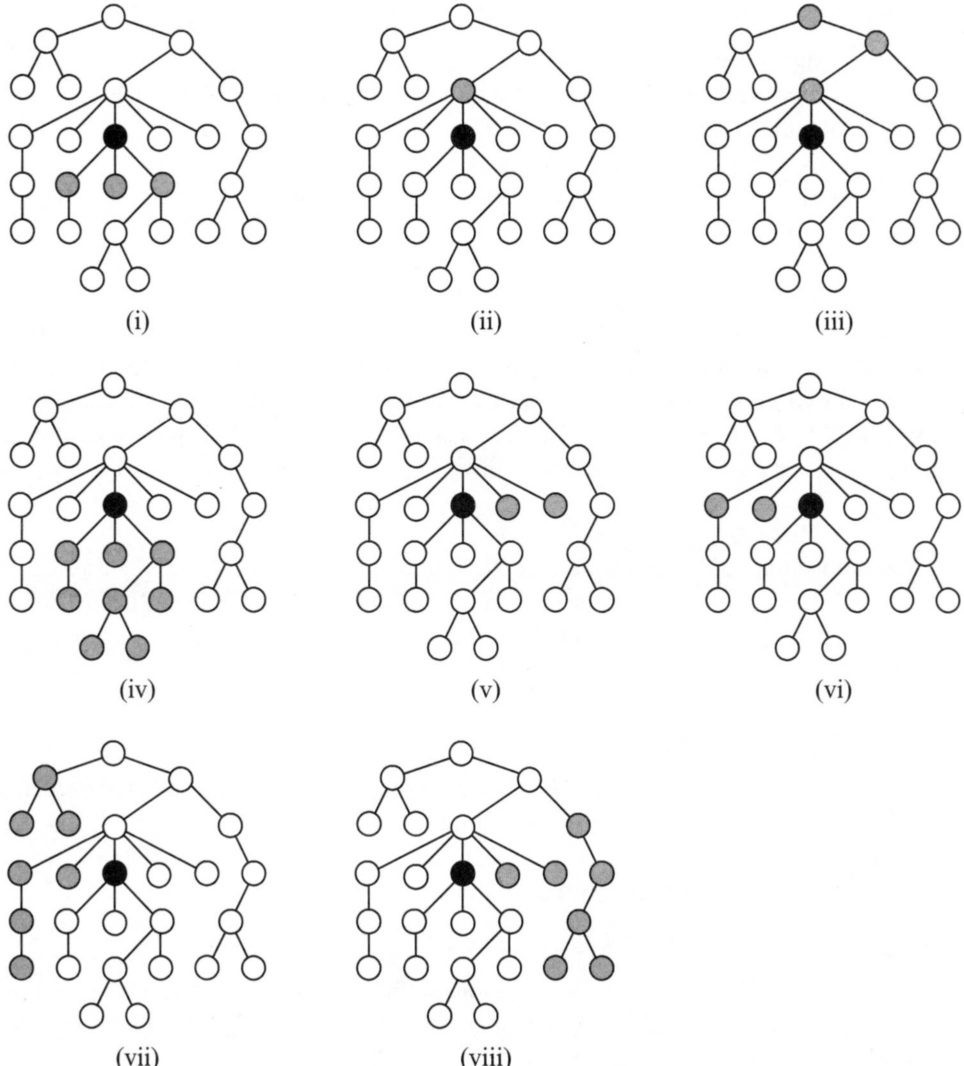

Figure 10.1 The meaning of XPath axes with respect to the context node (black) (i) child (ii) parent (iii) ancestor (iv) descendant (v) following-sibling (vi) preceding-sibling (vii) preceding (viii) following

10.5 LOCATION PATHS AND STEPS

Information from an XML document is retrieved using an expression called *location path*. It is an important construct in XPath, though it is not a general grammatical construct as it uses a verbose syntax. There are also syntactic abbreviations for common XPath expressions, which make them concise. We shall first use unabbreviated syntax to explain the location path. The abbreviated syntax will be discussed in Section 10.7.

The result of a location path can be

- a single node
- an unordered collection of nodes called node-set. Node-set will not contain any duplicate node.
- a floating point number
- a Boolean value, i.e., either `true` or `false`
- a string or
- null.

The format of a location path looks very similar to the path expression used in a traditional file system, except that it can get much more complex and have more detailed syntax than directory paths. A location path, like a directory path, consists of one or more steps, called *location steps,* separated by forward slash(es) (/). These location steps are used to get the desired set of nodes from an XML document, just as we use successive directories in a file path to get the desired file. Following is an example of a location path:

```
/store/HDD[1]/make/text()
```

This location path consists of four location steps: `store`, `HDD[1]`, `make`, and `text()`. This location path selects the name of the manufacturer of the first hard disk stored in the XML document. The exact procedure for obtaining the information from an XML document is described in detail later. There are two types of location paths: *absolute* location path and *relative* location path.

10.5.1 Absolute Location Path

Like an absolute file path in Unix, a location path starts with a forward slash (/). Here, this leftmost forward slash represents the root node as it represents the root directory in a Unix-like file path. The rest of the location path consists of one or more location steps separated by forward slash(es) (/). An absolute location path looks as follows:

```
/step1/step2/step3/…
```

Here, `step1`, `step2`, `step3...` are locations steps and are evaluated in that order. For example, `/store/HDD` selects all children `HDD` elements of the `store` element, which is a child of the document root. It has two location steps: `store` and `HDD`.

10.5.2 Relative Location Path

Relative location path is always specified with respect to a current node called the *context node*. It means that the relative location path assumes that the context node is already selected and the location path is specified relative to this context node. It does not start with a slash (/). The rest of the location path consists of one or more location steps, separated by a forward slash (/). The relative location path looks as follows:

```
step1/step2/step3/…
```

Here, `step1`, `step2`, `step3...` are locations steps and are evaluated in that order. For example, `HDD/make` selects all children `make` elements, which are children of `HDD` elements, which are in turn children of the context node.

10.5.3 Location Step

Note that a location (absolute or relative) path consists of one or more location steps. Each location step selects a set of nodes relative to the context node. Each node in this set is then used as the context node for the next location step. Nodes selected in the next step for each context node obtained in the previous step are joined to form a composite set. This composite set is the set returned by the location path.

The anatomy of a location step is as follows:

```
axis::node-test[predicate1][predicate2]..
```

A location step has three parts: an optional axis, a note-test, and zero or more predicates. Consider the following location step.

```
axis          predicate
child::HDD[position()=1]
       node test
```

Here, `child` is the name of the axis, `HDD` is the node test, and `position()=1` is predicate. This location step selects the first HDD child element of the context node. Let us now discuss each of these three components of a location step.

10.5.3.1 Axis

It is one of the axes listed in Table 11.1. It represents the structural relationship between the context node and nodes selected by each location step. XPath provides an abbreviated syntax where one may not use the name of the axis. If none is specified, the `child` axis is assumed by the XPath processor. Consider the following location step:

```
axis
child::HDD[position()=1]
```

Here, `child` is the name of the axis. It specifies that the nodes selected will be children of the current node. For the location step **`descendant`**`::HDD`, `descendant` is the axis name. The axes `child` and `attributes` are used most of the time. Other axes are used far less often.

10.5.3.2 Node test

`node-test` specifies the name of the node to be selected. It is used to perform the initial filtration of the candidate nodes depending on their type and name. The name of the node test depends upon the type of the axis. If the `attribute` axis is specified, `node-test` represents the name of an attribute. Similarly, if the `namespace` axis is specified, `node-test` represents a namespace. In all other cases, `node-test` is a name of an element. The `node-test` * represents all element nodes. The axis and node test are separated by "::". Predicates are logical expressions used to further filter the selected nodes.

Following is an example of a location step.

```
child::HDD[position()=1]
       node test
```

Here, HDD is the node-test and is the name of an element as axis specified is neither an attribute axis nor a namespace axis. The position()=1 is the predicate. It selects the first HDD child node of the current node. In the location step, attribute::**type**, type is a node test and represents an attribute. The location step child::* selects all child elements of the context node. Similarly, attribute::* selects all attributes of the context node.

So far, we have described how to select elements, attributes, and namespace nodes. There are other kind of nodes in XPath tree. The following node tests are available for text, processing-instruction, and comment nodes: text(), processing-instruction(), and comment(), respectively. For example, child::text() selects all children text nodes of the context node. The processing-instruction() test may take an argument. It is true for any processing instruction that has a name equal to the value of the argument.

10.5.3.3 Predicate

Each location step selects a set of nodes relative to the context node. This set is obtained from the axis and node-test after refining it by the predicates (if any) one by one in the order specified. A predicate is written within []. Consider the following example:

```
              predicate
child::HDD[position()=1]
```

Here, child::HDD selects all children HDD nodes under the current node. However, position()=1 filters out all except the first one. Similarly, descendant::make selects all make nodes that are descendants of the current node. In this case, no predicate is mentioned.

10.6 NODE POSITION

Every node in a selected node set has a *position*. The way the position of a node in the node set is calculated depends upon the type of the axis used. If the forward axis is used, the position indicates the index of a node in a node set ordered in the document order. Similarly, if the reverse axis is used, it indicates the index in a node set ordered in the reverse document order. XPath provides the position() function to calculate the position of a node in the selected node set.

10.7 ABBREVIATED SYNTAX

XPath provides some abbreviated notations that are quite useful while writing common expressions. It sometimes makes XPath expressions concise. Table 10.2 lists some abbreviated notations and their meaning.

Table 10.2 Abbreviated notations and their meaning

Abbreviated syntax	Meaning
child::*	Selects all children elements of the context node. Also used as *
child::text()	Selects all children text nodes of context node
child::node()	Selects all children nodes of context node
HDD	If no axis is specified, child axis is assumed. It is equivalent to child::HDD
@	Attribute axis is abbreviated as @. Equivalent to attribute::
HDD[1]	HDD[position()=1]. Selects first HDD child of context node
//	Abbreviation of all descendant nodes and the context node itself. Equivalent to /descendant-or-self::node()/
.	Selects context node. Equivalent to self::node()
..	Selects parent node. Equivalent to parent::node()

10.8 XPATH EXAMPLES

In this section, we shall discuss some examples of XPath expressions.

- Selects the store element of the document root.

```
/child::store
```

- Selects all children HDD elements of the store element.

```
/child::store/child::HDD
```

- Selects the names of all HDD manufacturers

```
/child::store/child::HDD/child::make
```

- Selects all children HDD elements of the store element

```
/child::store/child::HDD/child::price[preceding-sibling::make='Samsung']
```

- Finds names of those manufacturers that manufacture both HDDs and monitors

```
//HDD/make[//monitor/make=.]
```

- Selects all SATA HDDs

```
//HDD[attribute::type='SATA']
```

- Selects all SATA HDDs

```
//HDD[@type='SATA']
```

- Selects all CRT color monitors

```
//monitor[@type='CRT' and @color='yes']
```

or

```
//monitor[@type='CRT'][@color='yes']
```

- Selects all LCD monitors whose price is less than 8000

```
//monitor[@type='LCD' and price < 8000]
```

or

```
//monitor[@type='LCD'][price < 8000]
```

- Finds the prices of 15 inch LCD monitors

```
//monitor[@type='LCD']/price[../size = 15]
```

or

```
//monitor[@type='LCD' and size = 15]/price
```

or

```
//monitor[@type='LCD'][size = 15]/price
```

- Finds the prices of 15 inch LCD monitors manufactured by LG

```
//monitor[@type='LCD' and size = 15 and make='LG']/price
```

or

```
//monitor[@type='LCD'][size = 15][make='LG']/price
```

or

```
//monitor[@type='LCD'][size = 15]/price[../make='LG']
```

- Finds all Samsung products

```
//*[make='Samsung']
//HDD[make='Samsung'] | //monitor[make='Samsung']
```

- Finds the minimum price of an 80 GB HDD

```
min(//HDD[capacity='80']/price)
```

- Finds the minimum price of a 17 inch LCD monitor

```
min(//monitor[@type='LCD' and size='17']/price)
```

10.9 XPATH OPERATORS

XPath provides a set of operators to combine expressions to write more complex queries. Table 10.3 summarizes the XPath operators with their meaning.

Table 10.3 XPath operators

Arithmatic Operators	
Operator	**Meaning**
+	Adds two numbers
-	Subtracts one number from another
*	Multiplies two numbers
div	Performs floating-point division of two numbers
mod	Returns floating-point remainder after dividing one number by another
Boolean Operators	
Operator	**Meaning**
=	Checks whether two expressions are equal
!=	Checks whether two expressions are not equal

(Contd.)

(Contd.)

<table>
<tr><td><</td><td>Checks whether the first expression is less than the second. Within an attribute it must be written as "lt;"</td></tr>
<tr><td><=</td><td>Checks whether the first expression is less than or equal to the second. Within an attribute, it must be written as "lt;="</td></tr>
<tr><td>></td><td>Checks whether the first expression is greater than the second. Within an attribute it must be written as "gt;"</td></tr>
<tr><td>>=</td><td>Checks whether the first expression is greater than or equal to the second. Within an attribute, it must be written as "gt;="</td></tr>
<tr><td>and</td><td>Checks whether both the first and second expressions are true. Second expression is not evaluated, if first one is false</td></tr>
<tr><td>or</td><td>Checks whether either the first or second expressions is true. Second expression is not evaluated, if first one is true</td></tr>
<tr><th colspan="2">Expression operators</th></tr>
<tr><th>Operator</th><th>Meaning</th></tr>
<tr><td>.</td><td>Abbreviation of self axis</td></tr>
<tr><td>..</td><td>Abbreviation of parent axis</td></tr>
<tr><td>/</td><td>Used to separate location steps in a location path</td></tr>
<tr><td>//</td><td>Abbreviation of descendant-or-self axis</td></tr>
<tr><td>@</td><td>Abbreviation of attribute axis</td></tr>
<tr><td>|</td><td>Union operator. Performs union operation between two expressions</td></tr>
<tr><td>[]</td><td>Predicate operator. XPath predicates are written within '[' and ']'</td></tr>
<tr><td>$</td><td>Variable operator. It is used to specify that a symbol is a variable</td></tr>
</table>

10.9.1 Operator Precedence

If multiple operators are used in an XPath expression, the operator having higher precedence is evaluated first. The XPath operator precedence rule (highest precedence left) is shown in Figure 10.2.

Figure 10.2 XPath operator precedence rule

10.10 XPATH EXPRESSIONS

As stated earlier, an XPath query string to retrieve information from XML document is called *expression*. Depending upon their functionality, expressions are categorized as *sequence expression, range expression, filter expression, arithmetic expression, comparison expression, logical expression, for expression, conditional expression, and quantified expression.* The following section describes each of these expressions one by one.

10.10.1 Sequence Expression

It is said that XPath 2.0 is a language for processing sequences. This is because XPath 2.0 treats everything as a sequence. XPath 2.0 uses some basic rules that are fundamental to the way it works.

It is necessary and prerequisite to always remember these basic rules for clear understanding and appreciation of XPath 2.0.

As mentioned in XPath 2.0, everything is a sequence. Even a single value is treated as a sequence of one value. So, whenever it is specified that the result of an expression is "a node", what it means is a "sequence of a single node". XPath 2.0 does not make any distinction between these two. The only thing that has to be remembered is that everything in XPath 2.0 is a sequence.

In XPath 2.0, one way to create a sequence is to specify zero or more expressions enclosed in parenthesis and separated by the comma operator (,). For example, the result of the following expression is a sequence of four integers.

```
(3, 4, 2, 1)
```

An empty sequence is a sequence having no item and is represented as `()`.

Unlike the node set used in XPath 1.0, a sequence is an ordered collection of items. So, the sequences `(3, 4, 2, 1)` and `(1, 2, 3, 4)` are different. Each item is assigned a position number based on its ordinal position. The position starts with 1.

A sequence can have duplicate items. So, the following sequence is valid.

```
(1, 2, 2, 3, 4, 5, 2, 4, 6)
```

Nested sequence is not allowed. This means that a sequence can never be an item in another sequence. In such a case, the resulting sequence is obtained by concatenating those sequence items. For example, the result of the expression `(2, (3, 4), (2, 4, 6), (), (4))` is the sequence `(2, 3, 4, 2, 4, 6, 4)`.

The items of a sequence need not be integers; any atomic value is allowed to be an item. For example, the following example creates a sequence of all `salary` children of the `employee` element.

```
(//employee/salary)
```

Bound variables can also be used to create sequences. Consider the variable `$sal` bound to a value 20000.

```
($sal)
```

This expression creates the sequence `(20000)`.

10.10.2 Range Expression

XPath 2.0 provides a *range expression* that can be used to create a sequence of consecutive integers. The general syntax of range expression is as follows:

```
start to end
```

The result of this range expression is a sequence of integers from `start` to `end` in increasing order. Note that, if `start` is greater than `end`, or any one or both of the operands are empty, the result of the range expression is empty. If `start` is equal to `end`, the result is a sequence having one element. For example, the range expression `4 to 8` results in the sequence `(4, 5, 6, 7, 8)`. The expression `8 to 4` results in an empty [`()`] sequence, whereas the expression `4 to 4` results in the sequence `(4)`.

A range expression can be used in a sequence to create a resultant sequence.

```
(1, 2, 3 to 5, 4 to 6, 8)
```

The result of this expression is the sequence `(1, 2, 3, 4, 5, 4, 5, 6, 8)`.

10.10.3 Filter Expression

XPath 1.0 uses predicates to refine node sets. This concept is extended in XPath 2.0 and can be used to refine a sequence of arbitrary items. The syntax is as usual.

```
seq[predicate1][predicate]…
```

Each predicate is converted to its *effective Boolean values* using the rules described in Section 10.10.7. The context item is referred to in predicates, using a dot (.). The usual functions can also be used in predicates. Consider the following example.

```
(1 to 10)[. mod  2 = 0]
```

This example creates a sequence of even integers from 1 to 10, i.e., `(2, 4, 6, 8)`. The following expression creates a sequence `('XPath', 'XML')`.

```
('XPath', 'XML', 'HTML' )[starts-with(. , 'X')]
```

Multiple predicates can be used to get the desired sequence. The following expression creates the sequence `(2, 4, 6, 8,)`, which contains the first four even numbers from 1 to 100.

```
(1 to 100 )[. mod 2 = 0][position() &lt;= 4]
```

Note that predicates do not commute. So, the expression `(1 to 100 )[position() <= 4][. mod 2 = 0]` is not the same as the previous expression since the later expression creates the sequence `(2, 4)`, which is different from the sequence created by the former expression.

10.10.4 Set Operations

XPath 2.0 provides operators to perform set operations on sequences of nodes. There are four such operators: `|`, `union`, `intersect`, and `except`. The `|` and `union` operators are identical. They have their usual meaning. Duplicate nodes are eliminated from the resultant set based on node identity. Consider the existence of three nodes X, Y, and Z. Table 10.4 summarizes the set operations.

Table 10.4 XPath 2.0 set operators

<table>
<tr><th>Operator</th><th>Meaning</th><th>Example</th><th>Result</th></tr>
<tr><td>|</td><td>Union</td><td>(X, Y) | (X, Z)</td><td>(X, Y, Z)</td></tr>
<tr><td>Union</td><td>Union</td><td>(X,) union (Z, Y)</td><td>(X, Z, Y)</td></tr>
<tr><td rowspan="2">Intersect</td><td rowspan="2">Intersection</td><td>(X, Y) intersect (X, Z)</td><td>(Z)</td></tr>
<tr><td>(X, Y) intersect (Z)</td><td>()</td></tr>
<tr><td rowspan="2">Except</td><td rowspan="2">Difference</td><td>(X, Y) except (Y, Z)</td><td>(X)</td></tr>
<tr><td>(X, Y) except (X, Y)</td><td>()</td></tr>
</table>

10.10.4.1 XPath 1.0 and XPath 2.0

In XPath 1.0, a collection of nodes is represented by node-sets. The concept of node-sets is extended and generalized in XPath 2.0. We have seen that XPath 2.0 sequence can contain nodes. Unlike node-sets, sequences are ordered and contain duplicate nodes. Such sequences replace the concept of node-sets in XPath 1.0. For backward compatibility, an XPath 2.0 path expression returns the sequence of nodes in the document order, which is the default order used to process node-sets. This way, using only a sequence, XPath 2.0 makes itself compatible with XPath 1.0.

10.10.5 Arithmetic Expression

XPath supports various operators for performing standard arithmetic operations. Following is a list of arithmetic operators available, with their meaning and result. These operators follow standard precedence rules. For example, unary operators have higher precedence than binary operators, subject to the use of parenthesis of course.

Table 10.5 XPath arithmetic operators

Operator	Meaning	Example	Result	Operator	Meaning	Example	Result
+	Addition	3+2	5	idiv	Integer Division	3 idiv 2	1
–	Subtraction	2–3	–1	mod	Modulo	5 mod 3	2
*	Multiplication	3*2	6	–	Unary Minus	–2	–2
Div	Division	3 div 2	1.5	+	Unary Plus	+2	2

Since the operators –, div, idiv, and mod may occur as a part of an operand, the necessary white space must be inserted for proper evaluation of an arithmetic expression. For example, `3 div 2` is a valid expression, but `3div 2` is not, due to the lack of white space between `3` and `div`. Similarly, `$total-salary - $total-tax` and `$total-salary -$total-tax` are valid expressions, but `$total-salary- $total-tax` and `$total-salary-$total-tax` are not.

Operands of the correct type with respect to an operator must be provided. Unexpected types will cause run-time errors.

10.10.6 Comparison Expression

The XPath comparison expression allows comparing two values. There are three types of comparison expressions: *value comparison*, *general comparison*, and *node comparison*.

10.10.6.1 Value comparison

XPath provides the following value comparison operators: `eq`, `ne`, `lt`, `gt`, `le`, and `ge`. They are used to compare two single (atomic) values. Table 10.6 summarizes their meaning.

Table 10.6 XPath comparison operators

Operator	Meaning	Example
Eq	Equal to	//HDD[1]/make/text() eq 'Samsung'
Ne	Not equal to	//monitor[1]/@type ne 'LCD'

(Contd.)

(Contd.)

Lt	Less than	//HDD[1]/price/text() lt '2000'
Gt	Greater than	//monitor[1]/size/text() gt '15'
Le	Less than or equal to	//HDD[1]/price/text() le '2000'
Ge	Greater than or equal to	//monitor[1]/size/text() ge '15'

Value comparison operators cannot take empty operands or operands having more than one atomic value. If such operands are supplied, errors will occur when they are evaluated.

10.10.6.2 General comparison

XPath provides the following value comparison operators: =, !=, <, >, <=, and >=. They are used to compare two arbitrary values. Table 10.7 summarizes their meaning.

Table 10.7 XPath General comparison operators

Operator	Meaning	Example	Result
=	Equal to	(1, 2) = (2, 3)	true
!=	Not equal to	(1, 2) != (2, 3)	true
<	Less than	(3, 4) < (3,3)	false
>	Greater than	(3, 4) < (3,3)	false
<=	Less than or equal to	(3, 4) <= (3,3)	true
>=	Greater than or equal to	(3, 4) >= (3,3)	true

General comparison operators can take operands as sequences of atomic values. In such a case, the result is `true` if there exists at least one pair of atomic values, one taken from the first sequence and the other taken from the second sequence, for which the corresponding comparison holds. If there is no such pair, the result is `false`. For example, the result of (1, 2) = (2, 3) is true as the second element of the first sequence and the first element of the second sequence are equal.

Note that = and != are not inverse of each other. For example, `(1, 2) = (2, 3)` and `(1, 2) != (2, 3)` both result in the value `true`.

Escaping rules for special characters must be followed when using these operators in an XML document. For example, '<' must be written as '<' and '>=' must be written as '>='.

10.10.6.3 Node comparison

XPath provides comparison operators to compare nodes based on their identity or order of appearance in an XML document. There are three node comparison operators: `is`, <<, and >>. The operator `is` results true if both the operands evaluate to exactly the same single node. The operator << returns `true`, if the left operand precedes the right operand in the document order, otherwise it returns `false`. The operator >> returns `true`, if the right operand precedes the left operand in the document order, otherwise it returns `false`. Table 10.8 illustrates the node comparison operators with examples.

Table 10.8 XPath node comparison operators

Operator	Meaning	Example	Result
is	Identity	//HDD[1] is //HDD[position()=1]	true
		//HDD[2] is //HDD[make='Samsung' and @type='ATA']	false
<<	Left precedes right	//HDD[1] << //HDD[2]	true
		//HDD[1] << //HDD[1]	false
<<	Right precedes left	//HDD[2] >> //HDD[position()=1]	true
		//HDD[1] >> //HDD[2]	false

10.10.7 Logical Expression

There are two logical operators in XPath: `and` and `or`. They have the usual meanings. They are binary operators and expect two Boolean values as operands. If the operands are not Boolean, it is first necessary to find their *effective Boolean values*. The following rules are used to evaluate each operand's *effective Boolean value*:

- An empty sequence yields the value `false`.
- A non-empty sequence whose first item is a node yields `true`.
- The value of an operand whose type is derived from `boolean` yields the value as it is.
- A non-empty `string` yields `true` and an empty `string` yields `false`.
- A non-zero number and the number 0 yield `true` and `false`, respectively.
- All other cases yield type error.

In addition to these Boolean operators, XPath provides three useful functions `not()`, `true()`, and `false()`. The function `not()` takes a single Boolean value and inverts it, whereas the functions `true()` and `false()` returns the constants `true` and `false`, respectively.

10.10.8 For Expression

The XPath `for` expression allows iteration through a sequence of values. The general syntax of the `for` expression is as follows:

```
for $var in exp1 return exp2
```

where, `exp1` is a sequence of items to be iterated, called *binding sequence*, `var` is the loop variable, which will assume each item in the binding sequence, called *range variable*. `Exp2` is an expression evaluated for each item bound to var. The result of the `for` expression is a sequence obtained by concatenating the value of `expr2` for each item in `expr1`. Consider the following `for` expression:

```
for $i in (1, 2, 3, 4) return $i*$i
```

This `for` expression results in the sequence `1 4 9 16`. Similarly, the following expression produces the sequence of those companies that manufacture HDD.

```
for $i in distinct-values(//HDD/make) return $i
```

The result of this expression is `Samsung Seagate`. The following expression finds the lowest price among a set of HDDs.

```
for $i in min(//HDD/price) return $i
```

`for` expressions having multiple range variables are possible. In this case, more than one in-clause is specified. The syntax of such expressions is as follows:

```
for $var1 in exp1 [, $var1 in exp2, [$var1 in exp2],…] return exp3
```

Consider the following `for` expression having two range variables.

```
for $i in (1 to 5), $j in (1 to $i) return $j
```

This expression is first expanded as a nested `for` expression as follows:

```
for $i in (1 to 5) return for $j in (1 to $i) return $j
```

The result of this `for` expression is `1 1 2 1 2 3 1 2 3 4 1 2 3 4 5`. The following expression returns those HDDs, made by Seagate, whose price is equal to the price of the HDDs made by Samsung.

```
for $i in //HDD[make='Samsung'] return
   for $j in //HDD[make='Seagate' and price=$i/price] return $j
```

The following example produces items grouped by their manufacturer name.

```
for $i in distinct-values(//*/make) return ($i, //*[make=$i])
```

10.10.9 Conditional Expression

A conditional expression allows users to select between two choices, depending upon a logical expression called *test expression*. The general syntax of a conditional expression is as follows:

```
if (test-expression) then then-expression else else-expression
```

To find the result of a conditional expression, the *effective boolean value* of test-expression is first determined using the rules described in Section 10.10.7. If the Boolean condition is evaluated to true, the value of *then-expression* is evaluated and returned. Otherwise, the value of *else-expression* is evaluated and returned.

```
if ($emp/salary &lt;= 100000)
   then $emp/salary*0.01
   else 1000+($emp/salary - 100000)*0.02
```

Given the salary of an employee, this conditional expression returns the income tax of an employee. The following conditional expression returns the total income tax of all employees, to be deposited by the company.

```
sum(
   for $emp in (//employee) return
      if ($emp/salary &lt;= 100000)
         then $emp/salary*0.01
         else 1000+($emp/salary - 100000)*0.02
)
```

10.10.10 Quantified Expression

XPath quantified expressions allow us to perform *existential* and *universal* quantification. Existential quantification is used to check if some condition is true for at least one member of a set. Universal quantification is used to check if some condition is true for all members of a set. The value of any quantified expression is a Boolean (true/false) value. The general form of a quantified expression is as follows:

```
some|every $var in sequence-expression satisfies condition-expression
```

Consider the following universal quantified expression:

```
every $marks in //student[name='Kaushik']/marks satisfies $marks >=50
```

This expression returns `true` if all marks obtained by `Kaushik` in different subjects are greater than or equal to `50`. This expression can also be written using an existential quantified expression as follows:

```
some $marks in //student[name='Kaushik']/marks satisfies $marks < 50
```

A quantified expression can be combined with a conditional expression to get a concrete result. Following is an example.

```
if(every $marks in //student[name='Kaushik']/marks satisfies $marks >=50)
then 'passed' else 'failed'
```

This universal quantified expression can be expressed as using a traditional construct as follows:

```
empty(for $i in //student[name='Kaushik']/makrs return if($i >= 50) then
() else false())
```

Similarly, the existential construct can also be rewritten as follows:

```
empty(for $i in //student[name='Kaushik']/makrs return if($i &lt; 50) then
false() else ())
```

These examples show that quantified expressions do not add any power to the XPath language. They just makes things convenient.

10.11 BUILT-IN FUNCTIONS

XPath also provides a rich set of functions to manipulate numbers, strings, and Booleans. They can be categorized into four groups depending on the data types they operate on.

10.11.1 Node Functions

Node functions are XPath functions related to nodes in the XPath tree. These functions operate on a context node. They allow us to find the position of a node in a node set, count the number of nodes in a node set, etc. The most common XPath node functions are given in Table 10.9:

Table 10.9 Most common XPath node functions

Function	Description	Example	Return Value
position	Finds position of context node in a node set	//HDD[position()=1]	First HDD element
last	Determines last index in a node set	//HDD[position()=last()]	Last HDD element
count	Counts number of nodes in a node set	count(//HDD)	3

10.11.2 String Functions

XPath provides a rich set of functions to manipulate strings. Most common XPath string functions are given in Table 10.10.

Table 10.10 Most common XPath string functions

Function	Description	Example	Return Value
concat	Concatenates two or more strings together	concat('X','Path')	'XPath'
		concat('W','3','C')	'W3C'
starts-with	Checks if a string begins with another string	starts-with('W3C','W')	true()
ends-with	Checks if a string ends with another string	ends-with('XPath','path')	false()
contains	Checks if a string contains another string	contains('XPath','Path')	true()
substring-before	Returns substring that appears before another string	substring-before('XPath','Path')	'X'
substring-after	Returns substring that appears after another string	substring-after('XPath','X')	'Path'
substring	Retrieves a substring of specified length starting at a an index within another string	substring('XPath',2)	'Path'
		substring('XPath',2,2)	'Pa'
string-length	Returns the length of a string	string-length('XPath')	5
string-join	Concatenates two or more strings with specified delimiter	string-join(('XPath','functions'),' ')	'XPath 'functions'
		string-join(('X','M','L'),'-')	'X-M-L'
upper-case	Returns specified string with upper case letters	upper-case('XPath')	'XPATH'
lower-case	Returns specified string with lower case letters	lower-case('XPath')	'xpath'
replace	Replaces a substring within a string by another	replace('XPath','Path','ML')	'XML'
normalize-space	Removes leading and trailing white spaces and replaces one or more white spaces by one white space	normalize-space('XPath expr')	'XPath expr'
tokenize	Breaks specified string into sequence of tokens	tokenize('XML DTD XSL',' ')	('XML','DTD','XSL')

10.11.3 Boolean Functions

Table 10.11 lists the XPath Boolean functions.

Table 10.11 XPath Boolean functions

Function	Description	Example	Return Value
true	Returns Boolean value true	true()	true
false	Returns Boolean value false	false()	false
not	Negates boolean value specified	not(true)	false
		not(false)	true

10.11.3.1 Number functions

Table 10.12 lists the XPath number functions.

Table 10.12 XPath number functions

Function	Description	Example	Return Value
ceiling	Returns smallest integer not less than the value specified	ceiling(2.6)	3
floor	Returns largest integer not larger than the value specified	floor(2.6)	2
round	Rounds decimal value to the nearest integer	round(2.4)	2
		round(2.5)	3
abs	Returns absolute value of the value specified	abs(-3.5)	3.5
sum	Adds a set of numeric values	sum((2,3,4))	9
min	Returns minimum value among a set of numbers	min((3,4,1,2))	1
max	Returns maximum value among a set of numbers	max((3,4,1,2))	4
avg	Returns average of a set of values	avg((3,4,1,2))	2.5

10.11.4 Conversion Functions

Table 10.13 lists the XPath conversion functions.

Table 10.13 XPath conversion functions

Function	Description	Example	Return Value
number	Converts specified argument to integer	number('12')	12

10.11.5 Sequence Functions

Table 10.14 lists the XPath sequence functions.

Table 10.14 XPath sequence functions

Function	Description	Example	Return Value
empty	Checks if given sequence is empty or not	empty((1,2,4))	false()
		empty(())	true()
exists	Checks if there exists any element in the given sequence	exists((1,2,4))	true()
		exists(())	false()
index-of	Returns a sequence of indices where the specified number occurs in the specified sequence	index-of((2,3,2,2,4),2)	(1, 3, 4)
		index-of((2,3,4),5)	()

(Contd.)

(Contd.)

distinct-values	Removes duplicate values from given sequence	distinct-values((1,2,2,3,4,4))	(1, 2, 3, 4)
insert-before	Inserts a sequence into another sequence before a specified position	insert-before((1,2,5), 1, (3,4))	(3, 4, 1, 2, 5)
		insert-before((1,2,5), 2, (3,4))	(1, 3, 4, 2, 5)
remove	Removes an item from specified sequence at specified position	remove((3,4,5), 1)	(4, 5)
		remove((3,4,5), 0)	(3, 4, 5)
reverse	Reverses the order of items in a sequence	reverse((3,4,5))	(5, 4, 3)
subsequence	Returns a subsequence from the specified sequence and position(s)	subsequence((3,4,5,6), 2)	(4, 5, 6)
		subsequence((3,4,5,6), 1, 2)	(3, 4)

KEYWORDS

Abbreviated syntax: Shorthand XPath expression, quite useful while writing common expressions.

Absolute location path: It starts with a forward slash (/). The rest of the location path consists of one or more location steps separated by a forward slash (/).

Arithmetic Expression: Used to perform standard arithmetic operations

Axes: The structural relationships among nodes in the XPath tree are represented by components called axes.

Comparison Expression: A comparison expression that allows the comparion of two values.

Conditional Expression: A conditional expression allows users to select between two choices, depending upon a logical expression called *test expression.*

Filter expression: An XPath expression used to refine a sequence of arbitrary items.

For Expression: It allows iteration through a sequence of values.

Location Path: Basic building blocks of XPath expressions used to retrieve information from XML documents.

Location Step: A location path consists of one or more location steps separated by (/).

Logical Expression: Logical expressions are used to perform logical operations

Node Position: Every node in a selected node set has a *position.* The way the position of a node in the node set is calculated depends upon the type of the axis used.

Node test: A set of nodes to be selected.

Predicate: A phrase used to refine a set of nodes obtained from the previous step.

Quantified Expression: XPath quantified expressions allow us to perform *existential* and *universal* quantification.

Range expression: An XPath expression used to create a sequence of consecutive integers.

Relative location path: Relative location path is always specified with respect to a current node called the *context node.*

Sequence expression: An XPath expression used to create a sequence of elements

Set operations: Used to perform set operations on sequences of nodes

XPath Expression: An XPath query string used to retrieve information from XML document is called *expression.*

SUMMARY

DOM allows application programs to navigate XML documents. However, it seems to be difficult to retrieve information from an XML document. XPath is one of the major query languages used to retrieve information from XML documents. XPath is a major part of XSLT. XPath is a simple text-based and language-neutral technique, standardized by the W3C and used to navigate XML documents. XPath is a query language for XML documents as opposed to SQL for relational databases. XPath is the most common out of many XML Path languages. Its primary purpose is to select elements, attributes and other information from XML documents using XPath expressions, which are implementation-independent. The real power of XML is not in storing the data, but in the ability to use XPath expressions to retrieve complex subsets of data. In addition to this, it also provides rich sets of interfaces to manipulate numbers, strings, and Booleans. XPath is used in various technologies such as XSLT, XQuery, and XPointer, etc.

XPath uses a hierarchical tree structure consisting of different kinds of nodes to represent XML documents. The relationships among nodes are represented by axes. Each axis represents a specific relationship. There are two types of axes: forward axis and reverse axis. An axis that represents nodes after the context node is called forward axis. Otherwise the axis is called reverse axis. The axis `following` is an example of the forward axis whereas the axis `ancestor` is a reverse axis.

The query used to retrieve information from an XML document is called XPath expression. Two fundamental concepts are involved in XPath: location path and location step. A location path, which is the basic building block of the XPath expression, consists of one or more location steps. A location path may be absolute or relative.

A location path consists of an axis, a node test and zero or more predicates. The result of each location step is a set of nodes. Predicates are used to further filter nodes. XPath also provides abbreviated expressions useful for writing common expressions.

Every node in a selected node set has a position. XPath provides the `position()` function to calculate the position of a node in the selected node set.

XPath provides some abbreviated notations that are quite useful while writing common expressions.

Operators are used to form more complex XPath expressions. There are three types of operators: arithmetic operators, Boolean operators, and expression operators.

XPath expressions, depending upon the usage, may be categorized as sequence expressions, range expressions, filter expressions, and so on. A sequence expression, which is fundamental in XPath 2.0, is used to generate a sequence of elements. XPath 2.0 supports some programming constructs that can be used to retrieve more complex information from XML documents.

XPath also supports traditional operators to perform arithmetic, comparison, and logical operations.

XPath provides a rich set of functions for accessing and manipulating nodes, strings, and numbers.

WEB RESOURCES

`http://www.w3.org/TR/xpath`
XML Path Language (XPath) Version 1.0

`http://www.w3.org/TR/xpath20/`
XML Path Language (XPath) 2.0

EXERCISES

Multiple Choice Questions

1. XPath is a language used to find information in a
   (a) text file (b) XML document
   (c) HTML document (d) XQuery document

2. Which of the following is a major part of W3C's XSLT standard?
   (a) XPath (b) XPointer
   (c) XQuery (d) XLink

3. XPath is a language used to navigate through
   (a) files
   (b) directories
   (c) elements and attributes of an XML document
   (d) different pages

4. Which of these are based on XPath expressions?
   (a) XQuery and XML
   (b) XQuery and XLink
   (c) XQuery and XPointer
   (d) XLink and XPointer

5. Which of the following is true regarding XPath?
   (a) It is a Microsoft standard
   (b) It is not a W3C standard
   (c) It does not belong to any standard
   (d) It is a W3C standard

6. Which of the following are not supported by XPath?
   (a) Character values functions
   (b) Sequence manipulation functions
   (c) String values functions
   (d) Node manipulation functions

7. Which of the following is used to select a set of nodes in XPath?
   (a) Location steps (b) Location path
   (c) Both a and b (d) URL

8. Which of the following uses XPath expressions?
   (a) XLink documents (b) XSL documents
   (c) XML documents (d) XSLT documents

9. Which of the following support the same set of operators and functions?
   (a) XQuery 2.0 and XPath 1.0
   (b) XQuery 2.0 and XPath 2.0
   (c) XQuery 1.0 and XPath 2.0
   (d) XQuery 1.0 and XPath 1.0

10. Which of the following XPath expressions selects first four p elements in the document?
   (a) (//p)[index()<=4]
   (b) (//p)[order()<=4]
   (c) (//p)[position()<=4]
   (d) (//p)[last()<=4]

11. Which of the following is not a kind of XPath node?
   (a) Namespace (b) Instruction
   (c) Comment (d) Processing-instruction

12. Which of the following XPath expressions selects all *color* attributes in the XML document?
   (a) /color (b) //@color
   (c) /@color (d) //color

13. Which of the following is not a valid XPath expression?
   (a) // (b) $ (c) / (d) @

14. In XPath, predicates are used to find
   (a) the child of a specific node
   (b) the root node
   (c) the parent of a specific node
   (d) a specific set of nodes

15. Which of the following is not a valid XPath axis?
   (a) attribute (b) followed
   (c) ancestor (d) child

16. Which of the following is a valid XPath axis?
   (a) followed (b) previous
   (c) next (d) parent

17. In XPath, the `following` axis contains
   (a) all the descendants of the node
   (b) all the children of the node
   (c) all the nodes that appear after the current node is opened
   (d) all the nodes that appear after the current node is closed

18. The axis `following-sibling` contains
   (a) nodes that have a common parent
   (b) nodes that have a common parent and the same name
   (c) nodes that have a common ancestor and the same name
   {d) nodes that have a common ancestor

19. What is the result of count(//*) for the following XML document?

```
<?xml version="1.0"?>
<company>
    <employee id="23RF4DEG">
        <name>Kate</name>
        <salary currency="$">100000</salary>
    </employee>
</ company >
```

   (a) 3 (b) 4 (c) 5 (d) 6

20. In XPath, the descendant-or-self axis contains
   (a) descendants of the context node
   (b) all the nodes after the context node
   (c) the context node and the descendants of the context node.
   (d) all siblings after the context node

Review Questions

1. Rewrite the following XPath expressions, without backward axes (i.e., no parent, ancestor, ancestor-or-self, preceding, and preceding-sibling axes).

```
/descendant::price/preceding::name
/child::journal/child::editor/parent::*
/descendant::name[ancestor::journal]
/descendant::name[preceding-sibling:
:name]/parent::authors/
ancestor::journal/child::title
```

2. Consider the genealogical tree of the descendants of a person as an XML document with the following DTD:

```
<!ELEMENT person (name, (son |
daughter)*, alive?)>
<!ELEMENT son (name, (son |
daughter)*, alive?)>
<!ELEMENT daughter (name, (son |
daughter)* alive?)>
<!ELEMENT name (#PCDATA)>
<!ELEMENT alive (#PCDATA)>
```

Rewrite the following XPath expression, such that it does not contain any backward axes.

```
/descendant::son[child::alive]
[not ancestor::daughter=/
descendant::daughter]
[not preceding-sibling::son/
child::alive]
[not preceding-sibling::son/
descendant::son
   [child::alive]
   [not ancestor::daughter=/
descendant::daughter]
]
```

3. Give location path expressions for each of the following nodes with respect to the context node:
   (a) the context node
   (b) all children element of the context node
   (c) all children named 'x'
   (d) all ancestors of the context node
   (e) all ancestors named 'x'
   (f) the third element child
   (g) the third child named 'y'
   (h) the closest ancestor named 'x'
   (i) the most remote ancestor named 'x'
   (j) the immediately following sibling element
   (k) the immediately preceding sibling element
   (l) the closest following sibling named 'x'
   (m) the closest preceding sibling named 'x'
   (n) the seventh element among all siblings of the context node
   (o) the first child named 'x' of the third ancestor named 'x'
   (p) the second-closest ancestor named 'x' whose attribute 'val' is equal to 'a'
   (q) the closest ancestor that has a child named 'y' with a 'val' attribute of 'b'
   (r) the last following sibling named 'x'
   (s) all elements in the document with a 'val' attribute of 'd'
   (t) the first and last children with a 'val' attribute of 'c'

4. For a context node, the parent axis contains the same set of nodes as the value of the XPath expression `ancestor::node()[1]`. In a same way, provide for each of the following XPath axes an alternative expression that evaluates to the set of nodes belonging to the axis.
   (a) ancestor
   (b) ancestor-or-self
   (c) child
   (d) descendant
   (e) descendant-or-self
   (f) following
   (g) preceding
   (h) self

5. Write the longform of the XPath expression for each of the following abbreviated XPath expressions:
   (a) firstname
   (b) text()
   (c) *
   (d) @*
   (e) @name
   (f) .//firstname
   (g) */para
   (h) chapter//para
   (i) para[1]
   (j) //para
   (k) para[@type="warning"]
   (l) *[name()='chapter' or name()='appendix'

6. Write the XPath expression for each of the following:

(a) Find the document root.

(b) Find all children elements of the context node.

(c) Find all children text nodes of the context node.

(d) Find the x element children of the context node.

(e) Find all the children of the context node.

(f) Find all the attributes of the context node.

(g) Find the y attribute of the context node.

(h) Find the x element descendants of the context node.

(i) Find all y ancestors of the context node.

(j) Find the div ancestors of the context node and, if the context node is a div element, the context node as well.

(k) Find all para element descendants of the context node and, if the context node is a para element, the context node as well.

(l) Find all para element descendants of the chapter element children of the context node.

(m) Find all para grandchildren of the context node.

(n) Find all the item elements that have a parent "p" and that are in the same document as the context node.

(o) Find all the para elements in the same document as the context node.

(p) Find all the para children of the context node other than the first para child of the context node.

(q) Find the first para child of the context node.

(r) Find the last para child of the context node.

(s) Find the last but one para child of the context node.

(t) Find the next chapter sibling of the context node.

(u) Find the previous chapter sibling of the context node.

(v) Find the fifteenth figure element in the document.

(w) Find the fifth section of the second chapter of the doc document element.

(x) Find all para children of the context node that have a type attribute with value 'warning'.

(y) Find the second para child of the context node that has a type attribute with value 'warning'.

(z) Find the fourth para child of the context node if that child has a type attribute with value 'warning'.

(aa) Find the chapter children of the context node that have one or more title children with string-value equal to 'Introduction'.

(bb) Find the chapter children of the context node that have one or more title children.

(cc) Find the chapter and appendix children of the context node.

(dd) Find the last chapter or appendix child of the context node.

11 XML TRANSFORMATION

Key Objectives

After completing this chapter readers will be able to—

- **understand the purpose of XSLT**
- **distinguish between XSL-FO and XSLT**
- **understand the structure of an XSLT document**
- **get an idea about commonly used XSLT elements and their functions**
- **learn key concepts such as recursive template, functions, and variables**
- **understand how to write dynamic XSLT documents**

11.1 INTRODUCTION

XML documents contain self-describing and structured data. The meaning to the data is given and relationship among data is described by creating custom tags. The set of tags and their structure varies widely in different applications. Web browsers cannot display such non-HTML files as they have no prior knowledge about the meaning of the set of tags used in different XML documents. So, it becomes mandatory to generate an HTML version of this XML file, which can then safely be displayed by web browsers. Figure 11.1 illustrates this.

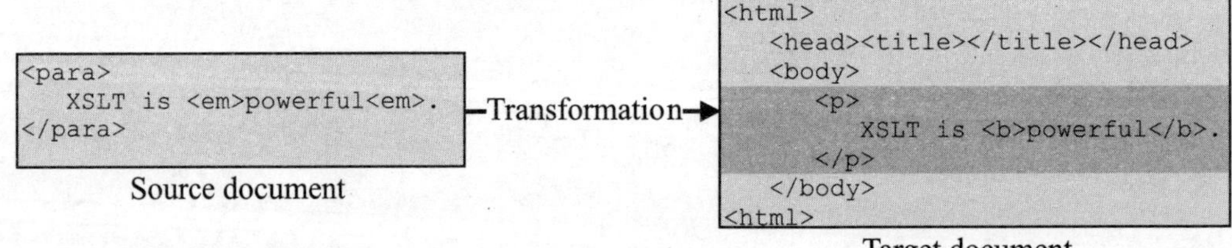

Figure 11.1 XML to HTML transformation using XSLT

Users may also want to generate new XML documents from one or more existing XML documents, for further processing or sharing of data between different applications. Consider the XML document `employee.xml`, which contains detailed information about all employees in a company. The manager of this company may not want to disclose sensitive information such as bank account number, date of birth, etc. to others.

One possible solution is to generate a separate XML document [Figure 11.2] from `employee.xml` such that the former contains only insensitive data. XSLT comes into play in this scenario.

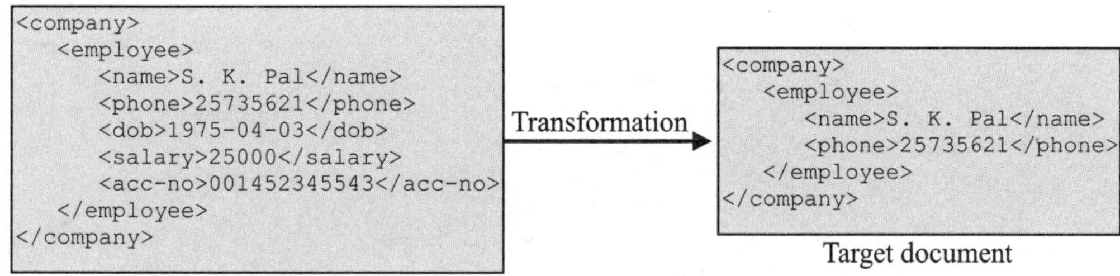

Figure 11.2 XML to XML transformation using XSLT

It is sometimes required to change the structure of an XML document. Consider the following XML document, `emp.xml`.

```
<?xml version='1.0'?>
<employee>
   <name>K. Pal</name>
   <sex>male</sex>
   <status>single</status>
   <salary basic='1500' DA='1000'/>
</employee>
```

In this example, marital status and sex of an employee is given by the elements `<status>` and `<sex>`, respectively whereas salary is given by the two attributes `basic` and `DA` of the `<salary>` element. Now consider another representation of the same information.

```
<?xml version='1.0'?>
<employee profile='male single'>
   <name>K. Pal</name>
   <salary>
      <basic>1500</basic>
      <DA>1000</DA>
   </salary>
</employee>
```

In this example, information such as marital status and sex of an employee is given by the `profile` attribute of the `<employee>` element whereas basic salary and DA are represented by the two elements, `<basic>` and `<DA>`. These two XML documents roughly contain the same information but in different structures. One possible solution is to write a transformation code in a traditional programming language. Following is a sample Java code for such a transformation.

```
import org.w3c.dom.*;
import javax.xml.parsers.*;
public class Translate {
   public static void main(String args[]) {
      try {
         DocumentBuilderFactory factory = DocumentBuilderFactory.newInstance();
         String profile="", status="", sex="", name="", basic="", DA="";
         Document source = factory.newDocumentBuilder().parse("emp2.xml");
         NodeList nodes = source.getElementsByTagName("employee");
         NodeList children = nodes.item(0).getChildNodes();
         for(int j=1;j<children.getLength();j+=1) {
            Node n = children.item(j);
            if(n.getNodeName().equals("status"))
               status+=n.getChildNodes().item(0).getNodeValue();
            if(n.getNodeName().equals("sex"))
               sex+=n.getChildNodes().item(0).getNodeValue();
            profile=status+" "+sex;
            if(n.getNodeName().equals("name"))
               name=n.getChildNodes().item(0).getNodeValue();
            if(n.getNodeName().equals("salary")) {
               for(int k= 0 ;k<n.getAttributes().getLength();k++) {
                  if(n.getAttributes().item(k).getNodeName().equals("basic"))
                     basic = n.getAttributes().item(k).getNodeValue();
                  if(n.getAttributes().item(k).getNodeName().equals("DA"))
                     DA = n.getAttributes().item(k).getNodeValue();
               }
            }
         }
         System.out.println("<?xml version='1.0'?>");
         System.out.println("<employee profile='"+profile+"'>");
         System.out.println("<name>"+name+"</name>");
         System.out.println("<salary><basic>"+basic+"</basic>");
         System.out.println("<DA>"+DA+"</DA></salary>");
         System.out.println("</employee>");
      }catch(Exception e) {e.printStackTrace();}
   }
}
```

Use the following commands to generate the class file `Translate.class` and execute it.

```
javac Translate.java
java Translate > out.xml
```

This piece of code is not easily readable by humans. Moreover, any changes in the source XML document would require significant change in the Java source code and need recompilation and rerun. This makes the entire thing tedious and almost practically impossible.

On the other hand, the following XSLT (**X**ML **S**tylesheet **L**anguage **T**ransformation) document performs the same translation as the previous Java program.

```
<?xml version='1.0'?>
<xsl:transform version='2.0' xmlns:xsl='http://www.w3.org/1999/XSL/
Transform'>
```

```
    <xsl:template match='/employee'>
        <xsl:element name='employee'>
            <xsl:attribute name='profile' select='concat(status, " ", sex)' />
            <name><xsl:value-of select='name' /></name>
            <salary>
                <basic><xsl:value-of select='salary/@basic' /></basic>
                <DA><xsl:value-of select='salary/@DA' /></DA>
            </salary>
        </xsl:element>
    </xsl:template>
</xsl:transform>
```

This code is not only smaller, but also readable to the users who are new to XSLT. Figure 11.3 describes the transformation process pictorially. In this chapter, we shall discuss how to write XSL files to do various tasks such as data reformatting, data suppression, addition of new content, copying information, etc.

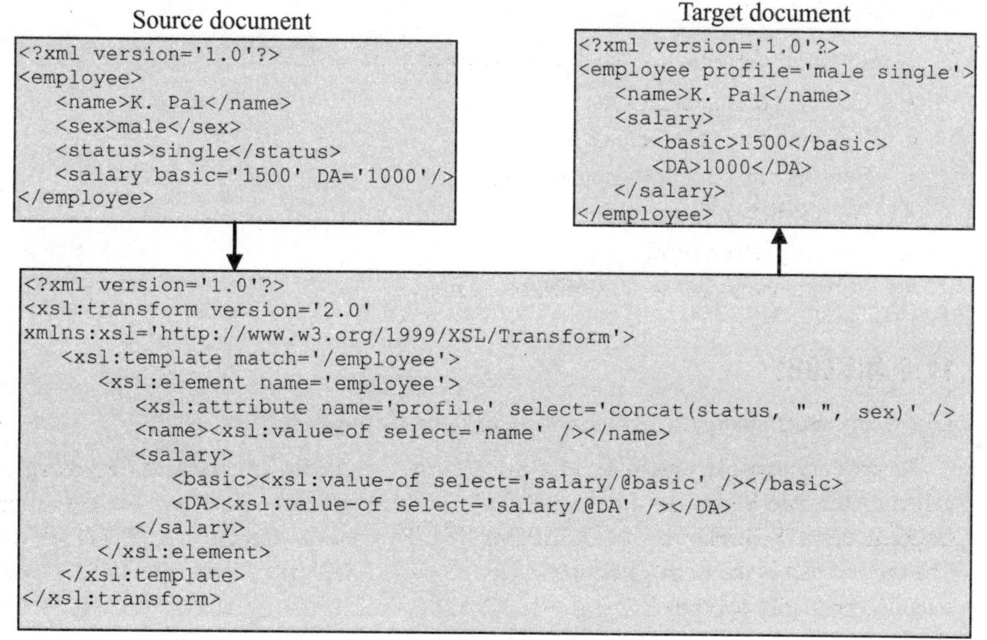
Source document
<?xml version='1.0'?>
<employee>
<name>K. Pal</name>
<sex>male</sex>
<status>single</status>
<salary basic='1500' DA='1000'/>
</employee>
Target document
<?xml version='1.0'?>
<employee profile='male single'>
<name>K. Pal</name>
<salary>
<basic>1500</basic>
<DA>1000</DA>
</salary>
</employee>
<?xml version='1.0'?>
<xsl:transform version='2.0'
xmlns:xsl='http://www.w3.org/1999/XSL/Transform'>
<xsl:template match='/employee'>
<xsl:element name='employee'>
<xsl:attribute name='profile' select='concat(status, " ", sex)' />
<name><xsl:value-of select='name' /></name>
<salary>
<basic><xsl:value-of select='salary/@basic' /></basic>
<DA><xsl:value-of select='salary/@DA' /></DA>
</salary>
</xsl:element>
</xsl:template>
</xsl:transform>
XSLT document

Figure 11.3 Data reformatting using XSLT

Figure 11.4 shows the role of XSLT in document publishing.

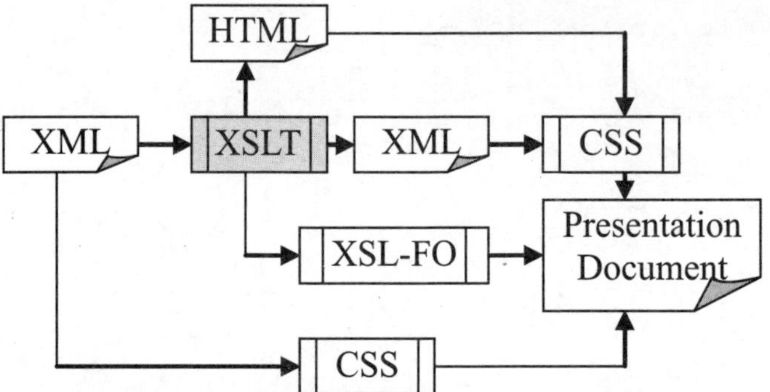

Figure 11.4 Role of XSLT in document publishing

An XSLT file transforms an XML file into another XML file. An XSLT processor generates a document tree from a source XML document and converts this to a result tree by executing the instructions specified in the XSLT file. The resultant XML file may be an XHTML file, which a web browser can understand or a WML (**W**ireless **M**arkup **L**anguage) file, which a cellular phone can display.

In general the following tasks can be performed using XSLT:

- Constant text generation
- Reformatting of information
- Sensitive information suppression
- Adding new information
- Copying information
- Sorting document with respect to a criteria

11.2 HISTORY

Like many other standards, XSLT was developed by the W3C.

Its primary purpose was to develop a platform- and media-independent formatting language called eXtensible Stylesheet Language (XSL). It has two parts. The first one is the formatting language called XSL FOrmatting (XSLFO or XSL-FO), used to format an XML/HTML document. The second part is the transformation language, called XSL Transformation (XSLT), which was intended primarily for translating source XML documents to target XML/HTML documents.

The first formal proposal by the W3C for standardizing such a language came on 21 August 1997 and can be found at http://www.w3.org/TR/NOTE-XSL.html. This first proposal contains many of the key concepts of XSLT. However, when it finally emerged, the syntax was virtually unrecognizable.

In May 1998, Norman Walsh produced a requirements summary to help the W3C make an assessment of the proposal.

Keeping those requirements in mind, the W3C published the first Working Draft of XSL on 18 August 1998. After that, the language started to evolve and gradually converged to its final form on 16 November 1999.

11.3 STYLESHEET STRUCTURE

XSLT files are themselves XML documents. So, these documents must adhere to the well-formedness constraint. The W3C defined the exact syntax of an XSLT 2.0 document by an XML schema, which is publicly available at

```
http://www.w3.org/2005/02/schema-for-xslt20.xsd
```

Being an XML document, an XSLT file starts with an XML declaration as follows:

```
<?xml version='1.0' ?>
```

Every XSLT file must have a root element. Either of the root elements `<stylesheet>` or `<transform>` can be used. The W3C specification states that they are identical. Everything about the element `<transform>` applies equally to `<stylesheet>`. Following are sample structures of an XSLT document.

```
<?xml version='1.0' ?>
<xsl:stylesheet version='2.0' xmlns:xsl='http://www.w3.org/1999/XSL/Transform'>
  ...
</xsl:stylesheet>
```

or

```
<?xml version='1.0' ?>
<xsl:transform version='2.0' xmlns:xsl='http://www.w3.org/1999/XSL/Transform'>
  ...
</xsl:transform>
```

The elements `<stylesheet>` or `<transform>` must have the attribute `version` and the namespace attribute `xmlns`. The attribute `version` indicates the version of XSLT being used. It can have values '1.0' or '2.0'. Most modern browsers only support XSLT 1.0. XSLT 2.0 is implemented in most good XSLT processors, including Saxon and Xalan. The namespace attribute `xmlns` must have the value `http://www.w3.org/1999/XSL/Transform` that distinguishes XSLT elements from other elements. Any suitable prefix can be used. We shall use the prefix `xsl` for XSLT elements throughout this book.

There are different ways to apply an XSLT document to an XML document. One way is to add a link to the XML document which points to the actual XSLT file and lets the browsers do the transformation. This linking declaration is placed after XML declaration. Following is an example of such a declaration:

```
<?xml version='1.0' ?>
<?xml-stylesheet type='text/xsl' href='AnXSLTFile.xsl'?>
<root>
  ...
</root>
```

The element `<xml-stylesheet>` has two attributes: `type` and `href`. The attribute `type` specifies the type of the file being linked to. The value of this attribute is set to `text/xsl` to indicate that it is an XSLT file. The attribute `href` specifies the URI of the stylesheet file.

Most of the modern browsers do not support XSLT 2.0, which provides better functionality. Moreover, we may just want the resultant XML document for further processing rather than for displaying in the browser. In either case, XSLT processors can be used to make this transformation and get the desired result. These processors typically take an XML document and an XSLT file as arguments and generate an output depending on the instruction given in the XSLT file. The exact procedure of transformation will be discussed in Section 11.6.

Figure 11.5 shows the steps involved in the transformation.

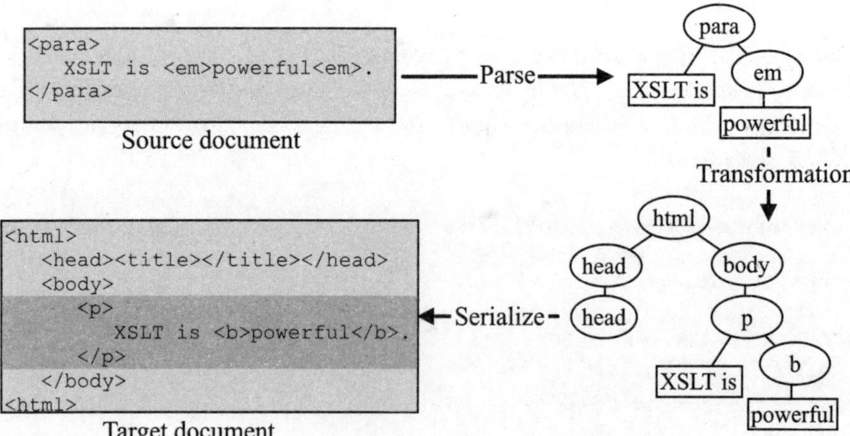

Figure 11.5 XSLT steps

11.4 XSLT ELEMENTS

An XSLT file contains elements from Table 11.1, which instruct the processor how an XML document is to be transformed.

Table 11.1 XSLT elements

analyze-string	apply-imports	apply-templates	attribute	attribute-set
call-template	character-map	choose	comment	copy
copy-of	decimal-format	element	fallback	for-each
for-each-group	function	if	import	import-schema
include	key	message	namespace-alias	number
otherwise	output	param	perform-sort	preserve-space
processing-instruction	result-document	sort	strip-space	stylesheet
template	text	transform	value-of	variable
when	with-param			

An XSLT file may contain elements that are not defined by XSLT. In such cases, an XSLT processor does not process these non-XSLT elements and add them to the output in the same order they occurred in the source XSLT document. This means that the transformed XML document may use the original markups as well as new markups.

11.5 TEMPLATE RULES

An XSLT document is all about template rules. A template specifies a rule and an instruction, which is executed when the rule matches. The rule is specified by the XSLT `<template>` element. It has the attribute `match`, which specifies the pattern. The value of the `match` attribute is a subset of the XPath expression. The XPath expression is not only used for the match attribute, but also in several other places in an XSLT document. XSLT is a major application area of XPath.

A template typically looks like this:

```
<xsl:template match='XPath expression'>
   Instruction to be followed
</xsl:template>
```

Consider a simple XSLT document containing a single template rule.

```
<?xml version='1.0' ?>
<xsl:transform version='2.0' xmlns:xsl='http://www.w3.org/1999/XSL/Transform' >
   <xsl:output method='html' />
   <xsl:template match='/'>
      Hello world!
   </xsl:template>
</xsl:transform>
```

This XSLT document contains a single template rule. It has a `match` attribute with the XPath expression "/", which matches the document root of any XML document. The instruction within this template specifies that the string `Hello world!` has to be added to the output. So, the result of any XML document transformed by this XSLT document is a single line:

```
Hello world!.
```

The result of this example is simply a line of text. Let us write a more complex XSLT file that generates an HTML file.

```
<?xml version='1.0' ?>
<xsl:transform version='2.0' xmlns:xsl='http://www.w3.org/1999/XSL/Transform' >
   <xsl:template match='/'>
      <html>
         <head><title>Simple template</title></head>
         <body>
            <h1>Hello world!</h1>
         </body>
      </html>
   </xsl:template>
</xsl:transform>
```

This stylesheet produces the following result if applied on any XML document:

```
<html>
  <head><title>Simple template</title></head>
  <body>
```

```
        <h1>Hello world!</h1>
    </body>
</html>
```

These XSLT documents do not do any useful task; they just show how a template rule can be used. Moreover, each of these XSLT documents has one template. A typical XSLT document contains many templates.

11.6 XSLT PROCESSORS

There are several XSLT 2.0 processors freely available on the web. In this book, we shall discuss installation and usage of two popular Java XSLT processors: Saxon and Xalan.

11.6.1 Saxon

SAXON is a popular and powerful XSLT processor developed by Michael Kay of Saxonica Limited. The information about this product can be found from the site `http://saxon.sourceforge.net/`. The latest version of Saxon is version 9.2. The following three versions are available: Saxon-HE (home edition), Saxon-PE (professional edition), and Saxon-EE (enterprise edition). Out of these three editions, Saxon-HE is an open source product available under the Mozilla Public License. It provides implementations of XSLT 2.0, XQuery 1.0, and XPath 2.0 at the basic level of conformance defined by the W3C. It is available for both Java and .NET.

Download the latest version of SAXON XSLT and XQuery processor for Java from `http://saxon.sourceforge.net/`. Typically, you will download a .zip file. Unzip the file in a directory. You will find a .jar file in the unzipped directory. This jar file contains necessary Java class files for the XSLT processor. Typically, we use the class `net.sf.saxon.Transform`.

Use the following command to perform the transformation. Make sure that the jar file is in your classpath.

```
java -cp saxon9.jar net.sf.saxon.Transform xmlFile XSLTFile
```

11.6.2 Xalan

Xalan-Java by Apache is also a commonly used XSLT processor for transforming XML documents into HTML, text, or other XML document types. It implements XSL Transformations (XSLT) Version 1.0 and XML Path Language (XPath) Version 1.0. This processor can be used from the command line, in an applet or a servlet, or as a module in another program.

Download the appropriate version of this XSLT processor from `http://www.apache.org/dyn/closer.cgi/xml/xalan-j`. Unzip the file and put it in a directory. You will find the `xalan.jar` file that contains the necessary Java classes for the XSLT processor.

Use the following command to perform the transformation. Make sure that the jar file is in your classpath.

```
java -cp xalan.jar org.apache.xalan.xslt.Process -IN xmlFile -XSL XSLTFile
-OUT outFile
```

11.7 SELECTING VALUE

So far, we have added constant text to the result. The value of a node can also be added. This is done using the element `<value-of>`. The node(s) to be selected is specified using the `select` attribute. Table 11.2 shows the values of different node types.

Table 11.2 Values of different node types

Node type	Node value	Node type	Node value
Text	The text of the node; essentially the node itself	Namespace	The URI of the namespace
Element	Concatenation of values of all text descendants	Comment	Anything between <!—and -->
Attribute	Attribute value without quotation marks	Processing instruction	Anything between <? and ?>

The *value* [Table 11.2] of a node depends on the type of the node. For example, the value of a text node is the text itself whereas the value of an element node is the concatenation of values of all text descendants. If multiple nodes are selected by the `select` attribute, the value is the concatenation of values of those selected nodes. Consider the following simple XML document.

```
<article>
   <title>Swarm intelligence</title>
</article>
```

One can now extract the value of the `title` element using the `<value-of>` element as follows:

```
<?xml version='1.0' ?>
<xsl:transform version='2.0' xmlns:xsl='http://www.w3.org/1999/XSL/Transform' >
   <xsl:template match='/'>
      Title: <xsl:value-of select='article/title' />
   </xsl:template>
</xsl:transform>
```

This XSLT file, on applying the previous XML document produces the following result.

```
Title: Swarm intelligence
```

Nodes selected by a relative XPath expression used in the `select` attribute of the `<value-of>` element are relative to the nodes selected by the `match` attribute of the enclosing template.

XSLT has another element <copy-of>, which returns all selected elements including nested elements and text. Consider the following XSLT document.

```
<?xml version='1.0' ?>
<xsl:transform version='2.0' xmlns:xsl='http://www.w3.org/1999/XSL/Transform' >
   <xsl:template match='/'>
      <xsl:copy-of select='.' />
   </xsl:template>
</xsl:transform>
```

When you apply this XSLT document to any XML document, it produces the same XML document. This is because, when the root element (/) is selected, `<copy-of>` copies the root element together with all child elements recursively.

11.8 APPLYING TEMPLATES

We have seen that if a node matches with a template's pattern, the template's action part is processed. It is also possible to instruct the XSLT processor to process other template rules (if any). This is done using the <apply-templates> element.

```
<?xml version='1.0' ?>
<xsl:transform version='2.0' xmlns:xsl='http://www.w3.org/1999/XSL/Transform' >
   <xsl:template match='/'>
      <xsl:apply-templates />
   </xsl:template>
</xsl:transform>
```

This example states that whenever a document root is encountered, the XSLT processor has to process all templates that match with the document root's children nodes. The XSLT engine, in turn, compares each child element of the document root against templates in the stylesheet and if a match is found, it processes the corresponding template. The matched node's template itself may contain <apply-templates> elements to search for other matches.

The element <apply-templates> has the attribute select, whose value is an XPath expression that can be used to select an arbitrary set of nodes to be processed. If none is specified (as in this case), all child elements, text, comment, and processing instruction nodes of the context node are selected. However, namespace and attribute nodes are not selected.

```
<?xml version='1.0' ?>
<xsl:transform version='2.0' xmlns:xsl='http://www.w3.org/1999/XSL/Transform' >
   <xsl:template match='/'>
      <xsl:apply-templates select='//HDD' />
   </xsl:template>
</xsl:transform>
```

In this example, if a document root is encountered, the XSLT processor processes all templates that match with HDD elements.

11.9 PROCESSING SEQUENCE AND DEFAULT TEMPLATES

When an XSLT processor is supplied an XML document for transformation using an XSLT document, it first creates a document tree. Processing always starts from the document root of this tree. So, the XSLT processor looks for a template for it. If no template is found for the document root, the XSLT processor provides a default template. This default template for the document root looks like this:

```
<xsl:template match='/'>
   <xsl:apply-templates/>
</xsl:template>
```

The action of this default template indicates that templates that match all of its children have also to be processed. If no template is specified for a child, the XSLT processor will provide a default one on behalf of that child and process it. This default template looks exactly like the document root's default template. It instructs the XSLT processor to process its children the same way the template for a document root does. This way, processing continues in a depth-first manner. The behavior of a default template can be overridden by explicity specifying that template. The behavior of the default template for any element node looks as follows:

```
<xsl:template match='*'>
   <xsl:apply-templates/>
</xsl:template>
```

The default template for text nodes looks as follows:

```
<xsl:template match='text()'>
   <xsl:value-of select='.'/>
</xsl:template>
```

Table 11.3 gives the exact behavior of these default templates.

Table 11.3 Default templates and their behavior

Template	Behavior	Template	Behavior
Root	Process templates for its children	Text	Output text value
Element	Process templates for its children	Processing instruction	Do nothing
Attribute	Output attribute name and value	Comment	Do nothing

Consider the following XSLT document.

```
//TCPFactServer.java
<?xml version='1.0' ?>
<xsl:transform version='2.0' xmlns:xsl='http://www.w3.org/1999/XSL/Transform' >
</xsl:transform>
```

Note that no template is specified here. However, this is a valid XSLT document. What will be the result if we use this document to transform an XML document? If you carefully observe the behavior of default templates, you will understand that ultimately templates for all text nodes will be processed. A default template for a text node simply outputs the text value. The result of this template will be the concatenation of all text values stored in the XML document.

Note that attributes are not treated as children. So, default templates for attributes are not called unless they are explicitly referenced.

11.10 NAMED TEMPLATES

XSLT named templates resemble the functions in any procedural programming language. The XSLT `<template>` element has a `name` attribute, which can be used to give a name to a template. Once a template is created this way, it can be called by using the `<call-template>` element and specifying its name. Consider the following example:

```
<?xml version='1.0' ?>
<xsl:transform version='2.0' xmlns:xsl='http://www.w3.org/1999/XSL/Transform' >
   <xsl:output method='html' />
   <xsl:template match='/'>
      <xsl:call-template name='header' />
   </xsl:template>
```

```
    <xsl:template name='header'>
      <title>XSLT</title>
    </xsl:template>
</xsl:transform>
```

This example simply illustrates the syntax of the named template. A named template is useful if a particular task has to done repeatedly. It is generally used in conjunction with the `param` element, which allows us to pass a parameter to a named template. The passing of a template parameter is described in Section 11.13.

11.11 REPETITION

XSLT allows the `<for-each>` construct, which can be used to process a set of instructions repeatedly for different items in a sequence. The attribute `select` evaluates a sequence of nodes. For each of the elements in this sequence, instructions under the `<for-each>` element are processed. Note that it is not a loop; so jumping out of it does not make any sense.

Consider the following XML document, `book.xml`.

```
<store>
   <book title='Communication Networks'>
      <author>Alberto Leon-Garcia</author>
      <author>Indra Widjaja</author>
      <price>400</price>
   </book>
      <book title='The Java Programming Language'>
      <author>Arnold Gosling Holmes</author>
      <price>350</price>
   </book>
</store>
```

In this example, a book may have any number of authors. It is difficult for an XSLT document writer to extract the names of all authors without any prior knowledge. The `<for-each>` construct can help much in this regard.

```
<?xml version='1.0' ?>
<xsl:transform version='2.0' xmlns:xsl='http://www.w3.org/1999/XSL/Transform' >
   <xsl:template match='//book'>
      Title: <xsl:value-of select='@title' />
      <xsl:for-each select='author'>
         Author: <xsl:value-of select='.' />
      </xsl:for-each>
   </xsl:template>
</xsl:transform>
```

The result of this XSLT document is as follows:

```
Title: Communication Networks
Author: Alberto Leon-Garcia
Author: Indra Widjaja

Title: The Java Programming Language
Author: Arnold Gosling Holmes
```

Consider the following XML document, `hdd.xml`.

```
<?xml version="1.0" encoding="UTF-8"?>
<store>
   <HDD type="ATA">
      <make>Samsung</make>
      <capacity>80</capacity>
      <speed>7200</speed>
      <price>1600</price>
   </HDD><HDD type="SATA">
      <make>Samsung</make>
      <capacity>160</capacity>
      <speed>7200</speed>
      <price>2200</price>
   </HDD><HDD type="SATA">
      <make>Seagate</make>
      <capacity>80</capacity>
      <speed>7200</speed>
      <price>1600</price>
   </HDD>
</store>
```

Now, consider the following XSLT file `for-each.xsl`, which extracts the information from this XML document and generates an HTML document.

```
<?xml version='1.0' ?>
<xsl:transform version='2.0' xmlns:xsl='http://www.w3.org/1999/XSL/Transform' >
   <xsl:output method='html' />
   <xsl:template match='/'>
   <html><body><table border='1'>
      <caption>Available Hard disks</caption>
      <tr>
         <th>Make</th>
         <th>Capacity</th>
         <th>Speed</th>
         <th>Price</th>
      </tr>
      <xsl:for-each select='.//HDD'>
         <tr>
         <td><xsl:value-of select='make'/></td>
         <td><xsl:value-of select='capacity'/></td>
         <td><xsl:value-of select='speed'/></td>
         <td><xsl:value-of select='price'/></td>
         </tr>
      </xsl:for-each>
   </table></body></html>
   </xsl:template>
</xsl:transform>
```

If you translate the XML document `hdd.xml` using this XSLT file, it generates the following result shown in Figure 11.6:

```
C:\Windows\system32\cmd.exe
E:\Books\WebTechnologies\11. XSLT>java -cp saxon9.jar net.sf.saxon.
Transform hdd.xml for-each.xsl
<html>
   <body>
      <table border="1">
         <caption>Available Hard disks</caption>
         <tr>
            <th>Make</th>
            <th>Capacity</th>
            <th>Speed</th>
            <th>Price</th>
         </tr>
         <tr>
            <td>Samsung</td>
            <td>80</td>
            <td>7200</td>
            <td>1600</td>
         </tr>
         <tr>
            <td>Samsung</td>
            <td>160</td>
            <td>7200</td>
            <td>2200</td>
         </tr>
         <tr>
            <td>Seagate</td>
            <td>80</td>
            <td>7200</td>
            <td>1600</td>
         </tr>
      </table>
   </body>
</html>
E:\Books\WebTechnologies\11. XSLT>
```

Figure 11.6 XSLT for-each construct demonstration

You can save this output to the HTML file `hdd.html` as follows:

```
java -cp saxon9.jar net.sf.saxon.Transform hdd.xml for-each.xsl > hdd.htm
```

Now, if you see this `hdd.htm` file in Internet explorer, it looks as shown in Figure 11.7.

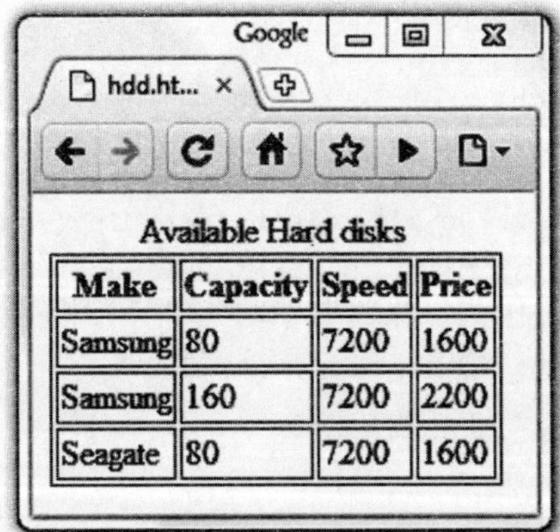

Figure 11.7 Converting XML document to HTML document using XSLT

Nested <for-each> elements are also possible. For example, this example could also have been written using the nested <for-each> element as follows:

```
<?xml version='1.0' ?>
<xsl:transform version='2.0' xmlns:xsl='http://www.w3.org/1999/XSL/Transform' >
   <xsl:output method='html' />
   <xsl:template match='/'>
   <html><body><table border='1'>
      <caption>Available Hard disks</caption>
      <tr>
         <th>Make</th>
         <th>Capacity</th>
         <th>Speed</th>
         <th>Price</th>
      </tr>
      <xsl:for-each select='.//HDD'>
         <tr>
            <xsl:for-each select='./*'>
               <td><xsl:value-of select='.'/></td>
            </xsl:for-each>
         </tr>
      </xsl:for-each>
   </table></body></html>
   </xsl:template>
</xsl:transform>
```

It generates exactly the same result as before.

11.12 CONDITIONAL PROCESSING

There are two types of branching constructs in XSLT: <if> and <choose>.

11.12.1 Using if

The XSLT <if> element has the attribute `test`, which takes a Boolean expression. If the effective Boolean value of this expression is evaluated to `true`, the action under the <if> construct is followed. The general syntax of the <if> construct is as follows:

```
<xsl:if test='somecondition'>
   do something here
</xsl:if>
```

The following XMLT file extracts information about only that book having the title "Communication Networks".

```
<?xml version='1.0' ?>
<xsl:transform version='2.0' xmlns:xsl='http://www.w3.org/1999/XSL/Transform' >
   <xsl:template match='//book'>
      <xsl:if test='@title="Communication Networks"' >
         Title: <xsl:value-of select='@title' />
         Price: Rs. <xsl:value-of select='price' />
      </xsl:if>
   </xsl:template>
</xsl:transform>
```

If it is applied on our book.xml file, the output looks like this:

```
Title: Communication Networks
Price: Rs. 400
```

11.12.2 Using Choose

The XSLT <choose> element allows us to select a particular condition among a set of conditions specified by the <when> element. The general format of the <choose> construct is this:

```
<xsl:choose>
   <xsl:when test='expression_1'>…</xsl:when>
   <xsl:when test='expression_2'>…<xsl:when>
   …
   <xsl:when test='expression_n'>…<xsl:when>
   <xsl:otherwise>…</otherwise>
</xsl:choose>
```

Consider the following XML file result.xml, containing the marks of different students.

```
<result>
   <student roll='01'><marks>80</marks></student>
   <student roll='02'><marks>92</marks></student>
   <student roll='03'><marks>75</marks></student>
   <student roll='04'><marks>45</marks></student>
   <student roll='05'><marks>60</marks></student>
</result>
```

The following XSLT document, choose-result.xsl, demonstrates how to use the <choose> construct.

```
<?xml version='1.0' ?>
<xsl:transform version='2.0' xmlns:xsl='http://www.w3.org/1999/XSL/Transform' >
   <xsl:template match='/'>
Roll Grade
<xsl:for-each select='//student'>
         <xsl:value-of select='@roll' /><xsl:text>    </xsl:text>
         <xsl:choose>
            <xsl:when test='marks &gt; 80 and marks &lt;= 100'>A</xsl:when>
            <xsl:when test='marks &gt; 50 and marks &lt;= 80'>B</xsl:when>
            <xsl:otherwise>F</xsl:otherwise>
         </xsl:choose>
<xsl:text>
</xsl:text>
      </xsl:for-each>
   </xsl:template>
</xsl:transform>
```

The choose-result.xsl file translates the result.xml file as follows:

```
Roll Grade
01   B
02   A
03   B
04   F
05   B
```

11.13 VARIABLES AND PARAMETERS

It was mentioned earlier that named templates resemble the functions in any procedural programming language. Like a function, a named template may accept arguments. Formal parameters are declared within a template using the <param> element as follows.

```
<xsl:template name='add'>
   <xsl:param name='a' />
   <xsl:param name='b' />
   <xsl:value-of select='$a+$b' />
</xsl:template>
```

This example defines the named template add, which takes two parameters, a and b. The purpose of this template is to add the two arguments taken and add the result to the output. Arguments can then be passed to the template using the <with-param> element during the template call.

```
<xsl:call-template name='add' >
   <xsl:with-param name='a' select='2' />
   <xsl:with-param name='b' select='4' />
</xsl:call-template>
```

This code segment calls the template add with parameters 2 and 4. Inside the template add, parameters a and b will be initialized by values 2 and 4, respectively. It then adds them and outputs the result. If this XSLT is applied on any XML document, the output will be 6.

The scope of a formal parameter is the template enclosing it. Formal parameters declared this way are variables and can be accessed using the following syntax:

```
$variableName
```

XSLT allows us to declare and use variables. Consider the following XSLT file variable.xsl.

```
<?xml version='1.0' ?>
<xsl:transform version='2.0' xmlns:xsl='http://www.w3.org/1999/XSL/Transform' >
   <xsl:output method='html' />
   <xsl:template match='/'>
      <xsl:variable name='a'>4</xsl:variable>
      <xsl:variable name='b'>3</xsl:variable>
      <xsl:value-of select='$a+$b' />
   </xsl:template>
</xsl:transform>
```

This XSLT document declares two variables, a and b with values 4 and 3, respectively. The variables can be used within the template using the <value-of> element and the select attribute. It outputs the value 7, on applying it on any XML document.

11.13.1 Recursive Template

XSLT also allows us to write recursive templates. The following example illustrates this.

```
<?xml version='1.0' ?>
<xsl:transform version='2.0' xmlns:xsl='http://www.w3.org/1999/XSL/Transform' >
   <xsl:output method='html' />
   <xsl:template match='/'>
```

```
        <xsl:call-template name='fact' >
           <xsl:with-param name='n' select='6' />
        </xsl:call-template>
     </xsl:template>

     <xsl:template name='fact'>
        <xsl:param name='n' />
        <xsl:if test='$n le 1'>1</xsl:if>
        <xsl:if test='$n gt 1'>
           <xsl:variable name='m'>
              <xsl:call-template name='fact'>
                 <xsl:with-param name='n' select='$n - 1' />
              </xsl:call-template>
           </xsl:variable>
           <xsl:value-of select='$n*$m' />
        </xsl:if>
     </xsl:template>
  </xsl:transform>
```

The XMLT document calculates and outputs the factorial of the number 6 recursively.

11.13.2 Attribute Value Templates

In XSLT, certain attributes of some elements can be set to an expression computed at runtime. Such attributes are called Attribute Value Templates. The expression used to set the attribute is written between "{" and "}" curly braces as follows:

```
<article title='{@title}' />
```

11.14 CREATING NODES AND SEQUENCES

XSLT allows us to directly create custom nodes such as element nodes, text nodes, etc. or sequences of nodes and atomic values that appear in the output. The name of the nodes created this way may be determined at run time.

11.14.1 Creating Element Nodes

An element node is created using the XSLT `<element>` tag. The content of the created element is whatever is generated between the starting and closing `<element>` tags. If an element has attributes, they are declared using the `<attribute>` tag described in the next section.

```
<xsl:element name='greeting'>
Hello World!
</xsl:element>
```

This code creates the element `greeting`.

```
<greeting>Hello World!</greeting>
```

The mandatory attribute `name` specifies the name of the generated element. This is one of the Attribute Value Templates and can be set to an expression computed at runtime.

```
<?xml version='1.0' ?>
<xsl:transform version='2.0' xmlns:xsl='http://www.w3.org/1999/XSL/Transform' >
   <xsl:output method='xml' />
   <xsl:template match='*'>
      <xsl:element name='{name()}' >
         <xsl:for-each select="@*" >
            <xsl:element name='{name()}'>
               <xsl:value-of select='.' />
            </xsl:element>
         </xsl:for-each>
         <xsl:apply-templates />
      </xsl:element>
   </xsl:template>
</xsl:transform>
```

This XSLT file converts all attribute nodes in any XML document to element nodes. For example, it converts the following XML document

```
<?xml version="1.0" encoding="utf-8"?>
<employee>
   <name>K. Pal</name>
   <sex>male</sex>
   <status>single</status>
   <salary basic='1500' DA='1000'/>
</employee>
```

to

```
<?xml version="1.0" encoding="UTF-8"?><employee>
   <name>K. Pal</name>
   <sex>male</sex>
   <status>single</status>
   <salary><basic>1500</basic><DA>1000</DA></salary>
</employee>
```

11.14.2 Creating Attribute Nodes

An attribute of an element is created using the enclosed `<attribute>` tag in XSLT. The mandatory attribute `name` specifies the name of the generated attribute. The value is indicated by the content of the `<attribute>` element. This is also an Attribute Value Templates and can be set to an expression computed at runtime.

```
<xsl:element name='greeting'>
   <xsl:attribute name='lang'>en</xsl:attribute>
   Hello World!
</xsl:element>
```

This code segment creates the element `greeting` with the attribute `lang`.

```
<greeting lang='en'>Hello World!</greeting>
```

The XSLT `<attribute>` construct is useful when we want to add an attribute to either a dynamically generated element or a literal result element. This element must appear immediately after the starting tag of the enclosing element. If attributes are created with the same name, the last one takes the precedence.

The XSLT <attribute> element has the attribute `select`, which can also be used to indicate the value of an attribute. In this case, the value of the select attribute is an XPath expression. The value of the resulting sequence for this XPath expression is computed as follows:

- The sequence is atomized.
- The final value is calculated by concatenating the resulting strings.

So, this attribute element could have been written as

```
<xsl:attribute name='lang' select='"en"' />
```

The named collection of attributes can be created using the <attribute-set> element. This named attribute set can then be used in <copy>, <element>, or another element using the `use-attribute-sets` attribute. The value of `use-attribute-sets` is a list of names of attribute sets, separated by white spaces. An attribute set cannot use itself.

```
<xsl:transform version='2.0' xmlns:xsl='http://www.w3.org/1999/XSL/Transform' >
   <xsl:attribute-set name='profile'>
      <xsl:attribute name='sex' select='"male"' />
      <xsl:attribute name='status' select='"double"' />
   </xsl:attribute-set>
   <xsl:template match='/'>
      <xsl:element name='employee' use-attribute-sets='profile'>
         U. K. Roy
      </xsl:element>
   </xsl:template>
</xsl:transform>
```

This creates the following element.

```
<employee sex='male' status='double'>U. K. Roy</employee>
```

Attributes can be added to the literal result element using the same procedure. These attributes can be overridden by adding them explicitly.

```
<employee status='single' xsl:use-attribute-sets='profile' />
```

This code generates the following result:

```
<employee sex='male' status='single'/>
```

The value of an attribute can be overridden further using the <attribute> element.

```
<employee status='single' xsl:use-attribute-sets='profile' >
   <xsl:attribute name='status' select='"divorced"' />
</employee>
```

This results in the following element.

```
<employee sex='male' status='divorced'/>
```

11.14.3 Creating Text Nodes

Generally, an XSLT processor outputs text that appears in the stylesheet. However, extra white spaces are not preserved in such a case. Secondly, special characters such as < and & are represented in text by the escape character sequences "<" and "&", respectively. For this reason, XSLT provides the <text> element to add literal text to the result.

The general format for outputting text is as follows:

```
<xsl:text [disable-output-escaping='yes|no']>text_contents</xsl:text>
```

The following example generates the single character "&".

```
<xsl:text disable-output-escaping='yes'>&amp;</xsl:text>
```

Similarly, the following code creates the string "Web Technology" preserving the space between "Web" and "Technology".

```
<xsl:value-of select='"Web"' />
<xsl:text> </xsl:text>
<xsl:value-of select='"Technology"' />
```

11.14.4 Creating Document Nodes

XSLT allows us to create a new document node using the <document> element. For example, the following code creates a temporary document node, which is stored in a variable named "tempTree".

```
<xsl:variable name="tempTree" as="document-node()">
  <xsl:document>
    <xsl:apply-templates/>
  </xsl:document>
</xsl:variable>
```

11.14.5 Creating Processing Instruction

A processing instruction is added in the result using the <processing-instruction> element. The most popular use of this <processing-instruction> element is to insert the <stylesheet> element in the output HTML/XML document. Consider the following example.

```
<xsl:processing-instruction name="xml-stylesheet">
      <xsl:text>href="sort.xsl" type="text/xsl"</xsl:text>
   </xsl:processing-instruction>
```

This code adds a processing instruction at the place of this <processing-instruction> as follows:

```
<?xml-stylesheet href="sort.xsl" type="text/xsl"?>
```

Following is a concrete example:

```
<?xml version='1.0' ?>
<xsl:transform version='2.0' xmlns:xsl='http://www.w3.org/1999/XSL/Transform' >
   <xsl:output method='xml' />
   <xsl:template match='/'>
      <xsl:processing-instruction name="xml-stylesheet">
         <xsl:text>href="hello.xsl" type="text/xsl"</xsl:text>
      </xsl:processing-instruction>
      <html>
         <head><title>Simple template</title></head>
         <body>
```

```
            <h1>Hello world!</h1>
         </body>
      </html>
   </xsl:template>
</xsl:transform>
```

It generates the following HTML document with the XSL file `hello.xsl` referenced from it.

```
<?xml version="1.0" encoding="UTF-8"?>
<?xml-stylesheet href="hello.xsl" type="text/xsl"?>
<html>
   <head><title>Simple template</title></head>
   <body>
      <h1>Hello world!</h1>
   </body>
</html>
```

11.14.6 Creating Comments

A comment is added using the XSLT `<comment>` element. The comment text is put in the starting and ending `<comment>` tags.

```
<xsl:comment> U. K. Roy </xsl:comment>
```

This code generates the following comment in the output.

```
<!-- U. K. Roy -->
```

Any space after the starting tag and before the ending tag is preserved in the comment.

11.15 COPYING NODES

The `<copy>` element copies the current node to the output. If the node is an element node, its namespace nodes are copied automatically, but the attributes and children of the element nodes are not copied automatically. Consider the simple SML document:

```
<article>
   <title>Swarm intelligence</title>
</article>
```

Now, consider the following XSLT document.

```
<xsl:transform
      xmlns:xsl='http://www.w3.org/1999/XSL/Transform' version='2.0'>
   <xsl:template match="/article">
      <xsl:copy />
   </xsl:template>
</xsl:transform>
```

This XSLT document has only one explicit template that matches with the root element, i.e., the `<article>` element. The `<copy>` element indicates that the current element `<article>` is to be copied. Since, no other action is taken, nothing else is added to the output. So, the result is as follows:

```
<article/>
```

Now, consider the following XSLT document:

```
<xsl:transform
        xmlns:xsl='http://www.w3.org/1999/XSL/Transform' version='2.0'>
   <xsl:template match="/article">
   <xsl:copy>
      <xsl:apply-templates />
   </xsl:copy>
   </xsl:template>
   <xsl:template match="/article/title">
   <xsl:copy />
   </xsl:template>
</xsl:transform>
```

This produces the following result:

```
<article>
   <title/>
</article>
```

What is the importance of this <copy> element? Suppose, we want to write an XSLT document which, when applied on an XML document, generates the XML document itself. This type of XSLT documents are called identity templates. The XSLT <copy> element can be used to write such an identity template. Following is an example:

```
<xsl:stylesheet
        xmlns:xsl='http://www.w3.org/1999/XSL/Transform' version='2.0'>
   <xsl:template match="@*|node()">
     <xsl:copy>
        <xsl:apply-templates select="@*|node()"/>
     </xsl:copy>
   </xsl:template>
</xsl:stylesheet>
```

This XSLT document has a single explicit template that matches every node including attribute, processing instruction, and comment node. When it matches the root element of any XML document, the <copy> element adds it to the output and applies the same template for attributes and children. This procedure continues recursively until no node is left. The output is effectively an exact copy of the XML document.

11.16 GROUPING

XSLT allows us to group related items based on common values. Consider the following XML document.

```
<?xml version='1.0'?>
<employees>
   <employee name='B. C. Dhara' dept='IT' />
   <employee name='U. K. Roy' dept='IT' />
   <employee name='S. Ghosh' dept='CSE' />
   <employee name='N. Mukherjee' dept='CSE' />
   <employee name='P. K. Das' dept='CSE' />
   <employee name='S. Roy' dept='SMCC' />
```

```
    <employee name='G. Roy' dept='SMCC' />
    <employee name='P. Bhaumik' dept='IT' />
    <employee name='S. Chattopadhyay' dept='IT' />
</employees>
```

What happens if somebody wants to print the name of all employees, grouped by their department name? Following is the solution.

```
<?xml version='1.0' ?>
<xsl:transform version='2.0' xmlns:xsl='http://www.w3.org/1999/XSL/Transform' >
   <xsl:output method='html' />

   <xsl:template match='/employees'>
      <xsl:for-each-group select="employee" group-by="@dept">
<xsl:text>
</xsl:text>
      <xsl:value-of select="current-grouping-key()"/>
         <xsl:for-each select="current-group()">
   <xsl:text>
   </xsl:text>
               <xsl:value-of select="@name"/>
         </xsl:for-each>
      </xsl:for-each-group>
   </xsl:template>
</xsl:transform>
```

The `<for-each-group>` enumerates group items based either on common values of a grouping key or a pattern specified by the `group-by` attribute. The `current-group()` function returns the current group item in the iteration and the `current-grouping-key()` returns the common key of the current group. The rest of the code is easy to understand.

The output looks like this:

```
IT
         B. C. Dhara
         U. K. Roy
         P. Bhaumik
         S. Chattopadhyay
CSE
         S. Ghosh
         N. Mukherjee
         P. K. Das
SMCC
         S. Roy
         G. Roy
```

11.17 SORTING

We can sort a group of similar elements using the XSLT `<sort>` element. The attributes of the `<sort>` element describe how to perform sorting. For example, sorting can be done alphabetically or numerically, based on single or multiple keys in increasing or decreasing order. The attribute `select` is used to specify the sorting key. The `order` attribute specifies the order and can have values `ascending` (default) or `descending`. The first `<sort>` element specifies the primary sorting key and subsequent <sort> elements specify secondary and other keys. The type (number/text) of the data to be sorted can be specified using the attribute data-type.

The following example sorts the list of HDDs with respect to their prices.

```
<?xml version='1.0' ?>
<xsl:transform version='2.0' xmlns:xsl='http://www.w3.org/1999/XSL/Transform' >
  <xsl:output method='html' />
  <xsl:template match='/' >
    <html><head><title>Sort Demo</title></head><body><table border='1'>
    <caption>Available HDDs</caption>
    <tr><th>Make</th><th>Capacity(GB)</th><th>Price(INR)</th></tr>
    <xsl:for-each select='//HDD'>
      <xsl:sort select='price' data-type='number'/>
      <tr>
        <td><xsl:value-of select='make'/></td>
        <td><xsl:value-of select='capacity'/></td>
        <td><xsl:value-of select='price'/></td>
      </tr>
    </xsl:for-each>
    </table></body></html>
  </xsl:template>
</xsl:transform>
```

It generates the following HTML document.

```
<html>
   <head>
      <meta http-equiv="Content-Type" content="text/html; charset=UTF-8">
      <title>Sort Demo</title>
   </head>
   <body>
      <table border="1">
         <caption>Available HDDs</caption>
         <tr>
            <th>Make</th>
            <th>Capacity(GB)</th>
            <th>Price(INR)</th>
         </tr>
         <tr>
            <td>Samsung</td>
            <td>80</td>
            <td>1600</td>
         </tr>
         <tr>
            <td>Seagate</td>
            <td>80</td>
            <td>1600</td>
         </tr>
         <tr>
            <td>Samsung</td>
            <td>160</td>
            <td>2200</td>
         </tr>
      </table>
   </body>
</html>
```

If you view this document, it looks as shown in Figure 11.8.

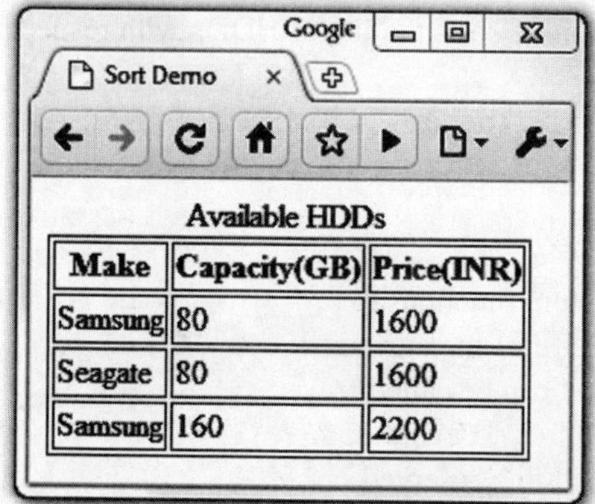

Figure 11.8 Demonstration of XSLT sort construct

11.18 NUMBERING

The XSLT `<number>` element allows us to insert and format a number into the result tree. Consider the XML document taken in Section 11.16. We can add numbers to the output as follows:

```
<?xml version='1.0' ?>
<xsl:transform version='2.0' xmlns:xsl='http://www.w3.org/1999/XSL/Transform' >
  <xsl:output method='html' />

  <xsl:template match='/employees'>
    <xsl:for-each-group select="employee" group-by="@dept">
<xsl:text>
</xsl:text>
<xsl:number value="position()"/>. <xsl:value-of select="current-grouping-key()"/>
      <xsl:for-each select="current-group()">

  <xsl:text>
  </xsl:text>
<xsl:number value="position()" />. <xsl:value-of select="@name"/>
      </xsl:for-each>
    </xsl:for-each-group>
  </xsl:template>
</xsl:transform>
```

The output will now look like this:

```
1. IT
      1. B. C. Dhara
      2. U. K. Roy
      3. P. Bhaumik
      4. S. Chattopadhyay
```

```
2. CSE
        1. S. Ghosh
        2. N. Mukherjee
        3. P. K. Das
3. SMCC
        1. S. Roy
        2. G. Roy
```

11.19 FUNCTIONS

XSLT also allows custom functions to be defined in a stylesheet. A function is defined using the <function> element. It has the attribute name, which specifies the name of the function. Once a function is defined, it can be called from any XPath expression. The function name must have a prefix. This is required to avoid conflict with any function from the default namespace. A prefix cannot be bound to a reserved namespace.

The <function> element must be defined as a top-level element in the stylesheet. The following example illustrates the uses of this element.

```
<?xml version='1.0' ?>
<xsl:transform version='2.0' xmlns:xsl='http://www.w3.org/1999/XSL/Transform'
xmlns:f='http://www.jusl.ac.in'>
   <xsl:function name='f:fact' >
      <xsl:param name='n' />
      <xsl:value-of select='if ($n le 1) then 1 else $n*f:fact($n - 1)' />
     </xsl:function>
   <xsl:template match='/'>
n n!
<xsl:for-each select='2 to 5' >
<xsl:value-of select='.' /><xsl:text> </xsl:text>
<xsl:value-of select='f:fact(.)' />
<xsl:text>
</xsl:text>
      </xsl:for-each>
     </xsl:template>
</xsl:transform>
```

This example produces the following result:

```
n n!
2 2
3 6
4 24
5 120
```

11.20 HANDLING MULTIPLE DOCUMENTS

XSLT allows us to work with multiple input documents or multiple output documents or both. In addition to the main document, multiple additional output documents (called subsidiary documents), can be created using the <result-document> element. The href attribute of the <result-document> element specifies the location of the subsidiary document. The content of the subsidiary document is the content of the corresponding <result-document> element.

```
<?xml version='1.0' ?>
<xsl:transform version='2.0' xmlns:xsl='http://www.w3.org/1999/XSL/Transform' >
  <xsl:output method='xml' />
  <xsl:template match='/'>
    <xsl:result-document href='hdd.xml'>
    <store>
      <xsl:copy-of select='//HDD'/>
    </store>
    </xsl:result-document>
    <xsl:result-document href='monitor.xml'>
    <store>
      <xsl:copy-of select='//monitor'/>
    </store>
    </xsl:result-document>
  </xsl:template>
</xsl:transform>
```

This XSLT document splits the file `store.xml` into two files, `hdd.xml` and `monitor.xml`. The file `hdd.xml` contains the information about all hard disk drives as follows:

```
<?xml version='1.0' encoding='UTF-8'?>
<store>
  <HDD type='ATA'>
    <make>Samsung</make>
    <capacity>80</capacity>
    <speed>7200</speed>
    <price>1600</price>
  </HDD>
  <HDD type='SATA'>
    <make>Samsung</make>
    <capacity>160</capacity>
    <speed>7200</speed>
    <price>2200</price>
  </HDD>
  <HDD type='SATA'>
    <make>Seagate</make>
    <capacity>80</capacity>
    <speed>7200</speed>
    <price>1600</price>
  </HDD>
</store>
```

The file `monitor.xml` contains the following information.

```
<?xml version='1.0' encoding='UTF-8'?>
<store>
  <monitor type='LCD' color='yes'>
    <make>LG</make>
    <price>7500</price>
    <size>15</size>
    <resolution>1280x800</resolution>
   </monitor><monitor type='LCD' color='yes'>
    <make>Samsung</make>
    <price>8000</price>
    <size>17</size>
```

```
      <resolution>1280x800</resolution>
   </monitor><monitor type='CRT' color='yes'>
      <make>LG</make>
      <price>4000</price>
      <size>15</size>
      <resolution>1024x768</resolution>
   </monitor>
   <monitor type='CRT' color='no'>
      <make>LG</make>
      <price>3500</price>
      <size>15</size>
      <resolution>1024x768</resolution>
   </monitor>
</store>
```

An XSLT does not allow the transformation of multiple input documents simultaneously. So, an XSLT stylesheet may take at most one input document. However, it can read additional documents using the XPath function `doc()`.The following XSLT document merges these two XML documents to form a single XML document.

```
<?xml version='1.0' ?>
<xsl:transform version='2.0' xmlns:xsl='http://www.w3.org/1999/XSL/Transform' >
   <xsl:output method='xml' />
   <xsl:template match='/store'>
      <store>
         <xsl:copy-of select='HDD'  />
         <xsl:copy-of select='doc("monitor.xml")/store/monitor' />
      </store>
   </xsl:template>
</xsl:transform>
```

It takes `hdd.xml` as the input document, reads another XML document `monitor.xml` using the XPath function `doc`, and finally merges these two.

11.21 INCLUDING AND IMPORTING STYLESHEETS

The XSLT `<include>` and `<import>` elements allow us to reuse existing stylesheets in other XSLT documents. The element `<include>` effectively copies the content of an XSLT document specified by its `href` attribute, into another XSLT document.

Suppose the content of `header.xsl` is

```
<?xml version='1.0' ?>
<xsl:transform version='2.0' xmlns:xsl='http://www.w3.org/1999/XSL/Transform' >
   <xsl:template name='header' >
      <xsl:param name='h' />
      <title><xsl:value-of select='$h' /></title>
   </xsl:template>
</xsl:transform>
```

and the content of `footer.xsl` is

```
<?xml version='1.0' ?>
<xsl:transform version='2.0' xmlns:xsl='http://www.w3.org/1999/XSL/Transform' >
   <xsl:template name='footer' >
      <xsl:param name='f' />
      <pageno><xsl:value-of select='$f' /></pageno>
   </xsl:template>
</xsl:transform>
```

The following example illustrates the use of include.

```
<?xml version='1.0' ?>
<xsl:transform version='2.0' xmlns:xsl='http://www.w3.org/1999/XSL/Transform' >
   <xsl:output method='html' />
   <xsl:include href='header.xsl' />
   <xsl:include href='footer.xsl' />

   <xsl:template match='/' >
      <xsl:call-template name='header' >
         <xsl:with-param name='h' select='"XSLT"' />
      </xsl:call-template>
      This is a page
      <xsl:call-template name='footer' >
         <xsl:with-param name='f' select='"1"' />
      </xsl:call-template>
   </xsl:template>
</xsl:transform>
```

Had the content of header.xsl and footer.xsl been copied in place of their respective <include> elements, it would have worked in the same way. The result of this XSLT document is

```
<title>XSLT</title>
   This is a page
<pageno>1</pageno>
```

It is not possible to include the same document more than once, either directly or indirectly. A stylesheet cannot also include itself. Either case will lead to a duplication error. The <include> element must be used as a top-level element, i.e., it must be a child of the <stylesheet> or <transform> elements.

The templates defined in including and included documents have equal importance. So, if there is any ambiguous template rule, the XSLT processor will identify it. Consequently, some warning/error message will be given.

The element <import> can also be used to add XSLT documents to other documents. However, definitions of templates defined in imported documents may be overridden in importing documents. This is a powerful way to exploit existing stylesheets. The <import> elements must also be children of the <stylesheet> or <transform> elements and must occur before all other elements. This XSLT document, if written using the <import> element, looks as follows:

```
<?xml version='1.0' ?>
<xsl:transform version='2.0' xmlns:xsl='http://www.w3.org/1999/XSL/Transform' >
   <xsl:output method='html' />
   <xsl:import href='header.xsl' />
   <xsl:import href='footer.xsl' />
```

```
    <xsl:template match='/' >
        <xsl:call-template name='header' >
            <xsl:with-param name='h' select='"XSLT"' />
        </xsl:call-template>
        This is a page
        <xsl:call-template name='footer' >
            <xsl:with-param name='f' select='"1"' />
        </xsl:call-template>
    </xsl:template>
</xsl:transform>
```

Needless to say, it generates the same output.

11.22 NAMESPACE ALIAS AND DYNAMIC STYLESHEET

The XSLT element `<namespace-alias>` allows us to create an alias for a namespace prefix. The general syntax of such an element is as follows:

```
<xsl:namespace-alias
   stylesheet-prefix = 'prefix' | '#default'
   result-prefix = 'prefix' | '#default'
/>
```

The element `<namespace-alias>` instructs the XSLT processor to substitute the prefix specified by the `stylesheet-prefix` attribute with the prefix specified by the `result-prefix` attribute, while producing the output. For example, if the following example is encountered, the XSLT processor replaces the prefix `source` by `target` in the result tree.

```
<xsl:namespace-alias  stylesheet-prefix = 'source' result-prefix = 'target'/>
```

The primary purpose of this element is to produce an XSLT document as a result of a transformation.

Elements that use XSLT namespace are treated as XSLT elements and are processed accordingly. For example, `<xsl:template>` is an XSLT element. Such XSLT elements are not added to the output. However, if a user really wants to add one such element that uses XSLT namespace to the output, how can he/she do this? The XSLT `<namespace-alias>` element helps in this regard.

Consider the following example, which shows an e-mail message written in English:

```
<?xml version='1.0' encoding='utf-8'?>
<email>
   <subject>Remainder</subject>
   <from>u_roy@it.jusl.ac.in</from>
   <to>parama@it.jusl.ac.in</to>
   <message>Return my book</message>
</email>
```

One may want to translate this e-mail message to some foreign language such as German. To do this, mapping from English to German is needed, which is described in the following XML document:

```
<?xml version='1.0' encoding='utf-8'?>
<mapping targetLanguage='German'>
```

```
    <email>email</email>
    <subject>thema</subject>
    <to>nach</to>
    <from>von</from>
    <message>Mitteilung</message>
</mapping>
```

With this mapping, it is possible to write an XSLT stylesheet that generates an XSLT document that transforms an e-mail message written in English to German language. The result document is itself an XSLT document, which contains elements that use XSLT namespace. Such elements cannot be produced using literal elements. The element `<namespace-alias>` can be used to do this very easily as follows:

```
<?xml version='1.0' ?>
<xsl:transform version='2.0' xmlns:xsl='http://www.w3.org/1999/XSL/Transform'
xmlns:out='http://mail.jusl.ac.in'>
    <xsl:namespace-alias stylesheet-prefix='out' result-prefix='xsl' />
    <xsl:template match='/mapping'>
        <out:transform version='2.0'>
            <out:output method='xml' indent='yes' />
            <xsl:for-each select='./*'>
                <out:template match='{name()}' >
                    <out:element name='{.}'>
                        <xsl:if test='name() ne "email"'>
                            <out:value-of select='.'/>
                        </xsl:if>
                        <xsl:if test='name() eq "email"'>
                            <out:apply-templates />
                        </xsl:if>
                    </out:element>
                </out:template>
            </xsl:for-each>
        </out:transform>
    </xsl:template>
</xsl:transform>
```

The elements that will be added to the output use the prefix `out` specified by the attribute `stylesheet-prefix`. The element `<namespace-alias>` states that the prefix `xsl` specified by the `result-prefix` attribute is an alias of the prefix `out` and that `xsl` must be used instead of `out` in the output tree. This way elements in the resultant document can use XSLT namespace.

If an XML document containing the mapping information from English to German is supplied as input, this stylesheet generates an XSLT document as follows:

```
<?xml version='1.0' encoding='UTF-8'?>
<xsl:transform xmlns:xsl='http://www.w3.org/1999/XSL/Transform' version='2.0'>
    <xsl:output method='xml' indent='yes' />
    <xsl:template match='email'>
        <xsl:element name='email'>
            <xsl:apply-templates />
        </xsl:element>
    </xsl:template>
    <xsl:template match='subject'>
```

```
        <xsl:element name='thema'>
            <xsl:value-of select='.' />
        </xsl:element>
    </xsl:template>
    <xsl:template match='to'>
        <xsl:element name='nach'>
            <xsl:value-of select='.' />
        </xsl:element>
    </xsl:template>
    <xsl:template match='from'>
        <xsl:element name='von'>
            <xsl:value-of select='.' />
        </xsl:element>
    </xsl:template>
    <xsl:template match='message'>
        <xsl:element name='Mitteilung'>
            <xsl:value-of select='.' />
        </xsl:element>
    </xsl:template>
</xsl:transform>
```

This resultant XSLT document translates an English email to corresponding German email as follows.

```
<?xml version='1.0' encoding='UTF-8'?>
<email>
    <thema>Remainder</thema>
    <von>u_roy@it.jusl.ac.in</von>
    <nach>parama@it.jusl.ac.in</nach>
    <Mitteilung>Return my book</Mitteilung>
</email>
```

Similarly, another transformation document can be produced dynamically for the following mapping file, which maps English to French.

```
<?xml version='1.0' encoding='utf-8'?>
<mapping targetLanguage='French'>
    <email>courriel</email>
    <subject>sujet</subject>
    <to>au</to>
    <from>de</from>
    <message>message</message>
</mapping>
```

The resultant XSLT document translates English email to French as follows:

```
<?xml version='1.0' encoding='utf-8'?>
<mapping>
    <email>courriel</email>
    <subject>sujet</subject>
    <to>au</to>
    <from>de</from>
    <message>message</message>
</mapping>
```

The element `namespace-alias` must be defined as a top-level element, i.e., it must be the child of the `stylesheet` element. There must be one `namespace-alias` element per namespace.

KEYWORDS

Attribute Value template: In XSLT, certain attributes of some elements can be set to an expression computed at runtime. Such attributes are called Attribute Value Templates.

Choice: The XSLT <choose> element allows us to select a particular condition among a set of conditions specified by the <when> element.

Conditional Processing: Processing is done depending on some condition. There are two types of branching construct in XSLT: <if> and <choose>.

Default template: If no template is provided in an XSLT document, the XSLT processor provides a default template for it.

Dynamic Stylesheet: An XSLT document that generates another XSLT document.

Grouping: XSLT allows us to group a related items based on common values.

Importing Stylesheet: The element `<import>` inserts XSLT documents into other documents; definitions of templates defined in imported documents may be overridden in importing documents.

Including stylesheet: The element `<include>` effectively copies the content of an XSLT document specified by its href attribute into another XSLT document.

Named template: A template that has a name, which can be used to call the template.

Namespace alias: The XSLT element `<namespace-alias>` allows us to create an alias for a namespace prefix.

Recursive template: A template that calls itself.

Repetition: XSLT allows the <for-each> construct, which can be used to process a set of instructions repeatedly for different items in a sequence.

Sorting: We can sort a group of similar elements using the XSLT <sort> element.

Template rule: A template specifies a rule and an instruction, which is executed when the rule matches.

XSLT processor: A program that understands XSLT documents and follows instructions written in them.

SUMMARY

XML documents contain self-describing and structured data. Users may also want to generate new XML documents from one or more existing XML documents for further processing or sharing of data between different applications. XSLT documents perform various tasks such as data reformatting, data suppression, addition of new content, copying information, etc.

An XSLT file transforms an XML file into another XML file. An XSLT processor generates a document tree from a source XML document and converts this to a result tree by executing the instructions specified in the XSLT file. The resultant XML file may be an XHTML file, which a web browser can understand or a WML (Wireless Markup Language) file, which a cellular phone can display.

An XSLT document is an XML document. Consequently, it starts with an XML declaration. The root element is either `<transform>` or `<stylesheet>`. There are different ways to apply an XSLT document to an XML document. One way is to add a link to the XML document, which points to the actual XSLT file and lets the browsers do the transformation.

An XSLT document basically consists of one or more template rules. A template specifies a rule and an instruction, which is executed when the rule matches. When an XSLT processor is supplied an XML document for transformation using an XSLT document, it first creates a document tree. Processing always starts from the document root of this tree. So, the XSLT processor looks for a template for it. If no template is found for the document root, the XSLT processor provides a default template.

XSLT named templates resemble the functions in any procedural programming language. It can be called repeatedly to perform the same task with different parameters.

XSLT also support important constructs such as looping, conditional processing, variables and parameters, recursive template, and functions. XSLT also allows us to add different types of elements to the result tree.

WEB RESOURCES

http://www.w3.org/TR/xslt
XSL Transformations (XSLT) Version 1.0

http://www.w3.org/TR/xslt20/
XSL Transformations (XSLT) Version 2.0

http://www.w3.org/TR/xslt20/#changes
Changes from XSLT 1.0

http://en.wikipedia.org/wiki/XSLT
XSLT

EXERCISES

Multiple Choice Questions

1. Which of the following statements is false?
   (a) XSLT is written in XML
   (b) XSLT uses XPath
   (c) XSLT is not a W3C Recommendation
   (d) XSLT is a subset of XSL

2. The `<choose>` element contains
   (a) a sequence of `<when>` elements followed by an optional `<otherwise>` element
   (b) one `<when>` element followed by a required `<otherwise>` element
   (c) one `<when>` element followed by an optional `<otherwise>` element
   (d) a sequence of `<when>` elements followed by a required `<otherwise>` element

3. Which of the following attributes is a valid attribute of the `<if>` element?
   (a) verify (b) check
   (c) select (d) test

4. Which of the following statements is true regarding the match attribute of the `<template>` element?
   (a) Selects elements for which a template is applied
   (b) Creates a variable
   (c) Selects a variable
   (d) Selects a case

5. The element `<sort>` is used
   (a) similarly to switch in other programming languages
   (b) inside `xsl:apply-templates` and `xsl:for-each` elements
   (c) inside `xsl:template` to select the elements the template is applied to
   (d) never; `sort` is an attribute, not an element

6. What does the element `<attribute>` do?
   (a) It generates an attribute in the destination document
   (b) It matches an attribute node in the source document
   (c) It associates an attribute to an element
   (d) Nothing; it does not exist

7. Which of the following syntaxes is the correct usage of the `<output>` element?
   (a) <xsl:output method='xml' indent='no'/>
   (b) <xsl:output method='html' indent='no'/>
   (c) <xsl:output method='text' indent='no'/>
   (d) All of them

8. Which is the correct syntax of the `union` operator?
   (a) <xsl:apply-templates select='/head/title & /book/title' />
   (b) <xsl:apply-templates select='/head/title OR /book/title' />
   (c) <xsl:apply-templates select='/head/title AND /book/title' />
   (d) <xsl:apply-templates select='/head/title | /book/title' />

9. Which of the following types of variables you can declare in XSLT?
   (a) Local variables only
   (b) Global variables only
   (c) Both local and global variables
   (d) None of the above

10. What is the full form of XSLT?
   (a) EXtendable Style Language Translation
   (b) EXtensible Stylesheet Language Transformation
   (c) EXtensible Style Language Transformation
   (d) EXtendable Stylesheet Language Translation

11. In an XSLT document, the matching rule is called
    (a) specification (b) syntax
    (c) rule (d) template

12. Which of the following axes is used by XSLT?
    (a) grand-parent (b) ancestor
    (c) child (d) descendant-or-self

13. Which of the following constructs is used for conditional processing?
    (a) ifelse (b) check (c) test (d) if

14. Which of the following characters is used before an attribute to access it?
    (a) % (b) $ (c) @ (d) &

15. Which of the following constructs is used for looping in XSLT?
    (a) while (b) for-each
    (c) do-while d) for

16. Which of the following constructs is used to select one among several possibilities?
    (a) select (b) choose
    (c) pickup (d) doSelect

17. Which of the following elements is used to insert formatted numbers in the output?
    (a) number (b) no
    (c) doNumber (d) format

18. Which of following elements is a valid element in XSLT?
    (a) than (b) where (c) when (d) which

19. Which of the following functions returns the number of nodes present in an argument node set?
    (a) find (b) number
    (c) counter (d) count

20. What does the following XSLT output?

```
<xsl:text disable-output-
escaping="yes">
  <!-- hello -->
</xsl:text>
```

    (a) hello
    (b) <!-- hello -->
    (c) <!-- hello -->
    (d) It will not output anything

21. Which of the following is a valid XSLT element?
    (a) copy-by (b) copy-of
    (c) copy-for (d) copy-with

Review Questions

1. Describe the structure of an XSLT document.
2. How do you link an XSLT file with an XML/HTML file?
3. What is the purpose of template rule?
4. What is the difference between value-of and copy-of?
5. An XSLT file is said to be an identity template if it is applied to an XML document producing the XML document itself. Write such an identity template.
6. Describe the processing sequence of templates written in an XSLT file.
7. Write the default template for element and text nodes.
8. How do you create a named template? How do you call it?
9. How do you pass parameters to named templates?
10. Discuss the syntax of the choose construct with examples.
11. How do you declare global variables? How do you access them?
12. Write a named template that takes two integer parameters and returns their sum.
13. Write a recursive template that takes one integer and returns the factorial of that number.
14. What are attribute value templates? Give examples.
15. Discuss how to create different types of nodes?
16. Explain how to group a set of related items in XSLT.
17. How do you perform numeric sorting in descending order?
18. Write a function that takes a single integer and returns the factorial of that number.
19. What is the difference between the <include> and <import> elements in XSLT?
20. Describe the notion of a dynamic style sheet. Mention its importance.

12 OTHER XML TECHNOLOGIES

KEY OBJECTIVES

After completing this chapter readers will be able to—

- **get an idea about four XML Technologies XLink, XPointer, XQuery, and XSL-FO**
- **learn how to create hyperlinks in XML documents**
- **learn basic syntax and semantics of XQuery language**
- **learn how to write basic queries to retrieve information from XML documents**
- **understand how to handle multiple XML documents in XQuery**
- **learn how to display XML documents using CSS and XSL-FO**

12.1 INTRODUCTION

In this chapter, we shall discuss four additional XML technologies, namely, XLink, XPointer, XQuery, and XSL-FO. Out of these technologies, XQuery and XSL-FO are widely used. We shall primarily focus on XQuery and XSL-FO.

12.2 XLINK

It allows us to create a standard way of inserting hyperlinks in XML documents. In June 2001, XLink became a W3C Recommendation.

In HTML documents, hyperlinks are created using the `<a>` tag. However, the same does not work in XML. In XML, we create hyperlinks by putting a marker on elements that we want to make hyperlinks. Following is an example:

```
<?xml version="1.0"?>
<?xml-stylesheet type="text/css" href="simple.css"?>
<links xmlns:xlink="http://www.w3.org/1999/xlink">

<jumail xlink:type="simple"
xlink:href="http://mail.jusl.ac.in">JU Mail</jumail>
```

```
<W3CHome xlink:type="simple"
xlink:href="http://www.w3.org">Visit W3C</W3CHome>

</links>
```

To use XLink, you must declare the namespace "http://www.w3.org/1999/xlink" for it at the top of the document. The `href` attribute of the `<jumail>` element indicates that it is a hyperlink and the `type` attribute indicates that it is a simple link. Figure 12.1 shows the result.

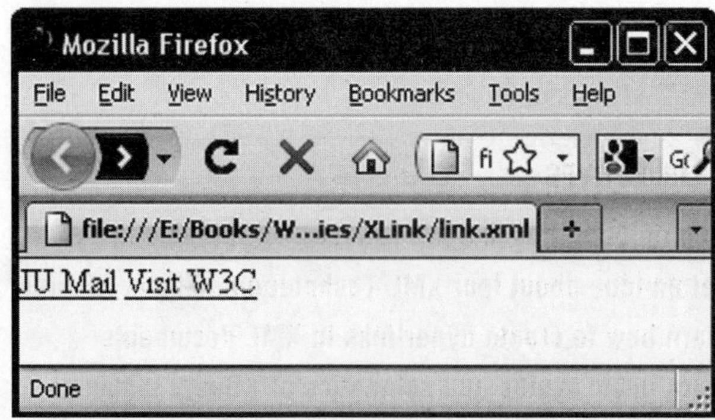

Figure 12.1 XLink used in an XML document

Unfortunately, most web browsers do not support XLink. The Firefox browser does include support for simple XLink links. So, we can create links in Firefox using XLink.

12.3 XPOINTER

XPointer resembles a bookmark in HTML. It allows us to select specific parts in the XML document. The following example illustrates this:

```
<?xml version="1.0"?>
<?xml-stylesheet type="text/css" href="simple.css"?>
<links xmlns:xlink="http://www.w3.org/1999/xlink">

<XQuery xlink:type="simple"
xlink:href="XTechnology.xml#id('XQuery')">XQuery</XQuery>

<XPath xlink:type="simple"
xlink:href="XTechnology.xml#id('XPath')">XPath</XPath>

</links>
```

This XML document provides two links: XQuery and XPath. When a user clicks on the first link, the `XTechnology.xml` file is loaded with the element having id “XQuery” as the first element.

12.4 XQUERY

One of the novel applications of XML documents is their use as relational databases. In fact, XML documents act as general databases. So, like SQL, which is a query language for relational databases, we also need a query language for XML documents. XQuery is nothing but one such query language.

12.4.1 XQuery and XPath

Note that, XPath can also extract information from XML documents. However, it has some limitations. For example, it cannot add anything to the result by itself. XQuery was designed to overcome these limitations keeping the strengths of XPath. The current version, XQuery 1.0, is a strict superset of Xpath 2.0. It means that every XPath 2.0 expression is also an XQuery 1.0 expression. In fact, many XPath expressions look like queries and they can extract fairly complex information from XML documents. XQuery basically adds the power of joining information from different sources and generating new XML documents. XPath only supports built-in functions. However, XQuery supports user-defined functions and thus allows arbitrary computations.

12.4.2 XQuery and XSLT

XQuery and XSLT have many concepts in common. In fact, as far as expressive power is concerned, one can be converted to the other. Both are designed to combine and transform XML documents. However, they differ vastly in their design. XQuery resembles SQL, whereas XSLT was influenced by CSS. Technically, they also use different philosophies. XSLT uses recursive procedure for traversing XML documents. On the other hand, users of the XQuery language must handle recursion explicitly.

In the following sections, we shall discuss the basic programming constructs of XQuery. In Section 12.4.3, we shall discuss the basic building blocks of XQuery. XQuery is an extension of XPath. Some of the basic concepts of XQuery can be found in Chapter 10. We shall discuss only those topics that are specific to XQuery.

12.4.3 XQuery Processor

Before discussing anything about XQuery, let us discuss how to process an XQuery and how to see the output. Many XQuery processors are freely available in the market. We shall use the well-known Saxon XQuery processor throughout this chapter. The Saxon XQuery processor is a part of the Saxon XPath/XSLT processor, which was used in Chapters 10 and 11. We also discussed how to download this processor in Chapter 10 (XPath).

The class file `net.sf.saxon.Query` is actually the XQuery processor. Suppose, you have written an XQuery in the file `"simple.xq"`. Process the query using the following command:

```
java -cp saxon9.jar net.sf.saxon.Query simple.xq
```

The Saxon XQuery processor will process the query written in the `simple.xq` file and display the result on the screen. The output can also be saved in a file. The processor has many options using which you can customize your query. This command assumes that the `saxon9.jar` file is placed in the same directory where the file containing XQuery is kept. If you have placed the `saxon9.jar` file anywhere else, specify the full path name.

12.4.4 Comments

Comments start and end with "smiley faces". Here is an example:

```
(: This is a comment :)
```

12.4.5 Literals

There are three types of numeric literals in XQuery:

- integer — number having only digits
- decimal — number having digits and a single decimal point
- double — floating-point number containing an `e` or `E`

They correspond to the XML Schema types `integer`, `decimal`, and `double`. Following are some examples of integer literals:

```
2    -2   +2
```

Following are some examples of decimal literals:

```
2.3  +2.3 -2.3
```

Following are some examples of double literals:

```
2.3e4   +2.3e4   -2.3e4  2.3E4    +2.3E4     -2.3E4
```

String literals are delimited by apostrophes or quotation marks as follows:

```
'a string'
"another string"
```

Apostrophes may occur between quotation marks and vice versa.

```
'a  "string"'
"another  'string'"
```

A string literal may contain entity references.

```
'&lt;para&gt;This  is  a  simple  paragraph.&lt;/para&gt;'
```

12.4.6 Input Documents

In this chapter, we shall discuss basics of XQuery with two XML documents, `HDD.xml` and `monitor.xml`. Two XML documents are used to demonstrate that XQuery can handle multiple XML documents. They contain specifications about different Hard Disk Drives (HDDs) and computer monitors, respectively. Here is the content of `HDD.xml`:

```
<?xml version='1.0'?>
<store>
   <HDD type='ATA'>
      <make>Samsung</make>
      <capacity>80</capacity>
      <speed>7200</speed>
      <price>1600</price>
   </HDD>
```

```
    <HDD type='SATA'>
       <make>Samsung</make>
       <capacity>160</capacity>
       <speed>7200</speed>
       <price>2200</price>
    </HDD>
    <HDD type='SATA'>
       <make>Seagate</make>
       <capacity>80</capacity>
       <speed>7200</speed>
       <price>1500</price>
    </HDD>
</store>
```

Here is the content of the `monitor.xml` file:

```
<?xml version='1.0'?>
<store>
    <monitor type='LCD' color='yes'>
       <make>LG</make>
       <price>7500</price>
       <size>15</size>
       <resolution>1280x800</resolution>
    </monitor>
    <monitor type='LCD' color='yes'>
       <make>Samsung</make>
       <price>8000</price>
       <size>17</size>
       <resolution>1280x800</resolution>
    </monitor>
    <monitor type='CRT' color='yes'>
       <make>LG</make>
       <price>4000</price>
       <size>15</size>
       <resolution>1024x768</resolution>
    </monitor>
    <monitor type='CRT' color='no'>
       <make>LG</make>
       <price>3500</price>
       <size>15</size>
       <resolution>1024x768</resolution>
    </monitor>
</store>
```

12.4.7 Input Functions

There are two input functions used frequently to create documents to be queried:

`doc(uri)`

This built-in function returns the document node corresponding to a document specified by the **U**niversal **R**esource **I**dentifier (URI). For example, for the XML file `HDD.xml`, `doc("HDD.xml")` returns a document node. Other nodes can be referred relative to this node. For instance, `doc("HDD.xml")/store` refers to the root node. All XPath/XQuery expressions can now be used to get the desired sequence of nodes. The concepts of location steps, location path, predicates are same as in XPath. So, we shall directly go to the XQuery-specific features.

```
collection(uri)
```

It returns a sequence of nodes that is associated with a document specified by the URI.

12.4.8 Constructors

XQuery not only extracts information from existing XML documents, but also produces XML documents. For example, the following line creates the `<greeting>` element.

```
<greeting>Hello World!</greeting>
```

In general, nodes are created using XQuery constructs called *constructors*. In this example, we have used an element constructor.

XQuery also provides an explicit constructor to create a document node. For example, `document { }` creates an empty document node. The following example creates an XML document using document constructor and other constructors:

```
document {
<!-- an email message, the comma used at the end is mandatory -->,
<email lang="en">
   <from>john@it.jusl.ac.in</from>
   <to>jane@it.jusl.ac.in</to>
   <subject>Remainder</subject>
   <body>Please return my book on Monday</body>
</email>
}
```

The result of an XQuery may be inserted in constructors using curly braces {} as follows:

```
<example>
   <para> Here is a query. </para>
   <query> doc("HDD.xml")//HDD[1]/make </query>
   <para> Here is the result of the above query.</para>
   <result>{ doc("HDD.xml")//HDD[1]/make }</result>
</example>
```

In this example, the result of the XQuery expression `doc("HDD.xml")//HDD[1]/make` is inserted. This generates the following output:

```
<?xml version="1.0" encoding="UTF-8"?>
<example>
   <para> Here is a query. </para>
   <query> doc("HDD.xml")//HDD[1]/make </query>
   <para> Here is the result of the above query.</para>
   <result>
      <make>Samsung</make>
   </result>
</example>
```

Element and attribute constructors have alternative syntaxes. The following example essentially generates the same email message as discussed previously:

```
element email {
   attribute lang { "en" },
   element from { "john@it.jusl.ac.in" },
```

```
    element to { "jane@it.jusl.ac.in" },
    element subject { "Remainder" },
    element body { "Please return my book on Monday" }
}
```

12.4.9 FLWOR Expression

One of the powerful features of XQuery is FLWOR (pronounced as flower) expressions. These expressions resemble The SELECT-FROM-WHERE...statements in SQL. Each letter in the phrase "FLWOR" stands for the first letter of the clauses that may occur in a FLWOR expression:

- `for` — binds items in a sequence generated by the given expression to a given variable one by one
- `let` — binds the result of an entire expression to a variable to be used later
- `where` — filters tuples keeping only those tuples that satisfy the given condition
- `order by` — sorts the items generated by other clauses
- `return` — for each tuple, it creates the result of the FLWOR expression.

A FLWOR expression consists of one or more `for` or `let` clauses in arbitrary order, followed by an optional `where` clause, an optional `order by` clause, and a mandatory `return` clause.

A variable is preceded by a `$` sign. Variable names follow the usual naming rules. So, `$count`, `$i`, `$x`, `$sum`, and `$avg` are all valid variable names. A variable binding done by the `for` and `let` clauses is called a *tuple*. For example, following is a simple FLWOR expression that returns the price of each HDD that has the capacity 80 GB:

```
for $hdd in doc("HDD.xml")//HDD
where $hdd/capacity = 80
return $hdd/price
```

The `for` clause in this example creates a series of tuples. Each tuple contains the variable `$hdd` bound to one HDD from a sequence generated by the expression `doc("HDD.xml")//HDD`. The `where` clause checks if `$hdd/capacity` is equal to `80`. The `return` clause returns `$hdd/price` if the tuple satisfies the condition. Save this query in the file `simple.xq` and use the following command.

```
java -cp saxon9.jar net.sf.saxon.Query simple.xq
```

The result of this command is shown as follows:

```
<price>1600</price>
<price>1500</price>
```

12.4.9.1 The for and let clauses

The `for` and `let` clauses in the FLWOR expression create tuples that are used by other clauses. So, every FLWOR expression must have at least one `for` or `let` clause. In this section, we shall discuss how various combinations of the `for` and `let` clauses generate tuples.

Consider the following expression:

```
for $v in (1, 2, 3)
   return <tuple><v>{ $v }</v></tuple>
```

In this query, the variable `$v` assumes one value from the sequence `(1, 2, 3)` at a time in that order and the `return` clause displays the result in terms of tuples.

```
<tuple><v>1</v></tuple>
<tuple><v>2</v></tuple>
<tuple><v>3</v></tuple>
```

The `let` clause, unlike the `for` clause, binds a variable to the entire result of an expression. Therefore, it generates a single tuple. Consider this example with the `let` clause.

```
let $v := (1, 2, 3)
   return <tuple><v>{ $v }</v></tuple>
```

This generates the following result.

```
<tuple><v>1 2 3</v></tuple>
```

The nested `for` clause may be possible.

```
for $v in (1, 2)
   for $w in (3, 4)
      return <tuple><v>{ $v }</v><w>{ $w }</w></tuple>
```

In this query, for each value of `$v`, `$w` assumes a value from the sequence `(1, 2, 3)`. So, this query effectively generates all possible combinations of `(1, 2)` and `(2, 3)`, called *Cartesian product* as follows:

```
<tuple><v>1</v><w>3</w></tuple>
<tuple><v>1</v><w>4</w></tuple>
<tuple><v>2</v><w>3</w></tuple>
<tuple><v>2</v><w>4</w></tuple>
```

This query could have been written like this:

```
for $v in (1, 2), $w in (3, 4)
  return <tuple><v>{ $v }</v><w>{ $w }</w></tuple>
```

Like the nested `for` clause, the nested `let` clause is also possible:

```
let $v := (1, 2)
   let $w := (3, 4)
      return <tuple><v>{ $v }</v><w>{ $w }</w></tuple>
```

Since each `let` clause generates one tuple, this query generates only one tuple as follows:

```
<tuple><v>1 2</v><w>3 4</w></tuple>
```

The `for` and `let` clauses may be combined to form a more complex expression. The following example uses one `for` and one `let` clause.

```
for $v in (1, 2)
   let $w := (3, 4)
      return <tuple><v>{ $v }</v><w>{ $w }</w></tuple>
```

It generates the following result.

```
<tuple><v>1</v><w>3 4</w></tuple>
<tuple><v>2</v><w>3 4</w></tuple>
```

The following code is another query that also combines the `for` and `let` clauses.

```
for $hdd in doc("HDD.xml")//HDD
   let $make := $hdd/make
   let $price := $hdd/price
   let $capacity := $hdd/capacity
      return <HDD>{ $make, $price, $capacity }</HDD>
```

This generates the following result.

```
<?xml version="1.0" encoding="UTF-8"?>
<HDD>
    <make>Samsung</make>
    <price>1600</price>
    <capacity>80</capacity>
</HDD>
<HDD>
    <make>Samsung</make>
    <price>2200</price>
    <capacity>160</capacity>
</HDD>
<HDD>
    <make>Seagate</make>
    <price>1500</price>
    <capacity>80</capacity>
</HDD>
```

The query shows the lists of manufacturers of HDDs, together with their capacity and price.

12.4.9.2 The where clause

A `where` clause keeps those tuples that satisfy a given condition.

```
for $v in (1, 2, 3, 4, 5, 6)
   where $v mod 2 = 0
      return <tuple><even>{ $v }</even></tuple>
```

In this query, the variable `$v` assumes all the values from 1 to 6, but the `where` clause retains those values that are divisible by 2. It results in the following:

```
<tuple><even>2</even></tuple>
<tuple><even>4</even></tuple>
<tuple><even>6</even></tuple>
```

The following query lists those manufacturers that have HDDs having price less than Rs. 2000.

```
for $hdd in doc("HDD.xml")//HDD
   where $hdd/price < 2000
      return $hdd/make
```

It generates the following result:

```
<make>Samsung</make>
<make>Seagate</make>
```

12.4.9.3 The order by clause

The `order by` clause sorts the tuples before the `return` clause generates the result. The following query sorts HDDs by their prices.

```
for $hdd in doc("HDD.xml")//HDD
   order by $hdd/price
      return  <HDD>{ $hdd/make, $hdd/capacity, $hdd/price }</HDD>
```

It results in the following output:

```
<HDD>
    <make>Seagate</make>
    <capacity>80</capacity>
    <price>1500</price>
</HDD>
<HDD>
    <make>Samsung</make>
    <capacity>80</capacity>
    <price>1600</price>
</HDD>
<HDD>
    <make>Samsung</make>
    <capacity>160</capacity>
    <price>2200</price>
</HDD>
```

The `order by` clause allows us to specify sorting criteria. The criteria tells the query processor whether to sort in `ascending` or `descending` order or to perform `stable` sorting or how to compare two values, etc. Consider the following expression.

```
for $hdd in doc("HDD.xml")//HDD
   order by $hdd/price ascending, $hdd/capacity descending
      return $hdd
```

This query sorts the HDDs by prices in ascending order, then by capacity in descending order.

The `order by` clause may use data not used by the `return` clause.

```
for $hdd in doc("HDD.xml")//HDD
   let $type := $hdd/@type
      order by $type descending
         return $hdd
```

This query sorts the HDDs in descending order with respect to their `type` attribute. The following example shows how to perform stable sorting.

```
for $hdd in doc("HDD.xml")//HDD
   let $type := $hdd/@type
   stable order by $type descending
      return $hdd
```

12.4.9.4 The return clause

The XQuery `return` clause is used to generate output. Like all other clauses, it can also have expressions. The most common expression used in the `return` clause is the element constructor:

```
for $make in distinct-values(doc("HDD.xml")//make)
  return <manufacturer>{ $make} </manufacturer>
```

It uses element constructors to show manufacturers of HDDs. It generates the following result.

```
<manufacturer>Samsung</manufacturer>
<manufacturer>Seagate</manufacturer>
```

The purpose of the built-in function `distinct-values()` is to eliminate duplicate tuples. We shall discuss about this function later in this section.

The order of elements may be changed in the `return` clause. The following example demonstrates this:

```
for $hdd in doc("HDD.xml")//HDD
  return <HDD>{ $hdd/price, $hdd/capacity, $hdd/make }</HDD>
```

This query changes the order of `<price>`, `<capacity>`, and `<make>` elements. It outputs the following result:

```
<HDD>
    <price>1600</price>
    <capacity>80</capacity>
    <make>Samsung</make>
</HDD>
<HDD>
    <price>2200</price>
    <capacity>160</capacity>
    <make>Samsung</make>
</HDD>
<HDD>
    <price>1500</price>
    <capacity>80</capacity>
    <make>Seagate</make>
</HDD>
```

12.4.9.5 The positional variable at

The position of a sequence can be retrieved using positional variables. The following query returns HDDs after adding the attribute `serial`, which numbers them.

```
for $hdd at $sr in doc("HDD.xml")//HDD
  return <HDD serial="{$sr}">{$hdd/make, $hdd/capacity}</HDD>
```

Here is the result of this query:

```
<HDD serial="1">
    <make>Samsung</make>
    <capacity>80</capacity>
</HDD>
<HDD serial="2">
```

```
        <make>Samsung</make>
        <capacity>160</capacity>
    </HDD>
    <HDD serial="3">
        <make>Seagate</make>
        <capacity>80</capacity>
    </HDD>
```

12.4.9.6 Distinct values

The set of tuples generated by some expressions may often have duplicate values. Consider the following query, which finds HDD manufacturers:

```
for $make in doc("HDD.xml")//make
   return $make
```

It outputs the following result, which contains duplicate tuples.

```
<make>Samsung</make>
<make>Samsung</make>
<make>Seagate</make>
```

The `distinct-values()` function can be used to eliminate duplicate tuples as follows:

```
for $make in distinct-values(doc("HDD.xml")//make)
   return <make>{ $make }</make>
```

This outputs the following result, which does not contain any duplicate tuple.

```
<make>Samsung</make>
<make>Seagate</make>
```

12.4.9.7 Join

One of the greatest powers of XQuery is that it can process and combine information from different sources to generate the desired result. The following query results in a list of manufacturers that manufacture HDDs as well as monitors.

```
for $hdd in doc("HDD.xml")//HDD
for $monitor in doc("monitor.xml")//monitor
   where $hdd/make = $monitor/make
      return $hdd/make

<?xml version="1.0" encoding="UTF-8"?>
<make>Samsung</make>
<make>Samsung</make>
```

We can use the `distinct-values()` function to remove duplicate tuples as follows:

```
distinct-values(for $hdd in doc("HDD.xml")//HDD
for $monitor in doc("monitor.xml")//monitor
   where $hdd/make = $monitor/make
      return $hdd/make)
```

This generates the following result:

```
Samsung
```

Following is a more complex query:

```
for $make in distinct-values(doc("HDD.xml")//make)
return <manufacturer name="{ $make }">
   {
      for $h in doc("HDD.xml")//HDD
      where $make = $h/make
      return <HDD>{ $h/price, $h/capacity, $h/speed }</HDD>
   }
   {
   for $m in doc("monitor.xml")//monitor
      where $make = $m/make
      return <monitor>{ $m/price, $m/size, $m/resolution }</monitor>
   }
</manufacturer>
```

This query lists all manufacturers that manufacture HDDs; if a manufacturer manufactures monitors, it also includes that information. Note that this is nothing but *left outer join* used in SQL. This query generates the following result.

```
<manufacturer name="Samsung">
   <HDD>
      <price>1600</price>
      <capacity>80</capacity>
      <speed>7200</speed>
   </HDD>
   <HDD>
      <price>2200</price>
      <capacity>160</capacity>
      <speed>7200</speed>
   </HDD>
   <monitor>
      <price>8000</price>
      <size>17</size>
      <resolution>1280x800</resolution>
   </monitor>
</manufacturer>
<manufacturer name="Seagate">
   <HDD>
      <price>1500</price>
      <capacity>80</capacity>
      <speed>7200</speed>
   </HDD>
</manufacturer>
```

12.4.9.8 Changing hierarchy

XQuery also allows the production of new documents where the hierarchy of nodes are changed. The following query outputs a list of manufacturers with items produced by them.

```
<manufacturers>
{
for $make in distinct-values(doc("HDD.xml")//make)
```

```
return <manufacturer name="{ $make }">
  {
     for $h in doc("HDD.xml")//HDD
     where $make = $h/make
     return <HDD type="{$h/@type}">{ $h/price, $h/capacity, $h/speed }</HDD>
  }
</manufacturer>
}
</manufacturers>
```

It results in the following output:

```
<manufacturers>
    <manufacturer name="Samsung">
      <HDD type="ATA">
          <price>1600</price>
          <capacity>80</capacity>
          <speed>7200</speed>
      </HDD>
      <HDD type="SATA">
          <price>2200</price>
          <capacity>160</capacity>
          <speed>7200</speed>
      </HDD>
    </manufacturer>
    <manufacturer name="Seagate">
      <HDD type="SATA">
          <price>1500</price>
          <capacity>80</capacity>
          <speed>7200</speed>
      </HDD>
    </manufacturer>
</manufacturers>
```

This query effectively represents the same information as `HDD.xml` but in a different format. The root element is now `<manufacturers>` instead of `<store>`. In `HDD.xml`, `<make>` was a child element of `<HDD>`. Now, `<HDD>` is a child element of `<manufacturer>`.

12.4.9.9 Quantifiers

Sometimes it is needed to check if at least one or every item in a sequence satisfies a condition. They are implemented using the *existential quantifier* `some` and *universal quantifier* `every`, respectively. Following is an example using existential quantifier:

```
for $make in distinct-values(doc("HDD.xml")//make)
where some $h in doc("HDD.xml")//HDD[make=$make]
satisfies ($h/capacity=160)
return $make
```

This query finds manufacturers that manufacture 160 GB HDD. The `some` quantifier in the `where` clause checks to see if there is at least one HDD made by a manufacturer that `satisfies` the specified condition. Here is the result of this query:

```
Samsung
```

This query could also have been written as follows:

```
distinct-values(for $hdd in doc("HDD.xml")//HDD
where $hdd/capacity = "160"
return $hdd/make)
```

Following is an example using universal quantifier:

```
for $make in distinct-values(doc("HDD.xml")//make)
where every $h in doc("HDD.xml")//HDD[make=$make]
satisfies ($h/capacity=80)
return $make
```

This results in the following:

```
Seagate
```

12.4.9.10 Conditional expression

XQuery also allows us to perform different operations depending on a Boolean condition. The following query illustrates this.

```
for $m in doc("monitor.xml")//monitor
return
<monitor>
{
$m/make, $m/size, $m/resolution
}
<type>
{
if ($m/@color = "yes") then
   "color"
else
   "blackAndWhite"
}
</type>
</monitor>
```

In this query, if the value of the `color` attribute is “yes” the `<type>color</type>` is returned otherwise `<type>blackAndWhite</type>` is returned. It generates the following result:

```
<monitor>
   <make>LG</make>
   <size>15</size>
   <resolution>1280x800</resolution>
   <type>color</type>
</monitor>
<monitor>
   <make>Samsung</make>
   <size>17</size>
   <resolution>1280x800</resolution>
   <type>color</type>
</monitor>
<monitor>
   <make>LG</make>
   <size>15</size>
```

```
    <resolution>1024x768</resolution>
    <type>color</type>
  </monitor>
  <monitor>
    <make>LG</make>
    <size>15</size>
    <resolution>1024x768</resolution>
    <type>blackAndWhite</type>
  </monitor>
```

12.4.9.11 Operators

Like other languages, XQuery provides the usual arithmetic and comparison operators. It also provides sequence operators to manipulate them. We have already used some of them. In this section, let us discuss the rest.

Before discussing various operators, let us discuss two fundamental concepts: *typed value extraction* and *atomization.*

If an operand is an element or its type is not known, the operator first extracts the value of the operand. This extracted value, which has a type, is called *typed value*. The operation can then be performed. The type is determined by the context. If the document is governed by a W3C XML Schema, the extracted value will have whatever type has been specified to the element by the schema.

XQuery provides a function called `data()`, which may be used to extract the typed value of an element. For example, the following function returns the value 4.

```
data(<price type="xs:double">20</price>)
```

Typed value extraction is applicable only for a single item. Atomization is a more general procedure where typed value is extracted from a number of items. For example, the following query performs atomization for every item in a sequence of elements.

```
data(doc("HDD.xml")//price)
```

The result of this query is

```
1600 2200 1600
```

Arithmetic Operators

The following arithmetic operators are available in XQuery:

```
+ -  * div     idiv     mod
```

The `idiv` operator expects integer arguments. It returns an integer value after rounding off the result. All operators have their conventional meaning.

If an operand has no type, arithmetic operators try to cast it as a double. An error occurs if casting fails. The following query uses the addition operator.

```
for $h in doc("HDD.xml")//HDD[make="Samsung" and capacity="80" and @type="ATA"]
for $m in doc("monitor.xml")//monitor[make="Samsung" and size="17" and
@color="yes"]
return <price>{ $h/price + $m/price }</price>
```

This query calculates the price of 80 GB ATA HDD and 17" color monitor made by Samsung. The $h/price and $m/price are elements. The typed value of these elements is first extracted and then addition is performed. The result is shown as follows:

```
<price>9600</price>
```

Comparison operators

XQuery supports four types of comparison operators: *value comparison*, *general comparison*, *node comparison,* and *order comparison*. The value comparison and general comparison operators [Figure 12.1] are closely related, although there are significant differences. We shall highlight them later in this section.

The value comparison operators compare two atomic values. Atomization is performed if an operand is a node. If an operand is un-typed, it is treated as a string. Here is an example:

```
for $h in doc("HDD.xml")//HDD
where $h/price lt "2000"
return $h/price
```

Table 12.1 shows XQuery comparison operators.

Table 12.1 XQuery comparison operators

Value Comparison Operators	General Comparison Operators
eq, ne, lt, le, gt, ge	=, !=, <, <=, >, >=

Value comparison operator expects two operands of the same type. This means that a string can be compared with another string, an integer can be compared with another integer, and so on. Note that, in this example, `$h/price` is an element. So, the first atomization is done to convert it to atomic values. Since it is also un-typed, string type is assumed. So, it expects the other operand to be a string. That is why the value 2000 is provided as "2000". The following query is invalid.

```
for $h in doc("HDD.xml")//HDD
where $h/price lt 2000
return $h/price
```

Since `$h/price` is un-typed, it is converted to the string type. So, the other operand must be of string type or `$h/price` must be converted to the same type as the operand on the right. The following query is valid:

```
for $h in doc("HDD.xml")//HDD
where xs:integer($h/price) lt 2000
return $h/price
```

So is

```
for $h in doc("HDD.xml")//HDD
```

```
where xs:integer($h/price) lt xs:string(2000)
return $h/price
```

If the value 2000 is specified as "2000", the string comparison will be performed and may give a wrong result.

Empty sequences are considered as nulls. If a sequence contains more than one item, it is an error. So, the following query is invalid as `$s/HDD/capacity` generates a sequence of multiple nodes.

```
for $s in doc("HDD.xml")/store
where $s/HDD/capacity eq 80
return $s/HDD/make
```

The general comparison operator may be used instead.

```
for $s in doc("HDD.xml")/store
where $s/HDD/capacity = 80
return $s/HDD/make
```

The one difference between value comparison and general comparison operators is that the general comparison operators may compare two sequences. It returns `true` if any value of the left sequence matches any value of the right sequence. The general comparison operators try to convert *required* type to perform comparison. So, the following query is valid.

```
for $h in doc("HDD.xml")//HDD
where $h/price < 2000
return $h/price
```

The `$h/price` is implicitly converted to the integer type.

There are two types of node comparison operators: `is` and `is not`. They test whether two expressions evaluate to the same node. Consider the following query.

```
let $hdd1 := for $h in doc("HDD.xml")//HDD
      where $h/@type = "ATA"
      return $h
let $hdd2 := for $h in doc("HDD.xml")//HDD
      where $h/make = "Samsung" and $h/capacity = 80
      return $h
return $hdd1 is $hdd2
```

It evaluates to `true` as `$hdd1` and `$hdd2` refer to the same node.

XQuery provides two operators `<<` and `>>` to check the order of nodes in the document. The expression `$x << $y` evaluates to true if `$x` occurs before `$y` in the document. Similarly, `$x >> $y` evaluates to true if `$y` occurs before `$x` in the document.

Sequence Operators

XQuery supports three sequence operators: `union` or `|`, `intersect`, and `except`. The union operator has two forms: `|` and `union`. This operator takes two sequences and returns a sequence containing elements from both the sequences. The following example returns all `<HDD>` and `<monitor>` elements.

```
for $item in (doc("HDD.xml")//HDD | doc("monitor.xml")//monitor)
return $item
```

The `intersect` operator takes two sequences and returns a sequence containing nodes that are common in both the sequences. The following query illustrates this:

```
let $make1 := for $h in  doc("HDD.xml")//HDD
      where $h/make = "Samsung"
      return $h/make
let $make2 := for $h in  doc("HDD.xml")//HDD
      where $h/price < 2000
      return $h/make
return $make1 intersect $make2
```

It outputs the following result:

```
<make>Samsung</make>
```

The `except` operator takes two input sequences and returns a sequence that are present in the first sequence but not in the second sequence. The following query illustrates this:

```
for $h in  doc("HDD.xml")//HDD
return <HDD> { $h/* except $h/speed } </HDD>
```

It generates the following output:

```
<HDD>
   <make>Samsung</make>
   <capacity>80</capacity>
   <price>1600</price>
</HDD>
<HDD>
   <make>Samsung</make>
   <capacity>160</capacity>
   <price>2200</price>
</HDD>
<HDD>
   <make>Seagate</make>
   <capacity>80</capacity>
   <price>1500</price>
</HDD>
```

12.4.9.12 Built-in functions

XQuery 1.0 supports all the functions as specified by XPath 2.0. Some of the functions were discussed in Chapter 10 (XPath). A detailed list of XQuery functions and their syntax can be found on the W3C site http://www.w3.org/2005/02/xpath-functions.

12.4.9.13 User-defined functions

XQuery allows us to write our custom functions. When a query becomes large and complex and is used many times, it is a good idea to put it in a function. This function can then be reused repeatedly. Following is a function declaration that takes the name of a manufacturer as an argument and returns a list of HDDs manufactured by it.

```
declare namespace ukr="http://www.jusl.ac.in";
declare function ukr:HDD_By_make($make as xs:string) as element()* {
for $h in doc("HDD.xml")//HDD
where $h/make = $make
return $h
};
```

Once this function is defined, it can be called as usual. The following query finds the list of HDDs manufactured by those manufacturers that also manufacture monitors.

```
for $make in doc("monitor.xml")//make
return ukr:HDD_By_make($make)
```

Here is the sample output:

```
<HDD type="ATA">
   <make>Samsung</make>
   <capacity>80</capacity>
   <speed>7200</speed>
   <price>1600</price>
</HDD>
<HDD type="SATA">
   <make>Samsung</make>
   <capacity>160</capacity>
   <speed>7200</speed>
   <price>2200</price>
</HDD>
```

12.4.9.14 Variable definition

XQuery allows us to define variables that are available at any point after they are declared. For example, if the list of HDDs is used several times in a query, the list can be stored in a variable as follows:

```
declare variable $HDDs := doc("HDD.xml")//HDD ;
for $h in $HDDs
return $h
```

12.5 DISPLAYING XML

Remember that XML documents contain custom tags created by different users at different times. Browsers do not have any idea about these tags. So, if XML documents are opened in a browser, the browser displays all tags together with the content of those tags. How can we display only XML data in the browser?

There are many ways to display an XML document in the browser. In the following sections, we shall discuss two commonly used methods to display XML data.

12.5.1 CSS

One of the ways to view XML documents in a browser is using Cascading Style Sheets. Cascading Style Sheets allow us to define every aspect of an XML document from size and color of the text to the background and position of non-text objects. Style sheets for XML documents are written in the same way as we do for HTML documents. Consider the following XML document `contact.xml`:

```
<?xml version="1.0"?>
<employees>
   <employee>
      <name>Ramesh</name>
      <phone>9831962261</phone>
      <email>ramesh12@gmail.com</email>
   </employee>
   <employee>
      <name>Megha</name>
      <phone>9051635758</phone>
      <email>megha@yahoo.com</email>
   </employee>
   <employee>
      <name>Arjun</name>
      <phone>9734835915</phone>
      <email>arjun121@rediffmail.com</email>
   </employee>
   <employee>
      <name>Rupa</name>
      <phone>9441804070</phone>
      <email>rupa25@gmail.com</email>
   </employee>
</employees>
```

We can write the style sheet `contact.css` as follows:

```
name {
   display: block;
   margin-top: 10pt;
   font-size: 11pt;
   color: #FF0000;
   margin-left: 10pt;
}
phone {
   display: block;
   color: #0000FF;
   margin-left: 30pt;
}
email {
   font-style: italic;
   display: block;
   color: #000000;
   margin-left: 30pt;
}
```

Now, insert the following line in the `contact.xml` file after the XML declaration:

```
<?xml-stylesheet href="contact.css" title="Modern" media="screen"
type="text/css"?>
```

We can now open the `contact.xml` file in any browser. Figure 12.2 shows the result when the file `contact.xml` is opened in Google Chrome.

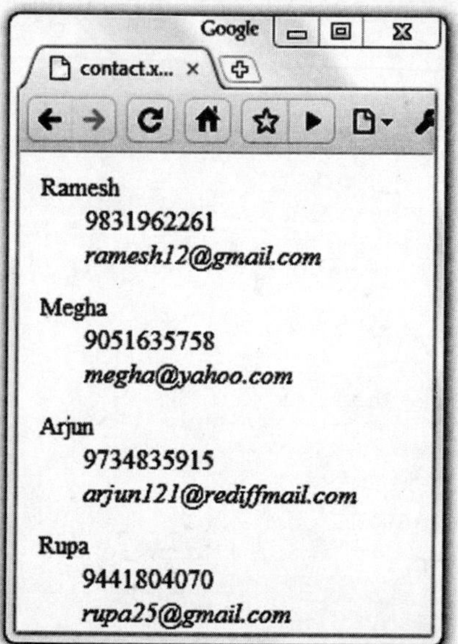

Figure 12.2 Viewing XML document using CSS

12.5.1.1 Positioning

CSS also allows us to place elements in desired positions. We can also place an element behind another, and specify what to do when an element's content is too large.

Elements can be positioned using the properties: *left*, *right*, *top*, and *bottom*. However, we must set the property position properly. It can have values *fixed*, *relative*, and *absolute*. Consider the following CSS file:

```
name {
   display: block;
   margin-top: 10pt;
   font-size: 16pt;
   color: #FF0000;
   margin-left: 10pt;
}

phone {
   position: relative;
   top: -25px;
   left: 100px;
}

email {
   position: relative;
   top: -10px;
   left: 40px;
   font-style: italic;
}
```

If we apply this style sheet to the previous XML document, it generates the output as shown in Figure 12.3.

Figure 12.3 CSS positioning

12.5.2 XSL-FO

XSL-FO is an acronym of eXtensible Stylesheet Language Formatting Objects. It is used to format XML data for output to screen, paper, and other media. Let us write the simplest XSL-FO document, which displays the string "Hello World!"

```
<?xml version="1.0" encoding="UTF-8"?>
<fo:root xmlns:fo="http://www.w3.org/1999/XSL/Format">
   <fo:layout-master-set>
      <fo:simple-page-master master-name="my-page">
         <fo:region-body margin="1in"/>
      </fo:simple-page-master>
   </fo:layout-master-set>
   <fo:page-sequence master-reference="my-page">
      <fo:flow flow-name="xsl-region-body">
         <fo:block>Hello World!</fo:block>
      </fo:flow>
   </fo:page-sequence>
</fo:root>
```

Typically, an XSL-FO document is generated from an input XML document by XSLT transformation. Consider the following XML document, `greeting.xml`.

```
<?xml version='1.0' ?>
<greeting>Hello World!</greeting>
```

This XML file can be converted to the given XSL-FO document using the following XSLT document, `greeting.xsl`.

```
<?xml version='1.0' ?>
<xsl:transform version='2.0' xmlns:xsl='http://www.w3.org/1999/XSL/Transform' >
   <xsl:output method='xml' />
   <xsl:template match='/'>
      <fo:root xmlns:fo="http://www.w3.org/1999/XSL/Format">
         <fo:layout-master-set>
            <fo:simple-page-master master-name="my-page">
               <fo:region-body margin="1in"/>
            </fo:simple-page-master>
         </fo:layout-master-set>
         <fo:page-sequence master-reference="my-page">
            <fo:flow flow-name="xsl-region-body">
               <fo:block><xsl:value-of select="."/></fo:block>
            </fo:flow>
         </fo:page-sequence>
      </fo:root>
   </xsl:template>
</xsl:transform>
```

Finally, the XSL-FO document can be converted to the desired format such as pdf using the XSL-FO processor. One such XSL-FO processor is Apache FOP (Formatting Object Processor) based on Java. This can be downloaded from the site `http://xmlgraphics.apache.org/fop/`. Use the following command to get the pdf file corresponding to the XML document.

```
fop -xml greeting.xml -xsl greeting.xsl -pdf greeting.pdf
```

This command converts the XML document to the corresponding XSL-FO using the `greeting.xsl` transformation file and finally converts the XSL-FO document to the `greeting.pdf` file.

Alternatively, you can use the following commands.

```
java -cp saxon9.jar net.sf.saxon.Transform -o:greeting.fo greeting.xml
greeting.xsl

fop greeting.fo greeting.pdf
```

Figure 12.4 shows the result.

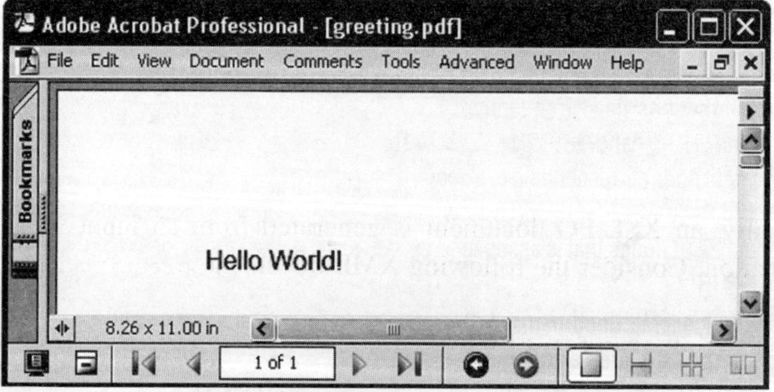

Figure 12.4 Displaying XML using XSL-FO

KEYWORDS

Constructors: XQuery constructs used to generate elements, attributes, etc.

FLWOR expression: An acronym of `for`, `let`, `where`, `order by`, and `return` expressions used in XQuery.

For clause: The `for` clause in the FLWOR expression creates tuples that are used by other clauses.

Let clause: The `let` clause in the FLWOR expression creates a single tuple.

Order by clause: The `order by` clause sorts the tuples before the `return` clause generates the result.

Positional variable: A positional variable returns the position of an item in a sequence.

Return clause: The XQuery `return` clause is used to generate output.

Where clause: The `where` clause filters the tuples, keeping only those tuples that satisfy a given condition.

XLink: It allows us to create a standard way of inserting hyperlinks in XML documents.

XPointer: XPointer acts as a bookmark in HTML and allows us to select more specific parts in the XML document.

XQuery Processor: A software that understands queries written in XQuery language and can generate output as specified in the query.

SUMMARY

In this chapter, we discussed four XML technologies, namely, XLink, XPointer, XQuery, and XSL-FO. Out of these four technologies, we primarily focused on XQuery which is widely used.

It allows us to create a standard way of inserting hyperlinks in XML documents. In June 2001, XLink became a W3C Recommendation.

XPointer resembles bookmarks in HTML. It allows us to select specific parts in the XML document.

XQuery was designed to overcome the limitations keeping only the strengths of XPath. XQuery basically resembles SQL in relational databases. XQuery and XSLT have many concepts in common. However, they differ vastly in their design.

An XQuery processor checks the syntax of the query and performs actions as specified in the query. Many such processors are freely available on the web. One frequently used processor is the Saxon XQuery processor.

There are two input functions used frequently to create documents to be queried: `doc()` and `collection()`. The former returns the document node corresponding to a document specified by the Universal Resource Identifier (URI), whereas the latter returns a sequence of nodes that is associated with a document specified by a URI.

XQuery can also produce XML documents. XQuery also provides an explicit constructor to create document nodes.

One of the powerful features of XQuery is FLWOR (pronounced as flower) expressions. The FLWOR expressions resemble The SELECT-FROM-WHERE...statements in SQL. Each letter in the phrase "FLWOR" stands for the first letter of the clauses that may occur in a FLWOR expression: `for`, `let`, `where`, `order by`, and `return` as follows:

- `for` — binds items in a sequence generated by the given expression to a given variable one by one
- `let` — binds the result of an entire expression to a variable to be used later
- `where` — filters tuples keeping only those tuples that satisfy the given condition
- `order by` — sorts the items generated by other clauses
- `return` — for each tuple, it creates the result of the FLWOR expression.

A FLWOR expression consists of one or more `for` or `let` clauses in arbitrary order, followed by an optional `where` clause, an optional `order` by clause, and a mandatory return clause.

Sometimes it is needed to check if at least one or every item in a sequence satisfies a condition. They are implemented using existential quantifier `some` and universal quantifier `every`, respectively.

XQuery also allows us to perform different operations depending on a Boolean condition.

XQuery allows us to define variables that are available at any point after they are declared. Like other languages, XQuery provides the usual arithmetic and comparison operators. It also provides sequence operators to manipulate them.

XSL-FO is used to format XML data for outputting to screen, paper, and other media.

WEB RESOURCES

http://www.w3.org/xml/Query.html.
W3C XML Query (XQuery)

http://www.w3.org/TR/xquery/
XQuery 1.0: An XML Query Language, W3C Recommendation 23 January 2007

http://www.w3.org/TR/xpath-functions/
XQuery 1.0 and XPath 2.0 Functions and Operators

http://www.w3.org/TR/2001/REC-xsl-20011015/
Extensible Stylesheet Language (XSL), Version 1.0

EXERCISES

Multiple Choice Questions

1. Which of the following does XQuery use as its base language?
   (a) XPath (b) XHTML
   (c) XSL (d) XSLT

2. XQuery is a language for finding and extracting information from
   (a) Image files (b) XML documents
   (c) tables (d) HTML pages

3. XQuery is a query language for
   (a) XSL (b) XML
   (c) XSLT (d) XHTML

4. Which of the following does XQuery resemble?
   (a) Oracle (b) MySQL
   (c) SQL (d) PL/SQL

5. Which of the following combinations shares the same data model and supports the same functions and operators?
   (a) XQuery 1.0 and XPath 2.0
   (b) XQuery 1.1 and XPath 2.0
   (c) XQuery 1.0 and XPath 1.0
   (d) XQuery 1.0.1 and XPath 2.0.1

6. For which of these can XQuery not be used?
   (a) Search Web documents for relevant information
   (b) Generate summary reports
   (c) Transform XML data to XHTML
   (d) Specify the structure of XML documents

7. Which of these is not a valid node type in XQuery?
   (a) number (b) namespace
   (c) attribute (d) element

8. Which of the following is used to filter the extracted data from XML documents?
   (a) eliminate (b) predicates
   (c) filter (d) limit

9. Which of the following clauses is used to specify the filter criteria?
   (a) let clause (b) For clause
   (c) where clause (d) order by clause

10. $x is an
    (a) Element (b) Attribute
    (c) XQuery (d) Variable

11. What is the full form of FLWOR?
    (a) for, let, where as, object, record
    (b) foreach, let, where as, order, return
    (c) for, let, when, order by, return
    (d) for, let, where, order by, return

12. Which function is used to create a document node?
    (a) fopen() (b) doc()
    (c) fileOpen() (d) open()

13. Which of the following is correct syntax?
    (a) doc(HDD.xml); (b) doc('HDD.xml')
    (c) doc("HDD.xml"); (d) doc("HDD.xml")

14. How many types of nodes are present in XQuery?
(a) 6 (b) 7 (c) 8 (d) 9

15. Which of the following is true regarding the `order by` clause?
(a) Places all elements in the XML document in descending order
(b) Places all elements in the XML document in ascending order
(c) Places all return values in ascending order by default
(d) Places all return values in descending order by default

16. The `where` clause
(a) Specifies the filter criteria
(b) Returns the result
(c) Locates the XML document
(d) Locates the output file

17. Which of the following is called the document node or root node?
(a) leaf (b) root
(c) child (d) middle-level nodes

18. Which of the following are known as atomic values?
(a) root node
(b) leaf nodes
(c) node with no parent or children
(d) parent nodes

19. Nodes that have the same parent are called
(a) elements (b) children
(c) siblings (d) descendants

20. A node's children, children's children, etc. are called
(a) descendants (b) siblings
(c) parent (d) ancestors

Review Questions

1. Write a function that transforms all attributes into elements, with the attribute value as text inside the element.
2. Consider the following document:

```
<graph>
<arc start="a" end="b">
<arc start="a" end="c">
<arc start="b" end="c">
<arc start="c" end="d">
</graph>
```

Write a function that computes the transitive closure of graphs given in this format. The transitive closure is the graph that connects two nodes if there is a path between them. For this graph, the result of the function should be:

```
<graph>
<arc start="a" end="b">
<arc start="a" end="c">
<arc start="b" end="c">
<arc start="c" end="d">
<arc start="a" end="d">
<arc start="b" end="d">
</graph>
```

3. What is the full form of FLWOR? Discuss the functionality of each clause that can occur in a FLWOR expression.
4. How are various conditional operations performed?
5. What is the difference between the `for` and `let` clause in the FLWOR expression?
6. Show with examples how to perform stable sort.
7. Show with examples how to perform sorting in descending order.
8. Show with examples how to perform sorting with respect to multiple fields.
9. How can you eliminate duplicate tuples?
10. What is the role of the `doc()` function?

Part III

Client-side Programming

- JavaScript
- JavaScript and HTML DOM
- Advanced JavaScript and HTML Forms
- JavaScript Regular Expression
- AJAX
- Applets

13 JAVASCRIPT

KEY OBJECTIVES

After completing this chapter readers will be able to—

- **embed JavaScript code in an HTML document**
- **handle browsers that do not support a JavaScript version**
- **understand the syntax and semantics of the JavaScript programming language**
- **get an idea about key concepts such as variables, control structures, etc.**
- **create arrays, functions, and objects**
- **use built-in objects such as `Math`, `Array`, `Function`, `Object`, `String`, and `Date`**

13.1 INTRODUCTION

This chapter on the JavaScript programming language is primarily targeted for those who have some exposure to an object-oriented programming language.

We shall not cover the basic concepts of the JavaScript programming language here. Instead, we shall start from an advanced stage and illustrate the JavaScript-specific concepts and methodologies. Let us first take a look at the evolution of the JavaScript programming language.

The **W**orld **W**ide **W**eb (WWW) was introduced in the early 1990s. The **H**yper**T**ext **M**arkup **L**anguage (HTML), which is used to write web pages, deals only with the design aspect. As a consequence, all web pages, at that time, were static. There was no way to change the appearance of the web pages once they were loaded. Visitors could not interact with the pages. To provide dynamic and interactive web pages, some form of programming language was necessary. The statements (scripts) would change the appearance of the web pages and respond to user actions even after loading the pages. In order to interpret these scripts, an engine needs to be embedded within the browser that runs in the client's computer.

13.1.1 History of JavaScript

The first scripting language was first introduced by Brendan Eich, a member of the Netscape 2 group, in early 1996 to provide dynamicity and interactivity to web pages. This first version, capable of being embedded in web pages, could only process numbers and modify HTML form contents. During the development phase, it was known as *Mocha*, then as *LiveWire* and even later as *LiveScript*. The name "LiveScript" was chosen because the browser itself could interpret on the fly without requiring the code to be compiled. When it was released, it was renamed *JavaScript* to capitalize its name due to tremendous popularity of Sun Microsystems's Java programming language at that time. Note that in many cases, JavaScript and Java code may appear to be similar, but they are completely different languages and serve entirely different purposes. Confusion between the two languages started because of this naming convention. JavaScript could reference links, forms, and anchors as children of the `document` object as well as form elements. The way, JavaScript was used to reference them, became known as DOM level 0.

In the same year, a standard was produced by the **E**uropean **C**omputer **M**anufacturers **A**ssociation (ECMA) and was known as ECMAScript. This standard only specified the core JavaScript syntax. The details of DOM level 0 were not standardized. Later in the same year, Netscape 3 released JavaScript 1.1 following the ECMA standard. This could change the location of images. This could also reference images as children of the `document` object, which makes DOM level 0 complete.

In 1997, the ECMAScript standard was updated and Netscape 4 released a modified version, JavaScript 1.2. JavaScript programmers were able to change styles of HTML elements, especially their visibility and position. This concept was highly appreciated by the W3C and was adopted in CSS 2 specification. The concept of layered DOM started.

In the same year, due to widespread acceptance, Microsoft introduced its own proprietary language, called *JScript* to avoid trademark issues, as a part of Internet Explorer 4. It could reference any part of the document and change any CSS style, including some CSS 2 styles. Programmers were offered additional extensions, e.g., transitions and filters. It was so versatile and reliable that the W3C decided to incorporate a major portion of this proprietary DOM in their future DOM recommendations.

Netscape, in mid 1998, also released a new version, JavaScript 1.3, based on their layered DOM. Netscape was unable to remove bugs from this new version and decided to produce its new version with the help of open source community. The open source community decided to rewrite a new version, JavaScript 1.5 (JavaScript 1.4 was a server-side JavaScript), according to the W3C specifications.

In 1999, Microsoft introduced an updated version of JScript (equivalent to JavaScript 1.5) with much greater functionality, as a part of Internet Explorer 5. It was based on proprietary DOM and supported ECMAScript 3 standard and major recommendations of W3C DOM 1. With this new version, almost everything could be done. It supported event handling, adding, modifying, and removing HTML elements and their attributes and styles even after loading the page. Internet Explorer became popular as it supported other scripting languages such as VBScript.

13.1.2 Inserting JavaScript Code

JavaScript code is executed from within HTML documents. So, your web pages will not only contain HTML tags, but also the JavaScript statements (called *scripts*). There are two ways to insert JavaScript code into an HTML file. One way to insert JavaScript code is to embed it directly within the `<script>` and `</script>` tag pair. The `<script>` tag notifies the browser that everything contained within is script and is to be interpreted by a suitable interpreter.

```
<script language="JavaScript">
  JavaScript code
</script>
```

The *optional* attribute `language` specifies the programming language used for scripting. There are many languages available in the market for scripting. Common languages are JavaScript and VBScript. In this book, we shall use JavaScript. So, the `language` attribute will have the value `JavaScript`. This attribute basically instructs the browser which interpreter to use for interpretation. If nothing is specified, `JavaScript` is assumed by the browser. However, it is recommended that an interpreter be specified explicitly always.

There are many versions of each scripting language. For example, JavaScript has versions 1.0, 1.1, 1.2, 1.3, and so on. Some browsers support only specific versions of a language. The author of the web page may also specify the specific version of the language used.

```
<script language="JavaScript1.1">
  JavaScript code
</script>
```

Note that there is no space between the language name and its version. The browser checks the version information and ignores the script altogether if it does not have an interpreter for the specified version.

The version number should be selected carefully as browsers may ignore scripts if it does not support the specified version. Authors should not increase the version number unnecessarily unless a tag defined in that version is used.

In this way, you may insert as many scripts as you want in an HTML document. All scripts ultimately form a single program in the order declared. Finally, the interpreter will interpret all statements of the program from top to bottom.

Another way to insert JavaScript code is to place it in an external source file and refer to it from an HTML file. This external source file generally has the extension `.js`. A source file contains only JavaScript statements without any `script` tag or other HTML tags. The tag `<script>` has the attribute `src`, which may be used to refer to an external JavaScript source file.

```
<script language="JavaScript" src="source.js">
</script>
```

The attribute `src` specifies the location of the JavaScript source file (`source.js` in our case). It can be an absolute or relative path name or a URL. In this example, `src` specifies the relative path of the JavaScript source file `source.js`. This file must be placed in the same directory, which contains the HTML file. Multiple JavaScript source files may be used, if necessary. Use a separate `<script>` tag for this purpose. This way, you can also insert as many scripts as you want in the HTML document.

When using a JavaScript source file, the browser ignores any JavaScript statement within the `<script>` and `</script>` tags. So, do not write anything between the opening and closing `<script>` tag.

So, we have seen that there are two ways to incorporate JavaScript code in an HTML file. Which one should we use?

It is easy and time-saving to embed JavaScript code directly into the HTML file if the code is fairly short. It avoids the relatively long procedure of inserting a source file. Sometimes, JavaScript source files are cached by some browsers. In such a case, any modification made in the source file will not be visible until the cache is cleared or a new browser window is opened. Embedded JavaScript code is not cached and changes are visible immediately. So, during the development phase, it is a good idea to embed JavaScript code directly into HTML documents.

However, if the JavaScript code is fairly long, it is easy to use the source file. It has many distinct advantages.

- This makes the HTML file neater and cleaner. Too much JavaScript code makes it large and unreadable.
- The same JavaScript source file can be reused in many HTML files. Common functions can be placed in a source file, instead of inserting them in each HTML file that uses them. Any changes to the source file reflect immediately in all HTML files that refer it.
- The JavaScript code remains hidden if the browser is not compatible with it. Incompatible embedded JavaScript code is displayed as if it is normal text. However, embedded JavaScript code can be placed within comment to avoid this problem.

A typical HTML file makes use of both the styles. By making a proper combination of these two, one can have finer granularity. It is believed that using a source file, the JavaScript code can be made hidden. However, this is not true as JavaScript code can be viewed by knowing the name of the source file and specifying the complete URL of the source file in the address bar of the browser's window even if the source file is used.

Each JavaScript code segment is executed in the order in which it appears. In other words, all JavaScript code segments are combined to form a single JavaScript program. So, variables and functions declared in former segments are available in later segments, but the opposite is not true.

13.1.3 First JavaScript Program

So far, we have discussed, how to insert JavaScript code in an HTML file. Let us now write our first JavaScript program by embedding the code directly in the web page.

```
<html>
   <head>
      <title>My first JavaScript program</title>
   </head>
   <body>
      <script language="JavaScript">
         document.writeln("Hello world!");
      </script>
   </body>
</html>
```

This web page, once loaded in the browser's window, simply prints the message `Hello world!` on the screen, as shown in Figure 13.1.

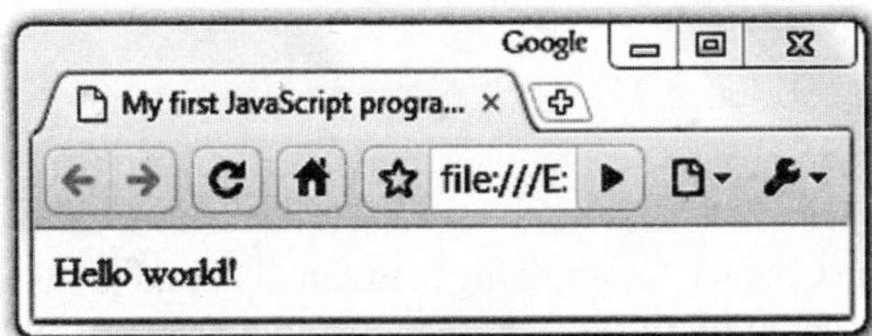

Figure 13.1 First JavaScript program

This JavaScript program does not do much, but is a complete program used only for demonstration purposes. Let us now discuss some other features.

13.1.4 Adding Comments

Adding comments to programs is considered to be a good practice. Comments are used for documentation. They help readers to understand the meaning of the code. Comments, when encountered by the interpreter, are not treated as programming statements and are ignored altogether. Like any other programming language, JavaScript also allows comments. Comments are of two types: *line comment* and *block comment*.

A line comment starts with `//`. The entire line is treated as a comment line and is skipped. Following is an example of a line comment.

```
//This is a line comment and it will be ignored.
```

Line comments are useful for comments that are smaller in size.

A block comment starts with `/*` and ends with `*/`. Everything within these opening and closing character sequences is ignored.

```
/*
This is a block comment.
This will also be ignored
*/
```

Block comments may span multiple lines. These are useful for long comments.

13.1.5 Browser Incompatibility

If a JavaScript code is embedded directly within an HTML file and a browser is not compatible with the scripting language and version specified, it does not interpret the code. However, in this case, everything within the `<script>` and `</script>` tags is treated as normal text. As a consequence, the browser displays the JavaScript statements in its window. This is sometimes ugly and interrupts normal viewing of web pages.

To hide embedded JavaScript code from incompatible browsers, an HTML comment may be used. In this case, embedded JavaScript code segments are inserted into HTML comments as follows:

```
<script language="JavaScript1.1">
   <!--
      JavaScript code
   -->
</script>
```

As mentioned in Chapter 3, everything between `<!--` and `-->` is treated as an HTML comment and will not be rendered on the screen. Incompatible browsers will ignore the JavaScript code and hand it over to the rendering engine for rendering. Since, the code is embedded within HTML comments, the rendering engine will not render the code on the screen. This is exactly what we want. Compatible browsers do not display JavaScript code at all. Instead, they interpret the JavaScript code using a scripting engine.

Another way to hide JavaScript code is to use JavaScript source files that are ignored by incompatible browsers and not rendered on the screen.

However, it is a good idea to display a suitable error message if the browser is not compatible. The message may include the browser's name and version number required to successfully interpret the JavaScript code used in the HTML page. This may help the user to use/upgrade to the correct browser. This is accomplished using the `<noscript>` and `</noscript>` tag pair. Everything within `<noscript>` and `</noscript>` is displayed on the screen if the browser does not support the scripting language and version specified. This tag is a part of the HTML specification and usually follows the `<script>` tag. Here is one example:

```
<script language="JavaScript1.1">
   <!--
      JavaScript code
   -->
</script>
<noscript>
   Internet Explorer 4.0 or higher is required to view this HTML page.
Please upgrade your browser version and try again.
</noscript>
```

If users are not using browsers compatible with JavaScript 1.1, a message will be displayed on the screen. Users may then take necessary actions to view the page correctly.

13.1.6 Placement of JavaScript Code

JavaScript code may be placed anywhere in an HTML file. It is interpreted in the order in which it appears. HTML tags are also rendered according to their document order. A function must be declared before it is called. This is true for variables as well. This suggests us to write JavaScript functions and declare global variables within the head section, which is rendered before the body section. Other JavaScript statements, including function calls, can be placed anywhere within the body tag. This ensures that a function is called after it is defined. This also ensures that a variable is used after it is created. The following code demonstrates this:

```
<html>
   <head>
      <title>My first JavaScript program</title>
      <script language="JavaScript">
         //Function declaration
         function hello() {
            document.writeln("Hello world!");
         }
      </script>
   </head>
   <body>
      <script language="JavaScript">
         //Function call
         hello();
         //Other JavaScript statements
      </script>
   </body>
</html>
```

Figure 13.2 shows the placement of JavaScript functions.

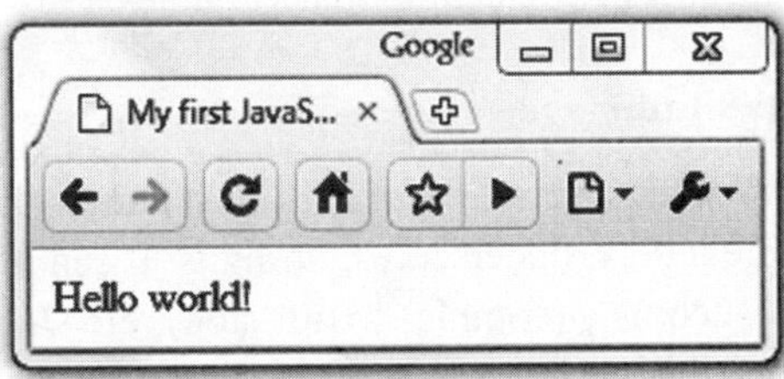

Figure 13.2 Placing JavaScript functions

However, the placement of JavaScript code depends entirely on the programmer. Usually, functions are declared in the head section and other statements are placed in the body section.

13.1.7 JavaScript Keywords

The set of keywords, some of which are not currently in use, is shown in Table 13.1.

Table 13.1 JavaScript keywords

abstract	boolean	break	byte	case	catch
char	class	const	continue	debugger	default
delete	do	double	else	enum	export
extends	false	final	finally	float	for
function	goto	if	implements	import	in
instanceof	int	interface	long	native	new
null	package	private	protected	public	return
short	static	super	switch	synchronized	this
throw	throws	transient	true	try	typeof
var	void	volatile	while	with	

13.2 VARIABLES

Programming means manipulation of data. Data are stored in variables. JavaScript, like other programming languages, allows us to create and manipulate variables. However, JavaScript variables are different from other variables in the sense that they are un-typed. There are other differences as well. The differences are so peculiar that JavaScript is sometimes considered a strange language. We shall figure out some of them in due course. Let us discuss about the variables here.

It was just mentioned that JavaScript variables are un-typed. This means that no type keyword is used during a variable declaration. However, this does not mean that variables do not have any type. The type of a variable, at any instant, is determined by its content. It may change from time to time as the content changes. Does it sound strange? You may think, as long as correct operation is performed on a variable (which should be), it works fine. However, it is the programmers' responsibility to remember a variable's type and perform correct operations on them.

A variable can be a *local* (to a function) or *global*. A local variable is declared in a function using the keyword `var`. Variables declared without the `var` keyword is always global even if they are created within a narrower scope, such as within a function. Variables declared using the `var` keyword in the outermost scope are also global variables.

13.2.1 Naming Convention

The name of a variable cannot be a *keyword*. It must start with a letter or an underscore ("_") followed by zero or more letters, underscores, or digits. It can never contain white spaces, or any punctuation characters such as , (comma) . (full stop), etc. JavaScript, unlike HTML, is case-sensitive. So, `count`, `COUNT`, and `Count` are separate variable names. Some new versions of browsers also allow variables names to start with the "$" sign. However, it is recommended not to use the "$" sign at the beginning of a variable name to avoid incompatibility. Officially, there is no limit on the number of characters in a variable name.

13.2.2 Local Variables

Local variables are declared within a function or a block. The general syntax for creating a local variable is as follows:

```
var variable = value;
```

The keyword `var` specifies that the variable is a local variable and is visible within the scope in which it is declared. Here are some examples:

```
var sum = 0;                 //number
var msg = "Hello World!";    //string
var found = false;           //boolean
var month = "April";         //string
```

The variable type is indicated beside each variable. Note that the type of a variable may change as content changes. Like in other programming languages, several variables may be declared in a single line as follows:

```
var sum = 0, msg = "Hello World!", found = false, month = "April";
```

All four variables, which differ in their type, are declared in a single line. A variable is said to be undefined if no value is assigned to it. For example, the following variable `count`, is undefined.

```
var count; //undefined
```

Working with undefined variables is illegal. For this reason, it is always safe assigning a value to a variable during declaration. The value of the variable may be changed later, if necessary. The value of an undefined variable may also be assigned later.

```
count = 0; //now count is defined
```

Now, the variable `count` is defined and (valid) operations may be performed upon it.

13.2.3 Global Variables

A global variable is created without the keyword `var`. It is created by assigning a value to it. The general syntax is

```
variable = value;
```

Here are some examples:

```
x = 1;
lang = "JavaScript";
flag = true;
```

Note that variables created this way, even within a narrower scope, are global variables. These variables are created as soon as the block is executed and become visible from that instant. This statement indicates that global variables may be created from within a function that has a limited scope. The exact procedure for creating global variables from within a function and its consequence will be described in Section 13.8.8.

No new variable is created if the variable is already declared. For example, the following statement does not create a new variable; it just assigns a new value to `x`.

```
x = 10;
```

Variables created this way can never be undefined and hence are safe to use.

13.2.4 Functions and Global Variables

A global variable is created without using the keyword `var`. Such a declaration can be placed anywhere within the script. It is also possible to make such declarations within a function. This means that creating a global variable is possible even within a function. The lifetime of this global variable starts as soon as the function is called and the variable is created. Once this global variable is created, it is now accessible by other JavaScript statements. The following example illustrates this:

```
function avg(a, b, c) {
   sum = a + b + c;
   average = sum / 3;
```

```
}
avg(2, 3, 4);     //sum and average get created here. sum is 9, average is 3
avg(1, 2, 3);     //sum is 6, average is 2
```

This is a unique feature of the JavaScript programming language. This is another reason why JavaScript is known as a strange language. The possibility of creating global variables from within a function makes some programming constructs critical especially when writing recursive functions. Extra care must be taken to write recursive functions. We shall discus about this in detail in Section 13.8.8.

13.2.5 typeof Operator

As mentioned earlier, the type of a variable is determined by its content.

```
var x = 0;                    //number
var msg = "Hello World!";     //string
var found = false;            //boolean
var month = "April";          //string
```

The type of the variable `x` is number, whereas the type of `found` is boolean, and that of `msg` and `month` is string. The type of a variable may change from time to time. So far, the type of the variable `x` is number. The following changes the type of the previously declared variable `x` to string.

```
x = "abc";                    //string
```

The type of a variable can be determined at any instant of time by using the `typeof` operator. The `typeof` operator returns a string describing the type of a value. Table 13.2 shows the return value of the `typeof` operator on applying different values.

Table 13.2 typeof operator

Type	Typeof	Type	Typeof
Object	'object'	String	'string'
Function	'function'	Boolean	'boolean'
Array	'object'	Null	'object'
Number	'number'	Undefined	'undefined'

The following JavaScript code segment illustrates this:

```
var pi = 3.142;
var t = typeof(pi);                 //t is 'number'
var greeting = "Hello World! ";
t = typeof(greeting);               //t is 'string'
var found = false;
t = typeof(found);                  //t is 'boolean'
var x;
t = typeof(x);                      //t is 'undefined'
```

It is always safe to check the type of a variable before performing an operation on it. The following example illustrates this:

```
var v = 12;
if(typeof(v) == 'number') {
  if(v % 2 == 0)
    alert('even');
  else
    alert('odd');
}
else alert('not a number');
```

The remainder operation (%) can only be performed on variables of type number.

13.3 LITERALS

JavaScript supports the following data types:

- String
- Number
- Boolean
- Function
- Object

13.3.1 String Data Type

A string value consists of a sequence of zero or more *Unicode* characters (e.g., alphabetic, numeric, punctuation marks, etc.). Usually a string value is used to represent text in JavaScript. A *string literal* is a string value written within a matching pair of double quotation ("") or single quotation ('') marks. Following are some examples of string literals:

```
"Hello World!"
'JavaScript programming language'
"What's your name?"
'"JavaScript" and "Java" are two different languages'
```

Note that, single quotation marks may occur in a string surrounded by double quotation marks and vice versa. However, the escape character (\) may be used to include single and double quotation marks in the string literal. For example, the last two string literals may also be written as

```
"What\"s your name?"
'\'JavaScript\' and \'Java\' are two different languages'
```

A string with no character is an empty string. JavaScript does not support character data type. A character value is represented as a string of one character.

13.3.2 Numeric Data Type

A variable of type number may hold an integer or a real number. JavaScript does not differentiate between an integer and a real number. All numbers are represented using the "64-bit double precision IEEE 754" standard.

JavaScript provides a special value `NaN` (Not a Number) that represents an error condition. Many JavaScript functions return this value, if the argument cannot be converted to a number. It can never be checked against any other number including itself. The function `isNaN` may be used instead.

13.3.2.1 Integers

Integers may be written either in decimal, hexadecimal, or octal notation. Hexadecimal and octal numbers cannot have any fractional part. Examples of decimal integer literals are

```
2, 100, 0 -1, -200
```

A hexadecimal integer literal starts with "0x" or "0X". They indicate that the base of this number is 16. These numbers may contain digits as well as alphabetic characters A through F either in uppercase or in lowercase. The character A represents the decimal number 10, B represents the decimal number 11, and so on. Following are examples of hexadecimal integer literals:

```
0x4, -0x2, 0xFF, 0X10, 0XA2
```

Hexadecimal numbers cannot have any fractional part. So, the following numbers are invalid:

```
0x2.3, 0x4.5e2
```

However, the following number is valid. This is because the character 'e' is not treated as exponentiation. It is the hexadecimal character e.

```
0x3e2
```

In addition to decimal and hexadecimal integers, JavaScript also supports octal notation. Octal integers start with 0 and may contain digits 0 through 7. Following are some examples of octal integer literals:

```
04, 05, 010, -02, 00, 012
```

The following number is invalid because the digit 8 is not a valid octal digit. Octal digits are 0 through 7.

```
038
```

Octal numbers also cannot have any fractional part. So, the following numbers are also invalid:

```
03.4, .00.005, 03e2
```

13.3.2.2 Floating point numbers

Floating-point numbers are written using base 10. They may have fractional parts separated by a decimal point. Scientific notation is also allowed. Following are some valid floating point numbers:

```
.001, 0.01, 3.4, 4, -2, 2e2, 2.3e4, 2e-3, 4.5e-2
```

The range of floating point numbers is from ±1.7976931348623157e308 to ±5e-324. Everything greater than 1.7976931348623157e308 is treated as `Infinity` and everything less than –1.7976931348623157e308 is treated as `-Infinity`. They behave exactly like mathematical infinity. Anything divided by `Infinity` is 0 (zero) and anything multiplied by `Infinity` is `Infinity`. Similarly, every positive number smaller than 5e–324 and every negative number greater than –5e-324 is treated as 0.

13.3.3 Boolean Data Type

A Boolean type variable can have only two values: `true` or `false`.

```
result = 2 < 3;                    //result is true
result = 2 > 3;                    //result is false
```

A non-zero value is treated as `true` and 0 is treated as the boolean value `false`.

```
var x = -1;
if (x)...            //evaluates to true
var x = 2;
if (x)...            //evaluates to true
var x = 0;
if (x)...            //evaluates to false
```

13.4 OPERATORS

JavaScript supports most of the traditional operators, which are grouped depending on their functionality, as follows:

- Arithmetic operators
- Assignment operators
- Relational operators
- Logical operators
- Bitwise operators

A built-in object, `Math`, is also provided to handle more sophisticated mathematical functions and constants. Frequently used properties are shown in Table 13.3.

Table 13.3 JavaScript math object properties

Properties	Meaning	Value
PI	The value of Pi	3.141592653589793
E	The base of natural logarithm e	2.718281828459045
LN2	Natural Logarithm of 2	0.6931471805599453
LN10	Natural Logarithm of 10	2.302585092994046
LOG2E	Base 2 logarithm of e	1.4426950408889633
LOG10E	Base 10 logarithm of e	0.4342944819032518
SQRT2	Square root of 2	1.4142135623730951
SQRT1_2	Square root of ½	0.7071067811865476

Frequently used JavaScript `Math` object methods are shown in Table 13.4.

Table 13.4 JavaScript math object methods

Methods	Meaning	Example	Result
max(a, b)	Returns larger of a and b	Math.max(2, 3)	3
min(a, b)	Returns smaller of a and b	Math.min(2, 3)	2
Round(a)	Rounds .5 up. Returns nearest integer.	Math.round(2.3)	2
		Math.round(2.8)	3
		Math.round(2.5)	3
ceil(a)	Round up. Returns the smallest integer greater than or equal to a	Math.ceil(2.3)	3
		Math.ceil(2.8)	3
floor(a)	Round down. Returns the largest integer smaller than or equal to a	Math.floor(2.3)	2
		Math.floor(2.8)	2
exp(a)	Returns e^a	Math.exp(1)	2.718281828459045
pow(a, b)	Returns a^b	Math.pow(2, 3)	8
		Math.pow(2, 3.2)	9.18958683997628
		Math.pow(2.3, 3)	12.166999999999996
		Math.pow(2.3, 3.2)	14.372392707920498
abs(a)	Returns absolute value of a	Math.abs(2)	2
		Math.abs(–2)	–2
log(a)	Returns natural logarithm of a	Math.log(2)	0.6931471805599453
		Math.log(0)	–Infinity
		Math.log(1)	0
random()	Returns a pseudorandom number between 0 and 1	Math.random()	Any number between 0 and 1
sqrt(a)	Returns square root of a	Math.sqrt(2)	1.4142135623730951
sin(a)	Returns sin of a (a is in radians)	Math.sin((22/7)/4)	0.7073302780849811
cos(a)	Returns cos of a (a is in radians)	Math.cos((22/7)/4)	0.706883213624587
tan(a)	Returns tan of a (a is in radians)	Math.tan((22/7)/4)	1.0006324445845895
asin(a)	Returns arc sin of a (a is in radians)	Math.asin(1)	1.5707963267948965
acos(a)	Returns arc cos of a (a is in radians)	Math.acos(1)	0
atan(a)	Returns arc tan of a (a is in radians)	Math.atan(1)	0.7853981633974483

The JavaScript arithmetic operators are given in Table 13.5.

Table 13.5 JavaScript arithmetic operators

+	–	*	/	%
++	--	– (unary minus)	+ (unary plus)	

13.4.1 Arithmetic Operators

The following operators are provided to perform arithmetic operations between variables.

- **+ operator**

It performs numeric addition.

```
var result = 2 + 3;                       //result is 5
```

It can also concatenate strings.

```
result = "Hello " + "World!";             //result is "Hello World!"
```

If mixed operands are used, it always performs concatenation. In such a case, numeric operands are first converted to string value and then string concatenation is performed.

```
result = 2 + "MB";                        //result is "2MB"
result = "P" + 4;                         //result is "P4"
```

If multiple addition operations are used in an expression, they are evaluated from left to right.

```
result = "Y" + 2 + "K";                   //result is "Y2K"
result = 2 + 3 + "K";                     //result is (2+3)+"K" = "5K"
result = "K" + 2 + 3;                     //result is ("K"+2)+3 = "K23"
result = "Age: " + 32 + "<br>";           //result is "Age: 32<br>"
msg = "Hello World!";
result = "<b>" + msg  + "</b>";           //result is "<b>Hello World!</b>"
width = 100;
line = '<hr width="' + width + '">'; //line is '<hr width="100">'
```

- **– operator**

This operator performs subtraction operation. The following examples illustrate this:

```
result = 3 - 2;                           //result is 1
result = 2 - 3;                           //result is -1
result = 3.6 - 1.3;                       //result is 2.3
result = -3.6 - 1.3;                      //result is -4.9
```

If string operands are used, the JavaScript engine tries to convert them into numeric values. If conversion is successful, subtraction operation is performed. Otherwise `NaN` (**N**ot **a** **N**umber) is returned for the expression.

```
result = 3 - "2";                         //result is 1
result = "3" - "2";                       //result is 1
result = "3.6" - "1.3";                   //result is 2.3
result = "2K" - 3;                        //result is NaN
```

- *** operator**

It performs multiplication of numeric operands. The following examples illustrate this:

```
result = 3 * 2;                           //result is 6
result = -2 * 3;                          //result is -6
result = -1.5 * 0.5;                      //result is -0.75
```

If string operands are used, the JavaScript engine tries to convert them into numeric values. If conversion is successful, multiplication operation is performed, otherwise `NaN` is returned for the expression.

```
result = 3 * "2";                         //result is 6
result = "3" * "2";                       //result is 6
result = "-1.5" * "0.5";                  //result is -0.75
result = "2k" * 3;                        //result is NaN
```

- **/ operator**

It performs division of numeric operands. See the following examples:

```
result = 5 / 2;                          //result is 2.5
result = -2 / 5;                         //result is -0.4
result = 2 / 0;                          //result is Infinity
result = -2 / 0;                         //result is -Infinity
result = 0 / 0;                          //result is NaN
result = 0 / 2;                          //result is 0
```

Remember, JavaScript internally represents integers as floating point numbers. So, the result of `5/2` will be `2.5`, a floating point number.

If string operands are used, the JavaScript engine tries to convert them into numeric values. If conversion is successful, division operation is performed. Otherwise `NaN` is returned for the expression. See the following examples:

```
result = 5 / "2";                        //result is 2.5
result = "5" / "2";                      //result is 2.5
result = "2k" / 2;                       //result is NaN
```

- **% operator**

This is a binary modulus operator, which returns a remainder.

```
result = 5 % 2;                          //result is 1
result = -5 % 2                          //result is -1
result = 5 % -2;                         //result is 1
result = -5 % -2;                        //result is -1
result = 2 % 0;                          //result is NaN
result = 0 % 0;                          //result is NaN
result = 0 % 2;                          //result is 0
```

If string operands are used, the JavaScript engine tries to convert them into numbers. If successful, a remainder is returned, otherwise `NaN` is returned. The following examples illustrate this:

```
result = 5 % "2";                        //result is 1
result = "5" % "2";                      //result is 1
result = "-5" % "2";                     //result is -1
result = "2k" % 2;                       //result is NaN
```

- **++ operator**

The unary increment operator increments the value of the operand by one. It has two types depending upon its usage: *pre increment* and *post increment*. The pre increment version (written before the operand, e.g., ++x) returns the final value (i.e., after incrementing the value) of the operand. Post increment (written after the operand, e.g., x++ returns the initial value (i.e., before incrementing the value) of the operand. The following examples illustrate this:

```
x = 1;
x++;                                     //x is 2;
++x;                                     //x is 3;
y = ++x;                                 //x is 4, y is 4
y = x++;                                 //x is 5, y is 4
```

- **-- operator**

The unary decrement operator decrements the value of the operand by one. It also has two types depending upon its usage: *pre decrement* and *post decrement*. The pre decrement version (written before the operand, e.g., --x) returns the final value (i.e., after decrementing the value) of the operand. Post decrement (written after the operand, e.g., x--) returns the initial value (i.e., before decrementing the value) of the operand. The following examples illustrate this:

```
x = 5;
x--;                          //x is 4;
—x;                           //x is 3;
y = --x;                      //x is 2, y is 2
y = x--;                      //x is 1, y is 2
```

- **– (unary minus) operator**

This operator is used to negate a number.

```
result = -1;                  //result is -1;
result = - -2.3;              //result is 2.3;
```

It is also used to convert a non-number value (such as a string) to a number. Unsuccessful conversion results in the value `NaN`.

```
result  = -"1";               //string to number conversion, result is -1
result  = -"2.3";             //string to number conversion, result is -2.3
result  = -"2K";              //result is NaN
```

- **+ (unary plus) operator**

This operator does nothing except converting a non-number value (such as a string) to a number. Unsuccessful conversion results in the value `NaN`.

```
result = +1;                  //result is 1;
result  = +"1";               //string to number conversion, result is 1
result = + -2.3;              //result is -2.3;
result  = +"2.3";             //string to number conversion, result is 2.3
result  = +"2K";              //result is NaN
```

13.4.1.1 Operator precedence

If an arithmetic expression contains different operators, the operator precedence rule determines the order in which they are evaluated. Operators having higher precedence are evaluated before operators having lower precedence. JavaScript arithmetic operators have the precedence rule shown in Table 13.6.

Table 13.6 JavaScript arithmetic operator precedence rule

Precedence	Operators
Lowest	+, –
	*, /, %
Highest	++, – –
	–(unary), +(unary)

For example, in the expression 2+3*4, there are two different operators + and * having different precedence. The multiplication operator (*) has higher precedence than the addition operator (+). So, the multiplication operation is performed first and then addition is done; this results in the value 14.

13.4.1.2 Associativity

Arithmetic operators are *left-to-right* associative when operators of the same precedence are chained.

```
result = 6 / 2 * 3;            //result is 9
```

In the following example, the division operation is performed first; the result will be 3. This value will then be multiplied by 3 resulting in the value 9.

However, the order may be overridden using parenthesis.

```
result = 6 / (2 * 3);          //result is 1
```

In this case, multiplication will be performed first resulting in the value 6. This value will be treated as denominator and division will be performed resulting in the value 1.

The order of execution does not always affect the result. The following expression will produce the same result, irrespective of which operation is performed first. However, as far as the JavaScript language is concerned, multiplication (*) is performed first.

```
result = 3 * 4 / 2;            //result is 6
```

13.4.2 Assignment Operators

The following operators are provided to assign values to variables. The primary assignment operator (=) is a binary operator that assigns the value of the operand on its right hand to the operand on its left. So, in the expression `a = b`, the value of `b` is assigned to `a`. JavaScript also provides different assignment operators in compressed form for traditional operations. Assuming `a = 3`, and `b = 2`, Table 13.7 illustrates different assignment operators.

Table 13.7 JavaScript assignment operators

<table>
<tr><th>Operator</th><th>Example</th><th>Meaning</th><th>Result</th><th>Operator</th><th>Example</th><th>Meaning</th><th>Result</th></tr>
<tr><td>+=</td><td>a += b</td><td>a = a + b</td><td>5</td><td>>>=</td><td>a >>= b</td><td>a = a >> b</td><td>0</td></tr>
<tr><td>–=</td><td>a –= b</td><td>a = a – b</td><td>1</td><td>>>>=</td><td>a >>>= b</td><td>a = a >>> b</td><td>0</td></tr>
<tr><td>*=</td><td>a *= b</td><td>a = a * b</td><td>6</td><td>&=</td><td>a &= b</td><td>a = a & b</td><td>2</td></tr>
<tr><td>/=</td><td>a /= b</td><td>a = a / b</td><td>1.5</td><td>|=</td><td>a |= b</td><td>a = a | b</td><td>3</td></tr>
<tr><td>%=</td><td>a %= b</td><td>a = a % b</td><td>1</td><td>^=</td><td>a ^= b</td><td>a = a ^ b</td><td>1</td></tr>
<tr><td><<=</td><td>a <<= b</td><td>a = a << b</td><td>12</td><td></td><td></td><td></td><td></td></tr>
</table>

13.4.3 Relational Operators

Relational operators [Table 13.8] are binary operators that test the relationship between two operands and return a boolean value (i.e., either `true` or `false`).

Table 13.8 JavaScript relational operators

==	!=	<	<=	>
>=	===	!=	In	instanceof

- **==(equal) and != (not equal) operator**

The equal (==) operator returns `true`, if both operands are equal. On the other hand, not equal (!=) operator returns `true` if the operands are not equal.

The equal and not equal operators work differently on different data types. They test equality (or inequality) by *value* for boolean, numeric, and string types. This means that two operands are equal (or identical) only if they have the same *value*. For example, two strings are equal only if they have exactly the same characters.

On the other hand, arrays, functions, and objects are tested *by reference*. It means that two references to arrays, functions, or objects are equal only if they *refer to* the same array, function, or object. So, two separate arrays are never equal even if they have the same elements.

```
a = [1, 2, 3, 4];
b = [1, 2, 3, 4];
var result = a == b;    //result is false, a and b are different arrays
b = a;
result = a == b; //result is true, a and b point to same array
```

If you want to check whether two separate objects have the same set of properties or two different arrays contain the same elements, you have to test individual properties or elements for sameness. Note that, if properties or elements are themselves objects or arrays, you have to test them using exactly the same procedure.

What happens if two operands are not of the same type? In this case, both operands perform conversions before testing equality, according to the following rules:

- A boolean operand is converted to a numeric value before testing. The values `false` and `true` are converted to 0 and 1, respectively.
- If one operand is numeric and the other is a string, the string operand is converted to a number before testing.
- If one operand is a string and the other is an object, the object operand is converted to a string using the `toString()` method of object before testing.
- If one operand is numeric and the other is an object, the object is converted to a number before testing.
- The 'undefined' and 'null' values cannot be converted into any other values for testing. They are equal.
- If either operand is `NaN`, the equal operator returns `false` and the not equal to operator returns `true`.
- The equal operator returns false even if both operands are `NaN`. This is because, by rule, `NaN` is not equal to `NaN`.

Table 13.9 shows some examples.

Table 13.9 Relational operators examples

Expression	Value	Expression	Value	Expression	Value
false == false	true	2==2	true	false == "1"	false
true == true	true	2==3	false	false == "0"	true
false == true	true	2!=3	true	null == undefined	true
false == 0	true	"abc" == "xyz"	false	"NaN" == NaN	false
false == 1	false	"abc" != "xyz"	true	5 == NaN	false
true == 1	true	"5" == 5	true	NaN == NaN	false
true == 0	false	"5" != 5	false	NaN != NaN	true
true == 2	false	true == "1"	true	undefined == 0	false
false != false	false	true == "0"	false	undefined == 1	false
false != true	true	true != "0"	true	null == 0	false

- **===(identical) and !==(not identical) operator**

These operators are the same as their counterparts, i.e., equal to and not equal to operators, except that no conversion is performed if two operands are not of the same type.

```
var result = 5 === "5";     //result is false
result = "5" === "5";       //result is true
result = false == 0;        //result is false
```

- **comparison operators (>, <, >=, <=)**

Comparison operators [Table 13.10] work only on numeric or string operands.

Table 13.10 Comparison operators examples

Operator	Description
>	Returns true if left-hand operand is **greater** than the right-hand operand
<	Returns true if left-hand operand is **less** than the right-hand operand
>=	Returns true if left-hand operand is **greater than or equal to** than the right-hand operand
<=	Returns true if left-hand operand is **less than or equal to** than the right-hand operand

- **in operator**

This binary operator returns `true` if the left-hand operand is a property of the right-hand operand. The left-hand operand should be a string and the right-hand operand should be an object or an array. The following examples illustrate this:

```
var p =  {x : 0, y : 0 };
result = "x" in p;  //result is true
result = "y" in p;  //result is true
result = "z " in p; //result is false
```

- **instanceof operator**

This binary operator expects the left-hand operand to be an object and the right-hand operand to be the name of a class. It returns `true` if the object is an instance of the class and `false` otherwise.

```
var p =  {x : 0, y : 0 };
result = p instanceof Object; //result is true, all objects are instances of
                                Object
```

```
result = p instanceof Date; //result is false, p is not a Date object
result = p instanceof Array; //result is false, p is not an Array object
a = [1, 2, 3];
result = a instanceof Array; //result is true, a is an Array object
result = a instanceof Function; //result is false, a is not a Function object
f = function(a, b) {return a + b;}
result = f instanceof Function; //result is true, f is a Function object
result = f instanceof Object;   //result is true, all objects are
instances of Object
```

13.4.4 Logical Operators

Logical operators typically operate on boolean values, which are either `true` or `false`. The following logical operators are available:

```
&&, ||, !
```

Table 13.11 shows the truth table for logical operators.

Table 13.11 JavaScript logical operators

a	b	Result		
		a && b	a || b	!a
false	false	false	false	true
false	true	false	true	
true	false	false	true	false
true	true	true	true	

What happens if operands are not boolean values? In this case, both && and || actually return the value of one of their operands.

To understand this, let us understand the concept of "truthy" and "falsy". An empty string (' '), the number 0, null, `NaN`, a boolean `false`, and undefined variables are all "falsy". Everything else is "truthy".

In general, the && operator checks the first operand. If it is falsy, the && operator returns the whole expression. Otherwise, it returns the second operand. The following examples illustrate this:

```
var result = false && true; //result is false
result = 0 && true;         //result is 0, 0 is falsy
result = null && true;      //result is null, null is falsy
result = NaN && true;       //result is NaN, NaN is falsy
result = '' && true;        //result is '', '' is falsy
result = undefined && true; //result is undefined, undefined is falsy
result = 1 && true;         //result is true, 1 is truthy
result = 1 && false;        //result is false, 1 is truthy
result = 1 && 2;            //result is 2, 1 is truthy
result = 1 && 0;            //result is 0, 1 is truthy
result = 1 && [1, 2, 3];    //result is 1,2,3 , 1 is truthy
result = "first" && "second"; //result is "second", "first" is truthy
result = "first" && NaN;    //result is NaN, "first" is truthy
```

In general, the || operator checks the first operand. If it is truthy, the || operator returns the whole expression. Otherwise, it returns the second operand. The following examples illustrate this:

```
var result = false || true;  //result is true
result = 0 || true;          //result is true, 0 is falsy
result = null || true;       //result is true, null is falsy
result = NaN || true;        //result is true, NaN is falsy
result = '' || true;         //result is true, '' is falsy
result = undefined || true;  //result is true, undefined is falsy
result = 1 || true;          //result is 1, 1 is truthy
result = [1, 2, 3] || false; //result is 1,2,3 , [1, 2, 3] is truthy
result = "abc" || 2;         //result is "abc", "abc" is truthy
result = 2 || 0;             //result is 2, 2 is truthy
result = true || [1, 2, 3];  //result is true
result = "first" || "second"; //result is "first", "first" is truthy
```

The ! operator, unlike the && and || operators, converts the value of its operand into a boolean. If the operand is truthy, it returns `false`, otherwise it returns `true`. The following examples illustrate this:

```
var result = ! (false || true); //result is false
result = ! (false || false);    //result is true
result = ! (false || null);     //result is true
result = ! (false || "second"); //result is false
```

13.4.5 Bitwise Operators

Table 13.12 summarizes JavaScript's bitwise operators.

Table 13.12 JavaScript bitwise operators

Operator	Meaning	Usage	Description
&	Bitwise AND	`a & b`	Returns 1 in each bit position if corresponding bits of a and b are 1; returns 0 otherwise
|	Bitwise OR	`a | b`	Returns 0 in each bit position if corresponding bits of a and b are 0; returns 1 otherwise
^	Bitwise XOR	`a ^ b`	Returns 0 in each bit position if corresponding bits of a and b are identical; returns1 otherwise
~	Bitwise NOT	`~ a`	Inverts the bits of its operand
<<	Left shift	`a << b`	Left-shifts a, b times (< 32) filling zeros from the right.
>>	Sign-propagating right shift	`a >> b`	Right-shifts a, b times (< 32) discarding bits shifted off.
>>>	Zero-fill right shift	`a >>> b`	Right-shifts a, b times (< 32) discarding bits shifted off, and shifting in zeros from the left.

13.4.6 Operator Precedence

Table 13.13 summarizes JavaScript's operator precedence and associativity.

Table 13.13 JavaScript operators precedence and associativity

Operators	Precedence Level	Associativity
. (dot—member reference), [] (bracket—property reference), new, ()	1	Left to right
++, – –	2	Right to left
+ (unary), – (unary), ~ (bitwise not), ! (not), delete , typeof, void	3	Right to left

(Contd.)

(Contd.)

*, /, %	4	Left to right
+ (addition), – (subtraction)	5	Left to right
<<, >>, >>>	6	Left to right
<, <=, >, >=, instanceof, in	7	Left to right
==, !=, ===, !==	8	Left to right
&	9	Left to right
^	10	Left to right
|	11	Left to right
&&	12	Left to right
||	13	Left to right
?:	14	Right to left
=, *=, /=, %=, +=, –=, <<==, >>==, >>>=, &=, ^=, |=	15	Right to left
, (comma)	16	Left to right

13.5 CONTROL STRUCTURE

In this section, we shall quickly cover how to change the control of execution in a program. There are two ways to change the control structures of a program.

13.5.1 for

The `for` loop is used to execute a set of instructions repeatedly. It takes the following form:

```
for ( [initial exp.]; [condition]; [update exp] ) {
   statements
}
```

The expression `initial exp` is evaluated only the first time. Then the condition is always checked at the beginning of each loop. If the condition is true the body of the `for` loop indicated by the curly braces, is executed. At the end of the body, the expression `update exp` is executed, where a loop variable is typically updated. Then the condition is checked once again and the same procedure is followed. Consider the following example.

```
for(i = 0; i < 10; i++)
  document.writeln(i + ' ');
```

The result of this piece of code is shown in Figure 13.3.

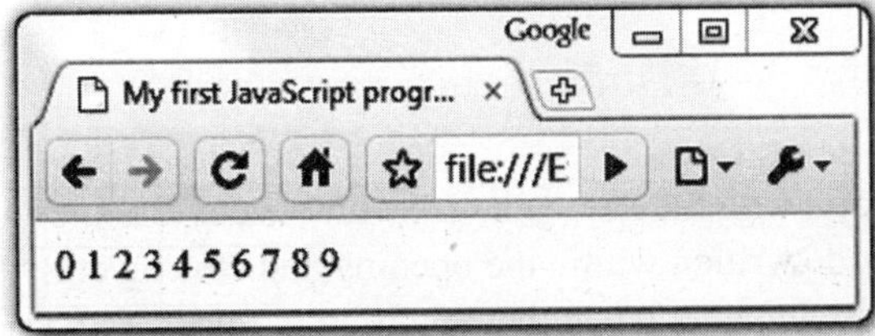

Figure 13.3 JavaScript for loop demonstration

13.5.2 while

The `while` loop is used to execute a block of statements as long as a given condition is true. It takes the following form:

```
while (condition) {
   statements
}
```

The condition is evaluated at the beginning of each loop. If the condition is true, the body is executed. Otherwise, the control of execution comes to the end of the `while` loop. At the end of the body, a variable is typically updated, which makes the condition false after a number of iterations.

The following example does exactly the same thing as the previous `for` loop.

```
i = 0;
while(i < 10) {
    document.writeln(i + ' ');
    i++;
}
```

13.5.3 do-while

The `do-while` loop is exactly the same as the `while` loop except that the condition is specified at the end of the body. It takes the following form:

```
do {
   statements
} while (condition)
```

The following example does exactly the same thing as the previous `while` loop.

```
i = 0;
do {
   document.writeln(i + ' ');
   i++;
}while(i < 10);
```

Unlike the `while` loop, the body of the `do-while` loop is executed at least once, irrespective of the specified condition.

13.6 CONDITIONAL STATEMENTS

A conditional statement takes the following form:

```
if (condition) {
   some JavaScript code
}
```

An `if` statement starts with the keyword "if" with the condition(s) listed in parenthesis. If the condition is true, the code written within the opening and closing curly braces is executed. If you want to execute some statements when the condition is false, the corresponding `else` part may be inserted as follows:

```
if (condition) {
   some JavaScript code
}
else {
   some JavaScript code
}
```

Consider the following example:

```
var x = 2;
if ( x%2 == 0 ) {
   alert("even");
}
else {
   alert("odd");
}
```

In this piece of code, the expression `x%2 == 0` evaluates to `true` and the `if` block is executed. It displays the message "even" in the alert dialog box.

Nested `if` and `else` statements are also possible.

13.7 ARRAYS

JavaScript arrays are different from arrays in other languages. Traditionally, an array is considered to be a collection of homogeneous items. It means an array cannot contain dissimilar items. For example, an array cannot simultaneously contain an integer element and a string element. All the items must be of similar type. However for different items, different arrays may be created. JavaScript does not follow this concept at all. A JavaScript array may contain heterogeneous items. These arrays are similar to structure variables, except that they can be accessed randomly with the array name and the index (not necessarily an integer). That is why JavaScript arrays are sometimes called *associative* arrays. This is another aspect in which JavaScript is different from other languages.

13.7.1 Array Literal

An array variable may be created by assigning an array literal to it. An array literal is written using square brackets with array elements separated by commas (,) as follows:

var anArray = [$element_0$, $element_1$, ..., $element_N$];

Here are some examples.

```
var odds = [1, 3, 5, 7];
var vowels = ['a', 'e', 'i', 'o', 'u'];
var bools = [true, false];
var colors = ["red", "yellow", "green", "blue"];
var empty = [];
```

Elements are accessed using the array name and the index (ordinal number) of the element written within square brackets. For example, `colors[2]`, `odds[3]`, `vowels[1]`, etc. The array index starts with `0`. So, `odds[0]` is `1`, `colors[0]` is `"red"`, and `vowels[0]` is `'a'`.

A JavaScript array literal may contain undefined elements.

```
var colors = ["red", , , "green", "blue"];
```

This array has five elements, `colors[0]` through `colors[4]`. However, the values of `colors[1]` and `colors[2]` have not been specified so far and hence, are undefined. The length of this array is 5 (five). Consider the following array declaration:

```
var colors = ["red", , , "green", "blue",];
```

The single comma (,) at the end of the array literal is ignored. So, this declaration is identical with the previous declaration. It still has 5 (five) elements of which `color[1]` and `color[2]` are undefined.

The traditional `for` loop can be used to iterate through an array. JavaScript arrays are objects and provide several useful properties and methods to work with it. The property `length` specifies the size of the array. We shall discuss array properties and methods in Sections 13.7.4 and 13.7.5, respectively.

```
var odds = [1, 3, 5, 7];
var sum = 0;
for(i = 0; i < odds.length; i++)
   sum += odds[i];
document.writeln(sum);
```

As mentioned earlier in this section, a JavaScript array may contain heterogeneous elements. One can declare an array that contains various information about an employee such as name, age, marital status, and salary. The declaration of such an array will look like this:

```
var employee = ["John", 24, false, 18000];
                   ↑     ↑    ↑      ↑
                 name   age married salary
```

```
▪   employee[0] contains name              //string
▪   employee[1] contains age               //number
▪   employee[2] contains married info      //boolean
▪   employee[3] contains salary            //number
```

The array variable `employee` has four elements: `employee[0]` through `employee[3]`. `employee[0]` is of string type, `employee[2]` is of boolean type and the rest of the elements are of number type.

JavaScript arrays are dynamic in nature. It means that elements can be added and deleted as and when required. For efficient memory usage, an array should contain only those elements that are actually required. Determining array size in advance during the creation of the array is also a major problem. JavaScript dynamic arrays eliminate all these problems.

```
var primes = [2, 3, 5, 7];   //length 4
primes[4] = 11;              //length 5, adds an element at the end
```

This code segment first creates an array of length 4. It then adds an element to the end of the array which changes array size to 5. The following statement also adds an element at the end.

```
primes[primes.length] = 13; //length 6, adds an element at the end
```

In general, if a value is assigned to an array element that has not yet been created, the corresponding element as well as all the uncreated elements that precede it are created automatically.

```
primes[8] = 23;  //length 9
```

This example adds an element at the index 8, which changes the array length to 9. The elements `primes[6]` and `primes[7]` are created automatically but are yet undefined.

13.7.2 Using Constructors

In JavaScript, an array is an object. JavaScript provides constructors to create arrays. There are three versions of array constructors:

```
Array();
Array(number of elements);
Array(comma separated list of elements);
```

The first constructor does not take any argument and creates an empty array (i.e., an array of length zero). Elements may be added later as and when needed.

```
var colors = new Array();     //array of length zero
```

This code segment creates an array of length zero. Now, consider the following statement:

```
colors[2] = "blue";           //length 3
```

This statement adds an element to the location `colors[2]`. What about `colors[0]` and `colors[1]`? Do they exist? If they exist, what are their values? Let us answer each of these questions one by one.

This statement not only creates element `color[2]` but also the elements `colors[0]` and `colors[1]`. The length of the array `colors` then becomes 3. Note that, the values of `colors[0]` and `colors[1]` are yet undefined. However, their values may be assigned later, if necessary, using the following syntax:

```
colors[0] = "red";
colors[1] = "green";
```

In general, if a value is assigned to an index i that is greater than or equal to the length of the array, the size of the array increases to (i+1). Creating an array this way is useful if the number of elements is not known during the declaration of the array. Consider the following question:

Find all prime numbers from 2 to 50 and put them in an array named `primes`.

Note that the number of prime numbers from 2 to 50 is not known in advance. Accordingly, the size of the array `primes` cannot be mentioned. The JavaScript `Array()` constructor can help in this regard, as an arbitrary number of elements may be added to this array even after the creation of the array. The following example illustrates this:

```
<!—primes.htm—->
<html>
   <head>
```

```
        <title>Dynamic Array Demo</title>
    </head>
    <body>
      <script language = "JavaScript">
         var primes = new Array();              //create an empty array
         for(var i = 2; i < 50; i++) {
            var prime = true;
            for(var k = 2; k < i; k++)
               if(i%k == 0) {
                  prime = false;
                  break;
               }
            if(prime == true)
               primes[primes.length] = i;     //add i at the end
         }
         for(i = 0; i < primes.length; i++)
            document.writeln(primes[i]);
      </script>
    </body>
</html>
```

In this example, an array `primes` of length 0 is created first. As prime numbers are found, they are added to the end of this array. Finally, all elements of this array are printed. Figure 13.4 shows the result.

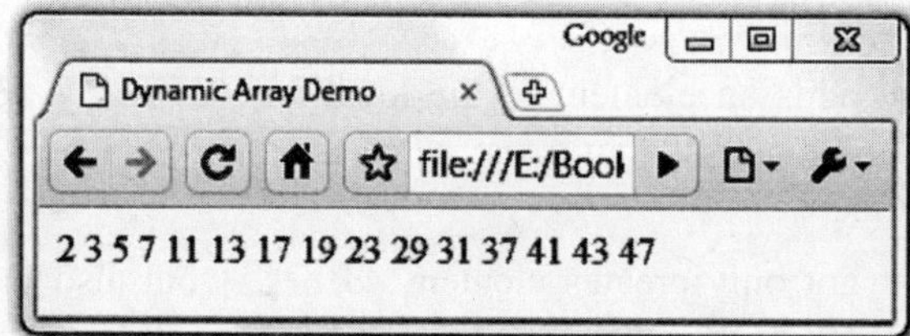

Figure 13.4 JavaScript dynamic array demonstration

Programmers may also specify the initial length of the array during creation, as follows:

```
colors = new Array(2);
```

This creates the array `colors` of initial length 2. Note that so far, no values have been assigned to the elements `colors[0]` and `colors[1]`. So, these elements are yet undefined. Elements may be assigned later as required.

```
colors[0] = "red";
colors[1] = "green";
```

Elements can also be added dynamically on demand.

```
colors[3] = "violet";        //length 4
```

This code segment adds an element to the location 3. The element `colors[2]` is automatically added.

Programmers may also explicitly specify the elements of an array during its creation. The length of the array will be the number of elements specified.

```
var manufacturers = new Array("Maruti", "Tata", "Ford");
```

This creates an array of length 3, where

```
manufacturers[0] is "Maruti"
manufacturers[1] is "Tata"
manufacturers[2] is "Ford"
```

An array created in this fashion is called a *dense* array, as each element in this array is defined and has a value.

If a single argument is passed to the array constructor and if it is not an integer, an array of length 1 is created. This happens because in such a case the last overloaded version of the array constructor is used. Accordingly, the value of this element will be the value specified. The maximum length possible for an array is 4,294,967,295.

13.7.3 Multi-dimensional arrays

Multi-dimensional arrays are created in exactly the same way as one-dimensional arrays. However, elements in a multi-dimensional array are themselves arrays.

```
<!--multi-dimensionalArray.htm-->
<html>
   <head>
      <title>Multi-dimensional Array Demo</title>
   </head>
   <body>
      <script language = "JavaScript">
         var emp1 = ["John", 24, false, 18000];
         var emp2 = ["Kate", 28, false, 28000];
         var emps = [emp1, emp2];
         var totalSalary = 0;
         for(i = 0; i < emps.length; i++)
            totalSalary += emps[i][3];
         document.writeln(totalSalary);
      </script>
   </body>
</html>
```

The array `emps` is a one-dimensional array of two elements. The only notable thing is that each of the two elements `emps[0]` and `emps[1]` is again a one-dimensional array. So, `emps[0][0]` is "John" and `emps[0][1]` is 24, and so on. Note that all the elements of the `emps` array need not be identical.

13.7.4 Properties

Table 13.14 shows the properties that are available on an array object.

Table 13.14 JavaScript array property summary

Property	Description
length	Returns the number of elements in an array
constructor	Returns the function that created the array object
prototype	Allows us to add properties and methods to an array object

13.7.5 Array methods

JavaScript has several useful built-in methods [Table 13.15] for manipulation of arrays.

Table 13.15 JavaScript array methods summary

Method	Description
reverse	reverses array elements
concat	joins two or more arrays
sort	sorts the elements of an array
push	appends one or more element at the end
pop	removes and returns the last element
shift	removes and returns the first element
unshift	adds one or more elements at the beginning
join	puts all the elements separated by a specified delimiter (default is ',') of an array into a string.
indexOf	returns the first index of the specified element
lastIndexOf	returns the last index of the specified element
slice	returns selected elements

reverse()

This method reverses (transposes) the order of the array elements. The original array is modified.

```
<!--reverse.htm-->
<html>
   <head>
      <title>Reverse Demo</title>
   </head>
   <body>
      <script language = "JavaScript">
         var a = [1, 7, 3, 5, 9, 4, 2, 6];
         document.write("Before reverse: ");
         for(i=0;i<a.length;i++)
            document.writeln(a[i]);
         a.reverse();
         document.write("<br>After reverse: ");
         for(i=0;i<a.length;i++)
            document.writeln(a[i]);
      </script>
   </body>
</html>
```

The result is shown in Figure 13.5.

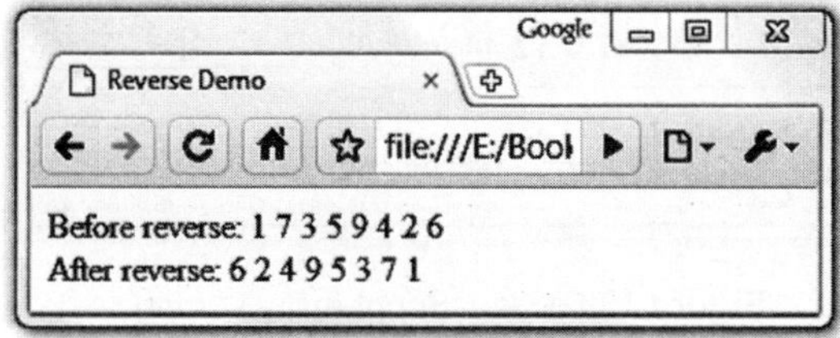

Figure 13.5 JavaScript array reversing

concat()

This method concatenates other arrays and elements with the existing array and returns a new array.

```
var a = [1, 3], b = [5, 7, 9], c = [11, 13];
var d = a.concat(b);              //d is [1, 3, 5, 7, 9]
var e = a.concat(5, 7, 9);        //e is [1, 3, 5, 7, 9]
var f = a.concat(b, c);           //f is [1, 3, 5, 7, 9, 11, 13]
var g = a.concat(b, c, 15, 17);   //g is [1, 3, 5, 7, 9, 11, 13, 15, 17]
```

The original array is not modified.

sort([sortFunction])

This method takes an optional parameter. If nothing is specified, it sorts the array alphanumerically (lexicographically) in ascending order. The following example illustrates this:

```
<!--sortAlphanumeric.html-->
<html>
   <head>
      <title>Alphanumeric Sort Demo</title>
   </head>
   <body>
      <script language = "JavaScript">
         var protocols = ["SMTP", "HTTP", "FTP", "HTTPS"];
         document.write("Before sorting: ");
         for(i = 0; i < protocols.length; i++)
            document.writeln(protocols[i]);
         protocols.sort();
         document.write("<br>After sorting: ");
         for(i = 0; i < protocols.length; i++)
            document.writeln(protocols[i]);
      </script>
   </body>
</html>
```

This code produces the result as shown in Figure 13.6.

Figure 13.6 JavaScript array sorting

The sorting criteria may be specified explicitly while calling the function `sort()`. This sorting criteria is specified as a function (we call it *criteria function*). The function `sort` makes use of this function to sort array elements. The criteria function should take two parameters, say `x` and `y` and return an integer. For any two elements `x` and `y` in the array, the function `sort()` decides if the element `x` should precede the element `y` based on the return value of the criteria function as follows:

- If return value is less than `0`, `x` must precede `y`.
- If return value is `0`, `x` and `y` are considered to be equal and nothing is done.
- If return value is greater than `0`, `y` must precede `x`.

This simple idea can be used to sort an array numerically either in ascending order or in descending order. The following example sorts the array numerically in ascending order.

```
function criteria(x, y) {
   return x - y;
}
var a = [1, 7, 30, 5, 9, 12, 20, 6];
a.sort(criteria);
```

In a sorted array of integers in ascending order, if the element `x` precedes the element `y`, then `x` is smaller than `y`. Therefore, the expression `x - y` is less than zero, which may be used by the function `sort()` to sort the array elements in ascending order. This simple idea is used in the code segment just discussed. Anonymous functions may also be used during the function call, as follows:

```
var a = [1, 7, 30, 5, 9, 12, 20, 6];
a.sort(function criteria(x, y) { return x - y; });
```

The following example sorts the array numerically in descending order. Here, the expression `y - x` is used instead of the expression `x - y`.

```
var a = [1, 7, 30, 5, 9, 12, 20, 6];
a.sort(function criteria(x, y) { return y - x; });
```

If the array elements are not numeric, the criteria function may be written as follows:

```
function criteria(x, y) {
   if ( x should precede y ) return -1;
   if ( y should precede x ) return 1;
   return 0;
}
```

pop()

It removes the last element and returns it. The original array is modified. The `length` property is decreased by 1.

```
var a = [1, 3, 5, 7];
var e = a.pop();              //e is 7 and a is [1, 3, 5]
```

The value of `e` is `7` and the array now becomes `1, 3, 5.`

push(value1, value2, ...)

Elements specified are added at the end of the array in the order specified and the new length of the array is returned. The original array is modified.

```
var a = [1, 3];
var l = a.push(5);            //a is [1, 3, 5] and l is 3
                              // equivalent to a[a.length] = 5;
l = a.push(7, 9);             //a is [1, 3, 5, 7, 9] and l is 5
```

The array `a` finally becomes `1, 3, 5, 7, 9.`

shift()

It removes the first element and returns it. The Original array is modified. The length of the array is decreased by 1.

```
var a = [1, 3, 5, 7];
var e = a.shift();            //e is 1 and a is [3, 5, 7]
```

The value of `e` is `1` and the array now becomes `3, 5, 7.`

unshift()

The elements specified are added at the beginning in the order specified and the new length of the array is returned. The original array is modified.

```
var a = [7, 9];
var l = a.unshift(1, 3, 5); //a is [1, 3, 5, 7, 9] and l is 5
```

The array `a` finally becomes `1, 3, 5, 7, 9.`

join()

It returns a string consisting of all element of the array separated by a specified delimiter. If no delimiter is passed, "," is assumed.

```
var a = [1, 3, 5, 7];
var str = a.join();         //str is "1,3,5,7"
str = a.join(":");          //str is "1:3:5:7"
```

The array is not modified.

indexOf()

It returns the first index of the specified element if it is found and –1 if the element is not found. An optional starting index (default is 0) may be specified. This method is a part of the JavaScript ECMA-262 standard and may not be present in other implementations.

lastIndexOf()

It returns the last index of the specified element if it is found and –1 if the element is not found. The array is searched in reverse order. An optional starting index (default is the last index, i.e., one less than the array length) may be specified. This method is a part of the JavaScript ECMA-262 standard and may not be present in other implementations.

slice()

It returns a sequence of elements from an array. It takes an integer argument that indicates the starting index of the array. An optional end index (default is last index) may also be passed to indicate the ending index of the array. The original array is not modified.

```
var a = [0, 1, 2, 3, 4, 5, 6, 7];
var b = a.slice(1, 3);      // b is [1, 2]
var c = a.slice(3);         //c is [2, 3, 4, 5, 6, 7]
```

If the second argument is negative, the actual index is calculated by subtracting it from the last index.

```
var d = a.slice(2, -3);    //d is [2, 3, 4]
```

pslice()

It returns and removes a sequence of elements. The general syntax is as follows:

```
splice(startIndex, [howMany, element1, element2…elementn]);
splice(startIndex, howMany, [element1, element2…elementn]);
```

It takes an integer argument that specifies the starting index of the sequence. An optional number of elements (default is 0) to be removed may also be specified. This method may be used to insert elements in the location from where the sequence is removed.

```
var a = [1, 2, 3, 4, 5];
var b = a.splice(1, 2);           //a is [1, 4, 5] and b is [2, 3]
var c = a.splice(1, 1, 2, 3);     //a is [1, 2, 3, 5] and c is [4]
```

13.8 FUNCTIONS

A function is a segment of code that performs, when called, a particular "function". In general, a function takes zero or more inputs (called parameters) from users, performs a particular task depending on the value of the parameters and optionally returns a value to the caller. Parameters allow us to perform different operations at different times using the same function.

A function is first declared specifying the details of the function such as its name, set of parameters (if any) it accepts, and tasks it performs. Following is the general syntax of declaring a function.

```
function functionName([parameters]) {
   functionBody
}
```

The keyword `function` is used to declare a function. It indicates that a function is going to be defined. The identifier following it is the name of the function, that will be used later to call this function. The comma-separated list of parameters that the function may take are written within parenthesis. The actual task of the function is specified within the function body. The body of the function, indicated by curly braces, may contain any JavaScript statements including another function declaration and function calls to itself and others. JavaScript functions are not as powerful as C/C++ functions, but are powerful enough to fulfil the requirements of current web pages.

The following is a declaration of the function `add`, which performs addition of two numbers passed as arguments and returns the result.

function name   parameters

```
function add(x, y) {
   return (x + y);        } body
}
```

So far, we have only declared the function. The function body is not executed until it is called. Internally an object with the name `add` is created. The implementation of functions as objects will be discussed in Section 13.8.2. A declared function is called using its name and passing parameters within parenthesis. If the function returns a value, it may be stored in a separate variable or may be processed further. The following statement calls the function `add` with arguments `2` and `3`. The function executes its body and returns `5`.

```
var result = add(2, 3);          //result is 5
```

The arguments of a function may be anything including strings, Booleans, objects, or even other functions.

13.8.1 Function Literal

A function literal may also be used to create a function.

```
var add = function(x, y) {
   return (x + y);
};
```

The syntax used here may appear strange. Remember, the general way of declaring a variable is

```
var variable = value;
```

The same syntax is used here. An entire function definition is used in place of `value`. The function, declared this way, does not have any name and is consequently called *unnamed* (or anonymous) function. A question may arise immediately that if the function does not have a name, how do you call it? There is a reference (`add` in our case) that refers to the function. This reference may be used to call the function. This function is exactly the same as it was declared previously and may be called using the usual syntax.

```
var result = add(2, 3);
```

A named function may also be used as a function literal.

```
var add = function sum(x, y) {
   return (x + y);
};
```

This function may now be referred using two names: `add` and `sum`. Both point to the same function code.

```
var result1 = add(2, 3);
var result2 = sum(2, 3);
```

The ability to declare functions this way allows us to add methods to an object even after the object is created. More about this in Section 13.9.6. The previous examples show that the JavaScript function names are similar to the function pointers in the C/C++ programming language. Let us see function name and function code as follows:

```
function square(x) {
   return x*x;
}
sqr = square;
```

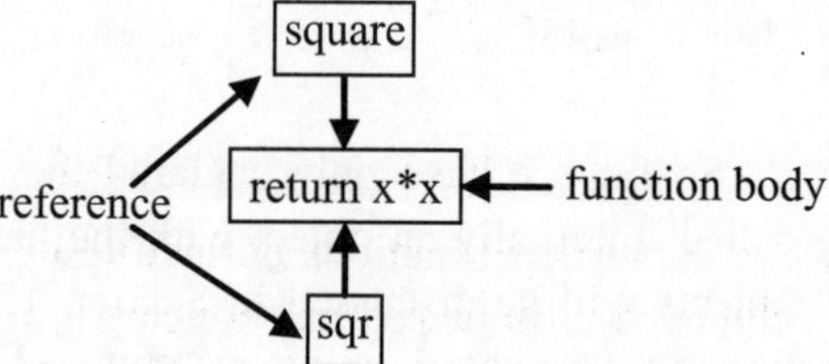

In this example, the identifiers `square` and `sqr` are nothing but references to the function body. So, the function body can be called using either of these two identifiers as follows:

```
square(2);    //calls function body with 2
sqr(2);       //calls function body with 2
```

13.8.2 Function Constructor

JavaScript functions are objects called *function objects*. A function object may be created dynamically using the usual syntax used to create other objects. Following is the general syntax that uses `Function` constructor and `new` operator to create such function objects:

```
var f = new Function([param1, param2,..., paramn,] body);
```

The constructor `Function` accepts a number of string arguments, the last of which is the function body. All others represent the parameters that the function may take. Following is an example.

```
var add = new Function("x", "y", "return x+y");
```

parameters   function body

This defines a function that takes two arguments and returns the result after addition of these two arguments. The body may contain many JavaScript statements, separated by a semicolon (;). Each argument, except the last one that corresponds to body of the function, must be a JavaScript identifier or a comma-separated list of such identifiers. So, the function definition could have been written as

```
var add = new Function("x, y", "return x+y");
```

This function definition is exactly the same as the following function definition, except that it uses a constructor and is available locally.

```
function add(x, y) {
   return x + y;
}
```

Accordingly, this function may be called using the usual syntax, as follows:

```
var result = add(2, 3);             //result is 5
```

Functions defined this way have no name and hence are called anonymous functions. The identifier `add` is associated with it later, after the creation of the function. If a function does not take any argument, the `Function` constructor takes a single argument that corresponds to the function body.

```
var greeting = new Function("return 'Hello world!'");    //function definition
greeting();       //function call
```

Note that functions defined this way are less efficient than ordinary functions. Ordinary functions are parsed only once. However, function objects created this way are parsed every time they are called. So, it is recommended not to use the `Function` constructor without any strong and valid reason.

13.8.3 Dynamic Function Creation

Consider the following function.

```
function create (op) {
   return new Function("a", "b", "returna" + op + "b;");
}
```

The function `create()` takes the name of a binary operator as a parameter, creates a function using the `Function` constructor, and returns it. So, newer and newer functions can be created dynamically using the function `create` depending upon the argument passed, as follows:

```
var add = create("+");        // creates "add" function
var subtract = create("-"); // creates "subtract" function
```

Functions created using the `create()` function may be called in the usual way as follows:

```
result = add(10, 2);          // result is 12
result = subtract(10, 2);     // result is 8
```

13.8.4 Anonymous Functions

Functions without a name are called *anonymous* functions. Anonymous functions are useful in many situations particularly when you want to temporarily use a function that is not intended to be used anywhere else. Since anonymous functions have no name, they are called during creation or passed to another function that calls them. There are several ways to create anonymous functions.

```
new Function("alert('Hello world!')")();
new Function("msg", "alert(msg)")('Hello World!');
Function("alert('Hello world!')")();
Function("msg", "alert(msg)")('Hello World!');

(function() {alert('Hello World!');})();
(function(msg) {alert(msg);})('Hello World!');

var result = new Function("x", "y", "return x > y")(2, 3);
result = Function("x", "y", "return x > y")(2, 3);
result = (function(x, y) {return x > y;})(2, 3);
```

Let us discuss a practical usage of an anonymous function. Suppose, we want to write a generic function to sort arrays of any type of elements. The function will take two arguments: an array and another a function that specifies the sorting criteria. The user will specify the different sorting criteria as functions for different types of elements. This way, it is possible to write a function that will work for all types of elements. The following function uses the bubble sort algorithm to sort an array.

```
function sort(arr, criteria) {
  for(var i = 0; i < arr.length; i++)
    for(var j = 0; j < arr.length - i - 1; j++)
      if(criteria(arr[j], arr[j+1])) {
        var temp = arr[j];
        arr[j] = arr[j+1];
        arr[j+1] = temp;
      }
}
```

Once this function is available, an array may be sorted in ascending or descending order. The only thing we have to do is to specify a separate function in each case. It is a good idea to use an anonymous function because the function will not be used anywhere else.

```
var x = [5, 2, 7, 3, 9, 1];
sort(x, function(a, b) { return a > b; });      //sort in ascending order
```

This sorts the array in ascending order. The anonymous function, in this case, returns `true` if the first argument is greater than the second argument, and `false` otherwise. The array will become:

```
1, 2, 3, 5, 7, 9
```

The array may be sorted in descending order using the following criteria:

```
sort(x, function(a, b) { return a < b; });     //sort in descending order
```

The array will become

```
9, 7, 5, 3, 2, 1
```

Note that a similar idea could have been implemented for the use of the `sort()` method on an array object.

```
var a = [1, 7, 30, 5, 9, 12, 20, 6];
a.sort(function(x, y) {  return x - y; });    //sort in ascending order
a.sort(function(x, y) {  return y - x; });    //sort in descending order
```

Anonymous functions may even be recursive. However, how will a function that does not have any name call itself? Every function object has the property `arguments`, which can be used to call itself. The following code shows an anonymous recursive function to calculate the factorial of a number.

```
var result =  ( function(n) {
                  if(n <= 1)
                     return 1;
                  else
                     return n*arguments.callee(n-1)
               }
              )(4);          //result is 24
```

13.8.5 Parameter Passing

JavaScript allows the passing of parameters to a function, by value only. If a parameter is passed to a function and the value of the parameter is changed within the function, this change is not reflected outside the function. The following example illustrates this:

```
function halveIt(a) {
   a = a / 2;
}

var x = 4;
halveIt(x);
document.writeln('x = ' + x);
```

What do you expect? What will be the value of `x` after calling the function `halveIt`? It shows the value `4`. The variable `x` is not halved by the function `halveIt`. The formal parameter `a` is local to the function `halveIt` where it is halved, but this changes does not reflect on the actual argument `x`. This is exactly what parameter passing by value means. If JavaScript had used pass by reference, the value of `x` would have changed to `2`.

Objects are also passed by value only. Consider the following function.

```
function change(x) {
   x = 4;
}
```

The definition of the function is simple and ideal for checking the parameter passing mechanism. It expects a single argument and changes its value to `4`.

```
var a = [1, 2, 3];
var b = "aString";
change(a);
document.writeln('a = ' + a);
change(b);
document.writeln('b = ' + b);
```

When executed, following is displayed. It displays the original value of a and b as shown in Figure 13.7.

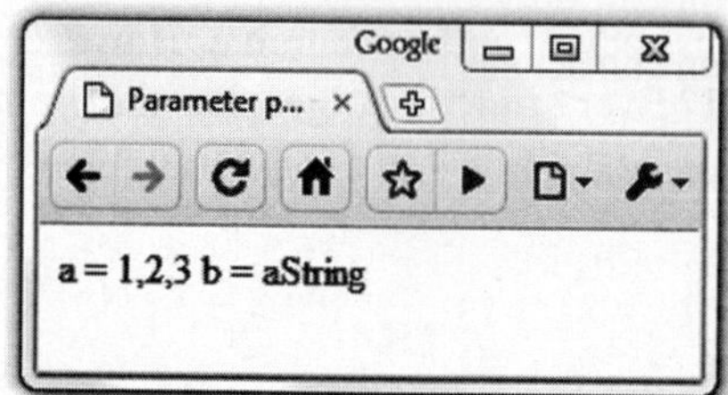

Figure 13.7 Passing objects to functions in JavaScript

The function did not change these objects. If JavaScript had used pass by reference, the values of a and b would have changed. So, JavaScript uses only one parameter passing mechanism, *pass-by-value,* for all variables including objects.

13.8.6 Function Pointer

The name of a function, in JavaScript, is nothing but a reference to the function body. Consider the following named function.

```
function square(x) {
   return x*x;
}
```

The identifier square is actually a reference to the function body. So this reference is used to create other references as follows:

```
f = square;
```

Now, f and square both points to the same function. Both can be used to call the function as follows:

```
f(2);           //call through f
square(3);      //call through square
```

13.8.7 Inner/nested Functions

JavaScript allows us to declare a function within another function. The ability of declaring a function inside another one is not common in programming languages. Except JavaScript, the only known language that supports this facility is C# version 2.0. The following example shows an inner/nested function.

```
function outer() {
   ...
   function inner() {
      ...
   }
}
```

The function `inner()` is a nested function of `outer()`. The nested (inner) function is private to its containing (outer) function. The following properties hold for nested functions:

- The inner function can only be accessed only from statements in the outer function.
- The inner function can access the variables that have been declared in the outer function.

The following example demonstrates this:

```
function average(a, b) {
   function half(x) {
      return x/2;
   }
   return half(a)+half(b);
}
result = average(2,4);
a = half(4);    //error
```

The arguments and variables of the outer function are accessible from the inner function. However, the arguments and variables of the inner function are not accessible from the outer function. The following example illustrates this:

```
function outer(a, b) {
   var outerx = 4;                   //global
   function inner() {
      var innerx = 2;                //local
      document.writeln(outerx);      //OK
      document.writeln(innerx);      //OK
   }
   document.writeln(outerx);         //OK
   document.writeln(innerx);         //error
}
```

However, if the inner function creates any global variable, the outer function can access it. The following example illustrates this:

```
function outer(a, b) {
   var outerx = 4;                   //local
   function inner() {
      innerx = 2;                    //global
      document.writeln(outerx);      //OK
      document.writeln(innerx);      //OK
   }
   inner();
   document.writeln(outerx);         //OK
   document.writeln(innerx);         //OK
}
```

We can declare a global function and a nested function with the same name. Consider the following example:

```
function half(x) {
   return x/2;
```

```
}
function average(a, b) {
   function half(x) {
      return x/2;
   }
   return half(a)+half(b);    //local half()
}
result = half(4);    //global half()
```

When the function `average()` calls the function `half()`, the local `half()` is called. However, when it is called from outside of the `average()` function, the global version of `half()` is called.

13.8.7.1 Closure

The interesting part of the inner function is that an inner function continues its execution even after the parent functions have returned. Consider the following example.

```
function outer() {
   function inner() {
      status = new Date();
   }
   setInterval(inner, 1000);
}
outer();
```

This example calls the `outer()` function. The outer function then uses the `setInterval()` method in the JavaScript `window` object and terminates. The `setInterval()` method takes two parameters: a function name and a time interval in milliseconds. The `setInterval()` method calls the specified function after the specified interval. So, in this case the function `inner()` is called every 1 second (1000 milliseconds). The `inner()` function simply displays the current date and time at the status bar of the window. So, even if the `outer()` function terminates, the `inner()` function continues to execute.

13.8.8 Global Variables and Functions

Remember, a variable declared without the keyword `var` is always a global one. This allows us to create a global variable from within a function. Let us take a simple example to illustrate this:

```
function f(a) {
   x = a;                          //x is global
}
f(3);
document.writeln('x = '+x);     //x is defined and has value 3;
```

This example only shows how to create a global variable. The variable `x` is a global variable and is created when the function is called for the first time. Subsequent call of `f()` does not create a new variable; instead the variable already created is used. The result is shown in Figure 13.8(i).

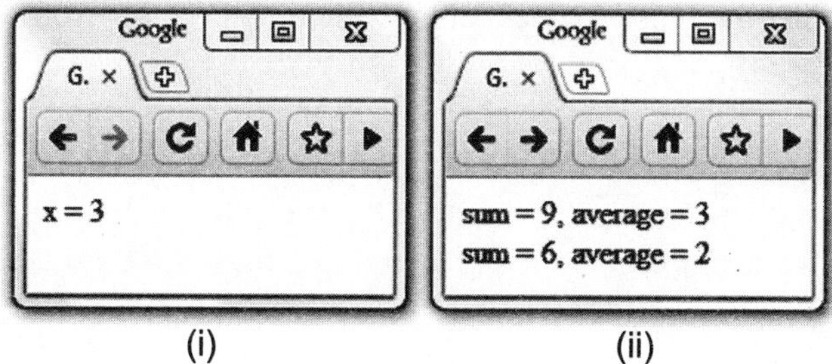

(i) (ii)

Figure 13.8 Creating global variables from within the function

Following is another example that demonstrates how to create global variables from within a function:

```
function avg(a, b, c) {
   sum = a + b + c;
   average = sum / 3;
   return average;
}
avg(2, 3, 4);                    //global variable average is created here
document.writeln('<br>sum = ' + sum + ', average = ' + average);
avg(1, 2, 3);
document.writeln('<br>sum = ' + sum + ', average = ' + average);
```

The result is shown in Figure 13.8(ii).

The ability to declare global variables may introduce unintentional programming errors. Consider the following script.

```
function fact(n) {
   prod = 1;
   for(var i = 2; i <= n; i++)              //this is local i
      prod *= i;
   return prod;
}
for(i = 1; i <= 6; i++)
   document.writeln(i + '! = ' + fact(i) + ', ');
```

This program is written to display the factorial of all numbers from 1 to 6. Note that, the variables i declared within the function and outside the function are different. It produces the result shown in Figure 13.9.

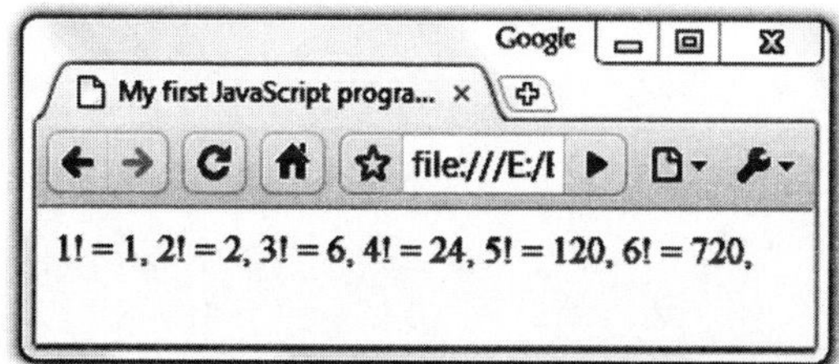

Figure 13.9 Recursive function in JavaScript

Now, consider the function declaration without the var keyword before i:

```
function fact(n) {
   prod = 1;
   for(i = 2; i <= n; i++)                   //this is global i
      prod *= i;
   return prod;
}
for(i = 1; i <= 6; i++)
   document.writeln(i + '! = ' + fact(i) + ', ');
```

It does not produce the factorial of all numbers from 1 to 6, but produces the result shown in Figure 13.10.

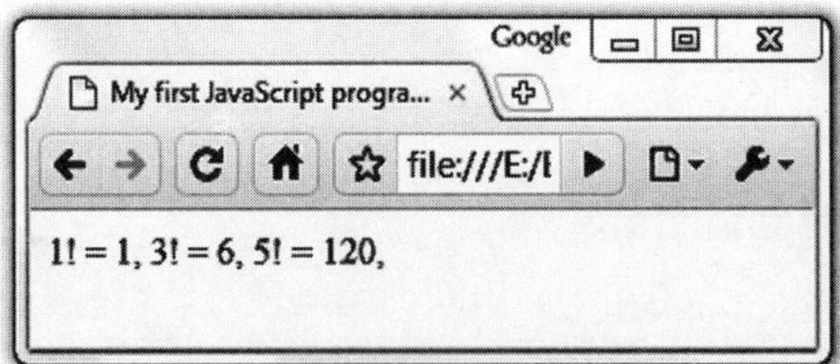

Figure 13.10 Recursive functions and local variables in JavaScript

What is wrong with this program? In this case, the variable i declared within the for loop is a global one, which is manipulated inside the function and hence is the result. Some recursive function may not work if a local variable is not used. Be careful when you are writing a recursive function in JavaScript. Following is a wrong example of recursive function to calculate Fibonacci numbers.

```
function fib(n) {
  if(n == 0 || n == 1) return 1;
  else {
    a = fib(n-1);
    b = fib(n-2);
    return a + b;
  }
}
```

The correct one is

```
function fib(n) {
  if(n == 0 || n == 1) return 1;
  else {
    var a = fib(n-1);
    var b = fib(n-2);
    return a + b;
  }
}
```

Formal parameters declared without the keyword var are always local. The following parameter declaration is incorrect.

```
function add(var x) {
   //...
}
```

JavaScript will treat the entire word "var x" as the name of a parameter, which is an incorrect variable name due to the presence of a space. Hence, it is illegal.

13.9 OBJECTS

An object is a collection of related properties and methods. Properties represent features and methods represent actions that may be performed upon those objects. These properties may be primitive data type or may be objects themselves. JavaScript objects are different from C++/Java objects. Properties and methods can be added at any time even after the creation of an object. As a consequence, objects of the same class may have different sets of properties and methods. Though constructors are available, they are significantly different from the same in other OOP languages.

13.9.1 Using Object Literal

The easiest and straightforward way to create an object is to use an object literal. It is a robust method that creates objects on the fly. An object literal is a comma-separated list of name–value pairs written within a pair of curly braces. The name and its value are separated by ":". The general syntax is as follows:

$\texttt{objectName = \{property}_1\texttt{ : value}_1\texttt{, property}_2\texttt{ : value}_2\texttt{, ... , property}_n\texttt{ : value}_n\texttt{\};}$

where, `objectName` is the name of the object created and `property1, property2, ...` are the names of the properties of this object, and `value1, value2, ...` are their corresponding values. Consider the following example.

```
p = {x : 2, y : 3};
```

It creates an object `p` having two properties, `x` and `y` which have values `2` and `3`, respectively. Once an object is created, its properties may be accessed using the dot (.) operator as follows:

```
objectName.propertuName
```

So, properties of the object `p` may be accessed using `p.x` and `p.y`. Properties may also be added later.

```
p.color = "red";
```

The object `p` now has three properties `x`, `y`, and `color`.

Following are some other examples:

```
aCircle = {x : 2, y : 3, radius : 10};
anotherCircle = {center : {x : 2, y : 3}, radius : 10};
aRectangle = {topLeft : {x : 4, y : 5}, rightBottom : {x : 8, y : 9}};
empty = {};
aStudent = {name : "Rohit", roll : 0422, age : 20, marks : [80, 84, 85, 86]};
hdd = {manufacturer : "Seagate", size : 250, speed : 7200, price : 1500};
origin = {x : 0, y : 0, move : function(a, b) { this.x += a; this.y += b; }};
```

13.9.2 for/in

JavaScript provides a `for/in` construct, which allows us to iterate through the array elements or properties of an object. The general syntax for such a `for/in` construct is

```
for (loopVariable in object) {
   code to execute
}
```

The variable `loopVariable` will assume the value of each property of the object specified. This value can then be used in the block under the `for` loop.

```
var origin = new Object();
origin.x = 0;
origin.y = 0;
for(i in origin)
   document.writeln(i + '=' + origin[i]);
origin.x = 2;
for(i in origin)
   document.writeln(i + '=' + origin[i]);
```

Array elements may also be obtained through the same procedure. The variable `loopVariable` in such a case will assume all valid indices (for which the element is defined) of the array one by one that may be used to obtain the array elements.

```
var odds = [1, 3];
odds[4] = 9;
for (i in odds)
   document.writeln('<br>odds['+i + ']=' + odds[i]);
```

This generates the following result:

```
odds[0]=1
odds[1]=3
odds[4]=9
```

The advantage of using this construct for an array is that it always returns a valid element and can be passed anywhere else safely for further processing. The `for` loop iterates through the array even if some elements are not defined.

```
for (i = 0; i < odds.length; i++)
   document.writeln('<br>odds['+i + ']=' + odds[i]);
```

This code segment generates the following:

```
odds[0]=1
odds[1]=3
odds[2]=undefined
odds[3]=undefined
odds[4]=9
```

Note that the `for/in` construct enumerates all the properties in an arbitrary order. So, the property that is defined first may not appear first.

13.9.3 Constructor Functions

A class in JavaScript is defined by a function, which acts as the constructor for the class. Objects are created with the help of this constructor function and the `new` operator. Following is the class definition for the class `Point`.

```
function Point() {
}
```

This constructor function can be used to create new objects.

```
origin = new Point();        //or simply origin = new Point;
```

The object created is empty [Figure 13.11(i)]. New properties may be added now.

```
origin.x = 0;
origin.y = 0;
```

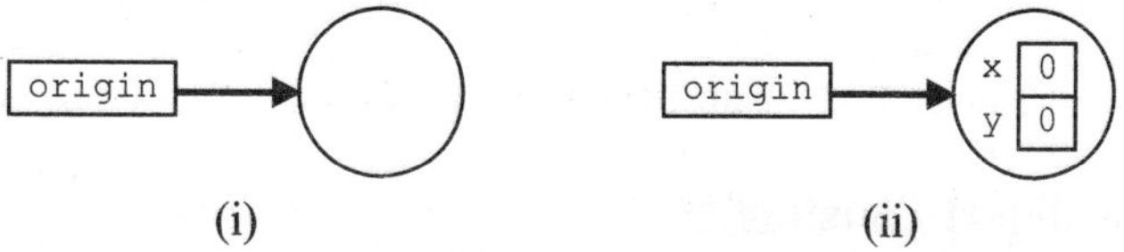

Figure 13.11 (i) Empty object (ii) With two propertied added

Now, the object origin has two properties `origin.x` and `origin.y` whose values are both 0 [Figure 13.11(ii)]. This way, you may create as many objects as you want and may add any number of properties to this object.

13.9.4 this keyword

The constructor used in the previous section creates an empty object and is not useful. You must add some properties to this object to work with it. Alternatively, a parameterized constructor may be used, during the creation of an object, to add some common properties and set their values. Other properties may be added later on a per-object basis as well as per-class basis, as and when needed.

```
function Point(x, y) {
   this.x = x;
   this.y = y;
}
```

Internally, a reference to the newly created object is passed to the constructor. The constructor has a reference `this` that refers to the newly created object for which the constructor was invoked. The `this` reference may be used to access the object's properties and methods.

```
p = new Point(2, 3);
pixel = new Point(100, 100);
```

When the object `p` is created using `new` and the constructor `Point`, a reference to p is passed to the constructor `Point`. Inside the constructor, the reference `this` is initialized by the reference passed to the constructor. So, `this` refers to the object `p` now and `this.x` and `this.y` refer to p.x and p.y, respectively. Similarly, when the object pixel is created, this.x and this.y refer to pixel.x and pixel.y, respectively.

Every object created this way will have two properties, x and y. Properties may be added on a per-object basis.

```
pixel.color = "red";
```

The object pixel now has one additional property color, but p has only two. Properties may also be added on a per-class basis.

```
Point.prototype.color = "green";
```

This code segment adds the property to all Point objects created so far and objects that will be created later. However, if this property is already added to a Point object (pixel in our case), this code has no effect.

```
p1 = new Point(4, 5);
```

The objects p, pixel, and p1 all have three properties now: x, y, and color.

13.9.5 Using Object Constructor

Another simple way to create empty objects is to use JavaScript's Object constructor and new operator.

```
var o = new Object();        //or simply o = new Object;
```

This creates an empty object. You can now add newer and newer properties to this object.

```
o.x = 4;
o.y = 5;
```

Two properties, namely, x and y are added to the object o. Note that if a property already exists, it is not added. However, the operation is performed.

13.9.6 Adding New Methods

A method may be added using a similar syntax inside the constructor during creation or outside after creation. Methods may be named or unnamed and typically operate on the this object. If a method is named, it is defined separately otherwise it is created during association. Adding a named method is a two-step procedure:

- Define the function
- Associate it within the constructor during object creation or make this association later.

The following code segment associates a method inside the constructor.

```
function computeArea() {
   return (3.14159 * this.radius* this.radius);
}
function Circle(x, y, r) {
   this.x = x;
```

```
    this.y = y;
    this.radius = r;
    this.area = computeArea;
}
```

Once the function computeArea is associated with the property area, it may be called as follows:

```
var c = new Circle(1, 2, 3);
var result = c.area();
```

The object and its member function are represented as shown in Figure 13.12. Note that the function computeArea operates on an object and consequently, it must be called on an object. So, the following function call is invalid.

```
result = computeArea();
```

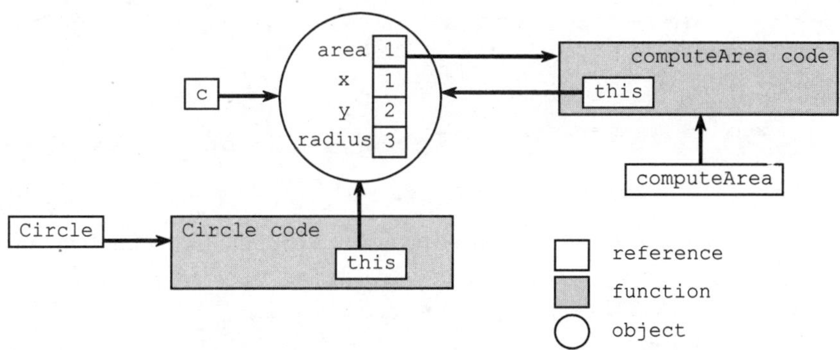

Figure 13.12 JavaScript object representation

In general, if a function operates on the this object, it must be called only on an object to get the desired functionality. Following is also invalid as computeArea does not exist on c.

```
result = c.computeArea(); //invalid method call, computeArea does not exist
```

It was mentioned that a method may be added to an object after its creation. Consider the following constructor function.

```
function Circle(x, y, r) {
    this.x = x;
    this.y = y;
    this.radius = r;
}
var c1 = new Circle(1, 2, 3);
var c2 = new Circle(2, 3, 4);
```

The objects c1 and c2 have no methods so far. The following code adds a method to c1.

```
c1.area = computeArea;
```

This method may be called as follows:

```
var result = c1.area();
```

The object `c2` does not yet have any method. This shows that methods may also be added per-object basis. However, methods may also be added to `c2`.

```
c2.getArea = computeArea;
```

The object `c2` now has a method `getArea()` and may be called as follows:

```
result = c2.getArea();
```

13.9.7 Function Overloading

As mentioned earlier, JavaScript functions are objects. Every function has the member variable `arguments`, which is an object that contains the parameters passed to the function. This member variable may be used to access the parameters passed to the function without the parameters being declared in the function. The total number of arguments may be obtained using the `length` property of the `arguments` array. Consider the following function declaration.

```
function add() {
   var sum = 0;
   var items = arguments.length;
   for (i = 0;i < items;i++)
      sum += arguments[i];
   return sum;
}
```

This function can add any number of parameters. So, the following function calls are valid.

```
var result = add(2, 3);          //result is 5
result = add(2, 3, 4);           //result is 9
result = add(2, 3, 4, 5);        //result is 14
```

Is this not similar to function overloading? Just one function allows us to add as many numbers as we want.

JavaScript functions are not polymorphic. Declaring different functions with the same name is allowed, but only the last function definition will always be used for any function call. JavaScript does not distinguish functions with respect to the number of parameters declared within them. So, the following two functions are treated the same in JavaScript.

```
function f() {
}
function f(x) {
}
```

Remember, the name of a function is a like a pointer. Declaring different functions with the same name will override the pointer. As a result, only the last function declaration will persist. Consider the following function declaration.

```
function add(x, y) {
   return x + y;
}
var result = add(2, 3, 4);
function add(x, y, z) {
```

```
    return x + y + z;
}
result = add(2, 3, 4);
```

In both the cases, the last function will be called.

13.9.8 Objects as Associative Array

Property of an object is usually accessed using the dot (.) operator as follows:

```
objectName.propertyName
```

JavaScript allows us to access the property of an object using array notation as follows:

```
objectName['propertyName']
```

For example, if `x` is a property of the object `p`, it is accessed as

```
p['x']
```

The syntax is exactly the same as used to access individual elements of an array. The only difference is that, here, the array index is a string instead of an integer. So, JavaScript objects behave like traditional arrays as long as accessing properties is concerned. Such arrays associate a unique key (the name of the property) with a value (the value of the property). To access the value (of a property), you specify the key. This concept resembles the concept of associative array, which returns, when a key is supplied, a value associated with that (unique) key.

What is the advantage of associative array objects? Since the property is provided as a string, the property name can be calculated in run-time. Consider the following scenario.

We have an array `users` containing the login names of different users and another array `passwords` that contains the corresponding passwords.

```
var users = ['user1', 'user2', 'user3', 'user4'];
var passwords = ['pass1', 'pass2', 'pass3', 'pass4'];
```

Suppose we want to add a property to an object for each of the users. The following code will not work properly.

```
for(var i = 0; i < users.length; i++) {
    user = users[i];
    db.user = passwords[i];
}
```

Every time the code

```
db.user = passwords[i];
```

is executed, JavaScript successfully creates the same property, `user`. So, after executing this code segment, only one property exists. We do not want it; we want one property per user. The associative array notation may help us in this regard. This code segment may be rewritten as follows:

```
for(var i = 0; i < users.length; i++)
    db[users[i]] = passwords[i];
```

What benefits do we get by adding a property for each user? Suppose a user provides its login name and password that are stored in variables `login` and `password`, respectively. The authentication code will look like this:

```
found = false;
for(var i = 0; i < users.length; i++)
   if(users[i] == login && passwords[i] == password) {
         found = true; //user authenticated
         break;
   }
if(found) {
   //user authenticated
}
else  {
   //not authenticated
}
```

As this piece of code traverses the array locations for a given user name, it may take significant time. The associative array notation makes it simple as follows:

```
if(db[login] == password) {
   //user authenticated
}
else {
   //not authenticated
}
```

13.9.9 Built-in Objects

JavaScript provides built-in objects: `Date`, `Math`, `String`, `Array`, and `Object`. We have already discussed about the `Math`, `Object`, and `Array` objects. In this section, we shall discuss the `Date` and `String` objects.

13.9.9.1 Date object

The `Date` object is used to work with date and time. It is useful to store dates, convert between date formats, and retrieve the current date and time. The `Date` object is created using any one of the following constructors:

`Date()`

// This creates a `Date` object with the current date and time of the browser's PC.

`Date("Month dd, yyyy hh:mm:ss")`

This creates a `Date` object, with the date specified by a date string in the format "Month dd, yyyy hh:mm:ss".

`Date("Month dd, yyyy")`

This creates a `Date` object with the date specified by a date string in the format "Month dd, yyyy".

`Date(yy,mm,dd,hh,mm,ss)`

This creates a `Date` object with the specified date and time.

`Date(yy,mm,dd)`

This creates a `Date` object with the specified date.

`Date(milliseconds)`

This creates a `Date` object with the date value represented by the number of milliseconds since midnight on Jan 1, 1970.

The following examples show how to create a `Date` object for each of the ways discussed:

```
x = new Date ( );
// This creates a Date object with current date and time of the browser's PC.
aDate = new Date("December 13, 2009 11:22:35");
aDate = new Date("December 13, 2009");
aDate = new Date(09,11,13,11,22,35);
aDate = new Date(09,11,13);
aDate = new Date(7600000);
```

The following methods are available to extract information from the `Date` object:

`getFullYear()`

Returns the 4-digit year component of the date. For example,

```
year = aDate.getFullYear();
```

`getMonth()`

Returns the month component (from 0 to 11) of the date as a number (0=January, 1=February, etc.). For example,

```
month = aDate.getMonth();
```

`getDate()`

Returns the date component of the date as a number from 1 to 31. For example,

```
date = aDate.getDate();
```

`getDay()`

Returns the day component (from 0 to 6) of the date as a number (0=Sunday, 1=Monday, etc.). For example,

```
day = aDate.getDay();
```

`getHours()`

Retrieves the hours component of the date as a number from 0 to 23. For example,

```
hour = aDate.getHours();
```

`getMinutes()`

Retrieves the minutes component of the date as a number from 0 to 59. For example,

```
minute = aDate.getMinutes();
```

`getSeconds()`

Retrieves the seconds component of the date as a number from 0 to 59. For example,

```
second = aDate.getSeconds();
```

`getMilliseconds()`

Retrieves the milliseconds component of the date as a number from 0 to 999. For example,

```
ms = aDate.getMilliseconds();
```

`getTimezoneOffset()`

Retrieves the time difference, in minutes, between the computer's local time and GMT. For example,

```
offset = aDate.getTimezoneOffset();
```

The following methods are available to set the components of the `Date` object:

`setFullYear()`

Sets the year component of the date using a 4-digit number.

```
aDate.setFullYear(2009);
```

`setMonth()`

Sets the month component of the date using a number from 0 to 11 (0=January, 1=February, etc.).

```
aDate.setMonth(10);
```

`setDate()`

Sets the day-of-month component of the date using a number from 1 to 31.

```
aDate.setDate(13);
```

`setHours()`

Sets the hours component of the date using a number from 0 to 23.

```
aDate.setHours(10);
```

`setMinutes()`

Sets the minutes component of the date using a number from 0 to 59.

```
aDate.setMinutes(15);
```

`setSeconds()`

Sets the seconds component of the date using a number from 0 to 59.

```
aDate.setSeconds(10);
```

`setMilliseconds()`

Sets the milliseconds component of the date using a number from 0 to 999.

```
aDate.setMilliseconds(100);
```

13.9.9.2 String objects

JavaScript `String` object allows us to store a sequence of characters (letters, numbers, spaces, and so on). A `String` object can be created using either a string literal or a string constructor.

```
lang = "JavaScript";
title = new String("Web Technologies");
```

The following methods are available to work with `String` objects.

`anchor()`

This method lets us create an HTML anchor element around a specified string. For example,

```
msg = "Hello World!";
document.writeln(msg.anchor("greeting"));
```

This code has the same effect as the following HTML:

```
<A NAME="greeting">Hello World!</A>
```

`big()`

This method lets us create an HTML `<big>` element around a specified string. For example,

```
msg = "Hello World!";
document.writeln(msg.big());
```

This code has the same effect as the following HTML:

```
<BIG>Hello World!</BIG>
```

`charAt(`*index*`)`

Returns the character at the specified index. The string index starts from zero. For example,

```
c = "Hello World!".charAt(6);    //c is 'W'
```

`charCodeAt(`*index*`)`

Returns the Unicode value of the character at the specified index. For example,

```
code = "Hello World!".charCodeAt(6);    //code is 87
```

`charCodeAt(`*index*`)`

Appends one or more strings at the end of the specified string and returns the resulting concatenated string. For example,

```
result = "Hello".concat(" ", "World!"); //result is "Hello World!"
```

`indexOf(searchText [, index])`

Searches the specified text for the first occurrence in the string. The search may be directed to start from a specified `index`. If the search is successful, it returns the index of the first character of the occurrence of `searchText` in the string. Otherwise it returns –1. For example,

```
msg = "Hello World!";
i = msg.indexOf("World"); //i is 6
i = msg.indexOf("Hi");          //i is -1
```

`lastIndexOf(searchText [, index])`

Searches the specified text backwards for the last occurrence in the string. The search may be directed to start from a specified `index`. If the search is successful, it returns the index of the first character of the occurrence of `searchText` in the string. Otherwise it returns –1. For example,

```
msg = "Hello World!";
i = msg.lastIndexOf("l"); //i is 9
i = msg.indexOf("Hi");          //i is -1
```

`match()`

It attempts to match the specified string/regular expression in the context string and returns an array of matched strings. We will cover regular expressions in detail in Chapter 16.

The following regular expression modifiers may be used:

- g — get all matches
- m — search over multiple lines of text
- i — case-insensitive search

The following example illustrates this:

```
msg = "Hello World!";
arr = msg.match(/l/);  //arr is l
arr = msg.match(/l/g); //arr is l,l,l
```

`replace(expression [, replacementText|function])`

Replaces the substring that matches the regular expression with the specified replacement text or the return value of a function and finally returns the modified string. The original string is not modified. The usual regular expression modifier may be used. The following examples illustrate this:

```
msg = "Hello World!";
result = msg.replace(/Hello/, "Hi"); //result is "Hi World!"
result = msg.replace(/!/, "!!!!!");  //result is "Hi World!!!!!"
```

`search(expression)`

It is the same as the `indexOf()` function, except that it can take a regular expression. For example,

```
msg = "Hello World!";
i = msg.search("World"); //i is 6
i = msg.search("Hi");    //i is -1
i = msg.search(/l/);     //i is 2
```

`slice(start [, end ])`

Extracts the substring of the string between the specified indices. If the end index is not specified, it retrieves a substring to the end of the string. For example,

```
msg = "Hello World!";
str = msg.slice(0, 5); //str is "Hello"
str = msg.slice(0);    //str is "Hello World!"
str = msg.slice(6, 12); //str is "World!"
```

`split(delimiter [, count])`

Splits the context string into an array of substring delimited by the specified delimiter. The optional `count` parameter indicates how many times the split should occur. If it is omitted, the split occurs as many times as possible. For example,

```
msg = "Hello World!";
str = msg.split("");   //str is "H,e,l,l,o, ,W,o,r,l,d,!"
str = msg.split("o");  //str is "Hell, ,W,rld!"
```

`substr(start [, length])`

Returns a substring having `length` characters from a specified index. If `length` is omitted, then it returns the portion between the start and the end of the string. For example,

```
msg = "Hello World!";
str = msg.substr(0,5); //str is "Hello"
str = msg.substr(0);   //str is "Hello World!"
str = msg.substr(6);   //str is "World!"
```

`toUpperCase()`

Returns the string after converting all characters to upper case. For example,

```
msg = "Hello World!";
str = msg.toUpperCase();  //str is "HELLO WORLD!"
```

`toLowerCase()`

Returns the string after converting all characters to lower case. For example,

```
msg = "HELLO WORLD!";
str = msg.toLowerCase();  //str is "hello world!"
```

KEY WORDS

Anonymous function: A function without any name.

Array Constructor: A special function used to create arrays.

Array literal: An array literal is written using square brackets with array elements separated by commas (,).

Array object: In JavaScript, an array is an object called array object.

Array: An array is considered to be a collection of items.

Associative array: An array that returns a value corresponding to a specified key.

Closure: An inner function continues its execution even after the parent functions have returned.

Compatible browsers: Web browsers that can understand a specific JavaScript version.

Control structure: Used to change the control of execution in a program.

Dynamic function: A Function created at run-time.

For/in: JavaScript provides a for/in construct, which allows us to iterate through the array elements or the properties of an object.

Function constructor: A special function used to create functions.

Function object: In JavaScript, a function is an object called function object.

Function: A function is a segment of code that performs, when called, a particular "function".

Global Variables: Variables declared without using the `var` keyword anywhere in the script.

Inner function: A function declared within another function.

JavaScript source file: External file containing JavaScript statements to be incorporated in an HTML file.

Local variables: Variables declared using the `var` keyword within a function.

Math object: A built-in object to handle more sophisticated mathematical functions and constants.

Object literal: An object literal is a comma-separated list of name value pairs written within a pair of curly braces.

Operator precedence: If an arithmetic expression contains different operators, the operator precedence rule determines the order in which operators are evaluated.

Recursive function: A function that calls itself.

Typeof Operator: This operator returns the type of a variable as a string.

SUMMARY

We started this chapter with the evolution of the JavaScript programming language.

The HyperText Markup Language (HTML), which is used to write web pages, deals only with the design aspect. To provide dynamic and interactive web pages, some form of programming language is necessary. JavaScript is one such scripting language used to change the behavior and appearance of web pages dynamically.

A JavaScript program typically runs within a compatible web browser. There are two ways to insert JavaScript code into an HTML file. One way is to embed it directly within the `<script>` and `</script>` tag pair. Another way is to place it in an external source file and refer to it from an HTML file. It is easy and time-saving to embed JavaScript code directly into an HTML file if the code is fairly short. However, if the JavaScript code is fairly long, it is easy to use a source file.

A JavaScript code may be placed anywhere in the HTML document. Typically, functions are placed in the `<head>` section and other statements are placed in the `<body>` section. This ensures that a function is called after it is defined.

Like other programming languages, JavaScript also provides primary features such as the ability to create variables and write iterative and conditional instructions. However, it has some distinct features over other commonly used programming languages.

JavaScript variables are un-typed. It means that the type of a variable is not specified during the variable creation. Moreover, the type of variable may change from time to time as content changes. The actual type of a variable is determined using the `typeof` operator.

There are two types of variables: local and global. A local variable is created using the `var` keyword. Variables created without the `var` keyword is global. This indicates that creating a global variable is possible even within a function.

JavaScript support the following data types: `String`, `Number`, `Boolean`, `Function`, and `Object`. It also supports standard functions and operators.

JavaScript arrays are dynamic in nature and are special objects. Numerous methods are available to navigate and manipulate arrays.

JavaScript also supports recursive, nested, and anonymous functions. All objects are passed to functions by value. Functions are also special types of objects.

JavaScript is an Object-Oriented Language. All the objects that are created inherit the properties and methods of the super object `Object`. A typical feature of JavaScript objects is that properties and methods can be added on a per-object basis. This means, objects from the same class can have different number and types of properties and methods. However, properties and methods can also be added on a per-class basis.

We discussed how to create objects. We also discussed how to add and access properties and methods on a per-object and per-class basis. It provides a special `for/in` construct to find out a list of properties available on an object. Objects can be used as associative arrays. JavaScript also provides a set of useful built-in objects.

WEB RESOURCES

`http://en.wikipedia.org/wiki/JavaScript`
JavaScript

`http://www.ecma-international.org/publications/files/ECMA-ST/ECMA-262.pdf`
ECMA Language Specification, 5th Edition / December 2009

`http://www.ecmascript.org/es4/spec/overview.pdf`
Proposed ECMAScript 4th Edition—Language Overview

`http://msdn.microsoft.com/en-us/library/4tc5a343(VS.85).aspx`
Microsoft JScript Features - Non-ECMA (Windows Scripting - JScript)

`http://www.echoecho.com/javascript.htm`
JavaScript Tutorial

`http://www.wdvl.com/Style/JavaScript/Tutorial/`
JavaScript Tutorial for Programmers

EXERCISES

Multiple Choice Questions

1. Which of the following tags is used to insert JavaScript code?
   (a) <jscode> (b) <script>
   (c) <javascript> (d) <code>
2. Which of the following is the correct syntax to display "Hello World" on the screen?
   (a) document.write["Hello World"];
   (b) response.write("Hello World");
   (c) window.write ("Hello World");
   (d) document.write("Hello World");

3. What is the correct place to insert a JavaScript code?
   (a) The <head> section
   (b) The <body> section
   (c) Both the <head> section and the <body> section
   (d) None of the above

4. Which one of the following tags refers to an external script called "sample.js"?
   (a) <script name="sample.js" ></script>
   (b) <script src="sample.js"></script>
   (c) <script href="sample.js"></script>
   (d) <script target="sample.js"></script>

5. Which of the following pops up an alert box?
   (a) alert("Hello World");
   (b) show("Hello World");
   (c) msgBox("Hello World");
   (d) pop("Hello World")

6. What is the correct syntax to create a JavaScript function?
   (a) function:aFunction(){}
   (b) function aFunction(){}
   (c) create function aFunction(){}
   (d) new function aFunction() {}

7. How do you call a function named "aFunction"?
   (a) aFunction()
   (b) call function aFunction
   (c) call aFunction()
   (d) execute aFunction()

8. Which of the following is a JavaScript comment?
   (a) 'This is a comment'
   (b) <!--This is a comment-->
   (c) //This is a comment
   (d) "This is a comment"

9. Which of the following is a JavaScript multi-line comment?
   (a) /*This comment has more than one line*/
   (b) //This comment has more than one line//
   (c) <!--This comment has more than one line-->
   (d) "This comment has more than one line"

10. What is the correct syntax to create an array in JavaScript?
    (a) names = new Array("tom", "Jerry");
    (b) names = new Array{1:"tom", 2:"Jerry"};
    (c) names = new Array{"tom", "Jerry"};
    (d) names = new Array["tom", "Jerry"];

11. Which of the following would JavaScript assign to an un-initialized array element?
    (a) NaN (b) null
    (c) undefined (d) false

12. Which of the following is not a JavaScript operator?
    (a) new (b) this (c) delete (d) typeof

13. How do you add a property on a per-class basis?
    (a) Using prototype() method.
    (b) Using prototype property.
    (c) Using add() method
    (d) Using add property

14. Which of the following properties returns the number of arguments expected by a function?
    (a) arguments.length (b) Function.caller
    (c) Function.display (d) Function.parity

15. Which of the following calculates the area of a circle having radius r?
    (a) area = pi * r ^2;
    (b) area = Math.PI * r^2;
    (c) area = Math.PI * Math.sqr(r);
    (d) area = Math.PI * r * r;

16. Which loop executes at least once irrespective of the condition?
    (a) for (b) while
    (c) do while (d) none of them

17. Which of these is not a mathematical operator?
    (a) / (b) * (c) + (d) –

18. Which of the following keywords is used to return a value from a function?
    (a) return (b) pass
    (c) send (d) set

19. Which date method would you use to set a 4-digit year?
    (a) setyear() (b) setfullyear()
    (c) setYear() (d) setFullYear()

20. Which of the following is true if A and B are not equal?
    (a) if A not = b (b) if A != B
    (c) if (A not = B) (d) if (A != B)

21. Which of the following triggers an event automatically at regular intervals?
    (a) onload (b) setTimeout
    (c) setInterval (d) setAutomatic

22. What value is returned by getMonth() for the month of April?
    (a) 2 (b) 3 (c) 4 (d) 5

23. The first control statement in a for loop usually
    (a) sets the termination condition
    (b) increments a counter
    (c) creates a control variable
    (d) none of the above

24. What does the ++ operator do?
    (a) Adds two numbers together
    (b) Concatenates two text strings together
    (c) Adds 1 to a number
    (d) Adds 2 to a number

25. How will you change a date to one week later?
    (a) aDate.setDate(+7);
    (b) aDate.chgDate(7);
    (c) aDate.setDate(aDate.getDate()+7);
    (d) aDate.chgDate(aDate.getDate()+7);

26. A for loop contains
    (a) Single statement
    (b) Two statements
    (c) As many individual statements as you like
    (d) A function call

27. If a browser has Javascript turned off, it will
    (a) ignore all <script> and <noscript> tags
    (b) display the content of <script> tags
    (c) display the content of <noscript> tags
    (d) display the content of <script> and <noscript> tags

28. What does "=" do?
    (a) Compares two values
    (b) Exchanges two values
    (c) Makes the right-hand value equal to the left-hand value
    (d) Makes the left-hand value equal to the right-hand value

29. Which of the following JavaScript statements are correct definitions of an array?
    (a) var a = new Array[100]
    (b) a = new Array[1,2,3,4]
    (c) a = new Array(1,2,3,4)
    (d) a = new Array[]

30. Which of the following do JavaScript lines end with?
    (a) , (b) ; (c) : (d) .

31. Which of the following returns the first character of the string str?
    (a) str.charAt(0); (b) str.substring(1);
    (c) str.charAt(1); (d) str.charAt(2);

32. Which method is used to search for a substring?
    (a) str.substring(subString)
    (b) str.find(subString)
    (c) str.indexOf(subString)
    (d) str.indexOf(charAt(0))

Review Questions

1. Demonstrate how to create arrays in JavaScript.
2. How are objects created?
3. How do you create a function using function constructor?
4. How do you associate functions with objects using JavaScript?
5. How do you use strings as array indexes using JavaScript?
6. How do you convert numbers to strings using JavaScript?
7. What is the function of the === operator?
8. How will you use an array as a stack in JavaScript?
9. How do you create a `Date` object?

14 JAVASCRIPT AND HTML DOM

KEY OBJECTIVES

After completing this chapter readers will be able to—

- get an idea about predefined JavaScript objects for an HTML page
- get an idea about different properties and methods on some important JavaScript objects
- understand HTML DOM object hierarchy
- learn how to access HTML elements using DOM
- understand the JavaScript event handling mechanism
- learn about the W3C event propagation model
- learn how to manipulate HTML documents using DOM interfaces on the fly

14.1 PREDEFINED OBJECTS

In Chapter 13, we have discussed the basic language constructs of JavaScript. In this chapter, we shall discuss how to interact with the components of a web page using interfaces provided by the JavaScript programming language.

JavaScript allows us to access contents of web pages. The components of web pages are represented by objects that are organized in a hierarchical structure, called **D**ocument **O**bject **M**odel (DOM). The hierarchical structure is represented as a parent–child relationship. Child objects are basically properties of their parent objects. These objects have properties and methods that can be used to work with web pages. The top of the object hierarchy is the `window` object, which represents the entire browser window that displays the document. All other objects are direct or indirect children of this `window` object. JavaScript makes many objects accessible directly to the users for convenience. Examples of such important objects are `document`, `location`, and `history`.

14.1.1 The window Object

The `window` object is the top-level object in the object hierarchy. It represents the entire browser window. All other objects, which represent other components of the window (such as menu bar, title bar and status bar) are either direct children or indirect children (descendants).

This object has many useful properties that may be used to get information about the window. It also provides many useful methods that may be used to perform specific tasks. In Section 14.1.1.1, we shall describe some of the properties and methods of the `window` object, and their usage.

14.1.1.1 Properties

The `window` object provides numerous properties [Table 14.1] to get information about the window itself as well as different parts of the window such as menu bar, address bar, and status bar.

closed

This read-only Boolean property essentially indicates whether a window opened using the `window.open()` method is closed or not. It returns `true` if the window is closed, and `false` otherwise. Whenever a (child) window is opened (from another window), its `closed` property is initialized to `false`. When this newly-opened window is closed, its `closed` property is set to `true`. It is always safe to inspect this property before performing any operation on a (child) `window` object.

Suppose the developer of a web page has decided to provide help information in a separate window. For this purpose, the web page contains a help button, which when clicked, opens a new window containing help information. The parent window opens a new window and maintains a reference to it. If the help window is already opened, instead of opening a new window, the existing window is focused on. Note that if the help window is closed, no operation is valid and if so done, the parent window may face some problem and may stop responding. So, before performing any operation on a `window` object, it is safe to test its `closed` property and take appropriate action. The following example illustrates this.

```
<html>
   <head>
      <title>window.closed demo</title>
   </head>
   <body onLoad="win_help=null;">
      <input type="button" value="Help" onCLick="doHelp()">
      <script language="JavaScript">
         function doOpen() {
            win_help = window.open("","","width=200,height=100");
         }
         function doHelp() {
            if(win_help != null )
               if(!win_help.closed) win_help.focus();
               else doOpen();
            else doOpen();
         }
      </script>
   </body>
</html>
```

You may not understand all the features used in this example. We shall discuss them in detail in the following sections.

defaultStatus

Specifies the default message in the window's status bar when the window is loaded.

name

A unique name used to reference the window.

document

An object that contains information about the current document displayed in the window. Its properties and methods are discussed in Section 14.7.9.

history

An object that contains the URLs visited so far by users in this window. Its properties and methods are described separately in Sections 14.1.3.1 and 14.1.3.2, respectively.

location

An object that contains information about the current URL. Its properties and methods are described separately in Sections 14.1.2.1 and 14.1.2, respectively.

event

An object that contains information about the event that occurred last. It is accessible only from event handlers. Its properties and methods are described in Section 14.5.2.

frames

This is an array containing all frames in the current window. Note that all frames are themselves windows. They are accessed as `frames[0]`, `frames[1]`, `frames[2]`,.... They have the same set of properties and methods as a window. The `length` property of `frames` indicates the number of frames.

length

The number of frames the window contains.

navigator

An object that contains the information about the browser application. Its properties and methods are described in Section 14.1.4.

screen

Refers to the `screen` object associated with the window.

screenLeft, screenTop

They specify the x and y coordinates, respectively, of the window, relative to the user's monitor screen. These properties are specific to the Internet Explorer.

window

A global object that refers to the current window.

self

This object is a synonym for the current window.

top

A reference to the top-level window in the object hierarchy.

parent

A reference to the parent window whose frameset contains the current frame.

opener

A reference to the window from which the current window was opened using the `open()` method.

status

It contains the message of the status bar of the window.

Table 14.1 summarizes the properties of the `window` object.

Table 14.1 Properties of the `window` object

Property name	Description
closed	Returns a Boolean value that indicates whether the window has been closed or not
defaultStatus	Default message displayed in the browser status bar
document	Document currently being displayed in the context window
event	Keeps track of various events that occur on the page
frames	Array of frame objects this window contains
history	Object that contains information about the URLs visited within the window so far
length	Returns the number of frames contained in this window
location	Object that contains information on the current URL
name	Contains the name of the corresponding window object
navigator	Represents the browser
opener	Reference to the window that opened this window via window.open(). Null for top-level window
parent	Reference to the parent window containing this frame when working with frames
screen	Object that encapsulates the screen where the window is displayed and contains information about the window
screenLeft	Specifies the x coordinate of the window relative to the user's monitor screen
screenTop	Specifies the y coordinate of the window relative to the user's monitor screen
self	Reference to the current window
Status	Specifies a temporary message to display in the browser status bar in place of the default. Disabled in many browsers.
Top	Reference to the top-level window when working with multiple frames
Window	Reference to the current window

14.1.1.2 Methods

Following are the commonly used methods of the `window` object.

alert(msg)

It pops up an alert dialog box. A string, which is passed to the `alert()` function, is displayed in the dialog box. If the argument is not a string, it is first converted into a string and then displayed.

```
function show() {
   alert("Hi! Today is " + new Date());
}

<button onClick="show()">Time</button>
```

This page has a button with the caption "Time". If the user clicks this button, the current system date and time are displayed in a dialog box [Figure 14.1].

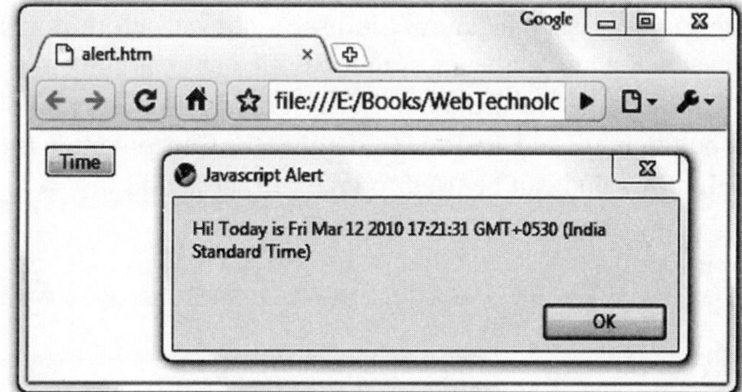

Figure 14.1 alert() method on window object demonstration

blur()

This function takes the focus away from the window on which the `blur()` method is invoked. It takes the following form:

```
window.blur();
```

close()

This method closes the browser window on which it is invoked. The only thing you need to have, to close a window, is a reference to it. If `win` refers to some window, use the following code to close it.

```
win.close();
```

The following code creates a button, which when clicked, closes the current window.

```
<script language="JavaScript">
   function doClose() {
      //do necessary things
```

```
        window.close();      //or simply close()
    }
</script>

<button onClick="doClose()">Close</button>
```

The following web page has a button captioned "Open". When this button is clicked, a new identical window is opened and the original window is closed.

```
<script language="JavaScript">
    function doOpen() {
        //do necessary things
        win = window.open(location.href);
        win.opener.close();
    }
</script>

<button onClick="doOpen()">Open</button>
```

confirm(msg)

Sometimes it is necessary to know the user's choice before doing any crucial task. This method pops up a dialog box with a message specified as an argument and an OK/Cancel button. The user may choose either of these two buttons depending on its choice. The method returns `true` if the OK button is clicked, and `false` if either the Cancel button is clicked or the dialog box is closed. This return value can be used to take further action.

```
<script language="JavaScript">
    function doClose() {
        msg = "Current window will be closed.\nDo you want to proceed?";
        state = confirm(msg);
        if(state) {
            alert("You pressed OK button");
            window.close();
        }
        else alert("You pressed Cancel button");
    }
</script>

<button onClick="doClose()">Close</button>
```

This code creates a button with the caption "Close". If this button is clicked, a dialog box appears [Figure 14.2(i)] asking whether the user really wants to close the window. If the user confirms by pressing the OK button, the window is actually closed.

Following is another example:

```
<script language="JavaScript">
    function logout() {
    if(confirm("Are you sure you want to logout?"))
        location.href='logout.htm';
    }
</script>
<input type="button" value="Logout" onClick="logout()">
```

If the user presses "Logout" button, a dialog box appears [Figure 14.2(ii)] for confirmation. On confirmation, another page "logout.htm" is loaded.

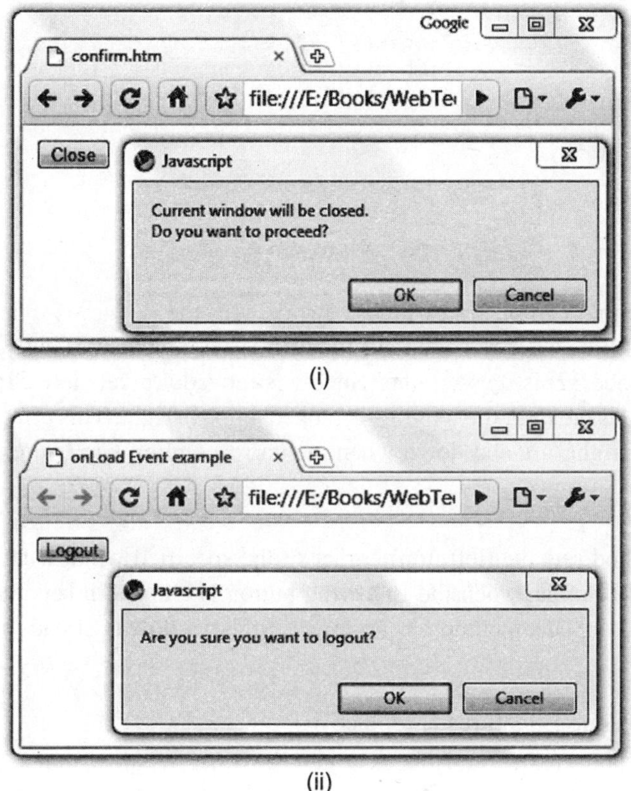

Figure 14.2 confirm() method on window object demonstration

focus()

This method gives the focus to the specified window.

```
<button onCLick="opener.focus();">Goto parent window</button>
```

When the button captioned "Goto parent window" is clicked, the parent window gets focus.

moveBy(dx, dy)

This method changes the position of the specified window by a specified number of pixels. It essentially adds `dx` to the `screenLeft` property and `dy` to `screenTop`, and finally places the window in a position as indicated by the `screenLeft` and `screenTop` properties. The value of offsets may be positive or negative.

```
<html>
   <head>
      <title>moveBy demo</title>
```

```
    </head>
    <body onKeyDown="f()">
        <script language="JavaScript">
            function f() {
                switch(event.keyCode) {
                    case 37:moveBy(-4, 0);break;
                    case 39:moveBy(4, 0);break;
                    case 38:moveBy(0, -4);break;
                    case 40:moveBy(0, 4);break;
                }
            }
        </script>
    </body>
</html>
```

This example demonstrates how to work with the `moveBy()` method. It captures the key pressed, identifies the key code, and moves the window accordingly. For example, if the left arrow key (code 37) is pressed, the window is moved 4 pixels left. Similarly, if the right arrow key (code 39) is pressed, the window is moved 4 pixels right. This effectively causes the window to move left, right, up, and down when the corresponding key is pressed.

moveTo(x, y)

This method sets the (left, top) corner of the specified window to the specified coordinates x and y. For example, when the following button is clicked, it sets the (left, top) corner of the window to (0,0). This method has no effect if the window is already in its designated position.

```
<input type="button" onClick="moveTo(0,0)" value="MoveTo">
```

open([url [, name [, features [, replace]]]])

This method creates and opens a new browser window and returns a reference to this window. It takes numerous arguments. All arguments are optional. The optional argument `url` is the URL of the web page to be opened in the new window. If no URL is specified, a new window with the URL `about:blank` is opened.

The second optional argument, `name`, is a string denoting name of the new window or an attribute denoting the target window of the URL to be loaded. It can have the following values:

- `_blank` — Default value. Indicates that the URL is to be loaded in a new window.
- `_self` — Indicates that the URL is to be loaded in the current window. This essentially replaces the current page.
- `_parent` — Indicates that the URL is to be loaded in the parent window.
- `_top` — Indicates that the URL is to be loaded in the top-level window.

The third optional argument specifies the features and attributes the newly created (name is either a string or `_blank`) window will have. It is a comma-separated list of items, each of which takes the form `feature=value`. The value is either yes/no (1/0) or an integer (pixels). The commonly used features and attributes are shown in Table 14.2.

Table 14.2 The window features

Feature	Description	Possible values
toolbar	Whether or not the window contains a toolbar. Default is yes.	yes|no|1|0
titlebar	Whether or not the window contains a title bar. Default is yes. If the calling application is not an HTML application or a trusted dialog box, the request is ignored.	
status	Whether or not the window contains a status bar. Default is yes.	
scrollbars	Whether or not the window contains a scroll bar. Default is yes.	
resizable	Whether or not the size of the window can be changed. Default is yes.	
menubar	Whether or not the window contains a menu bar. Default is yes.	
location	Whether or not the window contains an address bar. Default is yes.	
directories	Whether or not the window contains directory buttons. Default is yes.	
channelmode	Whether or not to display the window in theater mode. Default is no.	
fullscreen	Whether or not to display the browser in full-screen mode. The feature channelmode must have the value yes. Default is no.	
width	Width of the window. Smallest possible value is 100.	An integer
height	Height of the window. Smallest possible value is 100.	
left	Position of left edge of the window	
top	Position of top edge of the window	

The last argument indicates whether or not to create a new entry in the history list. The value `true` indicates that the current URL will be replaced by a new URL and the value `false` indicates that a new entry is created for the new URL in the history list.

The following example demonstrates how to create a new window using the `open()` method on the `window` object.

```
<html>
   <head>
      <title>window.open demo</title>
   </head>
   <body>
      <script language = "JavaScript">
         function showReport() {
            var features = "toolbar=no,menubar=no, resizable=no";
            win = open("report.htm","test", features);
         }
      </script>
      <input type="button" value="Report" onClick="showReport()">
   </body>
</html>
```

This HTML document has a single button captioned “showReport”. When this button is clicked, the `showReport()` function is executed. This function creates a new window with the name “test” and loads the HTML page `report.htm` in it.

print()

This method opens a print dialog box that helps users to print the contents of the specified window. The following code creates a button captioned "Print", which when clicked, opens the print dialog box.

```
<button onClick="print()">Print</button>
```

prompt(msg, [input])

This method is used to interact with the users. It takes the message as an argument and prompts the user with an input box [Figure 14.3] to enter the data. It returns the data entered by the user.

```
name = prompt("Enter your name", "");
alert('Hi, ' + name);
```

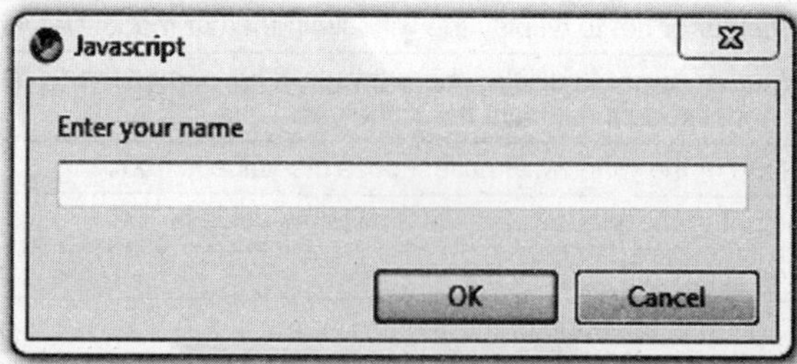

Figure 14.3 prompt() method on window object demonstration

resizeBy(dx, dy)

This method resizes the context window by the specified amount in pixels in the horizontal and vertical directions.

resizeTo(x, y)

It resizes the context window to the specified pixel values.

scrollBy(dx, dy)

This method on the `window` object scrolls the window by the specified amount in pixels along the horizontal and vertical directions.

scrollTo(x, y)

It scrolls the window to the specified pixel values.

setInterval(code, interval, [lang])

This method executes a certain piece of specified `code`, at regular intervals, specified in milliseconds by `interval`. The `code` may be a function name or any valid statement(s) written in the language specified by the optional `lang` argument, which can have the values: `JavaScript`, `Jscript`, or `VBScript`. The `setInterval()` method essentially creates a new periodic timer. This timer expires after every specified `interval`. Whenever the time expires, the code is executed.

This procedure continues until it is stopped using the `clearInterval()` method. The `setInterval()` method returns a unique integer that represents the ID of the newly created timer. The `clearInterval()` method takes this ID as an argument to stop the timer.

```
<button onClick="setInterval('status = new Date();',1000);">Start</button>
```

This code segment creates a button captioned "Start" which when clicked, starts a periodic timer with a period of 1000 milliseconds. When the timer expires, the following code is executed.

```
status = new Date();
```

This statement displays the current date and time on the status bar of the window. Consequently, a clock continues to run in the status bar of the window.

A separate function could have been specified in the `setInterval()` method, as follows:

```
<script language="JavaScript">
  function showTime() {
    status = new Date();
  }
</script>

<button onClick="setInterval('showTime()',1000);">Start</button>
```

In this example, when the button is clicked, a timer starts. Every time the timer expires after 1000 milliseconds, the `showTime()` function is executed, which sets the `status` to the current system date and time.

clearInterval(ID)

It is used to stop the timer created using the `setInterval()` method. So, the `code` that was set to execute periodically after a specified interval using `setInterval()` will not be executed any more. To identify a specific timer to be stopped, the `clearInterval()` method uses the ID returned by the `setInterval()` method.

```
<script language="JavaScript">
  function showTime() {
    status = new Date();
  }
</script>

<button onClick="timeID=setInterval('showTime()',1000);">Start</button>
<button onClick="clearInterval(timeID);">Stop</button>
```

This code segment, creates a button captioned "Start" which when clicked, starts a clock to run in the status bar of the window. The ID of the timer is stored in the global variable `timeID`. Whenever the button captioned "Stop" is clicked, the timer having the ID `timeID` is stopped. So, the function `showTime()` is not called further and consequently, the clock is stopped.

setTimeout(code, interval, [lang])

This is similar to the `setInterval()` method, except that it starts a simple timer, which expires only once after the specified `interval` in milliseconds. So, it executes a certain piece of specified `code` only once. The `setTimeout()` method, like the `setInterval()` method, returns a unique integer that represents the ID of the newly created timer.

For example, if the `setTimeout()` is called as follows, a timer that expires after 5 seconds is started and consequently an alert dialog box appears. After expiry of the timer, it stops forever.

```
setTimeout("alert('5 seconds have elapsed') ", 5000);
```

This code displays a clock on the status bar.

```
function clock() {
   status = new Date();
   setTimeout("clock()", 1000);
}
</script></Head>
<body onLoad="clock()">
</body>
```

In this example, the `clock()` function is called when the page is loaded. The `clock()` function sets a timer to call itself. So, after 1 second the `clock()` function is called again and a timer is also set. This process continues and the clock continues to run.

The `setTimeout()` method may be used to redirect a web page to another page after a specific interval. It is likely that you have seen web pages that display a message such as "…redirecting in 5 seconds…". The web page possibly uses the following mechanism.

```
<html>
   <head>
      <script language="JavaScript">
         function go() {
            location.href='somepage.htm';
         }
      </script>
   </head>
   <body onLoad="timeId=setTimeout('go()',5000)">
      Web page has been moved. Redirecting in 5 seconds...
   </body>
</html>
```

This web page, when loaded, sets a timer that expires after 5 seconds. When the timer expires, the `go()` function is called, which redirects to another page, `somepage.htm`.

clearTimeout(ID)

It is similar to the `clearInterval()` method except that it stops the timer started by the `setTimeout()` method. The `clearInterval()` method uses the ID returned by the `setInterval()` method to identify a specific timer to be stopped.

```
<html>
   <head>
      <script language="JavaScript">
         function logout() {
            location.href='logout.htm';
         }
         function reset() {
```

```
                clearTimeout(timeId);
                timeId = setTimeout('logout()',60000)
            }
        </script>
    </head>
    <body onKeyPress="reset()" onMouseMove="reset()"
onLoad="timeId=setTimeout('logout()',60000)">
    </body>
</html>
```

This web page is redirected to another page if the user remains idle for 1 minute. A timer is started whenever the page is loaded (`load` event) for the first time and its ID is stored in the variable `timeId`. Whenever the mouse is moved or some key is pressed (i.e., the user performs some action), the timer is stopped (cleared) and a fresh timer is started. If nothing happens within 1 minute, the timer expires and the `logout()` function is called, which loads another page, `logout.htm`.

This concept could also have been implemented using the `setInterval()` and `clearInterval()` methods as follows:

```
<html>
    <head>
        <script language="JavaScript">
            function logout() {
                location.href='logout.htm';
            }
            function reset() {
                clearInterval(timeId);
                timeId = setInterval('logout()',60000)
            }
        </script>
    </head>
    <body onKeyPress="reset()" onMouseMove="reset()"
onLoad="timeId=setInterval('logout()',60000)">
    </body>
</html>
```

stop()

This method, added in JavaScript 1.2, stops the current window from downloading and rendering the current page. This is equivalent to clicking the browser's stop button.

```
<input type="button" value="Stop" onClick="window.stop()">
```

Table 14.3 lists the methods of the `window` object.

Table 14.3 Methods of the `window` object

Method name	Description
alert(msg)	Displays a dialog box with a specified message and an OK button
blur()	Removes focus from this window
clearInterval(ID)	Cancels a timeout that was set using the setInterval() method

(Contd.)

(Contd.)

clearTimeout(ID)	Cancels a timeout that was set using the setTimeout() method
close()	Closes this window
confirm(msg)	Displays a dialog box with the specified message and OK and Cancel buttons.
focus()	Gives focus to this window
moveBy(dx, dy)	Moves this window by the specified number of pixels
moveTo(x, y)	Moves the top-left corner of the window to the specified screen coordinates
open(URL, [name], [features], [replace])	Opens a new browser window
print()	Prints the contents of the window or frame
prompt(msg, [input])	Displays a dialog box with a message and an input field. Returns the data supplied by the visitor
resizeBy(dx, dy)	Resizes an entire window by moving the window's bottom-right corner by the specified number of pixels
resizeTo(x, y)	Resizes an entire window to the specified outer height and width
scrollBy(dx, dy)	Scrolls the viewing area of a window by the specified amount
scrollTo(x, y)	Scrolls the viewing area of the window to the specified coordinates, such that the specified point becomes the top-left corner
setInterval(func, interval, [args])	Executes a specified function every time a specified number of milliseconds elapses
setTimeout("func", interval, [args])	Executes a specified function once after a specified number of milliseconds has elapses
stop()	Stops the current download

14.1.2 The location Object

The JavaScript `window` object has a property `location` (accessed by `window.location` or simply `location`), which encapsulates the current URL that is displayed in the visitor's browser. This object has several useful properties and methods that may be used to inspect or change different fields of a URL or even change the entire URL. The properties and methods of the `location` object along with brief descriptions are shown in Table 14.4. We have taken the URL `http://127.0.0.1:8080/wt/location.htm?x=2&y=3#top` to describe its different fields.

Table 14.4 Properties and methods of the `location` object

Properties		
Property name	**Description**	**Value**
href	The entire URL	http://127.0.0.1:8080/wt/location.htm?x=2&y=3#top
hostname	URL host section	127.0.0.1
host	URL's hostname and port section	127.0.0.1:8080
port	URL's port section	8080
pathname	URL's pathname section	/wt/location.htm
search	URL's query string portion	?x=2&y=3

(Contd.)

(Contd.)

protocol	URL protocol name including ":"	http:
hash	URL anchor	#top
Methods		
Method name	**Description**	
reload()	Current URL is reloaded. Equivalent to pressing browser's refresh button. The argument true ignores the browser's cache and forces a reload	
replace(URL)	Loads the specified URL by replacing the current one. Does not affect the browser's history	

14.1.2.1 Reading location object properties

The following code segment reads all the properties of the `location` object and displays them.

```
<html>
   <head>
      <title>Location object demo</title>
   </head>
   <body>
      <script language="JavaScript">
         for(i in location)
            document.writeln(i + " : " + location[i] + "<br>");
      </script>
   </body>
</html>
```

This generates the output shown in Figure 14.4 for the following URL:

```
http://127.0.0.1:8080/wt/location.htm?x=2&y=3
```

14.1.2.2 Changing location object

The `location` object allows us to change individual properties or the entire URL using the following syntax.

```
location.propertyName = value;
```

For example, the following code segment loads the new URL `http://www.google.com`.

```
location.href = "http://www.google.com";
```

This URL is stored in the browser's history, which may be accessed using the browser's back button. If you want to overwrite the previous URL with a new one, use the following.

```
location.replace("http://www.google.com");
```

To reload this page, the following code is used:

```
location.reload();
```

The `reload()` method reloads the current document, i.e., the one that is contained in the `location.href` property. Figure 14.4 shows the properties of the Javascript `location` object.

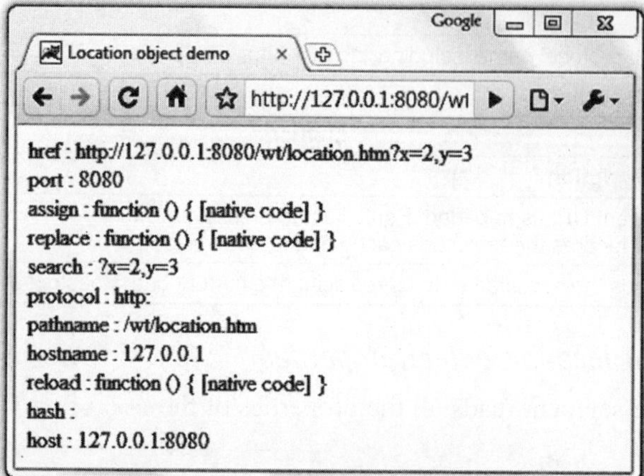

Figure 14.4 JavaScript location object properties

14.1.3 The history Object

The JavaScript `window` object has another important property `history` (accessed as `window.history` or simply `history`), which stores information about URLs already visited from the browser's window. The list of properties and methods of the `history` object along with their brief descriptions are given in Table 14.5.

Table 14.5 Properties and methods of the `history` object

Properties	
Property name	**Description**
current	Current document URL (Netscape-only property)
length	Number of entries of the history object
next	Next URL in the history object (Netscape-only property)
previous	Previous URL in the history object (Netscape-only property)
Methods	
Method name	**Description**
back()	Loads previous URL in the history list
forward()	Loads next URL in the history list
Go(relPos I string)	Loads a specific URL in the history list. The relPos indicates number of places to go, relative to the current position. String argument indicates the specific URL to be loaded.

14.1.3.1 Properties

current

This property refers to the complete URL of the current entry of the `history` object. The general syntax to access the `current` property of the `history` object is as follows:

```
history.current
```

length

This property of the `history` object returns the number of entries in the `history` object. The general syntax to access the `length` property of the `history` object is as follows:

```
history.length
```

The following example demonstrates how to use the `length` property:

```
<html>
   <head><title>history.length demo</title></head>
   <body>
      <script language="JavaScript">
         var len = history.length;
         document.write("The total number of pages visited : " + len);
      </script>
   </body>
</html>
```

The output of this program is

```
The total number of pages visited : 4
```

next

The `next` property of the `history` object refers to the URL of the next entry in the history list. It is undefined if there is no entry after the current entry.

previous

The `previous` property of the `history` object refers to the URL of the previous entry in the history list. It is undefined if there is no entry before the current entry.

14.1.3.2 Methods

back()

This method is used to load the previous URL (if any) in the browser's history. Calling this method is equivalent to pressing the browser's back button. It has no effect if the history does not contain any previous URL.

```
history.back();
```

forward()

Used to load the next URL (if any) in the browser's history. Calling this method is equivalent to pressing the browser's forward button. It has no effect if the history does not contain the next URL.

```
history.forward();
```

go()

This takes a single argument (either integer or string).

```
history.go(relPos|string);
```

The integer argument indicates the number of places to go, relative to the current position, to retrieve the desired URL. Positive and negative numbers indicate forward and backward directions, respectively. For example, `go(1)` loads the next URL and is equivalent to `forward()` and `go(-1)` loads the previous URL and is equivalent to `back()`. Similarly, `go(-3)` loads the URL three positions back, relative to the current position, and is equivalent to pressing the back button three times. `go(0)` has no effect. The string argument represents a specific URL.

14.1.4 The navigator Object

The `window` object has another important child object, `navigator`, which contains information about the client's browser such as its name and version. Remember that some JavaScript codes do not work on some old browsers. One good idea is to identify the name and version of the visitor's browser and accordingly send the appropriate code. This way, web pages can be made smart enough to function in different browsers. The `navigator` object can be used for this purpose. The list of properties and methods of the `navigator` object is shown in Table 14.6.

Table 14.6 JavaScript navigator object properties and methods

Properties		
Property	**Meaning**	**Value**
appCodeName	code name of the browser	Mozilla
appName	name of the browser	Microsoft Internet Explorer
appMinorVersion	Minor version number of the browser	;SP2;
cpuClass	Type of CPU	x86
platform	OS (Operating System) in which the browser is running	Win32
plugins	Array of plugins installed in the browser (NS and Firefox only)	[object]
systemLanguage	Language being used by the system (IE only)	en-us
userLanguage	Language the user is using (IE only)	en-us
appVersion	version of the browser	4.0 (compatible; MSIE 6.0; Windows NT 5.1; SV1; GTB6)
userAgent	Detailed information about the browser, which will be added in the HTTP protocol used for data transfer from browser to the server	Mozilla/4.0 (compatible; MSIE 6.0; Windows NT 5.1; SV1; GTB6)
onLine	Boolean value of true or false	True
cookieEnabled	Boolean value of true or false depending on whether cookies are enabled in the browser	True
mimeTypes	Array of mimeTypes supported by the browser (NS and Firefox only.)	
Methods		
Method	**Meaning**	**Return Value**
javaEnabled	Indicates whether the browser is Java-enabled or not	True
taintEnabled	Indicates whether the browser is taint-enabled (a security protection mechanism for data) or not	False

The following code retrieves all the properties of the `navigator` object.

```
for(i in window.navigator)
   document.writeln(i + " : " + window.navigator[i] + "<br>");
document.writeln('javaEnabled : ' + navigator.javaEnabled() + '<br>');
document.writeln('taintEnabled : ' + navigator.taintEnabled() + '<br>');
```

This generates the output shown in Figure 14.5.

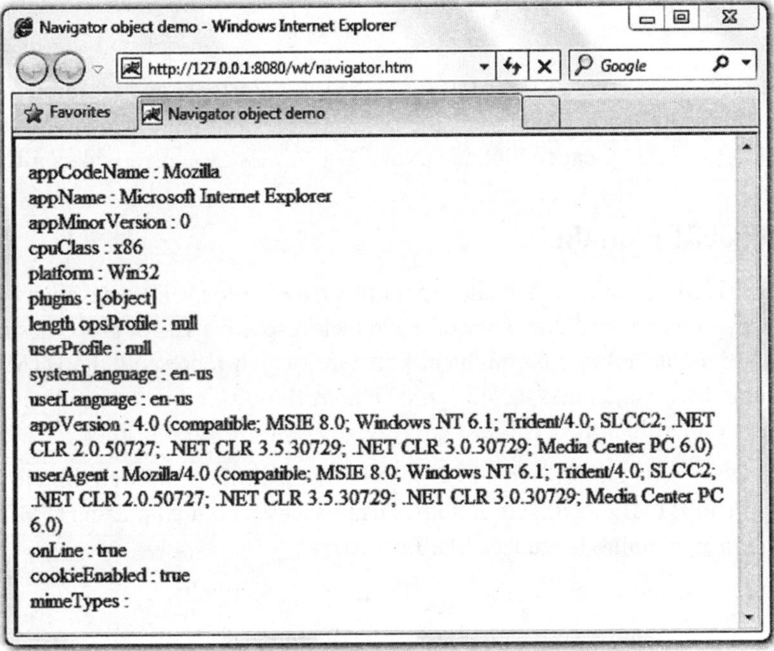

Figure 14.5 JavaScript navigator object properties

14.1.5 Browser Detection

Website visitors use different types of browsers with different versions. One major problem is that different browsers respond differently to different scripts. However, client-side scripts should give the same output for all browsers.

Knowing information about the browser being used by the user is sometimes very helpful to the application developer. For example, an application developer can develop a web page in such a way that an appropriate version of the web page is loaded depending upon the browser used.

The `navigator` object can be used to retrieve different properties of the browser. All properties are not supported by all browsers. However, we can use some common properties to identify the browser used and its version.

The following example illustrates this:

```
<html>
   <head>
      <title>Browser detection</title>
   </head>
```

```
    <body>
        <p>This is a paragraph</p>
        <script language="JavaScript">
            var name = navigator.appName;
            if (name == "Microsoft Internet Explorer")
                location.href="ie_version.html";
            if (name == "Netscape")
                location.href="nn_version.html";
        </script>
    </body>
</html>
```

The browser name is retrieved using `navigator.appName` and is stored in the variable `name`. If it is "Microsoft Internet Explorer", the `ie_version.html` page is loaded and if it is "Netscape", the `nn_version.html` page is loaded. Note that `window.location` takes a URL value.

14.2 OBJECT HIERARCHY

When an HTML document is loaded in a browser, the browser creates many JavaScript objects, which vary in their types. These objects have their respective sets of properties and methods. These objects are organized in a hierarchical structure, which represents the HTML document itself. This hierarchy is sometimes called *instance hierarchy*, as it is concerned with specific instances of objects rather than their classes.

The **D**ocument **O**bject **M**odel (DOM) is the road map through which we can locate any element in an HTML document. It allows us to access and manipulate HTML documents on the fly using programming languages like JavaScript.

Figure 14.6 shows the JavaScript HTML object hierarchy.

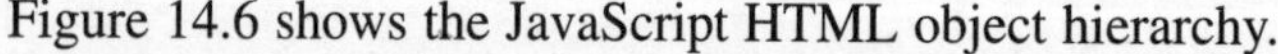

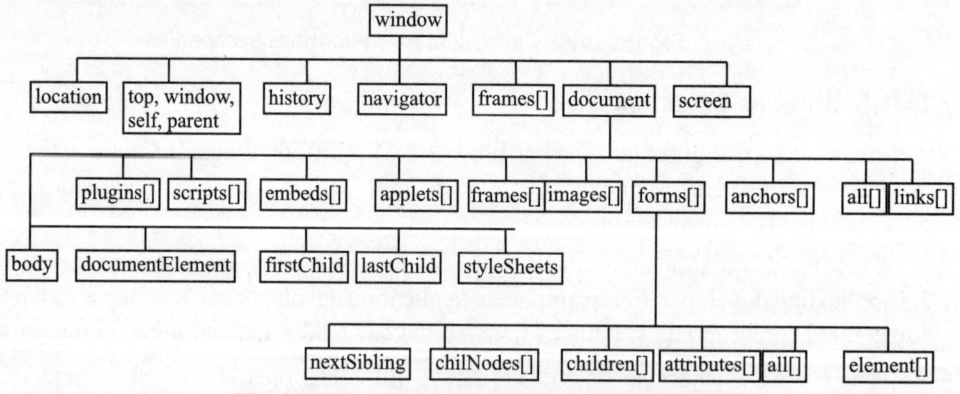

Figure 14.6 JavaScript HTML object hierarchy

14.3 ACCESSING OBJECTS

Many JavaScript objects are containers of other objects. Similarly, many JavaScript objects are contained in other objects. So, a container-to-contained object relationship is present, but not a class-and-subclass relationship.

The top-level object is `window`. So, it can be accessed directly by its name. Any other object can be referenced by its names, prefixed by the names of all the objects that contain it, in order, separated by dots (.).

For example, the `window` object contains the `document` object, which can be referred to as `window.document`. The `document` object, in turn, contains the `body` object. So, the `body` object can be referred to as `window.document.body`. If the `document` object contains two forms, they can be accessed as `window.document.body.forms[0]` and `window.document.body.forms[1]`.

JavaScript allows us a shorthand notation to access objects that are directly contained by the `window` object. These objects can be referred to directly without prefixing the `window` object. For example, `location`, `history`, `document`, etc. Similarly, methods on window objects can be accessed directly without using the `window` object. For example, `alert()`, `confirm()`, `open()`, etc.

14.4 EVENTS

In many previous examples, we have used JavaScript event handlers. Let us now discuss what they are and how to use them.

The basic purpose of JavaScript is to add interactivity to your web pages. This interactivity is provided by responding to user actions. It means that whenever users performs some tasks, it reacts by executing a piece of code. The set of tasks that users may perform on a web page are called *interactive events* or simply *events*. For example, when users click a button on a web page, a `click` event occurs. The button is called the *source* of the event. Other events may also occur due to other user tasks such as moving the mouse pointer on a hyperlink (`mouseOver` event), submitting a form (`submit` event), a keystroke (`keyPress` event), pressing a mouse button (`mouseDown` event), and so on. There are some events (known as *non-interactive* events) that are not caused by users. For example, a `load` event occurs automatically every time a web page is loaded in the browser.

For each element of a web page, users may perform a specific set of tasks. This means that a specific task may be performed on some specific elements. For example, the event `change` may occur for a selection list, but not for a button. Similarly, the `load` event is associated with only the `body` tag. So, an element may only be the source of a specific set of events.

14.5 EVENT HANDLERS

JavaScript identifies an event and takes an action by executing some piece of code. The procedure of taking actions is called *event handling*. The specific JavaScript code that takes the action (i.e., handles the event) is called *event handler*. An event handler may be any valid JavaScript statements. In JavaScript, the handler of an event is usually provided as a function. An event handler may be *interactive* or *non-interactive,* depending upon the type of the event it handles.

The source waits for an event to occur. We associate a handler with an event. When that event takes place, JavaScript identifies the event and executes its handler. Here, the event works as a trigger and the handler is triggered by the event.

The handler `eventHandler` of the event `evnt` for some element `ele` is specified by assigning it to the property of the element. The name of the property for the event `evnt` takes the following form:

```
onEvnt
```

For example, the name of the property for the event `click` is `onClick`. Similarly, `onMouseOver` is the name of the property for the `mouseOver` event. Note that the name of the property is case-insensitive. So `onClick`, `onclick`, `OnClick`, and `Onclick` are the same. However, conventionally, we use the `onClick` property for the `click` event.

There are many ways to add a handler to an event. The straightforward way is to specify it in the tag as follows:

```
                                     event
<input type="button" value="clickMe" onClick="alert('You clicked me');">
                                              Event handler
```

This tells the JavaScript engine that when the event `click` occurs, the handler having the single statement `alert('You clicked me');` should be executed. In general, to associate the handler `eventHandler` with the event `eventName`, the following syntax is used.

```
onEventName="eventHandler"
```

`EventName` must be one of the possible events for the tag. Using JavaScript code, this can be done as follows:

```
element.onEventName=eventHandler;
```

where, `element` is the source of the event.

A list of common events along with their source is given in Table 14.7.

Table 14.7 JavaScript events and their sources

Event name	Occurs when	Applicable to
click	mouse is clicked on an object	button, checkbox, radio, link, reset, submit, text, textarea, body
focus	Element gets focus	select, text, textarea
blur	Element loses focus	checkbox, radio, select, text, textarea
change	Content of an element is changed	select, text, textarea, file
error	Error occurs during loading of a document or an image	Image
abort	Loading of an image is interrupted	Image
load	Page or image has loaded completely	Window, image
mouseOver	mouse pointer is moved over an element	link, text, button, textarea, radio
mouseOut	mouse pointer is moved off an element	link, text, button, textarea, radio
select	text is selected	text, textarea
submit	HTML form is submitted	Form

(Contd.)

(Contd.)

unload	Window is closed	Window
mouseDown	Mouse button is pressed	Button, Document, Link
mouseUp	Mouse button is released	Button, Document, Link
mouseMove	Mouse pointer is moved	None
reset	Reset button of a form is clicked	Form
resize	Window or frame is resized	Window
keyPress	Keyboard key is pressed or held down	Document, Image, Link, TextArea
keyDown	Keyboard key is pressed	Document, Image, Link, TextArea
keyUp	Keyboard key is released	Document, Image, Link, TextArea
dblClick	User double clicks an object	Document, Image, Link, TextArea
move	User or script moves a window or frame	Window

The following example demonstrates how to work with a submit event.

```
<html>
<head><title>onSubmit Demo</title></head>
<body>
<script language="JavaScript">
function doCheck() {
   if(frmLogin.login.value == "") {
      alert('login field can never be blank');
      return false;
   }
   if(frmLogin.password.value == "") {
      alert('password field can never be blank');
      return false;
   }
   return true;
}
</script>
<form name="frmLogin" action="login.jsp" method="post" onSubmit="return
doCheck()">
Login: <input type="text" name="login"><br>
Password: <input type="password" name="password"><br>
<input type="submit" name="submit" value="Submit">
<input type="reset" name="reset" value="Reset">
</form>
</body>
</html>
```

This HTML document contains a text field and a password field to accept login name and password of the user, respectively. It also has a submit button and a reset button. Usually, users enter their login name and password and click the submit button for login. This information is then sent to the server-side script, `login.jsp`. However, we must be sure that valid information is being passed to `login.jsp` so that it does not malfunction.

To check that the user has entered valid data in the login and password fields, we have specified a handler for the submit event.

```
onSubmit="return doCheck()"
```

The handler of the submit event is nothing but the function `doCheck()`. When the user clicks the submit button (i.e., submits the form), the associated handler `doCheck()` gets invoked. Inside the handler function, we have performed simple data verification. A diagnostic error message is displayed in an alert box if the user has not entered the data correctly.

The handler returns a Boolean value. It returns `true` if the user has entered proper data. Otherwise, it returns `false`. The meaning of the `return` keyword in this code is as follows:

If the handler returns `true`, load the page specified by the `action` attribute of the `<form>` element. Otherwise, do nothing.

Figure 14.7 shows a sample output.

Figure 14.7 Submit event demonstration

The following example demonstrates how to work with a load event.

```
<html>
<head><title>OnLoad Demo</title></head>
<body onLoad="frmLogin.login.focus();">
<form name="frmLogin">
Login: <input type="text" name="login"><br>
Password: <input type="password" name="password"><br>
<input type="submit" name="submit" value="Submit">
<input type="reset" name="reset" value="Reset">
</form>
</body>
</html>
```

This HTML document provides a login interface to the user. It has one text field, one password field, one submit button, and one reset button. The text field is used to accept the login name of a user. This field is typically filled up the first time. So, when the page is loaded, this field should get focused so that user can enter the login name in the text field.

To fulfill this requirement, a handler is specified for the load event. When the page is loaded, this handler gets called. The handler makes the text field focused using the following code:

```
frmLogin.login.focus();
```

The text field (name is "login") is a child of the `<form>` element (name is "frmLogin"). So, the text field can be accessed as

```
frmLogin.login
```

The `focus()` method of the text field simply makes it focused.

Figure 14.8 shows a sample output.

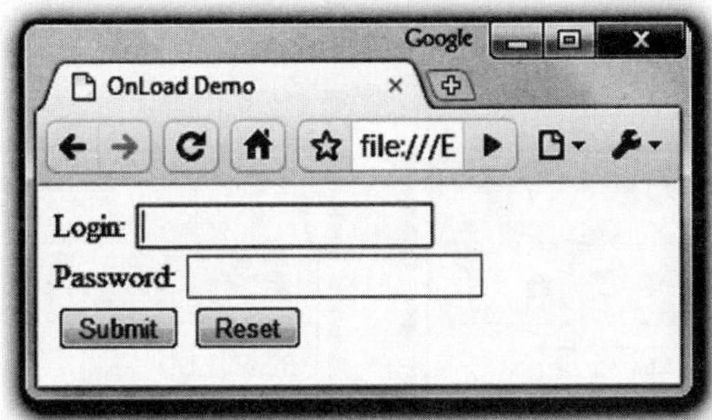

Figure 14.8 Load event demonstration

Note that the text field is focused.

The following example shows how to work with a change event that occurs when a different item in the selection list is selected.

```
<body onLoad="update()">
   Item:
   <select id="item" onChange="update()">
      <option value="HDD">HDD</option>
      <option value="Monitor">Monitor</option>
   </select><br>
   Model:
   <select id="spec">
   </select><br>
</body>
<script language="JavaScript">
function update() {
   db = new Object();
   db["HDD"] = ["40 GB", "80 GB", "150 GB", "250 GB"];
   db["Monitor"] = ['15"', '17"', '19"', '21"'];
   name = document.getElementById("item").value;
   value = document.getElementById("spec");
   value.innerHTML = "";
   for(i in db[name])
      value.innerHTML += "<option>" + db[name][i] + "</option>";
}
</script>
```

This HTML document has two selection lists, one having the id "item" and the other having the id "spec". The first selection list is used to select an item such as "HDD" or "Monitor". The second selection list is used to select a specific model of the item previously selected. However, this second selection list should be populated when the user selects an item using the first list.

To implement this idea, we have specified a handler for the `change` event for the first selection list. When the user changes the selection, this handler gets called. In this handler, the second selection list is populated.

Figure 14.9 shows a sample output for this HTML document.

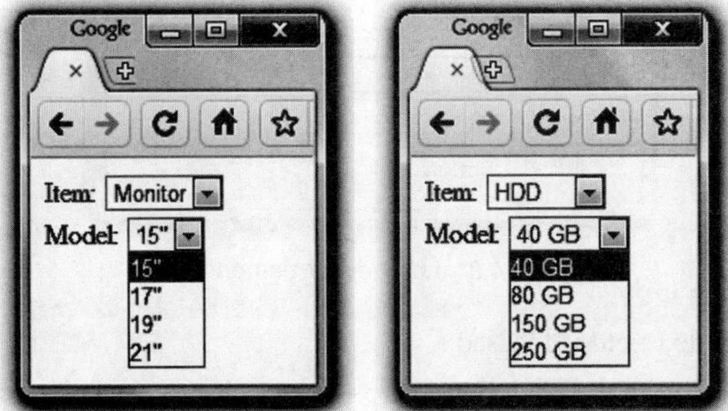

Figure 14.9 Change event demonstration

14.5.1 Event Object

In JavaScript, an event is represented as a global object called `event` object. This `event` object encapsulates the state of an event such as location of the mouse pointer and left or right button pressed for a mouse event, Unicode of the key pressed for a key event, and so on. The `event` object is available only when an event occurs. So, only event handlers can access this `event` object.

Consider the following example:

```
<html>
   <head><title>event object demo</title></head>
   <body onClick="handler()">
      <script language="JavaScript">
         function handler() {
         alert('You clicked at (' + event.clientX + ',' + event.clientY + ')');
         }
      </script>
   </body>
</html>
```

The HTML page in Figure 14.10 shows the x and y coordinates of the location where the mouse is clicked.

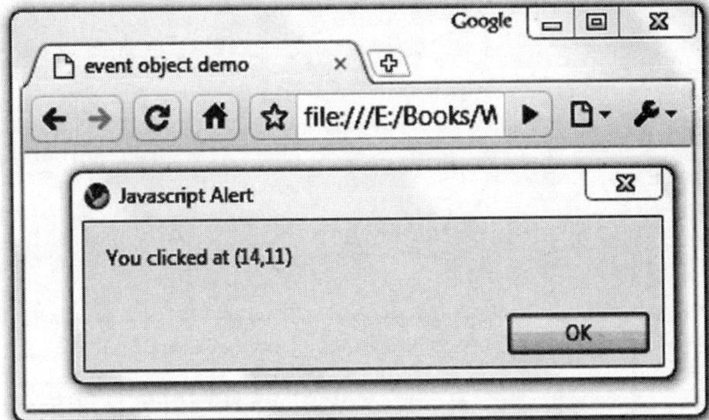

Figure 14.10 MouseClick event demonstration

The following code segment displays the Unicode character and its key code.

```
<html>
   <head>
      <title>keyCode</title>
   </head>
   <body onkeydown="showKey();">
   </body>
   <script>
      function showKey() {
         var str = 'key pressed : ' + String.fromCharCode(event.keyCode);
         str = str + ', key code : ' + event.keyCode;
         status = str;
      }
   </script>
</html>
```

Figure 14.11 shows a sample output when the key 'A' is pressed.

Figure 14.11 keyPress event demonstration

The following example demonstrates how to detect whether a key has been held down or not.

```
<html>
   <head><title>event repeat demo</title></head>
   <body onKeyDown="process();">
      <script language="JavaScript">
         function process() {
```

```
                if (event.repeat == true)
                    alert("You have held down a key");
            }
        </script>
    </body>
</html>
```

Figure 14.12 shows a sample result when the key 'A' was held down.

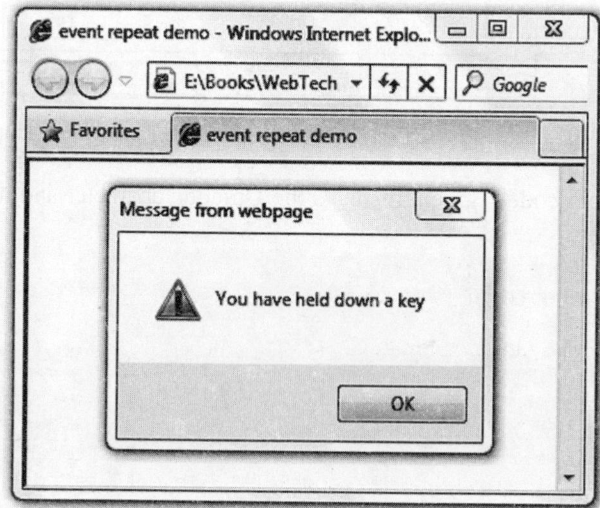

Figure 14.12 Repeat event demonstration

Table 14.8 shows a list of properties available on the `event` object.

Table 14.8 JavaScript event object properties

Property	Meaning
srcElement	Element that caused the event
type	Name of the event
altKey	Indicates whether alt key was pressed
altLeft	Indicates whether left alt key was pressed
ctrlKey	Indicates whether ctrl key was pressed
ctrlLeft	Indicates whether left ctrl key was pressed
shiftKey	Indicates whether shift key was pressed
shiftLeft	Indicates whether left shift key was pressed
button	Indicates the mouse button pressed by the user. 1—left, 2—middle, 4—right
keyCode	Unicode value of the key pressed
cancelBubble	Indicates whether the current event should bubble up the hierarchy of event handlers
clientX	x-coordinate of the mouse pointer, relative to the document
clientY	y-coordinate of the mouse pointer, relative to the document

(Contd.)

(Contd.)

fromElement	Indicates the element the mouse was left from for events such as mouseover and mouseout
nextPage	Indicates the position of the next page within a print template
offsetX	x-coordinate of the mouse pointer relative to the object firing the event
offsetY	y-coordinate of the mouse pointer relative to the object firing the event
screenX	x-coordinate of the mouse pointer, relative to the screen
screenY	y-coordinate of the mouse pointer, relative to the screen
propertyName	Name of the property that has changed on the object
reason	Result of data transfer from a data source. 0 — Successfully, 1 — Aborted, 2 — Error
recordset	Reference to the default record set in a data source
repeat	Indicates whether the user keeps the key depressed and the system's key repeat starts up.
returnValue	Indicates whether the event is cancelled (true) or not (false)
srcUrn	The Universal Resource Name (URN) of the behavior that fired the event
toElement	Indicates the element the mouse is entering for events such as mouseover and mouseout
wheelDelta	Distance and direction in which the wheel button has rolled
x	Returns the x-coordinate (in pixels) of the mouse pointer, relative to a relatively positioned parent element
y	Returns the y-coordinate (in pixels) of the mouse pointer, relative to a relatively positioned parent element

14.5.2 Advanced Event Handling

Suppose the element `inner` is declared inside another element `outer` [Figure 14.13]. Both `inner` and `outer` elements have their respective handlers for the `click` event. What happens if a user clicks on the `inner` element? Since `inner` is written inside `outer`, clicking on `inner` also means clicking on `outer`. This means that the `click` event will occur on `inner` as well as on `outer`. Consequently, handlers for `inner` as well as `outer` will be triggered. Figure 14.13 shows nested elements. What is the order in which these two events occurs? In other words, which handler will be called first?

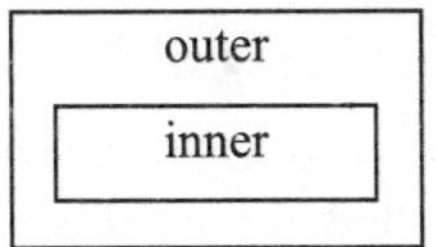

Figure 14.13 Nested elements

The order in which events occur depends on the underlying event *propagation model.* Two such models exist: *event bubbling* and *event capturing*.

14.5.2.1 W3C event propagation model

W3C provides a specification for the event handling mechanism called *event propagation model.* According to this specification, an event handling mechanism has two phases: *event capturing* and *event bubbling* and they *always* occur in the order specified. For each of these two steps, a separate handler may be registered.

Conceptually, whenever an event occurs on multiple elements, it starts from the outermost source element and propagates downwards until it reaches the innermost source element of the event. All the handlers that are set for the capturing phase are executed on its way. This is called *event capturing*.

After reaching the innermost source element of the event, it changes its direction and moves up (bubbles up) until it reaches to the outermost element. Like the capturing phase, all the handlers that are set for the bubbling phase are also executed on its way. This phase is called *event bubbling*.

The W3C event propagation model is described pictorially in Figure 14.14.

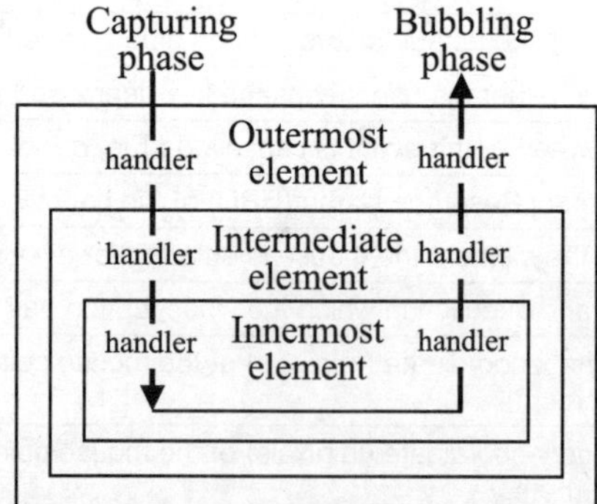

Figure 14.14 W3C event propagation model

Note that the event continues to propagate even if there is no handler registered for an element. However, the propagation of the event may be stopped at any time.

As mentioned earlier, a separate handler may be registered for each phase. Not all browsers allow us to register a handler for the capturing phase. For example, Microsoft's Internet Explorer does not support registering handler for the capturing phase. However, all browsers provide interfaces that allow us to register a handler for the bubbling phase. The traditional method of handler registration is nothing but registration for the bubbling phase.

```
someElement.onSomeEvent = someHandler;
```

This piece of code registers `someHandler` for the event `someEvent` on `someElement` for the bubbling phase. Similarly, the following code does essentially the same thing.

```
<someElement onSomeEvent="someHandler">
```

Consider the following HTML document.

```
<html>
   <head>
      <title>Event Demo</title>
      <script language="JavaScript">
         function handler_body() {
            alert('You clicked on body');
         }
         function handler_p() {
            alert('You clicked on p');
```

```
            }
        </script
    </head>
    <body onClick="handler_body()">
        <p onClick="handler_p()">A paragraph</p>
    </body>
</html>
```

The event handling mechanism that we use usually is described in Figure 14.15.

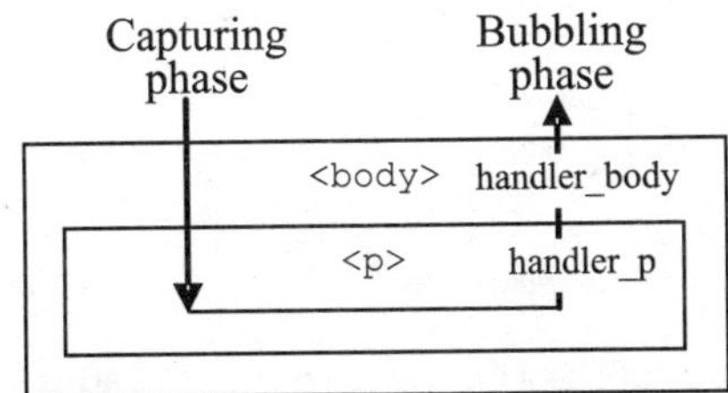

Figure 14.15 Traditional event handling

Now suppose the user clicks on `<p>`. Which handler will be called? `handler_body()` or `handler_p()` or both? The answer is both. Why? Let us discuss.

In this HTML document, the `<p>` element is written inside the `<body>` element. Both have a handler for the `click` event. Note that handlers are registered for the `click` event for `<body>` and `<p>` inline [Figure 14.15]. So, these handlers are set for the bubbling phase. No handler is registered for the capturing phase. Now, if the user clicks on `<p>`, a `click` event will occur on `<p>` as well as on `<body>`. The `click` event will start propagating from the `<body>` element (outermost element) and reaches the `<p>` element (innermost element) during the capturing phase. Since no handler is registered for capturing, nothing is executed during this phase. The `click` event then bubbles up from `<p>` to `<body>`. During this phase, along the path of propagation of `click` event, two handlers are registered. When the `click` event first propagates through the `<p>` element, the handler `handler_p()` is executed. The `click` event then passes through the `<body>` element and the handler `handler_body()` is executed.

How to register an event for the capturing phase then?

W3C provides the method `addEventListener()` on an element that can be used to register a handler for both the capturing and bubbling phases, as follows:

```
someElement.addEventListener('eventName', eventHandler, flag);
```

This method, like traditional registration, registers a handler for an event except that a specific event propagation model can be chosen. The method `addEventListener()` takes three arguments, `eventName` is the name of the event to be handled, `eventHandler` is the handler to be registered on this element; the boolean `flag` indicates whether this handler is a part of the capturing or bubbling phases. If `true` is specifed, this handler is set for the capturing phase. Otherwise, it is set for the bubbling phase.

The following example illustrates event capturing:

```
<html>
   <head>
      <title>Event Capturing Demo</title>
      <script language="JavaScript">
         function handler_body() {
            alert('You clicked on body');
         }
         function handler_p() {
            alert('You clicked on p');
         }
         function handler_div() {
            alert('You clicked on div');
         }
         function register() {
            document.getElementById("para1").addEventListener('click',
handler_p, true);
            document.getElementById("div1").addEventListener('click',
handler_div, true);
            document.body.addEventListener('click', handler_body, true);
         }
      </script
   </head>
   <body>
      <div id="div1">
         <p id="para1">A paragraph</p><br>
      </div>
      <script language="JavaScript">
         register();
      </script>
   </body>
</html>
```

In this example we have used the getElementById() method of the document object to obtain a reference to the element. The document object refers to the current document. This method and object are actually a part of JavaScript DOM which we shall discuss later in Section 14.7 in detail. For now, just remember that the getElementById() method takes an id of an element and returns an element having that id.

The last argument of the addEventListener() method is specified as true for all handlers. It means all handlers are registered for the capturing phase [Figure 14.16]. If the user clicks on <p>, following happens:

- Event propagation starts in the capturing phase from the outermost element, which is the <body> element.
- It then traverses the <div> element and finally reaches the <p> element. On its way, there are three handlers registered for the capturing phase. So, handler_body(), handler_div(), and handler_p() get executed in that order.
- After reaching the event at <p>, the bubbling phase starts. However, on its way, it cannot find any handler registered for the bubbling phase. So, none is executed.

Consider the following handler registration:

```
document.getElementById("para1").addEventListener('click', handler_p, false);
document.getElementById("div1").addEventListener('click', handler_div, false);
document.body.addEventListener('click', handler_body, false);
```

In this case all the handlers are registered for the bubbling phase [Figure 14.17].

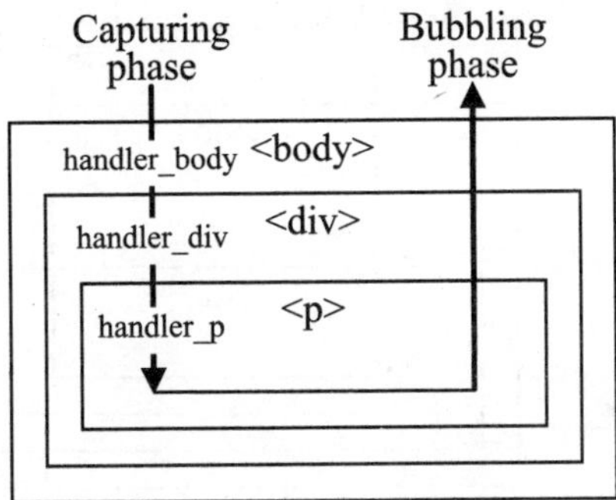

Figure 14.16 Event capturing

If the user clicks on <p>, the following happens:

- Event propagation starts in the capturing phase from the outermost element (<body> in our case) and reaches <p>. During this propagation, no event handler is registered for the capturing phase and hence nothing happens.
- After reaching <p>, the bubbling phase starts. This time, three handlers are registered and they are called in this order: `handler_p()`, `handler_div()`, and `handler_body()`.

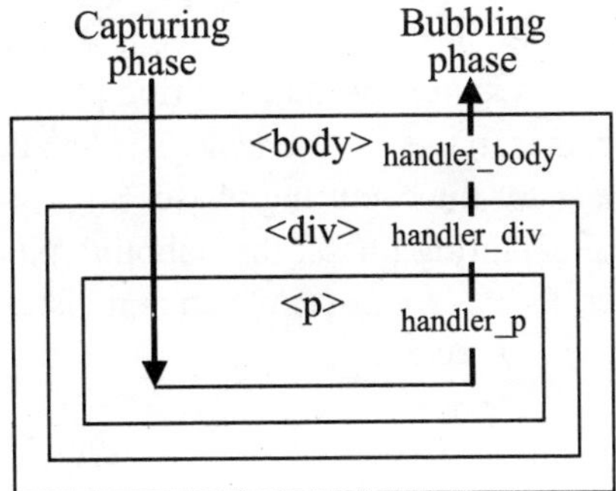

Figure 14.17 Event bubbling

What happens if the handlers are registered as shown in the following?

```
document.getElementById("para1").addEventListener('click', handler_p, true);
document.getElementById("div1").addEventListener('click', handler_div, true);
document.body.addEventListener('click', handler_body, false);
```

If the user clicks on <p>, following happens:

- Again, the capturing phase starts from <body>. However, the handler registered for the click event in <body> is *not* for the capturing phase. So, nothing happens this time.

- Two handlers `handler_div()` and `handler_p()`, which are registered for the capturing phase on `<div>` and `<p>` elements, respectively are executed in the order specified.
- At the end of the capturing phase, the bubbling phase starts and the event, on its way, finds one handler `handler_body()`, which is registered for the capturing event in `<body>`. This handler is then executed [Figure 14.18].

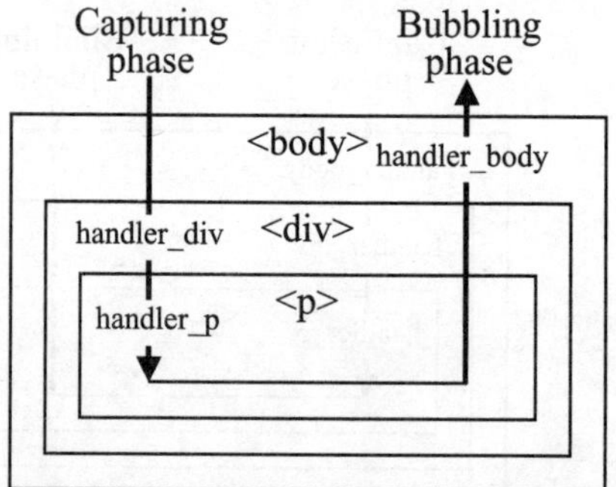

Figure 14.18 Event capturing and bubbling

Consider the following handler registration:

```
document.getElementById("para1").addEventListener('click', handler_p, true);
document.getElementById("div1").addEventListener('click', handler_div, false);
document.body.addEventListener('click', handler_body, true);
```

If the user clicks on `<p>`, following happens:

- Again, the capturing phase starts from `<body>`. The handler `handler_body()` is registered for the `click` event in `<body>` for the capturing phase. So, it is executed.
- The event then comes in the `<div>` element. However, the handler registered for the `click` event in `<div>` is *not* for the capturing phase. So, nothing happens this time.
- The event then comes in the `<p>` element. The handler `handler_p()` is registered for the `click` event in `<p>` for the capturing phase. So, it is executed.
- At the end of the capturing phase, the bubbling phase starts and the event, on its way, finds one handler, `handler_div()`, which is registered for the bubbling event in `<div>`. This handler is then executed.

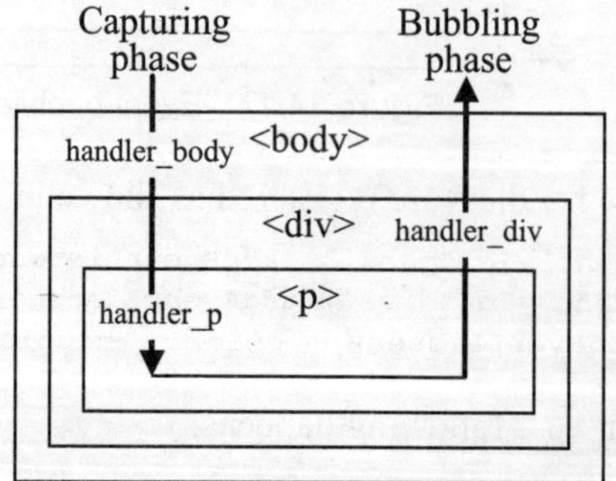

Figure 14.19 Event capturing and bubbling

Two event handlers may be registered on an element for some event, one for the capturing phase and the other for the bubbling phase. The following example illustrates this.

```
document.getElementById("para1").addEventListener('click', handler_p, true);
document.getElementById("div1").addEventListener('click', handler1_div, true);
document.getElementById("div1").addEventListener('click', handler2_div, false);
document.body.addEventListener('click', handler_body, true);
```

Here, two handlers are registered on the `<div>` element. The handler `handler1_div()` is registered for the capturing phase, whereas the handler `handler2_div()` is registered for the bubbling phase. Figure 14.20 describes this situation pictorially.

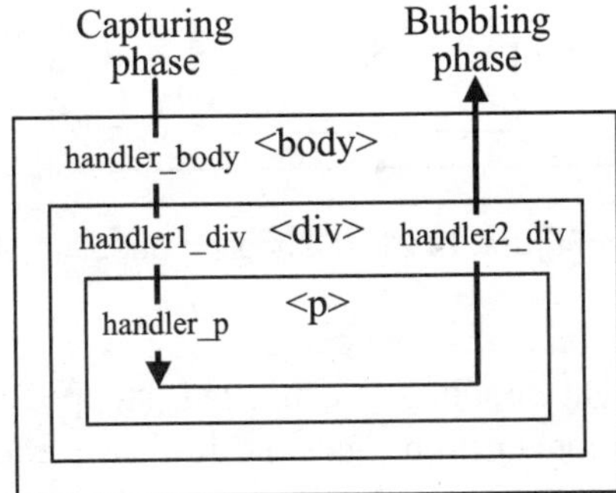

Figure 14.20 Event capturing and bubbling

The event handlers will be called in this order: `handler_body`, `handler1_div`, `handler_p`, and `handler2_div`.

14.5.2.2 Preventing event propagation

Sometimes, developers want to turn an event bubbling off to avoid interference among methods as well as to save system resources [Figure 14.21]. Moreover, browsers have to check every ancestor element for a handler that may take significant time. However, the upward movement (bubbling) of an event may be cancelled inside any handler. This is done by setting the `cancelBubble` property of the event object to true as follows:

```
window.event.cancelBubble = true;
```

In short, the following code can be used:

```
event.cancelBubble = true;
```

Consider the following example:

```
<html>
   <head>
      <title>Event Demo</title>
      <script language="JavaScript">
         function handler_body() {
            alert('You clicked on body');
         }
         function handler_p() {
            alert('You clicked on p');
```

```
                event.cancelBubble = true;
            }
        </script
    </head>
    <body onClick="handler_body()">
        <p onClick="handler_p()">A paragraph</p>
    </body>
</html>
```

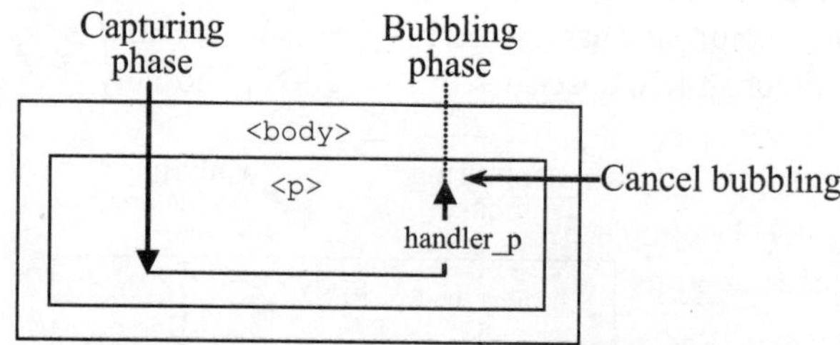

Figure 14.21 Canceling bubbling of an event

When the user clicks on a `<p>` element, a `click` event occurs, which triggers `handler_p()`. Inside `handler_p()`, event bubbling is cancelled (stopped) by setting `cancelBubble` to `true`. So, the event bubble no longer propagates, no further events occur and consequently no event handler is called further.

Use the following method for the browsers that use the W3C model of event propagation.

```
window.event.stopPropagation()
```

This prevents propagation of the event in the bubbling phase. Event propagation in the capturing phase can never be stopped.

Note that event capturing and bubbling always happens. In most cases, only one event handler is registered for a single event. Practically, you hardly find any situation where it is necessary to let a bubbling event be handled by many handlers. If several things happen with a single action, the visitor might get confused. Moreover, things get complicated and it is recommended not to use multiple event handlers without a strong reason.

14.6 MULTIPLE WINDOWS AND FRAMES

In chapter 4, we discussed how to create multiple frames in a web page. In this section, we shall discuss how to handle multiple frames using JavaScript.

In JavaScript, a frame is treated as a separate window. So, a frame has the same set of properties and methods as a window. So, we can control a frame exactly like a regular window. We can refer to a form field contained in a frame from another frame, or change the background of one frame from another frame.

Consider the following HTML page `parent.htm`.

```
<html>
    <frameset cols="20%,80%">
```

```
      <frame name="left" src="left.htm">
      <frame name="right" src="right.htm">
   </frameset>
</html>
```

This HTML document has two frames with names "left" and "right". The left frame has the associated HTML page "left.htm" and the right frame has "right.htm".

Every frame has a `parent` frame (window) in which the frame is contained. Since the task of the parent frame is to simply contain other frames, there is no need to refer to other frames from the parent. However, one frame may refer to other frames. To do this, you must start with the parent frame. Once you have a reference to the parent frame, you can refer to other frames using the dot (.) operator and the frame's name, i.e., HTML `name` attribute value which is specified in the parent page (frameset page). For example, to access the `right` frame from the `left` frame, use `parent.right`. Then all the properties of methods of the `right` frame can be accessed from the `left` frame.

Framesets are treated as arrays. So, the regular array notation or associative array notation may also be used. For example, `parent.right` may be written as `parent[1]` or `parent["right"]`.

Following is the source of the `left.htm` page. The page `right.htm` is a blank page.

```
<script language="JavaScript">
   function set(color) {
      parent.right.document.bgColor = color;
   }
</script>

<a href="JavaScript:set('blue')">Blue</a><br>
<a href="JavaScript:set('red')">Red</a><br>
```

The `left.htm` page has two anchor tags: Blue and Red. When the user clicks on Red anchor, the `set()` function is called. Inside the `set()` function, the "left" frame changes the background color of the right frame. The meaning of the variables in the left frame is as follows:

`parent` — a reference to the parent frame

`parent.right` — a reference to the right frame

`parent.right.document` — a reference to the `document` object of the right frame

`parent.right.document.bgcolor` — the background color property of the document of the right frame.

A sample output is shown in Figure 14.22.

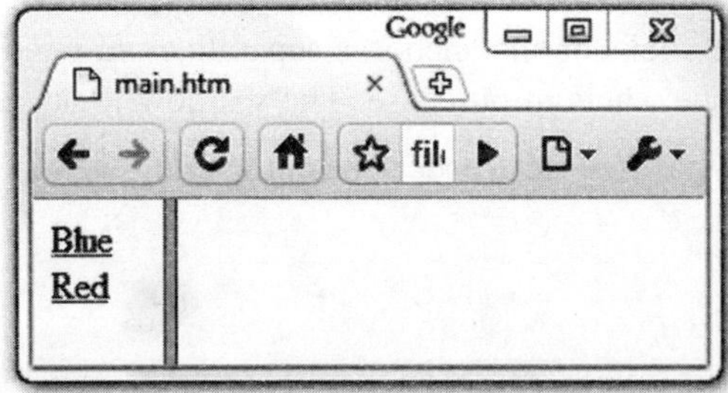

Figure 14.22 Working with multiple frames

The frame need not be embedded in another window. It may be a separate window. The following example demonstrates how to work with multiple windows.

Consider the following HTML document buy.htm.

```
<html>
   <head><title>Multiple window demo</title></head>
   <body>
      <script language = "JavaScript">
         function openWin() {
            w1 = window.open('ShareCode1.htm',
'win1',"toolbar=no,menubar=no,width=250,height=120,resizable=no");
         }
      </script>
      <form name="myForm" action="buy.jsp">
         Share Code <input type="text" name="code">
         <a href="JavaScript:openWin()">Find</a>
         <br>Quantity <input type="text" name="quantity">
         <br><input type="submit" name="buy" value="Buy">
      </form>
   </body>
</html>
```

This simple page is designed to provide an interface to the users to buy shares. It looks as shown in Figure 14.23.

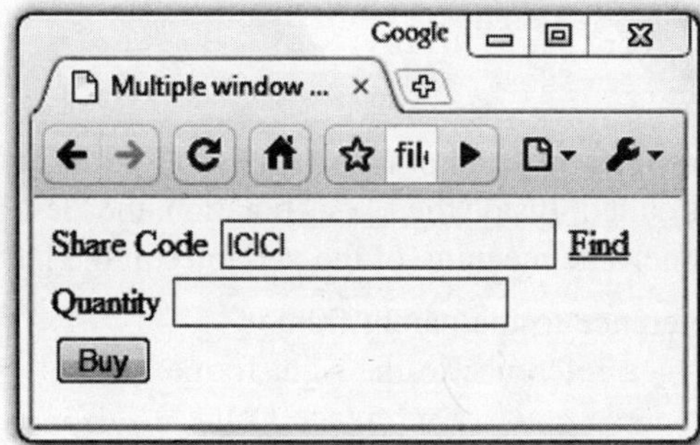

Figure 14.23 Interface to buy shares

The HTML page expects the code and quantity of shares to buy. What is the exact code of the shares the user wants to buy? The user may not know it exactly. Well, we can help the user. Just beside the text field for the share code, an anchor tag is provided, which helps in finding the share code. When the user clicks on the anchor, a separate child window appears, where the user can select the share he/she wants to purchase. The window looks as shown in Figure 14.24 (i).

The user can now easily select a code to be purchased. The source code of this HTML document is shown as follows:

```
<html>
   <head><title>child window</title></head>
   <body>
      <script language="javascript">
```

```
            function set(val) {
                opener.document.myForm.code.value=val;
                close();
            }
        </script>
        <a href="JavaScript:set('ICICI')">ICICI</a>-ICICI Bank<br>
        <a href="JavaScript:set('IDEA')">IDEA</a>-Idea Cellular<br>
        <a href="JavaScript:set('IDBI')">IDBI</a>-IDBI Bank
    </body>
</html>
```

When the user clicks on an item in this child window, the `set()` function gets called, which accesses the text field of the parent window and sets the code as follows:

```
opener.document.myForm.code.value = val;
```

The meaning of the variables in the child window is as follows:

`opener` — a reference to the window that opened this window
`opener.document` — a reference to the opener's `document` object
`opener.document.myForm` — a reference to the form element of opener's document
`opener.document.myForm.code` — the text field for share code in the opener window
`opener.document.myForm.code` — the value of the text field for share code in the opener window

The parent window will then look as shown in Figure 14.24 (ii). The user can now specify the quantity and buy the share. We have not shown here how to implement the buying procedure.

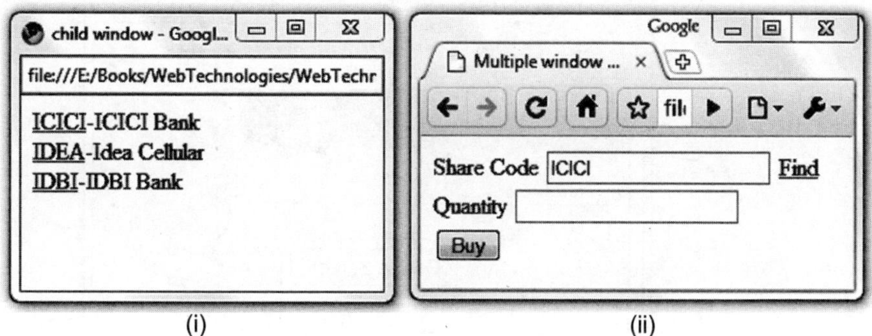

Figure 14.24 Selecting a code of a share

14.6.1 Scripting Iframes

In this section, we shall describe and demonstrate how to interact and manipulate iframes using JavaScript. JavaScript allows us to

- change properties (such as position, size, and background color) of an iframe element from a document
- communicate with the document from an iframe

- obtain information from an iframe
- passing parameters to an iframe

Inline frames or iframes are blocks used to load separate HTML documents into an existing HTML document. An iframe may appear anywhere in the document. Both JavaScript and CSS may be used to manipulate properties of an iframe.

Iframes can also be referenced in the same way that frames are referenced, using the frames array, i.e., `document.frames`. An iframe can access the contained document using its `parent` property. The following example illustrates how to access an iframe.

```
<html>
  <head><title>Multiple window demo</title></head>
  <body>
    <script language = "JavaScript">
      function show(url) {
        document.frames[0].location=url;
      }
    </script>
    <iframe id="panel" scrolling="yes" width="300" height="200"></iframe>
    <br><a href="JavaScript:show('http://www.yahoo.com')">Yahoo</a>
    <br><a href="JavaScript:show('http://www.google.com')">Google</a>
  </body>
</html>
```

A sample output is shown in Figure 14.25.

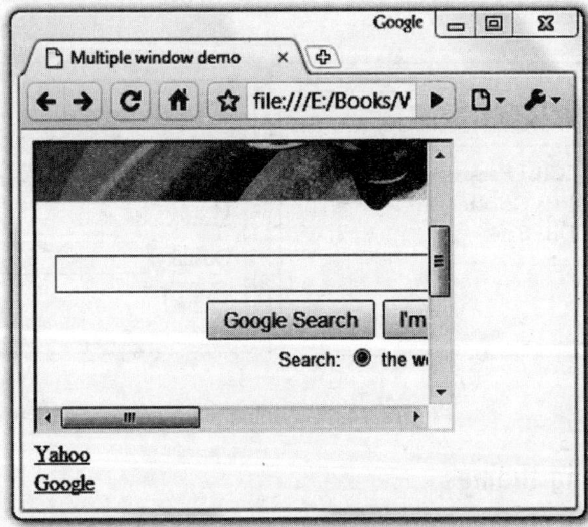

Figure 14.25 Accessing Iframes

14.7 DOM

In this chapter, we shall focus on HTML DOM only. The HTML DOM tree corresponding to an HTML document consists of a set of nodes, each of which represents some part of the HTML document. All elements, their attributes, and their containing text may be accessed through this DOM tree, using the interfaces provided in the HTML DOM specification. Moreover, the content of an HTML document may be modified or deleted, or new content may be added to the document.

An HTML document is represented as a DOM tree by the browsers. Browsers traverse the DOM tree and render the document on the screen. Like other programming languages, JavaScript also provides a mechanism to navigate and manipulate the HTML DOM tree. Since browsers use the DOM tree to render documents on the screen, the appearance of a web page may be changed by directly manipulating the underlying DOM tree through the JavaScript programming language dynamically.

We shall first describe how an HTML document is represented as a DOM tree. We shall then discuss what interfaces and facilities are provided by JavaScript to access and manipulate HTML document through the underlying DOM tree.

As mentioned earlier, an HTML document is represented as a DOM tree; to be precise, it is like a "forest" or "grove" that can have zero or more trees. The root of this tree represents the `html` element. In addition to DOM interfaces, JavaScript provides additional facilities to access an HTML DOM tree. The `document` object represents the entire HTML document. JavaScript also allows us to access the `<html>` and `<body>` elements of an HTML document directly. The object `document.documentElement` and `document.body` refer to the `<html>` and `<body>` elements, respectively.

Consider the following HTML page.

```
<html>
   <head>
      <title>Blank page</title>
   </head>
   <body>
   </body>
</html>
```

This HTML document is represented in DOM as follows:

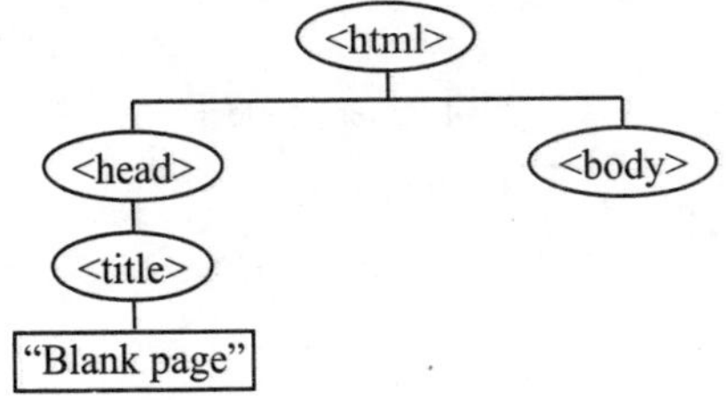

The following document segment is represented in DOM as follows:

```
<p>This is a paragraph</p>
```

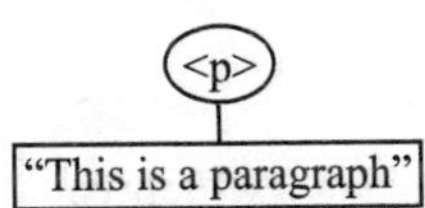

An element is represented as an element type node. The text content of an element is represented as a separate text type node which is a child of the embedding element node. If an element has mixed content, each component is represented as a separate node. The following example shows a mixed element and its corresponding DOM tree.

```
<p>This is a <b>paragraph</b></p>
```

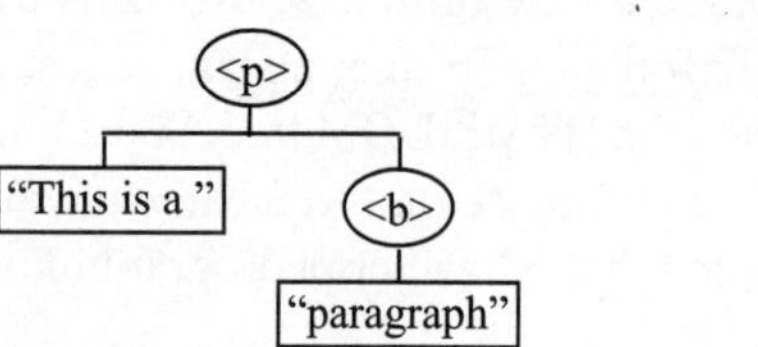

The element <p> has two children, one text node that holds the text "This is a" and another element node <b>. The text "paragraph" is stored in a separate child text node of <b>. Attributes are represented as attribute type nodes, as follows:

```
<p align="right">This is a <b>paragraph</b></p>
```

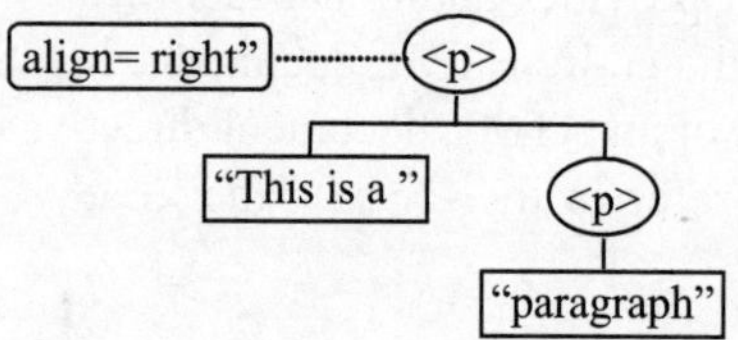


```
<html>
   <head>
      <title>Blank page</title>
   </head>
   <body>
      <p align="right">This is a <b>paragraph</b></p>
   </body>
</html>
```

Here is the complete document tree.

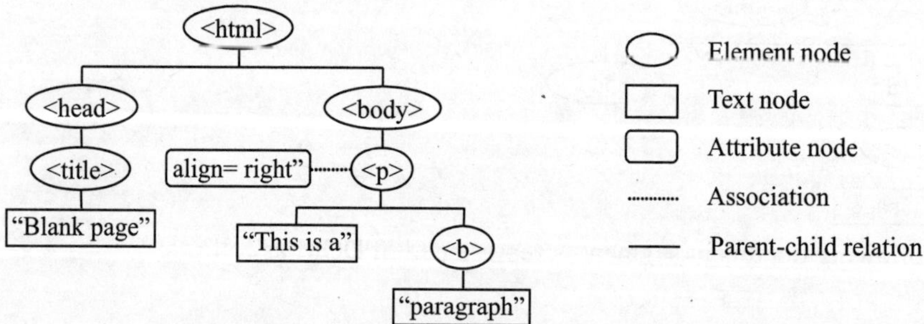

14.7.1 Node Methods

In DOM, every object is a Node. It has the method `hasChildNodes()`, which can be used to inspect whether it has any child nodes or not.

hasChildNodes()

This method returns a Boolean value, which indicates whether the context node has child nodes (true) or not (false). Consider the following HTML page segment:

```
<html>
   <head>
      <title></title>
   </head>
   <body>
      <p></p>
   </body>
<html>
```

The following code returns `true` as the `<html>` element (`document.documentElement`) has two children `<head>` and `<body>`.

```
document.documentElement.hasChildNodes()
```

However, the following code returns false as the element `<p>` (`document.body.firstChild`) has no child.

```
document.body.firstChild.hasChildNodes()
```

14.7.2 Navigating DOM Tree

The JavaScript HTML DOM interface provides facilities to access some elements in an HTML page. `document.documentElement` and `document.body` are two such nodes that refer to the `<html>` and `<body>` elements, respectively. In addition, DOM provides the following methods in the `document` object to get references to other elements.

getElementById(id)

We can refer to a particular element using the method `getElementById()` available on the `document` object, as follows.

```
var ref = document.getElementById(ID);
```

The method `getElementById()` takes the `ID` of an element and returns a reference to the element with this `ID`. The element may be used anywhere in the document. For example, the `login` in the following code segment refers to the `<input>` element having the id `txtLogin`.

```
var login = document.getElementById("txtLogin");
```

The declaration of such an element will look like this:

```
<input type="text" id="txtLogin">
```

This method can be used only if the `id` attribute is defined on the element. The value of the `id` attribute of an element must be unique. Once a reference to this element is obtained, all properties and methods may be accessed through this reference.

Since the `getElementById()` method returns a node irrespective of its position, it is a good idea to use it to find elements during the development phase when the elements change their position frequently.

getElementsByTagName(name)

Sometimes, programmers want to get all elements having a particular name. The method `getElementsByTagName()` returns an array of all elements with the specified tag name.

```
var paraElements = document.getElementsByTagName("p");
```

The array `paraElements` contains all `p` elements in the document. Individual elements may be obtained as `paraElements[0]`, `paraElements[1]`,.... The following method call returns a reference to the `title` element since an HTML document contains only one `<title>` element.

```
var title = document.getElementsByTagName("title");
```

The following method call returns an array of all tags.

```
var allElements = getElementsByTagName("*");
```

14.7.3 Creating Nodes

JavaScript HTML DOM provides a method on the `document` object to create different types of elements. These elements will probably be added to other elements.

14.7.3.1 Creating element node

The method `createElement()` on the `document` object is used to create an element with the name specified as an argument.

```
createElement(elementName)
```

For example, the following code creates a `<p>` element.

```
var newPara = document.createElement("p");
```

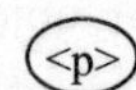

The element node created is empty. Child nodes may be added subsequently.

14.7.3.2 Creating text node

The method `createTextNode()` on the `document` object is used to create a text node. The text of the node is specified as an argument.

```
createTextNode(text)
```

The following code segment creates a text node whose value is `"This a new paragraph"`

```
var newText = document.createTextNode("This a new paragraph");
```

"This is a paragraph"

14.7.3.3 Creating attribute node

The method `createAttribute()` on the `document` object is used to create an attribute type node. The name of the attribute is specified as an argument.

```
createAttribute(attributeName)
```

The following code segment creates an attribute node with the name "width".

```
att = document.createAttribute("width");
```

The attribute created does not have any value yet. The value can be set using the `nodeValue` property of the attribute node as follows:

```
att.nodeValue = "100";
```

The attribute "width" now has the value "100". This attribute can then be attached to another element. The following example demonstrates this:

```
<html>
  <head><title>createAttribute demo</title></head>
  <body>
    <hr id="line">
    <script language="JavaScript">
      att = document.createAttribute("width");
      att.nodeValue = "100";
      rule = document.getElementById("line");
      rule.setAttributeNode(att);
    </script>
  </body>
</html>
```

14.7.3.4 Creating comment node

The method `createComment()` on the `document` object is used to create a comment node. The comment text is specified as an argument.

```
createComment(commentText)
```

For example, the following code creates a comment with the text "This is a simple comment".

```
document.createComment("This is a simple comment");
```

14.7.4 Adding Nodes

The method `appendChild()` adds (appends) the specified node as the last child of the context node.

```
appendChild(newNode)
```

If the node to be appended has any child nodes, they will remain attached. If `newNode` exists, it is first removed. The following example illustrates this.

```
<html>
  <head>
    <title>appendChild demo</title>
  </head>
  <body>
    <p>This is a paragraph</p>
    <script language="JavaScript">
      var newPara = document.createElement("p");
      var newText = document.createTextNode("This a new paragraph");
      newPara.appendChild(newText);
```

```
            document.body.appendChild(newPara);
        </script>
    </body>
</html>
```

This code segment appends a new text node having the text `"This a new paragraph"` to `p` element and finally adds the `p` element to the `body` element at the end. This is equivalent to adding the element `<p>This a new paragraph</p>` at the end of the `<body>` tag [Figure 14.26].

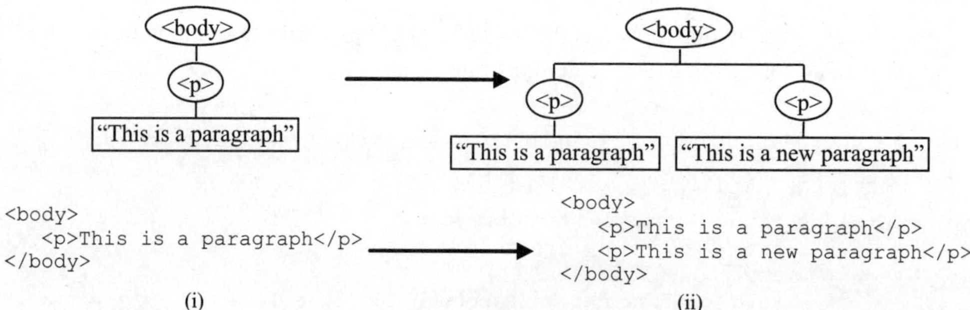


```
<body>
    <p>This is a paragraph</p>
</body>
```

(i)

```
<body>
    <p>This is a paragraph</p>
    <p>This is a new paragraph</p>
</body>
```

(ii)

Figure 14.26 Appending a node (i) before appending (ii) after appending

The result of this html document is shown in Figure 14.27.

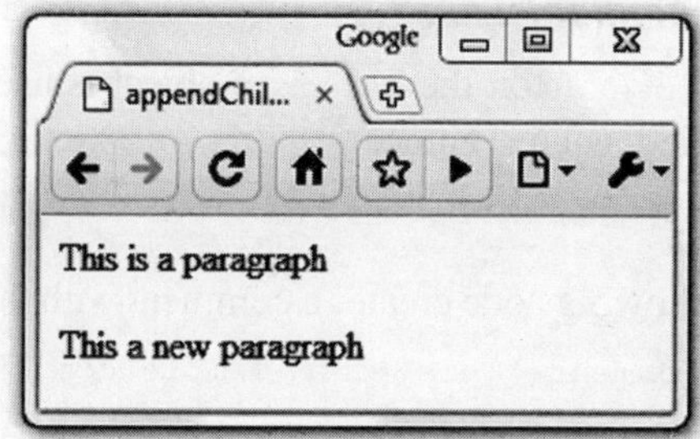

Figure 14.27 Appending a node (example)

14.7.5 Inserting Nodes

The `document` object has the method `insertBefore()`, which is similar to the `appendChild()` method, except that it adds a specified node `newNode` before a specified reference node `referenceNode` in the list of children of the context node. If `referenceNode` does not exist, `newNode` is added at the end of the list of children.

```
insertBefore(newNode, referenceNode)
```

The following example illustrates this.

```
<html>
    <head>
        <title>insertBefore demo</title>
    </head>
```

```
    <body>
       <p>This is a paragraph</p>
       <script language="JavaScript">
          var referenceNode = document.body.firstChild;
          var newPara = document.createElement("p");
          var newText = document.createTextNode("This a new paragraph");
          newPara.appendChild(newText);
          document.body.insertBefore(newPara, referenceNode);
       </script>
    </body>
</html>
```

This code segment creates a new text node having the text `"This a new paragraph"` and a `p` element and appends the text node to the `p` element. Finally, it adds the `p` element to the `body` element at the beginning. It is equivalent to adding the element `<p>This a new paragraph</p>` at the beginning of the `<body>` tag [Figure 14.28].

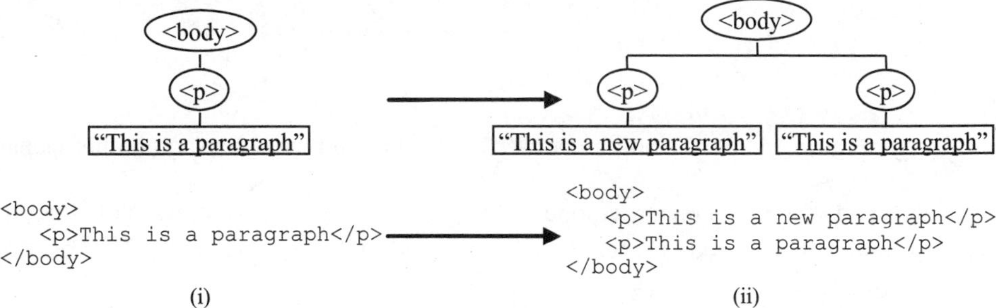

Figure 14.28 Inserting a node (i) before inserting (ii) after inserting

The result is shown in Figure 14.29.

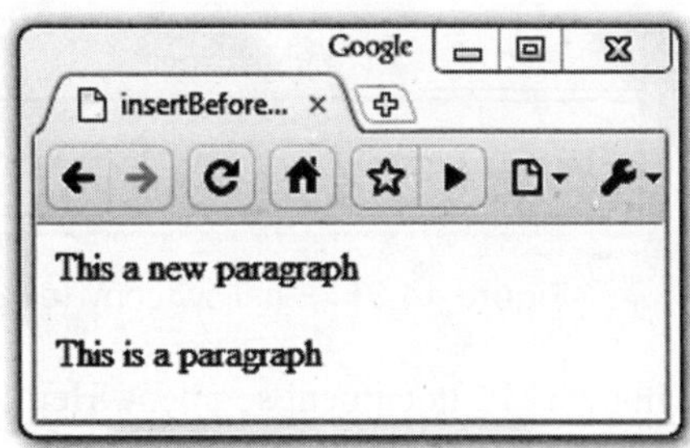

Figure 14.29 Inserting a node (example)

14.7.6 Cloning Nodes

The method `cloneNode()` returns a copy of the context node and serves as a copy constructor for the nodes.

```
cloneNode(copyType)
```

It takes a Boolean argument to indicate whether to perform deep copy or not. If `false` is specified, only the node and its attributes are copied [Figure 14.30], but nothing under this node is copied. If `true` is specified, the node and its attributes, all of its child nodes and attributes, and their child nodes and attributes are copied recursively [Figure 14.30]. The cloned copy has no parent. The cloned sub-tree, except the `EntityReference` clone is mutable.

```
var para = document.body.firstChild;
var newPara = para.cloneNode(false);          //shallow copy
document.body.appendChild(newPara);
```

<body>
<p>
"This is a paragraph"

<body>
<p> <p>
"This is a paragraph"

```
<body>
   <p>This is a paragraph</p>
</body>
```

(i)

```
<body>
   <p>This is a paragraph</p>
   <p></p>
</body>
```

(ii)

Figure 14.30 Cloning a node—shallow copy (i) before cloning (ii) after cloning

This code segment creates a clone of the `p` node using shallow copy. Note that the text node is not copied. This `p` node is then added at the end of the `body` element. The result is shown in Figure 14.31.

Figure 14.31 Shallow copy (example)

Consider the following HTML document segment. Here, a clone of the `p` element is copied using the deep copy mechanism [Figure 14.32]. In this case, everything below the `p` element is also copied.

```
var para = document.body.firstChild;
var newPara = para.cloneNode(true);          //deep copy
document.body.appendChild(newPara);
```

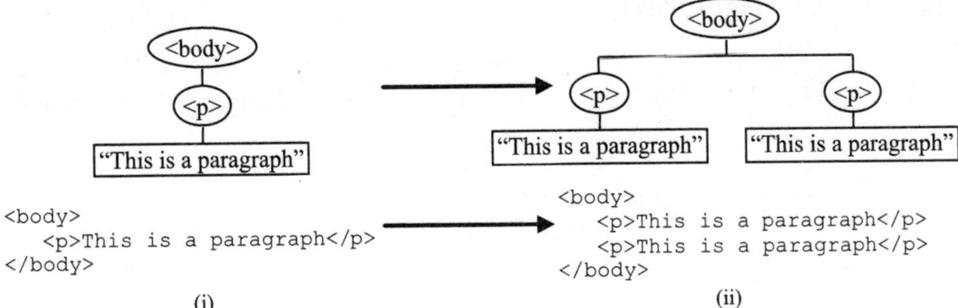

Figure 14.32 Cloning a node—deep copy (i) before cloning (ii) after cloning

The result is shown in Figure 14.33.

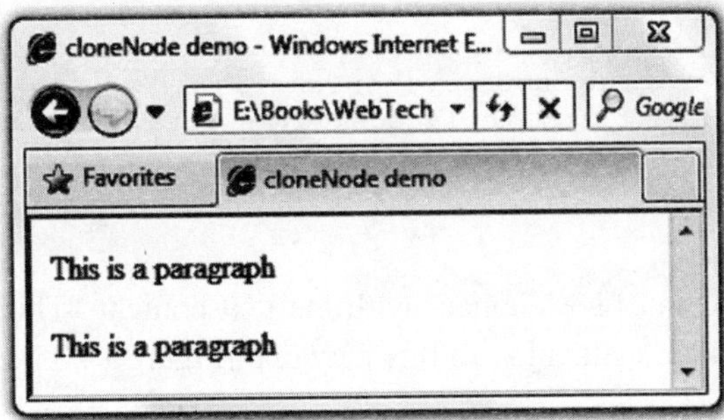

Figure 14.33 Deep copy (example)

14.7.7 Removing Nodes

The method `removeChild()` of a node removes a specified child from the context node and returns it.

```
removeChild(node)
```

The Following example illustrates this.

```
var child = document.body.firstChild;
document.body.removeChild(child);
```

This piece of code removes the first child of the `body` element.

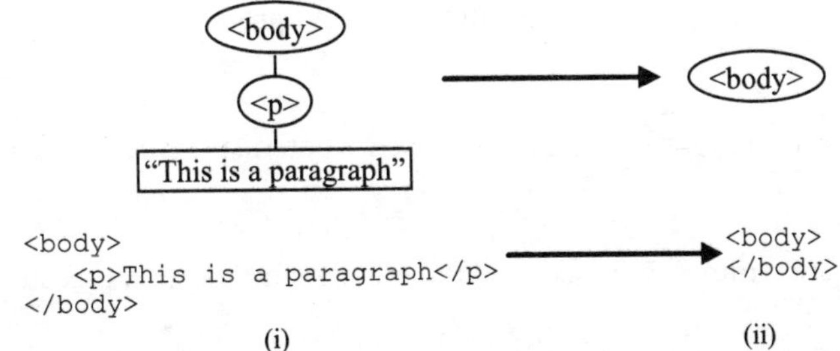

Figure 14.34 Removing a node (i) before removing (ii) after removing

14.7.8 Replacing Nodes

The method `replaceChild()` of a node replaces `oldChildNode` with the `newChildNode` and returns `oldChildNode`. If `newChildNode` already exists in the tree, it is first removed.

```
replaceChild(newChildNode, oldChildNode)
```

The following example illustrates this.

```
<html>
   <head>
      <title>replaceChild demo</title>
   </head>
   <body>
      <p>This is a paragraph</p>
      <script language="JavaScript">
         var oldPara = document.body.firstChild;
         var newPara = document.createElement("p");
         var newText = document.createTextNode("This is a new paragraph");
         newPara.appendChild(newText);
         document.body.replaceChild(newPara, oldPara);
      </script>
   </body>
</html>
```

This segment creates a `p` element with the text content "This is a new paragraph". It then replaces the existing `p` element with this new one [Figure 14.35].

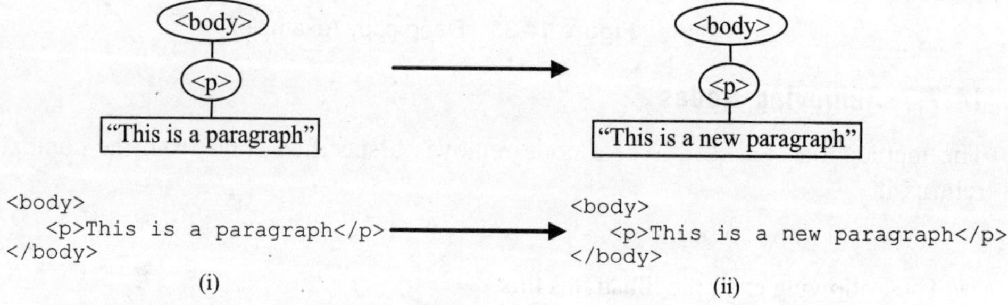

Figure 14.35 Replacing a node (i) before replacing (ii) after replacing

14.7.9 The Document Object Properties

The JavaScript `document` object has many properties that are considerably useful to web application developers. In this section, we shall discuss some properties of the `document` object.

`alinkcolor`

This property defines the color to be used when displaying activated links in the document.

`anchors`

An array containing references to all named anchor objects present in the current document.

`applets`
An array containing references to all Java applet objects embedded into the current document.

`bgColor`
It indicates the background color of the document.

`fgColor`
It indicates the foreground color (i.e., the color of the text in the document).

`cookie`
This property is a string that contains information about all cookies that are associated with the specified document.

`domain`
This is a read/write property that indicates the domain name of the server from which the document originated.

`embeds`
It is an array containing references to all the embedded objects in the current document.

`forms`
An array of the form objects contained in the current document.

`images`
This is an array containing references to all the Image objects in the current document.

`lastModified`
The date on which the document was last modified.

`linkColor`
It indicates the color to be used when displaying hyperlinks in the document.

`links`
This property is an array containing references to all the **Area** and **Link** objects in the current document.

`referrer`
The URL of the document from which the current document is reached.

`title`
The title of the document as defined between the `<title></title>` tags.

`URL`
The URL of the current document.

vlinkColor

The property indicates the color to be used when displaying links in the document that have already been visited by the current user.

14.7.10 Dynamic Content Properties

Manipulating an HTML document using the DOM interface is sometimes tedious. Let us take an example to explain this. Suppose we want to insert a <p> element inside a <div> element as shown here.

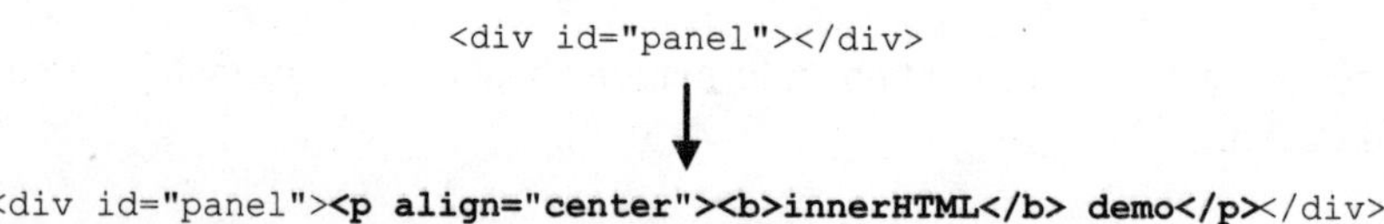

The JavaScript code that does this looks like this:

```
var newPara = document.createElement("p");
att = document.createAttribute("align");
att.nodeValue = "center";
newPara.setAttributeNode(att);
var b = document.createElement("b");
var bTxt = document.createTextNode("innerHTML");
b.appendChild(bTxt);
newPara.appendChild(b);
var txt = document.createTextNode(" demo");
newPara.appendChild(txt);
document.getElementById("panel").appendChild(newPara);
```

Is this code not large and complex? What happens then if you want to insert a table having 10 rows and 10 columns in it?

JavaScript HTML DOM provides a straightforward way to do the same using innerHTML property. This innerHTML property of each element defines both text and HTML code that occur between that element's opening and closing tags. The general syntax for accessing this property is as follows:

```
element.innerHTML [ = sHTML ]
```

Here, sHTML is a string that specifies the content of the element. This string is typically an HTML string.

This task can be done using a one line statement as follows:

```
document.getElementById("panel").innerHTML = '<p align="center"><b>innerHTML
</b> demo</p>';
```

This way the innerHTML property can save a lot of time and can be used to manipulate HTML documents on the fly. The value of innerHTML need not be a string literal; it can be any variable or expression as long as it can be converted to a string and the string is a valid HTML code. For example, the following code displays the current date and time.

```
<html>
   <head><title>innerHTML demo</title></head>
   <body onLoad="setInterval('clock()',1000)">
      <div id="panel"></div>
      <script language="JavaScript">
         function clock() {
            document.getElementById("panel").innerHTML = new Date();
         }
      </script>
   </body>
</html>
```

The `innerHTML` property is read/write for all elements except the following, for which it is read-only:

```
COL, COLGROUP, FRAMESET, HTML, STYLE, TABLE, TBODY, TFOOT, THEAD, TITLE, TR
```

JavaScript HTML DOM provides other properties to change the content dynamically. They are described in Table 14.9.

Table 14.9 Dynamic content properties

Dynamic content properties of IE	
innerText	The complete textual content of an element.
outerText	It is Identical to innerText property, except when assigning a new value to it. In this case, the value replaces the element itself as well.
innerHTML	The complete content (including HTML tags, if any) of element `element`.
outerHTML	The complete content of an element, including the element itself.

Figure 14.36 describes them pictorially.

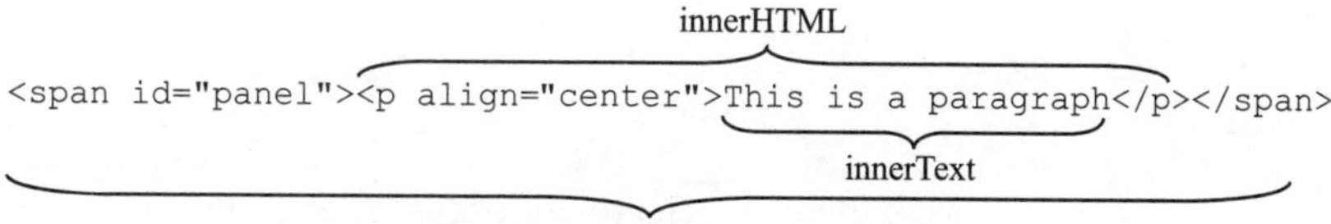

Figure 14.36 Dynamic content properties

The following program demonstrates the dynamic content properties:

```
<html>
   <head><title>dynamic content demo</title></head>
   <body>
      <span id="panel"><p align="center"><b>innerHTML</b> demo</p></span>
      innerHTML: <span id="panel1"></span><br>
      innerText: <span id="panel2"></span><br>
      outerHTML: <span id="panel3"></span><br>
      outerText: <span id="panel4"></span><br>
      <script language="JavaScript">
         d = document.getElementById("panel");
         d1 = document.getElementById("panel1");
         d2 = document.getElementById("panel2");
```

```
            d3 = document.getElementById("panel3");
            d4 = document.getElementById("panel4");
            d1.innerText = d.innerHTML;
            d2.innerText = d.innerText;
            d3.innerText = d.outerHTML;
            d4.innerText = d.outerText;
        </script>
    </body>
</html>
```

This results in the following:

```
innerHTML: <P align=center><B>innerHTML</B> demo</P>
innerText: innerHTML demo
outerHTML: <SPAN id=panel><P align=center><B>innerHTML</B> demo</P></SPAN>
outerText: innerHTML demo
```

Suppose you want to display the following HTML code on the screen.

```
<p align="center"><b>innerHTML</b> demo</p>
```

The innerHTML property will not help you as HTML tags are considered normally as a part of the element content. Consequently, those elements will not be displayed. The innerText property can be used. This property replaces special characters such as ‘<’, ‘&’, etc. with their corresponding entities. As a result, elements are displayed as they are. The following example illustrates this.

```
<html>
    <head><title>dynamic content demo</title></head>
    <body>
        <span id="panel"></span>
        <script language="JavaScript">
            str = "<p align=\"center\"><b>innerHTML</b> demo</p>";
            d = document.getElementById("panel");
            d.innerText = str;
        </script>
    </body>
</html>
```

The content of the <span> element effectively becomes as follows:

```
&lt;p align=&quot;center&quot;&gt;&lt;b&gt;innerHTML&lt;/b&gt; demo&lt;/p&gt;
```

14.7.11 Dynamic Content Methods

IE 4.0 introduced two useful methods on elements to insert text and HTML into existing content: insertAdjacentHTML() and insertAdjacentText()

They take the following form:

```
objectRef.insertAdjacentText(where, string)
objectRef.insertAdjacentHTML(where, string)
```

Each of these two methods takes two arguments. The second argument indicates the text/HTML to be inserted. If it is HTML, it must be valid and well-formed. Otherwise, the methods will fail. The first argument indicates the position of the text/HTML. It can have the following values:

`BeforeBegin`

It indicates that the text/HTML is to be inserted *immediately before* the context element. The text/HTML does not affect the formatting of the element as it resides outside the element's enclosing tags.

`AfterBegin`

It indicates that the text/HTML is to be inserted *immediately after* the element's start tag but before any other enclosed content. It inherits all the formatting properties of its enclosing element.

`BeforeEnd`

It indicates that the text/HTML is to be inserted *just before* the element's ending tag and after any other enclosed content. It inherits all the formatting properties of its enclosing element.

`AfterEnd`

It indicates that the text/HTML is to be inserted *immediately after* the context element. The text/HTML does not affect the formatting of the element as it resides outside the element's enclosing tags.

Let us consider the following `<p>` element.

```
<p>Banhi, <b id="hb">happy birthday</b></p>
```

Consider the following piece of code:

```
e = document.getElementById("hb");
e.insertAdjacentText("BeforeBegin", "very ");
```

It effectivly changes the `<p>` element to

```
<p>Banhi, very <b id="hb">happy birthday</b></p>
```

which displays like this:

Banhi, very **happy birthday**

Consider the following code:

```
e = document.getElementById("hb");
e.insertAdjacentText("AfterBegin", "very ");
```

It effectivly changes the `<p>` element to

```
<p>Banhi, <b id="hb">very happy birthday</b></p>
```

which displays like this:

Banhi, **very happy birthday**

Consider the following piece of code:

```
e = document.getElementById("hb");
e.insertAdjacentText("BeforeEnd", " to you ");
```

It effectivly changes the <p> element to

```
<p>Banhi, <b id="hb">happy birthday to you</b></p>
```

which displays like this:

Banhi, **happy birthday to you**

Consider the following code:

```
e = document.getElementById("hb");
e.insertAdjacentText("AfterEND", " to you");
```

It effectivly changes the <p> element to

```
<p>Banhi, <b id="hb">happy birthday</b> to you</p>
```

which displays like this:

Banhi, **happy birthday** to you

14.8 JAVASCRIPT AND XML

JavaScript also provides XML DOM interfaces to parse XML documents in a similar manner.

To access and manipulate an XML document, we have to create an XML DOM object first. JavaScript also has a built-in parser that reads an XML document and converts it into an XML DOM object. The following JavaScript function creates and returns an XML DOM object from an XML file.

```
function createFromFile(xmlFile) {
   try {
      xmlHttp = new XMLHttpRequest();
   }catch(e1) {
      try {
         xmlHttp = new ActiveXObject("Microsoft.XMLHTTP");
      }catch(e2) {
         try {
            xmlHttp = new ActiveXObject("Msxml2.XMLHTTP");
         }catch(e3) {
            alert('Can not load XML');
            return false;
         }
      }
   }
   xmlHttp.open("GET",xmlFile,false);
   xmlHttp.send(null);
   return xmlHttp.responseXML;
}
```

In IE, the HTML page must be opened using the HTTP URL. In other browsers, you can open it using the file URL also. The following function creates and returns an XML DOM object from an XML string.

```
function createFromString(xmlString) {
   try {
      parser = new DOMParser();
      xmlDoc = parser.parseFromString(xmlString,"text/xml");
   }catch(e1) {
      try {
         var xmlDoc = new ActiveXObject("Microsoft.XMLDOM");
         xmlDoc.async = "false";
         xmlDoc.loadXML(xmlString);
      }catch(e2) {
         alert('Can not load XML');
         return false;
      }
   }
   return xmlDoc;
}
```

Once you have obtained an XML DOM object, it can be used to access nodes in the DOM tree. Consider the following XML document `emp.xml`.

```
<?xml version="1.0"?>
<employees>
   <employee>
      <name>Parama Bhaumik</name>
      <phone>9831962261</phone>
      <email>parama@it.jusl.ac.in</email>
   </employee>
   <employee>
      <name>Banhishikha Roy</name>
      <phone>9051635758</phone>
      <email>banhishikha.roy@gmail.com</email>
   </employee>
   <employee>
      <name>Bibhas Chandra Dhara</name>
      <phone>9734835915</phone>
      <email>bibhas@it.jusl.ac.in</email>
   </employee>
   <employee>
      <name>Gitashri Mahapatra</name>
      <phone>9441804070</phone>
      <email>gitashri.m@gmail.com</email>
   </employee>
</employees>
```

The following HTML page parses the file and displays the content in tabular format:

```
<html>
   <head>
      <title>JavaScript and XML</title>
   </head>
   <body>
      <script language="JavaScript">
         function createFromFile(xmlFile) {
            try {
               xmlHttp = new XMLHttpRequest();
            }catch(e1) {
```

```
                try {
                    xmlHttp = new ActiveXObject("Microsoft.XMLHTTP");
                }catch(e2) {
                    try {
                        xmlHttp = new ActiveXObject("Msxml2.XMLHTTP");
                    }catch(e3) {
                        alert('Can not load XML');
                        return false;
                    }
                }
            }
            xmlHttp.open("GET",xmlFile,false);
            xmlHttp.send(null);
            return xmlHttp.responseXML;
        }

        doc = createFromFile("emp.xml");
        employees = doc.getElementsByTagName("employee");
        document.writeln("<table border=\"1\">");
        document.writeln("<tr><th>Name</th><th>Phone</th><th>email</th></tr>");
        for(i = 0; i < employees.length; i++) {
            document.writeln("<tr>");
            for(j = 0; j < employees[i].childNodes.length; j++) {
                if(employees[i].childNodes[j].nodeType == 1) {
                    value = employees[i].childNodes[j].childNodes[0].nodeValue;
                      document.writeln("<td>" + value + "</td>");
                }
            }
            document.writeln("</tr>");
        }
        document.writeln("</table>");
    </script>
  </body>
</html>
```

The output looks as shown in Figure 14.37.

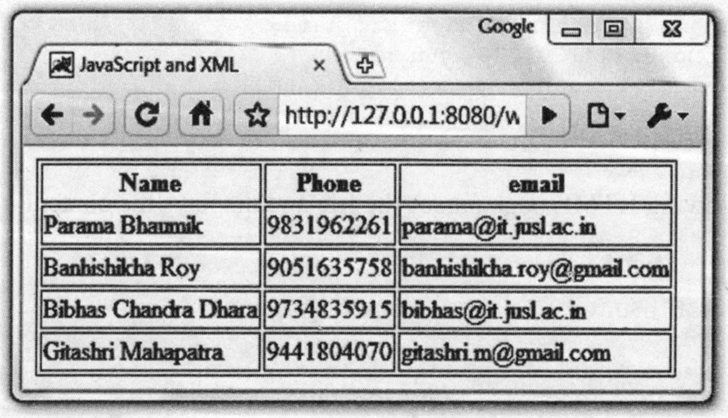

Name	Phone	email
Parama Bhaumik	9831962261	parama@it.jusl.ac.in
Banhishikha Roy	9051635758	banhishikha.roy@gmail.com
Bibhas Chandra Dhara	9734835915	bibhas@it.jusl.ac.in
Gitashri Mahapatra	9441804070	gitashri.m@gmail.com

Figure 14.37 Parsing and displaying XML document using JavaScript

KEYWORDS

addEventListener: A method to register an event handler for either the capturing phase or the bubbling phase.

Cloning nodes: The procedure for creating a copy of an existing node.

Document object: A child object of a window, which contains information about the current document displayed in the window.

DOM: The components of web pages are represented by objects that are organized in a hierarchical structure called Document Object Model (DOM).

Dynamic content properties: The properties that are used to change the content of HTML elements on the fly.

Dynamic content methods: The methods that are used to change the content of HTML elements on the fly.

Event bubbling: In this phase of event propagation, an event starts from the innermost source element and propagates upwards until it reaches the outermost source element of the event.

Event capturing: In this phase of event propagation, an event starts from the outermost source element and propagates downwards until it reaches the innermost source element of the event.

Event handler: The specific JavaScript code that takes action in response to an event

Event handling: The process of taking action against an event

Event object: A child object of a window, which contains the information about event that occurred last.

Event propagation model: The W3C specification for event handling.

Frames: A window contained in another window.

History object: An object that contains the URLs visited so far by users in this window.

Iframe: Inline frames or iframes are blocks used to load separate HTML documents into an existing HTML document.

Interactive events: Events that occur in response to some user actions.

Location object: An object that contains information about the current URL.

Navigator object: An object that contains information about the browser application.

Node: In DOM, every object is a Node.

Non-interactive events: Events that occur automatically without any user intervention.

Parent frame: The window that contains the current window.

Screen object: Refers to the screen object associated with the window.

Window object: The `window` object is the top-level object in the object hierarchy.

SUMMARY

In JavaScript, the components of web pages are represented by objects that are organized in a hierarchical structure called Document Object Model (DOM). The hierarchical structure is represented as a parent–child relationship. Child objects are basically properties of their parent object. These objects have properties and methods that can be used to work with web pages. The top of the object hierarchy is the `window` object, which represents the entire browser window that displays the document. All other objects are direct or indirect children of this `window` object. JavaScript makes many objects accessible directly to the users for convenience. Examples of such important objects are document, location, and history. Objects are referenced by their names, prefixed by the names of all the objects that contain them, in order, separated by dots (.).

The `window` object has many useful properties that may be used to get information about the window. It also provides many useful methods that may be used to perform specific tasks.

The `location` object encapsulates the current URL that is displayed in the visitor's browser. This object has several useful properties and methods that may be used to inspect or change different fields of a URL or even change the entire URL.

The `history` object keeps the information about the URLs already visited from browser's window.

The window object has another important child object navigator which contains information about the client's browser such as its name, version, and so on.

The set of tasks that users may perform on a web page are called interactive events or simply events. There are some events (known as non-interactive events) that are not caused by users. JavaScript identifies an event and takes an action by executing some piece of code. The process of taking action is called event handling. The specific JavaScript code that takes action (i.e., handles an event) is called event handler.

In JavaScript, an event is represented as a global object called `event` object. This `event` object encapsulates the state of an event such as location of the mouse pointer and left or right button pressed for a mouse event, Unicode of the key pressed for a key event, and so on. The `event` object is available only when an event occurs. So, only event handlers can access this `event` object.

The W3C event propagation model consists of two phases: event capturing and event bubbling. In the event capturing phase, an event starts from the outermost element and propagates downwards until it reaches the innermost element. In the event bubbling phase, an event starts from the innermost element and propagates upwards until it reaches to the outermost element.

JavaScript provides interfaces to access one frame/window from another.

Like other programming languages, JavaScript also provides a mechanism to navigate and manipulate the HTML DOM tree corresponding to an HTML document.

JavaScript also provides XML DOM interfaces to parse XML documents in a similar manner.

WEB RESOURCES

`http://www.howtocreate.co.uk/tutorials/javascript/domstructure`
DOM objects and methods

`http://www.w3.org/DOM/`
Document Object Model (DOM)

`http://www.w3.org/TR/REC-DOM-Level-1/level-one-html.html`
Document Object Model (HTML) Level 1

`http://www.quirksmode.org/js/introevents.html`
Introduction to Events

`http://webdevelopersjournal.com/articles/jsevents2/jsevents2.html`
Advanced JavaScript Event Handling

`http://en.wikibooks.org/wiki/JavaScript/Event_Handling`
JavaScript/Event Handling

`http://www.plus2net.com/javascript_tutorial/event.php`
Events in JavaScript

EXERCISES

Multiple Choice Questions

1. What is the full form of DOM?

(a) Distributed Object Model
(b) Document Object Model
(c) Dense Object Model
(d) Dynamic Object Model

2. Which of the following refers to the <html> element in an HTML document?

(a) document.body
(b) document.documentElement
(c) document.htmlElement
(d) document.rootElement

3. Which of the following objects is the root object in HTML DOM object hierarchy?

(a) document (b) navigator
(c) body (d) window

4. Which of the following is not a property of the window object?

(a) title (b) location
(c) history (d) document

5. Which of the following is not a method of the window object?

(a) alert() (b) move()
(c) confirm() (d) close()

6. What does the confirm() method of the window object return?
   (a) An integer (b) A string
   (c) A Boolean (d) An object

7. Which of the following methods executes a certain piece of code after a periodic interval?
   (a) setInterval() (b) setTimeout()
   (c) clearInterval() (d) clearTimeout()

8. Which of the following is not a property of the location object?
   (a) hostname (b) host
   (c) hash (d) url

9. Which of the following is a method of the location object?
   (a) go() (b) add()
   (c) reload() (d) delete()

10. Which of the following is not a property of the history object?
   (a) next (b) previous
   (c) up (d) current

11. Which of the following is not a method of the history object?
   (a) back() (b) up()
   (c) forward() (d) go()

12. Which of the following refers to the <body> element in an HTML page?
   (a) window.document
   (b) window.document.body
   (c) window.document.documentElement.
   (d) window.body

13. Which of the following represents the <head> element?
   (a) document.documentElement.firstChild
   (b) document.documentElement.childNodes[1]
   (c) document.body.firstChild
   (d) document.documentElement.lastChild

14. Which of the following is not a mouse event?
   (a) mouseup (b) mousedown
   (c) mousemove (d) mouseenter

15. The event object is accessible from
   (a) only event handlers
   (b) all functions
   (c) only handlers of keypress event
   (d) a function named event() only

16. Which of the following is not a property of the event object?
   (a) srcElement (b) targetElement
   (c) fromElement (d) toElement

17. How many phases are there in the W3C event propagation model?
   (a) 1 (b) 2 (c) 3 (d) 4

18. Which of the following methods on an element node is used to check whether it has any child nodes?
   (a) childNodes() (b) hasChildNodes()
   (c) checkChildNodes() (d) None of the above

19. Which of the following returns a reference of an element having the id "panel"?
   (a) getElementsByTagName("panel")
   (b) getElement("panel")
   (c) getElementByName("panel")
   (d) getElementById("panel")

20. Which of the following is not a valid argument of the insertAdjacentText() method?
   (a) BeforeBegin (b) AfterBegin
   (c) BeforeEnd (d) AtEnd

21. Which of the following is not a property of the document object?
   (a) alinkColor (b) bgColor
   (c) background (d) linkColor

22. What property is used to redirect a visitor to another page?
   (a) window.location.href
   (b) link.href
   (c) document.URL
   (d) .document.location.href

23. What is the name of the event that occurs when a user leaves an object ?
   (a) change (b) click
   (c) blur (d) abort

24. DOM represents a document as a
   (a) Tree (b) Array (c) Table (d) List

Review Questions

1. What is HTML DOM?
2. What is DOM?
3. What is DOM and how does it relate to XML?
4. Insert the following HTML code just after the <body> element using the DOM interface.
5. What is the difference between the innerHTML and innerText properties?
6. What is the difference between the innerHTML and outerHTML properties?
7. Describe the function of the method insertAdjacentText()?
8. Discuss the format of the method insertAdjacentHTML()?
9. What is the difference between the insertAdjacentText() and insertAdjacentHTML() methods?
10. Discuss the different methods that are available on the window.history property.

15 ADVANCED JAVASCRIPT AND HTML FORMS

KEY OBJECTIVES

After completing this chapter readers will be able to—

- **get an idea about the HTML form element and its purpose**
- **learn about different form elements**
- **write web pages using simple forms**
- **learn how to create forms dynamically**
- **learn how to generate dynamic tables**
- **get an idea about some advanced features of JavaScript**

15.1 FORM OBJECT AND ELEMENT

Forms are important building blocks of web pages. In this section, we shall discuss how to work with forms and the fields they contain.

15.1.1 Accessing Form Elements

The `document.forms` object is an array containing all the forms in a page. So, `document.forms[0]` is the first form, `document.forms[1]` is the second, and so on.

The child elements of a form may be accessed using the `elements` property of the form object. This is basically an array containing all the elements of the form. Individual elements can be accessed using either the ordinal number or the name of the element as an index. Note that the array of elements contains only form fields and not other elements such as `<br>`, `<p>`, `<div>`, and `<span>`. Consider a web page containing only one form, as follows:

```
<form name="frmLogin" id="frmLogin" action="login.jsp">
   Login: <input type="text" name="login"><br>
   Password: <input type="password" name="password" ><br>
   <input type="reset" value="Reset">
   <input type="button" value="Login">
</form>
```

The form has four form fields (`<br>` is not a form field). So, `document.forms[0].elements[0]` refers to the first text field, `document.forms[0].elements[3]` refers to the login button, and so on.

A reference to a particular form may be obtained using the `getElementById()` method on the `document` object. For example, the following statement refers to the form `frmLogin`, which we have just discussed.

```
frm = document.getElementById("frmLogin");
```

So, `frm.elements[0]` is now the first text field, `frm.elements[1]` is the second text field, and so on.

The name of the form fields may also be used to access them. For example, `frm.login` refers to the first form field and `frm.password` refers to the second form field. JavaScript associative array notation can also be used. For example, `frm.elements["login"]` and `frm.elements["password"]` refer to the first and second form fields, respectively.

15.1.2 Form Methods and Properties

JavaScript forms have methods and properties for dealing with them.

`submit()`

This method is used to submit a form through JavaScript. Note that the form may be submitted by clicking on its submit button. In that case, the handler (if any) for the submit event is called. Inside the handler of submit event, we first check whether all the form elements contain correct value. If the form passes this phase successfully, it can be submitted by calling its `submit()` method. In such a case, the URL specified by the `action` attribute (if any) is loaded. If no `action` attribute is specified, the URL of the current page is loaded.

To invoke the `submit()` method on a form object, we must have a reference to it. JavaScript HTML DOM or other methods may be used to get such a reference. For example, `document.forms[0]` refers to the first form. To submit this form, the following code is used.

```
document.forms[0].submit();
```

The important thing to remember is that the handler for the submit event is not called when a form is submitted using the `submit()` method in JavaScript. So, you should perform all desired tasks before applying this method.

`reset()`

This method sets the values of the form fields to their default values (i.e., the value that is specified by the `value` attribute of the form fields). Again, to invoke this method, you need to have a reference to the form element. It takes the following form:

```
document.forms[0].reset();
```

`action`

The `action` property of the form object is a read/write property that indicates the URL to be loaded when the form is submitted. To set the URL `check.jsp`, use the following:

```
document.forms[0].action = 'check.jsp';
```

The URL may be a relative or absolute URL. If a relative URL is used, the resource must be placed relative to the current page's directory.

15.2 ADVANCED JAVASCRIPT AND HTML

In this section, we shall discuss some advanced features of thc JavaScript programming language.

15.2.1 Conditional Compilation

The conditional compilation feature allows us to execute a certain piece of code, depending on whether IE or any other browser is used. Conditional compilation is activated by using the `@cc_on` statement and is ended with the `@` statement. These statements are written inside a comment. So, if the browser is IE, it parses the comment and executes the conditional compilation construct. Non-IE browsers simply ignore the comment. Consider the following example:

```
/*@cc_on
   alert("Hello, you are using IE");
@*/
```

The conditional compilation construct

```
@cc_on
   alert("Hello, you are using IE");
@
```

is written in the comment /* and */. So, IE executes the construct and other browsers ignore it. Inside IE, an alert box appears, but nothing appears in other browsers. Consider a more complex example:

```
/*@cc_on @*/
   alert("Hello world!");
   /*@if (@_jscript_version >= 4)
      alert("JavaScript version"+@_jscript_version);
   @else @*/
      alert("You are using either an older version of IE or non-IE browser");
/*@end @*/
```

The statement `alert("Hello world!")` is executed in all browsers. The statement `alert("JavaScript version"+@_jscript_version)` is executed if IE that supports JScript (MS version of JavaScript) version 4 or higher is used. The statement `alert("You are using either an older version of IE or non-IE browser")` is executed if a non-IE browser is used or IE that supports JScript version less than 4 is used.

15.2.2 Formatting Numbers

Sometimes we may want to display a specific number of digits after the decimal point. For example, we may want to display only two digits after the decimal point for currency data. JavaScript provides two functions on numbers to format them.

`toFixed(n)`

This function formats any number z for n number of digits after the decimal point. The number is rounded up and padded with zeros as and when necessary. The following example illustrates this:

```
no = 20.3246;
result = no.toFixed(3);        //result is 20.325, round up
result = no.toFixed(2);        //result is 20.32
```

```
result = no.toFixed(6);          //result is 20.324600, padded zeros
```

toPrecision(n)

This function formats any number z, so that it has exactly n number of total digits (i.e., digits before and after the decimal point). The number is rounded up and padded with zeros as and when necessary. The following example illustrates this:

```
no = 20.3246;
result = no.toPrecision(5);     //result is 20.325, round up
result = no.toPrecision(4);     //result is 20.32
result = no.toPrecision(8);     //result is 20.324600, padded zeros
```

15.2.3 Tabular Data Control

Microsoft Internet Explorer version 4 and above support a special ActiveX control called **T**abular **D**ata **C**ontrol (TDC). It allows us to access and display information stored in ASCII text files. TDC effectively provides simple database functions without any server-side script. Netscape requires a plug-in for TDC to work.

TDC is initialized with the HTML `<object>` tag, with the `classid` attribute set to "CLSID:333C7BC4-460F-11D0-BC04-0080C7055A83" as follows:

```
<object id="obj" classid="clsid:333c7bc4-460f-11d0-bc04-0080c7055a83">
...
</object>
```

The `<object>` element has a number of parameters that are specified by the `<param>` tags. The commonly used parameters are as follows:

- DataURL: The URL of the data file, e.g., `info.txt`.
- UseHeader: This Boolean parameter specifies whether the first line of the data contains column headers that can be referenced for their respective fields below. If `false` (default value) is specified, columns are retrieved as "Column1", "Column2", etc.
- TextQualifier: This optional parameter indicates the character that surrounds a field.
- FieldDelim: Specifies the field separator. The default delimiter is the comma (,).
- RowDelim: Specifies the end of the row character. The default character is the newline (NL) character.

Parameters are case insensitive. Now, consider an HTML page as follows:

```
<html>
  <head><title>TDC Demo</title>
  </head>
  <body>
    <object id="name" classid="clsid:333c7bc4-460f-11d0-bc04-0080c7055a83">
      <param name="DataURL" value="name.txt">
      <param name="UseHeader" value="TRUE">
      <param name="FieldDelim" value="|">
    </object>
    <span datasrc="#name" datafld="name"></span>,
    <span datasrc="#name" datafld="age"></span>
  </body>
</html>
```

This <object> element refers to the file name.txt. Make the following entry in this file:

```
name|age
B. S. Roy|32
U. K. Roy|33
```

The attribute datasrc of the <span> element specifies the data source to be used. This value is the value of the id attribute of some <object> element. The datafld attribute specifies the field to be displayed. The output will look like this:

```
B. S. Roy, 32
```

One problem of this page is that it can display only one row. One potential solution is to use the <span> tag inside the <table> tag. Following is an example:

```
<table DATASRC="#name" border="1">
   <thead>
      <th>Name</th>
      <th>Age</th>
   </thead>
   <tr>
      <td><span datafld="name"></span></td>
      <td><span datafld="age"></span></td>
   </tr>
</table>
```

The output will now look like this:

Name	Age
B. S. Roy	32
U. K. Roy	33

15.3 DATA ENTRY AND VALIDATION

Many websites provide forms to accept data from users. However, if users submit an incomplete form or provide incorrect data in form fields, it may create a problem in the server that operates on this form data.

We can avoid this problem, using a powerful JavaScript technique called "form validation". The basic idea behind the form validation is very simple. We provide a function to check the form data, supplied by the users. The function displays diagnostic information so that users can fix the error. In this section, we shall discuss how to perform basic form validation. In the next chapter, we shall discuss the same using regular expression, which is a powerful concept for data validation.

15.3.1 Checking a Non-empty Text/Password Field

This is the most common form of form validation. If a value of a text field/password field is "required" (such as login or password), make sure that the user has entered something there. Following is a simple example to validate the login form:

```
<html>
   <head><title>Form validation demo</title></head>
```

```
    <body>
      <script language="JavaScript">
        function validate(form) {
          msg = "";
          if(empty(form.login)) msg += "Login field cannot be empty\n";
          if(empty(form.password)) msg += "Password field can not be empty\n";
          if(msg == "") return true;
          else {
            alert(msg);
            return false;
          }
        }
        function empty(e) {
          var isEmpty = true;
          for(i = 0; i < e.value.length; i++)
            if(e.value.charAt(i) != ' ') {
              isEmpty = false;
              break;
            }
          return isEmpty;
        }
      </script>
      <form method='post' action='check.jsp' onSubmit='return validate(this)'>
        Login: <input type='text' name='login'><br />
        Password: <input type='password' name='password'><br />
        <input type='reset' value='Reset'>
        <input type='submit' value='Login'>
      </form>
    </body>
  </html>
```

In this example, the function `empty()` takes a text/password field and checks and returns a Boolean value indicating whether the field is empty (`true`) or not (`false`). Whenever the submit button is clicked (form is submitted), the click event handler function `validate()` gets called. This function checks whether the login field and password field are empty or not. For each empty field, it appends a string to the variable `msg`, initialized to the empty string. This function returns `true` if the string variable `msg` remains empty (i.e., all fields are filled in). Otherwise, it returns `false`. If the function `validate()` returns true, the form is actually submitted.

Figure 15.1 shows some sample outputs.

15.3.2 Restricting Length of Text/Password Field

You may have seen, when you fill up a form, login name and password must have some predefined number of characters. For example, a form may require the supplied password to be 6 to 8 characters long. Similarly, the login name may be 5 to 10 characters long. The following example demonstrates how to validate this constraint.

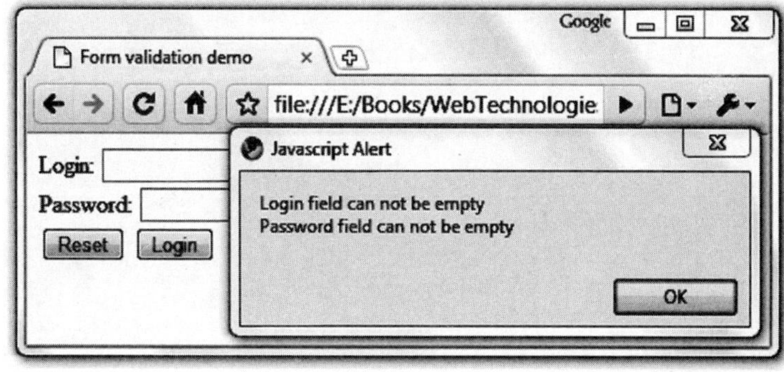

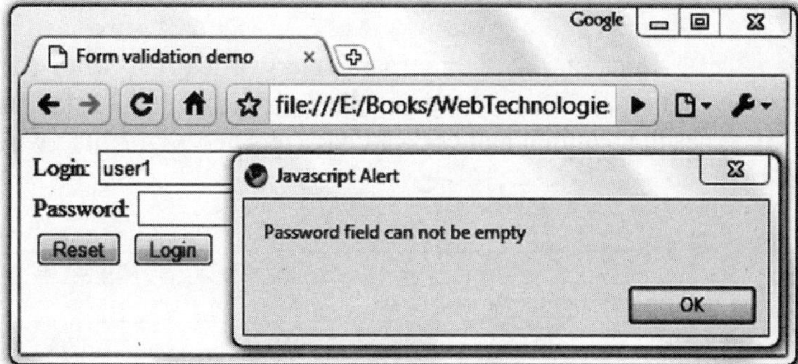

Figure 15.1 Validating text/password fields for emptiness

```
<html>
   <head><title>Form validation demo</title></head>
   <body>
      <script language="JavaScript">
         function validate(form) {
            msg = "";
            with(form) {
               if(!checkLen(login, 5, 10)) msg += "Login field must have 5-10
chars\n";
               if(!checkLen(password, 6, 8)) msg += "Password field have 6-8
chars\n";
            }
            if(msg == "") return true;
            else {
               alert(msg);
               return false;
            }
         }
         function checkLen(e, min, max) {
            if(!empty(e))
               if(e.value.length >= min && e.value.length <= max) return true;
            return false;
         }
         function empty(e) {
            var isEmpty = true;
            for(i = 0; i < e.value.length; i++)
```

```
                if(e.value.charAt(i) != ' ') {
                    isEmpty = false;
                    break;
                }
            return isEmpty;
        }
    </script>
    <form method='post' action='check.jsp' onSubmit='return validate(this)'>
        Select login: <input type='text' name='login'><br />
        Select password: <input type='password' name='password'><br />
        <input type='reset' value='Reset'>
        <input type='submit' value='Login'>
    </form>
  </body>
</html>
```

The `checkLen()` function takes three parameters, a text/password field and two integers, which indicate the minimum and maximum number of characters the field must have. This function returns `true` if it has the required numbers of characters and `false` otherwise. Figure 15.2 shows some sample outputs.

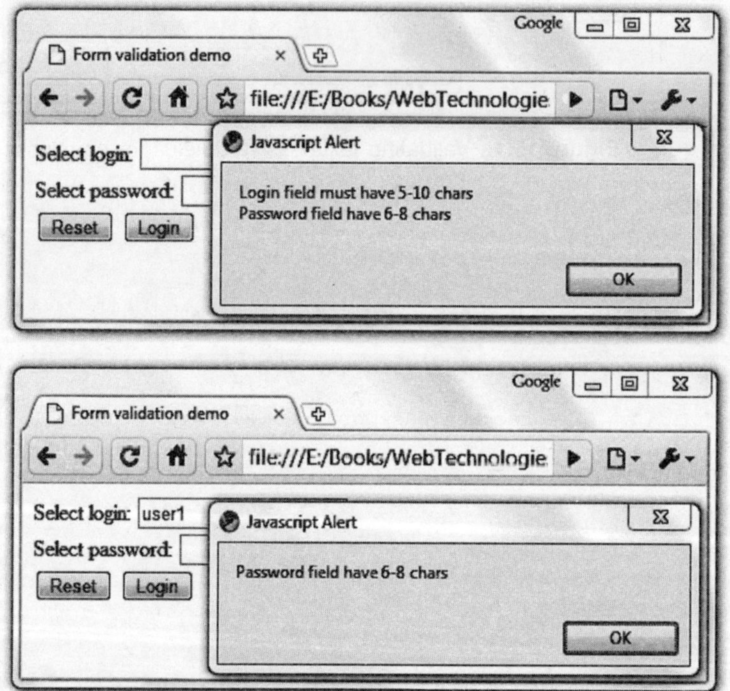

Figure 15.2 Validating length of text/password fields

15.4 TABLES AND FORMS

In this section, we shall discuss how to generate tables and forms dynamically. Think about an e-mail system that allows you to maintain an address book. It typically provides an interface where users can add entries to the address book. It also shows the entries in the address book in a tabular format. The table it uses grows and shrinks dynamically. Thc following example shows how to gencrate such tables dynamically.

```
<html>
   <head><title>Dynamic table demo</title></head>
   <body onLoad="displayForm('Search')">
      Address Book:<br>
      <input type='text' id='name'>
      <input type='text' id='email'>
      <input type='button' value='Add' onClick='add()'>
      <table id='tlb'>
         <tr><th>Name</th><th>Email</th></tr>
      </table>
      <script language="JavaScript">
         function add() {
            n = document.getElementById("name");
            e = document.getElementById("email");
            row = document.createElement("tr");
            col1 = document.createElement("td");
            col2 = document.createElement("td");
            txt = document.createTextNode(n.value);
            col1.appendChild(txt);
            txt = document.createTextNode(e.value);
            col2.appendChild(txt);
            row.appendChild(col1);
            row.appendChild(col2);
            t = document.getElementById("tlb");
            t.firstChild.appendChild(row);
            n.value = e.value = "";
         }
      </script>
   </body>
</html>
```

A sample output is shown in Figure 15.3.

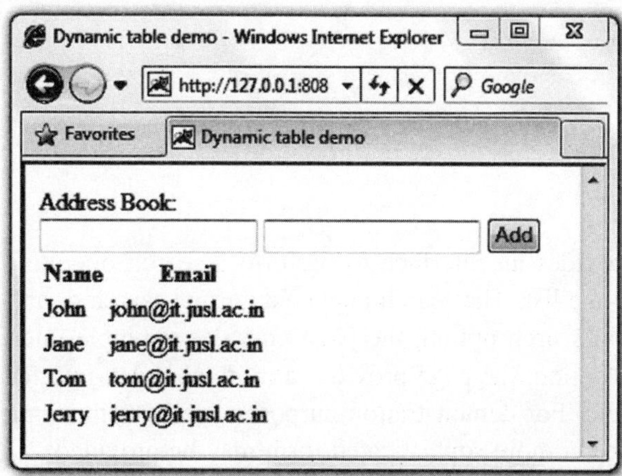

Figure 15.3 Dynamically generated tables

HTML forms are the primary and important components of most web-based applications. However, most often, the following problems occur:

- Forms can be very large having a large number of fields to be filled up by the user. Users may not be interested in all these fields. So, they may jump to another page.
- Users, in most cases, want to fill up a small form having a limited number of fields. If you provide a very large form, you are basically encouraging the users to go elsewhere.
- Form fields often require to conform to certain constrains and formats. Adding those constraints to web pages makes the page unappealing.

In this section, we shall discuss how to provide different forms to the users, depending on their requirement, dynamically.

Consider a web page where you can perform search operations. If you provide a very large form, the user will not use it. So, it is better to provide a small interface. If the user really wants to use a sophisticated interface, provide one such form dynamically. The following example demonstrates this.

```
<html>
   <head><title>Dynamic form demo</title></head>
   <body onLoad="displayForm('Search')">
      <script language="JavaScript">
         function displayForm(val) {
            frmArea = document.getElementById("panel");
            msg = "<form action='search.jsp'>";
            msg += "Search String: <input type='text' name='string'>";
            if(val == "Advanced Search")
               msg += "<br>Search in domain: <input type='text' name='domain'>";
            msg += "<br><input type='submit' value='Search' name='search'>";
            msg += "</form>";
            frmArea.innerHTML = msg;
         }
      </script>
      Select search option
      <select id="searchOption" onChange="displayForm(this.value)">
         <option value="Search">Search</option>
         <option value="Advanced Search">Advanced Search</option>
      </select>
      <span id="panel"></span>
   </body>
</html>
```

This page provides an interface to perform a search operation. It allows you to select a search option from a list. The search may be a normal search or an advanced search. If the user selects the normal search option, the page provides a simple interface. If the user selects the advanced search option, the page provides a more complex interface. In this case, it adds only one more text field. For demonstration purposes, we have made the form for advanced search simple. In practice, a more sophisticated form may be provided.

Figure 15.4 shows a simple and a complex form, both generated dynamically.

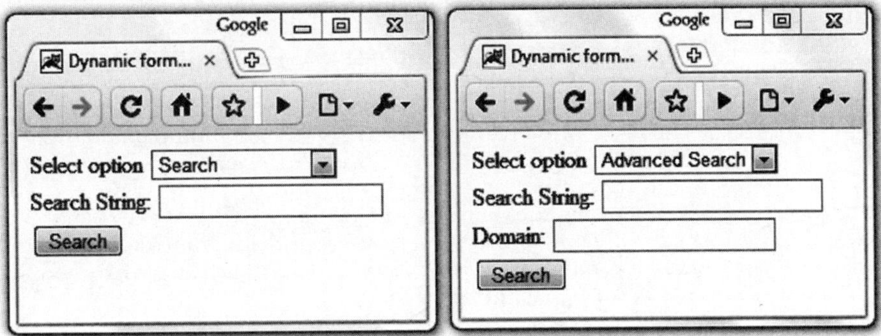

Figure 15.4 Dynamic form generation

15.5 DHTML WITH JAVASCRIPT

In this section, we shall discuss some advanced tricks to make HTML pages dynamic. We shall design a web page having two frames, one at the left and the other at the right. The left frame contains the table of content. When the user clicks on a particular topic, the content of that topic is shown in the right frame. The interesting part of this web page is that the table of content is shown as a tree with collapsing and expanding facility. Here is the source code of the web page `mail.html`.

```
<html>
   <head><title>Tree demo</title></head>
   <frameset cols="45%, *">
      <frame src="toc.html" />
      <frame name="right" />
   <frameset>
</html>
```

The content of the file `toc.html` is shown as follows:

```
<html>
   <head><title>TOC</title></head>
   <body>
      <script>
         function expand1(x) {
            if (x.innerText == "+") {
               var s = "<div style='position:relative; left:20;'>";
               s += "<div>";
               s += "<a onClick='expand1_1(this)'>+</a>";
               s += " Chapter 1.1 </div>";
               s += "<div>";
               s += "<a href='Chapter1_2.html' target='right'>";
               s += "Chapter 1.2 </a></div></div>";
               x.innerText = "-";
               x.parentElement.insertAdjacentHTML("BeforeEnd", s);
            }
            else x.parentElement.innerHTML="<a onClick='expand1(this)'>+</a>
Chapter 1";
         }
         function expand1_1(x) {
            if (x.innerText == "+") {
```

```
                    var s = "<div style='position:relative; left:20;'>"
                    s += "<div>";
                    s += "<a href='Chapter1_1_1.html' target='right'>";
                    s += "Chapter 1.1.1 </a></div>";
                    s += "<div>";
                    s += "<a href='Chapter1_1_2.html' target='right'>";
                    s += "Chapter 1.1.2 </a></div></div>";
                    x.innerText = "-";
                    x.parentElement.insertAdjacentHTML("BeforeEnd", s);
                }
                else x.parentElement.innerHTML="<a OnClick='expand1_1(this);
return false;'>+</a> Chapter 1";
            }
        </script>
        <div style ="position:relative">
        <div> <a href="preface.html" target="right">Preface </a></div>
        <div> <a onClick="expand1(this);" >+</a>  Chapter 1 </div>
        <div> <a href="Chapter2.html" target="right"> - Chapter 2 </a></div>
    <body>
</html>
```

The right frame is an empty page. Figure 15.5 shows some of the results of these web pages.

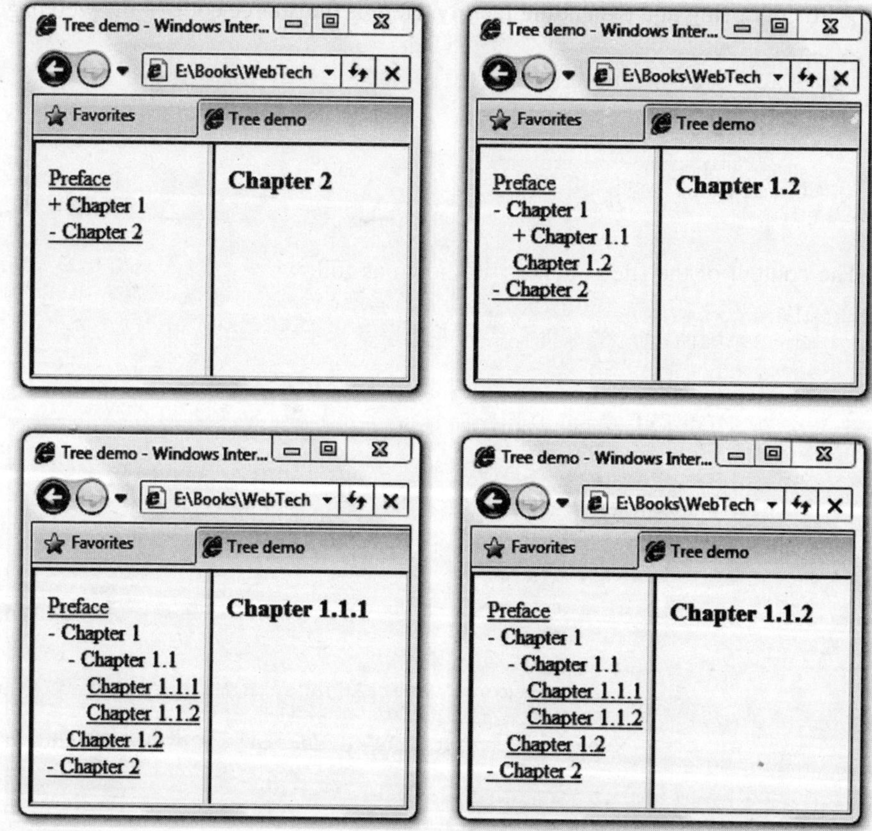

Figure 15.5 DHTML using JavaScript

15.5.1 Dynamic Script Loading

Often, an HTML page contains a large chunk of JavaScript code, either internally or externally. Not all these codes are executed all the time. So, it is not a good idea to load a large piece of code that will probably not get executed.

In this regard, JavaScript provides a facility that allows us to load JavaScript functions or codes on the fly. This is sometimes called "lazy loading".

There are many ways in which we can load JavaScript code on demand. In this section, we shall use a method where a `<script>` tag is created to load JavaScript code.

Suppose we want to load a JavaScript source file `simple.js`. The usual way to load (static load) this source file is to use the following script tag.

```
<script language="JavaScript" src="simple.js"></script>
```

The content of the file `simple.js` is as follows:

```
function show(msg) {
  alert(msg);
}
```

It contains a simple function `show()`, which takes a string and displays it in the alert dialog box. The `simple.js` file does not contain any important piece of code. Our purpose is to simply demonstrate how to load a JavaScript code dynamically. In practice, the JavaScript file to be loaded may contain any arbitrary piece of code.

To load the source file `simple.js`, we can create such a `<script>` element dynamically and add it to the `<body>` element. We can do this using the JavaScript code as follows:

```
var script= document.createElement('script');
script.language= 'JavaScript';
script.src= 'simple.js';
document.body.appendChild(script);
```

This code is typically executed in response to some event such as a click event. It effectively adds the following `<script>` element at the end of the body.

```
<script language="JavaScript" src="simple.js"></script>
```

If the `<body>` element already has a `<script>` element, we can set the src attribute of this `<script>` element to the source file to be loaded. Suppose `<body>` contains a `<script>` element as follows:

```
<script id="panel" language="JavaScript" />
```

We can write a simplified code as follows:

```
document.getElementById("panel").src = 'simple.js';
```

As soon as the `<script>` element is added to the `<body>` element, all code written in `simple.js` gets executed. Since `simple.js` defines only a function, nothing actually gets executed. However, since the `show()` function is now available in the page, we can call it explicitly. Make sure that the source file is fully loaded before calling the function. How do you identify that the source file is loaded completely? You can do this by adding the following lines to the previous code:

```
script.onreadystatechange = function () {
  if (script.readyState == 'complete') show('Hello World!');
}
```

The script loading procedure goes through a series of states. We have added a handler which gets called every time the state changes. Inside the handler, we have called the `show()` function when the state is 'complete'. In some browsers it does not work. So, we can try an alternative method as follows:

```
script.onload = show('Hello World!');
```

Now, the code is complete. When the user clicks on the button captioned "SayHello", the source code of `simple.js` is loaded and the function `show()` gets called. Here is the complete source code of the HTML file:

```
<html>
   <head>
      <title>Dynamic Script Loading demo</title>
   </head>
   <body>
      <script language="JavaScript">
         function load() {
            var script= document.createElement('script');
            script.language= 'JavaScript';
            try {
               script.onreadystatechange = function () {
                  if (script.readyState == 'complete') show('Hello World!');
               }
            }catch(e){
               try {
                  script.onload = show('Hello World!');
               }catch(e1){}
            }
            script.src= 'simple.js';
            document.body.appendChild(script);
         }
      </script>
      <input type="button" value="SayHello" onClick="load()" />
   </body>
</html>
```

Note that the file being loaded need not be a JavaScript source file. It may be anything including a server-side script. The only requirement is that the script return a valid JavaScript code.

This simple idea can be extended to implement the callback mechanism. Consider the following example:

```
<html>
   <head>
      <title>Callback demo</title>
      <script language="JavaScript">
```

```
         function load(name) {
            var se = document.createElement("script");
            se.src = 'callback.jsp?name='+name+'&func=callback';
            document.body.appendChild(se);
         }
         function callback(sText) {
            alert(sText);
         }
      </script>
   </head>
   <body>
      <input type="text" id="txtInput" value="User1" />
      <input type="button" value="Load" onclick="load(txtInput.value)" />
   </body>
</html>
```

This HTML document has a button captioned "Load" and a text field. When user clicks on this button, the associated handler `load()` gets called. The `load()` function calls a JSP page with two parameters: the string typed in the text field and the name of the function to be called. The JSP page simply generates a JavaScript code dynamically depending upon the parameters passed. For example, if for the following URL `http://127.0.0.1:8080/wt/DSL/callback.jsp?name=John&func=calback`, it generates the following JavaScript code:

```
calback('Hello John');
```

The JSP page looks like this:

```
<%
   response.setHeader("Pragma", "no-cache");
   String name = request.getParameter("name");
   String func = request.getParameter("func");
   String str = func+"('Hello "+name+"');";
   out.println(str);
%>
```

Figure 15.6 shows a sample output of this HTML file.

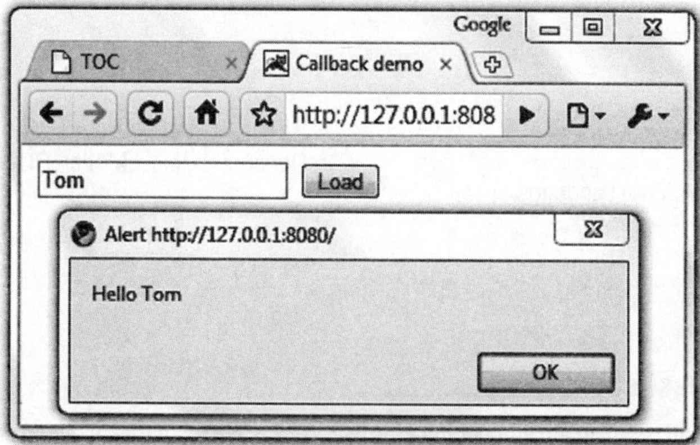

Figure 15.6 Dynamic script loading example

KEYWORDS

Callback: A mechanism where a server program invokes a method on the client side.

Conditional Compilation: In conditional compilation, certain piece of code is incorporated depending upon the browser used.

DHTML: A set of technologies used to make an HTML page interactive.

Dynamic Script Loading: A mechanism to load JavaScript code in an HTML page upon request.

Form element: Elements such as <input>, <select>, <button>, and <textarea> whose values are sent when the form is submitted.

Form validation: A procedure for checking whether form elements have data according to the given constraint.

Param: This element is used to pass parameters to the <object> tag.

readyState: Represents different states through which a script is loaded.

Submit event: This event occurs when the submit button in a form is clicked.

Reset Event: This event occurs when a reset button in a form is clicked.

TDC: It allows us to access and display information stored in an ASCII text file. TDC effectively provides simple database functions without any server-side script.

TextQualifier: This parameter indicates the character that surrounds a field.

UseHeader: Specifies whether the first line of the data contains column headers that can be referenced for their respective fields below.

SUMMARY

Forms are important building blocks of web pages. The `document.forms` array contains all the forms in the page. The child elements of a form may be accessed using the `elements` property, which is an array containing all the elements of the form. Individual elements can be accessed using either the ordinal number or the name of the element as an index.

JavaScript forms have methods and properties for dealing with them. Notable methods are `submit()` and `reset()`.

The conditional compilation feature allows us to execute a certain piece of code, depending on whether IE or any other browser is used. Conditional compilation is activated by using the @cc_on statement and is ended with the @ statement. These statements are written inside a comment.

JavaScript provides two functions on numbers to format them: `toFixed()` and `toPrecision()`.

Microsoft Internet Explorer version 4 and above support a special ActiveX control called Tabular Data Control (TDC). It allows us to access and display information stored in ASCII text files. TDC effectively provides simple database functions without any server-side script.

JavaScript's powerful form validation technique can be used to check whether the user has supplied proper data in the form fields.

JavaScript provides a facility called "lazy loading" that allows us to load JavaScript functions or codes on the fly.

WEB RESOURCES

`http://www.ecma-international.org/publications/standards/Ecma-262.htm`
Standard ECMA-262 ECMAScript Language Specification 3rd edition (December 1999)

`http://www.w3.org/DOM/`
Document Object Model (DOM)

EXERCISES

Multiple Choice Questions

1. Which of the following is not an attribute of the <form> element?
   (a) action (b) name (c) id (d) color

2. Which of the following attributes of the <form> element specifies the URL to be loaded when the form is submitted?
   (a) url (b) action (c) go (d) load

3. Which of the following is not a <form> element?

(a) <input> (b) <select>
(c)
 (d) <button>

4. What is the full form of TDC?

(a) Text Data Control
(b) Tabular Data Control
(c) Text Digital Communication
(d) Tabular Document Content

5. Which of the following is not a valid parameter name of the <object> element?

(a) DataURL (b) UseHeader
(c) FieldDelim (d) UseFooter

6. Which of the following attributes of the <script> tag refers to an external JavaScript source file?

(a) src (b) source (c) link (d) href

7. Which of the following creates the <script> element?

(a) document.createScript('script');
(b) document.createScript();
(c) document.createElement('script');
(d) document.createScriptElement('script');

8. What is the full form of DHTML?

(a) Dancing HTML (b) Dynamic HTML
(c) Distributed HTML (d) Data HTML

9. Which of the following events occurs when a form is submitted?

(a) go (b) submitted
(c) finished (d) submit

10. Which of the following functions is used to submit a form using JavaScript?

(a) doSubmit() (b) submit()
(c) formSubmit() (d) submitForm()

11. Which of the following statements is true?

(a) A document can have multiple forms.
(b) A form cannot have multiple submit buttons.
(c) A form can have multiple action attributes.
(d) The submit button must always have the caption "Submit".

12. What is the value of the redyState property of the <script> element when the script is completely loaded?

(a) loaded (b) finished
(c) done (d) complete

13. Which of the following is true?

(a) A dynamic script must be loaded in the <body> element
(b) The <body> element cannot have multiple dynamically loaded <script> elements.
(c) Dynamic scripts can save page loading time
(d) Dynamic scripts can save execution time

14. Which of the following is not a valid value of the position attribute?

(a) absolute (b) relative
(c) static (d) dynamic

15. Which of the following parameters of the insertAdjacentHTML() function does not affect the context element?

(a) BeforeBegin (b) AfterEnd
(c) AfterBegin (d) All of them

16. Which of the following elements is used to create a form?

(a) <createdForm> (b) <form>
(c) <HTMLForm> (d) <doForm>

17. Which of the following tags is used to create table headers?

(a) <insertHeader> (b) <header>
(c) <head> (d) <th>

18. Which of the following is used to create table caption?

(a) <caption> (b) <title>
(c) <tableCaption (d) <tableTitle>

19. Regarding JavaScript, which of the following is true?

(a) Programmed using Java language
(b) Can react to events
(c) Cannot read HTML elements
(d) Used to delete cookies

20. Client-side scripting is about "programming" the behavior of the

(a) Server (b) Browser
(c) html (d) All of the above

Review Questions

1. Mention advantages of dynamic script loading.
2. What are the advantages of the JavaScript callback mechanism?
3. Describe how an HTML form is created.
4. Which are form elements? Which are not form elements?
5. If an HTML page has multiple forms, how do you access them?
6. How do you access form elements?
7. What is the function of TDC in HTML?
8. Discuss how to handle runtime errors in JavaScript.
9. What is the importance of conditional compilation? How can it be implemented?
10. Write a function to check whether a text field contains more than 10 characters or not.

16 JAVASCRIPT REGULAR EXPRESSION

Key Objectives

After completing this chapter readers will be able to—

- understand what regular expressions are
- learn how to create and use simple regular expressions
- understand how a regular expression engine works
- get an idea about the functions available on strings and regular expressions
- learn how to validate form data using regular expressions

16.1 INTRODUCTION

Many web pages include HTML forms, which allow visitors to enter data such as visitors name, e-mail address, phone number, etc. Visitors may enter invalid data, either accidentally or for malicious purposes, even if sufficient hints are given. Sometimes, we may want to make sure that the data entered by the visitors into the website are valid before passing them to the server-side program.

Regular expressions have already become extremely powerful tools for many users, especially Unix and Perl programmers. JavaScript 1.2 also allows us to work with Perl-like regular expressions, which are part of the ECMA-262 standard of the language. They are basically used to perform pattern matching and searching and replacing of strings.

JavaScript code may be written explicitly to check data for validity. In many cases, solutions written in this way become very large, complex, and inefficient.

Regular expressions can help us in this regard. They can be used to check data against a pattern or a rule very easily. They are typically used in a web page to verify the input supplied by the user before sending them to the server. For example, it may be used to check whether an e-mail address or a phone number has been written correctly. It can easily ensure that the name of a person never contains a digit, or phone numbers contain only digits, dates supplied are valid, price of an item is a valid floating point number, and age of a person is a positive integer. This enables us to freely develop server applications as data that it will receive from client browsers are always in the correct form. Regular expressions reduce the amount of code significantly. As a programmer, you can save yourself lots of time and effort.

16.1.1 Creating Regular Expressions

A regular expression (regex for short) is a sequence or pattern of characters that specifies a rule. This rule may be very simple or fairly complex depending upon the situation. A regular expression engine typically takes a string and a regular expression and checks whether the string contains a match of the pattern specified. A match is a sequence of characters that corresponds to the regular expression. Special characters (meta characters) are also used to write a more complex regular expression. We shall first start with some simple regular expressions and then add more features in due course.

Each regular expression represents a set of strings that follows the rule specified in the regular expression. In JavaScript, regular expressions are objects. There are two ways to create regular expressions: using literals or using the constructor function `RegExp`. A literal for a regular expression in JavaScript is written within a pair of '/' and '/' characters. Following is the general syntax for creating a regular expression using a literal.

```
var exp = /pattern/;
```

The constructor function takes the following general form.

```
var exp = new RegExp("pattern");
```

A regular expression is created using a literal if the pattern is known to the author during the development of the script. Regular expressions created this way remain constant and exhibit better performance. On the other hand, the constructor `RegExp()` is used if the regular expression changes latter or it is not known in advance or it depends on another source.

Regular expressions are case sensitive by default. Some flags may be added to indicate case insensitivity and global searching. In this case, regular expressions are created as follows:

```
var exp = /pattern/flags;
```

or

```
var exp = new RegExp("pattern", "flags");
```

Here, possible values of flags are `g`, `i`, and `m`. They are used to indicate **g**lobal search, case-**i**nsensitive search, and **m**ulti-line search, respectively. Any combination of these flags may also be used.

A number of useful methods, which may be used for matching, searching, or replacing patterns are available on the regular expression objects.

16.1.1.1 Simple patterns

Some patterns are constructed using normal characters. They are used to find a direct match. The most basic regular expression is the one having a single literal character. For example, the regular expression `a` matches with the first occurrence of this character in any string. It matches with the character 'a' after 'J', in the string "J**a**vaScript".

This regular expression `a` can match with the second 'a' in "Jav**a**Script" too. However, it does so only when we tell the regular expression engine to continue searching through the string after the first match is found. In JavaScript, there are functions or mechanisms that we can use to give such instructions to continue searching through the string after the previous match has been found.

Similarly, the pattern `Script` matches with the strings "JavaScript", "JScript", and "VBScript" because they contain the character sequence 'Script'. However, it does not match with "Java" as it does not contain the pattern 'Script'.

16.1.1.2 Regular expression engine internals

What we mean by a regular expression *engine* is nothing but a software that can process regular expressions, trying to match the pattern with the specified string. It is usually a part of the language compiler; we do not use the engine directly. The language compiler, on our behalf, invokes the engine whenever needed. As usual, in the software world, different regex engines are implemented differently and are not compatible with each other.

Knowledge about how the regex engine works, and what it does and what it does not, enables us to write better regexes more easily. We can quickly figure out why a regex is not working properly as we expected. This may save a lot of guesswork and head scratching when writing complex regexes.

There are two types of regular expression engines: *regex-directed* engines and *text-directed* engines. Regex-directed engines have some distinct features such as lazy quantifiers and back references over text-directed engines and are more popular. JavaScript uses regex-directed engines. Tools that use text-directed engine include egrep, awk, lex, flex, and MySQL. In this chapter, we shall discuss only regex-directed engines.

We can easily identify whether a regex engine is regex-directed or text-directed. If an engine has features such as back references and/or lazy quantifiers, it is regex-directed. We can test this by applying the regex `Java|JavaScript` to the string "JavaScript". If the resulting match is only "Java", the engine is regex-directed. If the result is "JavaScript", then it is text-directed.

Let us now discuss step by step, how the regex engine actually works. This may appear a little boring, but it enables us to use the full power of regex and also helps us to avoid common mistakes.

The basic feature of a regex-directed engine is that it always returns the leftmost match, even if a "better" match exists later in the string. When we supply a regex and a string to the engine, it starts from the first character of the string. It tries to match this character with all possibilities of the regular expression at the first character. If there is a match, the engine takes the next character of the string and tries to match this character with all possibilities of the regular expression at the next character. This process continues until all the characters of the regex/string are exhausted or a match is failed.

If there is no match, the engine considers the next character of the string and starts the process all over again. The result of this process is the *leftmost* match.

Let us explain the procedure with a specific example. Suppose we supplied the regex `Java` and the following string to the regex engine.

```
The JScript, JavaScript and Java are different programming languages
```

The engine tries to match the first character 'J' in the regex with the first character 'T' in the string and fails. There are no other possibilities of the regex at this position. So, it tries to match 'J' with the 'h'. This fails too, as does matching the 'J' with the next character, 'e'. Arriving at the 5th character of the string, matches 'J'. The engine then tries to match the second character 'a' with the 6th character, 'S', but fails. Consequently, the engine understands that the regex cannot be matched starting at the 5th character of the string. So it continues with the 6th character, 'S', fails, and continues again. At the 14th character of the string, 'J' again matches with 'J'. The engine then attempts to match the rest of the characters of regex and finds that 'a' matches 'a', 'v' matches 'v', and 'a' matches 'a'. The entire regular expression matches starting at character 14. As soon as a match is found, the engine returns the index 14. It does not proceed beyond this point to check if there are any "better" matches. The first match is considered sufficient enough.

The regex-directed engine simply appears to work like a regular text search routine. You can follow the steps the engine takes, in your mind, while working with regexes. It may help you to check the result quickly.

16.1.1.3 Properties of regular expression

Each regular expression object has a set of properties that summarizes the information about the most recent search. They are updated by the following methods:

- exec() (a method on regular expression)
- match() (a method on string)
- test() (a method on regular expression)
- search() (a method on string)
- replace() (a method on string)
- split() (a method on string)

Table 16.1 shows all these read-only properties together with a short description.

Table 16.1 Properties of a regular expression object

Property	Description
$1, ..., $9	Parenthesized substring matches, if any
constructor	Specifies the function that creates an object's prototype
ignoreCase	Indicates whether or not to ignore case while attempting a match in a string
global	Indicates whether or not to match the regular expression only against the first or against all possible matches in a string
$* multiline	Indicates whether or not to search in strings across multiple lines
$_ input	Original string against which a regular expression is matched

(Contd.)

(Contd.)

Source	Text of the pattern
lastIndex	Zero-based index from which to start the next match
$& lastMatch	Last matched characters
$+ lastParen	Last parenthesized substring match, if any
$` leftContext	Substring preceding the most recent match
$' rightContext	Substring following the most recent match
prototype	Allows the addition of properties to all objects

16.1.1.4 Meta characters

Some characters used in the regular expressions have special meaning and are treated differently. They are used to write more complex regular expressions where a search for a match requires more than a direct match. For example, the characters `'^'` and `'$'` are used to indicate a string boundary. These characters are called *meta characters*. Following are examples of meta characters.

```
\  |  (  )  [  ^  $  *  +  ?  .
```

In JavaScript, the character '{' is treated as meta character, only if it is used as a part of an occurrence indicator such as `{1, 2}`.

Among these meta characters, the backslash (\) is special. To suppress the special meaning of these meta characters, a backslash (\) character must be used before them. For example, to suppress the meaning of `'*'`, the character sequence `\*` is used. If the meaning of a backslash character has to be suppressed too, another backslash character is used before it.

A backslash (\) in front of some alphanumeric characters also makes them meta characters. So, if you see an alphanumeric character preceded by a backslash, you must understand that it may not be a literal character, but may be a meta character that has special meaning. For example, \d represents a digit and \w represents an alphanumeric character.

Non-printable characters are also represented by a backslash. For example, `\t` represents tab, `\n` represents new line, and `\r` represents carriage return. Note that Unix text files use `\n` to indicate the end of line, whereas windows text files use `\r\n` for the same. Such meta characters together with their meaning are shown in Table 16.2.

Table 16.2 Meta characters

Meta characters	Meaning
\	Changes special characters to literals and some alphanumeric characters to meta characters
|	Matches a or b
()	Groups parts of the context expression
[]	Matches any character inside it

(Contd.)

(Contd.)

^	Indicates beginning of an expression
$	Indicates end of an expression
.	Any character except a new line, equivalent to [^\n] in Unix and [^\r\n] in Windows
\d	A digit (same as [0-9])
\D	A non-digit (same as [^0-9] or [^\d])
\w	A word (alphanumeric) character (same as [a-zA-Z_0-9])
\W	A non-word character (same as [^a-zA-Z_0-9] or [^\w])
\n	Linefeed, ASCII 0x0A
\r	Carriage return (0x0D)
\t	Tab (0x09)
\v	Vertical tab (0x0B)
\f	Form-feed (0x0C)
\0	Null character
[\b]	Backspace
\s	White space character (same as [\t\v\n\r\f])
\S	Non-white-space character (same as [^ \t\v\n\r\f])
\b	Matches a word boundary
\B	Matches non-word boundary
\cK	Matches control character K
\xhh	Matches characters with hexadecimal code hh
\uhhhh	Matches Unicode characters with hexadecimal code hhhh

If the ASCII value for a back slashed meta character is known, it may also be used in hexadecimal format. It takes the following form:

```
\xhh
```

Here, `hh` is the hexadecimal ASCII value of the character. For example, `\t` may be written as `\x09`, `\n` may be written as `\x0A`, and `\r` may be written as `\x0D`.

Control characters are also represented as back slashed character sequence in the following format:

```
\cK
```

Here, `K` is any character from uppercase `A (\x01)` through `Z (\x1A)`. For example, `Control+A` is represented by `\cA` and `Control+M` is represented by `\cM`. Note that `\cM` matches the carriage return. So, `\cM`, `\r`, and `\x0D` are equivalent.

Some regular expression engines support Unicode characters. In this case, use `\xhhhh` instead of `\xhh`. `hhhh` represents the Unicode value of the character. For example, use `\x00A3` to represent the pound (£) sign and `\x00A5` to represent the yen (¥) sign.

16.1.1.5 String anchoring

It is sometimes useful to specify whether a pattern must occur at the beginning or at the end of a string. This is called *string anchoring*. There are two characters that do not match any character; instead, they match a position. The *beginning* and *ending* position of a string are matched by the characters caret (^) and dollar ($), respectively.

The pattern `r` matches with "JavaScript", "**r**egular", and "exp**r**ession". However, `^r` matches only "**r**egular". This is because `^` matches the position before the first character in the string and `r` matches the first character. Similarly, `r$` matches only with "regula**r**". Suppose someone wants to write a regular expression to match a *single* digit and has written the same as follows:

```
\d
```

Note that no anchoring character is used here. It matches with 1, 3, 4, etc. as expected. However, unfortunately, it also matches with 12, 345, 254, 16523, and so on. The correct regular expression must be

```
^\d$
```

Since `\d` must be the first character and the last character, `^\d$` matches with only single digit numbers. It is recommended to use anchoring characters whenever necessary. Otherwise, the desired result may not be obtained.

Another string anchoring character is `\b`, which matches a word boundary. `\B` is its counterpart, which matches a non-word boundary. Let us discuss the importance of this anchoring character with examples.

Suppose, we want to search for "Java", which only appears as a whole word in a string. One might try the following regular expression.

```
/\sJava\s/
```

This pattern requires a space before and after the word "Java". This regex will work fine as long as the word "Java" does not appear at the beginning and at the end. Moreover, this returns a string "Java" after adding a space before and after it which is not desirable at all.

The anchoring character \b can help in this regard. The desired expression is:

```
/\bJava\b/
```

`\b` does not specify a character; it specifies the positions (before and after the word boundary) where a match can occur.

`\B` specifies a position that is not a word boundary. So, `/\BJScript/` matches with "JavaScript" but not with "JScript".

16.1.1.6 Character sets

A set (class) of characters is represented by square brackets `[` and `]`. This set matches a single character which is any one of the characters written within `[` and `]`. For example, `[aeiou]` matches with any vowel (in lower case). The order of characters in the set does not matter. Special characters may also be placed within [and].

```
[\d]                //any digits. Same as \d
[aeiouAEIOU]        //any vowel
[01]                //any binary digit
[01234567]          //any octal digit
```

A range of possible characters may be represented instead of writing them exhaustively. This is done by specifying the initial and final values separated by a hyphen (-) character.

```
[0-9]               //any digit from 0 to 9, same as \d and [\d]
[a-z]               //any lowercase alphabetic character
[A-Z]               //any uppercase alphabetic character
[0-7]               //any octal digit
[a-d]               //any lowercase character from a to d, hardly used
```

Multiple ranges may also be specified by writing them successively.

```
[a-zA-Z]            //any lowercase or uppercase alphabetic character
[0-9a-zA-Z]         //any alphanumeric character
[0-9_a-zA-Z]        //any alphanumeric character and character '_'(underscore).
                    //Same as \w and [\w]
[0-9a-fA-F]         //any hexadecimal digits, equivalent to [\da-fA-F]
```

If a character or character sequence cannot be a member of the set, it is preceded by a ^ character. Note that the character ^ has different meanings in different contexts. Remember, it is also used to specify the start of a string.

```
[^0-9]              //any character except digits. Same as \D and [^\d]
[^aeiouAEIOU]       //any character except vowels
```

To include ^ in the set, place it at the end. To include `]`, place it at the beginning. A backslash (\) may also be used to suppress the meaning of these characters. Other meta characters lose their meaning in the set.

Character sets may be combined with other patterns.

```
a[0-9]              //matches a0 to a9
a\[[0-9]]           //matches array locations a[0] to a[9]
```

Multiple sets may be joined to form a more general regular expression. For example, `[0-9][0-9]` matches any integer from 00 through 99.

16.1.1.7 Occurrence indicators

Occurrence indicators specify the number of times the preceding pattern must occur.

zero or more occurrences— *

It matches with a pattern zero or more times.

```
^[a-zA-Z]\w*$           //letter followed by zero or more letter or digits
^[0-9]\d*$              //decimal integer numbers
^[0-7][0-7]*$           //octal numbers
^[01][01]*$             //binary numbers
```

one or more occurrences— +

It matches with a pattern zero or more times.

```
^Chapter\d+$          //matches Chapter0, Chapter1, …
^0[xX][A-Fa-f0-9]+$ //hexadecimal numbers
^\s+$                 //one or more white space characters
^[01]+$               //binary numbers
^[0-7]+$              //octal numbers
^\d+$                 //integers
^\d+\.\d+$            //floating point numbers
```

zero or one occurrence— ?

It matches with a pattern zero or one time, which effectively makes a pattern optional. For example, in `^flavou?r$` the character `u` is optional. So, it matches with `flavour` as well as `flavor`. This occurrence indicator may be applied on several characters by putting them in parenthesis. `^Sun(day)?$` matches with `Sun` and `Sunday`. Similarly, `^Jan(uary)?$` matches with `Jan` and `January`.

n to m occurrences— {n, m}

Many regular expression engines including the one used by JavaScript supports additional occurrence indicators that allow patterns to match a specific number of times. They have the following form.

```
pattern{min, max}
```

Here, `min` and `max` indicate the minimum and maximum number of times the `pattern` may occur. See the following examples:

```
^\w{6,8}$           //matches any string having 6 to 8 alphanumeric
                    //characters, can be used for password
^\d{1,2}$           //any integer from 0 to 99
^flavou{0,1}r$      //zero or one u, same as ^flavou?r$
```

n or more occurrences {n,}

This is a special case of the previous indicator where maximum number of occurrence is infinite.

```
{1,}        //one or more times, same as +
{0,}        //zero or more times, same as *
```

Exactly n occurrences {n}

This specifies that the preceding pattern must occur exactly n (an integer) number of times. For example `\d{8}` specifies that the digit must occur exactly 8 times. Following are some other examples:

```
^\d{4}\-\d{2}\-\d{2}$ //matches a JavaScript date. must be in the yyyy-mm-dd
                      //format
^9\d{9}$              //matches a mobile number. Note that a mobile number
                      //always starts with the digit 9
^[0-9A-Z]{10}$        //Exactly 10 uppercase letters or digits. Matches
                      //Permanent Account Number (PAN) in India
^\d{6}$               //Matches PIN code
```

Table 16.3 summarizes the occurrence indicators.

Table 16.3 Occurrence indicators

Occurrence indicator	Example	Meaning
{n}	p{n}	Exactly n occurrences of p. p may be a single character or a pattern
{n,}	p{n,}	n or more times of p
{n,m}	p{n,m}	n to m times of p
*	p*	Zero or more times. Equivalent to {0,}
+	p+	One or more times. Equivalent to {1,}
?	p?	Zero or one time. Equivalent to {0,1}

16.1.1.8 Sub expressions

A part of a regular expression may be treated as a single unit and occurrence indicators may be applied on it. Everything written within parenthesis is treated as a single unit.

Consider the format of an email address which can be expressed as follows:

```
loginname@domainname(one or more '.domainname' )
```

The `domainname` may be represented as `\w+`. Then `.domainname` may be represented as `\.\w+`. Note that '.' is a special character (it represents any single character). So, we have added a '\' character before it to suppress its special meaning. This unit must occur one or more times. So, this entire sequence may be placed in parenthesis to treat this as a single unit. One or more occurrence indicators (+) may then be applied on it. If we consider that `loginname` consists of alphanumeric characters, the complete regular expression is as follows:

```
^\w+@\w+(\.\w+)+$
```

Parentheses may also be used to remember a match which may later be recalled. Such parentheses are called *capturing parentheses*. Capturing parentheses take the following form:

```
(pattern)
```

This regular expression matches `pattern` and remembers the match. The parenthesized pattern that matches (possibly many times) with a string may be recalled from the resulting array of elements `[1]`, `[2]`, `[3]`, ...

A non-capturing parenthesis is the one where matches are not remembered and hence cannot be recalled later. Non-capturing parentheses take the following form:

```
(?:pattern)
```

16.1.1.9 Look ahead

JavaScript supports a powerful regular expression construct, *look ahead*. Like anchoring, it does not match any characters. Instead, it represents a condition which decides whether a match has to be performed or not.

Look ahead has two variations: *positive look ahead* and *negative look ahead*. Positive look ahead asserts this: "attempt to match `pattern1` if it is followed by `pattern2`". For example, one may want to match a pattern if it is followed by "script".

Regular expressions with positive look ahead take the following form:

```
pattern1(?=pattern2)
```

The look ahead condition is written within parenthesis.

So, the pattern `\w+(?=Script)` matches with `JavaScript` and `VBScript`, but not with `Java` and `VB`.

```
var str = "JavaScript, Java, VBScript and VB are different languages";
var re = /\w+(?=Script)/g;
var result = str.match(re);
document.writeln(result + '<br>');
```

This generates the following output.

```
Java,VB
```

Similarly, `J\w+(?=Script)` matches with **Java**`Script`, **JScript**, and **Java**`Script`, but not with `JScript` and `VBScript`.

Negative look ahead regular expressions are written as:

```
pattern1(?!pattern2)
```

The look ahead condition is written within parenthesis. This means, attempt to match `pattern1` if it is not followed by `pattern2`. The following code finds the last word in a string of words (sentence).

```
var str = "JavaScript Java VBScript and VB are different languages";
var re = /\b\w+\b(?!( ))/g;
var result = str.match(re);
document.writeln(result + '<br>');
```

This produces the following result:

```
languages
```

Unfortunately, JavaScript does not support look behind.

16.1.1.10 Choice

Character sets allow us to match a single character among a set of characters. Choice performs a similar function but instead of a single character, it matches a single regular expression among many possible regular expressions. The general syntax is

```
sequence | sequence |...
```

For example, `JavaScript|VBScript|JScript` matches with any one of the regular expressions, `JavaScript`, `VBScript`, or `JScript`. Similarly, `(Java|VB|J)Script` matches with the same set of strings as before.

16.1.2 Usage

Regular expressions may be used for several purposes such as pattern matching, searching, replacing, and so on. Many methods are provided for this purpose. Some of these are methods on regular expression objects and some are on string objects.

16.1.2.1 Matching

You may sometimes want to know whether a string contains a pattern or not. The following methods are available to perform this task.

test

This is a method on a regular expression object. It takes a string argument, searches the pattern in the string, and returns `true` if a match is found anywhere. Otherwise, it returns `false`. It takes the following form:

```
regExp.test(string)
```

It is useful if you simply want to know whether a string contains a pattern or not.

```
var result = /C/.test("Java");       //result is false, there is no C in "Java"
result = /J/.test("Java");           //result is true, there is a J in "Java"
var isprice = /^\d*\.?\d{1,2}$/;
result = isprice.test("52.50");      //result is true
result = isprice.test("4.525");      //result is false
```

search

The JavaScript "String" object provides a method match that may also be used for searching a pattern in a string. Its task is similar to the `test()` method on regular expression objects but it returns the index of the search pattern found. It has the following form:

```
string.search(regExp)
```

It takes a regular expression as an argument and searches the pattern for a match in the string. For a successful search, it returns the zero-based index of the match and –1 otherwise.

```
var result = "Java".search(/C/);   //result is -1, there is no C in "Java"
result = "Java".search(/v/);       //result is 2, v matches at location 2
var regExp = /^\d*\.?\d{1,2}$/;
result = "52.50".search(regExp);   //result is 0, successful search
result = "4.525".search(regExp);   //result is -1, unsuccessful search
```

16.1.2.2 Searching

Sometimes, you may also want to know other information in addition to simply checking whether a string contains a pattern. The following methods are available to accomplish this.

exec

Similar to the `test()` method on regular expressions, but returns search information as an array for a successful search and `null` otherwise. It takes the following form:

```
regExp.exec(string)
```

Here, `regExp` is the name of the regular expression, which can be a literal or a variable and `string` is the string to be searched. The array returned by this method has the following properties:

```
index     zero based index of the last match in the string
input     original string
```

```
[0]         substring that was matched last
[1], [2], ...parenthesized substrings that matches(if any)
```

The method `exec()` changes the following properties of the regular expression object on which it is invoked.

```
Property    Meaning
lastIndex   index from which to start next match
ignoreCase  indicates whether the modifier i was used
global      indicates whether the modifier g was used
multiline   indicates whether the modifier m was used
source      text of the pattern
```

Consider the following script segment.

```
var re = /(.)(\w*)Script/;
var str = "JavaScript";
var resultArray = re.exec(str);
document.write('resultArray.index = ' + resultArray.index + '<br>');
document.write('resultArray.input = ' + resultArray.input + '<br>');
for(i = 0; i < resultArray.length; i++)
document.write('resultArray[' + i + '] = ' + resultArray[i] + '<br>');

document.write('lastIndex = ' + re.lastIndex + '<br>');
document.write('ignoreCase = ' + re.ignoreCase + '<br>');
document.write('global = ' + re.global + '<br>');
document.write('multiline = ' + re.multiline + '<br>');
document.write('source = ' + re.source + '<br>');
```

It generates the following result:

```
resultArray.index = 0
resultArray.input = JavaScript
resultArray[0] = JavaScript
resultArray[1] = J
resultArray[2] = ava
lastIndex = 10
ignoreCase = false
global = false
multiline = false
source = (.)(\w*)Script
```

match

This is a method on string objects and is similar to the `exec()` method on regular expression objects.

16.1.2.3 Replacing

The `replace()` method is used to replace a pattern in a string with another string. When the modifier `g` is used in the regular expression, the `replace()` method replaces all matches.

replace

This method is available on string objects. It takes the following form:

```
string.replace(regExp, replacementString);
```

Here, `regExp` is the regular expression, which can be a variable or a literal and `replacementString` is the string to be used for replacement. If the modifier `g` is used in the regular expression, this method replaces every match of the pattern. The following example illustrates the use of the `replace()` method.

```
var oldStr = "JavaScript and Java are two different languages";
newStr = oldStr.replace(/Java/g, "VB");
document.writeln('oldStr = ' + oldStr + '<br>newStr = ' + newStr + '<br>');
```

This generates the following result:

```
oldStr = JavaScript and Java are two different languages
newStr = VBScript and VB are two different languages
```

Parenthesized regular expressions may be used during the replacement procedure. Remember, parenthesized substrings may be recalled from the resulting array elements `[1]`, `[2]`, `[3]`, ... Those parenthesized substrings may be accessed from the script using `$1, $2, $3,…, $9`. The following example swaps the two words.

```
var re = /(\w+)\s(\w+)/;
var oldStr = "Java JavaScript";
var newStr = oldStr.replace(re, "$2 $1"); //newStr is "JavaScript Java"
```

Like `exec()`, this method changes the properties of regular expression objects.

split

This method takes a regular expression as a delimiter, splits a string into substrings, and returns those substrings as an array. If the pattern does not match at all, it returns the original string as a single substring. Since the delimiter used here is a pattern, it may be different for different substrings.

```
var str = "Java,JavaScript and VBScript are different languages";
result = str.split(/[ ,]/);
for(i = 0; i < result.length; i++)
document.write('result[' + i + '] = ' + result[i] + '<br>');
```

The array result contains all words separated by a blank space and comma (,) as follows:

```
result[0] = Java
result[1] = JavaScript
result[2] = and
result[3] = VBScript
result[4] = are
result[5] = different
result[6] = languages
```

The following example splits a string into characters.

```
var str = "regular expression";
result = str.split("");
document.write(result);
```

This results in the following:

```
r,e,g,u,l,a,r, ,e,x,p,r,e,s,s,i,o,n
```

16.1.2.4 Validating data

The following HTML page verifies the fields in a small registration form. The registration form has a text field and a password field to accept the preferred login name and password, respectively. It accepts those login names that start with a letter, followed by zero or more letters or digits. A regular expression for this pattern is shown as follows:

```
/^[a-zA-Z]\w*$/
```

The password should consist of 4 to 8 alphanumeric characters. The corresponding regular expression is as follows:

```
/^\w{4,8}$/
```

A handler for the `click` event is specified for the submit button. When the user clicks on the submit button, the handler function `check()` verifies whether the user has provided all the required data correctly. Accordingly, it displays a diagnostic error message.

```
<html>
   <head><title>Registration</title></head>
   <body>
      <script language="JavaScript1.2">
         msg = [];
         function conf(){
            return confirm("Do you want to reset all data");
         }
         function check() {
            var reLogin = /^[a-zA-Z]\w*$/;
            var rePassword = /^\w{4,8}$/;
            if(!reLogin.test(frmRegister.login.value))
               msg[msg.length] = "Invalid login.\nIt must consist of
letter(s) followed by letter(s) ot digit(s)\n";
            if(!rePassword.test(frmRegister.password.value))
               msg[msg.length] = "Invalid password.\nIt must have 4 to 8
alphanumeric characters";
            if(msg.length != 0) {
               var m = "";
               for(i=0;i<msg.length;i++)
                  m += msg[i];
               alert(m);
               msg = [];
               return false;
            }
            return true;
         }
      </script>
      <form name="frmRegister" action="register.jsp" method="post">
         Select login: <input type="text" name="login"><br>
         Select password: <input type="password" name="password"><br>
         <input type="reset" value="Reset" onClick="return conf();">
         <input type="submit" value="submit" onClick="return check()">
      </form>
   </body>
</html>
```

The following example validates the form step by step. Initially a global variable `flag` is set to `true`. Whenever a user enters data and goes to the next field, it checks if the data entered is correct. This is performed by specifying a handler for the blur `event`. If it is correct, it immediately displays the message "Ok" with green color at the end of the field. If it is wrong, it shows the error message "Error" with red color at the end of the field and sets the `flag` variable to false. When the user clicks on the submit button, the value of the flag variable is checked. A true value indicates that the form fields contain valid data. Otherwise one or more form fields contain invalid data.

```
<html>
   <head><title>Registration</title></head>
   <body>
      <form name="frmRegister" action="register.jsp" method="post">
         Select login: <input type="text" name="login"
onBlur="checkLogin(this)"><span id="lblogin"></span><br>
         Select password: <input type="password" name="password"
onBlur="checkPassword(this)"><span id="lbpassword"></span><br>
         <input type="reset" value="Reset" onClick="return conf();">
         <input type="submit" value="submit" onClick="return check();">
      </form>
      <script language="JavaScript1.2">
         function conf(){
            return confirm("Do you want to reset all data");
         }
         function check() {
            alert(flag);
            return true;
         }
         function checkLogin(o) {
            re = /^[a-zA-Z]\w*$/;
            set(re, o);
         }
         function checkPassword(o) {
            re = /^\w{4,8}$/;
            set(re, o);
         }
         function set(re, o) {
            e = document.getElementById('lb'+o.name);
            if (re.test(o.value)) {
               e.style.color='green';
               e.innerText=' Ok';
            }else {
               e.style.color='red';
               e.innerText=' Error';
               flag = false;
            }
         }
         flag = true;
         frmRegister.childNodes[1].focus();
      </script>
   </body>
</html>
```

KEYWORDS

Anchoring: Sometimes it is useful to specify that a pattern must occur at the beginning or at the end of a string. This is called string anchoring.

Character sets: A set (class) of characters is represented by square brackets, `[` and `]`. This set matches a single character, which is any one of the characters written within `[` and `]`.

Choice: A construct that allows us to match a single character among a set of characters.

Look ahead: A construct that represents a condition which decides whether a match has to be performed or not.

Matching: Procedure to check whether a string contains a pattern or not.

Meta characters: Some characters used in regular expressions have special meaning and are treated differently.

Occurrence Indicator: Occurrence indicators specify the number of times the preceding pattern must occur.

Pattern: A sequence of characters that represents a set of strings.

Regex-directed engines: Lazy regex engines that return by default only the first match of a pattern in a specified string.

Replacing: Procedure for substituting a pattern with another.

Searching: Procedure for finding other information in addition to simply checking whether a string contains a pattern.

Simple pattern: Some patterns are constructed using normal characters and are used to find a direct match.

Splitting: Procedure to break a string into substrings and return those substrings as an array.

Sub Expression: A part of a regular expression may be treated as a single unit and occurrence indicators may be applied on it.

Text-directed engines: Checks the best match of a pattern in a specified string.

SUMMARY

JavaScript 1.2 allows us to work with Perl-like regular expressions, which are part of the ECMA-262 standard of the language. They are basically used to perform pattern matching, searching, and replacing of strings.

A regular expression engine is nothing but a software that can process regular expressions, trying to match the pattern with the specified string. There are two types of regular expression engines: regex-directed engines and text-directed engines. JavaScript uses regex-directed engines.

There are two ways to create regular expressions: using a regular expression literal or using the constructor function `RegExp()`. Regular expressions created using literals exhibit better performance. On the other hand, the constructor `RegExp()` is used if the regular expression changes latter or is not known in advance or it depends on another source.

Each regular expression object has a set of properties that summarize the information about the most recent search.

Some characters used in the regular expressions have special meaning and are treated differently. They are used to write more complex regular expressions where a search for a match requires more than a direct match. These characters are called meta characters.

It is sometimes useful to specify that a pattern must occur at the beginning or at the end of a string. This is called string anchoring.

Occurrence indicators specify the number of times the preceding pattern must occur.

A part of a regular expression, called sub expression, may be treated as a single unit and occurrence indicators may be applied on it.

JavaScript supports a powerful regular expression construct, look ahead, which does not match any characters. Instead, it represents a condition that decides whether a match has to be performed or not.

Choice matches a single regular expression among many possible regular expressions.

The JavaScript "String" object provides a method match that may also be used for searching a pattern in a string.

WEB RESOURCES

http://www.regular-expressions.info/javascriptexample.html
JavaScript RegExp Example: Regular Expression Tester

http://www.zytrax.com/tech/web/regex.htm
Regular Expressions - User guide

http://www.webreference.com/js/column5/
Pattern Matching and Regular Expressions

http://en.wikipedia.org/wiki/Regular_expression
Regular expression

EXERCISES

Multiple Choice Questions

1. Which of the following functions is used to create a regular expression?
   (a) RegExp() (b) Expression()
   (c) Regular() (d) RegularExpression()

2. In JavaScript, regular expression literals are delimited by
   (a) | and | (b) \ and \
   (c) / and / (d) ^ and ^

3. Which of the following flags is invalid?
   (a) i (b) s (c) g (d) m

4. Which of the following regular expression engines is used by JavaScript?
   (a) Regular expression directed engine
   (b) Text directed engine
   (c) Both
   (d) None of the above

5. Which of the following is not a function of string?
   (a) test() (b) search()
   (c) replace() (d) split()

6. Which of the following is a function of regular expression?
   (a) exec() (b) match()
   (c) replace() (d) split()

7. Which of the following is not a meta character?
   (a) ((b) [(c) | (d) #

8. Which of the following is a meta character?
   (a) - (b) / (c) @ (d) .

9. Which of the following characters is used to match the beginning of a string?
   (a) $ (b) ^ (c) ~ (d) #

10. Which of the following characters is used to match the end of a string?
    (a) ^ (b) % (c) # (d) $

11. Which of the following is equivalent to \d?
    (a) [\d] (b) [0-9]
    (c) [0123456789] (d) All of the above

12. Which of the following is not equivalent to \d?
    (a) [\d] (b) [09]
    (c) [0123456789] (d) [0-9]

13. Which of the following represents an optional occurrence indicator?
    (a) * (b) +
    (c) ? (d) None of the above

14. Which of the following is equivalent to the ? occurrence Indicator?
    (a) {0,1} (b) {0,}
    (c) {1,} (d) None of the above

15. Which one of the following is equivalent to '*'?
    (a) {1,} (b) {0,}
    (c) {0,1} (d) None of the above

16. Which of the following represents exactly two occurrences of digits?
    (a) \d\d (b) \d{2}
    (c) [\d][\d] (d) all of the above

17. Which of the following is used to represent a sub expression?
    (a) [and] (b) (and)
    (c) { and } (d) < and >

18. Which of the following represents a positive look ahead regular expression?
    (a) pattern1(?!pattern2)
    (b) pattern1(?=pattern2)
    (c) pattern1(?|=pattern2)
    (d) pattern1(?==pattern2)

19. Which of the following represents a negative look ahead regular expression?
    (a) pattern1(?!pattern2)
    (b) pattern1(?=pattern2)
    (c) pattern1(?|=pattern2)
    (d) pattern1(?==pattern2)

20. Which of the following characters is used as a choice operator?
    (a) / (b) ^ (c) | (d) $

Review Questions

1. Distinguish between regular-expression-directed engine and text-directed engine.
2. What are the relative advantages of creating regular expressions using literals and constructor functions?
3. Mention the flags that can be used to control matching and searching.
4. What is meant by lazy regular expression engine?
5. Describe briefly the functionality of functions available on a regular expression object.
6. What are Meta characters?
7. Discuss the importance of string anchoring.
8. Discuss the different occurrence indicators available in JavaScript regular expressions.
9. What is a sub expression? Why is it used?
10. Explain the construct look ahead.
11. How many matches exist for this pattern?
    [135][246]
12. What regular expression special character(s) means "any character?"
13. What is wrong with this character class range? [A-z]
14. What string(s) does this regular expression match?
    August|April 5, 1908
15. Write a regular expression for the following:
    - All alphabetic characters
    - An e-mail address
    - A floating point number
    - A price up to 2 decimal digits
    - An IP address in dotted decimal notation. An IP address written in dotted decimal notation consists of 4 integers (from 0 to 255) separated by three dots (.)
    - An Ethernet address. An Ethernet address is written in the format hh-hh-hh-hh-hh-hh, where h is a hexadecimal number
    - Age
    - Name of a person
    - A telephone number
16. Write a JavaScript function to check if a string is only white space.

17 AJAX

Key Objectives

After completing this chapter readers will be able to—

- **understand the importance of AJAX technology**
- **learn how AJAX works**
- **send and retrieve HTTP requests and responses using JavaScript**
- **extract information using JavaScript XML DOM**
- **write interactive web applications using AJAX**

17.1 INTRODUCTION AND MARKETPLACE

AJAX is an acronym for **A**synchronous **J**avaScript **A**nd **X**ML. It is a technique for creating better, faster, and more interactive web applications with the help of XML, HTML, CSS, and JavaScript. Unlike classic web pages, which must load in their entirety if content changes, AJAX allows web pages to be updated asynchronously by fetching data from the server behind the scenes.

It provides a framework where JavaScript code can communicate with the server in a simple and standard way. AJAX commonly uses XML as the format for receiving server data, although any format, including plain text, can be used.

It is possible that you have already had a bitter experience while registering a new web site. Typically, it provides a large form to be filled up by you, with your preferred login name and other details. When you submit the form after filling up all the entries, it informs you that the preferred login name is not available and resets the entire form. You again fill up the form, and it again does the same thing. Think about a site that informs you immediately after entering the login name, whether it is available or not, thereby saving the time spent in filling up the entire form several times.

This idea can be extended to many other areas to provide additional functionality. Web applications using AJAX now act like desktop applications. It has become so popular over the years and that one hardly finds any web application being developed today without AJAX technology.

Many famous web applications now use AJAX technology. Following is a small list of such well-known web applications:

- Google Maps
- GMail
- Google

17.1.1 AJAX Benefits

Before AJAX, the client side of a web application could not communicate directly with the server without refreshing the page. AJAX makes this possible. AJAX allows the client and server of a web application to freely communicate with each other.

The primary purpose of AJAX is to modify the part of the web page already displayed in the browser's window without reloading the entire page. As it loads only the relevant portion instead of the entire page, it is faster than the traditional technologies.

AJAX allows JavaScript to communicate with the server *asynchronously*. JavaScript accepts a request from the user and sends it to the server using a separate thread. The user is free to do other things at that time. The response comes back, JavaScript code takes care about the response and displays the result (if any). This provides users a very friendly experience.

With the help of AJAX technology, we can make use of the power of a large number of client computers. It allows us to perform processing with data taken from server on the client computers. Therefore, it reduces the load on the server.

17.1.2 Basic Idea

Note that there is nothing new about AJAX technology. We request a file (possibly coded using technologies such as JSP, PHP, or ASP) using HTTP and receive a page as the response. This is exactly how the web works. The only thing AJAX does is that it allows us to make these requests and process the response using JavaScript.

Following is a typical sequence of actions that is executed by a web application to use AJAX technology:

- A user action, such as clicking on a button, triggers an event. This results in the calling of the associated event handler, which is very often a JavaScript function.
- Inside the handler, a special `XMLHttpRequest` object is created. This object is then configured with parameters such as the name of a *callback* function.
- The `XMLHttpRequest` object makes an asynchronous HTTP request to the web server for a designated resource.
- The resource is typically a server-side script written using JSP, ASP, PHP, etc. It receives the request, typically retrieves parameters and accesses the database if it needs to, and processes the data.
- The server-side script then returns data, typically as an XML document, to the original client-side page that made the request.
- The `XMLHttpRequest` object receives the XML data and invokes the callback function with this data.
- A JavaScript callback function catches the data, processes them, and updates the HTML DOM representing the page with the new data.

17.2 ENVIRONMENT REQUIRED

Though most of the currently available web browsers support AJAX technology, some do not. So, when you develop web applications using AJAX, you should check whether the browser running your application supports it. Here is the list of major browsers with their versions that support AJAX.

- Microsoft Internet Explorer 5 and above
- Mozilla Firefox 1.0 and above
- Netscape version 7.1 and above
- Apple Safari 1.2 and above
- Konqueror
- Opera 7.6 and above

17.3 ASYNCHRONOUS COMMUNICATION

The most interesting part of AJAX is that it allows users to fetch data from the web server asynchronously. However, what does "asynchronous" mean here? To understand this, let us recapitulate the HTTP protocol.

Remember that the HTTP protocol is a request–response protocol. It uses the client–server model of communication. In this protocol, a process (called server process or web server) runs (typically on port 80) and listens for incoming requests. We call this process 'server' as it provides 'service'. The most common service that it provides is sending resources (web pages) on request.

To get a service, for example, to get a web page, one can send an HTTP request to the web server according to the rules specified by HTTP. The server then accepts, processes, and understands the request and sends the response together with the data (if any) back to the process that made the request.

Figure 17.1 shows how AJAX technology works together to update a part of a page with new data from the server.

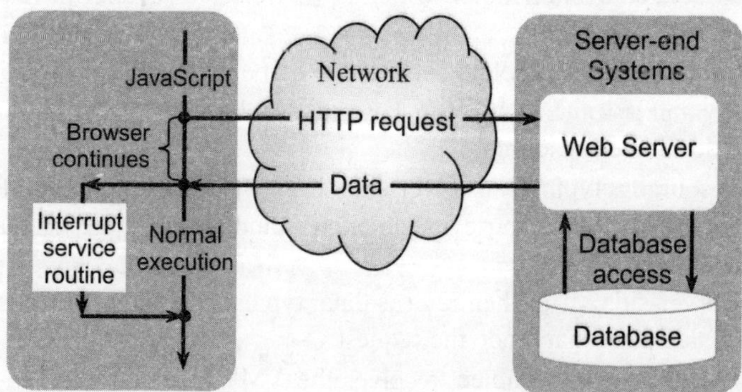

Figure 17.1 AJAX framework

JavaScript, like Java, also provides interfaces to work with the HTTP protocol, but in a slightly different way. We can use those interfaces to send a request to the web server and get the result. The result can then be processed and a specific portion of the web page can be modified.

The JavaScript HTTP interfaces are designed in such a way that it supports asynchronous communication. This means that when an HTTP request is sent [Figure 17.1] using these interfaces to the web server, the sender does not get blocked. It continues its normal execution as if nothing has happened. This is the "asynchronous" part of AJAX. Whenever the response comes back, the sender is interrupted. If the sender is configured properly before sending the request to the server, a JavaScript function (called callback service routine) or a piece of JavaScript code is executed as a part of this interrupt. The data returned by the server are processed in this function and a specific part of the web page is modified.

17.4 PROCESSING STEPS

To write an AJAX-based application, a programmer should follow the following three steps:

17.4.1 Create an `XMLHttpRequest` Object

The heart of the AJAX technology is the `XMLHttpRequest` object. It provides a set of useful properties and methods that are used to send HTTP request to and retrieve data from the web server. So, the first thing a programmer must do is to create an instance of the `XMLHttpRequest` object. Unfortunately, the procedure of creating such an instance is different for different browsers. We shall discuss methods to get such an object in different browsers such as Mozila, Opera, Safari, and Microsoft's Internet Explorer.

In browsers (such as Firefox, Opera, and Safari) except Microsoft's Internet Explorer, creating an `XMLHttpRequest` object is straightforward. Simply use the `XMLHttpRequest()` constructor to create the object. Here is an example.

```
xmlHttp = new XMLHttpRequest();
```

This piece of code attempts to create an `XMLHttpRequest` object using the constructor function `XMLHttpRequest()`. If it succeeds, an instance of the `XMLHttpRequest` object is created. If it fails, an exception is thrown and the program is terminated abruptly. This may happen for several reasons. It is possible that the browser used is Microsoft's Internet Explorer or that it does not support AJAX. If this happens, an alternative method should be used for the same. To avoid abnormal program termination, we can embed this piece of code in a `try–catch` block as follows:

```
try {
   xmlHttp = new XMLHttpRequest();
}catch(e) {
   //try other methods to obtain an XMLHttpRequest object.
}
```

Now, the program does not terminate abruptly. If anything goes wrong, the control comes to the catch block. In the catch block, we can try alternative methods to obtain an `XMLHttpRequest` object.

In Microsoft's Internet Explorer, an `XMLHttpRequest` object can be obtained using either of the following two methods.

```
xmlHttp = new ActiveXObject("Microsoft.XMLHTTP");
xmlHttp = new ActiveXObject("Msxml2.XMLHTTP");
```

These are also put in try–catch block to avoid abnormal program termination. So, the code to create an `XMLHttpRequest` object will finally look like this:

```
try {
   //try using non-IE browsers
   xmlHttp = new XMLHttpRequest();
}catch(e1) {
   try {
      //try first method of Internet Explorer
      xmlHttp = new ActiveXObject("Microsoft.XMLHTTP");
   }catch(e2) {
      try {
         //try second method of Internet Explorer
         xmlHttp = new ActiveXObject("Msxml2.XMLHTTP");
      }catch(e3) {
         //unable to create an XMLHttpRequest Object
         alert("Your browser does not support AJAX");
      }
   }
}
```

At this stage, if everything goes fine, an `XMLHttpRequest` object is created. The variable `xmlHttp` refers to this object.

17.4.2 Specify a Handler

When we use an asynchronous request, we cannot be sure when the response will come back. So, before we even think about sending the HTTP request to the web server, we must first specify a function (either named or unnamed) to be called when the HTTP response from the server comes back. We call this function "response handler". This function will receive information returned by the server, extract the desired data, and perform a specific task. The response handler is specified using the `onreadystatechange` property of the `xmlHttp` object. Here is an example.

```
// Create a function that will receive data sent by the server
function handler() {
   // code to extract and use data sent by the server
}
//specify the function handler() as the response handler.
xmlHttp.onreadystatechange = handler;
```

The handler may also be an anonymous function as follows:

```
xmlHttp.onreadystatechange = function () {
   // code to extract and use data sent by the server
}
```

The property, `onreadystatechange`, stores a function. As the name implies, every time the "ready state" changes this function gets executed. What is this "ready state" and what is its function here? The following section describes it.

17.4.3 AJAX `readyState` property

The process of communicating with the server, from sending an HTTP request to getting a response, involves several states. The state can be one of the following:

uninitialized, connection established, request sent, processing, completed, and response is ready.

These states occur in the order in which they are listed.

The `xmlHttp` object has a property called `readyState`, where the state of the HTTP request to be sent is stored. Each state is identified by a positive integer. The meaning of each ready state and its associated integer number is shown in Table 17.1.

Every time the state changes, the function indicated by the *onreadystatechange* property gets executed. In practice, we are particularly interested in the state *"completed"* because data (if any) are available only in this ready state. The *completed* state is represented by the integer 4. So, before doing anything, make sure that the state is *"completed"*, i.e., the value of the `readyState` property is 4. We add a conditional statement to check whether the state is *completed* or not.

```
function handler () {
   if(xmlHttp.readyState == 4) {   //if the request is complete
      // Get the data from the server's response
   }
   else {
      //request is not yet complete. So, response from server is not available.
   }
}
```

The response from the server can be retrieved from either the `responseText` or the `responseXML` property on the `XMLHttpRequest` object.

The AJAX `readyState` values for the various states are given in Table 17.1.

Table 17.1 AJAX readyState values

State	Value	Description
Un-initialized	0	After creating the XMLHttpRequest object, but before calling the open() method
Connection established	1	After calling the open() method, but before calling the send() method
Request sent	2	After calling the send() method
Processing	3	After calling the send() method but before getting the response
Completed and response is ready	4	After the request has been completed, and the response data have been completely received from the server.

The properties and methods of the `XMLHttpRequest` object are shown in Table 17.2.

Table 17.2 Properties of XMLHttpRequest object

Properties	Description
readyState	It indicates the state of the HTTP request to be sent to the server. The value of readyState property changes value from 0 to 4 during a request cycle
status	Returns the HTTP response status code (e.g., 200 for "OK" and 404 for "Not Found")
statusText	Returns the HTTP response status as a string (e.g., "OK" for 200 and "Not Found" for 404).
onreadystatechange	This is the method which is called every time ready state changes
responseText	Holds the response data from server as a string
responseXml	Holds the response data from server as an XML document, which can be parsed and processed using W3C DOM node tree methods and properties.

17.5 SENDING INFORMATION

Now that the response handler is ready, we can send the HTTP request to the server. Sending a request consists of two steps: *Opening a connection,* and *sending an HTTP request.*

17.5.1 Opening a Connection

Before sending an HTTP connection, we need to establish a TCP connection to the web server. The object `xmlHttp` has several overloaded methods to open a TCP connection to the server, as follows:

```
open( method, URL )
open( method, URL, async )
open( method, URL, async, userName )
open( method, URL, async, userName, password )
```

The most commonly used version is the second one, which takes three arguments:

- An HTTP method such as GET, POST, and HEAD
- The URL of the server resource
- A Boolean flag that indicates whether the request should be handled asynchronously (true) or synchronously (false)

A typical `open()` method call is as follows.

```
xmlHttp.open("GET", "getResult.jsp", true);
```

This function call shows that the HTTP GET method has to be used, that the URL of the resource is `getResult.jsp`, and that the request has to be handled asynchronously. URL-appended parameters may be passed to the server as follows:

```
xmlHttp.open("GET", "getResult.jsp?roll=1001", true);
```

17.5.2 Sending HTTP Request

Once the TCP connection is established, we can send the HTTP request to the server through this connection. The request is actually sent using the `send()` method on the `xmlHttp` object.

```
xmlHttp.send(null);
```

The value `null` is passed for the GET and HEAD methods. In such cases, parameters are appended to the URL and these parameters are added to the header of the HTTP request message. On the other hand, if the POST method is used, parameters are included in the body of the HTTP request message. In that case, we have to first set the `Content-Type` header to `"application/x-www-form-urlencoded;"` as follows:

```
xmlHttp.setRequestHeader("Content-Type", "application/x-www-form-urlencoded;");
```

It tells the server to retrieve data from the body of the HTTP request message. The actual parameters are included in the `send()` method as a name–value pair. So, the complete sequence for sending a request is

```
xmlHttp.open("POST", "getResult.jsp", true);
xmlHttp.setRequestHeader("Content-Type", "application/x-www-form-urlencoded;");
xmlHttp.send("roll=1001");
```

It is possible to send data in other formats, such as images or XML documents, using the POST method.

17.5.3 Method Type

Although several methods are specified in the HTTP specification, the most commonly supported and used methods are HEAD, GET, and POST.

HEAD

Remember, if the HEAD method is specified in the HTTP request, only the meta information about the URL is returned by the web server. So, if you want to get header information but not the resource body, use this method. A typical call will look like this:

```
xmlHttp.open("HEAD", "AJAXDemo.jsp", true);
```

The HTTP request is sent as follows:

```
xmlHttp.send(null);
```

The server response might look like this:

```
Server: Apache-Coyote/1.1
Content-Type: text/html
Content-Length: 84
Date: Tue, 13 Oct 2009 14:54:27 GMT
```

The headers may be retrieved as a single string using `getAllResponseHeaders()` on the `xmlHttp` object in the callback function.

GET

The HTTP GET method allows us to send parameters to the HTTP server as a part of the URL. The web server returns the header information as mentioned, together with the resource body. The parameters are sent as 'name=value' pairs separated by '&'. A typical call using the GET method looks like this:

```
xmlHttp.open("GET", "getResult.jsp?roll=1001&year=2009", true);
```

The HTTP request is sent as follows:

```
xmlHttp.send(null);
```

POST

In this case, parameters are not passed as a part of the URL; rather they are passed as a separate entity. A typical call using the POST method looks like this:

```
xmlHttp.open("POST", "update.jsp", true);
```

The HTTP request is sent somewhat differently in this case. Before sending the request you need to set the `Content-Type` header to "application/x-www-form-urlencoded;" as follows:

```
xmlHttp.setRequestHeader("Content-Type","application/x-www-form-urlencoded;");
```

It tells the server that the server should expect data that are specified in the `send()` method.

```
xmlHttp.send("name=Tom&designation=Lacturer&contact=9433880334");
```

The server application can extract those parameters for processing. Note that the HEAD and GET methods do not allow us to send parameters in this way. That is why the `null` value is passed.

17.5.4 URL

This is the URL of the server resource. Typically, it is a program written with any server-side technology such as JSP, ASP, and PHP, or a CGI technology. It may be a static HTML document also.

The URL may be absolute or relative. If a relative URL is used, make sure that the URL is locatable relative to the current web page from where the HTTP request is being sent.

17.5.5 Asynchronous and Synchronous Requests

The asynchronous flag is typically set to `true`. It makes the request asynchronous. In such a case, the browser can continue its normal execution [Figure 17.2(i)]. As a result, the user can interact with the browser even if the response is not complete. When the response comes back, a JavaScript function is executed, where we can process the data sent by the server.

The synchronous request (asynchronous flag set to `false`) leaves the browser in a waiting state until the response comes from the server and the service routine is executed [Figure 17.2(ii)]. During this time, the user cannot interact with the browser.

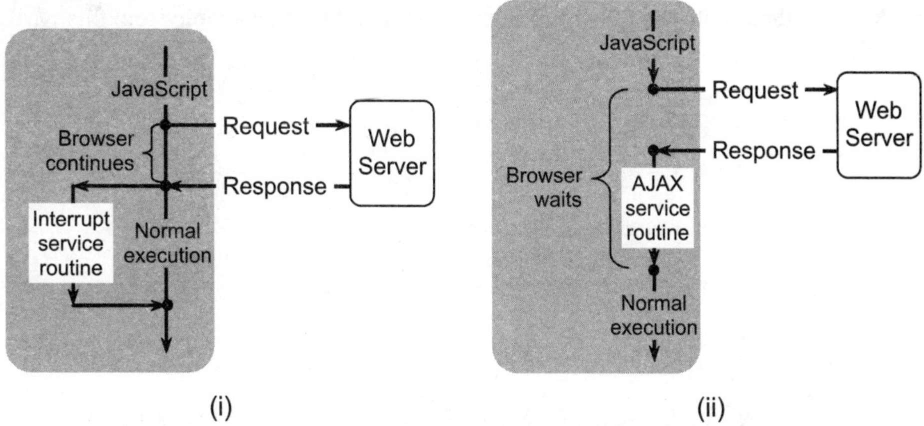

(i) (ii)

Figure 17.2 (i) Asynchronous request (ii) Synchrounous request

Table 17.3 shows the various `XMLHttpRequest` methods.

Table 17.3 XMLHttpRequest methods

Methods	Description

`open( method, URL )`
`open( method, URL, async )`
`open( method, URL, async, userName )`
`open( method, URL, async, userName, password )`
	Specifies the method, URL, and other optional attributes of a request.
	The method parameter is the HTTP method name such as "GET", "POST", and "HEAD".
	The "async" parameter specifies whether the request should be handled synchronously (true) or asynchronously (false).

`send("string")`	Sends the HTTP request to the server. null for a GET command (in native mode; null not passed with ActiveX)
`abort()`	Cancels the current request
`getAllResponseHeaders()`	Returns the complete set of HTTP headers as a string
`getResponseHeader(headerName)`	Returns the value of the specified HTTP header
`setRequestHeader(label, value)`	Adds a 'label: value' pair to the HTTP header to be sent

17.6 RETRIEVING INFORMATION

We can retrieve the server's response by using the `responseText` or `responseXml` properties. The response data may be a simple string or a complete XML document. If it is an XML document, JavaScript XML DOM may be used to retrieve information.

Consider that a server script returns an XML document as follows:

```
<info>
<country>India</country>
<population>1,161,580,000</population>
<percentage>17.15%</percentage>
<area>3,287,263</area>
<populationDensity>353</populationDensity>
</info>
```

We can then write the following JavaScript code to create a table from this XML document, as follows:

```
xmlDoc=new ActiveXObject("Microsoft.XMLDOM");
xmlDoc.loadXML(xmlHttp.responseText);
x = xmlDoc.getElementsByTagName("info")[0];
msg = '<table border="1" cellpadding="0" cellspacing="0">';
for(var i = 0; i < x.childNodes.length; i++) {
   name = x.childNodes[i].nodeName;
   value = x.childNodes[i].childNodes[0].nodeValue;
   msg += '<tr><td>'+name+'</td><td>'+value+'</td></tr>';
}
msg += '</table>';
document.getElementById('result').innerHTML = msg;
```

This generates the following HTML code table:

```
<table border="1" cellpadding="0" cellspacing="0"><tr><td>country</td>
<td>India</td></tr><tr><td>population</td><td>1,161,580,000</td></tr>
<tr><td>percentage</td><td>17.15%</td></tr><tr><td>area</td><td>3,287,263</
td></tr><tr><td>populationDensity</td><td>353</td></tr></table>
```

17.7 EXAMPLES

In this section, we shall discuss how to use AJAX technology in different practical situations.

17.7.1 Example 1

Here, we shall develop a small AJAX application. Consider the following HTML document `result.htm`.

```
<html>
   <head><title>AJAX Demo</title></head>
   <body>
      Enter Roll: <br>
      <input type='text' id='txtRoll' size="10" value='1001'/><br>
      <input type='button' value='getResult'  onClick='get()' />
      <span id='result'></span>
   </body>
</html>
```

It has one label "Enter roll", one text field, one button, and one `<span>` element. The small web page is intended for those users who want to know their result in an examination with a specified roll number. The user will provide the roll number in the text field. The AJAX will fill up the `<span>` element with the corresponding result upon clicking on the button captioned "getResult". We add a handler for the `click` event for this button.

```
<input type='button' value='getResult' onClick='get()' />
```

Inside the `get()` function, we first create an instance of the `XMLHttpRequest` object.

```
try {
   xmlHttp = new XMLHttpRequest();
}catch(e1) {
```

```
    try {
       xmlHttp = new ActiveXObject("Microsoft.XMLHTTP");
    }catch(e2) {
       try {
          xmlHttp = new ActiveXObject("Msxml2.XMLHTTP");
       }catch(e3) {
          alert('AJAX not supported');
          return false;
       }
    }
}
```

We then specify a function `processResponse()`, which will receive the data returned by the server. This is done by setting the `onreadystatechange` property of the `XMLHttpRequest` type object to the name of the function. We shall show the code of this function later in this section.

```
xmlHttp.onreadystatechange = processResponse;
```

Now, we can send an HTTP request to the server. However, before doing so, let us create the URL of the server. Suppose there exists a JSP page, `getResult.jsp`, that takes a roll number as an argument and returns the result. The result is a string: "Qualified", "Not qualified", or "Not found". We are assuming that the page `getResult.jsp` is placed in the same directory where `result.htm` is stored. The roll number is supplied by the user in the text box. So, we can get the value of the text box and form the URL by concatenating it.

```
var roll = document.getElementById('txtRoll').value;
var url = 'getResult.jsp?roll=' + roll;
```

To send an HTTP request to the server, we use the `open()` and `send()` methods. The `open()` method is used to create a TCP connection with the server. It takes three arguments. The first one indicates the HTTP method to be used. We shall use the HTTP GET method in our script. The second argument is the URL of the server-side program. The last argument indicates whether the request should be handled asynchronously (`true`).

```
xmlHttp.open("GET",url,true);
```

The request is actually sent off by the `send()` method.

```
xmlHttp.send(null);
```

We have to now specify what to do in the `processResponse()` function. Since the result is available when the request–response is complete (the value of the `readyState` property of the `XMLHttpRequest` object is 4), and the HTTP response status is 200 (OK), we add a conditional statement inside it.

```
if(xmlHttp.readyState == 4 && xmlhttp.status == 200) {
   //process result
}
```

The data sent by the server can be retrieved using the `responseText` property of `XMLHttpRequest`. We set the content of the `<span>` element with this data.

```
var sp = document.getElementById('result');
sp.innerText = xmlHttp.responseText;
```

Here is the complete HTML document, `result.htm`.

```
<html>
   <head><title>AJAX Demo</title>
      <script language="JavaScript">
         function get() {
            try {
               xmlHttp = new XMLHttpRequest();
            }catch(e1) {
               try {
                  xmlHttp = new ActiveXObject("Microsoft.XMLHTTP");
               }catch(e2) {
                  try {
                     xmlHttp = new ActiveXObject("Msxml2.XMLHTTP");
                  }catch(e3) {
                     alert('AJAX not supported');
                     return false;
                  }
               }
            }
            xmlHttp.onreadystatechange = processResponse;
            var roll = document.getElementById('txtRoll').value;
            var url = 'getResult.jsp?roll=' + roll;
            /* Set up the request */
            xmlHttp.open("GET",url,true);
            /* Send the POST request */
            xmlHttp.send(null);
         }
         /* The callback function */
         function processResponse() {
            if(xmlHttp.readyState == 4 && xmlHttp.status == 200) {
               var sp = document.getElementById('result');
               sp.innerText = xmlHttp.responseText;
            }
         }
      </script>
   </head>
   <body>
      Enter Roll: <br>
      <input type='text' id='txtRoll' size="10" value='1001'/><br>
      <input type='button' value='getResult'  onClick='get()' />
      <span id='result'></span>
   </body>
</html>
```

Some sample results, generated upon clicking on the button, are shown in Figure 17.3.

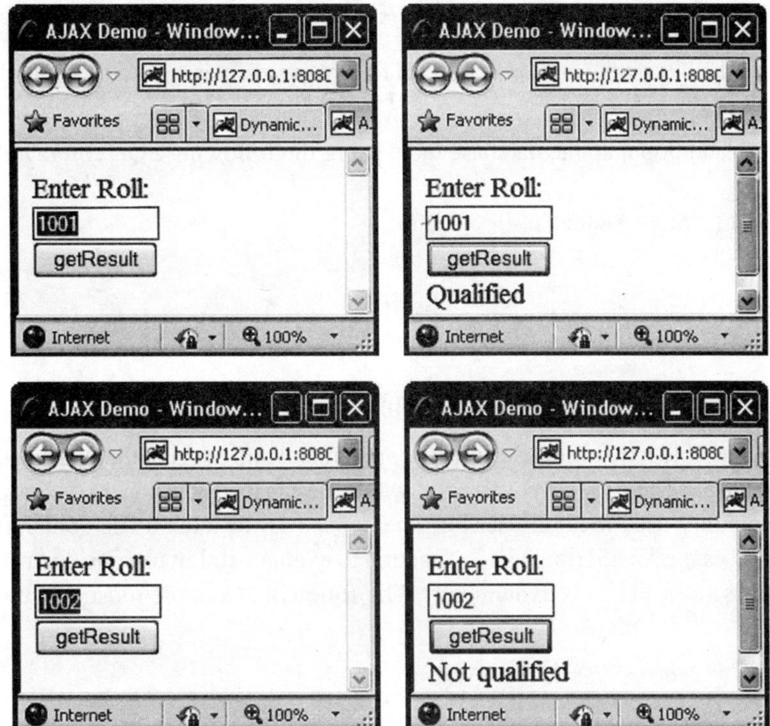

Figure 17.3 Retrieving result using AJAX

The code for `getResult.jsp` looks like this.

```
<%@page import="java.sql.*"%>
<%
  response.setDateHeader("Expires", -1);
  try {
    String driver = "org.gjt.mm.mysql.Driver";
    String url = "jdbc:mysql://thinkpad:3306/test";
    String user = "root", password = "nbuser";
    Class.forName(driver);
    Connection conn = DriverManager.getConnection(url, user, password);
    Statement stmt = conn.createStatement();
    String roll = request.getParameter("roll");
    String query = "select * from results where roll="+roll;
    ResultSet rs = stmt.executeQuery(query);
    String result = "Not found";
    if(rs.next())
      result = rs.getString("result");
    out.println(result);
  }catch(Exception e) {e.printStackTrace();out.println("Not found");}
%>
```

Note that most of the browsers cache pages and results. In such cases, if a user requests the same page before it expires, the cached result is returned. This cached result may not be consistent with the actual result stored in the database. To prevent caching, use the following instruction:

```
response.setDateHeader("Expires", -1);
```

It sets the "Expires" property of the HTTP response message to "1", which indicates that the page will never be cached.

Create and populate the database table using the following SQL commands.

```
CREATE TABLE results (
   roll      integer PRIMARY KEY,
   result       varchar(20)
);
INSERT INTO results VALUES(1001,'Qualified');
INSERT INTO results VALUES(1002,'Not qualified');
```

17.7.2 Using Dynamic Script Loading

It is also possible to load JavaScript code on demand and execute them. This is sometimes called "lazy loading". There are several ways in which we can load additional JavaScript code on demand. The commonly used method uses `XMLHttpRequest()` to fetch a file containing the JavaScript, and then uses the JavaScript `eval()` function to evaluate it. Let us consider an alternative method that creates `<script>` tags dynamically. The following example illustrates this.

```
<html>
   <head><title>Dynamic Script Loading Demo</title>
      <script type="text/javascript">
         function get() {
            var se = document.createElement("script");
            var roll = document.getElementById('txtRoll').value;
            var url = 'getResult.jsp?roll='+roll+'&func=callback';
            se.src = url ;
            document.body.appendChild(se);
         }
         function callback(responseText) {
            var sp = document.getElementById('result');
            sp.innerText = responseText;
         }
      </script>
   </head>
   <body>
      Enter Roll: <br>
      <input type='text' id='txtRoll' size="10" value='1001'/><br>
      <input type='button' value='getResult'  onClick='get()' /><br>
      <span id='result'></span>
   </body>
</html>
```

```
<%@page import="java.sql.*"%>
<%
   response.setDateHeader("Expires", -1);
   try {
      String driver = "org.gjt.mm.mysql.Driver";
```

```
        String url = "jdbc:mysql://thinkpad:3306/test";
        String user = "root", password = "nbuser";
        Class.forName(driver);
        Connection conn = DriverManager.getConnection(url, user, password);
        Statement stmt = conn.createStatement();
        String roll = request.getParameter("roll");
        String query = "select * from results where roll="+roll;
        ResultSet rs = stmt.executeQuery(query);

        String result = "Not found";
        if(rs.next())
           result = rs.getString("result");
        String func = request.getParameter("func");
        String str = func+"('"+result+"');";
        out.println(str);
     }catch(Exception e) {e.printStackTrace();out.println("Not found");}
%>
```

17.7.3 Example 2

This example demonstrates how a login page (`login.html`) performs user verification using AJAX technology, before forwarding the request to the actual page.

The login page has typically one text field and one password field, for the login name and password to be supplied by the user, and a submit button. When the user clicks on the submit button after supplying data in these two fields, the login page takes the login name and password and asks a JSP page, `login.jsp`, to verify the user information behind the scene before forwarding the request to the actual page. The page `login.jsp`, upon verification, returns a string ("OK", "Invalid login name", or "Invalid password") indicating the status of the verification. If anything goes wrong, the login page shows the information beside the corresponding text box, in red color, without refreshing the page. If the verification procedure succeeds, it forwards the request to another page, `home.jsp`.

Here is the source code for `login.htm`.

```
<html>
   <head><title>AJAX Demo</title>
      <script language="JavaScript">
         function check() {
            try {
               xmlHttp = new XMLHttpRequest();
            }catch(e1) {
               try {
                  xmlHttp = new ActiveXObject("Microsoft.XMLHTTP");
               }catch(e2) {
                  try {
                     xmlHttp = new ActiveXObject("Msxml2.XMLHTTP");
                  }catch(e3) {
                     alert('AJAX not supported');
```

```
                        return false;
                    }
                }
            }
            xmlHttp.onreadystatechange = processResponse;
            var login = document.getElementById('login').value;
            var password = document.getElementById('password').value;
            var url = 'login.jsp?login=' + login + '&password=' + password;
            xmlHttp.open("GET",url,true);
            xmlHttp.send(null);
        }
        function processResponse() {
            if(xmlHttp.readyState == 4 && xmlHttp.status == 200) {
                var res = xmlHttp.responseText.substr(2,
xmlHttp.responseText.length-1);
                eLogin = document.getElementById('lblogin');
                ePassword = document.getElementById('lbpassword');
                eLogin.innerText = "";
                ePassword.innerText = "";

                if(res == 'OK') {
                    frmLogin.action = 'home.jsp';
                    frmLogin.submit();
                }
                if(res == 'Invalid login name') {
                    eLogin.style.color='red';
                    eLogin.innerText=' Invalid Login';
                }
                if(res == 'Invalid password') {
                    ePassword.style.color='red';
                    ePassword.innerText=' Invalid password';
                }
            }
        }
    </script>
  </head>
  <body>
    <form name="frmLogin">
        Login: <input type="text" name="login"><span id="lblogin"></span><br>
        Password: <input type="password" name="password" ><span
id="lbpassword"></span><br>
        <input type="reset" value="Reset" onClick="return conf();">
        <input type="button" value="Login" onClick="check();">
    </form>
  </body>
</html>
```

Before writing the `login.jsp` page, create a table 'users' in MySQL 'test' database and insert data as shown in Figure 17.4.

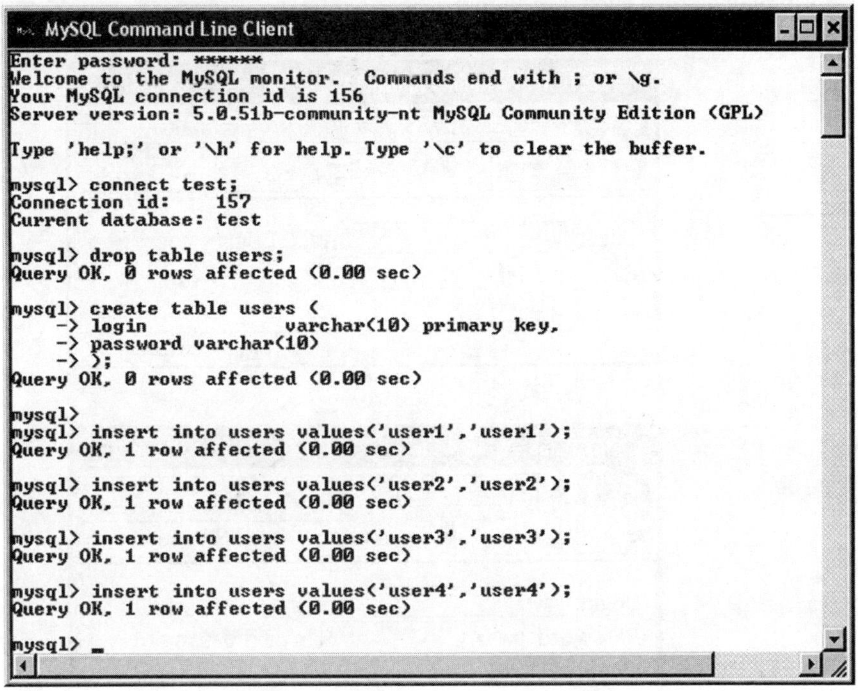

```
MySQL Command Line Client
Enter password: ******
Welcome to the MySQL monitor.  Commands end with ; or \g.
Your MySQL connection id is 156
Server version: 5.0.51b-community-nt MySQL Community Edition (GPL)

Type 'help;' or '\h' for help. Type '\c' to clear the buffer.

mysql> connect test;
Connection id:    157
Current database: test

mysql> drop table users;
Query OK, 0 rows affected (0.00 sec)

mysql> create table users (
    -> login           varchar(10) primary key,
    -> password varchar(10)
    -> );
Query OK, 0 rows affected (0.00 sec)

mysql>
mysql> insert into users values('user1','user1');
Query OK, 1 row affected (0.00 sec)

mysql> insert into users values('user2','user2');
Query OK, 1 row affected (0.00 sec)

mysql> insert into users values('user3','user3');
Query OK, 1 row affected (0.00 sec)

mysql> insert into users values('user4','user4');
Query OK, 1 row affected (0.00 sec)

mysql> _
```

Figure 17.4 Creating and populating 'users' table

The `login.jsp` page simply consults the table 'users' and returns a string that indicates the status of the user verification. Here is the source code of `login.jsp`.

```
<%@page import="java.sql.*"%>
<%
   response.setDateHeader("Expires", -1);
   try {
      String driver = "org.gjt.mm.mysql.Driver";
      String url = "jdbc:mysql://thinkpad:3306/test";
      String user = "root", password = "nbuser";
      Class.forName(driver);
      Connection con = DriverManager.getConnection(url, user, password);
      Statement stmt = con.createStatement();
      String login = request.getParameter("login");
      password = request.getParameter("password");
      String query = "select * from users where login='"+login+"'";
      ResultSet rs = stmt.executeQuery(query);
      if(rs.next()) {
         String pass = rs.getString("password");
         if(pass.equals(password))
            out.print("OK");
         else
            out.print("Invalid password");
      }
      else out.print("Invalid login name");
   }catch(Exception e) {e.printStackTrace();out.println("Invalid login name");}
%>
```

A sample output is shown in Figure 17.5.

Figure 17.5 User verification using AJAX (i) Invalid login name supplied (ii) Invalid password supplied

17.7.4 Example 3

This example (`info.htm`) provides a selection list consisting of the names of countries. When a user selects a country (change event), the info page `info.htm` consults a JSP page, `getInfo.jsp`, to get the information about this country selected. The `getInfo.jsp` page consults a database table and returns the result as an XML document. The `info.htm` page then extracts the necessary information, creates a table dynamically, and adds it to the `<div>` element with the id 'result'. Here is the source code of `info.htm`.

```
<html>
   <head><title></title>
      <script language="JavaScript">
         function getInfo(country) {
            try {
               xmlHttp = new XMLHttpRequest();
            }catch(e1) {
               try {
                  xmlHttp = new ActiveXObject("Microsoft.XMLHTTP");
               }catch(e2) {
```

```
                try {
                   xmlHttp = new ActiveXObject("Msxml2.XMLHTTP");
                }catch(e3) {
                   alert('AJAX not supported');
                   return false;
                }
             }
          }
          xmlHttp.onreadystatechange = processResponse;
          url = 'getInfo.jsp?country='+country;
          xmlHttp.open("GET",url,true);
          xmlHttp.send(null);
       }

       function processResponse() {
          if(xmlHttp.readyState == 4 && xmlHttp.status == 200) {
             try {
                xmlDoc=new ActiveXObject("Microsoft.XMLDOM");
                xmlDoc.loadXML(xmlHttp.responseText);
                x = xmlDoc.getElementsByTagName("info")[0];
                msg = '<table border="1" cellpadding="0" cellspacing="0">';
                for(var i = 0; i < x.childNodes.length; i++) {
                   name = x.childNodes[i].nodeName;
                   value = x.childNodes[i].childNodes[0].nodeValue;
                   msg += '<tr><td>'+name+'</td><td>'+value+'</td></tr>';
                }
                msg += '</table>';
                document.getElementById('result').innerHTML = msg;
             }catch(e) {alert(e);}
          }
       }
    </script>
 </head>
 <body>
    <select onChange="getInfo(this.value)">
       <option value="India">India</option>
       <option value="China">China</option>
       <option value="USA">USA</option>
    </select>
    <div id='result'></div>
 </body>
</html>
```

Before writing the getInfo.jsp page, create a table 'info' in the MySQL 'test' database and insert data as shown in Figure 17.6.

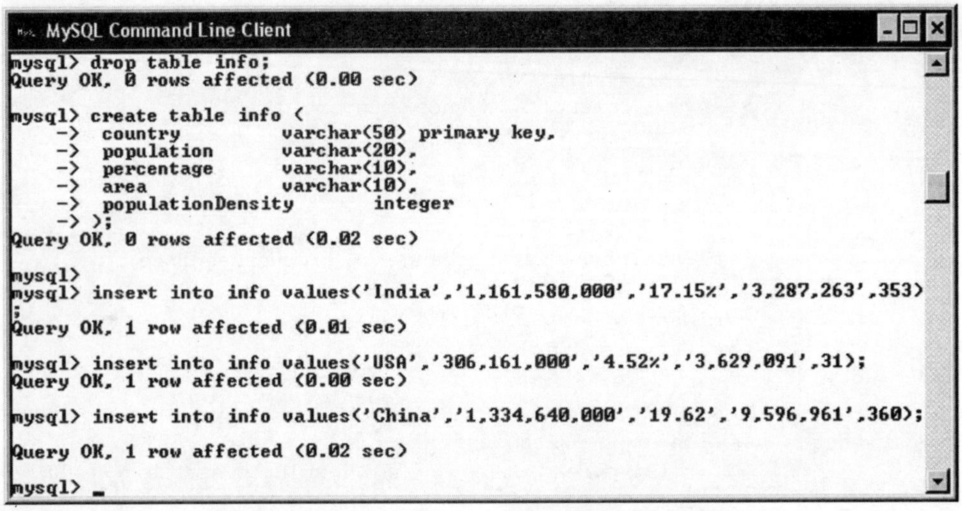

```
MySQL Command Line Client
mysql> drop table info;
Query OK, 0 rows affected (0.00 sec)

mysql> create table info (
    ->  country          varchar(50) primary key,
    ->  population       varchar(20),
    ->  percentage       varchar(10),
    ->  area             varchar(10),
    ->  populationDensity        integer
    -> );
Query OK, 0 rows affected (0.02 sec)

mysql>
mysql> insert into info values('India','1,161,580,000','17.15%','3,287,263',353)
;
Query OK, 1 row affected (0.01 sec)

mysql> insert into info values('USA','306,161,000','4.52%','3,629,091',31);
Query OK, 1 row affected (0.00 sec)

mysql> insert into info values('China','1,334,640,000','19.62','9,596,961',360);

Query OK, 1 row affected (0.02 sec)

mysql> _
```

Figure 17.6 Creating and populating 'info' table

Here is the source code of `getInfo.jsp`.

```
<%@page import="java.util.*, java.sql.*"%>
<%
   response.setHeader("Pragma", "no-cache");
   try {
      String driver = "org.gjt.mm.mysql.Driver";
      String url = "jdbc:mysql://thinkpad:3306/test";
      String user = "root", password = "nbuser";
      Class.forName(driver);
      Connection conn = DriverManager.getConnection(url, user, password);
      Statement stmt = conn.createStatement();

      String country = request.getParameter("country");

      ResultSet rs = stmt.executeQuery("select * from info where
country='"+country+"'");
      out.println("<info>");
      while(rs.next()) {
         String population = rs.getString("population");
         String percentage = rs.getString("percentage");
         String area = rs.getString("area");
         String populationDensity = rs.getString("populationDensity");


         out.println("<country>"+country+"</country>");
         out.println("<population>"+population+"</population>");
         out.println("<percentage>"+percentage+"</percentage>");
         out.println("<area>"+area+"</area>");
         out.println("<populationDensity>"+populationDensity+"</
populationDensity>");
      }
      out.println("</info>");
   }catch(Exception e) {e.printStackTrace();}
%>
```

A sample output is shown in Figure 17.7.

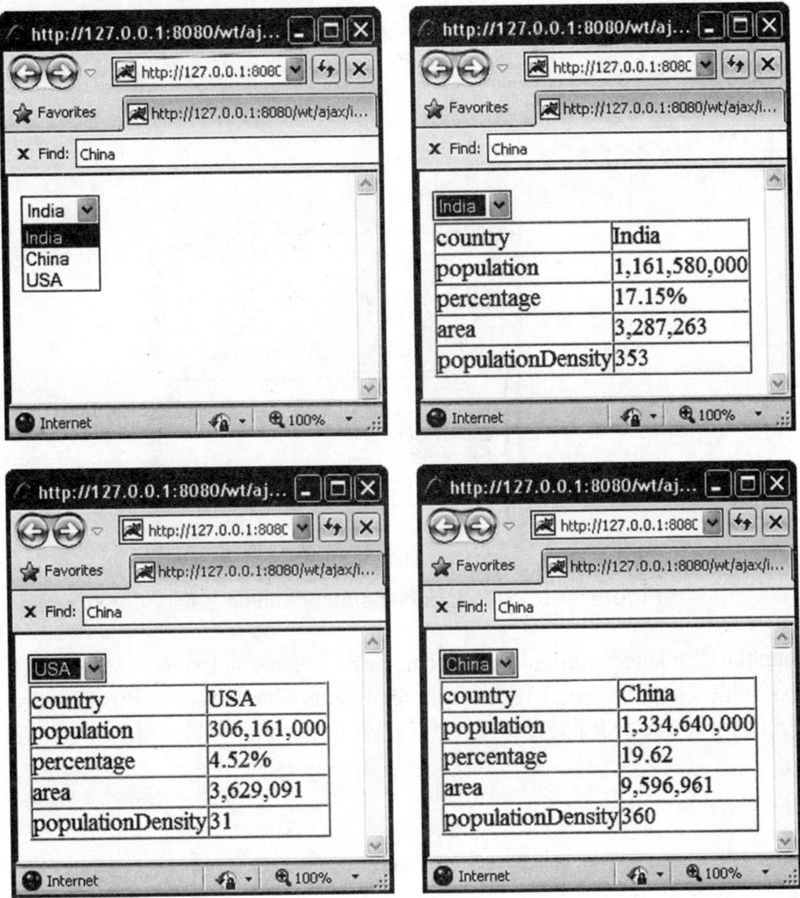

Figure 17.7 Getting information about countries using AJAX

17.8 USING XML

In the previous example, the server returns the result as a single string. If the server has to return much more information, XML is the best choice. In the next example, we shall use a JSP page that returns an XML document. It also demonstrates how to update employee information stored in the database server using AJAX technology without refreshing the page.

In this example, the HTML document provides a selection list [Figure 17.8] with a number of employee names. The HTML document looks like this.

```
<html>
   <head>
      <title>Update using AJAX</title>
   </head>
   <body>
```

```
        <select onChange="getInfo(this.value)">
           <option value="John">John</option>
           <option value="Jane">Jane</option>
           <option value="Tom">Tom</option>
           <option value="Jerry">Jerry</option>
        </select>
        <span id='panel'></span>
     </body>
  </html>
```

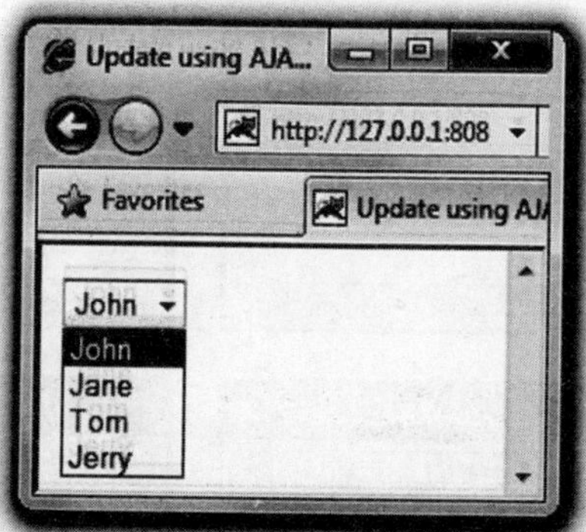

Figure 17.8 HTML document containing a list of employees

When the user selects (change event) an employee name from the selection list, the `getInfo()` function, which is the handler for the change event, gets called. In this function, AJAX sends an HTTP request to the JSP page `getEmp.jsp`, with the selected employee name as a parameter as follows.

```
function getInfo(emp) {
   try {
      xmlHttp = new XMLHttpRequest();
   }catch(e1) {
      try {
         xmlHttp = new ActiveXObject("Microsoft.XMLHTTP");
      }catch(e2) {
         try {
            xmlHttp = new ActiveXObject("Msxml2.XMLHTTP");
         }catch(e3) {
            alert('AJAX not supported');
            return false;
         }
      }
   }
   xmlHttp.onreadystatechange = processResponse;
   url = 'getEmp.jsp?name='+emp;
   xmlHttp.open("GET", url, true);
   xmlHttp.send(null);
}
```

It also specifies the function `processResponse()` as the callback function.

Given an employee name, the JSP page `getEmp.jsp` provides information such as name, designation, and contact number about that employee. This information is stored in the database. For this example, we shall use the MySQL database. A table `employee(name, designation, contact)` is created using the following SQL command.

```
CREATE TABLE employee (
   name        varchar(100)  PRIMARY KEY,
   designation varchar(50),
   contact     varchar(20)
);
```

Now, insert some data into the table using the following SQL commands.

```
INSERT INTO employee VALUES('John','Lecturer', '9433880334');
INSERT INTO employee VALUES('Jane','Sr. Lecturer', '9831962261');
INSERT INTO employee VALUES('Tom','Sr. Lecturer', '9433880334');
INSERT INTO employee VALUES('Jerry','Professor', '9830613450');
```

The JSP page, `getEmp.jsp`, takes a single parameter, name (the name of the employee), and retrieves the contact number and designation of the given employee from the database. It then creates and returns an XML document with this information. If it is invoked with the parameter `"John"` as `http://127.0.0.1:8080/wt/ajax/getEmp.jsp?name=John`, the following XML document is generated.

```
<?xml version="1.0" ?>
<employee>
  <name>John</name>
  <designation>Lecturer</designation>
  <contact>9433880334</contact>
</employee>
```

The code for `getEmp.jsp` is as follows.

```
<%@page import="java.sql.*"%>
<%
   response.setDateHeader("Expires", -1);
   try {
      String driver = "org.gjt.mm.mysql.Driver";
      String url = "jdbc:mysql://thinkpad:3306/test";
      String user = "root", password = "nbuser";
      Class.forName(driver);
      Connection conn = DriverManager.getConnection(url, user, password);
      Statement stmt = conn.createStatement();

      String name = request.getParameter("name");
      String query = "select * from employee where name='"+name+"'";

      ResultSet rs = stmt.executeQuery(query);
      out.println("<?xml version=\"1.0\"?>\n<employee>");
      rs.next();

      String contact = rs.getString("contact");
      String designation = rs.getString("designation");
```

```
        out.println("<name>"+name+"</name>");
        out.println("<designation>"+designation+"</designation>");
        out.println("<contact>"+contact+"</contact>");

        out.println("</employee>");

    }catch(Exception e) {e.printStackTrace();}
%>
```

Let us now discuss the code for the `processResponse()` method. JavaScript allows us to process XML documents according to the W3C DOM specification. This function parses the XML document upon receiving it from server, using DOM to get the desired information. For this XML document, it creates a table and a button as follows:

```
<table border="0">
    <tr>
        <td>name</td>
        <td><input type="text" id="name" value="John"></td>
    </tr>
    <tr>
        <td>designation</td>
        <td><input type="text" id="designation" value="Lecturer"></td>
    </tr>
    <tr>
        <td>contact</td>
        <td><input type="text" id="contact" value="9433880334"></td>
    </tr>
</table>
<button onClick="update()">Update</button>
```

This entire piece of HTML code is stored in the variable `msg` and then added to the `<span>` element having id "panel" using its `innerHTML` property. The code for the function `processResponse()` is as follows.

```
function processResponse() {
    if(xmlHttp.readyState == 4 && xmlHttp.status == 200) {
        try {
            xmlDoc=new ActiveXObject("Microsoft.XMLDOM");
            xmlDoc.loadXML(xmlHttp.responseText);
            children = xmlDoc.documentElement.childNodes;
            msg = '<table border="0">';
            for(var i = 0; i < children.length; i++) {
                name = children[i].nodeName;
                value = children[i].childNodes[0].nodeValue;
                msg += '<tr><td>'+name+'</td><td><input type="text" id="'+name+'"
value="'+value+'"></td></tr>';
            }
            msg += '</table><button onClick="update()">Update</button>';
            document.getElementById('panel').innerHTML = msg;
            document.getElementById("name").disabled = true;
        }catch(e) {alert(e);}
    }
}
```

The result is shown in Figure 17.9.

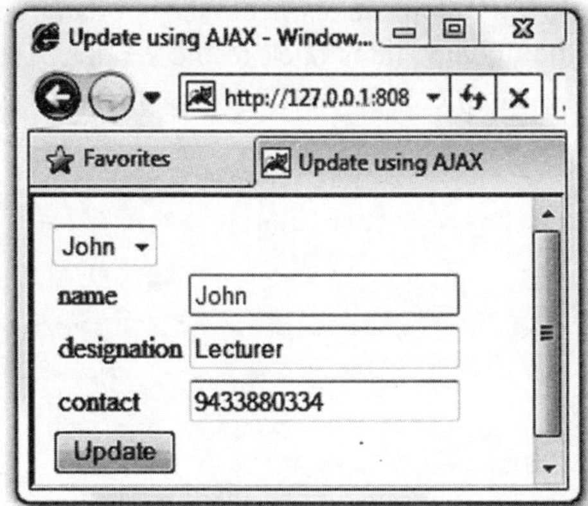

Figure 17.9 Retrieving employee information as an XML file

This interface [Figure 17.10] also allows users to edit information for this employee.

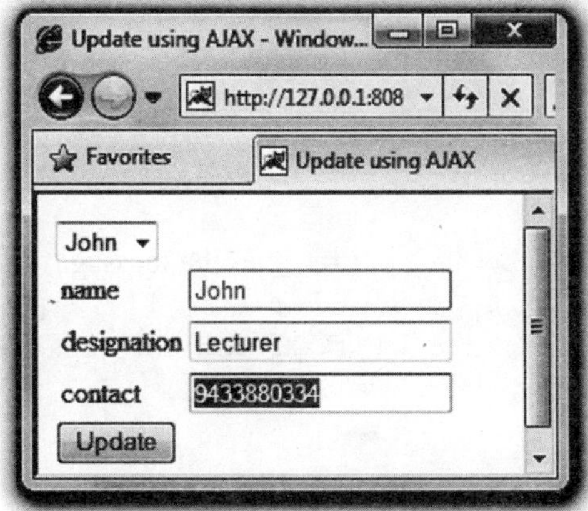

Figure 17.10 Editing employee information

The method `processResponse()` added a button captioned "Update". When this button is clicked on, the `update()` function gets called. The function `update()` extracts the edited designation and contact number, together with the employee name, and sends to the server for updates. It invokes the JSP page `updateEmp.jsp` with the information appended to it. It also specifies the `showMessage()` function as a callback function in this case.

```
function update() {
   n = document.getElementById("name").value;
   c = document.getElementById("contact").value;
   d = document.getElementById("designation").value;
   url = 'updateEmp.jsp?name='+n+'&contact='+c+'&designation='+d;
   xmlHttp.onreadystatechange = showMessage;
   xmlHttp.open("GET", url, true);
   xmlHttp.send(null);
}
```

The page `updateEmp.jsp` then makes necessary updates in the database table and sends a message representing the update status back to the sender. All these are accomplished without refreshing the page. The sample code for `updateEmp.jsp` is as follows.

```
<%@page import="java.sql.*"%>
<%
   response.setDateHeader("Expires", -1);

   try {
      String driver = "org.gjt.mm.mysql.Driver";
      String url = "jdbc:mysql://thinkpad:3306/test";
      String user = "root", password = "nbuser";
      Class.forName(driver);
      Connection conn = DriverManager.getConnection(url, user, password);
      Statement stmt = conn.createStatement();

      String name = request.getParameter("name");
      String contact = request.getParameter("contact");
      String designation = request.getParameter("designation");

      String query ="UPDATE employee SET contact='"+contact+"',
designation='"+designation+"' WHERE name='"+name+"'";
      stmt.executeUpdate(query);
      out.println("Updated successfully");

   }catch(Exception e) {e.printStackTrace();out.println("Failed to update");}
%>
```

When the function `showMessage()` receives the message, it displays it in an alert dialog box.

```
function showMessage() {
   if(xmlhttp.readyState == 4 && xmlhttp.status == 200)
      alert(xmlhttp.responseText);
}
```

The sample output is shown in Figure 17.11.

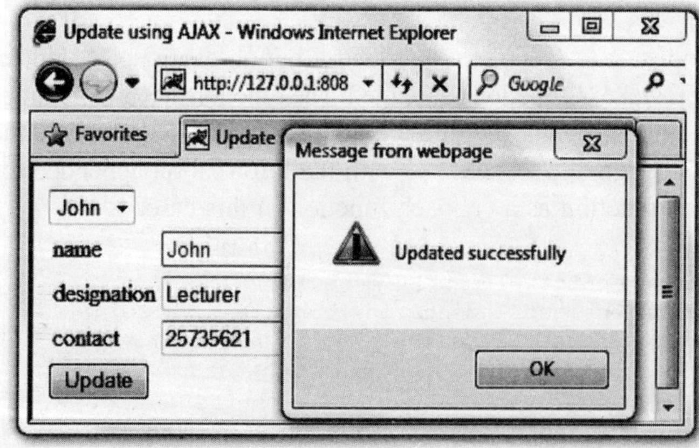

Figure 17.11 Saving employee information

KEYWORDS

Asynchronous communication: Ability to communicate with the server without blocking.

Callback function: The function that is called when the response comes back from the server.

Completed and response is ready state: Refers to the state that exists after the request has been completed, and the response data have been completely received from the server.

Connection established state: Refers to the state that exists after calling the `open()` method, but before calling the `send()` method.

Handler: The callback function as defined above is sometimes called as 'handler'.

onreadystatechange property: This property of the `XMLHttpRequest` object refers to the callback function, to be called when the response is received from the server.

Open method: Used to establish a TCP connection with the HTTP server.

Processing state: Refers to the state that exists after calling the `send()` method, but before getting the response.

Ready state: The process of communicating with the server, from sending an HTTP request to getting a response, involves several states called ready state.

readyState property: This property of the `XMLHttpRequest` object refers to the current state.

request sent state: Refers to the state that exists after calling the `send()` method.

responseText property: This property of the `XMLHttpRequest` object holds the response data from the server as a string.

responseXml property: The `XMLHttpRequest` object holds the response data from the server as an XML document, which can be parsed and processed using W3C DOM node tree methods and properties.

Send method: Used to send an HTTP request through the established connection.

status property: Refers to the HTTP response status from the server.

uninitialized state: Refers to the state that exists after creating the `XMLHttpRequest` object, but before calling the `open()` method.

XMLHttpRequest Object: The primary object in AJAX, which creates a framework to send and receive data to and from the server, respectively.

SUMMARY

AJAX is a technique for creating better, faster, and more interactive web applications with the help of XML, HTML, CSS, and JavaScript. It provides a framework where JavaScript code can communicate with the server in a simple and standard way. The most interesting part of AJAX is that it allows users to fetch data from the web server asynchronously. AJAX commonly uses XML as the format for receiving server data, although any format, including plain text, can be used. The primary purpose of AJAX is to modify the part of the web page already displayed in the browser's window, without reloading the entire page.

Though most of the currently available web browsers support AJAX technology, some do not. So, when we develop web applications using AJAX, we should check whether the browser running our application supports it.

The heart of the AJAX technology is the `XMLHttpRequest` object. It provides a set of useful properties and methods that are used to send HTTP request to and retrieve data from the web server. The procedure for creating an instance of the `XMLHttpRequest` object is different for different browsers.

Before sending a HTTP request to the web server, we must first specify a function to be called when the HTTP response from the server will come back. This function is called "response handler".

The process of communicating with the server, from sending an HTTP request to getting a response, involves several states: uninitialized, connection established, request sent, processing, completed and response is ready. Each state is identified by a positive integer.

To establish a TCP connection to the web server, the `open()` method on `XMLHttpRequest` type object is used. The HTTP request is sent to the server through this connection using the `send()` method on `XMLHttpRequest` type object.

The server's response is retrieved by using the `responseText` or `responseXml` properties on `XMLHttpRequest` type object.

WEB RESOURCES

http://www.w3.org/TR/XMLHttpRequest/
XMLHttpRequest, W3C Working Draft 19 November 2009

http://www.w3.org/TR/2000/WD-DOM-Level-1-20000929/
Document Object Model (DOM) Level 1 Specification (Second Edition), Version 1.0, W3C Working Draft 29 September, 2000

http://www.adaptivepath.com/ideas/essays/archives/000385.php
Ajax: A New Approach to Web Applications

http://www.wrox.com/WileyCDA/Section/id-303217.html
What is Ajax?

http://developer.apple.com/internet/webcontent/xmlhttpreq.html
Dynamic HTML and XML: The XMLHttpRequest Object

http://www.aaronsw.com/weblog/ajaxhistory
A Brief History of Ajax

http://tapestry.apache.org/tapestry4.1/ajax/json.html
JSON - JavaScript Object Notation

EXERCISES

Multiple Choice Questions

1. What is the full form of AJAX?
   (a) Asynchronous Java And XML
   (b) Asynchronous JavaScript And XML
   (c) Asynchronous JavaScript And XSL
   (d) Asynchronous Java And XML

2. Which of the following is the primary object type in AJAX?
   (a) AjaxHttp (b) XMLHttp
   (c) XMLHttpRequest (d) JavaScriptXML

3. Which of the following creates an XMLHttpRequest object in Microsoft's Internet Explorer?
   (a) xmlHttp = new ActiveXObject("Msxml2.XMLHttpRequest");
   (b) xmlHttp = new ActiveXObject("Msxml2.AJAX");
   (c) xmlHttp = new ActiveXObject("Msxml2.HTTPXML");
   (d) xmlHttp = new ActiveXObject("Msxml2.XMLHTTP");

4. Which of the following properties is used to specify a callback function?
   (a) onreadystatechange
   (b) oncallback
   (c) onreturn
   (d) onresponsereceived

5. Which of the following value is not a valid value of the readyState property?
   (a) 2 (b) 3 (c) 4 (d) 5

6. Which of the following values of the readyState property represents completed state?
   (a) 2 (b) 3 (c) 4 (d) 5

7. Which of the following properties of the XMLHttpRequest object is inspected to get the result from the server?
   (a) responseFromServer
   (b) responseText
   (c) response
   (d) textResponse

8. Which of the following functions is used to open a TCP connection to the server?
   (a) connect() (b) send()
   (c) doOpen() (d) open()

9. Which of the following functions is used to send an HTTP request to the server?
   (a) send() (b) pass()
   (c) doSend() (d) doPass()

10. What does the 'A' in AJAX stand for?
    (a) Autonomous (b) Advanced
    (c) Automatic (d) Asynchronous

11. What does the 'J' in AJAX stand for?
    (a) JavaScript (b) Java
    (c) Jscript (d) None of the above

12. Which of the following protocols is used by AJAX technology?
    (a) SMTP (b) FTP
    (c) HTTP (d) DNS

13. What does the 'X' in AJAX stand for?
    (a) XPath (b) XQuery
    (c) XSL (d) XML

14. Which one of these technologies is NOT used in AJAX?
    (a) CSS (b) DOM
    (c) DHTML (d) Flash

15. Which of the following functions is used to retrieve the HTTP response header?
    (a) getHeader() (b) getResponseHeader()
    (c) readHeader() (d) responseHeader()

16. Which of the following functions is used to set an HTTP request header?
    (a) setHeader()
    (b) requestHeader()
    (c) setRequestHeader()
    (d) readHeader()

17. Which of the following functions is used to retrieve all HTTP response headers?
    (a) getAll()
    (b) getHeaders()
    (c) getAllHeaders()
    (d) getAllResponseHeaders()

18. Which of the following HTTP methods can be used in AJAX?
    (a) GET (b) HEAD
    (c) POST (d) All of the above

19. Which of the following data formats is used by AJAX?
    (a) XML (b) JSON
    (c) Plain text (d) All of the above

20. Which of the following properties is used to retrieve the HTTP response status code?
    (a) status (b) statusText
    (c) statusCode (d) responseCode

Review Questions

1. What is the `XMLHttpRequest` object?
2. How do you get the `XMLHttpRequest` object?
3. How do you terminate the current `XMLHttpRequest`?
4. How do we create an `XMLHttpRequest` object for Internet Explorer? How is it different for other browsers?
5. What are the properties of the `XMLHttpRequest` object? What are the different values of readyState in AJAX?
6. What are limitations of AJAX technology?

18 APPLETS

Key Objectives

After completing this chapter readers will be able to—

- **understand the execution philosophy of applets**
- **understand the life cycle of an applet**
- **learn how to embed applets in HTML documents**
- **get an idea about methods available in the Applet class**
- **write basic applets**
- **understand the limitations of applets**

18.1 CLIENT-SIDE JAVA

Applets are nothing but Java programs that run usually within web browsers. They are typically embedded in an HTML page. A Java-enabled web browser downloads the class file of the applet together with the other parts of the web page from the web server and runs it in the client computer. Since applets run in the client computer, they are said to be client-side Java technology.

Unlike Java application programs, applets do not have any `main()` method. Instead, they have an `init()` method that can be used for a similar purpose. Applets do not have any constructor. The way instances of applets are created and run is completely different from the way objects are created in Java application programs. In this chapter, we shall focus on the structure of applets, their execution philosophy, and other applet-specific aspects.

18.2 LIFE CYCLE

An applet must be created by extending the `java.applet.Applet` class (Figure 18.1), which provides interfaces between the web browser and the applet. Java swing provides a special class, `javax.swing.JApplet`, which is a subclass of the `Applet` class. If you use swing components, you should create your applets by extending this `JApplet` class.

```
java.lang.Object
   java.awt.Component
      java.awt.Container
         java.awt.Panel
            java.applet.Applet
               javax.swing.JApplet
```

Figure 18.1 The applet class hierarchy

The class `Applet` provides a framework where your applets can run. It has a set of methods to control and supervise the execution of applets. These are called in a specific order during an applet's entire life cycle. A typical applet overrides these methods to do a designated task. Following is a brief description of these life cycle methods.

18.2.1 init()

This is the first method that gets called only once, when the applet is created and loaded by a web browser. Applets do not have any constructor. Since this method is called before all other methods, it can be used as a constructor. Consequently, the initialization code goes here. Usually, the piece of code that we write in the constructor is written here. Do not make this method large, resource-consuming, and computationally intensive. Otherwise, your applet will take a long time to load.

18.2.2 start()

This is the second method that gets called in the sequence. This starts the execution of an applet. It is also called every time an applet is restarted (revisited). If you want to perform a task after initialization, override this method. It is also overridden if a task has to be performed every time the web page containing the applet is revisited. It is also recommended to return from this method quickly. It is a good idea to start new threads, if you want to do any computationally intensive task.

18.2.3 paint()

This method is inherited from the `java.awt.Container` class. It is called when the applet starts its execution. This method is also called when the output of an applet is redrawn. There are several situations when an applet is redrawn.

- When the window containing the applet is minimized and restored
- When the applet's container window is overwritten by another window and is uncovered at some later point of time
- When the window containing this applet is moved/dragged to another location

This method takes a single argument of the type `Graphics`, which encapsulates the graphic window the applet is contained in. It has several useful methods that can be used to display something on the window.

18.2.4 stop()

This method is called when you switch to another window, leaving the current window containing the applet. So, you should suspend all threads that were started in the `start()` method so that they do not consume system resources. For example, if an applet shows some animation, you should suspend it when users are not viewing it.

18.2.5 destroy()

This method is called when the browser window containing the applet is closed (exited). Typically, you need not override this method. The `stop()` method calls this method after performing all the necessary tasks to shut down the applet. However, the method is still available to release other resources.

18.3 WRITING AN APPLET

Let us now write our first applet called `HelloWorld` which will display a simple message "Hello World!" on the screen. Following is the source code of the `HelloWorld` applet stored in the file `HelloWorld.java`.

```
//HelloWorld.java
public class HelloWorld extends java.applet.Applet {
     public void paint(java.awt.Graphics g) {
          g.drawString("Hello World!", 20, 20);
     }
}
```

Your applet must extend either the `java.applet.Applet` or the `javax.swing.JApplet` class. In this example, the class `HelloWorld` extends the `Applet` class and hence is an applet. It overrides only the `paint()` method to display a message on the screen. As mentioned earlier, the `paint()` method takes a `Graphics` object that represents the applet window. Numerous methods are available on this `Graphics` object, to display text and objects (such as circle, ellipse, line, and rectangle) on the screen. In this case, we have used the `drawString()` method, which takes three arguments: a string to be displayed on the screen and two integer arguments, which represent the x and y coordinates where the string is displayed.

18.4 COMPILING AN APPLET

Compiling an applet does not require any extra steps. Simply use the `javac` compiler bundled with the **J**ava **D**evelopment **K**it (JDK). Use the following command to compile our `HelloWorld` applet:

```
javac HelloWorld.java
```

This command generates a class file named `HelloWorld.class`, which contains the byte code for our `HelloWorld` applet. Make sure that the directory containing the `javac` compiler is included in your `PATH` environment variable.

18.5 THE APPLET TAG

Two HTML tags are used to work with applets: `<applet>` and `<param>`. An applet is typically embedded in an HTML document using the `<applet>` tag. The `<param>` tag is used to pass parameters to an applet. Some browsers provide the `<object>` or `<embed>` tag to include an applet. For more information, please see the documentation of your browser. The `<applet>` tag instructs the browser that an applet has to be loaded and executed using the **J**ava **R**untime **E**nvironment (JRE). It takes three mandatory attributes: `code`, `width`, and `height`. The `code` attribute specifies the class file for this applet to be instantiated. The `width` and `height` attributes indicate the width and height, respectively, of the applet window to be created. Create a simple HTML file, `HelloWorld.html`, as follows:

```
<!-- HelloWorld.html -->
<html>
   <head><title>Applet Demo</title></head>
   <body>
      <applet code="HelloWorld" height=50 width=150 >
      </applet>
   </body>
</html>
```

Now, open it in a browser. If the browser is Java-enabled, it understands the meaning of the `<applet>` tag. It loads the class file `HelloWorld.class` and executes it and places the result at the place of the `<applet>` tag. Note that the extension `.class` is not used in the `<applet>` tag. Put the `HelloWorld.class` file in the same directory as the `HelloWorld.html` file. If you want to deploy the applet on a web server, place these two files in the same folder. The result is shown in Figure 18.2.

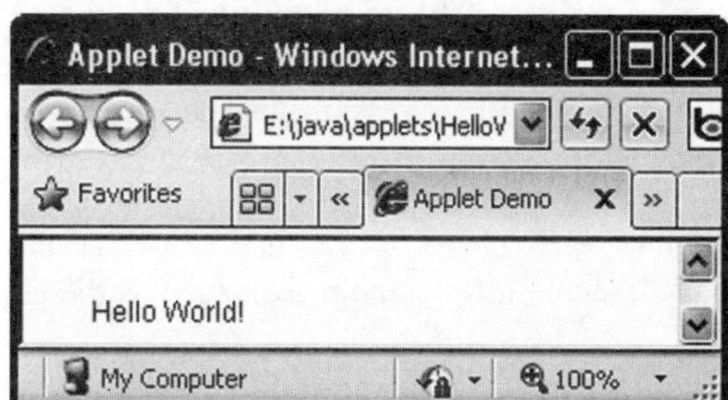

Figure 18.2 Result of HelloWorld applet

If you do not see the applet running, make sure that at least the **J**ava **2** **S**tandard **E**dition (J2SE) platform is installed in your client computer and linked with the browsers. Most often the browsers have their own **J**ava **R**untime **E**nvironment (JRE) to interpret applets. Alternatively, you can use the application `appletviewer`, which comes with JDK, as follows.

```
appletviewer HelloWorld.html
```

The output (Figure 18.3) now looks exactly the same except that it creates a window with a different appearance.

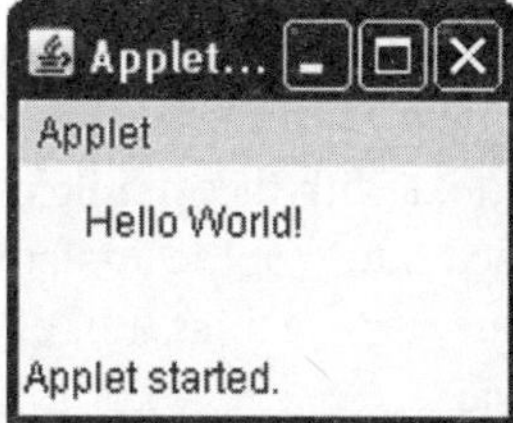

Figure 18.3 Result of HelloWorld applet using appletviewer

Note that the application `appletviewer` can be used for only testing purposes as it cannot download the class file from the remote web server.

The `<applet>` tag takes several other optional attributes. It takes the following general form:

```
<applet
   code='appletClassFile'
   [codebase='URLOfCodeBase']
   [alt='altervativeText']
   [name='NameOfApplet']
   width='width of Applet window in pixels'
   height='height of Applet window in pixels'
   [align='alignment']
   [vspace='pixels']
   [hspace='pixels']
```

The optional attributes are shown in square brackets. Let us discuss the functionality of each of these attributes.

`code` – This attribute specifies the name of the class file (without the extension `.class`) that contains the applet's byte code.

`codebase` – It specifies the base URL to be searched for the applet's executable class file. If nothing is mentioned, the directory from where the HTML document containing this applet was downloaded is assumed. In such cases, you must put the applet's class file and the HTML document in the same directory. However, different URLs may also be used with some restrictions.

`alt` – It specifies a message to be displayed if the browser has been able to understand the applet, but has failed to execute it for some reason such as the user turning off the applet.

`name` – This attribute specifies a name for an applet instance. Other applets use this name to find it and communicate with it.

`width` – It is the width of the applet window in pixels.

`height` – It is the height of the applet window in pixels.

`align` – It is used to adjust the position of an applet with respect to the surrounding text and images. It can have the following values:

- `left` — It puts the applet on the left side of the page and causes text to wrap around it.
- `right` — It puts the applet on the right side of the page and causes text to wrap around it.
- `top` — It aligns the top of the applet with the top of the text.
- `bottom` — It aligns the bottom of the applet with the bottom of the text.
- `middle` — This value works differently in different browsers. In some browsers, it aligns the middle of the text with the middle of the applet. In some other browsers, it aligns the bottom of the text with the middle of the applet window.
- `baseline` — It aligns the bottom of the applet with the baseline of the text. The baseline is the bottom line of characters such as a b, c, d, and e. Some letters such as g, j, and p dangle below this baseline.

`vspace` – It specifies the space to be left above and below of the applet window, in pixels.

`hspace` – It specifies the space to be left on the left and right of the applet window, in pixels.

18.6 SECURITY

Java applets were introduced a long time ago to provide animations in web pages. Applets are not architected for large applications. So, your applets should be small in size and should not perform computationally intensive tasks. Moreover, applets, after being downloaded from the server, run on the client machine. Several restrictions are introduced for security reasons. You should be aware of those limitations if you are going to develop applets. Applets should not be allowed to do the following:

- Reading, writing, creating, and destroying files on the local file system
- Sending sensitive information to other potentially vulnerable computers over the network
- Creating potentially destructive/malicious processes
- Writing virus programs that destroy your data or perform other malicious events.

Taking these points into consideration, many constraints are imposed, some of which are as follows:

Limitations on Read and Write

Applets cannot access (i.e., read from or write into) the local file system. This restriction is imposed on the applets to prevent searching and sending of valuable information, or even formatting of the hard disk, upon being downloaded onto the client's computer. Applets cannot create any file in the local file system.

Limitations on Connectivity

Applets cannot create any network connection or transfer data except the one from which they were downloaded. If it were allowed, the developer would be able to write malicious applets that send sensitive information from the client's computer to other computers.

Limitations on Native Library Access

Applets are not allowed to access native libraries from other languages such as C++ though Java applications do so. If this were allowed, there would be no way to prevent applets sitting on the client's computer from calling native methods that perform malicious actions.

Limitations on Process Creation

Applets are not allowed to spawn new processes from them. If this were allowed, users could write malicious applets that spawn too many new processes. These processes could make all the resources of the client computer busy. However, applets are allowed to create threads since threads belong to the same address space of the applet and cannot do much.

Limitations on Events

Applets cannot detect or handle events that occur outside the applet area.

18.7 UTILITY METHODS

The `Applet` class provides a set of useful methods (in addition to the five methods `init()`, `start()`, `paint()`, `stop()`, and `destroy()`) that can be used for different purposes. A brief description of commonly used methods is given here:

`isActive()` — Returns `true` if the applet is active, `false` otherwise. An applet becomes active just before the `start()` method is called and becomes inactive just before the `stop()` method is called.

`resize(int width, int height)` — Sets the size of the applet's window with the specified width and height.

`resize(Dimension new)` — Sets the size of the applet with the specified dimension.

`showStatus(String message)` — Displays the specified message in the status bar of the browser's window.

`getDocumentBase()` — Returns the URL of the document containing this applet.

`getCodeBase()` — Returns the URL of the base directory from which this applet was loaded.

`getParameter(String param)` — Returns the value of the specified parameter passed to this applet.

`getParameterInfo()` — Returns a two-dimensional array of strings that contains information about the parameters that this applet understands.

`getAppletContext()` — Returns a `java.applet.AppletContext` object that represents applet's context, which allows us to query, and affects applet's environment.

`getAppletInfo()` — Returns information about the applet as a string.

`getImage(URL url)` — Returns an `Image` object from the specified URL of the image.

`getImage(URL base, String name)` — Returns an `Image` object from the specified base URL and relative name of the image.

`newAudioClip(URL)` — Creates an `AudioClip` object specified by the URL.

`getAudioClip(URL)` — Returns an `AudioClip` object specified by the absolute URL argument.

`getAudioClip(URL, String)` — Returns an `AudioClip` object specified by the absolute base URL and relative name arguments.

`play(URL)` — Plays an audio clip specified by the absolute URL.

`play(URL, String)` — Plays an audio clip specified by the absolute base URL and a relative name.

18.8 USING STATUS BAR

You can display a short message on the status bar of the window using the `showStatus()` method. Consider the following applet:

```
//Status.java
public class Status extends java.applet.Applet {
   public void paint(java.awt.Graphics g) {
      setBackground(java.awt.Color.gray);
      g.drawString("This is in the applet window", 20, 30);
      showStatus("This is shown in the status window");
   }
}
```

Now, create an HTML document containing an `<applet>` tag as follows:

```
<applet code="Status" width="200" height="50">
</applet>
```

The appletviewer results the output as shown in Figure 18.4.

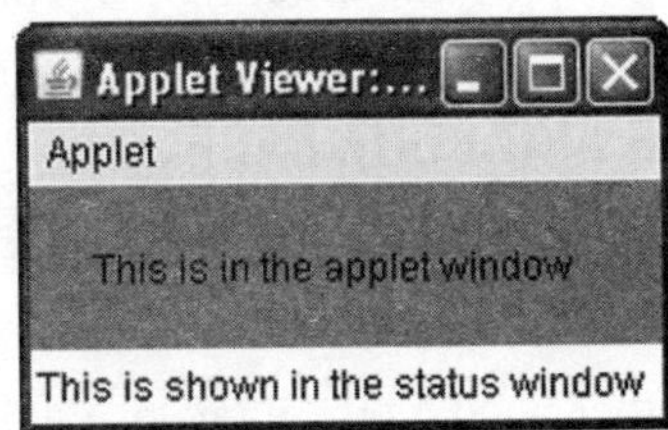

Figure 18.4 Displaying a message on the status bar

18.9 APPLETCONTEXT INTERFACE

The `Applet` API provides an interface, `java.applet.AppletContext`, which can be used to interact with the environment where the applet runs. For example, we can manipulate the containing web page, load a URL, interact with the JavaScript code embedded in the web page, communicate with other applets running in the same web page, and so on.

An `AppletContext` object is obtained using `getAppletContext()` on the `Applet` object. The prototype declaration of this method is as follows:

```
public java.applet.AppletContext getAppletContext();
```

The following code shows how to obtain an `AppletContext` object.

```
AppletContext ac = getAppletContext();
```

The `AppletContext` interface provides several useful methods, some of which are mentioned as follows:

`AudioClip getAudioClip(URL url);`

Returns an `AudioClip` object from the specified URL.

`Image getImage(URL url);`

Returns an `Image` object, which can be painted on the screen, from the specified URL.

`Applet getApplet(String appletName)`
Finds and returns an `Applet` object that exist in the same context, with the specified name.

`Enumeration getApplets();`
Finds and returns all applets that exist within the same context.

`void showDocument(URL url)`
Loads the specified URL in the current window.

`void showDocument(URL url, String targetWindow)`
Loads the specified URL in the specified window.

`void showStatus(String message)`
Displays a short message on the status bar.

`void setStream(String key, InputStream stream)`
Binds the specified stream with the specified key in this applet context.

`InputStream getStream(String key);`
Returns the stream associated with the specified key within this applet context.

`Iterator getStreamKeys();`
Returns a list of keys of the streams in this applet context.

18.10 DOCUMENT BASE AND CODE BASE

The document base is the URL of the HTML file containing this applet. The method `getDocumentBase()` returns this URL.

The code base, on the other hand, is the name of the base directory from where the applet's class file was loaded. The values of the document base and code base are the same, unless the `codebase` attribute of the `<applet>` tag is used.

Typically, a code base (if specified) refers to a subdirectory of the document base directory. This is because browsers restrict applets from accessing arbitrary URLs. If access permission is given to the document base, subdirectories have similar permissions. So, specifying a subdirectory as the code base is always safe. Consider the following applet (`Bases.java`), which displays the code base and document base.

```
//Bases.java
public class Bases extends java.applet.Applet {
   public void paint(java.awt.Graphics g) {
      g.drawString("Document base : " + getDocumentBase(), 20, 10);
      g.drawString("Code base : " + getCodeBase(), 20, 30);
   }
}
```

Now, compile this applet and create an HTML page containing the following:

```
<applet code="Bases" codebase="./applets" width="400" height="40">
</applet>
```

The result is shown in Figure 18.5.

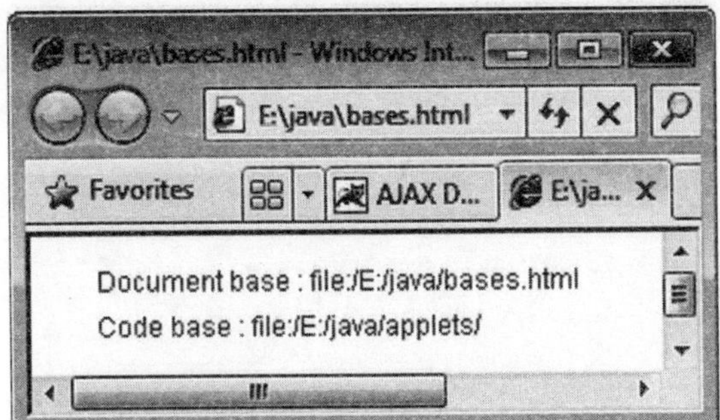

Figure 18.5 Document base and code base

18.11 PASSING PARAMETER

Like command line arguments, parameters can be passed to applets. Applets can access those parameters and customize their tasks. This helps applets to work with different situations without recompiling the source code.

Parameters are passed to the applet using the `<param>` child tag of the `<applet>` tag. Each <param> tag passes one parameter. It has two attributes, `name` and `value`. The `name` attribute indicates the name of the parameter to be passed and the `value` attribute specifies the value of the parameter. Consider the following code:

```
<applet code="ParamDemo" width="200" height="60">
   <param name="fontColor" value="FF0000">
   <param name="bgColor" value="EEEEEE">
</applet>
```

It calls the `ParamDemo` applet with two parameters `fontColor` and `bgColor`, whose values are “FF0000” and “EEEEEE”, respectively.

18.11.1 Retrieving Parameter

Parameters are retrieved from an applet using the `getParameter()` method. This methods takes the name of the parameter as an argument and returns the value of the parameter as a `String`. The prototype declaration of this method is as follows:

```
public java.lang.String getParameter(java.lang.String);
```

The following code shows how to retrieve the parameters using the `getParameter()` method.

```
//ParamDemo.java
import java.awt.*;
import java.applet.*;
public class ParamDemo extends Applet {
   String fontColor, bgColor;
   public void init() {
      fontColor = getParameter("fontColor");
      bgColor = getParameter("bgColor");
   }
   public void paint(Graphics g) {
```

```
        setBackground(color(bgColor));
        g.setColor(color(fontColor));
        g.drawString("Font Color :" + fontColor, 20, 20);
        g.drawString("Background color:" + bgColor, 20, 40);
    }
    public Color color(String color) {
        int c = Integer.parseInt(color, 16);
        int red = c / (256 * 256);
        int green = (c / 256) % 256;
        int blue = c % 256;
        return new Color(red, green, blue);
    }
}
```

The result is shown in Figure 18.6 (i). The following code results in the output as shown in Figure 18.6 (ii).

```
<applet code="ParamDemo" width="200" height="60">
   <param name="fontColor" value="FFFFFF">
   <param name="bgColor" value="AAAAAA">
</applet>
```

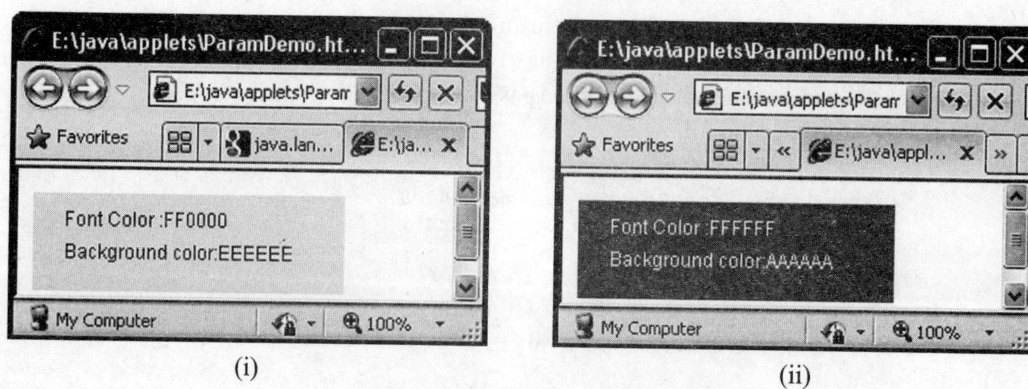

Figure 18.6 Parameter passing in applets

Note that the method `getParameter()` always returns the value of the specified parameter as a string. It is typically converted to the desired type. For example, in the `ParamDemo` applet, the value of the `fontColor` and `bgColor` parameters is a hexadecimal RGB value. To get the actual color from it, we have first converted it into an integer value using the `Integer.parseInt()` method. Then, we have extracted red, green, and blue components and finally created a color with these components.

18.12 EVENT HANDLING

The event handling mechanism is the same as the Java Application program. The following applet demonstrates this:

```
//MouseEventDemo.java
import java.awt.*;
import java.applet.*;
import java.awt.event.*;
public class MouseEventDemo extends Applet implements MouseListener {
   String msg = "";
   int x = 0, y = 0;
   public void init() {
      addMouseListener(this);
   }
   public void paint(Graphics g) {
      g.drawString(msg, x, y);
   }
   public void mouseClicked(MouseEvent me) {
      x = me.getX();
      y = me.getY();
      msg = "clicked";
      repaint();
   }
   public void mouseEntered(MouseEvent me) {
      x = y = 10;
      msg = "entered";
      repaint();
   }
   public void mouseExited(MouseEvent me) {
      x = y = 10;
      msg = "exited";
      repaint();
   }
   public void mousePressed(MouseEvent me) {
      x = me.getX();
      y = me.getY();
      msg = "pressed";
      repaint();
   }
   public void mouseReleased(MouseEvent me) {
      x = me.getX();
      y = me.getY();
      msg = "released";
      repaint();
   }
}
```

Now create the following applet, which results in the output shown in Figure 18.7.

```
<applet code="MouseEventDemo" width="200" height="50">
</applet>
```

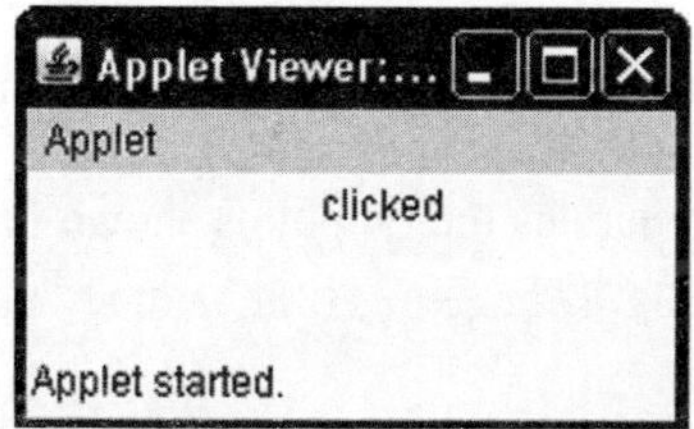

Figure 18.7 Event handling in applets

18.13 COMMUNICATION BETWEEN TWO APPLETS

It is possible to find other applets from within an applet and communicate with them. There are two ways an applet can find other applets.

Using `getApplet()` method

The `getApplet()` method on the `AppletContext` interface takes the following form:

```
Applet getApplet(String appletName);
```

The `getApplet()` method returns an `Applet` object with the specified name. The name of an applet is the one that is specified by the `name` attribute of the `<applet>` tag. Since the `getApplet()` method returns a generic `Applet` object, it is typically converted to your custom applet object. Suppose, the name of your applet class is `Server` and an instance is created with the name "server". A reference to this applet can be obtained from another applet `Client` as follows:

```
AppletContext ac = getAppletContext();
Server s = (Server) ac.getApplet("server");
```

Once a reference to an applet is obtained, methods can be invoked on it.

Using `getApplets()` method

The `getApplets()` method on the `AppletContext` interface takes the following form:

```
Enumeration getApplet(String appletName);
```

Essentially, it returns a list of all applets available in the same context as this applet. In the following code, e is a list of applets. We can now iterate through the list to get individual applets.

```
Enumeration e = getAppletContext().getApplets();
```

The following example shows how to find other applets.

```
//GetAppletDemo.java
import java.awt.*;
import java.applet.*;
public class GetAppletsDemo extends Applet {
   public void paint(Graphics g) {
      AppletContext ac = getAppletContext();
      java.util.Enumeration e = ac.getApplets();
      while (e.hasMoreElements()) {
         Applet a = (Applet) e.nextElement();
         g.drawString(a.toString() + " " + a.getClass().getName(), 20, 20);
      }
   }
}
```

The following applet generates the output as shown in Figure 18.8.

```
<applet code="GetAppletsDemo" width="500" height="40">
</applet>
```

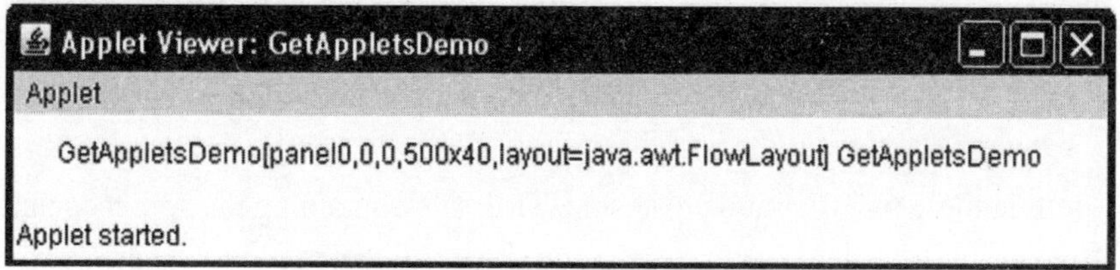

Figure 18.8 Finding all applets

18.13.1 A Sample Application

Now, let us develop a simple but elegant application that demonstrates how two applets communicate with each other. In this application, the applet `Client` sends an integer to another applet `Server`. The `Server` applet simply returns the square of the number. Finally, `Client` displays the result. The source code for the `Server` applet (`Server.java`) is as follows.

```
//Server.java
public class Server extends Applet {
   int val = 1, result = 0;
   public void paint(java.awt.Graphics g) {
      setBackground(java.awt.Color.LIGHT_GRAY);
      g.drawString("Server", 20, 20);
      g.drawString("received :" + String.valueOf(val), 20, 40);
      g.drawString("Sent  :" + String.valueOf(result), 20, 60);
   }
   public int sqr(int n) {
      val = n;
      result = n * n;
      repaint();
      return result;
   }
}
```

The `Server` applet has a public method `sqr()`, which takes an integer and returns its square. The `Client` applet will use this method to send an integer and get the result. The source code for the `Client` applet (`Client.java`) is as follows:

```
//Client.java
import java.awt.*;
import java.applet.*;
public class Client extends Applet {
   int n = 2, result;
   Server s;
   public void init() {
      String param = getParameter("calculator");
      AppletContext ac = getAppletContext();
      Server s = (Server) ac.getApplet(param);
   }
   public void paint(Graphics g) {
      setBackground(Color.LIGHT_GRAY);
      result = s.sqr(n);
      g.drawString("Client", 20, 20);
```

```
        g.drawString("Sent:  \n" + String.valueOf(n), 20, 40);
        g.drawString("Received:  " + String.valueOf(result), 20, 60);
    }
}
```

Compile these two files and create an HTML file containing the applet declaration as follows:

```
<applet code="Server" width="200" height="80" name="server">
</applet>

<applet code="Client" width="200" height="80" name="client">
<param name="calculator" value="server">
</applet>
```

Create a `Server` applet first, with the name "server". Now, create a `Client` applet and pass the parameter `calculator` with the value "server". The `Client` applet first gets the value of the parameter. It then finds the applet having this name. If you open this HTML document in a browser, it appears as shown in Figure 18.9.

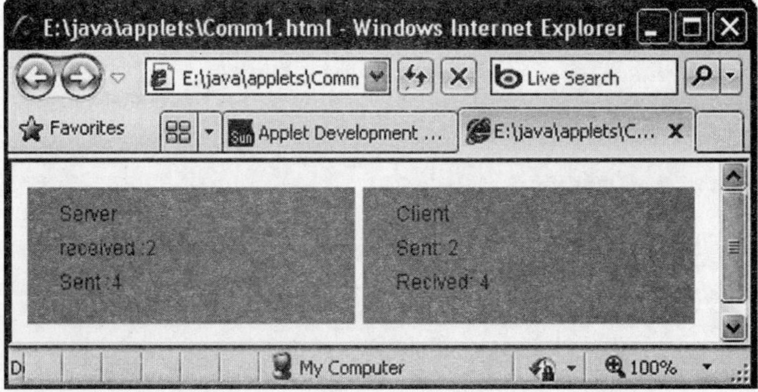

Figure 18.9 Communication between two applets

18.14 LOADING WEB PAGES

You can load a web page in the browser's window using the `showDocument()` method on the `AppletContext` object. It takes the following forms:

```
void showDocument(URL url)
void showDocument(URL url, String targetWindow)
```

The first form takes a URL argument and loads it in the current window. The second form allows us to load the URL in the specified window. The second argument can have the following values:

- `_blank` — Loads the URL in a new unnamed window
- `targetWindow` — Loads the URL in the window having the name `targetWindow`
- `_self` — Loads the URL in the window containing this applet
- `_parent` — Loads the URL of the parent window containing this applet
- `_top` — Loads the URL in the top-level window.

The following applet loads the URL `http://www.yahoo.com` in the applet's window.

```
/LoadDemo.java
import java.awt.*;
import java.applet.*;
import java.net.*;
public class LoadDemo extends Applet {
   AppletContext ac; URL url;
   public void start() {
     ac = getAppletContext();
     url = getCodeBase();
   }
   public void paint(Graphics g) {
      try {
            ac.showDocument(new URL("http://www.yahoo.com"));
      }catch(Exception e) {showStatus("URL not found");}
   }
}
```

The following applet declaration results in the output as shown in Figure 18.10.

```
<applet code="LoadDemo" width="200" height="80">
</applet>
```

Figure 18.10 Loading a URL using applet

KEYWORDS

Active Applets: Applets that are being viewed by the user.

Applet class: Base class of all applets.

Applet Communication: The process by which applets find other applets and exchange information.

Applet tag: It is an HTML tag used to embed applets in HTML documents.

AppletContext: It is the interface that provides methods to query and affect the environment where the applet is running.

Applet: Tiny java programs that run within the context of a web browser.

Appletviewer: An application provided by the JDK to view your applets without any browser.

Codebase: Code base is the name of the base directory from where the applet's class file was loaded.

Document base: The document base is URL of the HTML file that contains an applet.

Graphics: An object that represents the canvas of the applet.

Inactive Applets: Applets that are stopped possibly because the user selected another window.

JApplet: Swing extension of the `Applet` class.

Life Cycle: The stages through which an applet passes, from its creation to its destruction.

Param tag: It is used to pass parameters to the applets.

SUMMARY

We started this chapter with the execution philosophy of applets. Applets are tiny Java programs that run within the context of web browsers. They are embedded in HTML documents. Java-enabled web browsers download the class files for applets and execute them.

Every applet must extend the `java.applet.Applet` class, which provides interfaces to work with the applets. The `Applet` class has five life cycle methods: `init()`, `start()`, `paint()`, `stop()`, and `destroy()`. These methods are executed in that order, from the creation of an applet to its destruction. Our applet class should override these methods as and when necessary. We can also add other methods in the applet class.

Applets are compiled using the same procedure as Java application programs are compiled. HTML provides two tags to work with the applets: `<applet>` and `<param>`. The applets are embedded in an HTML document using the `<applet>` tag. It has several attributes that are used to customize applets.

Since applets are run in the client computer, restrictions are imposed on applets so that they cannot perform any malicious events. Developers of applets should be aware of these limitations.

The `<param>` tag, which is a child tag of the `<applet>` tag, is used to pass parameters to the applets. Applets can retrieve parameters using the `getParameter()` method. We described how to pass and retrieve parameters with extensive examples.

The `Applet` class also provides several other methods that are used to query and affect the properties of applets. Then we described the event handling mechanism in applets. Event handling in applets is exactly the same as in other Java AWT application programs.

Applets can find other applets and communicate with them. We developed a sample application consisting of two applets to demonstrate how applets can communicate.

An applet can load web pages in the browser's window using the `showDocument()` method.

WEB RESOURCES

`http://java.sun.com/docs/books/tutorial/deployment/applet/index.html`
Java Applets Tutorial

`http://java.sun.com/applets/`
Applets: Code samples and Apps.

`http://en.wikipedia.org/wiki/Applet`
Applets

EXERCISES

Multiple Choice Questions

1. What is an Applet?
   (a) The name of a database
   (b) A kind of fruit
   (c) A Java program that is run through a web browser
   (d) An interactive website

2. What is the difference between a Java Applet and a Java application program?
   (a) All the method in an applet class are private
   (b) Applets can create GUI, applications cannot
   (c) Applets are run in web browsers but applications are not
   (d) An application is a small program whereas an applet is large

3. What is the full form of AWT?
   (a) Adjust Window Table
   (b) Abstract Window Toolkit
   (c) Auto Window Transfer
   (d) Advanced Window Toolkit

4. Which one of the following is a valid declaration of an applet?
   (a) class AnApplet implements Applet {
   (b) public class AnApplet extends applet implements Runnable {
   (c) abstract class AnApplet extends java.applet.Applet {
   (d) public class AnApplet extends java.applet.Applet {

5. Why does an applet have no main() method?
   (a) The browser acts as the main. The applet provides methods for the browser
   (b) The paint() method is like the main method for an applet
   (c) Programs that do graphics do not need a main
   (d) Only simple programs need a main

6. Which of the following classes your applet must extend?
   (a) Component (b) Graphics
   (c) Applet (d) AWT

7. What is the function of the Graphics object?
   (a) It represents the canvas of the applet and provides drawing methods
   (b) It represents the status bar
   (c) It represents the entire screen of the computer monitor
   (d) It represents the applet background

8. Which of the following code is used to display the string "Hello World!" at X=20 Y=50 location? Assume that g holds a Graphics object reference.
   (a) g.println("Hello World!");
   (b) drawString("Hello World!", 20, 50);
   (c) g.drawString(20, 50, "Hello World!");
   (d) g.drawString("Hello World!", 20, 50);

9. Which of the following sets the background color of the applet to white?
   (a) setBackColor(gray);
   (b) setBackGround(gray);
   (c) setBackGround(Color.gray);
   (d) setBackColor(Color.gray);

10. Which of the following packages must be imported to get the class Applet?
    (a) java.applet.Applet (b) java.util.*
    (c) java.awt.* (d) javax.swing.*

11. Which of the following must be imported to get the most graphics components?
    (a) java.util.* (b) java.awt.*
    (c) java.Graphics (d) java.lang.*

12. Which of the following tags is used to pass parameters to applets?
    (a) <parameter> (b) <para>
    (c) <argc> (d) <param>

13. Which of the following tags is used to insert an applet into an HTML document?
    (a) <applet> (b) <body>
    (c) <insertapplet> (d) <embedapplet>

14. Which of the following methods is called by the browser when it wishes to display it on the monitor?
    (a) draw() (b) show()
    (c) display() (d) paint()

15. Can the source code for your applet be compiled by the usual javac compiler?
    (a) No, because applets have no main() method
    (b) Yes, if you are going to run it from the DOS prompt
    (c) Yes, an applet is just another class as far as the compiler is concerned
    (d) No, the web browser compiles the code

16. Which of the following methods is used to draw a rectangle filled in with the current color?
    (a) fillRect() (b) drawRect()
    (c) fillOval() (d) drawOval()

17. If you are using the Graphics object g and wish to change the pen color to blue, what should you do?
    (a) g.setPen(Color.blue)
    (b) setBackground(Color.blue)
    (c) g.setColor(Color.blue)
    (d) g.setBlue( )

18. Which of the following statements is true?
    (a) Applets have main() function
    (b) Applets cannot use System.out.print() method

(c) Applets are JavaScript programs
(d) Applets run within a web browser

19. Which of the following sequences is the correct order of method call?
(a) start(), init(), paint(), stop(), destroy()
(b) init(), paint(), start(), stop(), destroy()
(c) init(), start(), paint(), stop(), destroy()
(d) start(), init(), paint(), destroy(), stop()

20. Which of the following is not a method of the Applet class?
(a) move() (b) resize()
(c) play() (d) isActive()

Review Questions

1. What are applets?
2. Explain why applets do not have constructors.
3. Explain briefly the applet's life cycle methods?
4. What are the differences between Java applets and Java applications?
5. Write the steps involved in applet development.
6. Write the sequence of applet's life cycle methods in which they are called.
7. Demonstrate with example, how parameters are passed to applets.
8. Describe how parameters are retrieved from an applet.
9. Demonstrate with examples, how applets can communicate with each other.
10. Can applets on different pages communicate with each other?
11. How do you determine the width and height of an applet?
12. Show how URLs are loaded dynamically using applets.
13. Which classes and interfaces does the Applet class contain?
14. Which tags are used in HTML to display an applet?
15. Which methods are available to retrieve information about an applet?
16. Which method is used to display a string on the applet's window? Which function is this method included in?

Part IV

Server-side Programming

- Common Gateway Interface (CGI)
- Servlet
- Java Server Pages (JSP)
- Introduction to J2EE

19 COMMON GATEWAY INTERFACE (CGI)

KEY OBJECTIVES

After completing this chapter readers will be able to—

- **understand the concept of server-side programming**
- **get an idea about the execution philosophy of CGI programs**
- **get an overview about languages used to write CGI programs**
- **understand CGI environment variables and their importance**
- **write basic CGI programs using C/C++, Perl, Python, etc.**
- **learn how to retrieve parameters from CGI programs**
- **get an overview about the shortcomings of CGI programs**

19.1 INTERNET PROGRAMMING PARADIGM

Internet programming can be classified into two categories: *client-side programming* and *server-side programming*. In the client-side programming paradigm, programs/scripts are downloaded, interpreted, and executed by the browser. The author of the programs does not have any idea about the type and version of the browser used to execute them. So, if the browser is not compatible with the technology used, the content will not be presented properly. Let us take a specific example.

Applets are client-side programming technology, where special Java programs are embedded directly into web pages with the help of the `<applet>` tag. When a browser loads such a web page, the applet byte code is also downloaded and executed on the client side. If the browser uses an old Java Runtime Environment (JRE), applet byte code cannot be executed properly and the entire thing becomes garbled. Moreover, for large applets, download time becomes significant. Hence, this technology tends to be unacceptable. These issues have enforced businesses to use server-side programming.

19.2 SERVER-SIDE PROGRAMMING

Server-side programming solves the problem discussed in Section 19.1. The basic idea of this paradigm is that programs are executed in the web server. Hence, there is no issue of browser incompatibility or long download time. The web server sends web pages (containing simple code generated by those programs) that even an old browser can understand.

The Common Gateway Interface (CGI) is one of the important server-side programming techniques. The CGI connects a web server to an external application. Figure 19.1 shows the CGI architecture.

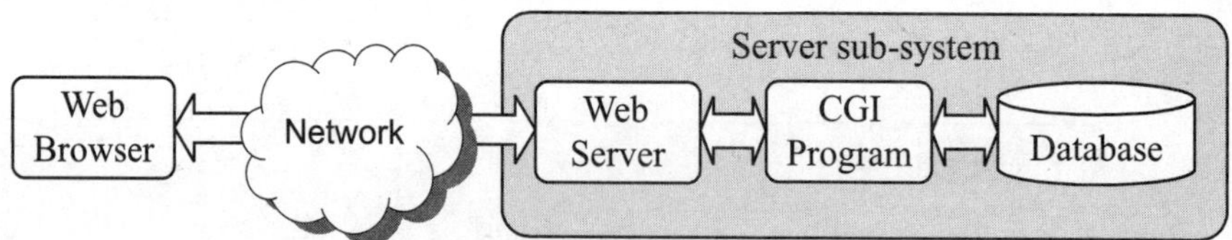

Figure 19.1 CGI Architecture

When a CGI-enabled web server receives a request for a CGI program, it does not send the file as it is. Instead, the web server executes [Figure 19.1] the program at the server end and sends the output back to the client, which is then displayed in the browser's window. This simple and elegant idea can be used to develop many powerful applications.

CGI has numerous advantages. Most of the web servers have built-in support for CGI. So, if you have your web server installed in your computer, you can start writing without any further effort.

Moreover, the CGI specification is independent of any programming language. It defines how information is transferred from a web server to an external application and from the external application to the web server. So, these external applications may be developed using a programming language that fits the application.

19.3 LANGUAGES FOR CGI

The most powerful feature of CGI technology is that virtually any programming language can be used to write CGI programs as long as it can read from a standard input and write to a standard output. Following are some popular CGI programming languages.

C/C++

C is one of the popular programming languages. It is well known for its extremely good performance. It is widely used on many different software platforms and is a primary language for CGI. There is virtually no computer architecture for which a C compiler does not exist.

C++ supports Object Oriented Programming (OOP) and is suitable for large complex applications. So, if your CGI program should handle a large problem, C++ is ideal.

Perl

This interpreted language provides powerful text processing and file manipulation facilities. Perl borrows features from other programming languages such as C, shell script (sh), AWK, and sed. Due to its flexibility and adaptability, it is widely used for CGI programming. It is also used for network programming, applications that require database access, system administration, and graphics programming.

Tcl

Tcl is a scripting language that was originated from "Tool Command Language", but is conventionally rendered as "Tcl". It is commonly used for CGI scripting as well as rapid prototyping, other scripted applications, GUIs, and testing.

Python

It is an interpreted, interactive, portable, Object Oriented Programming (OOP) language. Its significant power and clear syntax make Python an excellent instructional tool and ideal for **C**ommon **G**ateway **I**nterface (CGI) programming. Language features include modules, classes, very high level dynamic data types, and dynamic typing.

Unix/Linux Shell

A shell is a command line interpreter that provides an interface to the users, to execute their commands. Unix/Linux shell is extremely powerful for manipulating files, pattern searching, and matching, and is ideal for CGI scripting in the Unix/Linux platform.

19.3.1 Preferred Language

The commonly used languages are Perl, C/C++, and shell script. However, your choice depends on what you want to do because different languages have different specialized features. For example, Perl is extremely powerful for string and file manipulation while C/C++ is better for complex and larger programs.

It depends on your taste as well as the facilities available on your system. If you prefer a *programming language* such as C/C++ or Fortran, you have to compile the program and generate an executable code before it runs. The original source code is no longer needed. This allows you to hide your sensitive program code from others who have access to the CGI directory. Moreover, the programs are already compiled and they take less time to start servicing than an interpreted one.

On the other hand, if you use any *scripting language*, such as Perl, Tcl, or Unix/Linux shell, you need to keep the script itself in the "cgi-bin" directory. Many programmers prefer CGI scripts instead of programs, as scripts are easier to modify, debug, and maintain than typical compiled programs.

19.4 APPLICATIONS

There are numerous applications of the CGI. It is usually used to build database applications in conjunction with HTML forms. For example, suppose we want to "hook up" our database to the World Wide Web (WWW), so that people from all over the world can query it, all we need to do is write a CGI program that can access this database. The web server will execute this program to store information to the database and receive results from the database, which are then sent back to the client.

19.5 SERVER ENVIRONMENT

Most the web servers standardize the CGI mechanism. Usually, the directory "cgi-bin" exists under the web server's installation directory. The files in this directory are treated differently. Any file requested from this special "cgi-bin" directory is not simply read and sent. Instead, it is executed in the computer where the web server is installed. The output of this program is actually sent to the browser that requested this file. The program is an executable file of typically a Perl or Python script.

Though the "cgi-bin" directory is usually considered as the container of CGI scripts, most web servers allow us to specify other directories as the CGI directory.

Suppose that you have entered the following URL in the address bar of your browser:

```
http://192.168.1.2/cgi-bin/hello.pl
```

The web server recognizes the file `hello.pl`, which is nothing but a Perl script in the `cgi-bin` directory. It then executes `hello.pl` and sends the output of this script to the browser, which then displays it on the screen.

Though CGI programs are typically written on a Unix platform, you can also write your CGI programs in a Windows environment. For this purpose, you need a web server. Perl is the typical language used for CGI programs, but you can use C/C++ or Python as well. In this section, we shall discuss how to install and configure Apache and Perl on your computer running Windows. Once Apache and Perl are successfully installed, you can test your CGI programs using the address `http://locahost` in your own computer. This is quite useful to test your CGI programs locally before installing them in the actual server.

Download the installer file for Apache from `http://httpd.apache.org/download.cgi`. Now, install it by double clicking on the installer file. We are assuming that you have installed Apache in the directory "D:\Apache Software Foundation".

Now, download and install ActivePerl from `http://www.activestate.com/Products/ActivePerl/`
We are assuming that you have successfully installed Perl in the "D:\Perl" directory.

19.5.1 Configuring Apache

To enable CGI programs, you need to modify the Apache configuration file `httpd.conf`, which can be found in the `conf` directory under the apache installation directory. Go to the `<Directory>...</Directory>` section. Uncomment or add the following line:

```
Options MultiViews Indexes SymLinksIfOwnerMatch Includes ExecCGI
```

The `Options` specifies what options are available in this directory. `ExecCGI` enables the CGI scripting. Go to the `AddHandler` section and add or uncomment the following line.

```
AddHandler cgi-script .cgi .pl
```

This causes files with the extensions `.cgi` and `.pl` to be treated as CGI programs. Finally, save the configuration file and restart Apache. Ensure that the server restarted successfully by checking `http://localhost/` in your browser.

If everything goes well, your web server is ready to serve the CGI request. Save your CGI programs in the `cgi-bin` directory under the Apache installation directory.

Use the following line as the first line of your Perl program:

```
#!D:/perl/bin/perl.exe
```

This tells the web server where to find the Perl interpreter to interpret Perl programs.

19.6 ENVIRONMENT VARIABLES

In order to pass and retrieve parameters, web servers use several environment variables. The web server usually sets these environment variables before starting a CGI program. The CGI program can inspect those environment variables [Table 19.1] to retrieve information. Note that CGI environment variables are the primary source of information that server-side programs can use.

Table 19.1 CGI Environment Variables

Variable Name	Description
SERVER_NAME	The server's DNS name or IP Address
SERVER_SOFTWARE	The name and version of the web server software answering the request
GATEWAY_INTERFACE	The version of the CGI specification that the server complies with
SERVER_PROTOCOL	The HTTP version used by the server
SERVER_PORT	The port number used by the web server
CONTENT_TYPE	The type of the data of the content. It is used when the client is sending attached content to the server e.g., example file upload, etc.
CONTENT_LENGTH	The length of the query information in case of the POST method
HTTP_ACCEPT	The list of MIME types that the client can accept
HTTP_USER_AGENT	The browser name and version that the user is using to make this request
PATH	The value of PATH environment variable
QUERY_STRING	The URL-encoded information which follows the ? in the URL
REMOTE_ADDR	The IP address of the remote host that made the request
REMOTE_PORT	The port number from which the request was sent
REQUEST_METHOD	The HTTP method used in the request. The most common methods are GET, HEAD, and POST
SCRIPT_FILENAME	The full path of the CGI script being executed
SCRIPT_NAME	The relative path of the script being executed

The following Perl script prints available environment variables with their values.

```
#!D:/perl/bin/perl.exe
print "Content-type: text/html\n\n";
print "<table style=\"font-size:12; font-family:arial\" border=\"0\" >";
print "<caption>CGI variables</caption>";
foreach $var (sort(keys(%ENV))) {
   $val = $ENV{$var};
   print "<tr><td>${var}</td><td >${val}</td></tr>\n";
}
print "</table>";
```

Ignore the syntax of this Perl program. It simply iterates through the associative array variable ENV, which contains all the environment variables and prints their values in a tabular format. We shall discuss the syntax briefly in Section 19.9. The script results in the output shown in Figure 19.2.

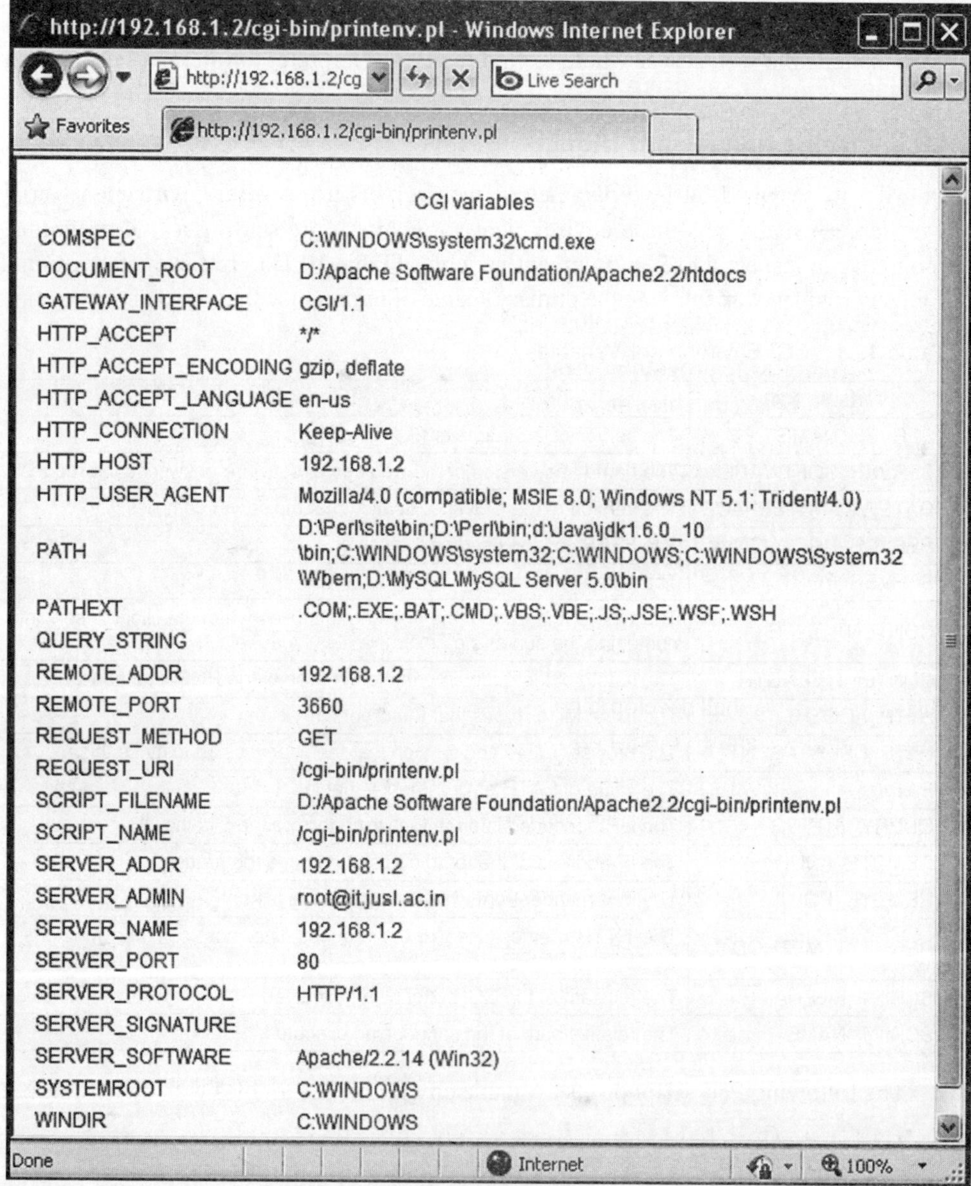

CGI variables

COMSPEC	C:\WINDOWS\system32\cmd.exe
DOCUMENT_ROOT	D:/Apache Software Foundation/Apache2.2/htdocs
GATEWAY_INTERFACE	CGI/1.1
HTTP_ACCEPT	*/*
HTTP_ACCEPT_ENCODING	gzip, deflate
HTTP_ACCEPT_LANGUAGE	en-us
HTTP_CONNECTION	Keep-Alive
HTTP_HOST	192.168.1.2
HTTP_USER_AGENT	Mozilla/4.0 (compatible; MSIE 8.0; Windows NT 5.1; Trident/4.0)
PATH	D:\Perl\site\bin;D:\Perl\bin;d:\Java\jdk1.6.0_10\bin;C:\WINDOWS\system32;C:\WINDOWS;C:\WINDOWS\System32\Wbem;D:\MySQL\MySQL Server 5.0\bin
PATHEXT	.COM;.EXE;.BAT;.CMD;.VBS;.VBE;.JS;.JSE;.WSF;.WSH
QUERY_STRING	
REMOTE_ADDR	192.168.1.2
REMOTE_PORT	3660
REQUEST_METHOD	GET
REQUEST_URI	/cgi-bin/printenv.pl
SCRIPT_FILENAME	D:/Apache Software Foundation/Apache2.2/cgi-bin/printenv.pl
SCRIPT_NAME	/cgi-bin/printenv.pl
SERVER_ADDR	192.168.1.2
SERVER_ADMIN	root@it.jusl.ac.in
SERVER_NAME	192.168.1.2
SERVER_PORT	80
SERVER_PROTOCOL	HTTP/1.1
SERVER_SIGNATURE	
SERVER_SOFTWARE	Apache/2.2.14 (Win32)
SYSTEMROOT	C:\WINDOWS
WINDIR	C:\WINDOWS

Figure 19.2 CGI environment variables

19.7 CGI BUILDING BLOCKS

Any CGI script basically consists of three steps:

- Read parameters passed to this script
- Process these parameters
- Write the HTML response to the standard output

19.8 CGI SCRIPTING USING C, SHELL SCRIPT

Writing CGI programs using C/C++ language is somehow different from writing them in shell script. Here, shell refers to the Unix/Linux shell. The Windows shell is not so powerful and is hardly used. Note that shell scripts are interpreted by the underlying shell. You simply need to mention which shell should be used to interpret your script in the first line of your script as follows:

```
#!/bin/bash
```

C/C++ programs are, on the other hand, compiled programs. Writing CGI programs using C/C++ basically consists of two steps:

- Compile the program to generate the executable file
- Put this executable file in the `cgi` directory.

Compiling a C/C++ program is different for different compilers. Ask your system administrator to know the compilation procedure of C/C++ programs. Moreover, C/C++ programs are not platform-independent. So, you must compile your program in the computer where the web server runs, using a suitable compiler available on that platform.

19.9 WRITING CGI PROGRAMS

In this section, we shall develop simple programs to display "Hello World!" using different languages such as Perl, C, and Python. Following is the program (`hello.pl`) written in Perl.

```
#!D:/perl/bin/perl.exe
print "Content-type: text/html\n\n";
print "<html>\n";
print "  <head><title>First Perl script</title></head>\n";
print "  <body>\n";
print "     <h2>Hello, World!</h2>\n";
print "  </body>\n";
print "</html>\n";
```

The script `hello.pl` is a simple script that prints a simple HTML document on the standard output, i.e., screen. The first line of any Perl script should look like this:

```
#!D:/perl/bin/perl.exe
```

The `#!` indicates that this is a script. The path `D:/perl/bin/perl.exe` refers to the full path name of the Perl interpreter to be used by the web server to execute the Perl script. However, this could be different in different systems. For a Unix or Linux OS, this is typically `/usr/bin/perl` or `/usr/local/bin/perl`. If you are not sure about the path, type "whereis perl" or "which perl" at the command prompt, it shows the path where the Perl interpreter is stored. Alternatively, ask the webmaster about the location of the Perl interpreter.

The remaining part consists of actual Perl statements. Before printing anything else, you should use the following line:

```
print "Content-type: text/html\n\n";
```

This prints `Content-type: text/html` followed by a blank line. This is sent as a HTTP response header, which specifies the type of the content to be displayed in the browser's screen. In our case, we shall send an HTML document and that is why the `Content-type` header is specified as `text/html`. This Perl program, except `Content-type` header, basically generates the following:

```
<html>
   <head><title>First Perl script</title></head>
   <body>
      <h2>Hello, World!</h2>
   </body>
</html>
```

If you enter the following URL, you will see the result shown in Figure 19.3.

```
http://192.168.1.2/cgi-bin/hello.pl
```

Here, 192.168.1.2 is the IP address of the computer where the web server is running. If you are testing your program locally, you can also use the following URL:

```
http://localhost/cgi-bin/hello.pl
```

Alternatively, you can use

```
http://127.0.0.1/cgi-bin/hello.pl
```

Figure 19.3 Hello world CGI program using perl

Let us now write a CGI program (`hello.c`) using C language for the same purpose.

```
//hello.c
int main() {
   printf("Content-type: text/html\n\n");
   printf("<html>\n");
   printf(" <head><title>First Perl script</title></head>\n");
   printf(" <body>\n");
   printf("    <h2>Hello, World!</h2>\n");
   printf(" </body>\n");
   printf("</html>\n");
  return 0;
}
```

Compile the program using a suitable compiler such as Microsoft's Visual C++. Microsoft's Visual C++ compiler will generate the executable file `hello.exe`. Rename this file to hello and put it in the CGI directory. If you are using the Unix/Linux platform, use the following command to compile the C program and generate an executable file:

```
gcc -o hello hello.c
```

It generates an executable file `hello`. Put this file in the CGI directory. Now, type the following URL, you will see the output shown in Figure 19.4.

```
http://192.168.1.2/cgi-bin/hello
```

Figure 19.4 Hello world CGI program using C

The following program is written in Python (`hello.cgi`) and generates the same output.

```
#!D:\Python31\python.exe
print("Content-type: text/html\n\n");
print("<html>");
print("  <head><title>Python demo<title></title></head>");
print("  <body>");
print("     Hello World!");
print("  </body>");
print("</html>");
```

The first line indicates the location of the Python interpreter. We are assuming that you have installed the Python in the "D:\Python31" directory. Put this file in the CGI directory and use the following URL to view the result.

```
http://192.168.1.2/cgi-bin/hello.cgi
```

19.9.1 Getting Arguments

In this section, we shall discuss how CGI programs can retrieve URL-encoded parameters passed to them. The parameters passed have the following characteristics:

- They are sent in the form of name–value pairs.
- Each name–value pair starts with an & sign.
- The name and value are separated by the equal (=) sign.

URL encoding changes some special characters to placeholders and replaces them with hexadecimal values. To retrieve the information, the CGI program should implement the following basic steps:

- Get the information from the proper environment variable, depending upon the method type. For example, we can retrieve information from the `QUERY_STRING` environment variable for the GET method.
- Change all placeholders to their correct values.
- Split each name–value pair.
- Convert hexadecimal values back to their original characters.
- Find the respective name and value.

The following C program (`add.c`) shows how to retrieve two parameter values. The program adds those two values and sends the result back to the client.

```
//add.c
#include <stdio.h>
#include <stdlib.h>
int main(void) {
   long a, b;
   printf("Content-Type:text/html\n\n");
   char *data = getenv("QUERY_STRING");
   sscanf(data,"a=%d&b=%d", &a, &b);
   printf("%d + %d = %ld", a, b, a + b);
   return 0;
}
```

Here, we first obtain the entire parameter information using the `getenv()` function. The individual parameters are then obtained using the `sscanf()` function. Compile the program to have an executable file add using the following command:

```
gcc -o add add.c
```

Now, use the following URL to test the program.

```
http://192.168.1.2/cgi-bin/add?a=3&b=4
```

The result is shown in Figure 19.5.

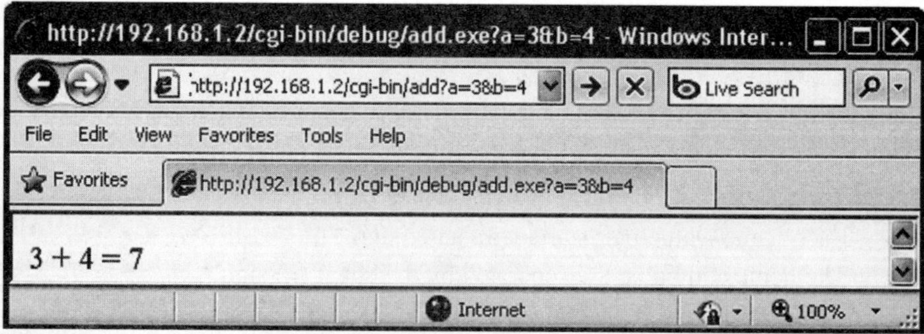

Figure 19.5 Retrieving parameters

Following is the equivalent Perl program.

```
#!D:/perl/bin/perl.exe
use CGI qw(:standard);
print "Content-type: text/html\n\n";
$a = param('a');
$b = param('b');
$c = $a + $b;
print "$a + $b = $c";
```

The following Perl script retrieves all parameters appended to the URL.

```
#!D:/perl/bin/perl.exe
print "Content-type:text/html\r\n\r\n";
$buffer = $ENV{'QUERY_STRING'};
@pairs = split(/&/, $buffer);
foreach $pair (@pairs)     {
   ($name, $value) = split(/=/, $pair);
   print "$name=$value<br>";
}
```

19.10 CGI SECURITY

The CGI technology allows users to run programs in a system remotely using their URLs. This may become vulnerable. Therefore, some security precautions need to be taken when CGI technology is used. Note that CGI programs are kept in a special directory, so that the web server can execute the program rather than just send them to the browser. This is the most important concept that CGI writers follow: The external users may try to use this concept to perform malicious events. The CGI directory is usually controlled by the webmaster, who should prohibit the average user from creating and running CGI programs. There are many ways to allow access to CGI scripts, but the webmaster decides how to set these up for you.

Although the CGI protocol is inherently secure, CGI scripts may become a major source of security holes. CGI scripts should be written with utmost care just as the server. The web administrator should not also trust the script writers and should not install arbitrary CGI scripts.

If you are a system administrator, a webmaster, or are otherwise involved with the administration of a network, you should create a security policy for your website. The following points should be taken into consideration while writing the security policy:

- Users who can access the system
- When they are allowed to use the system
- What operations they are allowed to perform
- A way to grant access to the system
- Acceptable permission to use the file system
- Procedure for monitoring the system
- Actions to be taken against suspected security breaches

19.11 ALTERNATIVES AND ENHANCEMENTS TO CGI

Each time the web server receives a CGI request, it starts a new process that serves the request. Starting a new process may take significant amount of time and memory than the actual task of generating the output. If users send CGI requests very frequently, they may quickly overwhelm the web server.

If the CGI program is an interpreted program such as Perl, Python, or shell script, it needs more time. We can use compiled programs such as C/C++, instead of scripting languages, to avoid overhead involved in interpretation.

The overhead in process creation may be reduced by using technology such as FastCGI or by using special extension modules provided by some web server.

FastCGI uses a single persistent process that handles many requests during its lifetime. This way, overhead involved in new process creation for every request may be avoided. Multiple simultaneous requests can be handled either by using multiple processes or using a single process with internal multiplexing. FastCGI allows web servers to perform simple operations, such as reading a file before the request is handed over to the FastCGI program. Some of the web servers that implement FastCGI are Apache HTTP Server, Microsoft IIS, Resin Application Server, Sun Java System Web Server, etc.

Another alternative to CGI is Simple Common Gateway Interface (SCGI), which is similar to FastCGI but easier to implement. In this technology, clients send requests to the SCGI server using an SCGI request message. The server sends the response back and closes the connection. Web servers that implement SCGI are Apache HTTP Server, Lighttpd, Cherokee, etc.

Another viable and effective solution to CGI is Java servlets. Servlets can avoid overhead involved in new process creation. Web servers load the servlet class when it starts up. The servlet can then serve many requests using a separate thread. Since threads are more lightweight than processes, servlets are more efficient than CGI programs.

Java Server Page (JSP) is an extension of Java servlet and is a potential solution to CGI technology. In the next two chapters, we shall discuss Java servlet and JSP, separately.

KEYWORDS

CGI alternatives: The competent technologies such as servlets, JSP, ASP, and PHP.

CGI directory: CGI programs are kept in some predefined special directory called CGI directory so that the web server knows that those programs must be executed, instead of being sent directly to the clients.

CGI Environment variables: The variables used to pass and retrieve information in CGI programs.

CGI Languages: The programming languages that can be used to write CGI programs.

Client-side programming: A programming paradigm where programs are executed in the client machine.

Common Gateway Interface: A standard that interfaces the HTTP server software with the CGI programs that run on the server.

Compiled CGI program: A program that is compiled to generate executable code, which acts as a CGI program.

Gateway program: A program that the web server contacts to process some request sent by the client.

Interpreted CGI program: A program whose statements are interpreted using an interpreter program.

SCGI: An extension to CGI called Simple Common Gateway Interface.

Server-side programming: A programming paradigm where programs are executed in the server machine.

SUMMARY

The Common Gateway Interface (CGI) is one of the popular server-side technologies. CGI has numerous advantages. Most of the web servers have built-in support for CGI. Moreover, the CGI specification is independent of any programming language; it defines how information is transferred from the web server to an external application and from the external application to the web server. So, these external applications may be developed using a programming language that fits the application.

When a CGI-enabled web server receives a request for a CGI program, it does not send the file as it is. Instead, the web server executes the program and sends the output back to the client, which is then displayed in the browser's window.

The most powerful feature of CGI technology is that virtually any programming language can be used to write the CGI program as long as it can read from a standard input and write to a standard output. Some examples are C/C++, Perl, Python, Tcl, shell, Ruby, etc. Compiled programs such as C/C++ run faster than interpreted programs. Interpreted programs, on the other hand, are easier to modify, debug, and maintain.

Most web servers standardize the CGI mechanism. Usually, the directory "cgi-bin" exists under the web server's installation directory. The files in this directory are treated differently. Any file requested from this special "cgi-bin" directory is not simply read and sent. Instead, it is executed in the computer where the web server is installed. The output of this program is actually sent to the browser that requested this file. The program usually is pure executable file of typically a Perl or Python script.

To pass and retrieve parameters, web servers use several environment variables. The web server usually sets these environment variables before starting a CGI program. The CGI program can inspect those environment variables to retrieve the information.

Since the CGI program can be written in almost all languages and in all platforms, the exact procedure for executing the CGI program varies from one platform/web server to another.

The CGI technology allows users to run programs in a system remotely using their URLs. This may become vulnerable. Therefore, some security precautions need to be taken when CGI technology is used.

WEB RESOURCES

`http://www.ietf.org/rfc/rfc3875.txt`
The Common Gateway Interface (CGI) Version 1.1

`http://hoohoo.ncsa.illinois.edu/cgi/`
The Common Gateway Interface

`http://www.w3.org/CGI/`
CGI: Common Gateway Interface

`http://www.fastcgi.com/devkit/doc/fcgi-spec.html`
FastCGI Specification

EXERCISES

Multiple Choice Questions

1. Server-side scripting is about "programming" the behavior of the
   (a) Server (b) Browser
   (c) HTML (d) All of the above

2. What is the full form of CGI?
   (a) Common Graphical Interface
   (b) Cascading Gateway Interface
   (c) Class Generator Instance
   (d) Common Gateway Interface

3. Which of the following defines how a web server communicates with external applications?
   (a) HTTP (b) CGI
   (c) SMTP (d) TCP/IP

4. Which of the following is true regarding CGI?
   (a) It is a client-side technology
   (b) It is the name of a browser
   (c) It is a server-side technology
   (d) It is a web server

5. Which of the following languages can be used as a CGI language?
   (a) C (b) C++
   (c) Perl (d) All of the above

6. Which of the following directories is usually used to store CGI programs?
   (a) cgi-bin (b) cgi
   (c) cgiprogs (d) bin

7. Which of the following environment variables is used to retrieve URL-encoded information?
   (a) QUERY (b) QUERY_STRING
   (c) PARAM (d) URL_ENCODE

8. What should be the value of Content-type to generate HTML documents?
   (a) text/html (b) text/plain
   (c) plain/text (d) plain/html

9. Whenever a web server receives a CGI request, it
   (a) Creates a new thread
   (b) Uses an existing process
   (c) Uses an existing thread
   (d) Creates a new process

10. Which of the following statements is true regarding CGI?
    (a) Compiled programs are faster than interpreted programs
    (b) Compiled programs are slower than interpreted programs
    (c) The source code is necessary for compiled programs
    (d) The source code is not necessary for interpreted programs

11. Which of the following is a compiled language?
    (a) C++ (b) Perl
    (c) Python (d) Shell

12. Which of the following is an interpreted language?
    (a) Tcl (b) Ruby
    (c) Visual Basic (d) All of the above

13. Which of the following headers should be set by a CGI script?
    (a) Value-type (b) Content
    (c) Content-type (d) Return-type

14. Which of the following CGI environment variables represents the port number used by the web server?
    (a) REMOTE_PORT (b) SERVER_PORT
    (c) PORT (d) HOST_PORT

15. Which of the following functions in C/C++ is used to retrieve the value of an environment variable?
    (a) env() (b) environment()
    (c) getenv() (d) getvariable()

16. Which of the following lines should be printed by a CGI program to generate an HTML document?
    (a) Content-type: html/text
    (b) Content-type: text/html
    (c) Return-type: text/html
    (d) Return-type: html/text

17. The first line of any CGI script should start with
    (a) $! (b) &!
    (c) @! (d) #!

18. Which of the following characters is used to separate a parameter from a URL?
    (a) ? (b) &
    (c) $ (d) %

19. Which of the following characters is used to separate a parameter name and its value?
    (a) ^ (b) $
    (c) = (d) &

20. Which of the following functions is used in Perl to print a string on the standard output?
    (a) print (b) show
    (c) display (d) out

Review Questions

1. How does server-side programming differ from client-side programming?
2. What are the relative advantages and disadvantages of compiled and interpreted programs in CGI?
3. Mention two names each of compiled and interpreted languages.
4. What are environment variables? Name two CGI environment variables.
5. What is the purpose of the Content-type header in CGI programs?
6. Can we use Java as the CGI language? If yes, how?
7. Mention two web servers that support CGI programming.
8. Describe how parameters are passed and retrieved in CGI programs.
9. What are the drawbacks of CGI technology? How can we overcome them?
10. Mention some of the alternatives of CGI technology.

20 SERVLET

Key Objectives

After completing this chapter readers will be able to—

- **get an idea about server-side technology**
- **understand the advantages of Java servlet technology over other similar technologies**
- **get an idea about the basic execution philosophy of servlets**
- **understand how to write, deploy, and invoke servlets**
- **learn how to install and configure Tomcat servlet engine**
- **learn how to use important concepts such as filters, session tracking, etc.**

20.1 SERVER-SIDE JAVA

Servlet is a Java technology for server-side programming. It is a Java module that runs inside a Java-enabled web server and services requests obtained from the web server. Servlets are not tied to a specific client–server protocol, but are most commonly used with HTTP. The word "servlet" is often used to mean "HTTP servlet". Execution of a servlet consists of four steps [Figure 20.1]:

- The client sends a request to the web server.
- The web server interprets it and forwards it to the corresponding servlet.
- The servlet processes the request, generates the output (if any), and sends it back to the web server.

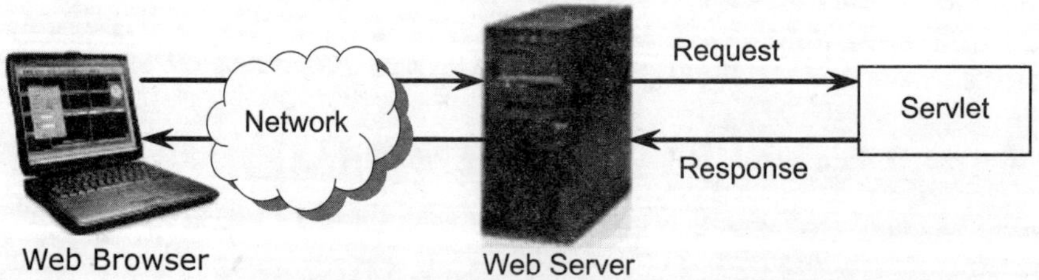

Figure 20.1 Execution of a Java servlet

- The web server sends the response back to the client. The browser then displays it on the screen.

It runs entirely within the **J**ava **V**irtual **M**achine (JVM). Since it runs on the server and generates simple output, which even older versions of browsers can interpret, there is no browser incompatibility.

20.2 ADVANTAGES OVER APPLETS

Applets, upon download from the server, run in the client's browser. They will function properly, provided a proper **J**ava **R**untime **E**nvironment (JRE) is installed in the client's browser. If the client uses old fashioned browsers and the applets use advanced features, the browsers may fail to execute them.

Servlets run on the server machine and usually generate simple HTML codes. So, even an older version of the browser can display these HTML pages correctly.

Applets cannot access local resources such as files and databases. Servlets, if configured properly, have full access to system resources. Therefore, servlets are more powerful than applets.

20.3 SERVLET ALTERNATIVES

There are several alternatives to servlets. However, each has its own set of problems. Some of the other server-side technologies are discussed briefly here.

20.3.1 Common Gateway Interface (CGI)

CGI is one of the most common server-side solutions. Although widely used, CGI scripting technology has a number of shortcomings, including platform dependence and lack of scalability. As described in Chapter 19, a CGI application is an independent program that receives requests from the web server and sends it back to the web server. Some of the common problems of this technology are as follows:

- A new process is created every time the web server receives a CGI request. Since a new process is created and initialized, it results in the delay of response time. Servers may also run out of memory if not configured properly.
- As mentioned earlier, a CGI application can be written in almost every language and most of them are not platform-independent. The common platform-independent language is Perl. Although Perl is a very powerful text processing language, for every request it requires a new interpreter to be started. This makes the overall response time longer.
- Since a CGI application is a completely separate process, if it terminates abnormally before responding, the web server has no way to identify what happened there.

20.3.2 Proprietary APIs

Many proprietary web servers have built-in support for server-side programming. Examples include Netscape's NSAPI, Microsoft's ISAPI, and O'Reilly's WSAPI. None of these APIs is free and the newer versions may not be backward compatible. Most of these are developed in C/C++ languages and hence can contain memory leaks and core dumps that can crash the web server.

20.3.3 Active Server Pages (ASP)

Microsoft's Active Server Pages (ASP) is another technology that supports server-side programming. Unfortunately, the only web server that supports this technology is Microsoft's Internet Information Server (IIS), which is not free. Although some third-party products support ASP, they are not free either.

20.3.4 Server-side JavaScript

Server-side JavaScript is another alternative to servlets. However, the only known servers that support it are Netscape's Enterprise and FastTrack servers. This ties you to a particular vendor.

20.4 SERVLET STRENGTHS

Java servlet technology has some distinct advantages over other competent technologies. Truly speaking, except JSP, no technology can compete with servlet technology. Following are some advantages of Java servlet technology.

20.4.1 Efficient

When a servlet gets loaded in the server, it remains in the server's memory as a single object instance. Each new request is then served by a lightweight Java thread spawned from the servlet. This is a much more efficient technique than creating a new process for every request, as done in CGI. Servlets also have more alternatives for optimizations, such as caching the previous computation and keeping database connections open.

20.4.2 Persistent

Servlets can maintain the session by using the session tracking/cookies, a mechanism that helps them track information from request to request. Critical information can also be saved to a persistent storage and can be retrieved from it when the servlet is loaded next time.

20.4.3 Portable

Servlets are written in Java and so they are portable across operating systems and server implementations. This allows servlets to be moved across new operating systems seamlessly. We can develop a servlet on a Windows machine running the Tomcat or any other server and later we can deploy that servlet effortlessly on any other operating system such as a Unix server running an iPlanet/Netscape application server. So, servlets are Write Once Run Anywhere (WORA) programs.

20.4.4 Robust

Since servlets can use the entire JDK, they can provide extremely robust solutions. Java has a very powerful exception handling mechanism and provides a garbage collector to handle memory leaks. It also has a very large and rich class library with network and file support, database access, distributed object components, DOM support, security, utility packages, etc.

20.4.5 Extensible

Servlets are nothing but Java technology, which is popular for its well-known features such as platform independence, garbage collection, exception handling, and extremely powerful utility packages. Servlets can also make use of Java's object orientation features, especially inheritance. A sub class inherits all the features of its super class. Additional features and methods can be added and hence it is easily extendable.

20.4.6 Secure

Servlets run in a Java-enabled web server. So, they can use security mechanisms from both the web server and the Java Security Manager.

20.4.7 Cost-effective

There are a number of free web servers available [Table 20.1] for personal and commercial use. Java Development Kit (JDK) is also free and can be downloaded from `http://java.sun.com`. So, applications can be developed practically without any cost.

Table 20.1 Standalone web server

Product	Source	Product	Source
Apache Web Server	Apache	Web Server	ZEUS
WebSphere Application Server	IBM	iPlanet	Netscape
Weblogic Application Server	BEA	J Application Server	GenStone
Resin	Caucho	Netscape Enterprise Server	Netscape
JRUN	Adobe	LiteWebServer	Gefion
Orion Application Server	Orion	Java Web Server	Sun
Oracle Application Server	Oracle	CtO-JStar	JavaOne
Dynamo Application Server	ATG	iServer	ServerTec
J2EE Server	Pramati	Domino Go WebServer	Lotus
AppServer	Borland	Java Servlet Server 2.0	Paperclips
Jetty	Eclipse Foundation	KonaSoft Enterprise Server	KonaSoft
Jigsaw Server	W3C	Enhydra	ObjectWeb

Table 20.2 also shows some other add-on software that support Java servlet technology.

Table 20.2 Add-on Servlet engine

Product	Source	Product	Source
Tomcat	Jakarta Project	JRun web server	Allaire
JServ	Java-Apache Project	ServletExec	New Atlanta

20.5 SERVLET ARCHITECTURE

Servlet architecture consists of two packages: `javax.servlet` and `javax.servlet.http`. The first package contains top-level interfaces and classes that are used and extended by all other servlets. The second package is provided for servlets that can handle HTTP requests. Figure 20.2 shows the Servlet architecture.

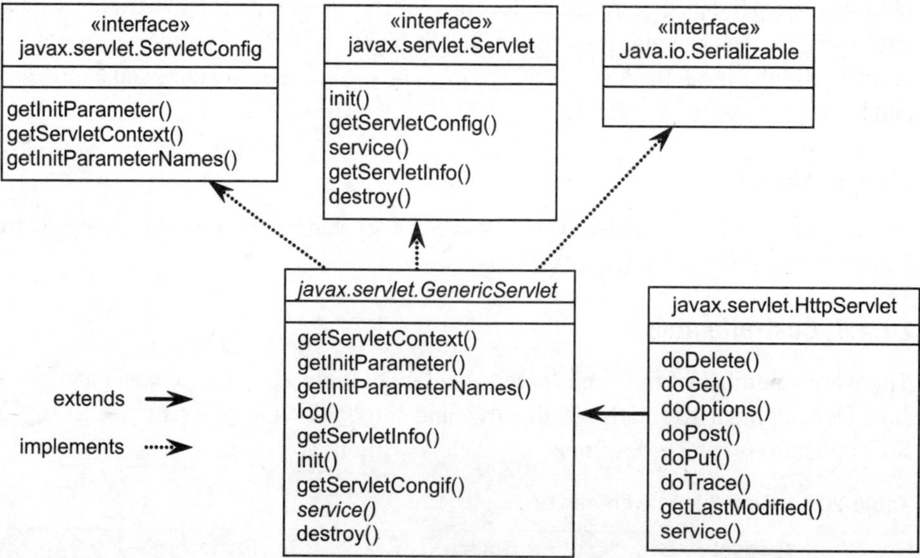

Figure 20.2 Servlet architecture

The top-level interface of the servlet architecture is `javax.servlet.Servlet`. It provides the basic functionalities of all the servlets that are created by implementing this interface directly or indirectly. For example, the `init()` method initializes the servlet, the `service()` method serves the client request, and the `destroy()` method shuts the servlet down.

20.6 SERVLET LIFE CYCLE

The container in which the servlet has been deployed supervises and controls the life cycle of a servlet. Typically, this container is nothing but a web server. When the container receives a request from a client and determines that the request should be handled by a servlet, it performs the following steps.

- If an instance of the target servlet does not exist, the container does the following:
  - Finds and loads the servlet class
  - Creates an instance of the servlet class
  - Calls the `init()` method on this servlet instance to initialize it
- Otherwise (i.e., if the target servlet exists), it invokes the `service()` method on it, passing a `ServletRequest` type object and a `ServletResponse` type object.
- If the container decides that the servlet is no longer needed, it removes and finalizes the servlet by calling the servlet's `destroy()` method.

20.6.1 init()

A servlet's life begins here. This method is called *only once* by the web container, just after it instantiates and loads the servlet. So, it is a good idea to read the persistent configuration data, initialize resources that will be used during the rest of the time, and perform any other one-time activity by overriding the `init()` method. Once the servlet is initialized, it becomes ready to handle the client's request. The prototype of the `init()` method is as follows:

```
void init(ServletConfig)
```

The web container passes a `ServletConfig` object, which contains the startup configuration for this servlet such as initialization parameters.

20.6.2 service()

This is the most important method, whose signature is as follows:

```
void service(ServletRequest request, ServletResponse response)
```

This method gets called each time the web container receives a request intended for this servlet. The web container calls the `service()` method on a servlet with two objects: a `ServletRequest` type object `request` and a `ServletResponse` type object `response`. The `request` object encapsulates the communication from the client to the server, while the `response` object encapsulates the communication from the servlet back to the client.

The `ServletRequest` interface provides methods to retrieve information sent by the clients. Similarly, the `ServletResponse` interface provides methods to send data to the clients.

20.6.3 destroy()

The method signature is as follows:

```
void destroy();
```

This method gets called when the web container uninstalls the servlet. This method is overridden to clean up the resources that were allocated to this servlet. It also makes sure that any persistent state is synchronized with the servlet's current in-memory state.

20.6.4 Other Methods

The `javax.servlet.Servlet` interface also provides the following methods to inspect the properties of a servlet at runtime.

`ServletConfig getServletConfig();`

Returns a `ServletConfig` object, which contains the initialization parameters and startup configuration used for this servlet.

`String getServletInfo();`

Returns a `String` object containing information about the servlet, such as its version, author, copyright, etc.

20.7 GENERICSERVLET AND HTTPSERVLET

The class `javax.servlet.GenericServlet` implements the `javax.servlet.Servlet` interface and, for convenience, the `javax.servlet.ServletConfig` interface. A servlet class is usually created by extending either the `GenericServlet` class or its descendant `javax.servlet.http.HttpServlet` class unless the servlet needs another class as a parent. If a servlet does need to be a subclass of another class, it must implement the `Servlet` interface directly. This would be necessary when, for example, RMI or CORBA objects act as servlets. In such a case, the servlet class must implement all the methods of the `Servlet` interface.

The `GenericServlet` class defines a generic protocol-independent servlet, in the sense that it can be extended to provide implementation of any protocol, such as HTTP, FTP, and SMTP.

The `GenericServlet` class was created to make writing servlets easier. It provides implementations of the life cycle methods `init()` and `destroy()`, as well as methods in the `ServletConfig` interface. The servlet writer has to implement only the `service()` method. This is required because it is the method that is called every time a client requests for the servlet. The prototype of this method is shown as follows.

```
public void service(javax.servlet.ServletRequest request,
        javax.servlet.ServletResponse response)
        throws javax.servlet.ServletException, java.io.IOException;
```

This method expects two arguments. `request` encapsulates the client request and is used to extract information from the client's request. On the other hand, `response` contains information to be sent back to the client.

The `HttpServlet` class extends `GenericServlet` and provides a framework for handling HTTP requests. Servlets that want to handle only HTTP requests are usually created by extending this class. It provides an implementation for the `service()` method. So, you do not have to implement the `service()` method if you extend the `HttpServlet` class. The `service()` method in the `HttpServlet` class reads the method type stored in the request and invokes a specific method based on this value. Specifically, if the method type is GET, it calls `doGet()`; if the method type is POST, it calls `doPost()`; and so on These are the methods that we need to override. The list of all such methods is given in Figure 20.3.

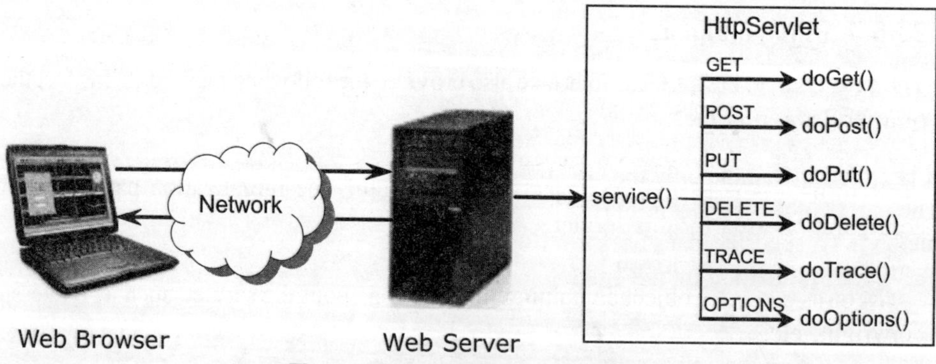

Figure 20.3 HttpServlet in action

Each of these methods takes two arguments: an `HttpServletRequest` type object and an `HttpServletResponse` type object. Following is the prototype of the `doGet()` method:

```
void doGet(HttpServletRequest request, HttpServletResponse response)
```

The `HttpServletRequest` interface extends the `ServletRequest` interface and provides all the functionalities of the `ServletRequest` interface. Additionally, it provides methods to retrieve HTTP headers, cookies sent, and other HTTP-specific information.

The `HttpServletResponse` interface extends the `ServletResponse` interface and provides all the functionalities of the `ServletResponse` interface. Additionally, it provides methods to send HTTP-specific information back to the client.

Servlets created by extending the `HttpServlet` class can handle multiple simultaneous requests. For each request, a thread is created, which runs its `service()` method. If you want to create a single-threaded servlet, your servlet must also implement the `SingleThreadModel` interface as follows:

```
public class SimpleServlet extends HttpServlet implements SingleThreadModel { }
```

The interface `SingleThreadModel` does not define any method. It is used to merely declare that the servlet should use a single thread.

20.8 FIRST SERVLET

Our first servlet is a simple servlet designed to handle the HTTP GET method. Create the following servlet `HelloWorldServlet.java` using any text editor.

```
import java.io.*;
import javax.servlet.*;
import javax.servlet.http.*;
public class HelloWorldServlet extends HttpServlet {
   public void doGet(HttpServletRequest request, HttpServletResponse response)
      throws IOException, ServletException {
      response.setContentType("text/html");
      PrintWriter out = response.getWriter();
      out.println("<html><head><title>Hello World Servlet</title></head>");
      out.println("<body>");
      out.println("<h1>Hello World!</h1>");
      out.println("</body></html>");
      out.close();
   }
}
```

The class `HelloWorldServlet` extends the `HttpServlet` class. So, it can handle HTTP requests. It is written to handle only the GET method. Therefore, only the `doGet()` method is overridden. The output of this servlet is an HTML document. This is mentioned using the `setContentType()` method. To send the data back to the client, a `PrintWriter` object is obtained by calling the `getWriter()` method on the `response` object. Finally, it sends an HTML document as follows:

```
<html><head><title>Hello World Servlet</title></head>
<body>
<h1>Hello World!</h1>
</body></html>
```

At the end, we close the `PrintWriter` object. It is not mandatory as the web container closes the `PrintWriter` or `ServletOutputStream` automatically, when the `service()` method returns. An explicit call to `close()` is useful when you want to perform some processing after responding to the client's request. This also tells the web container that the response is completed and the connection to the client may be closed as well.

20.8.1 Installing Apache Tomcat Web Server

Note that the procedure for installing servlets varies from web server to web server. Please refer to the documentation of your web server for definitive instructions. All the servlets are tested in this book using Apache's Tomcat web server. Tomcat is a lightweight, easily configurable free web server and is widely used by users who are new to servlets.

Let us now discuss how to install and configure the Tomcat web server.

Before installing Tomcat, make sure that you have installed either Java 6 Standard Edition (JDK 1.6) or Java 5 Standard Edition (JDK 1.5) in your computer. Download and install Java from `http://java.sun.com/javase/downloads/index.jsp`. Once you have installed, include the Java "bin" directory in the PATH environment variable. Additionally, create an environment variable JAVA_HOME and set it by the Java installation directory.

Download the necessary files from `http://tomcat.apache.org/download-60.cgi`. If you have downloaded an installer file, install it. If it is a `.zip` file or `.zip.tar` file, simply unzip it in a folder. We shall assume that you have installed Tomcat in the `D:\apache-tomcat-6.0.16` directory.

Tomcat has a predefined directory structure. A typical directory structure is shown in Figure 20.4.

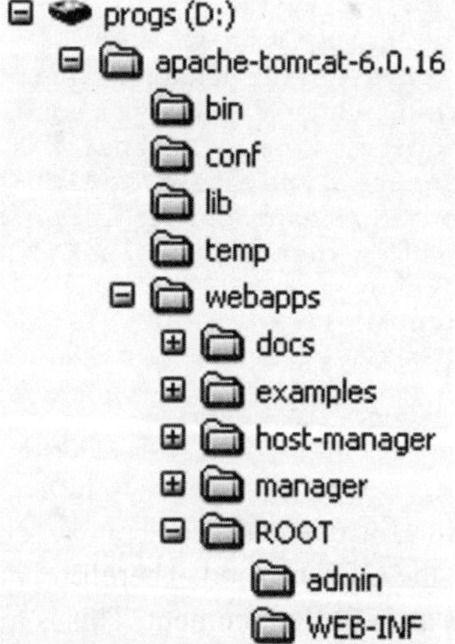

Figure 20.4 Tomcat directory structure

Suppose `$TOMCAT_HOME` represents the root of the Tomcat installation directory. According to Figure 20.4, it represents the `D:\apache-tomcat-6.0.16` directory. Following are some key Tomcat directories under `$TOMCAT_HOME`:

- \bin — Startup, shutdown, and other scripts. The *.bat (for Windows) files and Unix/Linux counterparts *.sh files.
- \conf — Configuration XML files. The primary configuration file is server.xml, which describes how the server starts, behaves and finds other information. All the information in the configuration files is loaded whenever the web server starts up. So, any change to the files needs a restart of the web server.
- \lib — Binary jar files are needed for the server to function. You should put your custom jar files in this directory. Tomcat can find them at runtime.
- \webapps — It contains web applications. The directory ROOT under it contains the default web application, which can be accessed using the URL http://192.168.1.2:8080, where 192.168.1.2 is the IP address of the computer where this web server is running. You should create your own directory under it. We shall create a directory wt (short for web technology) to put our servlet files. So, the document root of our website will be http://192.168.1.2:8080/wt.

20.8.2 Building and Installing Servlet

To compile our HelloWorldServlet.java file, servlet class files are required. Tomcat comes with a .jar file (servlet-api.jar for version 6.0.16) that contains necessary class files. You can find this jar file usually in the $TOMCAT_HOME\lib directory.

Compile the HelloWorldServlet.java using the following command:

```
javac -cp d:\apache-tomcat-6.0.16\lib\servlet-api.jar HelloWorldServlet.java
```

This generates the file HelloWorldServlet.class that contains the byte code for our servlet. Create the following directory structure.

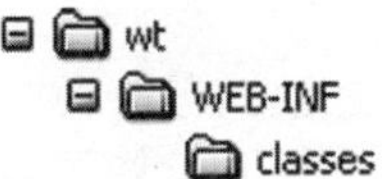

Put this HelloWorldServlet.class file in the $TOMCAT_HOME\webapps\wt\WEB-INF\classes directory.

The servlet class file is now ready to use. However, we have to inform the web server about the existence of this servlet and the URL that will be used to refer to this servlet. This is specified in the $TOMCAT_HOME\wt\WEB-INF\web.xml file, which is the configuration XML file for this website. If the file does not exist, create this file first.

Now, insert the following lines in this file. Some IDE provides interfaces to generate the same information. However, it is recommended to the beginners to do it manually. When you have sufficient knowledge about how to install servlets and how they work, you can use IDEs.

```
<servlet>
    <servlet-name>HelloWorld</servlet-name>
   <servlet-class>HelloWorldServlet</servlet-class>
</servlet>
```

This code maps the servlet class (`HelloWorldServlet.class`) file to a servlet name (`HelloWorld`). You then need to map this servlet name to a URL to be used to invoke this servlet. This is a URL relative to the document root for this website.

```
<servlet-mapping>
   <servlet-name>HelloWorld</servlet-name>
   <url-pattern>/servlet/HelloWorld</url-pattern>
</servlet-mapping>
```

In our case, the document root is `http://192.168.1.2:8080/wt`. So, the complete URL of this servlet will be `http://192.168.1.2:8080/wt/servlet/HelloWorld.`

20.8.3 Invoking Servlet

Invoking this servlet is very easy. Start the Tomcat web server. Type the following URL in the address bar of your web browser and press enter. Make sure that the computer where the web server runs is accessible from your computer.

```
http://192.168.1.2:8080/wt/servlet/HelloWorld
```

It generates the result shown in Figure 20.5.

Figure 20.5 HelloWorld servlet

20.9 PASSING PARAMETERS TO SERVLETS

There are two ways in which you can pass parameters to a servlet: using URL and using HTML form.

Passing parameters directly to a Servlet

Parameters can be passed to servlets directly using URL. In this case parameters and their values are attached directly to the URL when you use the URL to call the servlet. The URL and parameters are separated by '?' character. The character ? says "here are the parameters". Each parameter takes the form `name=value`. Multiple parameters are separated by the '&' character Consider the following URL.

```
http://192.168.1.2:8080/servlet/check?login=abc&password=xyz
```

In this example, two parameters are passed `login` and `password` whose values are `abc` and `xyz`, respectively.

Certain special characters such as space and quote (") are not allowed directly in the URL. These characters are encoded in the `%hh` format where `hh` is the hex code of the character. For example, `%20`, `%22`, and `%7E` represent the space, quote, and tilde (~) characters, respectively.

Passing parameters directly to a Servlet

One of the disadvantages of passing parameters using URLs is that users can view the parameter names with their values passed. So, it is not safe to send sensitive information using this method. Moreover, the number of parameters that we can pass is also limited. HTML forms can be used to pass parameters in a convenient way. The following HTML code can be used to pass the same information as the previous example.

```
<form method='post' action='http://192.168.1.2:8080/servlet/check'>
   Login:<input type='text' name='login'><br />
   Password:<input type='password' name='password'><br/>
   <input type='submit' value='Login'>
</form>
```

The POST method is used here. In this case, the values of all form fields are embedded in the body of the HTTP request message and hence cannot be viewed directly. However, servlets can retrieve them using the usual way.

20.10 RETRIEVING PARAMETERS

The three methods of the `ServletRequest` interface may be used to retrieve parameters. Their signatures are as follows:

```
public abstract java.lang.String getParameter(java.lang.String);
public abstract java.lang.String[] getParameterValues(java.lang.String);
public abstract java.util.Enumeration getParameterNames();
```

The `getParameter()` method returns the value of the specified parameter. Make sure that the parameter has exactly one value. If there are multiple parameters with the same name, use the `getParameterValues()` method, which returns an array of string values of the specified parameter.

The `getParameterNames()` method returns all the parameters as an enumeration. The values of the individual parameters can be obtained by iterating through the enumeration and using the `getParameter()` method for each of these parameters. The following example shows how to retrieve values of two parameters, `login` and `password`, and return back to the client.

```
import java.io.*;
import javax.servlet.*;
import javax.servlet.http.*;
public class GetParameterServlet extends HttpServlet {
   public void doPost(HttpServletRequest request, HttpServletResponse response)
      throws IOException, ServletException {
      response.setContentType("text/html");
```

```
        PrintWriter out = response.getWriter();
        out.println("<html><head><title>Hello World Servlet</title></head>");
        out.println("<body>");
        String login = request.getParameter("login");
        String password = request.getParameter("password");
        out.println("<h2> login:" + login + "<br>password:" + password + "</h2>");
        out.println("</body></html>");
    }
}
```

Compile the servlet, make the following entry in the `web.xml` file, and restart the web server.

```
<servlet>
    <servlet-name>GetParameter</servlet-name>
    <servlet-class>GetParameterServlet</servlet-class>
</servlet>
<servlet-mapping>
    <servlet-name>GetParameter</servlet-name>
    <url-pattern>/servlet/check</url-pattern>
</servlet-mapping>
```

Now, call this servlet from the form described before. The form output is shown in Figure 20.6 (i), while the response from the servlet is shown in Figure 20.6 (ii).

(i) (ii)

Figure 20.6 (i) Passing parameter (ii) Retrieving parameter

In practice, servlets hardly return the parameter with their values back to the client. Typically, they consult the database for further processing. In our case, the servlet will possibly verify the login name and password information against the information stored in the database and depending upon the result, either allow or disallow the user to login.

20.11 SERVER-SIDE INCLUDE

Server-Side Include (SSI) allows us to embed (include) servlets within HTML pages. The HTML files containing servlets typically have the extension `.shtml`. The web server understands this extension and forwards it to an internal servlet. This internal servlet parses the HTML document and executes the referenced servlets and sends the result back to the web server after merging it with the original HTML document. This lets us include dynamically generated content in an existing HTML file, without having to serve the entire page via a CGI program or other dynamic technologies.

Tomcat uses `org.apache.catalina.ssi.SSIServlet` as its internal servlet. To enable SSI support, remove the XML comments from around the SSI servlet and servlet-mapping configuration in `$TOMCAT_HOME/conf/web.xml`.

The syntax for including servlets in HTML documents varies widely from web server to web server. Tomcat SSI directives have the following syntax:

```
<!--#directive attribute="value" attribute="value" ... -->
```

Tomcat SSI directives are formatted like an HTML comment. So, if SSI is not correctly configured, the browser will ignore it. Otherwise, the directive will be replaced with its results.

echo

It just inserts the value of a variable. For example, the following directive inserts the value of the local date.

```
<!--#echo var="DATE_LOCAL" -->
```

This generates the following result:

```
Friday, 20-Nov-2009 20:50:28 IST
```

There are a number of standard variables, including all the environment variables that are available to servlets. Additionally, you can define your own variables with the `set` directive.

printenv

It returns the list of all defined variables.

```
<!--#printenv -->
```

It results in the following:

```
HTTP_USER_AGENT=Mozilla/4.0 (compatible; MSIE 8.0; Windows NT 5.1; Trident/4.0)
HTTP_ACCEPT_LANGUAGE=en-us HTTP_ACCEPT=*/* LAST_MODIFIED=11/20/09
DOCUMENT_URI=/wt/SSI.shtml HTTP_ACCEPT_ENCODING=gzip, deflate REMOTE_PORT=1482
SERVER_NAME=192.168.1.2 SERVER_SOFTWARE=Apache Tomcat/6.0.16 Java HotSpot(TM)
Client VM/11.0-b12 Windows XP SCRIPT_FILENAME=D:\ApacheTomcat6.0.16 on
Thinkpad\webapps\wt\SSI.shtml DATE_LOCAL=11/20/09 SERVER_ADDR=192.168.1.2
SERVER_PROTOCOL=HTTP/1.1 REQUEST_METHOD=GET DOCUMENT_NAME=SSI.shtml
SERVER_PORT=8080 SCRIPT_NAME=/SSI.shtml REMOTE_ADDR=192.168.1.2
DATE_GMT=11/20/09 REMOTE_HOST=192.168.1.2 HTTP_HOST=192.168.1.2:8080
HTTP_CONNECTION=Keep-Alive UNIQUE_ID=2BD24DA4115256FAA76B7E55168AFC28
QUERY_STRING= GATEWAY_INTERFACE=CGI/1.1 org.apache.catalina.ssi.SSIServlet=true
REQUEST_URI=/wt/SSI.shtml
```

config

We can use the `config` directive, with a `timefmt` attribute, to modify the formatting of the date and time as follows:

```
<!--#config timefmt="%A %B %d, %Y" -->
<!--#echo var="DATE_LOCAL" -->
```

This generates the following result:

```
Friday November 20, 2009
```

fsize

This directive returns the size of the file specified by the `file` attribute.

```
<!--#fsize file="SSI.shtml" -->
```

This directive returns the size of the file `SSI.shtml` in kilobytes.

flastmod

The last modification time of a file is inserted using `flastmod` directive whose `file` attribute specifies the file name. The following code inserts the last modification time of the file named `SSI.shtml`.

```
<!--#flastmod file="SSI.shtml" -->
```

You need to replace the `SSI.shtml` with the actual file name you want to refer to. Note that this piece of code does not give the last modification time of an arbitrary file. It is better to use the `echo` directive to print the value of the `LAST_MODIFIED` environment variable, which specifies the last modification time of the file where this directive is included.

```
<!--#echo var="LAST_MODIFIED" -->
```

include

The most common use of SSI is to include the result of a server-side program such as servlet or CGI. The following directive includes the result of our `HelloWorld` servlet in the place of the directive.

```
<!--#include virtual="servlet/HelloWorld" -->
```

The attribute `virtual` specifies the server-side script to be used. Note that the servlet URL used here is relative to the `.shtml` file containing this directive.

So, create a file `SSI.shtml` containing a single line as follows and put in the `$TOMCAT_HOME\webapps\wt` directory.

```
<!--#include virtual="servlet/HelloWorld" -->
```

It generates the same output as our `HelloWorld` servlet, as shown in Figure 20.7.

Figure 20.7 Using SSI

The `include` directive is useful if you want to insert the result of the same servlet in different pages. Use the following to insert a header in every page.

```
<!--#include virtual="/header.html" -->
```

Note that the `include` directive can insert the result of any type of file.

set

It is used for creating variables and setting their values for later use. The following directive creates a variable `SSI` with the value `"Server Side Include"`.

```
<!--#set var="SSI" value="Server Side Include" -->
```

Similarly, the following code creates a variable `sum` with the value `"0"`.

```
<!--#set var="sum" value="0" -->
```

20.12 COOKIES

HTTP is stateless. This means that every HTTP request is different from others. Sometimes, it is necessary to keep track of a sequence of related requests sent by a client to perform some designated task. This is called *session tracking*.

Cookies are one of the solutions to session tracking. A *cookie* is key–value pair created by the server and is installed in the client's browser when the client makes a request for the first time. Browsers also maintain a list of cookies installed in them and send them to the server as a part of subsequent HTTP requests. The server can then easily identify that this request is a part of a sequence of related requests. This way, cookies provide an elegant solution to session tracking.

The servlet API supports cookies. A cookie is represented using the `javax.servlet.http.Cookie` class and is created using the following constructor:

```
Cookie(String key, String value)
```

A cookie is added by the `addCookie()` method of the `HttpServletResponse` class. Similarly, the server can get all cookies sent by the web browser using the `getCookies()` method of the `HttpServletRequest` class.

```
import java.io.*;
import javax.servlet.*;
import javax.servlet.http.*;
public class CookieDemo extends HttpServlet {
   public void doGet(HttpServletRequest request, HttpServletResponse response)
      throws IOException, ServletException {
      PrintWriter out = response.getWriter();
      Cookie[] cookies = request.getCookies();
      boolean found = false;
      if (cookies != null) {
         for (int i = 0; i < cookies.length; i++) {
            if (cookies[i].getName().equals("session_started")) {
               found = true;
               out.print("You started this session on : " );
               out.println(cookies[i].getValue());        }
         }
      }
```

```
        if (!found) {
            String dt = (new java.util.Date()).toString();
            response.addCookie(new Cookie("session_started", dt));
            out.println("Welcome to out site...");
        }
    }
}
```

When a client makes the call for the first time, the web browser does not send any cookie. The servlet looks for the cookie with the name `"session_started"`. Naturally, it cannot find the cookie. It creates, installs, and sends a cookie with the name `"session_started"` using the following code.

```
response.addCookie(new Cookie("session_started", dt));
```

For subsequent calls, web browsers send this cookie with a request. Our servlet finds it, and retrieves the start time of this session and finally sends this value. So, when you access this servlet for the first time, you will see an output as shown in Figure 20.8 (i). Any subsequent request generates the output shown in Figure 20.8 (ii).

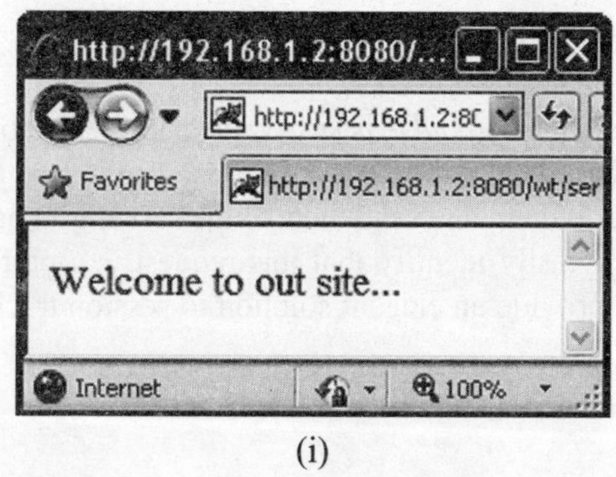

(i)

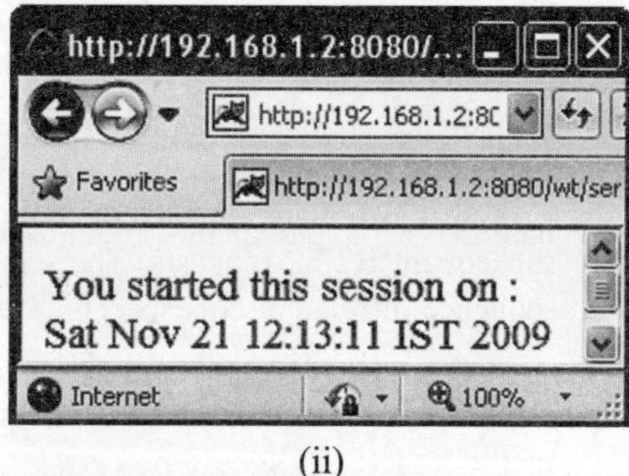

(ii)

Figure 20.8 (i) First access (ii) Subsequent access

20.12.1 Limitations of Cookies

Cookies work correctly, provided that the web browsers have enabled cookie support. In addition to the security concerns, there are some technical limitations:

- Cookies can carry small pieces of information and are not a standard way of communication.
- Some web browsers limit the number of cookies (typically 20 per web server) that can be installed. To avoid this problem, more than one block of information may be sent per cookie.
- The value of a cookie should never exceed 4 KB. If the value of a cookie is larger than 4 KB, it should be trimmed to fit.
- Cookies cannot identify a particular user. A user can be identified by a combination of user account, browser, and computer. So, users who have multiple accounts and use multiple computers/browsers have multiple sets of cookies. Consequently, cookies cannot differentiate between multiple browsers running in a single computer.
- Intruders can snoop, steal cookies, and attack sessions. This is called *session hijacking*.

20.13 FILTERS

Filters are objects that are installed between the client and the server to inspect requests and responses. They can transform the request or modify the response. Note that filters are not servlets and hence cannot create actual responses. Filters process requests before they reach a servlet and/or process responses after leaving a servlet. In general, a filter can do the following:

- Intercept and inspect requests before dispatching them to the servlets
- Modify requests' headers and data and discard or filter requests
- Intercept and inspect responses before dispatching them to the clients
- Modify requests' headers and data and discard or filter responses

A filter can work on behalf of a single servlet or a group of servlets. Similarly, zero or more servlets can be installed for a servlet.

A filter class must implement the `javax.servlet.Filter` interface, which provides a framework for the filtering mechanism. It defines the following method to be implemented by each filter class:

```
void init(FilterConfig config)
```

The web container calls this method once to install it and to set its configuration object. The filter can then start servicing. The `FilterConfig` interface defines methods to retrieve the filter's name, its `init` parameters and the underlying servlet context.

```
void defiler(ServletRequest request, ServletResponse response, FilterChain chain)
```

This method is called before dispatching the request to the servlet. It receives the current request as well as the `FilterChain` containing filters that will handle this request after it. In this method, the filter should process the request and take necessary actions. The filter should then call the `chain.doFilter()` method to handover the control to the next filter in this chain. Whenever the response comes back, this filter can do additional tasks on the response.

If the filter decides, it may not forward the request to the next filter; in this case, the request will not reach the servlet at all. In this way, filters can drop malicious requests intended for the servlet.

```
void destroy()
```

The method is called to uninstall the filter.

The following filter forwards only those requests that come from the host having the IP address "192.168.1.2". Requests from all other hosts are discarded.

```
import java.io.*;
import javax.servlet.*;
public class Firewall implements Filter {
   private FilterConfig config = null;
   public void init(FilterConfig config) throws ServletException {
      this.config = config;
   }
   public void doFilter(ServletRequest request, ServletResponse response,
      FilterChain chain) throws IOException, ServletException {
```

```
        if (request.getRemoteAddr().equals("192.168.1.2"))
            chain.doFilter(request, response);
    }
    public void destroy() {
        config = null;
    }
}
```

20.13.1 Deploying Filter

To use this filter, you must specify it in the `web.xml` file using the `<filter>` tag.

```
<filter>
    <filter-name>myFirewall</filter-name>
    <filter-class>Firewall</filter-class>
</filter>
```

This notifies the server that a filter named `myFirewall` is implemented in the `Firewall` class. Now, add the following lines in the `web.xml` file.

```
<filter-mapping>
    <filter-name>myFirewall</filter-name>
    <url-pattern>/HelloWorld</url-pattern>
</filter-mapping>
```

This code states that a filter has to be installed for the URL pattern `/HelloWorld` that corresponds to our `HelloWorld` servlet. Now, try accessing the `HelloWorld` servlet from the host 192.168.1.2. A response will be received as before. But, if the servlet is accessed from any machine other than 192.168.1.2, no response will be received.

20.14 PROBLEMS WITH SERVLET

Servlets are not useful for generating presentation content such as HTML. Consider the following piece of code.

```
out.println("<html>");
out.println(" <head>");
out.println("    <title>Hello World Servlet</title>");
out.println(" </head>");
out.println(" <body>");
out.println("    <h1>Hello World!</h1>");
out.println(" </body>");
out.println("</html>");
```

The purpose of the code is to generate the following HTML code.

```
<html>
  <head>
    <title>Hello World Servlet</title>
  </head>
  <body>
    <h1>Hello World!</h1>
  </body>
</html>
```

This is acceptable if you want to generate smaller HTML files. However, if the size of the HTML document is large, it is a tedious process to generate it.

Another drawback of the servlet over **J**ava **S**erver **P**ages (JSP) is that you have to recompile the source yourself after any modification is done. Moreover, the web server has to be restarted to get the effect of the modified code. However, JSP can perform these tasks automatically on our behalf.

Servlets often contain presentation logic as well as processing logic, which makes the code difficult to read, understand and extend. If the presentation logic changes, the servlet code has to be modified, recompiled, and redeployed.

20.15 SECURITY ISSUES

Different authors write servlets that are run using the resources of the server computer under the supervision of a web server. So, before installing servlets in the web server, make sure that they come from trusted sources. Certain access constraints should be imposed on the servlets depending on their sources.

The concept of *sandbox* may be incorporated. A *sandbox* is a container of servlets where restrictions are imposed. The administrator of the web server decides which servlets are given which permissions, so that they cannot compromise with the system's security.

In addition to these security issues, the author of the servlet should consider the following points:

- Take sufficient care while writing the file upload code. If not implanted carefully, users may fill the hard disk of the server by uploading large files.
- Review the code that accesses files/database based on the user input. For example, do not allow users to execute arbitrary SQL commands. If allowed, users may fire some harmful SQL commands that can delete database tables.
- Make sure that the request comes from an authorized user. Do not rely on the existence of a session variable.
- Make sure that you have not used the `System.exit()` method anywhere in your program. This will terminate the web server.
- Do not display sensitive parameter values in the web page.

KEYWORDS

Cookies: A cookie is a key–value pair used for session tracking.

Filters: Filters are objects that are installed between the client and the server to inspect requests and responses.

GenericServlet: The class `GenericServlet` implements the Servlet and ServletConfig interfaces and defines a generic protocol-independent servlet.

HTTP tunneling: A procedure for using other protocols through the HTTP protocol.

HttpServletRequest: An interface that represents an HTTP request from the client.

HttpServletResponse: An interface that represents an HTTP response from the servlet.

HttpServlet: The `HttpServlet` class extends `GenericServlet` and provides a framework for handling HTTP requests.

Life Cycle methods: The methods such as `init()`, `service()`, `destroy()` that run during the life cycle of a servlet.

Multi-threaded servlet: A servlet that can handle multiple simultaneous requests.

Server Side Include: Server-Side Include (SSI) allows us to embed (include) servlets within HTML pages, using SSI directives.

Servlet Chain: A sequence of servlets called in that order to accomplish some specific task.

Servlet interface: Top-level interface of the servlet architecture, which provides the basic functionalities of all servlets that are created by implementing this interface directly or indirectly.

Servlet life cycle: The set of states that a servlet goes through, from creation to destruction.

ServletConfig interface: Represents the configuration of a servlet.

ServletRequest: An interface that represents a request from the client.

ServletResponse: An interface that represents a response from the servlet.

Session Tracking: Keeping track of a sequence of requests sent by a client to perform some designated task.

Single-threaded servlet: A servlet that can service one request at a time.

Web container: The environment/engine where servlets or other server-side programs run.

SUMMARY

Servlet is a Java technology for server-side programming. A servlet is a Java module that runs inside a Java-enabled web server and services requests obtained from a web server.

Java servlet technology has some distinct advantages over other competent technologies in terms of efficiency, persistency, portability, robustness, extensibility, etc. Servlets run in the server machine and usually generate simple HTML codes. So, even a very old browser can display generated HTML pages correctly.

The basic servlet architecture consists of two packages: `javax.servlet` and `javax.servlet.http`. The first package contains top-level interfaces and classes that are used and extended by all other servlets. The second package is provided to use for servlets that can handle HTTP requests.

The container in which the servlet is deployed, supervises and controls the life cycle of a servlet. During its lifetime, methods such as `init()`, `service()`, and `destroy()` are called in some specific order.

The `GenericServlet` class defines a generic protocol-independent servlet in the sense that it can be extended to provide implementation of any protocol such as HTTP, FTP, and SMTP. On the other hand, `HttpServlet` class extends GenericServlet and provides a framework for handling HTTP requests.

There are two ways in which you can pass parameters to a servlet: using URL and using HTML form. One of the disadvantages of passing parameters using URLs is that users can view the parameter names with their values passed. So, it is not safe to send sensitive information using this method. Moreover, the number of parameters that we can pass is also limited. HTML forms can be used to pass parameters in a convenient way. The methods of the ServletRequest interface are used to retrieve parameters.

Server-Side Include (SSI) allows us to embed (include) servlets within HTML pages, using SSI directives. This lets us include dynamically generated content in an existing HTML file, without having to serve the entire page via a CGI program or other dynamic technologies.

Sometimes, it is necessary to keep track of a sequence of related requests sent by a client to perform some designated task. This is called session tracking. Cookies are one of the solutions to session tracking.

Filters are objects that are installed between clients and servers to inspect requests and responses. They can transform request or modify responses.

WEB RESOURCES

`http://java.sun.com/j2ee/tutorial/1_3-fcs/doc/Servlets.html`
Java Servlet Technology

EXERCISES

Multiple Choice Questions

1. Which one of the following methods is called first on a servlet?
   (a) start() (b) initialize()
   (c) init() (d) doInit()

2. Which of the following is the name of a web server?
   (a) Netscape (b) Borland
   (c) W3C (d) Tomcat

3. Which is the top-level class/interface in the servlet class hierarchy?
   (a) javax.servlet.Servlet
   (b) javax.servlet.HttpServlet
   (c) javax.servlet.GenericServlet
   (d) javax.servlet.TopServlet

4. Which of the following statements is false regarding servlets?
   (a) The init() function is called only once during the instantiation of the servlet
   (b) The HttpServlet class implements the Servlet interface
   (c) The HttpServlet can handle HTTP requests
   (d) The GenericServlet class implements the Servlet interface

5. A servlet is instantiated when
   (a) a client makes a request for the first time.
   (b) the web server starts up
   (c) the client makes a request
   (d) the source code is compiled

6. Which of the following interfaces a single threaded servlet must implement?
   (a) NoMultiThread
   (b) SingleThread
   (c) OneThreadModel
   (d) SingleThreadModel

7. How many arguments does the service() method take?
   (a) 1 (b) 2 (c) 3 (d) 4

8. Which of the following methods is used to retrieve the value of a specified parameter?
   (a) getParameter() (b) retrieveParameter()
   (c) parameter() (d) getParam()

9. Which of the following tags is used to make a named servlet?
   (a) <servlet-name> (b) <servlet-class>
   (c) <servlet> (d) <servlet-mapping>

10. Which of the following tags maps a named servlet to a URL pattern?
    (a) <servlet> (b) <servlet-name>
    (c) <servlet-class> (d) <servlet-mapping>

11. Which of the following SSI directives displays the value of a variable?
    (a) display (b) print
    (c) echo (d) show

12. What is the full form of SSI?
    (a) Server Side Include
    (b) Server Side Integration
    (c) Same Side Include
    (d) Same Side Integration

13. Which of the following SSI directive is used insert the content of a server-side program?
    (a) insert (b) include
    (c) paste (d) import

14. Which of the following methods is used to add a cookie to the response?
    (a) addCookie() (b) sendCookie()
    (c) installCookie() (d) insertCookie()

15. What is the name of the servlet configuration file?
    (a) servlet.xml (b) config.xml
    (c) web.xml (d) server.xml

16. Which of the following packages contains Servlet interface?
    (a) javax.server.servlet (b) javax.servlet
    (c) java.server.servlet (d) java.servlet

17. The servlet initialization parameters are specified in the ________ deployment descriptor file as part of a servlet element.
    (a) web.xml (b) web.doc
    (c) web.txt (d) web.ini

18. Which of the following identifies the correct method a servlet developer should use to retrieve data provided by the client?
    (a) getParameter() against the HttpServletRequest object
    (b) getInputStream() against the HttpServletRequest object
    (c) getBytes() against the HttpServletRequest object
    (d) getQueryString() against the HttpServletRequest object

19. Which package provides interfaces and classes for writing servlets?
    (a) javax.servlet (b) javax.java.servlet
    (c) javax.awt.servlet (d) javax.swing.servlet

20. The Web server that executes the servlet creates an ________ object and passes this to the servlet's service method (which, in turn, passes it to doGet or doPost).
    (a) HttpRequest (b) HttpResponse
    (c) Request (d) HttpServletResponce

21. Which method can be used to access the ServletConfig object?
    (a) getServletInfo()
    (b) getServletConfig()
    (c) getInitParameters()
    (d) getConfig()

Review Questions

1. What is a servlet?
2. What are the advantages of servlets over CGI?
3. What is the task of the javax.servlet.Servlet interface?
4. What are the two objects that a servlet receives when it accepts a call from a client?
5. What information does ServletRequest allow access to?
6. What type of constraints can ServletResponse interface set on the client?
7. Describe the life cycle of a servlet.
8. Describe how an HTTP Servlet handles its client requests.
9. Differentiate between the single-threaded and multi-threaded servlet model.
10. What are the differences between servlets and applets?
11. Mention some uses of Servlets.
12. How can you invoke other web resources such as servlets /JSPs?
13. How can you include other Resources in the Response?
14. What information does the ServletResponse interface give to the servlet methods for replying to the client?
15. What do you understand by servlet mapping?
16. What are the advantages of Cookies over URL rewriting?
17. What is session hijacking?

21 JAVA SERVER PAGES (JSP)

Key Objectives

After completing this chapter readers will be able to—

- understand the advantages of JSP technology over other competitive technologies
- learn the architecture of JSP pages and their execution philosophy
- get an idea about the different components of JSP pages
- get an overview about the methods used to track sessions
- create and use JavaBean components
- create and use custom tags
- learn how to use JDBC technology

21.1 INTRODUCTION AND MARKETPLACE

Java **S**erver **P**ages (JSP) is a server-side technology that enables web programmers to generate web pages dynamically in response to client requests. There are many server-side technologies for building dynamic web applications. However, JSP is the one that has pulled the attention of the web developers. There are several reasons for it.

JSP is nothing but high-level abstraction of Java servlet technology. It allows us to directly embed pure Java code in an HTML page. JSP pages run under the supervision of an environment called *web container*. The web container compiles the page on the server and generates a servlet, which is loaded in the Java Runtime Environment (JRE). The servlet serves the client requests in the usual way. This makes the development of web applications convenient, simple, and fast. Maintenance also becomes very easy.

JSP technology provides excellent server-side programming for web applications that need database access. JSP not only provides cross-web-server and cross-platform support, but also integrates the WYSIWYG (What You See Is What You Get) features of static HTML pages with the extreme power of Java technology.

JSP also allows us to separate the dynamic content of our web pages from the static HTML content. We can write regular HTML files in the usual way. We can then insert Java code for the dynamic parts using special tags, which usually start with <% and end with %>.

Usually, JSP files have the extension .jsp. They are also installed in a place where we can place our normal web pages. Many web servers let us define aliases for JSP pages or servlets. So, a URL that appears to reference an HTML file may actually point to a JSP page or servlet.

21.2 JSP AND HTTP

Java Server Pages specification extends the idea of Java servlet API, to provide a robust framework to developers of web applications for creating dynamic web content. Currently, JSP or servlet technology supports only HTTP. However, a developer may extend the idea of servlet or JSP to implement other protocols such as FTP or SMTP. Since JSP uses HTML, XML, and Java code, the applications are secure, fast, and independent of server platforms. It allows us to embed pure Java code in an HTML document. It is important to note that JSP specification has been defined on top of the Java servlet API. Consequently, it follows all servlet semantics and has all powers that the servlet has.

The life cycle and many of the capabilities, especially the dynamic aspects of JSP pages, are exactly the same as Java servlet technology. So, much of the discussion in this chapter refers to Chapter 20.

21.3 JSP ENGINES

To process JSP pages, a JSP engine is needed. It is interesting to note that what we know as the "JSP engine" is nothing but a specialized servlet, which runs under the supervision of the servlet engine. This JSP engine is typically connected with a web server or can be integrated inside a web server or an application server. Many such servers are freely available and can be downloaded for evaluation and/or development of web applications. Some of them are Tomcat, Java Web Server, WebLogic, and WebSphere.

Once you have downloaded and installed a JSP-capable web-server or application server in your machine, you need to know where to place the JSP files and how to access them from the web browser using the URL. We shall use the Tomcat JSP engine from Apache to test our JSP pages.

21.3.1 Tomcat

Tomcat implements servlet 2.2 and JSP 1.1 specifications. It is very easy to install and can be used as a small stand-alone server for developing and testing servlets and JSP pages. For large applications, it is integrated into the Apache Web server.

In this book, we shall use tomcat JSP engine to test our JSP pages. Following is a brief description of how to install Tomcat in your machine.

- Download the appropriate version of Tomcat from the Apache site `http://tomcat.apache.org/`
- Uncompress the file in a directory. If it is an installer file in Windows, install it in a directory by double clicking on the installer file.
- Set the environment variable JAVA_HOME to point to the root directory of your JDK hierarchy. For example, if the root directory of your JDK is `D:\Java\jdk1.6.0_10`, the JAVA_HOME environment variable should point to this directory. Also make sure that the directory (usually bin) containing the Java compiler and interpreter is in your PATH environment variable.
- Go to the bin directory under the tomcat installation directory and start Tomcat using the command-line command `startup.bat` (in Windows) or `startup.sh` (in Unix/Linux). If everything goes well, you will see an output in Windows as shown in Figure 21.1

Figure 21.1 Starting tomcat server

- Tomcat is now running on port 8080 by default. You can test it by using the URL `http://127.0.0.1:8080/` . The page shown in Figure 21.2 appears.

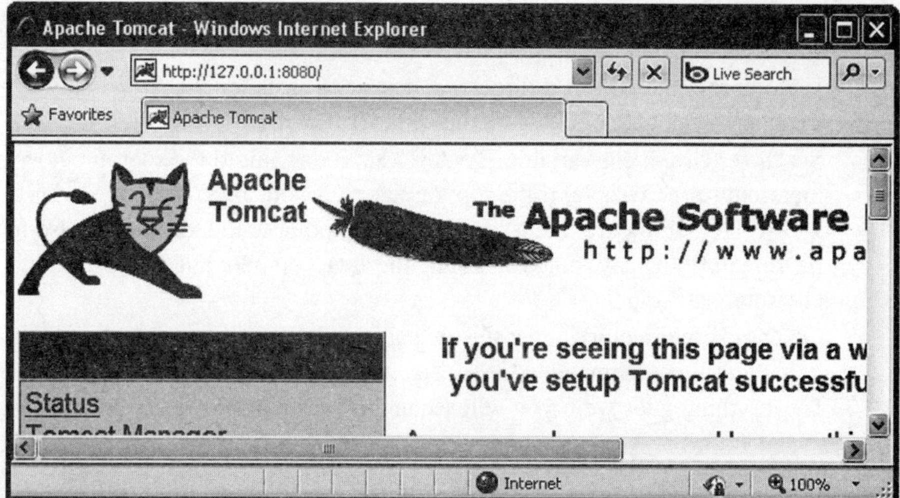

Figure 21.2 Tomcat home page

21.3.2 Java Web Server

The Java System Web Server by Sun is a leading web server that delivers secure infrastructure for medium and large business technologies and applications. Sun claims that it delivers 8x better performance than Apache 2.0 with Tomcat. It is available on all major operating systems and supports a wide range of technologies such as JSP and Java Servlet technologies, PHP, and CGI.

21.3.3 WebLogic

WebLogic by BEA Systems of San Jose, California, is a J2EE application server and also an HTTP server for Microsoft Windows, Unix/Linux, and other platforms. WebLogic supports DB2, Oracle, Microsoft SQL Server, and other JDBC-compliant databases.

The WebLogic server also includes the .NET framework for interoperability and allows integration of the following native components:

- CORBA connectivity
- COM+ Connectivity
- J2EE Connector Architecture
- IBM's WebSphere MQ connectivity
- Native JMS messaging for enterprise

Data Mapping functionality and Business Process Management are also included in WebLogic Server Process Edition.

21.3.4 WebSphere

IBM attempted to develop a software to set up, operate, and integrate electronic business applications that can work across multiple computing platforms, using Java-based web technologies. The result is WebSphere Application Server (WAS). It includes both the run-time components and the tools that can be used to develop robust and versatile applications that will run on WAS.

21.4 HOW JSP WORKS

When a client such as a web browser sends a request to a web server for a JSP file using a URL, the web server identifies the .jsp file extension in the URL and figures out that the requested resource is a Java Server Page. The web server hands over the request to a special servlet. This servlet checks whether the servlet corresponding to this JSP page exists or not. If the servlet does not exist, or exists but it is older than the JSP page, it performs the following:

- Translates the JSP source code into the servlet source code
- Compiles the servlet source code to generate a class file
- Loads the class file and creates an instance
- Initializes the servlet instance by calling the `jspInit()` method
- Invokes the `_jspService()` method, passing request and response objects

If the servlet exists and is not older than the corresponding JSP page requested, it does the following:

- If an instance is already running, it simply forwards the request to this instance.
- Otherwise, it loads the class file, creates an instance, initializes it, and forwards the request to this instance.

During development, one of the advantages of JSP pages over servlets is that the build process is automatically performed by the JSP engine. When a JSP file is requested for the first time, or if it is changed, the translation and compilation phase occurs. The subsequent requests for the JSP page directly go to the servlet byte code, which is already in the memory.

21.5 JSP AND SERVLET

Java servlet technology is an extremely powerful technology. However, when it is used to generate large, complex HTML code, it becomes a bit cumbersome.

In most servlets, a small piece of code is written to handle application logic and a large code is written using several `out.println()` statements that handle output formatting. Since the codes for application logic and formatting are closely tied, it is difficult to separate and reuse portions of the code when a different logic or output format is required.

JSP separates the static presentation templates from the logic, to generate the dynamic content by encapsulating it within external JavaBean components. These components are then instantiated and used in a JSP page using special tags and scriptlets. When the presentation template is changed by the web designer, the JSP engine recompiles the JSP page and reloads it in the **J**ava **R**untime **E**nvironment (JRE).

Another problem of servlets is that each time the servlet code is modified, it needs to be recompiled and the web server also needs to be restarted. The JSP engine takes care of all these issues automatically.

Whenever a JSP code is modified, the JSP engine identifies it and translates it into a new servlet. The servlet code is then compiled, loaded, and instantiated automatically. The servlet remains in the memory and serves requests subsequently without any delay.

JSP uses technologies based on reusable component engineering such as JavaBean component architecture and Enterprise JavaBean technology. So, JSP does not require significant developer expertise, like Java servlets. Consequently, in the application development life cycle, page designers can now play a major role. JSP pages can be moved easily across web servers and platforms, without any changes or significant effort.

For these reasons, web application developers turn towards JSP technology as an alternative to servlet technology.

21.5.1 Translation and Compilation

Every JSP page gets converted to a normal servlet behind the scene by the web container automatically. Figure 21.3 shows one such translation.

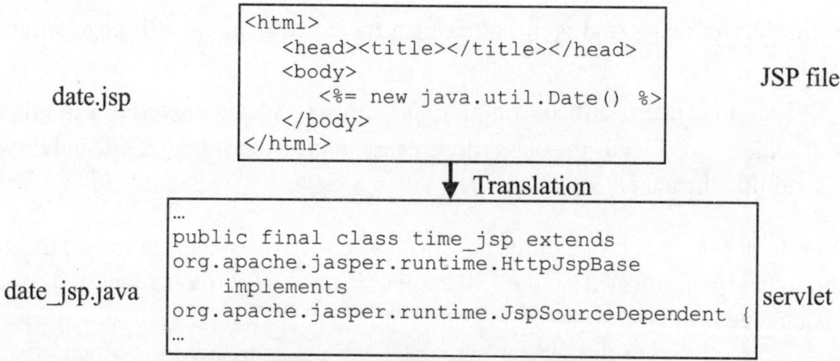

Figure 21.3 JSP to servlet translation

Each type of data in a JSP page is processed differently during the translation phase. The translation and compilation phases may result in errors. These errors (if any) are generated when a user requests the page for the first time.

The JSP engine returns a `ParseException`, if an error occurs during the translation phase. In such a case, the servlet source file will be empty or incomplete. The last incomplete line describes the cause of error in the JSP page. If an error occurs during the compilation phase, the JSP engine returns a `JasperException` and a message that describes the name of the JSP page's servlet and the line that caused the error.

Now, let us take a specific example to understand this translation procedure. Consider the following JSP page. You may not understand the syntax used in this file. We shall discuss it in the rest of this chapter.

```
<html>
   <head><title>Square table</title></head>
   <body>
      <table border="1">
```

```
        <caption>Temperature Conversion chart</caption>
        <tr><th>Celsius</th><th>Fahrenheit</th></tr>
      <%
        for(int c = 0; c <= 100; c+=20) {
          double f = (c*9)/5.0 + 32;
          out.println("<tr><td>" + c + "</td><td>" + f + "</td></tr>");
        }
      %>
      </table>
    </body>
  </html>
```

This is a simple JSP page that prints temperature conversion (from Celsius to Fahrenheit) chart. If you open this page in the Internet Explorer, it looks as shown in Figure 21.4.

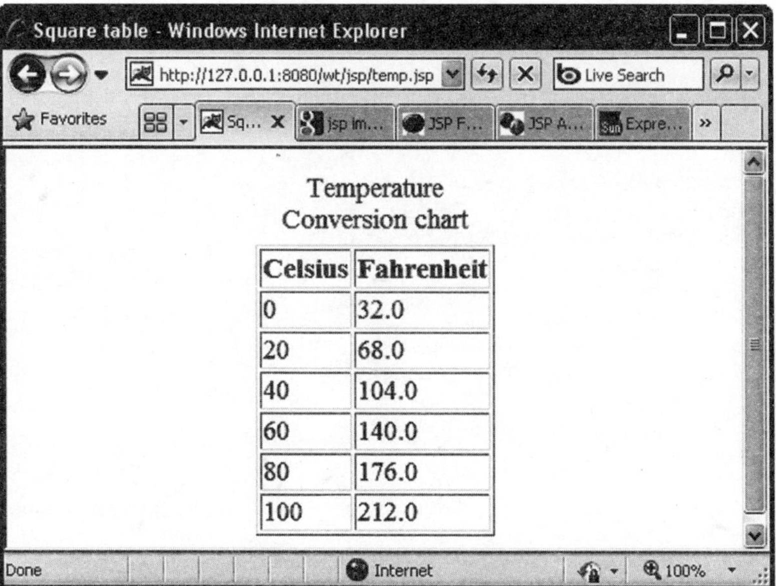

Figure 21.4 Temperature conversion chart

When you request this page for the first time, the JSP engine translates the JSP page into the following servlet source code.

```
package org.apache.jsp.jsp;

import javax.servlet.*;
import javax.servlet.http.*;
import javax.servlet.jsp.*;

public final class temp_jsp extends org.apache.jasper.runtime.HttpJspBase
    implements org.apache.jasper.runtime.JspSourceDependent {

  private static final JspFactory _jspxFactory = JspFactory.getDefaultFactory();

  private static java.util.List _jspx_dependants;
```

```
  private javax.el.ExpressionFactory _el_expressionfactory;
  private org.apache.AnnotationProcessor _jsp_annotationprocessor;

  public Object getDependants() {
    return _jspx_dependants;
  }

  public void _jspInit() {
    _el_expressionfactory =
_jspxFactory.getJspApplicationContext(getServletConfig().getServletContext()).
getExpressionFactory();
    _jsp_annotationprocessor = (org.apache.AnnotationProcessor)
getServletConfig().getServletContext().getAttribute(org.apache.AnnotationProcessor.
class.getName());
  }

  public void _jspDestroy() {
  }

  public void _jspService(HttpServletRequest request, HttpServletResponse response)
        throws java.io.IOException, ServletException {

    PageContext pageContext = null;
    HttpSession session = null;
    ServletContext application = null;
    ServletConfig config = null;
    JspWriter out = null;
    Object page = this;
    JspWriter _jspx_out = null;
    PageContext _jspx_page_context = null;


    try {
      response.setContentType("text/html");
      pageContext = _jspxFactory.getPageContext(this, request, response,
                null, true, 8192, true);
      _jspx_page_context = pageContext;
      application = pageContext.getServletContext();
      config = pageContext.getServletConfig();
      session = pageContext.getSession();
      out = pageContext.getOut();
      _jspx_out = out;

      out.write("<html>\r\n");
      out.write("\t<head><title>Square table</title></head>\r\n");
      out.write("\t<body>\r\n");
      out.write("\t\t<table border=\"1\">\r\n");
      out.write("\t\t\t<caption>Temperature Conversion chart</caption>\r\n");
      out.write("\t\t\t<tr><th>Celsius</th><th>Fahrenheit</th></tr>\r\n");
      out.write("\t\t");

        for(int c = 0; c <= 100; c+=20) {
           double f = (c*9)/5.0 + 32;
           out.println("<tr><td>" + c + "</td><td>" + f + "</td></tr>");
        }
```

```
        out.write("\r\n");
        out.write("\t\t</table>\r\n");
        out.write("\t</body>\r\n");
        out.write("</html>");
      } catch (Throwable t) {
        if (!(t instanceof SkipPageException)){
          out = _jspx_out;
          if (out != null && out.getBufferSize() != 0)
            try { out.clearBuffer(); } catch (java.io.IOException e) {}
          if (_jspx_page_context != null)
  _jspx_page_context.handlePageException(t);
        }
      } finally {
        _jspxFactory.releasePageContext(_jspx_page_context);
      }
    }
  }
```

The JSP page's servlet class extends `HttpJspBase`, which in turn implements the `Servlet` interface. In the generated servlet class, the methods `jspInit()`, `_jspService()`, and `jspDestroy()` correspond to the servlet life cycle methods `init()`, `service()`, and `destroy()`, respectively which were discussed in Chapter 20. The `_jspService()` method is responsible for serving client's requests. JSP specification prohibits the overriding of the `_jspService()` method. However, the developers are allowed to override the `jspInit()` and `jspDestroy()` methods within their JSP pages, to initialize and shut down servlets, respectively.

By default, the servlet container dispatches the `_jspService()` method using a separate thread to process concurrent client requests, as shown in Figure 21.5.

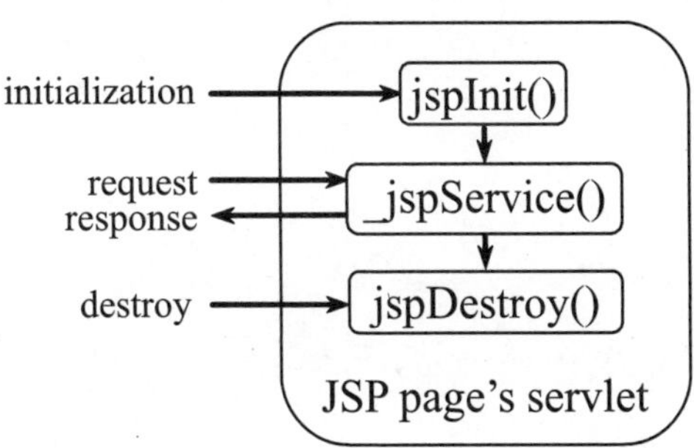

Figure 21.5 Life cycle of JSP's servlet

The static HTML part is simply printed to the output stream associated with the servlet's `service()` method. The code in <% and %> is copied in the `_jspService()` method.

21.6 ANATOMY OF A JSP PAGE

A JSP page basically consists of two parts: HTML/XML markups and JSP constructs. A large percent of your JSP page, in many cases, just consists of static HTML/XML components, known as *template text.* Consequently, we can create and maintain JSP pages using traditional HTML/XML tools.

We use three primary types of JSP constructs in a typical JSP page: *scripting elements*, *directives*, and *actions*.

Java code that will become an integral part of the resultant servlet is inserted using *scripting elements*. *Directives* let us control the overall structure and behavior of the generated servlet. *Actions* allow us to use existing components, and otherwise control the behavior of the JSP engine.

There are three kinds of scripting elements: *scriptlets*, *declarations*, and *expressions.* Scriptlets allow us to insert any Java-server-relevant API in the HTML or XML page provided that the syntax is correct. Declarations allow us to declare variable and methods. Expressions are used to print the value of a Java expression.

21.7 JSP SYNTAX

The syntax of JSP is almost similar to that of XML. ALL JSP tags must conform to the following general rules:

- Tags must have their matching end tags.
- Attributes must appear in the start tag,
- Attribute values in the tag must be quoted.

White spaces within the body text of a JSP page are preserved during the translation phase. To use special characters such as '%', add a '\' character before it. To use the '\' character, add another '\' character before it.

21.8 JSP COMPONENTS

A JSP page consists of the following components:

- Directives
- Declarations
- Expressions
- Scriptlets
- Actions

Table 21.1 lists some JSP tags and their meanings.

Table 21.1 JSP tags

JSP tag	Meaning
<%@...%>	Used for JSP directives such as page and include
<%=...%>	Used for JSP expressions
<%...%>	Used for JSP scriptlets that can contain arbitrary Java statements
<%!...%>	Used for variables, methods, and inner class declarations

21.8.1 Directives

A JSP page may contain instructions to be used by the JSP container to indicate how this page is interpreted and executed. Those instructions are called *directives*. Directives do not generate any output directly, but tell the JSP engine how to handle the JSP page. They are enclosed within the <%@ and %> tags. The commonly used directives are page, include, and taglib.

21.8.1.1 Page directive

Following is the syntax of the page directive:

```
<%@ page
    [ language="java" ]
    [ extends="package.class" ]
    [ import="{package.class | package.*}, ..." ]
    [ session="true | false" ]
    [ buffer="none | 8kb | sizekb" ]
    [ autoFlush="true | false" ]
    [ isThreadSafe="true | false" ]
    [ info="text" ]
    [ errorPage="relativeURL" ]
    [ contentType="MIMEType [ ;charset=characterSet ]"   |   "text/html ;
charset=ISO-8859-1" ]
        [ isErrorPage="true | false" ]
%>
```

The page directive has many attributes, which can be specified in any order. Multiple page directives may also be used, but in this case, except for the import attribute, no attribute should appear more than once. The code in boldface indicates the default values. Let us discuss the function of some attributes.

import

The value of this attribute is a list of fully qualified names of classes separated by commas (,), to be imported by the JSP file. To import all the classes of a package, use ".*" at the end of the package name. The following directive imports all the classes in the java.io and java.reflect packages and the class Vector that belongs to the java.util package.

```
<%@ page import="java.io.*, java.reflect.*, java.util.Vector" %>
```

The classes can then be referred from declarations, expressions, and scriptlets within the JSP document, without using the package prefix. You must import a class before using it. You can use import as many times as you wish in a JSP file. For example, the line of code we have just discussed can be written as three directives, as follows:

```
<%@ page import="java.io.*" %>
<%@ page import="java.reflect.*" %>
<%@ page import="java.util.Vector" %>
```

Those directives are converted to the corresponding import statement in the generated servlet file. You need not import the classes of the packages java.lang, javax.servlet, javax.servlet.http, and javax.servlet.jsp, as they are imported implicitly.

session

This attribute indicates whether the JSP file requires a HTTP session. The following syntax is used:

```
session="true | false"
```

If `true` is specified (this is the default value), the JSP file has a `session` object that refers to the current or new session. If the value is `false`, no `session` object is created.

If your JSP file does not require a session, the value should be set to `false` for performance consideration.

buffer

Syntax:

```
buffer="none | sizekb"
```

The `buffer` attribute indicates the size in kilobytes (default is 8kb) of the output buffer to be used by the JSP file. The value `none` indicates a buffer with zero size. In such a case, the output is written directly to the output stream of the response object of the servlet.

autoFlush

Syntax:

```
autoFlush="true | false"
```

The `autoFlush` attribute specifies whether the buffer should be flushed automatically (`true`) when it is full. If set to `false`, a buffer overflow exception is thrown when the buffer becomes full. The default value is `true`. The value of `autoFlush` can never be set to false when the buffer is set to none.

isThreadSafe

Syntax:

```
isThreadSafe="true | false"
```

This attribute indicates whether the JSP page can handle multiple threads simultaneously. If true (default value) is specified, the JSP container is allowed to send multiple concurrent client requests to this JSP page. In this case, we must ensure that the access to shared resources by multiple concurrent threads is effectively synchronized. If false is specified, the JSP container sends clients requests one by one using a single thread. This attribute basically provides information to the underlying servlet on whether it should implement the `SingleThreadModel` interface or not. Tomcat generates the following servlet class declaration if `false` is specified.

```
public final class ThreadDemo_jsp extends org.apache.jasper.runtime.HttpJspBase
    implements  org.apache.jasper.runtime.JspSourceDependent,
                SingleThreadModel
```

In this case, the JSP container loads multiple instances of the servlet in the memory. It then distributes concurrent client requests evenly among these servlet instances for processing in a round-robin fashion.

If `true` is specified, the following code is generated:

```
public final class ThreadDemo_jsp extends org.apache.jasper.runtime.HttpJspBase
    implements org.apache.jasper.runtime.JspSourceDependent
```

info

Syntax:

```
info="text"
```

It allows us to specify a descriptive information about the JSP page. This information can be retrieved using the `Servlet.getServletInfo()` method.

contentType

Syntax:

```
contentType="MIMEType [ ;charset=characterSet ]"
```

It specifies the MIME type and encoding used in the generated response to be sent to the client. MIME types and encoding supported by the JSP container can only be specified. The default MIME type and character encoding are `text/html` and `ISO-8859-1`, respectively.

errorPage and isErrorPage

Syntax:

```
errorPage="relativeURL"
isErrorPage="true | false"
```

When an uncaught exception occurs in a JSP page, the JSP container sends information explaining the exception, which is undesirable in commercial sites. The `errorPage` attribute specifies the relative path name of another JSP page to be displayed, in case an error occurs in the current page. In the error page, the `isErrorPage` attribute must be set to `true`. The error page can access the implicit `exception` variable that represents the exception that has occurred as well as other implicit variables. It can then send some message understandable by the clients, by consulting those objects.

21.8.1.2 Include directive

This directive inserts the content of a file in a JSP page, during the translation phase when the JSP page is compiled.

```
<%@ include file="relativeURL" %>
```

If the file to be included is an HTML or text file, its content is directly included in the place of the `include` directive. The following example includes an HTML file `header.html` in a JSP page.

```
<%@ include file="header.html" %>
```

If the included file is a JSP file, it is first translated and then included in the JSP page.

```
<%@ include file="login.jsp" %>
```

Make sure that the tags in the included file do not conflict with the tags used in including the JSP page. For example, if the including JSP page contains tags such as `<html>` and `<body>`, the included file must not contain those tags.

The include process is said to be static as the file is included at compilation time. JSP 1.1 specifies that once the JSP file is compiled any changes in the included file will not be reflected. However, some JSP containers, such as tomcat, recompile the JSP page if the included file changes.

21.8.2 Comments

Comments are used to document the JSP pages and can be inserted anywhere in the JSP page. The general syntax is as follows:

```
<%-- JSP comment --%>
```

Anything between `<%--` and `--%>` is ignored by the JSP engine and is not even added to the servlet's source code. Here is an example:

```
<%-- Prints current date and time --%>
<%= new java.util.Date(); %>
```

The Java-like comments may also be used in scriptlets and declarations. They are added to the servlet, but not interpreted and hence are not sent to the client.

```
<%
   //get all cookies
   Cookie[] cookies = request.getCookies();
   /*
   Following code checks whether the request contains
   a cookie having name "user"
   */
   String user = null;
   for(int i = 0; i < cookies.length; i++)
      if(cookies[i].getName().equals("user"))
         user = (String)cookies[i].getValue();
   if(user != null) {
      //proceed
   }
%>
```

The HTML comments are enclosed in `<!--` and `-->` and added to the servlet source code as well as to the response, but are not displayed on the client's screen. Consider the following code:

```
<!-- This page was generated at server on
<%= (new java.util.Date()) %>
-->
```

This generates the following HTML comment. This is sent to the client, but not displayed on the screen.

```
<!-- This page was generated at server on
Sat Dec 05 13:17:45 IST 2009
-->
```

21.8.3 Expressions

JSP 2.0 specification includes a new feature, "Expression". It is used to insert usually a small piece of data in a JSP page, without using the `out.print()` or `out.write()` statements. It is a faster, easier, and clearer way to display the values of variables/parameters/expressions in a JSP page. The general syntax of the JSP expression is as follows:

```
<%= expressions %>
```

The expression is embedded within the tag pair `<%=` and `%>`. Note that no semicolon is used at the end of the expression. The expression is evaluated, converted to a `String` and inserted in the place of the expression using an `out.print()` statement. For example, if we want to add 3 and 4 and display the result, we write the JSP expression as follows:

```
3 + 4 = <%= 3+4 %>
```

The expression is translated into the following Java statements in servlet source code.

```
out.write("3 + 4 = ");
out.print( 3+4 );
```

If everything works, you should see the following output:

```
3 + 4 = 7
```

The expression can be anything, as long as it can be converted to a string. For example, the following expression uses a `java.util.Date` object.

```
Date and time is : <%= new java.util.Date() %>
```

JSP expressions can be used as attribute values as well as tag names of JSP elements. Consider the following JSP code.

```
<%
   java.util.Date dt = new java.util.Date();
   String dateStr = dt.toString();
   String time = "currentTime";
%>
<<%= time %> value="<%= dateStr %>" />
```

This generates the following tag:

```
<currentTime value="Mon Nov 30 19:26:17 IST 2009" />
```

JSP also has the following XML equivalent for expression:

```
<jsp:expression>
   expressions
</jsp:expression>
```

21.8.4 Scriptlets

You can insert an arbitrary piece of Java code using the JSP *scriptlets* construct in a JSP page. This code will be inserted in the servlet's `_jspService()` method. Scriptlets are useful if you want to insert complex code which would otherwise be difficult using expressions. A scriptlet can contain any number of variables, class declarations, expressions, or other language statements. Scriptlets have the following form:

```
<% scriptlets %>
```

For example, the following scriptlet inserts the current date and time in the JSP page.

```
<%
   java.util.Date d = new java.util.Date();
   out.println("Date and time is : " + d);
%>
```

The resultant servlet code looks like this:

```
...
public final class scriptlet_jsp extends org.apache.jasper.runtime.HttpJspBase
    implements org.apache.jasper.runtime.JspSourceDependent {
...
  public void _jspService(HttpServletRequest request, HttpServletResponse
response)
        throws java.io.IOException, ServletException {
...

   java.util.Date d = new java.util.Date();
   out.println("Date and time is : " + d);
...
```

This results in the following:

```
Date and time is : Mon Nov 30 17:01:09 IST 2009
```

JSP also has the following XML equivalent for scriptlet:

```
<jsp:scriptlet>
   scriptlets
</jsp:scriptlet>
```

21.8.4.1 Conditional processing

Several scriptlets and templates can be merged, to do some designated task. The following example illustrates this:

```
<%
int no = (int)(Math.random()*10);
if(no % 2 == 0) {
%>
Even
<% } else { %>
Odd
<% } %>
```

This code gets converted into something like

```
int no = (int)(Math.random()*10);
if(no % 2 == 0) {

      out.write("\r\n");
      out.write("Even\r\n");
 } else {
      out.write("\r\n");
      out.write("Odd\r\n");
 }
```

21.8.5 Declarations

JSP *declarations* are used to declare one or more variables, methods, or inner classes, which can be used later in the JSP page. The syntax is as follows:

```
<%! declarations %>
```

Examples are

```
<%! int sum = 0; %>
<%! int x, y , z; %>
<%! java.util.Hashtable table = new java.util.Hashtable(); %>
```

These variable declarations are inserted into the body of the servlet class, i.e., outside the `_jspService()` method that processes the client requests. So, variables declared in this way become instance variables of the underlying servlet.

```
<%! int sum = 0; %>
```

This is translated in the servlet as follows:

```
...
public final class test_jsp extends org.apache.jasper.runtime.HttpJspBase
    implements org.apache.jasper.runtime.JspSourceDependent {
  int sum = 0;
  ...
  public void _jspService(HttpServletRequest request, HttpServletResponse
response)
        throws java.io.IOException, ServletException {
  ...
```

Note that variables created using *scriptlets* are local to the `_jspService()` method. Instance variables are created and initialized once the servlet is instantiated. This is sometimes useful, but sometimes not desirable. The following declarations create an instance variable, `lastLoaded`.

```
<%! java.util.Date lastLoaded =  new java.util.Date();%>
The servlet was last loaded on <b><%=lastLoaded%></b>
```

This generates the following result:

```
The servlet was last loaded on Sun Nov 29 00:01:43 IST 2009
```

Similarly, the following piece of code displays the number of times the JSP page is referred after the page is loaded.

```
<%! int count = 0;%>
This page is referred <%= ++count %> times after last modification
```

Variables generated using declarations are available in scriptlets. A declaration has the scope of entire translation unit. It is valid in the JSP file as well as in all the files included statically. Declarations are not valid in dynamically included files.

JSP also has the following XML equivalent for declaration:

```
<jsp:declaration>
   declarations
</jsp:declaration>
```

21.8.6 Scope of JSP Objects

In a JSP page, objects may be created using directives, actions, or scriptlets. Every object created in a JSP page has a scope. The scope of a JSP object is defined as the availability of that object for use from a particular place of the web application. There are four object scope: *page*, *request*, *session*, and *application*.

page

Objects having *page* scope can be accessed only from within the same page where they were created. JSP implicit objects `out`, `exception`, `response`, `pageContext`, `config`, and `page` have 'page' scope. We have discussed about implicit objects in the next section. JSP objects created using the `<jsp:useBean>` tag also have page scope.

request

A request can be served by more than one page. Objects having *request* scope can be accessed from any page that serves that request. The implicit object `request` has the *request* scope.

session

Objects having *session* scope are accessible from pages that belong to the same session from where they were created. The `session` implicit object has the *session* scope.

application

JSP objects that have *application* scope can be accessed from any page that belong to the same application. An example is `application` implicit object.

21.8.7 Implicit Objects

Web container allows us to directly access many useful objects defined in the `_jspService()` method of the JSP page's underlying servlet. These objects are called *implicit objects* as they are instantiated automatically. The *implicit objects* contain information about request, response, session, configuration, etc. Some implicit objects are described in Table 21.2.

Table 21.2 JSP Implicit Objects

Variable	Class	Description
out	javax.servlet.jsp.JspWriter	Output stream of the JSP page's servlet.
request	Subtype of javax.servlet.ServletRequest	Current client request being handled by the JSP page
response	Subtype of javax.servlet.ServletResponse	Response generated by the JSP page to be returned to the client
config	javax.servlet.ServletConfig	Initialization information of the JSP page's servlet
session	javax.servlet.http.HttpSession	Session object for the client
application	javax.servlet.ServletContext	Context of the JSP page's servlet and other web components contained in the same application.

(Contd.)

(Contd.)

exception	java.lang.Throwable	Represents error. Accessible only from an error page
page	java.lang.Object	Refers to JSP page's servlet processing the current request
pageContext	javax.servlet.jsp.PageContext	The context of the JSP page that provides APIs to manage the various scoped attributes. It is extensively used by the tag handlers.

request

This object refers to the `javax.servlet.http.HttpServletRequest` type object that is passed to the `_jspService()` method of the generated servlet. It represents the HTTP request made by a client to this JSP page. It is used to retrieve information sent by the client such as parameters, (using the `getParameter()` method), HTTP request type (GET, POST, HEAD, etc), and HTTP request headers (cookies, referrer, etc). This implicit object has request scope.

```
<%
   String name =request.getParameter("name");
   out.println("Hello " + name);
%>
```

For the URL `http://127.0.0.1:8080/wt/jsp/getParameterDemo.jsp?name=Monali`, it displays the following:

```
Hello Monali
```

A JSP page can retrieve parameters sent through an HTML form. Consider the following form:

```
<form method='post' action='jsp/add.jsp'>
<input type='text' name='a' size='4'>+
<input type='text' name='b' size='4'>
<input type='submit' value='Add'>
</form>
```

Here is the code for the `add.jsp` file.

```
<%
   int a = Integer.parseInt(request.getParameter("a"));
   int b = Integer.parseInt(request.getParameter("b"));
   out.println(a + " + " + b + " = " + (a + b));
%>
```

The result is shown in Figure 21.6.

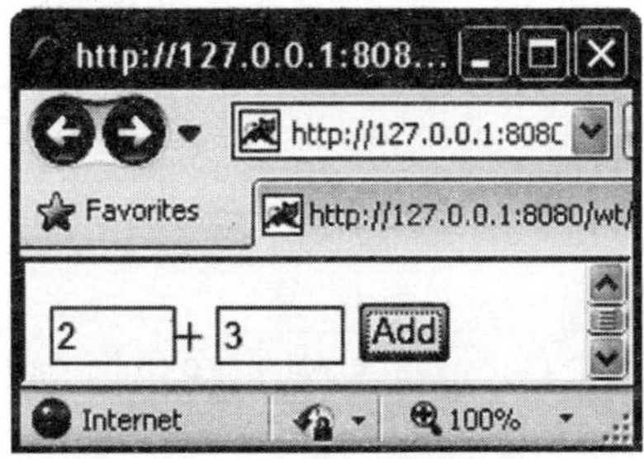

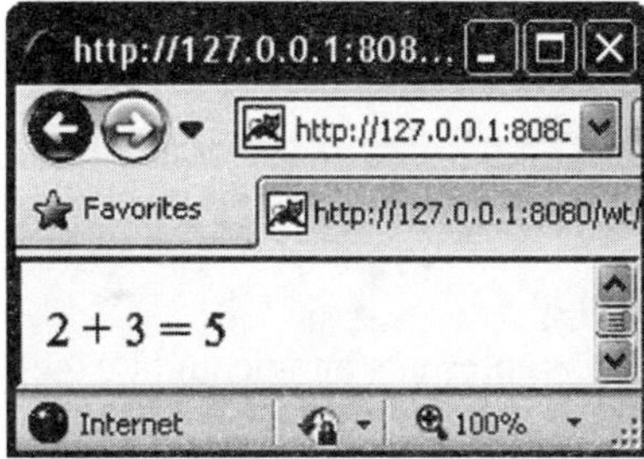

Figure 21.6 Retrieving form data from JSP page

response

This object refers to the `javax.servlet.http.HttpServletResponse` type object that is passed to the `_jspService()` method of the generated servlet. It represents the HTTP response to the client. This object is used to send information such as HTTP response header and cookies. This implicit object has page scope.

pageContext

This `javax.servlet.jsp.PageContext` type object refers to the current JSP page context. It is used to access information related to this page such as request, response, session, application, and underlying servlet configuration. This implicit object has page scope.

session

This `javax.servlet.http.HttpSession` type object refers to the session (if any) used by the JSP page. Note that no `session` object is created if the `session` attribute of the `page` directive is turned off and any attempt to refer to this object causes an error. It is used to access session-related information such as creation time and ID associated to this session. This implicit object has session scope.

application

This `javax.servlet.ServletContext` object refers to the underlying application and is used to share data among all pages under this application. This implicit object has application scope.

out

It denotes the character output stream that is used to send data back to the client. It is a buffered version of `java.io.PrintWriter` called `javax.servlet.jsp.JspWriter` type object. The object `out` is used only in scriptlets. This implicit object has page scope.

```
<% out.println("Hello World!"); %>
```

JSP expressions are placed in the output stream automatically and hence we do not use this `out` object there explicitly.

config

This `javax.servlet.ServletConfig` type object refers to the configuration of the underlying servlet. It is used to retrieve initial parameters, servlet name, etc. This implicit object has page scope.

page

This object refers to the JSP page itself. It can be used to call any instance of the JSP page's servlet. This implicit object has page scope.

exception

This represents an uncaught exception, which causes an error page to be called. This object is available in the JSP page for which the `isErrorPage` attribute of the `page` directive is set to `true`. This implicit object has page scope.

21.8.8 Variables, Methods, and Classes

Variables, methods, and classes can be declared in a JSP page. If they are declared in the declaration section, they become part of the class. For example, variables declared in the declaration section become instance variables and are accessible from any method of the JSP page's servlet class.

Consider the following variable declaration:

```
<%! double PI = 22/7.0; %>
```

The resultant servlet code will look like this:

```
...
public final class method_jsp extends org.apache.jasper.runtime.HttpJspBase
    implements org.apache.jasper.runtime.JspSourceDependent {
double PI = 22/7.0;
...
```

These variables are also shared among multiple threads. Classes and methods can be declared in a similar way as follows:

```
<%!
int add(int a, int b) {
   return a + b;
}
class AnInnerClass {
}
%>
```

The resultant servlet source code will look like this:

```
...
public final class method_jsp extends org.apache.jasper.runtime.HttpJspBase
    implements org.apache.jasper.runtime.JspSourceDependent {
int add(int a, int b) {
   return a + b;
}
class AnInnerClass {
}
...
```

Variables, methods, and classes declared in the declaration section are available in scriptlets. So, the following scriptlet is valid for this declaration.

```
<%out.println(add(2, 3));%>
```

It displays the following:

```
5
```

JSP allows us to declare variables and classes, but not methods, in the scriptlet section. Variables declared in the scriptlet section are local to the `_jspService()` method. They are created each time the client makes a request and destroyed after the request is over. Similarly, classes declared in the scriptlet section become inner classes of the `_jspService()` method. Consider the following code:

```
<%
double temp = 0;
```

```
class TempClass {
}
%>
```

The resultant servlet code looks like this:

```
...
public final class method_jsp extends org.apache.jasper.runtime.HttpJspBase
    implements org.apache.jasper.runtime.JspSourceDependent {
...
  public void _jspService(HttpServletRequest request, HttpServletResponse response)
       throws java.io.IOException, ServletException {
...
double temp = 0;
class TempClass {
}
```

21.8.8.1 Synchronization

Note that variables declared in the declaration section become instance variables. Instance variables become shared automatically among all request handling threads. You must write the code to access these variables synchronously. Consider the following piece of code:

```
<%!int n = 1;%>
<%
for (int i = 0; i < 5; i++) {
   out.println("Next integer: " + n++ + "<br>");
   Thread.sleep(500);
}
%>
```

The code is intended to print five consecutive integers. Each time this JSP page is invoked, it increments the instance variable n five times and displays the value. The code segment works fine if only one request is dispatched to this JSP page at a time. However, if two or more requests are sent to this JSP page, the result is not displayed correctly. To demonstrate this and to allow collision, an artificial delay is given. A sample output is shown in Figure 21.7, if two requests are sent simultaneously.

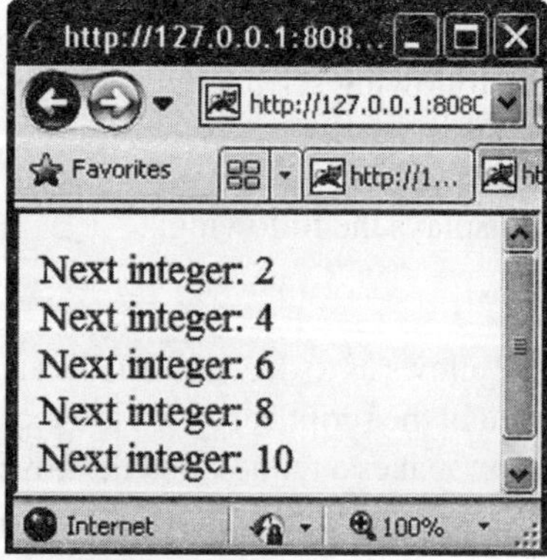

Figure 21.7 Accessing JSP page without synchronization

One of the solutions of this problem is to make the `for` loop atomic so that only one request can access it at a time.

```
<%!
   int n = 1;
   Object o = new Object();
%>
<%
synchronized(o) {
   for (int i = 0; i < 5; i++) {
      out.println("Next integer: " + n++ + "<br>");
      Thread.sleep(500);
   }
}
%>
```

Another way to solve this problem is to inform the JSP container that this page is not thread-safe, so that the container dispatches requests one by one.

```
<%@ page isThreadSafe="false" %>
<%!int n = 1; %>
<%
for (int i = 0; i < 5; i++) {
   out.println("Next integer: " + n++ + "<br>");
   Thread.sleep(500);
}
%>
```

In either case, the result will be correct.

21.8.9 Standard Actions

The JSP engine provides many built-in sophisticated functions to the programmers for easy development of the web applications. These functions include instantiating objects in a JSP page, communicating with other JSP pages and servlets, etc. JSP *actions* are nothing but XML tags that can be used in a JSP page to use these functions.

Note that the same thing can be achieved by writing Java code within scriptlets. However, JSP action tags are a convenient way to use those functions. They also promote component framework as well as application maintainability. The following section describes commonly used JSP action tags.

include

This action tag provides an alternative way to include a file in a JSP page. The general syntax of the `include` action tag is

```
<jsp:include page="relativeURL | <%=expression%>" flush="true" />
```

For example, the following code includes the file `header.jsp` in the current page:

```
<jsp:include page="header.jsp" />
```

It is similar to the include directive but instead of inserting the text of the included file in the original file at compilation time, it actually includes the target at run-time. It acts like a subroutine where the control is passed temporarily to the target. The control is then returned back to the original JSP page. The result of the included file is inserted in the place of <jsp:include> action in the original JSP page. Needless to say, the included file should be a JSP file, servlet, or any other dynamic program that can process the parameters. The optional attribute flush can only take the value true.

Let us illustrate with an example. Suppose the content of date.jsp is as follows:

```
Date and time: <%= new java.util.Date() %>
```

Now, consider the file include.jsp, which has included the date.jsp file using the <jsp:include> action tag as follows:

```
Before<br>
<jsp:include page="date.jsp" />
<br>After
```

This generates the following result:

```
Before
Date and time: Wed Dec 02 19:56:54 IST 2009
After
```

The value of the page attribute may be a dynamically generated file name. The following example illustrates this:

```
<%
String fileName = "sortByName.jsp";
String criteria = request.getParameter("sortCriteria");
if(criteria != null) fileName = criteria + ".jsp";
%>
<jsp:include page="<%=fileName%>" />
```

So, if the include.jsp page is invoked using the URL http://127.0.0.1:8080/wt/jsp/include.jsp?sortCriteria=sortByRoll, the include action effectively becomes:

```
<jsp:include page="sortByRoll.jsp" />
```

Note that the file sortByRoll.jsp must exist. Otherwise, an exception will be thrown. If the include.jsp page is invoked using the URL http://127.0.0.1:8080/wt/jsp/include.jsp, the include action effectively becomes

```
<jsp:include page="sortByName.jsp" />
```

param

The JSP <jsp:param> action allows us to append additional parameters to the current request. The general syntax is as follows:

```
<jsp:param name="parameterName" value="parameterValue | <%=expression%>" />
```

The name and value attributes of the <jsp:param> tag specify the case-sensitive name and value of the parameter, respectively.

It is typically used with the <jsp:include> and <jsp:forward> action tags. For example, the following code passes the control to the JSP page `process.jsp` temporarily, with two additional parameters, `user` and `sessionId`.

```
<jsp:include page="process.jsp">
   <jsp:param name="user" value="monali" />
   <jsp:param name="sessionId" value="12D43F3Q436N43" />
</jsp:include>
```

The value of the `value` attribute may be a dynamic value, but the value of the `name` attribute must be static. The following example illustrates this:

```
<% String user = request.getParameter("user"); %>
<jsp:include page="process.jsp">
   <jsp:param name="user" value="<%=user%>" />
   <jsp:param name="sessionId" value="<%=System.currentTimeMillis()%>" />
</jsp:include>
```

forward

This action tag hands over the current request to the specified page internally at the server side. If the current page has already generated any output, it is suppressed. The output will only be caused by the page that has handled the request last in the forward chain. The control is never returned to the original page. The general syntax of the JSP forward action tag is

```
<jsp:forward page="relativeURL | <%=expression%>" />
```

Consider the `forward.jsp` file, which forwards the current request to the `date.jsp` file using the <jsp:forward> action as follows:

```
Before<br>
<jsp:forward page="date.jsp" />
<br>After
```

This transfers the control to the `date.jsp` page. The result the file `forward.jsp` has generated so far (`Before<br>` in our case) is cleared. The output is due to the page `date.jsp` only, as follows.

```
Date and time: Wed Dec 02 20:03:00 IST 2009
```

Like the <jsp:include> action tag, the value of the `page` attribute of <jsp:forward> may be a dynamic file name. The following example illustrates this:

```
<% String mailbox = request.getParameter("mailbox") + ".jsp";%>
<jsp:forward page="<%=fileName%>" />
```

Additional parameters may be specified using the <jsp:param> action as follows:

```
<%
   String mailbox = request.getParameter("mailbox") + ".jsp";
   String user = request.getParameter("user");
%>
<jsp:forward page="<%=fileName%>" >
   <jsp:param name="user" value="<%=user%>" />
<jsp:forward>
```

plugin

The <jsp:plugin> action is used to generate an HTML file that can download the Java plug-in on demand and execute applets or JavaBeans. It is an alternative way to deploy applets through Java plug-in. Since JSP pages are dynamic in nature, the developers of web applications can make use of Java plug-in to generate browser-specific tags to insert applets on the fly in a much easier and flexible way.

The <jsp:plugin> action generates the embed or object tag for the applet to be executed, depending upon the browser used. When the JSP is translated, the <jsp:plugin> action element is substituted by either an <embed> or an <object> HTML tag. The following code specifies an applet.

```
<jsp:plugin type="applet" code="Message" >
<jsp:params>
    <jsp:param name="message" value="Hello World!"/>
</jsp:params>
<jsp:fallback>
        <p> Unable to start Plug-in. </p>
</jsp:fallback>
</jsp:plugin>
```

The type attribute of the <jsp:plugin> tag specifies the type (bean or applet) of plug-in to be used and the code attribute specifies the name of the file (without extension) containing the byte code for this plug-in. For example, the <jsp:plugin> action inserts an applet whose code can be found in the class file Message.class.

The <jsp:plugin> action tag has a similar set of attributes as the <applet> tag. The <jsp:params> and <jsp:param> actions are used to pass parameters to the plug-in. The <jsp:fallback> tag specifies the message to be displayed if the Java plug-in fails to start due to some unavoidable reason.

Here is the source code for the Message applet (Message.java).

```
public class Message extends java.applet.Applet {
   String msg;
   public void init() {
      msg = getParameter("message");
   }
   public void paint(java.awt.Graphics g) {
      g.drawString(msg, 20, 20);
   }
}
```

This applet takes a single parameter message and displays its value at location (20, 20) on the browser's screen, relative to the applet window.

As mentioned earlier, the web server generates either an <embed> or an <object> tag, depending upon the browser that requested the JSP page. For example, the following code is generated if Tomcat 6.0 is used as the web server and Internet Explorer 8.0 makes the request.

```
<object classid="clsid:8AD9C840-044E-11D1-B3E9-00805F499D93"
codebase="http://java.sun.com/products/plugin/1.2.2/jinstall-1_2_2-
win.cab#Version=1,2,2,0">
```

```
<param name="java_code" value="Message">
<param name="type" value="application/x-java-applet;">
<param name="message" value="Hello World!">
<comment>
<EMBED type="application/x-java-applet;"
pluginspage="http://java.sun.com/products/plugin/" java_code="Message"
message="Hello World!"/>
<noembed>

      <p> Unable to start Plug-in. </p>

</noembed>
</comment>
</object>
```

Though JSP specification includes the `<jsp:plugin>` action tag, different vendors may implement it differently. For detailed information, read the documentation of the web server.

useBean

It is used to instantiate a JavaBean object for later use. We shall discuss this action in Section 21.9.1 in detail.

setProperty

It is used to set a specified property of a JavaBean object. A detailed description of this action may be found in Section 21.9.2.

getProperty

It is used to get a specified property from a JavaBean object. This action has been discussed in Section 21.9.3 in detail.

21.8.10 Tag Extensions

One significant feature added in the JSP 1.1 specification is *tag extension*. It allows us to define and use custom tags in a JSP page exactly like other HTML/XML tags, using Java code. The JSP engine interprets them and invokes their functionality. So, Java programmers can provide application functionality in terms of custom tags, while web designers can use them as building blocks without any knowledge of Java programming. This way, JSP tag extensions provide a higher-level application-specific approach to the authors of HTML pages.

Though a similar functionality can be achieved using JavaBean technology, it lacks many features such as nesting, iteration, and cooperative actions. JSP tag extension allows us to express complex functionalities in a simple and convenient way.

21.8.10.1 Tag type

JSP specification defines the following tags, which we can create and use in a JSP file.

Simple Tags

Tags with no body or no attribute. Example:

```
<ukr:copyright>
```

Tags with attributes

Tags that have attributes but no body. Example:

```
<ukr:hello name="Monali" />
```

Tags with body

Tags that can contain other tags, scripting elements, and text between the start and end tags. Example:

```
<ukr:hello>
   <%= name%>
</ukr:hello>
```

Tags Defining Scripting Variables

Tags that can define scripting variables, which can be used in the scripts within the page. Example:

```
<ukr:animation id="logo" />
<% logo.start(); %>
```

Cooperating Tags

Tags that cooperate with each other by means of named shared objects. Example:

```
<ukr:tag1 id="obj1" />
<ukr:tag2 name="obj1" />
```

In this example, `tag1` creates a named object called `obj1`, which is later used by `tag2`.

21.8.10.2 Writing tags

In this section, we shall discuss how to define and use simple tags. The design and use of a custom tag has the following basic steps:

- Tag Definition
- Provide Tag Handler
- Deploy the tag
- Use the tag in the JSP file

Tag Definition

Before writing the functionality of a tag, you need to consider the following points:

- Tag Name—The name (and prefix) that will be used for the tag we are going to write
- Attributes—Whether the tag has any attribute and whether it is mandatory
- Nesting—Whether the tag contains any other child tag. A tag directly enclosing another tag is called the *parent* of the tag it encloses
- Body Content—Whether the tag contains anything (such as text) other than child tags

Provide Tag Handler

The functionality of a tag is implemented using a Java class called *tag handler*. Every tag handler must be created by directly or indirectly implementing the `javax.servlet.jsp.tagext.Tag` interface, which provides the framework of the JSP tag extension. In this section, we shall develop a simple tag named `<ukr:hello>`, which has a single optional attribute, `name`. The `<ukr:hello>` tag prints "Hello <name>" or "Hello World!" depending upon whether the attribute `name` is specified or not.

Note that the tag `<ukr:hello>` does not do much. It helps us understand the basic steps that we must follow to write a custom tag. In practice, custom tags will do complex tasks, but the procedure for developing such tags is exactly the same as the `<ukr:hello>` tag. After creating the `<ukr:hello>` tag, it is used in either of the following ways:

```
<ukr:hello name="Monali" />
```

This prints "Hello Monali".

```
<ukr:hello  />
```

This prints "Hello World!". Here is the complete source code for the hello tag handler (`HelloTag.java`).

```
package tag;
import javax.servlet.jsp.tagext.SimpleTagSupport;
import javax.servlet.jsp.JspException;
import javax.servlet.jsp.JspWriter;
import java.io.IOException;
public class HelloTag extends SimpleTagSupport {
   String name = "World!" ;
   public void doTag() throws JspException, IOException {
      JspWriter out = getJspContext().getOut();
      out.println("Hello " + name);
   }
   public void setName(String name) {
      this.name = name;
   }
}
```

Though each tag handler must implement the `javax.servlet.jsp.tagext.Tag` interface, it is convenient to use one of the default implementations, the `TagSupport` or `SimpleTagSuport` class. Our tag is one without any body and hence we have used the `SimpleTagSupport` class. Each tag handler must define some predefined methods [Table 21.3] that are called by the JSP engine. For example, the JSP engine calls the `doStartTag()` and `doEndTag()` methods when the start tag and the end tag, respectively, are encountered. The class `SimpleTagSupport` implements most of the work of a tag handler. The implementation of our class is simple, as it extends the `SimpleTagSupport` class. We have only implemented the `doTag()` method, which is called when the JSP engine encounters the start tag.

Table 21.3 Tag handler methods

Tag Handler Type	Methods
Simple	doStartTag, doEndTag, release
Attributes	doStartTag, doEndTag, set/getAttribute1...N
Body, No Interaction	doStartTag, doEndTag, release
Body, Interaction	doStartTag, doEndTag, release, doInitBody, doAfterBody

The hello tag has one attribute, `name`, whose value the handler must access. The JSP engine sets the value of an attribute `xxx` using the method `setXxx()` of the handler. This `setXxx()` method is invoked after the start tag, but before the body of the tag. So, we have inserted one method `setName()`, which will by used by the JSP engine to pass the value of the attribute `name`. Inside the handler, we have stored this value in a variable `name`. If a tag has multiple attributes, the corresponding tag handler must have separate set functions, one for each of these attributes.

Finally, we write the string "Hello" appended with the value of the `name` attribute to the servlet output stream. A reference to this output stream is obtained using the `getOut()` method on `javax.servlet.jsp.JspContext`, which is returned by the `getJspContext()` method.

Deploy the tag

Save this code in file `HelloTag.java` and put it in the application's `/WEB-INF/classes/tag` directory. To compile this file, we need the necessary tag classes that are provided as the jar file `jsp-api.jar`. This jar file can be found in the `lib` directory of Tomcat's installation directory. Make sure that this jar file is in your classpath during compilation. You can use the following command in the `/WEB-INF/classes/tag` directory to compile the `HelloTag.java` file.

```
javac -classpath ../../../../../lib/jsp-api.jar HelloTag.java
```

This will generate the `HelloTag.class` file in the `/WEB-INF/classes/tag` directory. If everything goes fine, restart the web server. The tag class is now ready to use.

Now, we have to map the tag `hello` with this tag handler class, `HelloTag`. This is done in an XML file called **T**ag **L**ibrary **D**escriptor (TLD). A TLD contains information about a tag library as well as each tag contained in the library. The JSP engine uses TLDs to validate tags used in the JSP pages. The Tag Library Descriptor is an XML document conforming to a DTD specified by Sun Microsystems.

We shall name our tag library file as `tags.tld` and put it in the application's `/WEB-INF/taglib` directory. For example, if the application's root directory is `wt`, put the `tags.tld` file in the `/wt/WEB-INF/taglib` directory. Make the following entry in the `tags.tld` file.

```
<?xml version="1.0"?>
<taglib>
   <tlib-version>1.0</tlib-version>
   <jsp-version>1.2</jsp-version>
   <short-name>Simple tag library</short-name>
   <tag>
      <description>Prints Hello 'name'</description>
      <name>hello</name>
```

```
        <tag-class>tag.HelloTag</tag-class>
        <body-content>empty</body-content>
        <attribute>
            <name>name</name>
            <required>false</required>
            <rtexprvalue>true</rtexprvalue>
        </attribute>
    </tag>
</taglib>
```

Each `<tag>` element in the TLD file describes a tag. The `<name>` element specifies the name of the tag that will be used in the JSP file. The `<tag-class>` element associates the handler class with this tag name. In this case, the `tag.HelloTag` class is the handler of the tag `hello`. Each `<attribute>` element specifies the attribute that can be used for this tag. Our tag can have only one attribute, `name`. The `<required>` element specifies whether the attribute is mandatory (`true`) or optional (`false`). A tag without a body must specify that its `body-content` is empty.

Use the tag in the JSP file

The tag `hello` is now ready to use. Use the following entry in the JSP page `tag.jsp` and put it in the applications root directory, i.e., `/wt` in our case.

```
<%@ taglib prefix="ukr" uri="/taglib/tags.tld" %>
<ukr:hello name="Monali"/>
```

The `taglib` directive includes a tag library whose tags will be used by the JSP page. It must appear before using any custom tags it refers to. The `uri` attribute specifies a URI that uniquely identifies the TLD. The `prefix` attribute specifies the prefix to be used for every tag defined in this TLD. The prefix distinguishes tags in one library from those in others, if they contain tags with the same name. Now, write the following URL in the address bar of your web browser and press enter.

```
http://127.0.0.1:8080/wt/tag.jsp
```

It displays

```
Hello Monali
```

For the following code

```
<%@ taglib prefix="ukr" uri="/taglib/tags.tld" %>
<ukr:hello />
```

The code

```
Hello World!
```

```
<%@ taglib prefix="ukr" uri="/taglib/tags.tld" %>
<%!String name="Kutu"; %>
<ukr:hello name="<%=name%>"/>
```

displays

```
Hello Kutu
```

21.8.11 Iterating a Tag Body

Sometimes, it is necessary to iterate a specific code several times. For example, suppose we want to generate a table containing integers and their factorial value. We can write scripts to do this, as follows:

```
for(int i = 2; i <= 6; i++) {
%>
<%=i%>!=<ukr:fact no="<%=i%>" /><br>
<%
}
%>
```

We have assumed that there exists a tag handler for `<ukr:fact>` as follows:

```
package tag;
import javax.servlet.jsp.tagext.SimpleTagSupport;
import javax.servlet.jsp.JspException;
import java.io.IOException;
import javax.servlet.jsp.JspWriter;
public class FactTag extends SimpleTagSupport {
   int no;
   public void doTag() throws JspException, IOException  {
      int prod = 1;
      for(int j = 1;j <= no; j++)
         prod *= j;
      JspWriter out = getJspContext().getOut();
      out.println(prod);
   }
   public void setNo(int no) {
      this.no = no;
   }
}
```

It would be better, if the same table uses the following code:

```
<ukr:FactTable start="2" end="6">
   ${count}! = ${fact}<br>
</ukr:FactTable>
```

We can reduce the amount of code in the scripting element by moving the flow control to the tag handlers. The basic idea is to write a tag called iteration tags that iterates its body.

The iteration tag retrieves two parameters start and end. It calculates the factorial of each number between these two numbers (both inclusive) and assigns them to a scripting variable. The body of the tag retrieves the numbers and their factorials from scripting variables. Here is the handler for the iteration tag.

```
package tag;
import javax.servlet.jsp.tagext.SimpleTagSupport;
import javax.servlet.jsp.JspException;
import java.io.IOException;
public class FactorialTag extends SimpleTagSupport {
   int start, end;
   public void doTag() throws JspException, IOException  {
```

```
        for(int i = start; i <= end; i++) {
            int prod = 1;
            for(int j = 1; j <= i; j++)
                prod *= j;
            getJspContext().setAttribute("count", String.valueOf(i) );
            getJspContext().setAttribute("fact", String.valueOf(prod) );
            getJspBody().invoke(null);
        }
    }
    public void setStart(int start) {
        this.start = start;
    }
    public void setEnd(int end) {
        this.end = end;
    }
}
```

This handler, in each iteration, stores the value of the integer and its factorial in the `count` and `fact` variable, respectively, using the following code.

```
getJspContext().setAttribute("count", String.valueOf(i) );
getJspContext().setAttribute("fact", String.valueOf(prod) );
```

The body of the tag is iterated as follows:

```
getJspBody().invoke(null);
```

Now, make the following entry in the `tags.tld` file.

```
<?xml version="1.0"?>
<taglib>
    <tlib-version>1.0</tlib-version>
    <jsp-version>1.2</jsp-version>
    <short-name>Simple tag library</short-name>
    <tag>
        <description>Calculates factorial from 'start' to 'end'</description>
        <name>FactTable</name>
        <tag-class>tag.FactorialTag</tag-class>
                <body-content>scriptless</body-content>
        <attribute>
            <name>start</name>
            <required>true</required>
            <rtexprvalue>true</rtexprvalue>
        </attribute>
        <attribute>
            <name>end</name>
            <required>true</required>
            <rtexprvalue>true</rtexprvalue>
        </attribute>
    </tag>
</taglib>
```

Obtaining the factorial tables is now very simple. Consider the following code.

```
<%@ taglib prefix="ukr" uri="/taglib/tags.tld" %>
Factorial table<br>
```

```
<ukr:FactTable start="2" end="6">
   ${count}! = ${fact}<br>
</ukr:FactTable>
```

In the body of the tag, the values of the count and fact variables are retrieved using expression language. Note that the JSP page does not contain a single piece of script. It is displayed as follows:

```
Factorial table
2! = 2
3! = 6
4! = 24
5! = 120
6! = 720
```

21.8.12 Sharing Data Between JSP Pages

All JSP pages participate in an HTTP session unless the `session` attribute of the `page` directive is set to `false`. An HTTP session is represented by the implicit object `session`. This `session` object has session scope and is thus shared among all the pages within the session.

This session object can be used as a shared repository of information such as beans and objects among JSP pages of the same session. For example, `login.jsp` page may store the user name in the session, while subsequent pages such as `home.jsp` can use it. Consider the code segment in `login.jsp`:

```
String user = request.getParameter("user");
session.setAttribute("user", user);
```

Now, see the code segment in `home.jsp`.

```
String user = (String)session.getAttribute("user");
```

21.9 BEANS

JavaBeans are reusable Java components that allow us to separate business logic from presentation logic. Technically, a JavaBean class is a Java class that meets the following requirements:

- It has a public, no argument constructor.
- It implements the `java.io.Serializable` or `java.io.Externalizable` interface.
- Its properties are accessible using methods that are written following a standard naming convention.

With this simple definition, properly designed beans can be used virtually in all Java environments such as JSP, servlet, applet, or even in Java applications. Note that most of the existing classes are already bean classes or they can be converted to bean classes very easily.

The methods of a bean must follow a naming convention. If the name of a bean property is `xxx`, the associate reader and writer method must have the name `getXxx()` and `setXxx()`, respectively. Following is a sample class declaration for JavaBean `Factorial`:

```
package bean;
public class Factorial implements java.io.Serializable {
   int n;
   public int getValue() {
      int prod = 1;
      for(int i = 2; i <= n; i++)
         prod *= i;
      return prod;
   }
   public void setValue(int v) {
      n = v;
   }
}
```

Since no constructor is defined explicitly in this class, a zero argument constructor is inserted in the `Factorial` class. The `Factorial` bean class has one property, `value`. So, the name of the reader method is `getValue()`. Similarly, the name of the writer method is `setValue()`. The name of the member variable need not be `value`; it is the property that we want to manipulate on a `Factorial` bean.

Save this code in the file `Factorial.java` and store it in the application's `/WEB-INF/classes/bean` directory. Compile the class exactly like other Java classes. Use the following command in the `/WEB-INF/classes/bean` directory.

```
javac Factorial.java
```

This generates a class file, `Factorial.class`. If everything goes fine, restart the tomcat web server. Tomcat loads all the class files under `/classes` directory and add its subdirectories to the CLASSPATH of the Java Runtime Environment (JRE). Those class files can now be used exactly like other Java classes.

There are three action elements that are used to work with beans.

21.9.1 useBean

A JSP action element `<jsp:useBean>` instantiates a JavaBean object into the JSP page. The syntax is

```
<jsp:useBean id="object_name" class="class_name" scope="page | request |
session |application" />
```

Here, the `id` attribute refers to the name of the object to be created and the attribute `class` specifies the name of the JavaBean class from which the object will be instantiated. The attribute `scope` specifies the area of visibility of the loaded bean. The effect of the `<jsp:useBean>` element is equivalent to instantiating an object as follows:

```
<% class_name object_name = new class_name(); %>
```

For example, to instantiate a Factorial bean in a JSP page, the following action is used:

```
<jsp:useBean id="fact" scope="page" class="bean.Factorial" />
```

This is equivalent to the following scriptlet:

```
<% bean.Factorial fact = new bean.Factorial(); %>
```

Once a bean object is loaded into a JSP page, we can use two other action elements to manipulate it.

21.9.2 setProperty

The `<jsp:setProperty>` action tag assigns a new value to the specified property of the specified bean object. It takes the following form:

```
<jsp:setProperty name="obj_name" property="prop_name" value="prop_value"/>
```

The object name, property name, and its value are specified by the `name`, `property`, and `value` attributes, respectively. This is equivalent to calling the `setProp_name()` method on the specified object `obj_name` as follows:

```
<% obj_name.setProp_name(prop_value); %>
```

To set a property of our bean object `fact`, we use the following:

```
<jsp:setProperty name="fact" property="value" value="5" />
```

The equivalent scriptlet is as follows:

```
<% fact.setValue(5); %>
```

21.9.3 getProperty

The `<jsp:getProperty>` action element retrieves the value of the specified property of the specified bean object. The value is converted to a string. It takes the following form:

```
<jsp:getProperty name="obj_name" property="prop_name"/>
```

The object name and its property name are specified by the `name` and `property` attributes, respectively. This is equivalent to calling the `getProp_name()` method on the specified object `obj_name` as follows:

```
<%= obj_name.getProp_name() %>
```

To get the value of the property `value` of our `fact` bean object, we use the following:

```
<jsp:getProperty name="fact" property="value" />
```

The equivalent scriptlet is as follows:

```
<%= fact.getValue() %>
```

21.9.4 Complete Example

Following is a complete JSP page:

```
<table border="1">
   <caption>Factorial table</caption>
   <tr><th width="50">n</th><th width="100">n!</th></tr>
```

```
    <jsp:useBean id="fact" scope="page" class="bean.Factorial" />
    <%
    for(int i = 2; i < 6; i++) {
    %>
    <jsp:setProperty name="fact" property="value" value="<%=i%>" />
    <tr><td><%=i%></td><td><jsp:getProperty name="fact" property="value"
    /></td></tr>
    <%
    }
    %>
</table>
```

It generates the output shown in Figure 21.8.

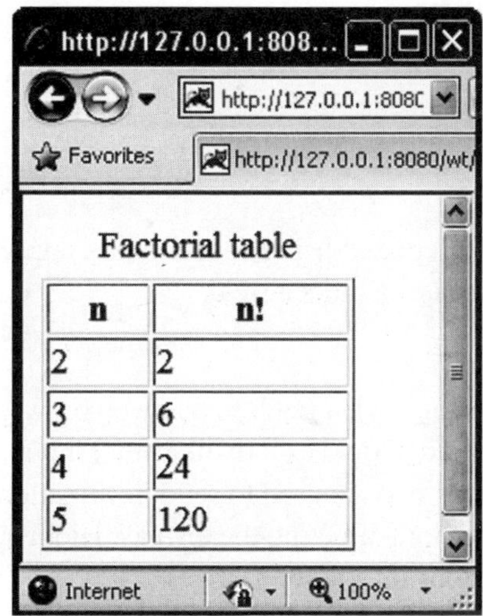

Figure 21.8 Using beans in JSP

21.9.5 Other Usage

Once a bean object is loaded into the page, it can be used exactly like other objects in scripting elements in the same JSP page. Consider the following code:

```
<jsp:useBean id="fact" scope="page" class="bean.Factorial" />
```

This is equivalent to the following instantiation:

```
<% bean.Factorial fact = new bean.Factorial(); %>
```

Now, the bean object can be accessed using its name, as follows:

```
<%fact.setValue(6);%>
<%=fact.getValue()%>
```

This displays the following output:

```
720
```

21.10 SESSION TRACKING

Since HTTP is a stateless protocol, the web server cannot remember previous requests. Consequently, the web server cannot relate the current request with the previous one. This creates a problem for some applications that require a sequence of related request–response cycles. Examples include online examination systems, email checking systems, and banking applications. How does the server know how many questions you have answered so far or when did you start the examination?

We shall use a simple application to demonstrate session tracking using different methods. In this application, the server initially dynamically generates an HTML file to display the integer 0, with two buttons captioned "prev" and "next". If the user clicks on the *next* button, the server sends the integer next to the one displayed. Similarly, when *prev* button is clicked, the server sends the integer previous to the one displayed.

Note that each time the server receives a request, it has to remember the number it sent in the previous step. Let us now discuss different methods used for session tracking.

21.10.1 Hidden Fields

An HTML hidden field is created using the `<input>` tag, with the `type` attribute `hidden`. For example, the following creates a hidden field.

```
<input type="hidden" name="user" value="monali" >
```

The interesting part about hidden fields is that web browsers do not display them, but send the name–value pair of each hidden field exactly like other input elements when the enclosing form is submitted. So, hidden fields may be used to send information back and forth between server and client to track sessions, without affecting the display. Hidden fields are ideal for applications that do not require a great deal of information.

Let us now implement the application mentioned, using hidden fields.

```
<%@page import="java.util.*"%>
<html>
   <head><title>Hidden field demo</title></head>
   <body>
      <%
         int current = 0;
         String last = request.getParameter("int");
         String button = request.getParameter("button");
         if(button != null) {
            if(button.equals("next"))
               current = Integer.parseInt(last) + 1;
            else
               current = Integer.parseInt(last) - 1;
         }
         out.println(current);
      %>
      <br>
      <form name="myForm" method="post">
         <input type="hidden" name="int" value="<%=current%>">
```

```
      <input type="submit" name="button" value="prev">
      <input type="submit" name="button" value="next">
    </form>
  </body>
</html>
```

In this method, the JSP page uses a single hidden field in the generated HTML file named "int". The value of this hidden field is the integer being sent currently. The hidden field, together with the two submit buttons captioned "prev" and "next", are put in a form. So, the web browser receives an HTML file like this:

```
<html>
  <head><title>Hidden field demo</title></head>
  <body>

      0

      <br>
      <form name="myForm" method="post">
        <input type="hidden" name="int" value="0">
        <input type="submit" name="button" value="prev">
        <input type="submit" name="button" value="next">
      </form>
  </body>
</html>
```

The HTTP `POST` method is used in the form and no `action` attribute is specified. When the user clicks any of the two submit buttons, the value of this hidden field (which is the integer currently displayed) is sent to the same JSP page behind the scene. The JSP page extracts this value and understands that this value was sent in response to the previous request. This way, the hidden field helps the JSP page to remember information sent earlier. It also determines the button whose click event generates this request. The JSP page can then easily calculate the value to be sent next, depending on the button clicked.

The advantage of this method is that it does not require any special support from the client's side. Hidden fields are supported by all browsers and underlying information propagation is absolutely transparent to the user.

Note that users can view the source code of the HTML page and consequently see the value of the hidden field. So, the JSP page should not pass sensitive information such as passwords in the hidden field.

21.10.2 URL Rewriting

This is another simple but elegant method to track sessions and is widely used. It does not require any special support from the web browser. Remember that HTTP allows us to pass information using HTTP URL. This method makes use of that concept. The session information is appended to the URL. Here is the solution using URL rewriting.

```
<%@page import="java.util.*"%>
<html>
   <head><title>URL rewriting demo</title></head>
   <body>
      <%
         int last = 0;
         String param = request.getParameter("int");
         if(param != null) last = Integer.parseInt(param);
            out.println(last);
      %>
      <br>
      <a href="intUrl.jsp?int=<%=last-1%>">prev</a>
      <a href="intUrl.jsp?int=<%=last+1%>">next</a>
   </body>
</html>
```

In this case, the JSP page generates and sets the URL to be called for the hyperlinks "prev" and "next". For example, the web gets this HTML page for the first time:

```
<html>
   <head><title>URL rewriting demo</title></head>
    <body>

0

<br>
<a href="intUrl.jsp?int=-1">prev</a>
<a href="intUrl.jsp?int=1">next</a>
    </body>
</html>
```

When a user clicks on the "prev" hyperlink, the integer that should be sent by the JSP page for this request is appended to the URL. The JSP page simply extracts this information and sends it back with the new URLs for those two hyperlinks. A similar sequence of events happen when a user clicks on the "next" button.

21.10.3 Cookies

This method requires support from the web browsers. In this method, session information is represented by a named token called *cookie*. The JSP page sends this cookie to the web browser. The browser must be configured properly to accept it. Upon receiving a cookie, the web browser installs it. This cookie is then sent back to the server with the subsequent requests. The JSP page can then extract session information from this cookie. This way, the server can identify a session.

By default, most browsers support cookies. However, due to security reasons, very often cookie support is disabled and in that case session management will not work correctly. Following is the JSP page for the application we discussed earlier.

```
<html>
   <head><title>Cookie demo</title></head>
   <body>
      <%
         int current = 0;
         Cookie cookie = null;
```

```
            Cookie[]   cookies = request.getCookies();
            if(cookies != null)
               for(int i = 0; i < cookies.length; i++)
                  if(cookies[i].getName().equals("last"))
                     cookie = cookies[i];
            if(cookie != null) {
               String button = request.getParameter("button");
               if(button != null) {
                  if(button.equals("next"))
                     current = Integer.parseInt(cookie.getValue()) + 1;
                  else
                     current = Integer.parseInt(cookie.getValue()) - 1;
               }
            }
            response.addCookie(new Cookie("last", String.valueOf(current)));
            out.println(current);
         %>
         <br>
         <form name="myForm" method="post">
            <input type="submit" name="button" value="prev">
            <input type="submit" name="button" value="next">
         </form>
      </body>
   </html>
```

The JSP page first looks for a cookie named "last". If it finds the cookie, the value of the cookie is obtained using the `getValue()` method. Depending on the button clicked, the integer to be sent next is calculated and stored in the variable `current`. This integer, together with a new cookie with the name "last" having the current value set is sent to the web browser. However, if the JSP page does not find any cookie with the name "last", which happens during the first time, it sends a new cookie having the value 0, which is the initial value of the variable `current`.

21.10.4 Session API

JSP technology (and its underlying servlet technology) provides a higher level approach for session tracking. The basic building block of this session API is the `javax.servlet.http.HttpSession` interface. The `HttpSession` objects are automatically associated with the client by the cookie mechanism. An `HttpSession` object is the one that persists during a session, until it times out or is shutdown by the JSP page participating in this session.

In a JSP page, an HTTP session is created by default if it is not suppressed by setting the `session` attribute of the `page` directive to `false` as follows.

```
<%@ page session="false" %>
```

This session can be accessed by the implicit object `session`. A JSP page may also create an `HttpSession` object explicitly, using the following method in `HttpServletRequest`.

```
HttpSession getSession(boolean create);
HttpSession getSession();
```

The first version takes a boolean parameter that indicates whether a new session has to be created if one does not exist. If the parameter is `true`, a new session is created if it does not exist.

Otherwise, the existing session object is returned. If the parameter is false, it returns the existing session object if it exists, and null otherwise. The second version simply calls the first version with the parameter `true`.

In the `HttpSession` object, we can store and retrieve key–value pair using `setAttribute()`, `getAttribute()`, and `getAttributes()` methods.

```
Object getAttribute(String key);
Enumeration getAttributeNames();
void setAttribute(String key, Object value);
```

The return type of the `getAttribute()` method is `Object`. So you must typecast it to the required type of data that was stored with a key in the session object. If the key specified in the `setAttribute()` method does not already exist in the session, the specified value is stored with this key. Otherwise, the old value is overwritten with the specified value.

The JSP engine uses the cookie mechanism to keep track of sessions. A session object is associated with usually a long alphanumeric ID. This session ID is sent to the client as a cookie with the name `JSESSIONID`, when the client makes a request for the first time using the HTTP response header `Set-Cookie`, as follows:

```
Set-Cookie: JSESSIONID=g52d15acu325dlw532h234
```

For subsequent requests, the client sends this cookie back to the server using the HTTP request header `Cookie` as follows:

```
Cookie: JSESSIONID=g52d15acu325dlw532h234
```

The server can then identify that this request has come from the same client. However, if the client does not accept cookies, this mechanism fails. In that case, programmers may use the URL rewriting mechanism, where each URL must have the session ID appended. The JSP engine, on behalf of programmers, provides a straightforward mechanism to implement URL rewriting. The `HttpServletResponse` object provides methods to append this session ID automatically. These methods identify whether the client is configured to accept cookies. They append the session ID only if the client does not accept cookies.

```
java.lang.String encodeURL(java.lang.String);
java.lang.String encodeRedirectURL(java.lang.String);
```

The `encodeRedirectURL()` method is used for the `sendRedirect()` and `encodeURL()` method is used for the rest to create such URLs.

Here is the solution of our application using `HttpSession` API:

```
<%@page import="java.util.*"%>
<html>
   <head><title>Hidden field demo</title></head>
   <body>
      <%
   int current = 0;
         String last = (String)session.getAttribute("last");
         if(last != null) {
```

```
            String button = request.getParameter("button");
               if(button != null) {
                  if(button.equals("next"))
                     current = Integer.parseInt(last) + 1;
                  else
                     current = Integer.parseInt(last) - 1;
               }
         }
         session.setAttribute("last", String.valueOf(current));
         out.println(current);
      %>
      <br>
      <form name="myForm" method="post">
         <input type="submit" name="button" value="prev">
         <input type="submit" name="button" value="next">
      </form>
   </body>
</html>
```

21.11 USERS PASSING CONTROL AND DATA BETWEEN PAGES

Sometimes, we need to hand over the control to another page, with the necessary data passed to it. In this section, we shall discuss how to pass control across pages with data passed to them.

21.11.1 Passing Control

Sometimes, a JSP page wants to pass the control to another server-side program for further processing. For example, in an e-mail application, the `login.jsp` page on user verification may want to forward the request to the `home.jsp` page. This is done using the `<jsp:forward>` action in the `login.jsp` page as follows:

```
String user = request.getParameter("user");
String password = request.getParameter("password");
//verify the user here
<jsp:forward page="home.jsp" />
```

Once the JSP engine encounters the `<jsp:forward>` action, it stops the processing of the current page and starts the processing of the page (called target page) specified by the `page` attribute. The rest of the original page is never processed further.

The `HttpServletRequest` and `HttpServletResponse` objects are passed to the target page. So, the target page can access all information passed to the original page. You can pass additional parameters to the target page using the `<jsp:param>` action as follows.

```
String user = request.getParameter("user");
String password = request.getParameter("password");
//verify the user here
double startTime = System.currentTimeMillis();
<jsp:forward page="home.jsp">
   <jsp:param name="startTime" value="<%=startTime%>" />
</jsp:forward>
```

The target page can access these parameters in the same way as the original parameters, using the `getParameter()` and/or `getParameterNames()` methods.

21.11.2 Passing Data

The scope of an object indicates from where the object is visible. JSP specification defines four types of scopes: `page`, `request`, `session`, and `application`. The objects having `page` scope are only available within the page. So, objects that are created with `page` scope in a page are not available in another page where the control is transferred using the `<jsp:forward>` action. If you make an object visible across multiple pages across the same request, create the object with `request` scope. The following example illustrates this.

```
<!--original.jsp-->
<jsp:useBean id="fact" scope="request" class="bean.Factorial" />
<%fact.setValue(5);%>
<jsp:forward page="new.jsp" />
```

This page creates a bean object with the `request` scope and sets the value property with 5. It then passes the control to the `new.jsp` page, which looks like this.

```
<!--new.jsp-->
<jsp:useBean id="fact" scope="request" class="bean.Factorial" />
<%=fact.getValue()%>
```

Since the bean was saved as the `request` scope in the `original.jsp` page, the `<jsp:useBean>` action in the `new.jsp` page finds and uses it.

For the URL `http://127.0.0.1:8080/wt/original.jsp`, the following is displayed:

```
120
```

Depending upon your requirement, you may create an object having any one of the four scopes.

21.12 SHARING SESSION AND APPLICATION DATA

The objects having `request` scope are available in all pages across a single request. However, sometimes objects should be shared among multiple requests.

Think about on online examination system. JSP pages requested from the same browser must share the same user name that was provided during the login procedure. This is required because different users have different sets of data such as expiry time, number of questions answered so far, number of correct answers, and so on. This type of information can be shared through `session` scope.

The objects having `session` scope are available to all pages requested by the same browser. The implicit object `session` is one such object. This session object can be used to store and retrieve other objects. So, objects may be shared across pages in the same session using this `session` object. Following is a code fragment used in `login.jsp`.

```
<!—login.jsp-->
<%
String user = request.getParameter("user");
String password = request.getParameter("password");
```

```
//verify the user here
double startTime = System.currentTimeMillis();
session.setAttribute(user, String.valueOf(startTime));

<jsp:forward page="exam.jsp" />
%>
```

It stores the time when the user starts its session in the session object and forwards the request to `exam.jsp`. The `exam.jsp` will be called many times by the user. The `exam.jsp` retrieves the start time for this user, checks whether the user has exhausted its time limit, and takes necessary actions.

```
String user1 = (String)session.getAttribute("user");

double startTime = Double.parseDouble((String)session.getAttribute("user"));
double currentTime = System.currentTimeMillis();
if(currentTime - startTime > 600000) { //duration is 10 minutes
   //the time is over, forward the request to the page logout.jsp
%>
<jsp:forward page="logout.jsp" />
<%
}
%>
```

Now, think about the same online examination system where different users are giving the examination using different browser windows, but using the same database. For efficiency purposes, information should be shared among pages even if the pages are requested by different users. This type of information can be shared through application scope.

The objects that have application scope are shared by all pages requested by any browser. One such implicit object is `application`. Consider the following code fragment in the `login.jsp` page:

```
Object obj = application.getAttribute("config");
if(obj == null) {
   ExamConfig conf = new ExamConfig();
   application.setAttribute("config", conf);
}
```

It looks for an object having the name "config" in the `application` object. If no such object exists, it creates an `ExamConfig` object and stores one such object in the `application` object. When the `ExamConfig` object is created, connection to the database is established. This database connection can now be shared by all other pages related to this application.

Here is the code fragment used in the `exam.jsp` page.

```
ExamConfig conf = (ExamConfig)application.getAttribute("config");
Statement stmt = conf.getConnection().createStatement();
//use stmt to fire SQL query
```

All requests that use the `exam.jsp` file can simply use the same object stored in the application object to get the `Statement` object and fire the SQL query.

21.13 DATABASE CONNECTIVITY

Most of the web applications need access to databases in the backend. **J**ava **D**ata**B**ase **C**onnectivity (JDBC) allows us to access databases through Java programs. It provides Java classes and interfaces to fire SQL and PL/SQL statements, process results (if any), and perform other operations common to databases. Since Java Server Pages can contain Java code embedded in them, it is also possible to access databases from Java Server Pages. The classes and interfaces for database connectivity are provided as a separate package, `java.sql`.

21.14 JDBC DRIVERS

A Java application can access almost all types of databases such as relational, object, and object-relational. The access to a specific database is accomplished using a set of Java interfaces, each of which is implemented by different vendors differently. A Java class that provides interfaces to a specific database is called JDBC driver. Each database has its own set of JDBC drivers. Users need not bother about the implementation of those Java classes. They can concentrate on developing database applications. Those drivers are provided (generally freely) by database vendors. This way, JDBC hides the underlying database architecture. JDBC drivers provided by database vendors convert database access requests to database-specific APIs.

JDBC drivers are classified into four categories depending upon the way they work.

21.14.1 JDBC-ODBC bridge (Type 1)

This is the *Type 1* driver. This type of drivers cannot talk to the database directly. It needs an intermediate ODBC (**O**pen **D**ata**B**ase **C**onnectivity) driver, with which it forms a kind of bridge. The driver translates JDBC function calls to ODBC method calls. ODBC makes use of native libraries of the operating system and is hence platform-dependent. For this mechanism to function correctly, the ODBC driver must be available in the client machine and must also be configured correctly, which is generally a long and tedious process. For this reason, the Type 1 driver is used for experimental purposes or when no other JDBC driver is available. Sun provides a Type 1 JDBC driver with JDK 1.1 or later.

21.14.2 Native-API, Partly Java (Type 2)

This is very similar to the Type 1 driver. However, it does not forward the JDBC call to the ODBC driver. Instead, it translates JDBC calls to database-specific native API calls. This driver is not a pure Java driver, as it interfaces with non-Java APIs that communicates with the database. This approach is a little bit faster than the earlier one, as it interfaces directly with the database through the native APIs. However, it has limitations similar to the previous one. This means that the client must have vendor-specific native APIs installed and configured in it.

21.14.3 Middleware, Pure Java (Type 3)

In this case, the JDBC driver forwards the JDBC calls to some middleware server using a database-independent network protocol. The middleware server acts as a *gateway* for multiple (possibly different) database servers and can use different database-specific protocols to connect to different database servers. This intermediate server sends each client request to a specific database. The results are then sent back to the intermediate server, which in turn sends the result back to the client. This approach hides the details of connections to the database servers and makes it possible to change the database servers without affecting the client.

21.14.4 Pure Java Driver (Type 4)

These types of drivers communicate with the database directly by making socket connections. It has distinct advantages over other mechanisms, in terms of performance and development time. Since it talks with the database server directly, no other subsidiary driver is needed. In this book, we shall use only the Type 4 driver. Figures 21.9 (i) and (ii) show the JDBC two-tier and three-tier architectures.

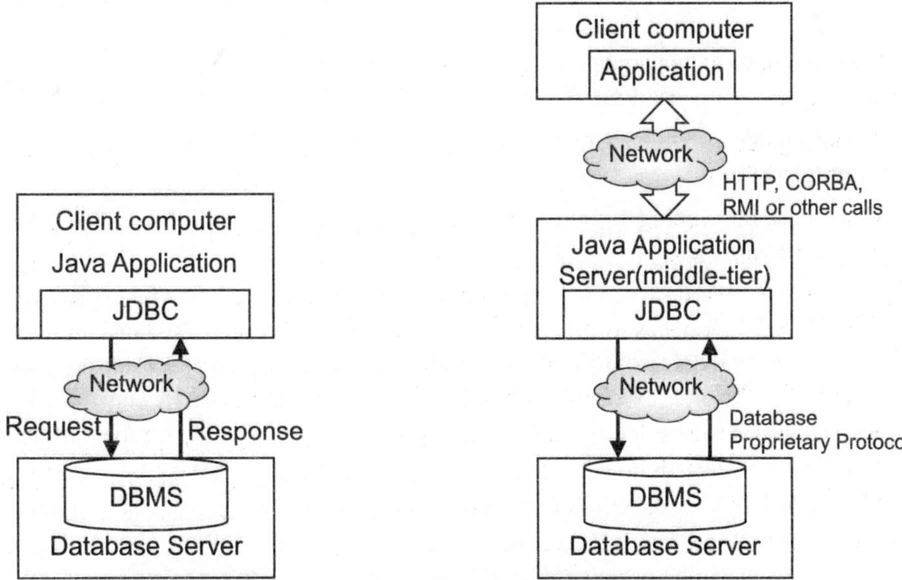

Figure 21.9 JDBC architecture (i) two tier (ii) three-tier

Table 21.4 gives the Java JDBC classes and interfaces.

Table 21.4 Java JDBC classes and interfaces

DriverManager	Connection	Statement
PreparedStatement	ResultSet	ResultSetMetaData
CallableStatement	DatabaseMetaData	

21.15 BASIC STEPS

The following basic steps are followed to work with JDBC:

- Loading a Driver

- Making a connection
- Executing an SQL statement

21.16 LOADING A DRIVER

You have to first download an appropriate driver depending upon the database you want to connect. Sun provides a Type 1 driver bundled with the JDK 1.1 or later. Other types of drivers are database-specific and must be downloaded.

The latest version, Type 4 MySQL JDBC driver, can be downloaded from the following site:

```
http://dev.mysql.com/downloads/connector/j/5.1.html
```

Download the .zip or .tar.gz file containing the binary file `mysql-connector-java-5.1.7-bin.jar`.

The latest version Type 4 JDBC driver for Oracle can be downloaded from the following site:

```
http://www.oracle.com/technology/software/tech/java/sqlj_jdbc/index.html
```

Download the appropriate driver depending upon the JDK and Oracle version you are using. For example, the binary driver file for Oracle 9i and JDK 1.4 or later is `ojdbc14.jar`.

Once you have downloaded the appropriate .jar file, put it in Tomcat's `lib` directory and restart the web server.

If you are developing simple Java database applications, put this .jar file in the `CLASSPATH` environment variable.

So far, we have downloaded and installed the JDBC driver. For it to start functioning, an instance of the driver has to be created and registered with the `DriverManager` class so that it can translate the JDBC call to the appropriate database call. The JDBC class `DriverManager` is an important class in the `java.sql` package. It interfaces between the Java application and the JDBC driver. This class manages the set of JDBC drivers installed on the system. It has many other useful methods, some of which will be discussed in Section 21.17.

One way to register a driver with the driver manager is to use the static method `forName` of the Java class `Class` with a driver class name as an argument. For example, the Type 1 driver provided by sun can be instantiated and registered with the driver manager as follows:

```
Class.forName("sun.jdbc.odbc.JdbcOdbcDriver");
```

The method `forName` creates an instance of the class whose name is specified as an argument using its default constructor. The instance created in this fashion must register itself with the `DriverManager` class. The .jar file for MySQL contains two driver class files with the name `Driver.class`, one in the `com.mysql.jdbc` package and the other in the `org.gjt.mm.mysql` package. So, you may use any one of the following:

```
Class.forName("com.mysql.jdbc.Driver");
Class.forName("org.gjt.mm.mysql.Driver");
```

One can perform this registration procedure by explicitly creating an instance and passing it to the static `registerDriver` method of the `DriverManager` class. The method `registerDriver()`

in turn registers the driver with the driver manager. Some JDBC vendors such as Oracle recommend the latter mechanism.

```
DriverManager.registerDriver(new oracle.jdbc.driver.OracleDriver());
```

A similar procedure can be followed for other drivers as well. The implementation of the MySQL driver file `com.mysql.jdbc.Driver` looks like this.

```
public class Driver extends NonRegisteringDriver implements java.sql.Driver{
   static {
      try {
         java.sql.DriverManager.registerDriver(new Driver());
      } catch (SQLException E) {
         throw new RuntimeException("Can't register driver!");
      }
   }
   public Driver() throws SQLException {}
}
```

Since the static block registers the driver with the driver manager automatically, only creating an instance is sufficient. So, one might use the following code as well:

```
new com.mysql.jdbc.Driver();
```

Now, the driver is ready to translate the JDBC call.

21.17 MAKING A CONNECTION

Once a driver is instantiated and registered with the driver manager, the connection to the database can be established using methods provided by the `DriverManager` class. For each connection created, `DriverManager` makes use of the appropriate driver registered to it. The following methods are available on the `DriverManager` class to establish a connection. All methods return a `Connection` object on successful creation of the connection.

```
public static Connection getConnection (String url, String login, String passwd)
public static Connection getConnection (String url)
public static Connection getConnection (String url, Properties)
```

The `Connection` object encapsulates the session/connection to a specific database. It is used to fire SQL statements as well as commit or roll back database transactions. It also allows us to collect useful information about the database dynamically and to write custom applications. Many connections can be established to a single database server or different database servers.

The primary argument that the `getConnection()` method takes is a database URL. This argument identifies a database uniquely. `DriverManager` uses this URL to find a suitable JDBC driver installed earlier, which recognizes the URL and uses this driver to connect to the corresponding database.

The URL always starts with `jdbc:`. The format of the rest of the JDBC URL varies widely for different databases. Some are mentioned in Table 21.4. The format of the MySQL JDBC URL is as follows:

```
jdbc:mysql://[host]:[port]/[database]
```

Here, `host` is the name (or IP address) of the machine running the database at the port number `port` and `database` is a name of a database. Suppose a MySQL database, `test`, is running in a machine, `thinkpad`, at port `3306`, the corresponding URL will be

```
jdbc:mysql://thinkpad:3306/test
```

A database connection can be established using this URL as follows:

```
Connection con = DriverManager.getConnection("jdbc:mysql://thinkpad:3306/test",
"root", "nbuser");
```

Similarly, the following code segment creates a database connection to the Oracle database `mirora` running in the machine `miroracle` at port `1521`.

```
Connection  con =
DriverManager.getConnection("jdbc:oracle:thin:@miroracle:1521:mirora", "scott",
"tiger");
```

Table 21.5 shows the JDBC URL formats.

Table 21.5 JDBC URL format

<table>
<tr><th colspan="3">MySQL</th></tr>
<tr><td>Jar file</td><td colspan="2">mysql-connector-java-nn-bin.jar</td></tr>
<tr><td>Download URL</td><td colspan="2">http://dev.mysql.com/downloads/connector/j/5.1.html</td></tr>
<tr><td>Driver</td><td colspan="2">com.mysql.jdbc.Driver</td></tr>
<tr><td>URL format</td><td colspan="2">jdbc:mysql://[host]:[port]/[database]</td></tr>
<tr><td rowspan="2">Sample URL</td><td colspan="2">jdbc:mysql://thinkpad:3306/test</td></tr>
<tr><td colspan="2">jdbc:mysql://localhost:3306/sample</td></tr>
<tr><th colspan="3">Oracle</th></tr>
<tr><td>Jar file</td><td colspan="2">ojdbc14.jar (Java 1.4)
ojdbc15.jar (Java 1.5)
ojdbc16.jar (Java 1.6)</td></tr>
<tr><td>Download URL</td><td colspan="2">http://www.oracle.com/technology/software/tech/java/sqlj_jdbc/index.html</td></tr>
<tr><td>Driver</td><td colspan="2">oracle.jdbc.driver.OracleDriver</td></tr>
<tr><td>URL format</td><td colspan="2">jdbc:oracle:[type]:@[host]:[port]:[service]
jdbc:oracle:[type]:[host]:[port]:[SID]
jdbc:oracle:[type]:[TNSName]</td></tr>
<tr><td rowspan="2">Sample URL</td><td>thin</td><td>jdbc:oracle:thin:@miroracle:1521: ORCL_SVC
jdbc:oracle:thin:@172.16.4.243:1521: ORCL_SID
jdbc:oracle:thin:@(description=(address=(host=localhost)(protocol=tcp)(port=152 1))(connect_data=(sid=ORCL)))
jdbc:oracle:thin:@TNS-NAME</td></tr>
<tr><td>Oci</td><td>jdbc:oracle:oci:@miroracle:1521: ORCL_SVC
jdbc:oracle:oci:@172.16.4.243:1521: ORCL_SID
jdbc:oracle:oci:@(description=(address=(host=localhost)(protocol=tcp)(port=1521))(connect_data=(sid=ORCL)))
jdbc:oracle:oci:@TNS-NAME</td></tr>
</table>

(Contd.)

(Contd.)

Sun JDBC–ODBC Bridge	
Jar file	Bundled with JDK
Driver	Sun.jdbc.odbc.JdbcOdbcDriver
URL format	JDBC:ODBC:[data source name]
Sample URL	JDBC:ODBC:test
DB2	
Jar file	db2jcc.jar
Download URL	http://www-01.ibm.com/software/data/db2/ad/java.html
Driver	Com.ibm.db2.jdbc.net.DB2Driver
URL format	Jdbc:db2://[host]:[port]/[database]
Sample URL	jdbc:db2://172.16.4.243:50000/test
Pervasive	
Jar file	pvjdbc2.jar
Driver	com.pervasive.jdbc.v2.Driver
Download URL	http://www.pervasive.com/developerzone/access_methods/jdbc.asp
URL format	jdbc:pervasive://[host]:[port]/[database]
Sample URL	jdbc:pervasive://thinkpad:1583/sample
PostgreSQL	
Jar file	postgresql-nn.jdbc3.jar
Download URL	http://jdbc.postgresql.org/download.html
Driver	org.postgresql.Driver
URL format	jdbc:postgresql://[host]:[port]/[database]
Sample URL	jdbc:postgresql://[localhost]:[5432]/[test]
JavaDB/Derby	
Jar file	derbyclient.jar
Download URL	http://db.apache.org/derby/derby_downloads.html
Driver	org.apache.derby.jdbc.ClientDriver
URL format	jdbc:derby:net://[host]:[port]/[database]
Sample URL	jdbc:derby:net://[172.16.4.243]:[1527]/[sample]

The second overloaded version of the `getConnection()` method takes only a string argument. This argument must contain URL information, together with other parameters such as user name and password. The parameters are passed as a name–value pair separated by "&" using the same syntax as the HTTP URL. The general syntax of such a URL is as follows:

```
basicURL?param1=value1&param2=value2…
```

Following is an example of such a string argument for the MySQL database.

```
jdbc:mysql://thinkpad:3306/test?user=root&password=nbuser
```

Alternatively, parameters can be put in a `java.util.Properties` object and the object can be passed to the `getConnection()` method. Following is an example using Properties.

```
String url = "jdbc:mysql://thinkpad:3306/test";
java.util.Properties p = new java.util.Properties();
p.setProperty("user", "root");
p.setProperty("password", "nbuser");
Connection con = DriverManager.getConnection(url, p);
```

21.18 EXECUTE AN SQL STATEMENT

Once a connection to the database is established, we can interact with the database. The `Connection` interface provides methods for obtaining different statement objects that are used to fire SQL statements via the established connection. The `Connection` object can be used for other purposes such as gathering database information, and committing or rolling back a transaction. The following section describes different types of statement objects and their functionality.

21.19 SQL STATEMENTS

The `Connection` interface defines the following methods to obtain statement objects.

```
Statement createStatement()
Statement createStatement(int resultSetType,
                          int resultSetConcurrency)
Statement createStatement(int resultSetType,
                          int resultSetConcurrency,
                          int resultSetHoldability)

PreparedStatement prepareStatement(java.lang.String)
PreparedStatement prepareStatement(String sql,
                                   int resultSetType,
                                   int resultSetConcurrency)
PreparedStatement prepareStatement(String sql,
                                   int resultSetType,
                                   int resultSetConcurrency,
                                   int resultSetHoldability)

CallableStatement prepareCall(java.lang.String)
CallableStatement prepareCall(String sql,
                              int resultSetType,
                              int resultSetConcurrency)
CallableStatement prepareCall(String sql,
                              int resultSetType,
                              int resultSetConcurrency,
                              int resultSetHoldability)
```

The JDBC `Statement`, `CallableStatement`, and `PreparedStatement` interfaces define the methods and properties that enable you to send SQL or PL/SQL commands and receive data from your database.

21.19.1 Simple Statement

The `Statement` interface is used to execute static SQL statements. A `Statement` object is instantiated using the `createStatement()` method on the `Connection` object as follows:

```
Statement stmt = con.createStatement();
```

This `Statement` object defines the following methods to fire different types of SQL commands on the database.

`executeUpdate()`

This method is used to execute DDL (CREATE, ALTER, and DROP), DML (INSERT, DELETE, UPDATE, etc.) and DCL statements. In general, if an SQL command changes the database, the `executeUpdate()` method is used. The return value of this method is the number of rows affected.

Assume that `stmt` is a `Statement` object. The following code segment first creates a table named `accounts`.

```
String create = "CREATE TABLE accounts (            "+
                "  accNum      integer  primary key, "+
                "  holderName  varchar(20),          "+
                "  balance     integer               "+
                ")";
stmt.executeUpdate(create);
```

Once the table is created, data can be inserted into it using the following code segment.

```
String insert = "INSERT INTO accounts VALUES(1,'Uttam K. Roy', 10000)";
stmt.executeUpdate(insert);
insert = "INSERT INTO accounts VALUES(2,'Bibhas Ch. Dhara', 20000)";
stmt.executeUpdate(insert);
```

`executeQuery()`

This is used for DQL statements such as SELECT. Remember, DQL statements only read data from database tables; it cannot change database tables. So, the return value of this method is a set of rows that is represented as a `ResultSet` object.

The result of the `executeQuery` method is stored in an object of type `ResultSet`. This result set object looks very much similar to a table and hence has a number of rows. A particular row is selected by setting a cursor associated with this result set. A cursor is something like a pointer to the rows. Once the cursor is set to a particular row, individual columns are retrieved using the methods provided by the `ResultSet` interface. The cursor is placed before the first row of result set when it is created first. JDBC 1.0 allows us to move the cursor only in the forward direction using the method `next()`. JDBC 2.0 allows us to move the cursor both forward and backward as well as to move to a specified row relative to the current row. These types of result sets are called scrollable result sets, which will be discussed in Section 21.22.

Since the cursor does not point to any row (it points to a position before the first row), users have the responsibility to set the cursor to a valid row to retrieve data from it. To retrieve data from a column, methods of the form `getX()` are used, where `X` is the data type of the column. Following is an example that retrieves information from the `accounts` table created earlier.

```
String query = "SELECT * FROM accounts";
ResultSet rs = stmt.executeQuery(query);
while(rs.next()) {
```

```
        out.println(rs.getString("accNum"));
        out.println(rs.getString("holderName"));
        out.println(rs.getString("balance"));
    }
```

`execute()`

Sometimes, users want to execute SQL statements whose type (DDL, DML, DCL, or DQL) is not known in advance. This may happen particularly when statements are obtained from another program. In that case, users cannot decide which method they should use. In such cases, the `execute()` method is used. It can be used to execute any SQL commands. Since it allows us to execute any SQL commands, the result can either be a `ResultSet` object or an integer. However, how does a user know it? Fortunately, this method returns a Boolean value, which indicates the return type. The return value `true` indicates that the result is a `ResultSet` object, which can be obtained by calling its `getResultSet()` method. On the other hand, if the return value is `false`, the result is an update count, which can be obtained by calling the `getUpdateCount()` method.

The following JSP page takes an arbitrary SQL statement as a parameter and fires this SQL statement on the database. Make sure that the MySQL JDBC driver is in the `/lib` directory under the Tomcat installation directory.

```
<%@page import="java.sql.*"%>
<%
    response.setHeader("Pragma", "no-cache");
    response.setHeader("Cache-Control", "no-cache");
    response.setDateHeader("Expires", -1);
    try {
        String query = request.getParameter("sql");
        if (query != null) {
            new com.mysql.jdbc.Driver();
            String url = "jdbc:mysql://thinkpad:3306/test";
            Connection con = DriverManager.getConnection(url, "root", "nbuser");
            Statement stmt = con.createStatement();
            if (stmt.execute(query) == false) {
                out.println(stmt.getUpdateCount() + " rows affected");
            }
            else {
                ResultSet rs = stmt.getResultSet();
                ResultSetMetaData md = rs.getMetaData();
                out.println("<table border=\"1\"><tr>");
                for (int i = 1; i <= md.getColumnCount(); i++) {
                    out.print("<th>" + md.getColumnName(i) + "</th>");
                }
                out.println("</tr>");
                while (rs.next()) {
                    out.println("<tr>");
                    for (int i = 1; i <= md.getColumnCount(); i++) {
                        out.print("<td>" + rs.getString(i) + "</td>");
                    }
                    out.println("</tr>");
                }
                out.println("</table>");
                rs.close();
            }
```

```
            stmt.close();
            con.close();
         }
      }
      catch (Exception e) {
         out.println(e);
      }
   %>
   <form name="sqlForm" method="post">
      SQL statement:<br><input type="text" name="sql" size="50"><br />
      <input type="reset"><input type="submit" value="Execute">
   </form>
```

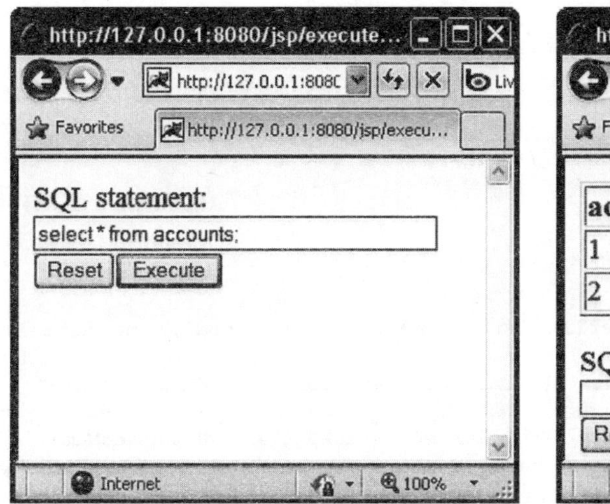

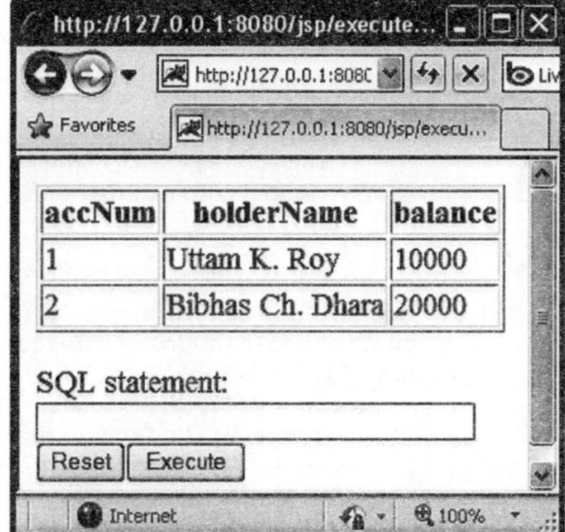

Figure 21.10 Executing SQL statements

Note that this JSP page allows you to fire any valid SQL query, including DML. So, the JSP page must perform user verification before providing this interface.

21.19.2 Atomic Transaction

The database transaction made by the `executeUpdate()` method is committed automatically. This may lead to data inconsistency if a series of related statements are executed. Consider the following simple table for a banking application.

```
   accounts(accNum, holderName, balance)
```

The bank manager wants to write a java program to transfer some amount of money `amount` from the source account `src` to the destination account `dst`. The basic task of this program will be to subtract `amount` from the source account balance and add `amount` to the destination account balance. A sample JSP page looks like this:

```
   <%@page import="java.sql.*"%>
   <%!
      Connection con;
      Statement stmt;
```

```
    String query;
    public void jspInit() {
       try {
          new com.mysql.jdbc.Driver();
          String url = "jdbc:mysql://thinkpad:3306/test";
          con = DriverManager.getConnection(url, "root", "nbuser");
          stmt = con.createStatement();
       }catch(Exception e) {}
    }
    public boolean transfer(int src, int dst, int amount) {
       try {
          query = "SELECT balance FROM accounts WHERE accNum=" + src;
          ResultSet rs = stmt.executeQuery(query);
          rs.next();
          int srcBal = rs.getInt("balance") - amount;
          query = "SELECT balance FROM accounts WHERE accNum=" + dst;
          rs = stmt.executeQuery(query);
          rs.next();
          int dstBal = rs.getInt("balance") + amount;
          return doTransfer(src, dst, srcBal, dstBal);
       } catch (SQLException e) {
          return false;
       }
    }
    public boolean doTransfer(int src, int dst, int srcBal, int dstBal) {
    try {
       query = "UPDATE accounts SET balance=" + srcBal + " WHERE accNum=" + src;
       stmt.executeUpdate(query);
       query = "UPDATE accounts SET balance=" + dstBal + " WHERE accNum=" + dst;
       //If anything goes wrong here, destination account will contain wrong
       //result.
       stmt.executeUpdate(query);
       return true;
    } catch (SQLException e) {
       return false;
    }
    }
%>
<%
try {
    int src = Integer.parseInt(request.getParameter("src"));
    int dst = Integer.parseInt(request.getParameter("dst"));
    int amount = Integer.parseInt(request.getParameter("amount"));
    transfer(src, dst, amount);
}catch(Exception e) {out.println(e);}
%>
```

Note that source and destination accounts must be updated atomically. However, if anything goes wrong after updating the source account and before updating the destination account in the `doTransfer()` method, the destination account will hold an incorrect balance.

This problem can be solved using the `autoCommit()` method available on the `Connection` object. First the `autoCommit` flag of the `Connection` object is set to false. At the end of execution of all related statements, the transaction is committed. If anything goes wrong during the execution of those statements, it can be caught and the transaction gets rolled back accordingly. This way a set of related operations can be performed atomically.

The correct `doTransfer()` method looks like this:

```
public boolean doTransfer(int src, int dst, int srcBal, int dstBal) {
   try {
      con.setAutoCommit(false);
      query = "UPDATE accounts SET balance=" + srcBal + " WHERE accNum=" + src;
      stmt.executeUpdate(query);
      query = "UPDATE accounts SET balance=" + dstBal + " WHERE accNum=" + dst;
      stmt.executeUpdate(query);
      con.commit();
      return true;
   } catch (SQLException e) {
      try {
         con.rollback();
      } catch (SQLException e1) {
      }
      return false;
   }
}
```

`executeBatch()`

This method allows us to execute a set of related commands as a whole. Commands to be fired on the database are added to the `Statement` object one by one using the method `addBatch()`. It is always safe to clear the `Statement` object using the method `clearBatch()` before adding any command to it. Once all commands are added, `executeBatch()` is called to send them as a unit to the database. The DBMS executes the commands in the order in which they were added. Finally, if all commands are successful, it returns an array of update counts. To allow correct error handling, we should always set auto-commit mode to `false` before beginning a batch command.

Following is the method `doTransfer`, rewritten using this mechanism.

```
public boolean doBatchTransfer(int src, int dst, int srcBal, int dstBal) {
  try {
    String query;
    con.setAutoCommit(false);
    stmt.clearBatch();
    query = "UPDATE accounts SET balance=" + srcBal + " WHERE accNum=" + src;
    stmt.addBatch(query);
    query = "UPDATE accounts SET balance=" + dstBal + " WHERE accNum=" + dst;
    stmt.addBatch(query);
    stmt.executeBatch();
    con.commit();
    return true;
  } catch (SQLException e) {
    try {
      con.rollback();
    } catch (SQLException e1) {
    }
    return false;
  }
}
```

Since all the commands are sent as a unit to the database for execution, it improves the performance significantly.

21.19.3 Pre-compiled Statement

When an SQL statement is fired to the database for execution using the `Statement` object the following steps get executed:

- DBMS checks the syntax of the statement being submitted.
- If the syntax is correct, it executes the statement.

DBMS compiles every statement unnecessarily, even if users want to execute the *same* SQL statement repeatedly with different data items. This creates significant overhead, which can be avoided using the `PreparedStatement` object.

A `PreparedStatement` object is created using the `prepareStatement()` method of the `Connection` object. An SQL statement with placeholders (?) is supplied to the method `Connection.prepareStatement()` when a `PreparedStatement` object is created. This SQL statement, together with the placeholders is sent to the DBMS. DMBS, in turn, compiles the statement and if everything is correct, a `PreparedStatement` object is created. This means that a `PreparedStatement` object contains an SQL statement whose syntax has already been checked and hence is called pre-compiled statement. This SQL statement is then fired repeatedly, with placeholders substituted by different data items. Note that `PreparedStatement` is useful only if the same SQL statement is executed repeatedly with different parameters. Otherwise, it behaves exactly like `Statement` and no benefit can be obtained.

The following example creates a `PreparedStatement` object:

```
PreparedStatement ps = con.prepareStatement("INSERT INTO user values(?,?)");
```

The SQL statement has two placeholders, whose values will be supplied whenever this statement is sent for execution. Placeholders are substituted using methods of the form `setX()`, where `X` is the data type of the value used to substitute. These methods take two parameters. The first parameter indicates the index of the placeholder to be substituted and the second one indicates the value to be used for substitution. The following example substitutes the first placeholder with "user1".

```
ps.setString(1, "user1");
```

Consider a file, `question.txt`, which contains questions of the form `question_no:question_string` as follows:

```
1:What is the full form of JDBC?
2:How is a PreparedStatement created?
...
```

The following example inserts questions and their numbers stored in this file in the table `questions`.

```
PreparedStatement ps = con.prepareStatement("INSERT INTO questions
values(?,?)");
```

```
BufferedReader br = new BufferedReader(new InputStreamReader(new
FileInputStream("question.txt")));
String line = br.readLine();
while (line != null) {
   StringTokenizer st = new StringTokenizer(line, ":");
   String qno = st.nextToken();
   String question = st.nextToken();
   ps.setString(1, qno);
   ps.setString(2, question);
   ps.executeUpdate();
   line = br.readLine();
}
```

`PreparedStatement` has another important role in executing parameterized SQL statements. Consider this solution using the `Statement` object.

```
Statement stmt = con.createStatement();
BufferedReader br = new BufferedReader(new InputStreamReader(new
FileInputStream(application.getRealPath("/")+"question.txt")));
String line = br.readLine();
while (line != null) {
   StringTokenizer st = new StringTokenizer(line, ":");
   String qno = st.nextToken();
   String question = st.nextToken();
   String query = "INSERT INTO questions values("+qno+",'"+question+"')";
   stmt.executeUpdate(query);
   line = br.readLine();
}
```

This code segment will work fine, provided the question does not contain characters such as "'". For example, if the file `question.txt` contains a line "3:What's JDBC?", the value of the query will be

```
INSERT INTO questions values(3,'What's JDBC?')
```

This is an invalid query due to the "'" character in the word "What's". If you try, you will get an error message like this:

```
com.mysql.jdbc.exceptions.jdbc4.MySQLSyntaxErrorException: You have an error
in your SQL syntax; check the manual that corresponds to your MySQL server
version for the right syntax to use near 's JDBC?')' at line 1
```

`PreparedStatement` can handle this situation very easily, as it treats the entire parameter as input. So, the example given using the `PreparedStatement` will work correctly in this case.

21.19.4 SQL Statements to Call Stored Procedures

JDBC also allows the calling of stored procedures that are stored in the database server. This is done using the `CallableStatement` object. A `CallableStatement` object is created using the `prepareCall()` method on a `Connection` object.

```
CallableStatement prepareCall(String)
```

The method `prepareCall()` takes a primary string parameter, which represents the procedure to be called, and returns a `CallableStatement` object, which is used to invoke stored procedures if the underlying database supports them. Here is an example:

```
String proCall = "{call changePassword(?, ?, ?)}";
CallableStatement cstmt = con.prepareCall(proCall);
```

The variable `cstmt` can now be used to call the stored procedure `changePassword`, which has three input parameters and no result parameter. Whether the ? placeholders are `IN`, `OUT`, or `INOUT` parameters depends on the definition of the stored procedure `changePassword`.

JDBC API allows the following syntax to call stored procedures:

```
{call procedure-name [(?, ?, ...)]}
```

For example, to call a stored procedure with no parameter and no return type, the following syntax is used:

```
{call procedure-name}
```

The following syntax is used to call a procedure that takes a single parameter:

```
{call procedure-name(?)}
```

If a procedure returns a value, the following syntax is used:

```
{? = call procedure-name (?, ?)}
```

Since MySQL procedures are not allowed to return values, the last format is not allowed in MySQL. The web developer must know what stored procedures are available in the underlying database. Before using any stored procedure, one can use the `supportsStoredProcedures()` method on the `DatabaseMetaData` object to verify if the underlying database supports the stored procedure. If it supports, the description of the stored procedures can be obtained using `getProcedures()` on the `DatabaseMetaData` object. Consider the following procedure created in MySQL.

```
CREATE PROCEDURE changePassword(IN loginName varchar(10), IN oldPassword
varchar(10), IN newPassword varchar(10))
BEGIN
  DECLARE old varchar(10);
  SELECT password INTO @old FROM users WHERE login=loginName;
  IF @old = oldPassword THEN
    UPDATE users SET password=newPassword WHERE login=loginName;
  END IF;
END;
```

This procedure changes the password of a specified user in the table `users`. It takes three parameters: the login id of the user whose password has to be changed, the old password, and a new password.

If you are using MySQL command prompt to create a procedure, you may face a problem. Note that the stored procedures use ";" as the delimiter. The default MySQL statement delimiter is also ";". This would make the SQL in the stored procedure syntactically invalid. The solution is to temporarily change the command-line utility delimiter using the following command;

```
DELIMITER //
```

In the end, change the delimiter to ";" if necessary.

The `IN` parameters are passed to a `CallableStatement` object using methods of the form `setXxx()`. For example, `setFloat()` and `setBoolean()` methods are used to pass `float` and `boolean` values, respectively.

The following code segment illustrates how to call this procedure.

```
<%@page import="java.sql.*"%>
<%
   try {
      new com.mysql.jdbc.Driver();
      String url = "jdbc:mysql://thinkpad:3306/test";
      Connection con = DriverManager.getConnection(url, "root", "nbuser");
      String proCall = "{call changePassword(?, ?, ?)}";
      CallableStatement cstmt = con.prepareCall(proCall);
      String login = request.getParameter("login");
      String oldPassword = request.getParameter("oldPassword");
      String newPassword = request.getParameter("newPassword");
      cstmt.setString(1, login);
      cstmt.setString(2, oldPassword);
      cstmt.setString(3, newPassword);
      if (cstmt.executeUpdate() > 0) {
         out.println("Password changed successfully");
      } else {
         out.println("Couldn't change password");
      }
      cstmt.close();
      conn.close();
   } catch (Exception e) {
      out.println(e);
   }
%>
```

The `CallableStatement` object also allows batch update exactly like `PreparedStatement`.

Following is an example:

```
String proCall = "{call changePassword(?, ?, ?)}";
CallableStatement cstmt = con.prepareCall(proCall);

cstmt.setString(1, "user1");
cstmt.setString(2, "user1");
cstmt.setString(3, "pass1");
cstmt.addBatch();

cstmt.setString(1, "user2");
cstmt.setString(2, "user2");
cstmt.setString(3, "pass2");
cstmt.addBatch();

int [] updateCounts = cstmt.executeBatch();
```

This example illustrates how to use batch update facility to associate two sets of parameters with a `CallableStatement` object.

21.20 RETRIEVING RESULT

A table of data is represented in the JDBC by the `ResultSet` interface. The `ResultSet` objects are usually generated by executing the SQL statements that query the database. A pointer points to a particular row of the `ResultSet` object at a time. This pointer is called *cursor*. The cursor is positioned before the first row when the `ResultSet` object is generated. To retrieve data from a row of `ResultSet`, the cursor must be positioned at the row. The `ResultSet` interface provides methods to move this cursor.

next()

- This method on the `ResultSet` object moves the cursor to the next row of the result set.
- It returns true/false depending upon whether there are more rows in the result set.

Since the `next()` method returns false when there are no more rows in the `ResultSet` object, it can be used in a while loop to iterate through the result set as follows:

```
String query = "SELECT * from users";
ResultSet rs = stmt.executeQuery(query);
while(rs.next()) {
   //process it
}
```

The `ResultSet` interface provides reader methods for retrieving column values from the row pointed to by the cursor. These have the form `getXxx()`, where `Xxx` is the name of the data type of the column. For example, if data types are string and int, the name of the reader methods are `getString()` and `getInt()`, respectively.

Values can be retrieved using either the column index or the name of the column. Using the column index, in general, is more efficient. The column index starts from 1. The following example illustrates how to retrieve data from a `ResultSet` object.

```
String query = "SELECT * from users";
ResultSet rs = stmt.executeQuery(query);
while(rs.next()) {
   String login = rs.getString("login");
   String password = rs.getString("password");
   System.out.println(login+"\t"+password);
}
```

21.21 GETTING DATABASE INFORMATION

Sometimes, it is necessary to know the capabilities of DataBase Management System (DBMS) before dealing with it. This is because different DBMSs often provide different features, implement them differently, and also use different data types. Moreover, the driver may also implement additional features on top of the DBMS. The `DatabaseMetaData` interface provides methods to collect comprehensive information about a DBMS. We can discover features a DBMS supports and develop our application accordingly. For example, before creating a table, one may want to know what data types are supported by this DBMS. User may also want to know whether the underlying DBMS supports batch update.

A `DatabaseMetaData` object is obtained using the `getMetaData()` method on the `Connection` object as follows:

```
DatabaseMetaData md = con.getMetaData();
```

We can then use various methods on this `DatabaseMetaData` object to collect the required information about the DBMS. Following is a list of commonly used methods:

`getDatabaseMetaData()`

Returns the `DatabaseMetaData` object, which contains detailed information about the underlying database. Some important methods of `DatabaseMetaData` are

`String getSQLKeywords()`

Returns keywords available

`getDatabaseProductName()`

Returns the name of the manufacturer

`getDatabaseProductVersion()`

Returns the current version

`getDriverName()`

Returns driver used

The following JSP page retrieves most of the MySQL database information.

```
<%@page import="java.sql.*, java.lang.reflect.*"%>
<%
   new com.mysql.jdbc.Driver();
   String url = "jdbc:mysql://thinkpad:3306/test";
   Connection con = DriverManager.getConnection(url, "root", "nbuser");
   DatabaseMetaData md = con.getMetaData();
   Method[] methods = md.getClass().getMethods();
   Object[] param = new Object[0];
   out.println("<table border=\"1\">");
   for (int i = 0; i < methods.length; i++) {
      if (methods[i].getParameterTypes().length == 0) {
         if (methods[i].getReturnType() == Boolean.TYPE ||
methods[i].getReturnType() == String.class) {
            out.println("<tr>");
            out.println("<td>"+methods[i].getName() + "</td>");
            out.println("<td>" + methods[i].invoke(md, param)+"</td>");
            out.println("</tr>");
         }
      }
   }
   out.println("</table>");
%>
```

The result of this page is shown in Table 21.9.

21.22 SCROLLABLE AND UPDATABLE RESULTSET

The result set returned so far by a query can be navigated in one direction (forward). Moreover the data the result sets contain are read-only. Any change to the result set does not affect the actual database.

Result sets can be *scrollable* in the sense that the cursor can be moved backward and forward. Additionally, a result set can be *updatable*, such that any change to the result set reflects in the database immediately. A result set can be scrollable as well as updatable. *Note that scrollable and updatable result sets incur significant overhead. So, such result sets should be created if the underlying application performs scrolling.*

In addition to *scrollability* and *updatability*, another important concept, called *sensitivity*, is defined. Sensitivity broadly answers the following question:

```
Can a result set see the changes that are made to the underlying database?
```

If a result cannot see any changes, it is said to be insensitive. Otherwise, the sensitivity of a result set is defined with respect to the database operation as well as the operating party. For example, a result set is said to be sensitive to update if it can see any update operation made on the underlying database. The sensitivity rules are shown in Table 21.6.

The `createStatement()` and `prepareStatement()` methods take extra parameters that specify the type of result returned by subsequent execution of SQL statements. The prototype of the `createStatement()` method to generate a scrollable and updatable result set is as follows:

```
Statement createStatement(int resultSetType, int resultSetConcurrency)
```

Here, scrollability and updatability are controlled by the parameters `resultSetType` and `resultSetConcurrency`, respectively.

21.22.1 Scrollability Type

The parameter `resultSetType` can assume the following static integer constants defined in `ResultSet`. Their meaning is as follows:

- `TYPE_FORWARD_ONLY`

  If this constant is used, the cursor starts at the first row and can only move forward.

- `TYPE_SCROLL_INSENSITIVE`

  All cursor positioning methods are enabled; the result set does not reflect changes made by others in the underlying table.

- `TYPE_SCROLL_SENSITIVE`

  All cursor positioning methods are enabled; the result set reflects changes made by others in the underlying table.

The visibility of internal and external changes to scrollable `ResultSet` in Oracle JDBC is shown in Table 21.6.

Table 21.6 Visibility of internal and external changes to scrollable result set in oracle JDBC

Scroll Type		TYPE_FORWARD_ONLY	TYPE_SCROLL_SENSITIVE	TYPE_SCROLL_INSENSITIVE
Internal	DELETE	No	Yes	Yes
	UPDATE	Yes	Yes	Yes
	INSERT	No	No	No
External	DELETE	No	No	No
	UPDATE	No	Yes	No
	INSERT	No	No	No

21.22.2 Concurrency Type

The parameter `resultSetConcurrency` can assume the following static integer constants defined in `ResultSet`. The following is a brief description:

- `CONCUR_READ_ONLY`

  The result set is not updatable.

- `CONCUR_UPDATABLE`

  Rows can be added and deleted; columns can be updated and are visible to others.

21.22.3 Examples

The following example creates a `Statement` object, whose methods will return scrollable, update insensitive, and read-only result sets.

```
Statement stmt = conn.createStatement(ResultSet.TYPE_SCROLL_INSENSITIVE,
ResultSet.CONCUR_READ_ONLY);
ResultSet rs = stmt.executeQuery("SELECT * FROM questions");
```

The `ResultSet` object `rs` is now scrollable, but update insensitive.

Originally, result sets could be navigated only in one direction (forward) and starting at only one position (the first row). In JDBC 2.0, the row pointer can be manipulated as if it were an array index. Some of the important methods available on the scrollable `ResultSet` object are shown in Table 21.7. The following examples demonstrate how to navigate a scrollable result set:

- Move the cursor forward by one row.

```
rs.next();
//or
rs.relative(1);
```

- Move the cursor backward by one row.

```
rs.previous();
//or
rs.relative(-1);
```

- Set the cursor before the first row.

```
rs.beforeFirst();
```

- Set the cursor after the last row.

```
rs.afterLast();
```

- Set the cursor at the first row (row 1).

```
rs.first();
//or
rs.absolute(1);
```

- Set the cursor at the last row.

```
rs.last();
//or
rs.absolute(-1);
```

- Set the cursor at the second row.

```
rs.absolute(2);
```

- Set the cursor at the second last row.

```
rs.absolute(-2);
```

- Move the cursor forward six rows from the current position.

```
rs.relative(6);
//Sets the cursor after the last row, if it goes beyond the last row
```

- Move the cursor backward four rows from the current position.

```
rs.relative(-4);
//Sets the cursor before the first row, if it goes before the first row
```

Table 21.7 Scrollable ResultSet methods

Method	Description
next()	Advances cursor to the next row
previous()	Moves cursor back one row
first()	Sets cursor to the first row
last()	Sets cursor to the last row
beforeFirst()	Sets cursor just before the first row
afterLast()	Sets cursor just after the last row
absolute(int rowNumber)	Sets the cursor to the specified row number. +ve and –ve numbers indicate positions relative to the position before first row and after last row, respectively. For example, 1 and –1 represent first and last row, respectively.
relative(int rows)	Forwards or reverses cursor the specified number of rows relative to the current position. +ve number indicates forwarding and –ve number indicates reversing. For example, relative(1) forwards the cursor one position, which is equivalent to next(). Similarly, relative(–1) moves the cursor one position back and is equivalent to previous(). It throws an SQLException if cursor points before the first row or after the last row.
moveToInsertRow()	Sets the cursor to a special row called "insert row" and remembers the current position before moving the cursor.
moveToCurrentRow()	Sets the cursor to the row from where the cursor was moved to "insert row" using moveToInsertRow().

The following example creates a `Statement` object, whose methods will return scrollable as well as external-update-insensitive and updatable result sets.

```
Statement stmt = conn.createStatement(ResultSet.TYPE_SCROLL_INSENSITIVE,
ResultSet.CONCUR_UPDATABLE);
ResultSet rs = stmt.executeQuery("SELECT * FROM questions");
```

To update a row in a database table, the following steps are used:

- Obtain an updatable result set.
- Move the cursor to the row to be updated using positioning methods available on the `ResultSet` object.
- Update the value of one or more columns in that row using the `updateXxx()` method on the `ResultSet` object, where `Xxx` is the data type of the column.
- Finally, update the database table using the `updateRow()` method.

The following example demonstrates how to update, insert, or delete a row from a database table using an updatable result set.

```
Statement stmt = conn.createStatement(ResultSet.TYPE_SCROLL_SENSITIVE,
ResultSet.CONCUR_UPDATABLE);
ResultSet rs = stmt.executeQuery("SELECT * FROM users");

//Updating existing row
rs.absolute(4);
rs.updateString("password","newPassword");
rs.updateRow();

//inseting new row
rs.moveToInsertRow();
rs.updateString(1, "anik");
rs.updateString(2, "anik123");
rs.insertRow();

//Deleting a row
rs.deleteRow()
```

The following JSP page changes the password of a specified user using the updatable result set.

```
<%@ page import="java.sql.*" %>
<%
   try {
      String login = request.getParameter("login");
      String oldPassword = request.getParameter("oldPassword");
      String newPassword = request.getParameter("newPassword");

      new com.mysql.jdbc.Driver();
      String url = "jdbc:mysql://thinkpad:3306/test";
      Connection con = DriverManager.getConnection(url, "root", "nbuser");
      Statement stmt = con.createStatement(ResultSet.TYPE_SCROLL_INSENSITIVE,
ResultSet.CONCUR_UPDATABLE);
```

```
        String query = "SELECT * FROM users WHERE login='" + login + "'";
        ResultSet rs = stmt.executeQuery(query);   //rs contains one row
        rs.next();                                 //set cursor at first row
        String password = rs.getString("password");
        if (password.equals(oldPassword)) {
            System.out.println(password);
            rs.updateString("password", newPassword); //update the password column
            rs.updateRow();                         //update database table
        }
    } catch (Exception e) {out.println(e); }
%>
```

The following example populates the table questions by inserting questions into the updatable result set.

```
<%@ page import="java.sql.*, java.io.*, java.util.*" %>
<%
    try {
        new com.mysql.jdbc.Driver();
        String url = "jdbc:mysql://thinkpad:3306/test";
        Connection con = DriverManager.getConnection(url, "root", "nbuser");
        Statement stmt = con.createStatement(ResultSet.TYPE_SCROLL_INSENSITIVE,
ResultSet.CONCUR_UPDATABLE);
        ResultSet rs = stmt.executeQuery("SELECT * FROM questions");
        BufferedReader br = new BufferedReader(new InputStreamReader(new
FileInputStream(application.getRealPath("/")+"question.txt")));
        String line = br.readLine();
        while (line != null) {
            StringTokenizer st = new StringTokenizer(line, ":");
            String qno = st.nextToken();
            String question = st.nextToken();

            rs.moveToInsertRow();
            rs.updateString(1, qno);
            rs.updateString(2, question);
            rs.insertRow();
            line = br.readLine();
        }
        br.close();
    } catch (Exception e) {out.println(e); }
%>
```

The following example creates a `Statement` object, whose methods will return scrollable as well as external-update-sensitive and updatable result sets.

```
Statement stmt = conn.createStatement(ResultSet.TYPE_SCROLL_SENSITIVE,
ResultSet.CONCUR_UPDATABLE);
ResultSet rs = stmt.executeQuery("SELECT * FROM questions");
```

In this case, if the database table is updated, it is reflected in the result set. Before retrieving data from a row, you should invoke the `refreshRow()` method of the `ResultSet` object so that it contains the updated row. The following JSP page shows how to use an updatable result set.

```
<%@page import="java.sql.*"%>
<%!
```

```
    Connection con;
    Statement stmt;
    ResultSet rs;
    String query;
    public void jspInit() {
       try {
          new com.mysql.jdbc.Driver();
          String url = "jdbc:mysql://thinkpad:3306/test";
          con = DriverManager.getConnection(url, "root", "nbuser");
          Statement stmt = con.createStatement(ResultSet.TYPE_SCROLL_SENSITIVE,
 ResultSet.CONCUR_UPDATABLE);
          query = "SELECT * FROM users";
          rs = stmt.executeQuery(query);
          System.out.println("loaded");

       }catch(Exception e) {}
    }
 %>
 <table border="1">
 <tr><th>Login name</th><th>Password</th></tr>
 <%
    try {
       response.setHeader("Pragma", "no-cache");
       response.setHeader("Cache-Control", "no-cache");
       response.setDateHeader("Expires", -1);

       rs.beforeFirst();
       while(rs.next()) {
          rs.refreshRow();
          out.println("<tr><td>" + rs.getString("login") + "</td>");
          out.println("<td>" + rs.getString("password")+"</td></tr>");
       }
    }catch(Exception e) {out.println(e);}
 %>
 </table>
```

This JSP page creates the `ResultSet` when this page is requested for the first time. The `ResultSet` is created in the `jspInit()` method. Consequently, it becomes an instance variable. For subsequent requests, it simply uses the `ResultSet` variable.

21.23 RESULT SET METADATA

The `ResultSetMetaData` object is used to retrieve information about the types and properties of the columns and other meta information about a `ResultSet` object. This is sometime very useful, if you do not know much about the underlying database table. A `ResultSetMetaData` object is obtained using the `getMetaData()` method on the `ResultSet` object as follows:

```
ResultSet rs = stmt.executeQuery("SELECT * FROM questions");
ResultSetMetaData rsmd = rs.getMetaData();
```

It can be used to get some useful information such as number of rows, number of columns, column names, and their type. Following are some commonly used methods on the `ResultSetMetaData` object:

`int getColumnCount()`

Returns the number of columns in the result

`String getColumnName(int)`

Returns the name of a column in a result set. Requires an integer argument indicating the position of the column within the result set

`int getColumnType(int)`

Returns the type of the specified column in the form of `java.sql.Types`

`String getColumnTypeName(int)`

Returns the type of the specified column as a string

`String getColumnClassName(int)`

Returns the fully qualified Java type name of the specified column

`int getPrecision(int)`

Returns the number of decimal positions

`int getScale(int)`

Returns the number of digits after the decimal position

`String getTableName(int)`

Returns the name of the column's underlying table

`int isNullable(int)`

Returns a constant indicating whether the specified column can have a NULL value

The following JSP page shows how to retrieve meta information from a `ResultSet` object.

```
<%@page import="java.sql.*, java.lang.reflect.*"%>
<%
   try {
      Class.forName("org.gjt.mm.mysql.Driver");
      String url = "jdbc:mysql://localhost:3306/test";
      Connection conn = DriverManager.getConnection(url, "root", "nbuser");
      Statement stmt = conn.createStatement();
      ResultSet rs = stmt.executeQuery("SELECT * FROM questions");
      ResultSetMetaData rsmd = rs.getMetaData();
      Object obj[] = new Object[1];
      Method[] methods = rsmd.getClass().getDeclaredMethods();
      out.println("<table border=\"0\"><tr><td>Method Name</td>");
      for(int j = 0; j < rsmd.getColumnCount(); j++)
         out.println("<td>" + rsmd.getColumnName(j+1) + "</td>");
      out.println("</tr>");
      for (int i = 0; i < methods.length; i++) {
      if(Modifier.isPublic(methods[i].getModifiers()))
         if (methods[i].getParameterTypes().length == 1) {
            if(!methods[i].getName().equals("isWrapperFor"))
               if(!methods[i].getName().equals("unwrap")) {
                  out.print("<tr><td>" + methods[i].getName() + "</td>");
                  for(int j=0;j<rsmd.getColumnCount();j++) {
                     obj[0] = new Integer(j+1);
                     out.print("<td>" + methods[i].invoke(rsmd,obj) +
"</td>");
```

```
                    }
                    out.println("</tr>");
                }
            }
        }
        out.println("<table>");
    }catch(Exception e) {e.printStackTrace();}
%>
```

A sample result for MySQL database is shown in Table 21.8.

Table 21.8 Result set metadata

Method Name	Qno	Question
isWritable	True	True
isCaseSensitive	False	False
getPrecision	11	200
getColumnDisplaySize	11	200
getTableName	Questions	Questions
getColumnLabel	Qno	Question
isAutoIncrement	False	False
getCatalogName	test	Test
getColumnClassName	java.lang.Integer	java.lang.String
getColumnType	4	12
getColumnTypeName	INT	VARCHAR
getScale	0	0
getSchemaName		
isCurrency	false	False
isDefinitelyWritable	true	True
isNullable	0	1
isSearchable	true	True
isSigned	true	False
getColumnCharacterEncoding	null	Null
getColumnCharacterSet	US-ASCII	Cp1252
isReadOnly	false	False
getColumnName	qno	Question

Table 21.9 Database metadata

Method Name	Return value
autoCommitFailureClosesAllResultSets	False
getDriverName	MySQL-AB JDBC Driver
supportsTransactions	True
getDriverVersion	mysql-connector-java-5.1.7 (Revision: ${svn.Revision})
getIdentifierQuoteString	`
allProceduresAreCallable	False

(Contd.)

(Contd.)

allTablesAreSelectable	False
dataDefinitionCausesTransactionCommit	True
dataDefinitionIgnoredInTransactions	false
doesMaxRowSizeIncludeBlobs	true
getCatalogSeparator	.
getCatalogTerm	database
getDatabaseProductName	MySQL
getDatabaseProductVersion	5.0.51b-community-nt
getExtraNameCharacters	#@
getNumericFunctions	ABS,ACOS,ASIN,ATAN,ATAN2,BIT_COUNT,CEILING,COS,COT,DEGREES,EXP,FLOOR,LOG,LOG10,MAX,MIN,MOD,PI,POW,POWER,RADIANS,RAND,ROUND,SIN,SQRT,TAN,TRUNCATE
getProcedureTerm	PROCEDURE
getSQLKeywords	ACCESSIBLE,ANALYZE,ASENSITIVE,BEFORE,BIGINT,BINARY,BLOB,CALL,CHANGE,CONDITION,DATABASE,DATABASES,DAY_HOUR,DAY_MICROSECOND,DAY_MINUTE,DAY_SECOND,DELAYED,DETERMINISTIC,DISTINCTROW,DIV,DUAL,EACH,ELSEIF,ENCLOSED,ESCAPED,EXIT,EXPLAIN,FLOAT4,FLOAT8,FORCE,FULLTEXT,HIGH_PRIORITY,HOUR_MICROSECOND,HOUR_MINUTE,HOUR_SECOND,IF,IGNORE,INFILE,INOUT,INT1,INT2,INT3,INT4,INT8,ITERATE,KEYS,KILL,LEAVE,LIMIT,LINEAR,LINES,LOAD,LOCALTIME,LOCALTIMESTAMP,LOCK,LONG,LONGBLOB,LONGTEXT,LOOP,LOW_PRIORITY,MEDIUMBLOB,MEDIUMINT,MEDIUMTEXT,MIDDLEINT,MINUTE_MICROSECOND,MINUTE_SECOND,MOD,MODIFIES,NO_WRITE_TO_BINLOG,OPTIMIZE,OPTIONALLY,OUT,OUTFILE,PURGE,RANGE,READS,READ_ONLY,READ_WRITE,REGEXP,RELEASE,RENAME,REPEAT,REPLACE,REQUIRE,RETURN,RLIKE,SCHEMAS,SECOND_MICROSECOND,SENSITIVE,SEPARATOR,SHOW,SPATIAL,SPECIFIC,SQLEXCEPTION,SQL_BIG_RESULT,SQL_CALC_FOUND_ROWS,SQL_SMALL_RESULT,SSL,STARTING,STRAIGHT_JOIN,TERMINATED,TINYBLOB,TINYINT,TINYTEXT,TRIGGER,UNDO,UNLOCK,UNSIGNED,USE,UTC_DATE,UTC_TIME,UTC_TIMESTAMP,VARBINARY,VARCHARACTER,WHILE,X509,XOR,YEAR_MONTH,ZEROFILL
getSchemaTerm	
getSearchStringEscape	\
getStringFunctions	ASCII,BIN,BIT_LENGTH,CHAR,CHARACTER_LENGTH,CHAR_LENGTH,CONCAT,CONCAT_WS,CONV,ELT,EXPORT_SET,FIELD,FIND_IN_SET,HEX,INSERT,INSTR,LCASE,LEFT,LENGTH,LOAD_FILE,LOCATE,LOCATE,LOWER,LPAD,LTRIM,MAKE_SET,MATCH,MID,OCT,OCTET_LENGTH,ORD,POSITION,QUOTE,REPEAT,REPLACE,REVERSE,RIGHT,RPAD,RTRIM,SOUNDEX,SPACE,STRCMP,SUBSTRING,SUBSTRING,SUBSTRING,SUBSTRING,SUBSTRING,SUBSTRING_INDEX,TRIM,UCASE,UPPER

(Contd.)

(Contd.)

getSystemFunctions	DATABASE,USER,SYSTEM_USER,SESSION_USER,PASSWORD,ENCRYPT,LAST_INSERT_ID,VERSION
getTimeDateFunctions	DAYOFWEEK,WEEKDAY,DAYOFMONTH,DAYOFYEAR,MONTH,DAYNAME,MONTHNAME,QUARTER,WEEK,YEAR,HOUR,MINUTE,SECOND,PERIOD_ADD,PERIOD_DIFF,TO_DAYS,FROM_DAYS,DATE_FORMAT,TIME_FORMAT,CURDATE,CURRENT_DATE,CURTIME,CURRENT_TIME,NOW,SYSDATE,CURRENT_TIMESTAMP,UNIX_TIMESTAMP,FROM_UNIXTIME,SEC_TO_TIME,TIME_TO_SEC
isCatalogAtStart	true
locatorsUpdateCopy	true
nullPlusNonNullIsNull	true
nullsAreSortedAtEnd	false
nullsAreSortedAtStart	false
nullsAreSortedHigh	false
nullsAreSortedLow	true
storesLowerCaseIdentifiers	true
storesLowerCaseQuotedIdentifiers	true
storesMixedCaseIdentifiers	false
storesMixedCaseQuotedIdentifiers	false
storesUpperCaseIdentifiers	false
storesUpperCaseQuotedIdentifiers	true
supportsANSI92EntryLevelSQL	true
supportsANSI92FullSQL	false
supportsANSI92IntermediateSQL	false
supportsAlterTableWithAddColumn	true
supportsAlterTableWithDropColumn	true
supportsBatchUpdates	true
supportsCatalogsInDataManipulation	true
supportsCatalogsInIndexDefinitions	true
supportsCatalogsInPrivilegeDefinitions	true
supportsCatalogsInProcedureCalls	True
supportsCatalogsInTableDefinitions	True
supportsColumnAliasing	True
supportsConvert	False
supportsCoreSQLGrammar	True
supportsCorrelatedSubqueries	True
supportsDataDefinitionAndDataManipulationTransactions	False
supportsDataManipulationTransactionsOnly	False
supportsDifferentTableCorrelationNames	True

(Contd.)

(Contd.)

supportsExpressionsInOrderBy	True
supportsExtendedSQLGrammar	False
supportsFullOuterJoins	False
supportsGetGeneratedKeys	True
supportsGroupBy	True
supportsGroupByBeyondSelect	True
supportsGroupByUnrelated	True
supportsIntegrityEnhancementFacility	False
supportsLikeEscapeClause	true
supportsLimitedOuterJoins	true
supportsMinimumSQLGrammar	true
supportsMixedCaseIdentifiers	false
supportsMixedCaseQuotedIdentifiers	false
supportsMultipleOpenResults	true
supportsMultipleResultSets	false
supportsMultipleTransactions	true
supportsNamedParameters	false
supportsNonNullableColumns	true
supportsOpenCursorsAcrossCommit	false
supportsOpenCursorsAcrossRollback	false
supportsOpenStatementsAcrossCommit	false
supportsOpenStatementsAcrossRollback	false
supportsOrderByUnrelated	false
supportsOuterJoins	true
supportsPositionedDelete	false
supportsPositionedUpdate	false
supportsSavepoints	true
supportsSchemasInDataManipulation	false
supportsSchemasInIndexDefinitions	false
supportsSchemasInPrivilegeDefinitions	false
supportsSchemasInProcedureCalls	false
supportsSchemasInTableDefinitions	false
supportsSelectForUpdate	true
supportsStatementPooling	false
supportsStoredFunctionsUsingCallSyntax	true
supportsStoredProcedures	true
supportsSubqueriesInComparisons	true
supportsSubqueriesInExists	true

(Contd.)

(Contd.)

supportsSubqueriesInIns	true
supportsSubqueriesInQuantifieds	true
supportsTableCorrelationNames	true
supportsUnion	true
supportsUnionAll	true
usesLocalFilePerTable	false
usesLocalFiles	false
providesQueryObjectGenerator	false
getURL	jdbc:mysql://thinkpad:3306/test
isReadOnly	false
getUserName	root@localhost
toString	com.mysql.jdbc.JDBC4DatabaseMetaData@5bf624

KEYWORDS

Actions: JSP actions are XML tags that can be used in a JSP page to use functions provided by the JSP engine.

Atomic Transaction: A transaction that either does not occur or occurs completely without any interleaving.

Bean: JavaBeans are reusable Java components, which allow us to separate business logic from presentation logic.

CallableStatement: Statements that are used to call stored procedures in a database.

Cookie: A name–value pair.

Database Metadata: An object that represents the meta information about a database.

DCL Statement: SQL statements typically used to control database tables.

DDL Statement: SQL statements typically used to create tables.

Declarations: JSP declarations are used to declare one or more variables, methods, or inner classes that can be used later in the JSP page.

Directives: Instructions used in the JSP page to inform the JSP engine how this page is interpreted and executed.

DML Statement: SQL statements typically used to manipulate tables such as insert and update.

DQL Statement: SQL statements typically used to read values from tables.

Expression: It is a faster, easier, and clearer way to display values of variables/parameters/expressions in a JSP page.

Implicit Objects: A web container allows us to directly access many useful objects defined in the `_jspService()` method of the JSP page's underlying servlet. These objects are called implicit objects.

JDBC: A Java framework that allows us to access databases through Java programs.

JSP Engine: A specialized servlet that supervises and controls the execution of JSP pages.

Plug-in: The `<jsp:plugin>` action is used to generate an HTML file that can download a Java plug-in on demand and execute applets or JavaBeans.

PreparedStatement: Pre-compiled statements used to fire parameterized queries.

Result Set Metadata: An object that represents the meta information about a result set.

ResultSet: The result of a DQL statement.

Scope: The scope of a JSP object is defined as the availability of that object for use from a particular place of the web application.

Scriptlets: Sections in a JSP page where we can insert an arbitrary piece of Java code.

Scrollable Result Set: A result set whose pointer (cursor) can be moved back and forth.

Session tracking: A procedure using which JSP pages can relate a sequence of requests.

Stored Procedure: Subroutine written using SQL.

Tag extension: It allows us to define and use custom tags in an JSP page exactly like other HTML/XML tags, using Java code.

Template text: The static HTML/XML components in a JSP page.

Translation: The procedure for converting a JSP page to its servlet source code.

Updatable Result Set: A result set that can be used directly to modify original database tables.

Web container: JSP pages run under the web server called web container.

SUMMARY

JSP allows us to directly embed Java code in the HTML pages. To process JSP pages, a JSP engine is needed. It is interesting to note that what we know as the "JSP engine" is nothing but a specialized servlet that runs under the supervision of the servlet engine. Commonly used JSP engines include Apache's Tomcat, Java Web Server, IBM's WebSphere, etc.

JSP technology was developed on top of servlet technology. The JSP pages are finally converted to servlets automatically.

A JSP page basically consists of static HTML/XML components called template text as well as JSP constructs. JSP constructs consist of directives, declarations, expressions, scriptlets, and actions.

A JSP page may contain instructions to be used by the JSP container to indicate how this page is interpreted and executed. Those instructions are called directives.

Expressions are used to insert usually small pieces of data in a JSP page without using `out.print()` or `out.write()` statements.

You can insert an arbitrary piece of Java code using JSP scriptlets construct in a JSP page.

JSP declarations are used to declare one or more variables, methods, or inner classes that can be used later in the JSP page.

JSP actions are XML tags that can be used in a JSP page to use functions provided by the JSP engine.

In a JSP page, objects may be created using directives, actions, or scriptlets. Every object created in a JSP page has a scope. The scope of a JSP object is defined as the availability of that object for use from a particular place of the web application. There are four object scopes: page, request, session, and application.

A web container allows us to directly access many useful objects defined in the `_jspService()` method of the JSP page's underlying servlet. These objects are called implicit objects as they are instantiated automatically. The implicit objects contain information about request, response, session, configuration, etc.

Variables, methods, and classes can be declared in a JSP page. If they are declared in the declaration section, they become part of the class.

JSP tag extension allows us to define and use custom tags in a JSP page exactly like other HTML/XML tags, using Java code.

JavaBeans are reusable Java components called beans which allow us to separate business logic from presentation logic. There are three action elements that are used to work with beans. A JSP action element `<jsp:useBean>` instantiates a JavaBean object into the JSP page. The `<jsp:setProperty>` action tag assigns a new value to the specified property of the specified bean object. The `<jsp:getProperty>` action element retrieves the value of the specified property of the specified bean object.

There are many ways to track sessions in JSP. Hidden fields may be used to send information back and forth between server and client to track sessions, without affecting the display. This is another simple but elegant method to track sessions and is widely used. Cookies are also used to track sessions. JSP technology (and its underlying servlet technology) provides a higher level approach for session tracking.

Most of the web applications need access to databases in the backend. Java DataBase Connectivity (JDBC) allows us to access databases through Java programs. A Java class that provides interfaces to a specific database is called JDBC driver. Each database has its own set of JDBC drivers. JDBC drivers are classified into four categories depending upon the way they work. The following basic steps are followed to work with JDBC: Loading a Driver, Making a connection, Execute SQL statement.

The `Statement` interface is used to execute static SQL statements. JDBC also allows calling stored procedures that are stored in the database server. This is done using the `CallableStatement` object. A table of data is represented in JDBC by the `ResultSet` interface. Result sets can be scrollable in the sense that the cursor can be moved backward and forward. The `DatabaseMetaData` interface provides methods to collect comprehensive information about a DBMS.

WEB RESOURCES

http://java.sun.com/products/jsp/
JavaServer Pages Technology

http://java.sun.com/products/jsp/syntax/2.0/syntaxref20.html
Java Server Pages (JSP) v2.0 Syntax Reference

http://java.sun.com/products/jsp/tutorial/TagLibrariesTOC.html
Tag Libraries Tutorial (v. 1.0)

http://en.wikipedia.org/wiki/Java_Server_Pages
JavaServer Pages

http://www.visualbuilder.com/jsp/tutorial/
JSP Tutorial Home

http://java.sun.com/products/jsp/archive.html
JavaServer Pages Specification 1.0

http://tomcat.apache.org/tomcat-6.0-doc/index.html
Apache Tomcat 6.0, Documentation Index

http://tomcat.apache.org/tomcat-5.5-doc/jasper-howto.html
Apache Tomcat 6.0, Jasper 2 JSP Engine How To

http://tomcat.apache.org/tomcat-6.0-doc/config/index.html
Apache Tomcat Configuration Reference

EXERCISES

Multiple Choice Questions

1. What is the full form of JSP?
   (a) Java Servlet Pages (b) Java Server Pages
   (c) Java Small Pages (d) Java Special Pages

2. Which of the following statements is true?
   (a) JSP and servlets are completely different technologies.
   (b) Servlets are built on JSP technology and all servlets are ultimately converted to JSP pages.
   (c) Servlet is a client-side technology, whereas JSP is server-side technology.
   (d) JSPs are built on servlet technology and all JSPs are ultimately translated to servlets.

3. What is the advantage of using RequestDispatcher over sendRedirect() to forward a request to another resource?
   (a) The RequestDispatcher does not use the reflection API.
   (b) sendRedirect() is no longer available in the current servlet API.
   (c) The RequestDispatcher does not require a round trip to the client, and thus is more efficient and allows the server to maintain request state.
   (d) sendRedirect() is not a cross-web server mechanism.

4. In which one of the following cases is the scriptlet better suited?
   (a) Code that handles cookies
   (b) Code that deals with logic that relates to database access
   (c) Code that deals with session management
   (d) Code that deals with logic that is common across requests

5. Which of the following handles a request first in a page-centric approach?
   (a) A JSP page (b) A session manager
   (c) A servlet (d) A JavaBean

6. Which of the following can be included using the JSP include action?
   (a) Servlet (b) Another JSP
   (c) Plain text file (d) All of the above

7. Which of the following is used to read parameters from a JSP page?
   (a) <jsp:getParam/> action
   (b) <jsp:param> action
   (c) request.getParameter() method
   (d) <jsp:readParam/> action

8. Which of the following is not a method of JSP's servlet?
   (a) _jspService() (b) jspDestroy()
   (c) jspService() (d) jspInit()

9. Which of the following JSP actions is used to include a file in another file?
   (a) <jsp:import> (b) <jsp:include>
   (c) <jsp:read> (d) <jsp:get>

10. What is a JSP page translated into?
   (a) CGI (b) Servlet
   (c) Applet (d) JavaBean

11. Which of the following is not true regarding cookies?
   (a) Cookie class has a two argument constructor
   (b) The response object is used to add a cookie
   (c) The request object is used to get the cookie
   (d) The request object is used for creating cookies

12. Which of the following scopes does the implicit object exception have?
   (a) page (b) request
   (c) session (d) application

13. Which of the following tags is used to override the JSP file's initialization method?
   (a) <%= %> (b) <%@ %>
   (c) <% %> (d) <%! %>

14. Which of the following scopes is not valid with respect to JavaBean in JSP?
   (a) request (b) response
   (c) session (d) application

15. Which of the following statements is true regarding HttpServletResponse.sendRedirect()?
   (a) Server itself redirects the current request
   (b) sendRedirect() executes on the client
   (c) Server sends a redirection instruction to the client
   (d) Server drops the current request

16. Which of the following tags is used for scriptlets?
   (a) <%= %> (b) <%@ %>
   (c) <% %> (d) <%! %>

17. Which of the following attributes of the page directive is used to indicate that the current page is an error page?
   (a) errorPage (b) isErrorPage
   (c) anErrorPage (d) pageError

18. Which of the following tags is used for expressions?
   (a) <%= %> (b) <%@ %>
   (c) <% %> (d) <%! %>

19. Which packages contain the JDBC classes?
   (a) java.db.sql and javax.db.sql
   (b) java.jdbc and javax.jdbc
   (c) java.db and javax.db
   (d) java.sql and javax.sql

20. Which of the following drivers converts JDBC calls into network protocol, to communicate with the database management system directly?
   (a) Type 1 driver (b) Type 2 driver
   (c) Type 3 driver (d) Type 4 driver

21. Which of the following types of objects is used to execute parameterized queries?
   (a) ParameterizedStatement
   (b) Statement
   (c) PreparedStatement
   (d) All of the above

22. Which of the following methods on the Statement object is used to execute DML statements?
   (a) executeInsert() (b) execute()
   (c) executeQuery() (d) executeDML()

23. Which type of driver makes a JDBC–ODBC bridge?
   (a) Type 1 driver (b) Type 2 driver
   (c) Type 3 driver (d) Type 4 driver

24. What is the meaning of ResultSet. TYPE_SCROLL_INSENSITIVE
   (a) This means that the ResultSet is insensitive to scrolling.
   (b) This means that the ResultSet is sensitive to scrolling, but insensitive to changes made by others.
   (c) This means that the ResultSet is insensitive to scrolling and insensitive to changes made by others.
   (d) This means that the ResultSet is sensitive to scrolling, but insensitive to updates, i.e., not updateable.

25. Which of the following SQL keywords is used to read data from a database table?

(a) SELECT (b) CHOOSE
(c) READ (d) EXTRACT

26. Which of the following statement objects is used to call a stored procedure in JDBC?

(a) Statement (b) PreparedStatement
(c) CallableStatement (d) ProcedureStatement

27. Which of the following objects is used to obtain the DatabaseMetaData object?

(a) Driver (b) DriverManager
(c) Connection (d) ResultSet

28. Which of the following methods is used to call a stored procedure in the database?

(a) execute() (b) executeProcedure()
(c) call() (d) run()

29. What will be the effect if we call the deleteRow() method on a ResultSet object?

(a) The row pointed to by the cursor is deleted from the ResultSet, but not from the database.
(b) The row pointed to by the cursor is deleted from the ResultSet and from the database
(c) The row pointed to by the cursor is deleted from the database, but not from the ResultSet.
(d) None of the above

30. If you want to work with a ResultSet, which of these methods will not work on PreparedStatement?

(a) execute() (b) executeQuery()
(c) executeUpdate() (d) All of the above

31. Which of the following characters is used as a placeholder in CallableStatement?

(a) $ (b) @ (c) ? (d) #

32. Which one of the following will not get the data from the first column of ResultSet rs, returned from executing the SQL statement: "SELECT login, password FROM USERS"?

(a) rs.getString(0) (b) rs.getString("login")
(c) rs.getString(1) (d) All of the above

33. Which of the following interfaces is used to control transactions?

(a) Statement (b) Connection
(c) ResultSet (d) DatabaseMetaData

34. Which one of the following represents the correct order?

(a) INSERT, INTO, SELECT, FROM, WHERE
(b) SELECT, FROM, WHERE, INSERT, INTO
(c) INTO, INSERT, VALUES, FROM, WHERE
(d) INSERT, INTO, WHERE, AND, VALUES

35. Which of the following is *not* a benefit of using JDBC?

(a) JDBC programs are tightly integrated with the server operating system.
(b) Systems built with JDBC are relatively easy to move to different platforms.
(c) JDBC programs can be written to connect with a wide variety of databases.
(d) JDBC programs are largely independent of the database to which they are connected.

36. In which of the following layers of the JDBC architecture does the JDBC–ODBC bridge reside?

(a) database layer
(b) client program layer
(c) both client program and database layers
(d) JDBC layer

37. Which database application model would an enterprise-wide solution most likely adopt?

(a) The monolithic model
(b) The two-tier model
(c) The three-tier model
(d) The n-tier model

38. Which code segment could execute the stored procedure "calculate()" located in a database server?

(a) Statement stmt = connection.createStatement();
stmt.execute("calculate()");
(b) CallableStatement cs = con.prepareCall("{call calculate}");
cs.executeQuery();
(c) PrepareStatement pstmt = connection.prepare Statement("calculate()");
pstmt.execute();
(d) Statement stmt = connection.createStatement();
stmt.executeStoredProcedure("calculate()");

Review Questions

1. What is the key difference between HttpServlet Response.sendRedirect() and <jsp:forward>?
2. What is the benefit of using JavaBeans to separate business logic from presentation markup within the JSP environment?
3. Write the differences between Type 2 and Type 3 drivers.
4. How do you to get the ResultSet of a stored procedure?
5. What is the purpose of the setAutoCommit( ) method on the Connection object?
6. How do you move the cursor in scrollable resultsets?
7. Describe the procedure we use to retrieve data from the ResultSet.
8. What are the three statements in JDBC and the differences between them?
9. How do you update a ResultSet programmatically?
10. Why do we use PreparedStatement instead of Statement?
11. What is stored procedure? How do you create a stored procedure?
12. How do you insert and delete a row programmatically?
13. What are batch updates? How are they useful?
14. What are the four types of JDBC driver?
15. How can you use PreparedStatement?

22 INTRODUCTION TO J2EE

KEY OBJECTIVES

After completing this chapter readers will be able to

- **have an idea about the technologies used in J2EE**
- **learn JavaBean technology and its advantages**
- **understand key JavaBean features such as Introspection, Customization, Persistence, etc**
- **get an idea about EJB component architecture**
- **learn Model–View–Controller architecture**
- **get an idea about struts framework**

22.1 OVERVIEW OF J2EE

Today, in the fast-moving and highly demanding world of e-commerce and Information Technology (IT), there is a tremendous need for low-cost, distributed applications (especially transactional applications) for enterprises. These distributed enterprise applications must be designed, implemented, and deployed in less time, with few resources and greater speed.

Fortunately, the Java 2 Enterprise Edition (J2EE) provides a component-based technology for the design, development, assembly, and deployment of low-cost and fast-track enterprise applications. The purpose of J2EE is to simplify the design and implementation of distributed enterprise applications. J2EE offers the following functionalities:

- Multi-tiered distributed application model
- Reusable components
- Flexible transaction control
- Web services support through integrated data interchange on Extensible Markup Language (XML)-based open standards and protocols
- Unified security model

Since J2EE solutions are basically Java-based, they are platform-independent and are not tied to a specific vendor or customer. Customers and vendors are free to select from a wide variety of products and components.

J2EE is not a single technology; it consists of a large set of technologies, some of which are mentioned as follows:

- Enterprise Java Beans (EJB)
- Java Servlets
- Java Server Pages (JSP)
- Java Message Service (JMS)
- Java Naming and Directory Interface (JNDI)
- Java-XML
- J2EE Connector Architecture
- Java Mail
- Java DataBase Connectivity (JDBC)
- Remote Method Invocation (RMI)
- CORBA
- RMI-IIOP

We have already covered some of these technologies in previous chapters. In this chapter, we shall discuss some other J2EE technologies, especially, JavaBean and EJB. In Chapter 21, an introduction to JavaBean technology was given. Since JavaBean is the fundamental component technology and is a basic building block of EJB, we must discuss this technology in detail.

22.2 INTRODUCTION TO JAVABEANS

JavaBean technology is a Java-based technology to design and develop reusable and platform-independent software components. These components can then be integrated virtually in all Java-compatible applications. JavaBean components are knows as *beans*. The appearance and features of a bean can be changed or customized using builder tools such as BeanBox and NetBeans.

A bean class is nothing but a usual Java class with the following requirements:

- It must have a public no-argument constructor.
- It has public accessor methods to read and write properties.
- It should implement `Serializable` or `Externalizable` interface.

So, virtually all Java classes are already bean classes or they can be converted to beans with a little effort. For example, following is an example of a bean class.

```
//Factorial.java
import java.io.*;
public class Factorial implements Serializable {
   protected int n;
   public int getN() {
      return n;
```

```
    }
    public void setN(int n) {
        this.n = n;
        long prod = 1;
        for(int i = 2; i <= n; i++)
            prod *= i;
        fact = prod;
    }
    protected long fact;
    public long getFact() {
        return fact;
    }
}
```

Here is another example of a bean class:

```
//State.java
import java.io.Serializable;
public class State implements Serializable {
    protected String state = "off";
    public String getState() {
        return state;
    }
    public void setState(String state) {
        this.state = state;
    }
}
```

Most often, JavaBeans have a GUI representation of themselves. For example, button, calculator, and calendar beans are expected to have a visual representation, so as to be useful. However, some beans do not have any visual representation, and are called *invisible* beans. Invisible beans include a spell checker, random number generator, and temperature monitor.

22.2.1 Properties

A bean typically has one or more *properties* that control appearance and behavior. Properties are discrete, named attributes of a bean. They constitute the data part of a bean's structure and represent the internal state of a bean. Properties allow us to isolate component state information into discrete pieces that can be easily modified.

In our `Factorial` bean, there are two properties: `n` and `fact`. The property `n` holds an integer value, whose factorial is stored in the property `fact`. Here, `n` is said to be independent property and `fact` is dependent on `n` as the value of `fact` can be calculated from `n`. There need not be such a relationship in all the cases. For example, in the `State` bean, there is only one property `state`. In general, a bean can have any number of properties.

22.2.2 Accessor Methods

The primary way to access bean properties is through accessor methods. An accessor method is a public method of the bean that directly reads or writes the value of a particular bean. For example, the `getN()` method of the `Factorial` bean returns the value of the property `n`. Similarly, `setN()` sets the value of `n`. For the `fact` property, only one method is provided, which returns the value of the property `fact`. In general, a property can have two methods associated with it. The methods that are responsible for reading property values are called *reader* methods. Similarly, methods that are responsible for changing property values are called *writer* methods.

22.3 BEAN BUILDER

Readymade applications are available that provide an environment in which we can build and test beans. Those tools are known as builder tools. Some of the popular bean builder tools are Sun's BeanBox and NetBeans, JBuilder, Borland's Delphi, etc.

A builder tool is able to display several beans simultaneously. It is also able to connect different beans together in a visual manner. So, we can manipulate a bean without writing any piece of code. Most builder tools have a palette of components from which developers can drag and drop components onto a graphical canvas.

The facilities supported by a bean builder vary widely, but there are some common features as follows:

- *Introspection*—ability to analyze a bean to discover properties, methods, and events.
- *Properties*—used for customization of the state of a bean
- *Events*—a way used by beans to tell the outside that something is happening, or to react to something that happened outside the bean
- *Customization*—a developer of a bean can customize the behavior and appearance of the bean within a builder tool.
- *Persistence*—a builder tool allows us to customize a bean, and have its state saved away and reloaded later

22.4 ADVANTAGES OF JAVABEANS

Before we discuss the features and facilities supported by JavaBean technology, let us understand what JavaSoft wanted to accomplish by developing this Java-based component technology. In this regard, we can refer to JavaSoft's own JavaBeans mission statement: "Write once, run anywhere, use everywhere". Let us examine each part of this statement to realize what JavaSoft had in mind.

Write Once

A good software component technology should encourage component developers to write code only once. The component should not require rewriting of code to add and/or improve features. Keeping this point in mind, JavaSoft developed JavaBean technology, which allows us to add or improve functionality in the existing code, without re-engineering the original code.

The concept of writing components once also adds sense in terms of version control. This means that developers can make changes to components incrementally instead of rewriting significant portions from scratch. This results in a steady improvement of functionality, which, in turn, dictates a more consistent software component development through increasing versions.

Run Anywhere

A software technology must be platform independent to have a realistic meaning in today's rapidly varying software environment. This refers to the capability of software components developed using a technology to be executed (run) in any environment. Fortunately, JavaBeans components are ultimately Java components. Consequently, cross-platform support comes automatically.

Good software components should also run across distributed network environments. This can be simply achieved using Java's powerful technology, Remote Method Invocation (RMI), Socket, and RMI-IIOP.

Use Everywhere

This is perhaps the most important part of the JavaSoft's JavaBean mission statement. Well-designed JavaBeans components are capable of being used in a wide range of situations, which include applications, other components, documents, websites, and application builder tools, and so on.

In addition to these key features, JavaBean technology has the following built-in features.

JavaBeans are compact components and can be transferred across a low-bandwidth Internet connection that facilitates a reasonable transfer time.

JavaBeans components are so simple that they are not only easy to use, but also easy to develop. Therefore, we can devote more time to embellishing components with interesting features than debugging them.

22.5 BDK INTROSPECTION

A bean builder usually uses Java core reflection API to discover methods of a bean. It then applies the design pattern to discover other bean features (such a properties and events). This procedure is known as *introspection.*

22.5.1 Design Patterns

The JavaBeans framework introduces a lot of rules for names to be used for classes and methods. They are collectively called *design patterns*.

Note that the conventions and design patterns are all optional. However, by following those conventions, we can create really useful beans that can be used within a builder tool as well as in other JavaBean-enabled environments. Builder tools such as BeanBox, NetBeans, and JBuilder use these conventions and design patterns to introspect a bean's properties, methods, and events. Consequently, they can provide an environment where we can customize bean features.

Suppose, a bean has a property called "xxx". JavaBean technology encourages us to use "getXxx" as the name of the reader method and "setXxx" as the name of the writer method. If the property happens to be a Boolean, the reader method could be named "isXxx". For example, our State bean has the property `state`. So, the reader method is "getState" and the writer method is "setState".

A `BeanInfo` class is a class that is used to provide information about a bean explicitly. To do this, a class is created implementing the `BeanInfo` interface. The name of this class should also follow a naming rule. The name of the `BeanInfo` class must be the name of the target bean, followed by the string "BeanInfo". For example, the name of the `BeanInfo` class for the bean `Person` must be "PersonBeanInfo".

Similarly, the name of the `Customizer` class (see Section 22.9) for the bean `MyBean` must be `MyBeanCustomizer`.

JavaBean API provides interfaces and classes that can be used to discover properties and methods of a bean dynamically. Following is brief description of those interfaces and classes:

`BeanInfo`

The `java.beans.BeanInfo` interface defines a set of methods that allow bean developers to provide information about their beans explicitly. By specifying `BeanInfo` for a bean component, a developer can hide methods, specify an icon for the toolbox, provide descriptive names for properties, define which properties are bound, etc.

`Introspector`

The `java.beans.Introspector` class provides descriptor classes (see Section 22.7) with information about properties, methods, and events of a bean.

The `getBeanInfo()` method of the Introspector class can be used by builder tools and other automated environments to provide detailed information about a bean. The `getBeanInfo()` method relies on the naming conventions for the bean's properties, events, and methods. A call to `getBeanInfo()` results in the introspection process analyzing the bean's classes and super classes. The following example finds the properties and methods of our `Factorial` bean.

```
//IntrospectionDemo.java
import java.beans.*;
public class IntrospectionDemo {
   public static void main( String[] args ) throws IntrospectionException  {
        BeanInfo info = Introspector.getBeanInfo( Factorial.class,
Object.class);
      System.out.println("properties: ");
      for ( PropertyDescriptor pd : info.getPropertyDescriptors() )
         System.out.println("  " + pd.getName());
      System.out.println("methods: ");
      for ( MethodDescriptor pd : info.getMethodDescriptors() )
         System.out.println("  " + pd.getName());
   }
}
```

It generates the output shown in Figure 22.1:

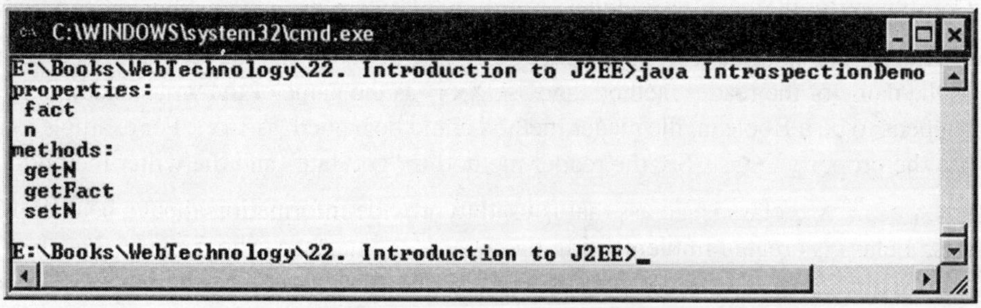

```
C:\WINDOWS\system32\cmd.exe
E:\Books\WebTechnology\22. Introduction to J2EE>java IntrospectionDemo
properties:
 fact
 n
methods:
 getN
 getFact
 setN

E:\Books\WebTechnology\22. Introduction to J2EE>_
```

Figure 22.1 Bean introspection

22.6 PROPERTIES

The properties of a bean represent and control its behavior and appearance. JavaBean API allows us to create the following primary property types.

22.6.1 Simple Properties

Simple properties of a bean are those that do not depend on other beans or control properties of another bean. Properties are typically declared as `private`. To access them, `get` and `set` methods are used. The names of the `get` and `set` methods follow specific rules, known as *design patterns*. JavaBean-enabled builder/tester tools (such as NetBeans and BeanBox) use these design patterns to do the following:

- Discover the properties of a bean
- Determine the types of the properties
- Display the properties in the property window
- Determine the read/write attribute of the properties
- Find the appropriate property editor for each property type
- Allow us to change the properties

Suppose a bean builder/tester tool encounters the following methods on a bean:

```
public int getValue() { ... }
public void setValue(int v) { ... }
```

The tool infers the following:

- There exists a property name `value`.
- Its type is `int`.
- It is readable and writable.
- It displays the value of this property in the property editor.
- Moreover, it finds the property editor that allows us to change the value of the property.

Creating a simple property

The following code is used in the bean to create the property `propertyName`:

```
private PropertyType propertyName = initialValue;
```

Providing a reader method

The following code is used to provide a reader method:

```
PropertyType getPropertyName() {
  return propertyName;
}
```

Providing a writer method

The following code is used to provide a writer method:

```
void getPropertyName(PropertyType value) {
```

```
    propertyName = value;
}
```

The following example shows how to create a simple property:

```
//MyBean.java
public class MyBean {
   private int value = 0;

   /**
    * Get the value of value
    *
    * @return the value of value
    */
   public int getValue() {
      return value;
   }

   /**
    * Set the value of value
    *
    * @param value new value of value
    */
   public void setValue(int value) {
      this.value = value;
   }
}
```

22.6.2 Bound Properties

Sometimes, when a property of a bean changes, you might want to notify another object about this change. This object typically reacts to the change by changing one of its properties. For example, consider two beans `Parent` and `Child`, each having two properties, `firstName` and `familyName`. The `familyName` property of `Child` and `Parent` must have the same value. So, whenever the `familyName` property of `Parent` changes, the `familyName` property of `Child` must also be changed to make them synchronized.

This synchronization can be implemented using the *bound* property. The accessor or modifier methods for a bound property are defined in the same way, except that whenever a bound property changes, a notification is sent to the interested listeners. Whenever a property of a bean changes, a "PropertyChange" event gets fired. The bean generating the event is called *source* bean. We can register one or more "Listener" objects with a source, so that these objects get notified when a bound property of the source bean is updated.

Bean Development Kit (BDK) provides special classes to accomplish coordination between the notifier and listener.

`PropertyChangeListener`

If an object is interested in being notified about the property changes of a source bean, its class must implement the `PropertyChangeListener` interface. This interface defines the following method:

```
void propertyChange(PropertyChangeEvent pce)
```

The listener's class must implement this method. If the listener is registered for a property change event, this method gets called when a bound property of the source bean changes. In this method, the listener object reacts to the property change by modifying one or more of its properties.

`PropertyChangeEvent`

A `PropertyChangeEvent` object is generated whenever a bound property of a bean changes. This object is then sent from the source bean to all registered `PropertyChangeListener` objects, as an argument of their respective `PropertyChange()` method. This class encapsulates the property change information. It provides several useful methods as follows:

`String getPropertyName()`

Returns the name of the property that was changed and caused this event firing

`Object getOldValue()`

Returns the value of the property as an object before it was changed. The bean writer should typecast it to the desired type.

`Object getNewValue()`

Returns the value of the property as an object after it was changed. The bean writer must typecast it to the desired type.

`PropertyChangeSupport`

This class is used by the beans having at least one bound property to keep track of registered listeners. It is also used to deliver `PropertyChangeEvent` objects to those registered listeners when a bound property changes. A source bean can instantiate this class as a member field or inherit the functionality of this class by extending it. Figure 22.2 gives the framework for bound property support.

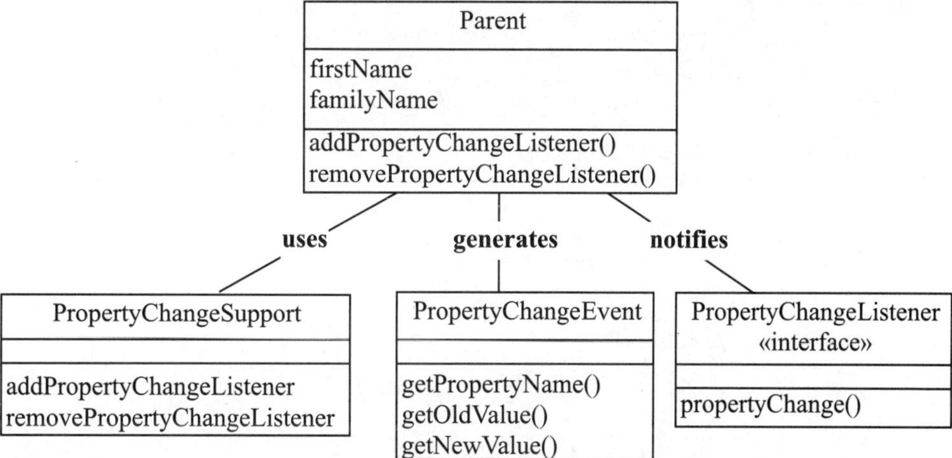

Figure 22.2 Bound property support framework

Let us now discuss how to write a bound property. The following class acts as a source bean.

```
//Parent.java
import java.beans.*;
public class Parent {
   private String firstName = "Uttam", familyName = "Roy";
   private PropertyChangeSupport pcs;
   public Parent() {
      pcs = new PropertyChangeSupport(this);
   }
   public String getFirstName() {
      return firstName;
   }
   public void setFirstName(String fname) {
      firstName = fname;
   }
   public String getFamilyName() {
      return familyName;
   }
   public void setFamilyName(String newFamilyName) {
      String oldFamilyName = familyName;
      familyName = newFamilyName;
      pcs.firePropertyChange("familyName", oldFamilyName, newFamilyName);
   }
   public void addPropertyChangeListener(PropertyChangeListener pcl) {
      pcs.addPropertyChangeListener(pcl);
   }
   public void removePropertyChangeListener(PropertyChangeListener pcl) {
      pcs.removePropertyChangeListener(pcl);
   }
}
```

The following bean is a listener that wants to be notified when the `familyName` property of the `Parent` bean changes. So, it implements the `PropertyChangeListener` interface and defines the method `propertyChange()`. In the `propertyChange()` method, it changes its own `familyName` property to the new value of the `familyName` property of the `Parent` bean by using the `getNewValue()` method on the `PropertyChangeEvent` object.

```
//Child.java
import java.beans.*;
public class Child implements PropertyChangeListener {
   private String firstName = "Rimisha", familyName = "Roy";
   public String getFirstName() {
      return firstName;
   }
   public void setFirstName(String fname) {
      firstName = fname;
   }
   public String getFamilyName() {
      return familyName;
   }
   public void setFamilyName(String fname) {
      familyName = fname;
   }
```

```
    public void propertyChange(PropertyChangeEvent pce) {
    if(pce.getPropertyName().equals("familyName"))
        setFamilyName((String)pce.getNewValue());

    }
}
```

For demonstration purposes, we have created the following Java application program. Typically, a bean builder (such as BeanBox provided by Sun) may be used.

```
//BoundDemo.java
public class BoundDemo {
    public static void main(String args[]) {
        Parent p = new Parent();
        Child c = new Child();
        p.addPropertyChangeListener(c);
        System.out.println("Before changing family name");
        System.out.println("Parent: " + p.getFirstName() + " " + p.getFamilyName());
        System.out.println("Child: " + c.getFirstName() + " " + c.getFamilyName());

        p.setFamilyName("Biswas");
        System.out.println("After changing family name of parent to 'Biswas'");
        System.out.println("Parent: " + p.getFirstName() + " " + p.getFamilyName());
        System.out.println("Child: " + c.getFirstName() + " " + c.getFamilyName());
    }
}
```

This program creates a `Parent` bean and a `Child` bean. The `Child` bean is then registered with the `Parent` bean. So, whenever the `familyName` property of the `Parent` bean changes, the `Child` bean gets notified and it can change its own `familyName` property. Finally, we have changed the `familyName` property of the `Parent` bean using the `setFamilyName()` method. We also have displayed the details of parent and child before and after changing the property. The output is as shown in Figure 22.3.

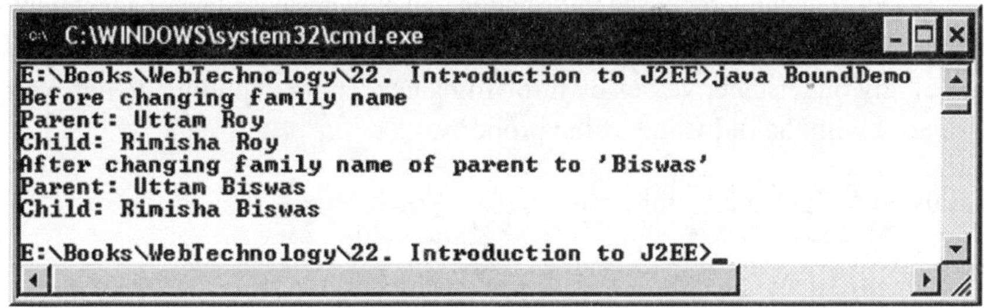

Figure 22.3 Bean bound property demo

22.6.3 Constrained Properties

A *constrained* property of a bean is a special type of property, which can be changed subject to prior permission taken from external object(s). External objects act as *vetoers* and exercise such authority in this case. For example, think about `Broker` and `ShareHolder` beans. The `Broker` can sell the shares at a rate provided that `ShareHolder` allows it to do so.

JavaBean API provides a mechanism very similar to the one used for the bound property, which allows other objects to veto the change of the source bean's property. The basic idea for implementing a constrained property is as follows:

- Store the old value of source bean's property if it is to be vetoed.
- Ask listeners (vetoers) of the new proposed value.
- Vetoers are authoritative to process this new value. They disallow by throwing an exception. Note that no exception is thrown if a vetoer gives the permission.
- If no listener vetoes the change, i.e., no exception is thrown, the property is set to the new value; optionally notify "PropertyChange" listeners, if any.

Three objects are involved in this process.

- The *source* bean containing one or more constrained property
- A listener object that accepts or rejects changes proposed by the source bean
- An `PropertyChangeEvent` object encapsulating the property change information

22.6.3.1 Implementing constrained property support

In the source bean, the accessor method for the constrained property is defined in the same way, except that it throws a `PropertyVetoException` as follows:

```
public void setPropertyName(PropertyType pt) throws PropertyVetoException{
   //method body
}
```

A source bean containing one or more constrained properties implements the following functionalities:

- Provides methods to add and remove `VetoableChangeListener` objects to register and unregister them so that they receive notification for property change proposal.
- When a property change is proposed, the source bean sends the `PropertyChangeEvent` object containing proposed information to the interested listeners. This should be done before the actual property change takes place. It allows listeners to accept or refuse a proposal.
- If any one listener vetoes by throwing an exception, continue to notify other listeners (if any) with the old value of the property.

JavaBean API provides a utility class, `VetoableChangeSupport`, similar to `PropertyChangeSupport`. The `VetoableChangeSupport` class provides the methods `addVetoableChangeListener()` and `removeVetoableChangeListener()` to add and remove `VetoableChangeListener` objects, respectively, and keeps track of such listeners. It also provides a method, `fireVetoableChange()`, to send the `PropertyChangeEvent` object to each registered listener when a property change is proposed.

The source bean can instantiate this class as a member field or inherit the functionality of this class by extending it. A `VetoableChangeSupport` object is instantiated as follows:

```
VetoableChangeSupport vcs = new VetoableChangeSupport(this);
```

22.6.3.2 Implementing constrained property listener

If an object's class wants to act as a vetoer, it must implement the `VetoableChangeListener` interface. This interface defines a single method as follows:

```
void vetoableChange(PropertyChangeEvent pce) throws PropertyVetoException;
```

A `VetoableChangeListener` must implement this method. This is the method where the vetoer exercises its power and agrees or disagrees with the proposal. In this method, the listener processes proposed property change and disagrees (vetoes) by throwing a `PropertyVetoException` exception. A typical code looks like this:

```
void vetoableChange(PropertyChangeEvent pce) throws PropertyVetoException{
   if(the_condition_is_not_fulfilled)
      throw new PropertyVetoException("NO", pce);
}
```

Figure 22.4 shows the constrained property support framework.

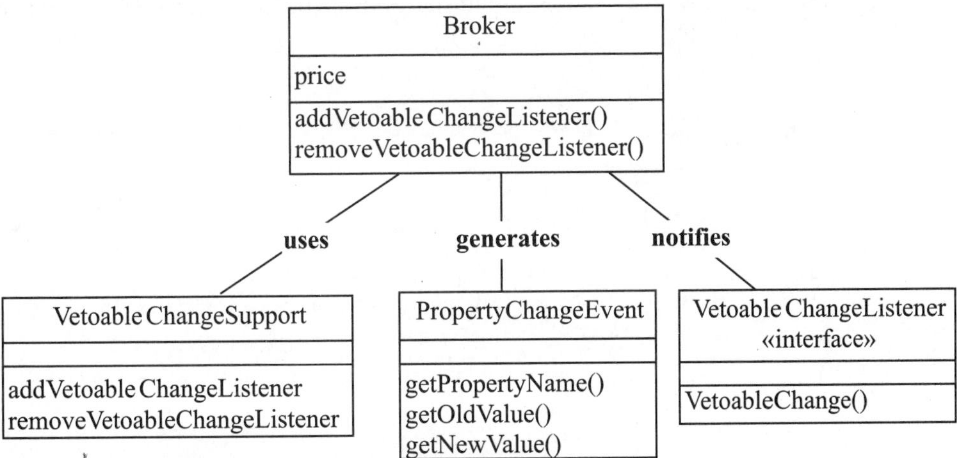

Figure 22.4 Constrained property support framework

22.6.3.3 Example

Let us now demonstrate the constrained property with our `Broker` and `ShareHolder` beans. The `Broker` is the source bean that has a single constrained property, `price`. A `Broker` can sell a share owned by a `ShareHolder`, provided that the `ShareHolder` object allows it. So, `Broker` should take permission before it sells the share. If the permission is given, it actually sells the shares. Otherwise, it does not do anything. Following is the source code of the `Broker` bean.

```
//Broker.java
import java.beans.*;
public class Broker {
   private float price = 10;
   private VetoableChangeSupport vcs;
   public Broker() {
      vcs = new VetoableChangeSupport(this);
   }
```

```
    public float getPrice() {
       return price;
    }
    public void setPrice(float newPrice) throws PropertyVetoException {
       float oldPrice = price;
       vcs.fireVetoableChange("price", oldPrice, newPrice);
       System.out.println("Setting new price limit");
       price = newPrice;
    }
    public void  addVetoableChangeListener(VetoableChangeListener pcl) {
       vcs.addVetoableChangeListener(pcl);
    }
    public void removeVetoableChangeListener(VetoableChangeListener pcl) {
       vcs.removeVetoableChangeListener(pcl);
    }
}
```

The `ShareHolder` is the listener bean. It decides whether the `Broker` can sell shares at the specified price. It allows the `Broker` selling shares if the proposed price is greater than or equal to Rs. 15. Otherwise, it disallows, by throwing the `PropertyVetoException` object. Here is the source code of `ShareHolder`.

```
//ShareHolder.java
import java.beans.*;
public class ShareHolder implements VetoableChangeListener {

    public void vetoableChange(PropertyChangeEvent pce) throws
PropertyVetoException {
       if(pce.getPropertyName().equals("price")) {
          float price = ((Float)pce.getNewValue()).floatValue();
          if(!price >= 15 ) throw new PropertyVetoException("NO", pce);
       }

    }
}
```

For demonstration purposes, we have created a Java application that creates a `Broker` and a `ShareHolder` bean. It then registers the `ShareHolder` with the `Broker` so that it receives notification for the property change proposal. Finally, it tries to change the price limit of the share passed as an argument.

```
public class ConstrainedDemo {
    public static void main(String args[]) {
       Broker b = new Broker();
       ShareHolder s = new ShareHolder();
       b.addVetoableChangeListener(s);
       float price = Float.parseFloat(args[0]);
       try {
          System.out.println("Old price limit: " + b.getPrice());

          b.setPrice(price);
          System.out.println("New price limit: " + b.getPrice());
       }catch(Exception e) {
```

```
            System.out.println("Ah! failed to set price at " + price);
        }
    }
}
```

Figure 22.5 shows a sample output.

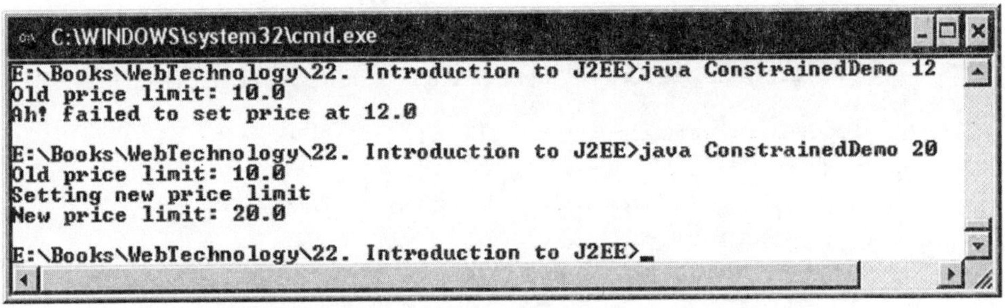

```
C:\WINDOWS\system32\cmd.exe
E:\Books\WebTechnology\22. Introduction to J2EE>java ConstrainedDemo 12
Old price limit: 10.0
Ah! failed to set price at 12.0

E:\Books\WebTechnology\22. Introduction to J2EE>java ConstrainedDemo 20
Old price limit: 10.0
Setting new price limit
New price limit: 20.0

E:\Books\WebTechnology\22. Introduction to J2EE>_
```

Figure 22.5 Bean constrained property demo

22.6.4 Indexed Properties

An index property is an array of properties. It can hold a range of values that can be accessed through accessor functions. To access an individual element, following methods are specified:

```
public PropertyElementType getPropertyName(int index)
public void setPropertyName(int index, PropertyElementType element)
```

The `get` method takes an array index and returns the element at that index. The `set` method takes two arguments: an index of the property array and its value, and sets the element at the specified index to the specified value. Methods to access the entire array are also specified as follows:

```
public PropertyElementType[] getPropertyName()
public void setPropertyName(PropertyElementType element[])
```

In this case, the `get` method returns the entire property array and the `set` method takes an entire array to be used to set the property array.

The following bean class stores the temperatures of the last seven days.

```
//TemperatureBean.java
public class TemperatureBean {
   private float[] temperatures = new float[7];
   /**
    * Get the value of temperatures
    *
    * @return the value of temperatures
    */
   public float[] getTemperatures() {
      return temperatures;
   }

   /**
    * Set the value of temperatures
    *
```

```
     * @param temperatures new value of temperatures
     */
    public void setTemperatures(float[] temperatures) {
       this.temperatures = temperatures;
    }

    /**
     * Get the value of temperatures at specified index
     *
     * @param index
     * @return the value of temperatures at specified index
     */
    public float getTemperatures(int index) {
       return this.temperatures[index];
    }

    /**
     * Set the value of temperatures at specified index.
     *
     * @param index
     * @param newTemperatures new value of temperatures at specified index
     */
    public void setTemperatures(int index, float newTemperatures) {
       this.temperatures[index] = newTemperatures;
    }
}
```

22.7 BEANINFO INTERFACE

A bean builder typically uses the *introspection* process to discover features (such as properties, methods, and events). In this case, the bean builder exposes all the features to the outside world.

We can also expose the bean's features by using an associated class explicitly. By doing this we obtain the following benefits:

- Hide features we do not want to disclose
- Provide more information about bean features
- Associate an icon with the target bean
- Group bean features into different categories such as normal and advanced groups
- Specify a customizer class
- Expose some bean features explicitly and others using Java reflection API

The features of a bean are exposed using a separate special class. This class must implement the `BeanInfo` interface. The `BeanInfo` interface defines several methods that can be used to inspect properties, methods, and events of a bean. Following is the declaration of the `BeanInfo` interface:

```
public interface java.beans.BeanInfo{
   public static final int ICON_COLOR_16x16;
   public static final int ICON_COLOR_32x32;
   public static final int ICON_MONO_16x16;
   public static final int ICON_MONO_32x32;
```

```
    public abstract java.beans.BeanDescriptor getBeanDescriptor();
    public abstract java.beans.EventSetDescriptor[] getEventSetDescriptors();
    public abstract int getDefaultEventIndex();
    public abstract java.beans.PropertyDescriptor[] getPropertyDescriptors();
    public abstract int getDefaultPropertyIndex();
    public abstract java.beans.MethodDescriptor[] getMethodDescriptors();
    public abstract java.beans.BeanInfo[] getAdditionalBeanInfo();
    public abstract java.awt.Image getIcon(int);
}
```

The BeanInfo interface uses several *descriptor* classes, each of which describes specific features. Following is a list of descriptors:

- `BeanDescriptor`—This descriptor class describes the bean's name, type, and its customizer class, if any.
- `PropertyDescriptor`—This descriptor encapsulates the target bean's properties.
- `MethodDescriptor`—This descriptor encapsulates the target bean's methods.
- `EventSetDescriptor`—This descriptor encapsulates the events that the target bean can fire.

Let us now write a `BeanInfo` class that describes the features of a bean. For this purpose, we shall first write a bean and show how the BeanBox extracts information of this bean. Consider the following bean class:

```
//Person.java
public class Person {
   private String name = "B. S. Roy";
   private String address = "Narayanpur, Kol-136";
   private String PAN = "AGCPR8830P";
   public String getName() {
      return name;
   }
   public void setName(String name) {
      this.name = name;
   }
   public String getAddress() {
      return address;
   }
   public String getPAN() {
      return PAN;
   }
   public void setPAN(String PAN) {
      this.PAN = PAN;
   }
   public void setAddress(String address) {
      this.address = address;
   }
}
```

The bean `Person` has three properties: `name`, `address`, and `PAN`. Each of the three properties has a `get` and a `set` method. Compile this bean using the following command:

```
java Person.java
```

Create a class file, `Person.class`. Create a manifest file, `manifest_person.mf`, as follows:

```
Manifest-Version: 1.0

Name: Person.class
Java-Bean: True
```

Place this file in the same directory as `Person.class`. Now, create a jar file, `person.jar`, using the following command:

```
jar cvfm person.jar manifest_person.mf Person.class
```

It typically generates the following output:

```
added manifest
adding: Person.class(in = 754) (out= 410)(deflated 45%)
```

The bean is now ready to test and use. Load the `person.jar` file in the Bean Box. Create an instance of the `Person` bean and view its properties. It looks as shown in Figure 22.6.

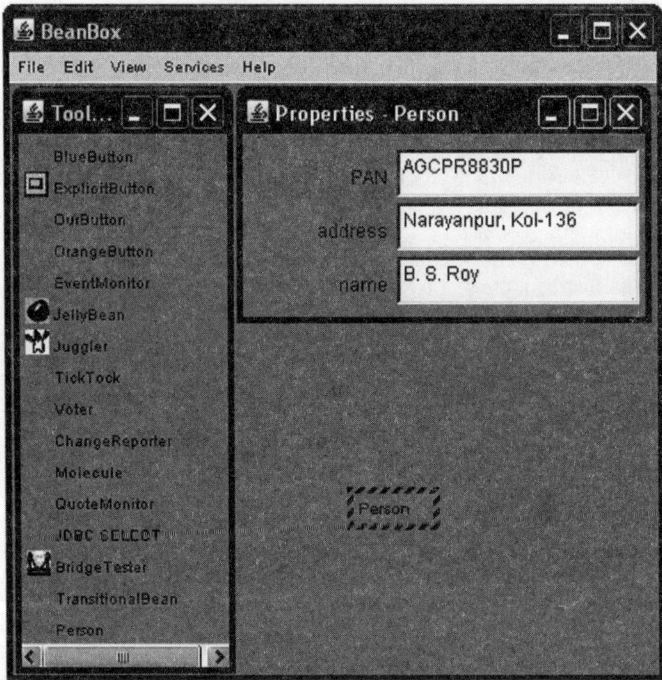

Figure 22.6 Bean introspection

As you can see, BeanBox shows all the properties of the `Person` bean. Suppose we do not disclose the `PAN` property of the `Person` bean, as it is sensitive information. For that purpose, we can write the `BeanInfo` class. Following is the source code of the `BeanInfo` class.

```
//PersonBeanInfo.java
import java.beans.*;
public class PersonBeanInfo extends SimpleBeanInfo {
```

```
    private Class personClass = Person.class;
    public PropertyDescriptor[] getPropertyDescriptors() {
       PropertyDescriptor name = null, address = null, PAN = null;
       try {
             name = new PropertyDescriptor("name", personClass);
          name.setDisplayName("Name:");
          name.setPreferred(true);

          address = new PropertyDescriptor("address", personClass);
          address.setDisplayName("Address:");
          address.setPreferred(true);
       } catch (IntrospectionException e) {}
       PropertyDescriptor[] result = {name, address};
       return result;
    }
}
```

To write a `BeanInfo` class, we need to give a name. The name of each `BeanInfo` class follows a naming rule. The name of the `BeanInfo` class of the target bean X must have the name `XBeanInfo`. For example, the name of the `BeanInfo` class of our `Person` bean must be `PersonBeanInfo`. The string "BeanInfo" is appended to the target bean class name.

Since the `BeanInfo` interface implements several methods, we have to implement all of them. Alternatively, a `BeanInfo` class can be created by sub-classing the `SimpleBeanInfo` class. The `SimpleBeanInfo` class is a convenient base class for the `BeanInfo` classes. It implements all the methods, but all are empty. So, the `SimpleBeanInfo` class does not disclose any property of the method at all. We can override a specific method, where we want to return specific information. Since we want to hide the PAN property, we have overridden only the `getPropertyDescriptors()` method. In this method, we have returned an array of only three properties.

Now, modify the manifest file, `manifest_person.mf`, as follows:

```
Manifest-Version: 1.0

Name: Person.class
Java-Bean: True

Name: PersonBeanInfo.class
Java-Bean: False
```

Create the `person.jar` file as shown in Figure 22.7.

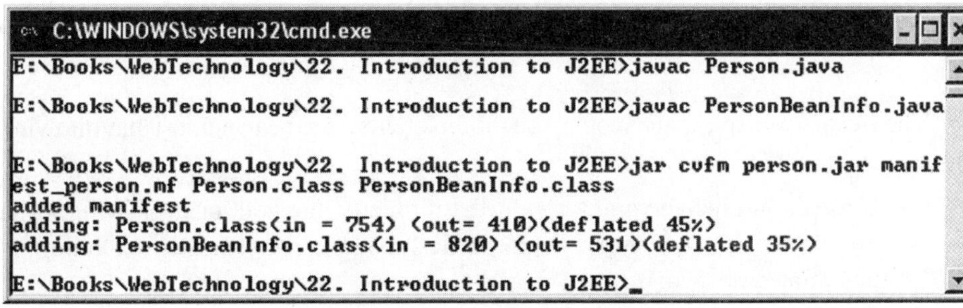

```
C:\WINDOWS\system32\cmd.exe
E:\Books\WebTechnology\22. Introduction to J2EE>javac Person.java

E:\Books\WebTechnology\22. Introduction to J2EE>javac PersonBeanInfo.java


E:\Books\WebTechnology\22. Introduction to J2EE>jar cvfm person.jar manif
est_person.mf Person.class PersonBeanInfo.class
added manifest
adding: Person.class(in = 754) (out= 410)(deflated 45%)
adding: PersonBeanInfo.class(in = 820) (out= 531)(deflated 35%)

E:\Books\WebTechnology\22. Introduction to J2EE>_
```

Figure 22.7 Bean introspection

Load the jar file in BeanBox and create a `Person` bean. You can see that only three properties are shown. The result is shown in Figure 22.8.

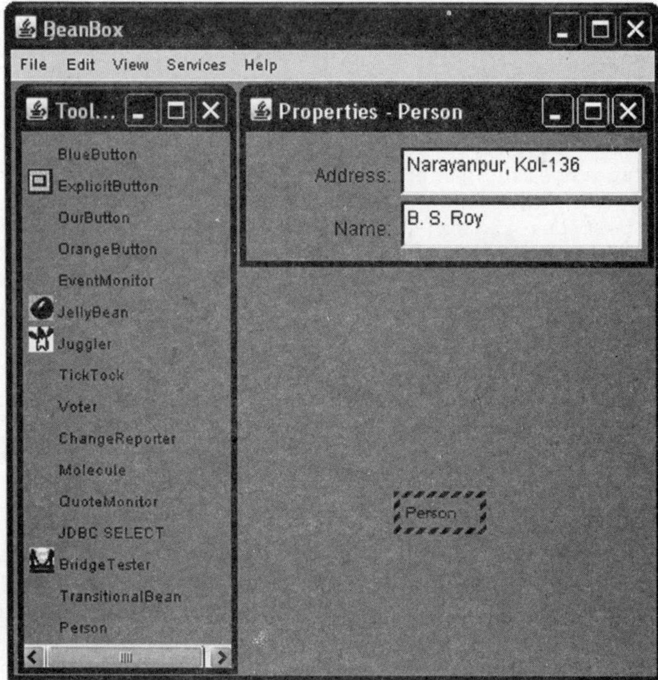

Figure 22.8 Bean introspection

We can also associate an icon with the bean. Override the `getIcon()` method as follows:

```
public java.awt.Image getIcon(int iconKind) {
    if (iconKind == BeanInfo.ICON_MONO_16x16 ||
            iconKind == BeanInfo.ICON_COLOR_16x16 ) {
        java.awt.Image img = loadImage("person16.gif");
        return img;
    }
    if (iconKind == BeanInfo.ICON_MONO_32x32 ||
            iconKind == BeanInfo.ICON_COLOR_32x32 ) {
        java.awt.Image img = loadImage("person32.gif");
        return img;
    }
    return null;
}
```

The BeanBox displays the icon in the toolbox before the bean name. The following important points can be noted:

- If we do not include a descriptor, that property, method, or event will *not* be exposed. So, we can selectively expose properties, methods, or events by excluding those we do not want disclosed.

- If a feature's `get` (for example, `getMethodDescriptor()`) method returns null, low-level Java reflection API is then used to extract that feature. This means that developer-defined as well as low-level reflection both can be used to discover the methods. If default methods of the `SimpleBeanInfo` class, which return null, are not overridden, low-level reflection is used for that feature.

22.8 PERSISTENCE

Sometimes, it is necessary to store the beans for later use. *Persistence* is a procedure to save a bean in non-volatile storage such as a file. The bean can be reconstructed and used later. The important point is that persistence allows bean developers to save the current state of the bean and retrieve the same at some later point of time.

To understand the importance of persistence, let us understand the life cycle of a bean. A bean is first created (possibly using a builder tool). Then its properties are accessed and/or manipulated by calling its public methods. After a degree of use, the bean is no longer needed, and is destroyed and removed from the memory. This is a typical life cycle of a bean. However, think about a situation where you have decided to complete your application temporarily but use of the bean is not yet over. You want the same bean with the state of the bean unchanged whenever the application is restarted later. Persistence is a procedure that does exactly what we have described here.

Let us consider a simple example. Consider the following `Factorial` bean.

```
//Factorial.java
import java.io.*;
public class Factorial implements Serializable {
   protected int n;
   public int getN() {
      return n;
   }
   public void setN(int n) {
      this.n = n;
      long prod = 1;
      for(int i = 2; i <= n; i++)
         prod *= i;
      fact = prod;
   }
   protected long fact;
   public long getFact() {
      return fact;
   }
}
```

This bean has two properties, `n` and `fact`. The property `n` has a `get` method and a `set` method and `fact` has only a `get` method. The `getFact()` method returns the factorial of `n`, which can be specified using the `setN()` method. So, this bean can be used to create a factorial table. Suppose we want to create a table containing factorial of numbers from 2 to 10. So, we can write a code like this:

```
Factorial f = new Factorial();
for(int i = 2; i <= 10; i++) {
   f.setN(i);
   System.out.println(i + "! = " + f.getFact()+ " ");
}
```

However, during the calculation, assume that an external interrupt may occur and in such a case, the application must be terminated. Before terminating, we must save the state of the bean so that we can retrieve the value of the integer up to which we calculated the factorial, so as to find the factorial of the rest of the integers. Java's Serialization procedure may be used to save and retrieve the state of a bean. An object is said to be serializable if its class implements the `Serializable` interface and all members are serializable. The `Serializable` interface does not define any method; it merely indicates that the class implementing it can be serialized. The following code shows how to save the state of a bean.

```
//SaveBean.java
import java.io.*;
public class SaveBean {
   public static void main(String args[]) {
      try {
         Factorial f = new Factorial();
         for(int i = 2; i < 10; i++) {
            f.setN(i);
            System.out.println(i + "! = " + f.getFact()+ " ");
            if(i > Math.random()*10 ) break;
         }
         //save the state of f now
         FileOutputStream fos = new FileOutputStream("out.dat");
         ObjectOutputStream oos = new ObjectOutputStream(fos);
         oos.writeObject(f);
         oos.close();
         System.out.println("Factorial bean saved in file out.dat");
      }catch(Exception e) {e.printStackTrace();}
   }
}
```

The following code demonstrates how to retrieve the bean with its original state.

```
//RetrieveBean.java
import java.io.*;
public class RetriveBean {
   public static void main(String args[]) {
      try {
         FileInputStream fis = new FileInputStream("out.dat");
         ObjectInputStream ois = new ObjectInputStream(fis);
         Factorial f1 = (Factorial)ois.readObject();
         ois.close();
         System.out.println("Factorial bean retrieved from file out.dat");
         for(int i = f1.getN()+1; i <= 10; i++) {
            f1.setN(i);
            System.out.println(i + "! = " + f1.getFact()+ " ");
         }
      }catch(Exception e) {e.printStackTrace();}
   }
}
```

Figure 22.9 shows a sample output that is obtained if you run these two applications.

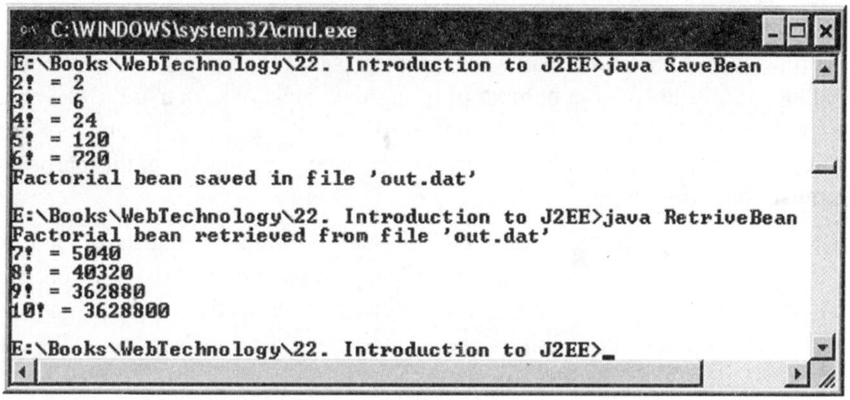

```
C:\WINDOWS\system32\cmd.exe
E:\Books\WebTechnology\22. Introduction to J2EE>java SaveBean
2! = 2
3! = 6
4! = 24
5! = 120
6! = 720
Factorial bean saved in file 'out.dat'

E:\Books\WebTechnology\22. Introduction to J2EE>java RetriveBean
Factorial bean retrieved from file 'out.dat'
7! = 5040
8! = 40320
9! = 362880
10! = 3628800

E:\Books\WebTechnology\22. Introduction to J2EE>_
```

Figure 22.9 Saving and retrieving bean

The JavaBean framework provides a utility class, `XMLEncoder`, which allows us to save a bean in XML format. The following example shows how to save a bean as an XML file:

```
XMLEncoder encoder = new XMLEncoder(
   new BufferedOutputStream(new FileOutputStream("fact.xml")));
encoder.writeObject( f );
encoder.close();
```

It creates the following XML document:

```
<?xml version="1.0" encoding="UTF-8"?>
<java version="1.6.0_10-beta" class="java.beans.XMLDecoder">
 <object class="Factorial">
  <void property="n">
   <int>6</int>
  </void>
 </object>
</java>
```

The bean can later be retrieved from this XML document using the following code:

```
XMLDecoder decoder = new XMLDecoder(
   new BufferedInputStream(new FileInputStream("fact.xml")));
f1 = (Factorial)decoder.readObject();
decoder.close();
```

The object `f1` refers to the original bean now.

22.9 CUSTOMIZER

Bean *customization* allows us to customize the appearance and behavior of a bean at design time, within a bean-compliant builder tool. There are two ways to customize a bean:

- Using a property editor
- Using Customizers

Property editors are usually supplied by the builder tool, although you can write your own property editor. In this section, we shall discuss how to customize a bean's appearance and behavior using customizers.

A property editor usually displays all properties that can be manipulated. Sometimes, it is not a good idea to display a large number of properties, most of which are irrelevant. A Customizer class gives us complete control to configure and edit beans. Customizers are used when a specific instruction is needed and property editors are too primitive for this purpose. A Customizer class must do the following:

- A Customizer must be some kind of AWT component that is suitable for display in a dialog box created by the BeanBox. So, it must extend `java.awt.Component` or one of its subclasses. Typically, the Customizer class extends `Panel`.
- It must implement the `Customizer` interface. This interface looks like this:

```
public interface java.beans.Customizer{
    public abstract void setObject(java.lang.Object);
    public abstract void addPropertyChangeListener(java.beans.PropertyCha
ngeListener);
    public abstract void removePropertyChangeListener(java.beans.Property
ChangeListener);
}
```

So, the Customizer class must implement those properties. It must also fire `PropertyChangeEvent` to all registered listeners when a change to the target Bean has occurred.

- Implement a default constructor
- Associate the customizer with its target class via `BeanInfo.getBeanDescriptor`

If a Bean that has an associated Customizer is dropped into the BeanBox, a "Customize..." item is added by the BeanBox in the Edit menu.

22.10 JAVABEANS API

JavaBean API provides a set of related interfaces and classes necessary to design and develop beans in a separate package, `java.beans`. Not all the classes and interfaces are used all the time to develop a bean. For example, the event classes are used by beans that fire property and vetoable change events. However, most of the classes in this package are used by a bean builder/editor. In particular, these classes and interfaces help the bean builder/editor to create user interfaces that the user can use to customize their beans. Tables 22.1, 22.2, and 22.3 respectively show the list of interfaces, classes, and exceptions, which are used to develop beans.

Table 22.1 Java bean interfaces

Interface Name	Description
AppletInitializer	It is designed to work in collusion with java.beans.Beans.instantiate.
BeanInfo	A bean implementor who wants to provide information about their bean explicitly may provide a class that implements this BeanInfo interface.

(Contd.)

(Contd.)

Customizer	It provides a complete custom GUI for customizing a target Java Bean.
DesignMode	It is intended to be implemented by, or delegated from, instances of BeanContext, in order to propagate to its nested hierarchy of BeanContextChild instances, the current "designTime" property.
ExceptionListener	It is notified of internal exceptions.
PropertyChangeListener	This event gets fired whenever a bean changes a "bound" property.
PropertyEditor	It provides support for GUIs that want to allow users to edit a property value of a given type.
VetoableChangeListener	This event gets fired whenever a bean changes a "constrained" property.
Visibility	A bean may be run on servers where a GUI is not available under some circumstances.

Table 22.2 Java bean classes

Class Name	Description
BeanDescriptor	It provides global information about a bean, including Java class and displayName.
Beans	It provides some general purpose methods to control beans.
DefaultPersistenceDelegate	It is an implementation of the abstract PersistenceDelegate class and is the delegate used by default for classes about which no information is available.
Encoder	A class that is used to create streams or files which encode the state of a JavaBean collection in terms of its public APIs.
EventHandler	It provides support for dynamically generating event listeners, whose methods execute a statement involving an incoming event object and a target object.
EventSetDescriptor	It describes a group of events that a specified Java bean fires.
Expression	It represents a primitive expression where a single method is applied to a target and a set of arguments to return a result.
FeatureDescriptor	It is the common baseclass for PropertyDescriptor, EventSetDescriptor, and MethodDescriptor, etc.
IndexedPropertyChangeEvent	This event gets delivered whenever a component that conforms to the JavaBeans specification (a "bean") changes a bound indexed property.
IndexedPropertyDescriptor	It describes a property that acts as an array and has an indexed read and/or indexed write method to access specific elements of the array.
Introspector	This class provides a standard way for buider tools to learn about the properties, methods, and events that a target Java Bean supports.
MethodDescriptor	It describes a particular method that a Java Bean supports for external access.
ParameterDescriptor	It allows bean implementors to provide additional information for each parameter.
PersistenceDelegate	It takes the responsibility for expressing the state of an instance of a given class in terms of the methods in the class's public API.
PropertyChangeEvent	This event is delivered when a "bound" or "constrained" property is changed.
PropertyChangeListenerProxy	It extends the EventListenerProxy to add a named PropertyChangeListener.
PropertyChangeSupport	It is a utility class that can be used by beans that support bound properties.

(Contd.)

(Contd.)

PropertyDescriptor	It describes a property that a Java Bean exports through accessor methods.
PropertyEditorManager	It is used to locate a property editor for any given type name.
PropertyEditorSupport	It helps to build property editors.
SimpleBeanInfo	This is a support class to make it easier for people to provide BeanInfo classes.
Statement	A Statement object represents a primitive statement in which a single method is applied to a target and a set of arguments.
VetoableChangeListenerProxy	It extends the EventListenerProxy specifically for associating a VetoableChangeListener with a "constrained" property.
VetoableChangeSupport	It is a utility class that is used by beans that support constrained properties.
XMLDecoder	The XMLDecoder class is used to read XML documents created using the XMLEncoder and is used just like ObjectInputStream.
XMLEncoder	The XMLEncoder class is a complementary alternative to ObjectOutputStream and can be used to generate a textual representation of a JavaBean in the same way that the ObjectOutputStream can be used to create binary representation of Serializable objects.

Table 22.3 Java bean exceptions

Exception Name	Description
IntrospectionException	It is thrown when an exception happens during Introspection.
PropertyVetoException	It is thrown when a proposed change to a property represents an unacceptable value.

22.11 EJB

Enterprise JavaBeans (EJB) is a Java-based comprehensive component architecture for design and development of world-class distributed modular enterprise applications. EJBs are not only platform-independent, but also they can run in any application server that implements EJB specifications. The EJB component architecture integrates several enterprise-level requirements such as distribution, transactions, security, messaging, persistence, and Enterprise Resource Planning (ERP) systems.

22.11.1 Benefits of EJB

Unlike other distributed component technologies such as CORBA and Java RMI, the EJB architecture hides most of the underlying system-level semantics such as instance management, object pooling, connection pooling, and thread management. The EJB container performs these tasks on behalf of us.

In the EJB architecture, beans contain the business logic, not the client. Therefore, the client developer can devote more time to the presentation of the client. Since clients do not have to implement business logic, they are thinner. This is very much required if devices running client applications are small and resource-constrainted.

EJBs are portable and can run on any EJB-compliant server.

It also provides us different types of components for business logic, session, persistence, and enterprise messages.

22.11.2 Usage Scenario

The EJB architecture should be used for those applications that have any of the following requirements:

- The applications must be scalable. The application's components need to be distributed across multiple machines to accommodate a large number of users. EJBs can run on different machines. Moreover, their location will remain transparent to the clients.
- Transactions are required to ensure data integrity. Enterprise beans allow us to perform transactions in a safe way. They also provide mechanisms for accessing shared objects concurrently.
- The application will have a wide variety of clients. Remote clients can easily locate enterprise beans using just a few lines of code. These clients can be thin, various, and numerous.

22.11.3 EJB Architecture

Before discussing the EJB architecture, let us understand the fundamental requirements of the distributed component architecture.

- It must provide mechanisms to instantiate the server-side and client-side proxies. A client-side proxy is created at the client side that represents the actual remote server object and acts as a proxy. A server-server side proxy, on the other hand, is created at the server-side. It must provide basic mechanism to accept client requests and delegate these requests to the object implementation.
- It must provide a mechanism that allows us to have a reference to the client-side proxy. Using this reference, clients invoke methods. The client-side proxy is responsible for communicating with the server-side proxy.
- It must support a mechanism that can be used to inform the system that a specific component is no longer needed.

To satisfy these requirements, the EJB architecture specifies two types of interfaces: `javax.ejb.EJBHome` and `javax.ejb.EJBObject`. The `javax.ejb.EJBHome` defines the methods that allow a remote client to create, find, and remove EJB objects, as well as home business methods that are not specific to a bean instance. On the other hand, `javax.ejb.EJBObject` defines methods that collectively provide the remote client view of an EJB object.

There are three kinds of beans in the EJB architecture: *Session Beans*, *Entity Beans,* and *Message Driven Beans*.

22.11.4 Session Beans

Session beans perform specific tasks for a client. They are plain remote objects meant for abstracting business logic.

A client invokes methods of the session bean to access an application, which is deployed on the EJB server. The session bean performs business tasks inside the server on behalf of the client, hiding all the complexities from the client.

A session bean, as its name suggests, can be considered as an interactive session. A session bean is not shared. It can handle a single client in the same way as an interactive session that has just one client. A session bean, like an interactive session, is also not persistent. This means that its state is not saved to a database. When the client finishes, its session bean is also terminated. There are two types of session beans: *stateless* and *stateful*.

22.11.4.1 Stateless session beans

A stateless session bean does not keep the state between client requests. When a client sends a request for method invocation, the EJB container assigns an instance of a stateless bean. During the method invocation, bean's instance variables may have a state, but that is valid only during the method invocation. When the client makes another request, the same instance may not be assigned to the client possibly due to the reason that it is already assigned to another client.

Since a stateless bean can be assigned to any client, it supports multiple clients. Therefore, to support the same number of clients, a lesser number of stateless session beans is required than stateful session beans. Session beans are useful for applications that have a large number of clients.

22.11.4.2 Stateful session beans

The state of a bean consists of values of its instance variable. Unlike stateless session beans, stateful session beans maintain their states. It means that a client sees the same state of the bean when it interacts with the stateful session bean through multiple method invocation. This is accomplished by assigning the same session bean to the client across multiple requests.

The stateful session bean loses its state when a client terminates. When the client terminates, the state is no longer necessary.

22.11.5 Entity Beans

Entity beans model real world business objects such as customers, orders, and products. They contain business logic that can be saved in a persistent storage for later use. The state of an entity bean persists beyond the lifetime of the application or the EJB server process. In J2EE, the persistency is obtained using a relational database. Usually, each entity bean has an underlying table in a relational database. Each instance of the bean corresponds to a row in that table.

Persistency can be obtained in two ways: *bean-managed* and *container-managed*. In the bean-managed persistency mechanism, the entity bean itself contains the code to save its state in the underlying table. On the other hand, in the container-managed persistence mechanism, the EJB container generates the necessary database access calls automatically.

Container-managed entity beans are not tied to a specific database. Therefore, you can redeploy the same entity bean on different J2EE servers that use different databases without modifying or recompiling the bean's code.

Multiple clients may share entity beans. So, entity beans work within transactions. The EJB container usually supports transaction management. In this case, you only have to specify the transaction attributes in the bean's deployment descriptor. The EJB container will take care of the rest of the procedure.

22.11.6 Message Driven Beans

A Message Driven Bean acts as a listener for the Java Message Service API, processing messages asynchronously. It is similar to an event listener, except that it receives messages instead of events.

The messages may be sent by a wide range of entities such as J2EE components, application clients, other enterprise beans, web components, JMS applications, or even systems that do not use J2EE technology. Message Driven Beans currently process only JMS (Java Message Service) messages, but provisions are left so that they can process other kinds of messages in the future.

The message-driven beans differ from session and entity beans in the sense that clients do not access message-driven beans through interfaces. Message Driven Beans and stateless session beans are similar with respect to the following points:

- They do not maintain state for a client. However, sometimes they can contain state across the handling of client messages such as an open database connection, an object reference to an enterprise bean object, or a JMS API connection.
- All instances are similar. The EJB container can use any instance to process a message. So, it can process multiple messages concurrently.
- One instance of a Message Driven Bean can handle multiple requests.

Note that, session and entity beans allow us to send and receive JMS messages. However, it happens in a synchronous way. We should not use synchronous 'send–receive', which are costly and blocking in a server-side component. Instead, message-driven beans can be used to send and receive messages asynchronously.

22.12 INTRODUCTION TO STRUTS FRAMEWORK

Struts is an application framework for developing Java EE web applications. This is an open-source framework and was originally developed by Craig McClanahan and donated to Apache. Fundamentally, it uses and extends Java servlet API and supports Model–View–Controller (MVC) architecture. It allows us to create flexible, extensible, and maintainable large web applications based on standard technologies, such as Java servlets, JSP, JavaBeans, resource bundles, and XML.

22.12.1 Basic Idea

In a Java EE-based web application, a client usually submits data to the server using the HTML form. These data are then handed over to a servlet or a Java Server Page, which processes them, typically interacts with the database, and finally processes the HTML output that is sent to the client. Since servlet as well as JSP technologies mix application logic with the presentation, they are inadequate for large web projects.

The primary task of struts is to separate application logic that interacts with the database, called *model* from HTML pages that are sent to the client, called *view* and instance that passes information between model and view, called *controller*. For this purpose, struts provides a controller as a servlet, called `ActionServlet`, and allows the writing of templates for the presentation (view), typically in terms of JSP. This special servlet acts as a switchboard to route requests from clients to the appropriate server page. This simple idea makes web applications much easier to design, develop, and maintain. Figure 22.10 describes the struts framework.

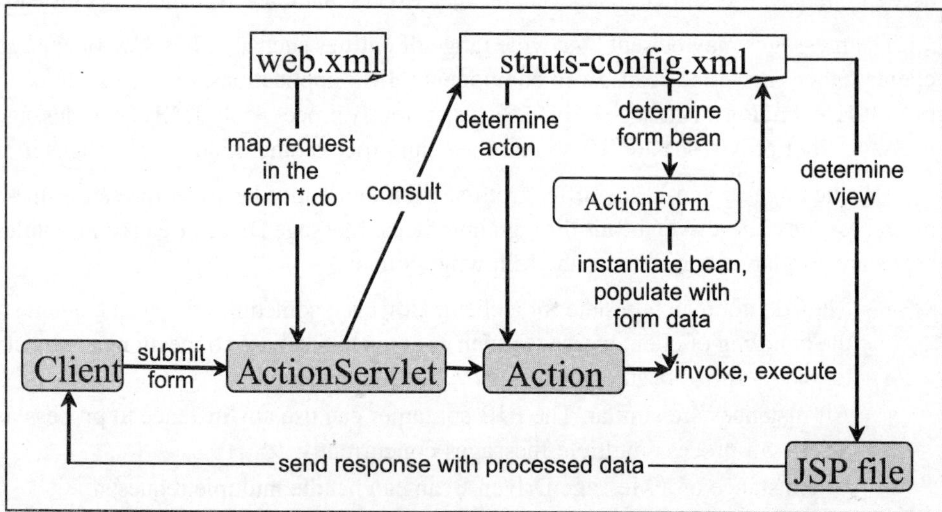

Figure 22.10 Struts framework

That was a high-level description of the struts framework. Let us now discuss the framework technically in more detail.

Every web application has an associated XML file (`WEB-INF/web.xml`) called deployment descriptor. This file must be configured by the web application developer. The deployment descriptor file specifies the configuration of the web application such as servlet mapping, parameter to those servlets, welcome pages, etc. This `web.xml` file is first configured to forward [Figure 22.9] all requests with a specified pattern (usually `*.do`) to the struts framework's `ActionServlet` using the following entry:

```
<servlet>
   <servlet-name>action</servlet-name>
      <servlet-class>org.apache.struts.action.ActionServlet</servlet-class>
      <init-param>
         <param-name>config</param-name>
         <param-value>/WEB-INF/struts-config.xml</param-value>
      </init-param>
      <init-param>
         <param-name>debug</param-name>
         <param-value>2</param-value>
      </init-param>
      <init-param>
         <param-name>detail</param-name>
         <param-value>2</param-value>
      </init-param>
      <load-on-startup>2</load-on-startup>
</servlet>
<servlet-mapping>
```

```
    <servlet-name>action</servlet-name>
    <url-pattern>*.do</url-pattern>
</servlet-mapping>
```

If you use an IDE such as NetBeans, these entries are automatically inserted. The `web.xml` file also specifies one or more configuration XML file (`struts-config.xml`) that the `ActionServlet` will consult. This `ActionServlet` performs switching functions as mentioned earlier.

Suppose we are developing a web application using `/myapp` as a location relative to the server's document root. In the `struts-config.xml` file, we associate paths with the controller components called Action classes. Following is an example:

```
<action-mappings>
    <action name="LoginForm" path="/login" scope="request"
    type="com.myapp.struts.LoginAction" validate="false">
    </action>
</action-mappings>
```

It specifies that the `ActionServlet` should invoke the controller component `com.myapp.struts.LoginAction` for the URL `http://myhost/myapp/login.do`. We also give a name to this association ("LoginForm" in our case) to refer to it further. Note that the `web.xml` file specified that for the **`*.do`** pattern URL, `ActionServlet` should be invoked by the web container. So, the **`.do`** in this URL causes the web container to invoke `ActionServlet` of the struts framework. This `ActionServlet` consults the `struts-config.xml` file and sees the path "login" and invokes `LoginAction`. The form data are temporarily stored in an `ActionForm` type bean. The developer has to write this bean by extending the `ActionForm` class explicitly. `Action` and `ActionForm` are bound using the `name` property of the `<form-bean>` tag. Following is an example:

```
<form-beans>
    <form-bean name="LoginForm" type="com.myapp.struts.LoginForm"/>
</form-beans>
```

This "LoginForm" is the name of the action defined earlier and `com.myapp.struts.LoginForm` is the `ActionForm` bean.

For each `Action`, we can specify the names of the resulting page(s) that has(ve) to be sent to the client as a result of that action. There can be more than one view as the result of an action. Typically, there are at least two: one for "success" and one for "failure". This is accomplished by returning a string from the `execute()` method of `Action` to the `ActionServlet`.

The action form, in turn, can retrieve data sent by the client from `ActionForm` bean. The following example illustrates this:

```
public class LoginAction extends org.apache.struts.action.Action {

    /* forward name="success" path="" */
    private final static String SUCCESS = "success1";
    /* forward name="failure" path="" */
    private final static String FAILURE = "failure";

    /**
      * This is the action called from the Struts framework.
```

```
     * @param mapping The ActionMapping used to select this instance.
     * @param form The optional ActionForm bean for this request.
     * @param request The HTTP Request we are processing.
     * @param response The HTTP Response we are processing.
     * @throws java.lang.Exception
     * @return
     */
    public ActionForward execute(ActionMapping mapping, ActionForm  form,
            HttpServletRequest request, HttpServletResponse response)
            throws Exception {
        // extract user data
       LoginForm formBean = (LoginForm) form;
       String name = formBean.getName();
       String email = formBean.getEmail();

       // perform validation
       if ((name == null) || // name parameter does not exist
          email == null || // email parameter does not exist
          name.equals("") || // name parameter is empty
          email.indexOf("@") == -1) {    // email lacks '@'
          formBean.setError();
          return mapping.findForward(FAILURE);
       }
       return mapping.findForward(SUCCESS);
    }
}
```

The parameter `mapping` in the `execute()` method refers to the `ActionServlet` and `form` refers to the associated `ActionForm` bean. The `Action` (the controller component) reports back to the `ActionServlet` using words like "success", "failure", "ready", "OK", "UserError", etc. We specify corresponding view pages in the configuration file as follows:

```
<action name="LoginForm" path="/login" scope="request"
type="com.myapp.struts.LoginAction" validate="false">
   <forward name="success" path="/success.jsp"/>
   <forward name="failure" path="/login.jsp"/>
</action>
```

The `ActionServlet` knows from the configuration file where to forward and what to show as a result. This has the added advantage of reconfiguration of the view layer by simply editing the XML configuration file.

The `ActionForm` beans can be validated ensuring that the user provides valid data in the form. The validation can be carried out on a per-session basis. It allows forms to span multiple pages of the View and Actions in the Controller.

Since the framework works on the server side, the client's view has to be composed at the server before sending it to the client. Typically, some sort of server-side technology such as JSP, Velocity, and XSLT is used for the view layer. Simple HTML files may be used to compose client's view. However, they cannot provide full advantage of all of the dynamic features.

KEYWORDS

Accessor methods: Public methods of a bean used to read and write bean properties.

Bean builder: A tool that is used to build and/or test beans.

BeanInfo interface: The `BeanInfo` interface defines several methods that can be used to inspect properties, methods, and events of a bean.

Bound property: A bound property of a bean is one which when changed, notifies one or more beans about this change.

Constraint property: A constrained property of a bean is a special type of property which can be changed subject to prior permission from external object(s).

Controller: Controls the Model and View components.

Customization: Bean customization allows us to customize the appearance and behavior of a bean at design time, within a bean-compliant builder tool.

Design Patterns: The JavaBeans framework introduces several rules for names to be used for classes and methods. They are collectively called design patterns.

EJB: Enterprise JavaBeans (EJB) is Java-based comprehensive component architecture for design and development of world-class distributed modular enterprise applications.

Entity Beans: Entity beans model real world business objects such as customers, orders, and products. They contain business logic that can be saved in a persistent storage for later use.

Indexed Property: An index property is an array of properties. It can hold a range of values that can be accessed through accessor functions.

Introspection: A procedure to discover properties, methods, and events of a bean dynamically.

Message Driven Beans: A Message Driven Bean acts as a listener for the Java Message Service API, processing messages asynchronously.

Model: Specific code that handles the business logic.

Persistence: Persistence is a procedure to save a bean in non-volatile storage such as a file. The bean can be reconstructed and used later.

Session Beans: Session beans perform specific tasks for a client. They are plain remote objects meant for abstracting business logic.

Stateful session beans: Stateful session beans maintain their states across client requests.

Stateless session beans: A stateless session bean does not keep the state between client requests.

View: Takes care of the appearance of web pages.

SUMMARY

J2EE is not a single technology; it consists of a large set of technologies.

JavaBean technology is a Java-based technology to design and develop reusable and platform-independent software components. These components can then be integrated virtually in all Java-compatible applications. JavaBean components are knows as beans. The appearance and features of a bean can be changed or customized using builder tools such as BeanBox and NetBeans. A bean class is nothing but a usual Java class with the following requirements:

- It must have a public no-argument constructor.
- It has public accessor methods to read and write properties.
- It should implement `Serializable` or `Externalizable` interface.

Properties control the behavior and appearance of a bean. Usually, beans are developed and tested using tools called bean builder. A bean builder provides several facilities to build a bean.

A bean builder usually uses Java core reflection API to discover the methods of a bean. It then applies design patterns to discover other bean features (such as properties and events). This procedure is known as introspection. The JavaBeans framework introduces a lot of rules for names to be used for classes and methods. They are collectively called design patterns. The different types of bean properties, namely, simple, bound constraint, and indexed properties were explained with extensive examples. JavaBean API provides interfaces and classes to discover properties, methods, and events of a bean. The `BeanInfo` interface defines several methods that can be used to inspect properties, methods, and events of a bean. Sometimes, it is necessary to store the beans for later use. Persistence is a procedure to save a bean in non-volatile storage such as a file. The bean can be reconstructed and used later.

Bean customization allows us to customize the appearance and behavior of a bean at design time, within a bean-compliant builder tool.

Enterprise JavaBeans (EJB) is Java-based comprehensive component architecture for design and development of world-class distributed modular enterprise applications. EJBs are not only platform-independent, but also run in any application server that implements EJB specification. The EJB component architecture integrates several enterprise-level requirements such as distribution, transactions, security, messaging, persistence, and Enterprise Resource Planning (ERP) systems. There are three kinds of beans in EJB architecture: Session Beans, Entity Beans, and Message Driven Beans.

Session beans perform specific tasks for a client. They are plain remote objects meant for abstracting business logic. A stateless session bean does not keep the state between client requests. Unlike stateless session beans, stateful session beans maintain their states. Entity beans contain business logic that can be saved in a persistent storage for later use. A Message Driven Bean acts as a listener for the Java Message Service API, processing messages asynchronously.

Struts is an application framework for developing Java EE web applications. It uses and extends Java servlet API and supports Model–View–Controller (MVC) architecture. It allows us to create flexible, extensible, and maintainable large web applications based on standard technologies, such as Java servlets, JSP, JavaBeans, resource bundles, and XML.

WEB RESOURCES

`http://java.sun.com/docs/books/tutorial/javabeans/`
Trail: JavaBeans

`http://java.sun.com/j2ee/1.4/docs/tutorial/doc/`
The J2EE 1.4 Tutorial

`http://www.ibm.com/developerworks/edu/j-dw-java-gsejb-i.html`
Getting started with Enterprise JavaBeans technology

`http://java.sun.com/j2ee/tutorial/1_3-fcs/doc/EJBConcepts.html`
Enterprise Beans

`http://struts.apache.org/`
Struts

`http://netbeans.org/kb/docs/web/quickstart-webapps-struts.html`
Introduction to the Struts Web Framework

`http://www.vaannila.com/struts-2/struts-2-tutorial/struts-2-tutorial.html`
Struts 2 Tutorial

EXERCISES

Multiple Choice Questions

1. How to make an instance variable into a JavaBean property?
   (a) Drop the Bean into the BeanBox property sheet
   (b) Specify get and set methods for the variable
   (c) Declare the instance variable public and static
   (d) Declare the instance variable private and let the BeanBox define get and set methods for the variable

2. JavaBean methods are all
   (a) Properties
   (b) Event listeners
   (c) Identical to methods of other Java classes
   (d) Events

3. Which of the following aspects do properties control?
   (a) How a JavaBean is compiled and dropped into the BeanBox (or other tool)
   (b) The tools you can use to customize a JavaBean
   (c) The communication between JavaBeans
   (d) A JavaBean's appearance and behavior

4. Which of the following is done using BeanBox's property tool?
   (a) Change the value of a Bean's property
   (b) Add new properties to a Bean
   (c) Delete a Bean's property
   (d) None of the above

5. Bound properties are associated with
   (a) propertyBound event
   (b) valueChanged event
   (c) valueBound event
   (d) propertyChange event

6. A property defined in a JavaBean typically
   (a) is declared as a private type
   (b) has a corresponding get method and set method
   (c) can be saved and retrieved at a later time
   (d) all of the above

7. A bean that receives events generated by a source bean is called
   (a) EventHandler Bean (b) Receiver Bean
   (c) Acceptor Bean (d) Listener Bean

8. The properties of a Bean
   (a) are defined by the Bean itself
   (b) may be inherited from Bean's super class
   (c) are analogous to instance variables
   (d) All of the above

9. Which of the following mechanisms is used to discover the bean's properties, methods, and events?
   (a) Persistence (b) Introspection
   (c) Customization (d) Event delegation

10. JavaBeans with constrained properties
   (a) instantiate an ActionListener object.
   (b) use methods of the VetoableChangeSupport class.
   (c) instantiate a ConstraintChangeSupport object.
   (d) None of the above

11. Which of the following executes EJB components?
   (a) A web server (b) An EJB container
   (c) A web browser (d) A database server

12. Which of the following interfaces is used to find and remove enterprise beans?
   (a) java.rmi.Home (b) javax.ejb.EJBObject
   (c) javax.ejb.EJBHome (d) javax.ejb.Object

13. Which of the following is used to create business objects?
   (a) javax.ejb.EntityBean
   (b) javax.ejb.Object
   (c) javax.ejb.SessionBean
   (d) javax.ejb.Business

14. What type of bean is used to embody application processing state information?
   (a) javax.ejb.StateBean
   (b) javax.ejb.Object
   (c) javax.ejb.EntityBean
   (d) javax.ejb.SessionBean

15. Which of the following interfaces must the enterprise bean implement so that an application can invoke its operations?
   (a) javax.ejb.EJBHome
   (b) javax.ejb.EntityBean
   (c) javax.rmi.Remote
   (d) javax.ejb.EJBObject

16. Which of the following is true about a Message-driven bean?
   (a) It has a remote interface.
   (b) It does not feature a component interface.
   (c) It has a local interface.
   (d) It has a client view.

17. What does the EJB architecture specify?
   (a) Distributed object components
   (b) Transactional components
   (c) Server-side components
   (d) All of the above

18. What happens when a reference to a remote method is passed?
   (a) A local copy of the remote object is passed.
   (b) The remote object reference is passed
   (c) The remote object's stub is passed
   (d) None of these

19. Each struts action element is uniquely identified by its
   (a) path attribute (b) name attribute
   (c) page attribute (d) input attribute

20. What is the full form of MVC
   (a) Multiple–View–Controller
   (b) Model–View–Cache
   (c) Multiple–View–Cache
   (d) Model–View–Controller

Review Questions

1. What are JavaBeans?
2. Mention the types of bean properties.
3. How do you create a bound property?
4. Explain with example bean design patterns.
5. How do you create a constrained property?
6. What do you mean by bean customization?
7. What is the purpose of the BeanInfo interface?
8. Explain the importance of bean persistence. How do you make a bean persistent?
9. What is Deployment Descriptor?
10. Mention the advantages of EJB over other component architectures.
11. What is the difference between Java Bean and Enterprise Java Bean?
12. What is a bean managed transaction?
13. What are the differences between stateless and stateful session beans?
14. How does a stateful session bean remember its client state?
15. What is the lifecycle of an Entity Bean?

APPENDIX

ANSWERS TO MULTIPLE CHOICE QUESTIONS

Chapter 1: Introduction to the Web

1. (b) **2.** (c) **3.** (d) **4.** (a) **5.** (c) **6.** (a) **7.** (b) **8.** (c) **9.** (b) **10.** (b) **11.** (c) **12.** (a) **13.** (b) **14.** (a) **15.** (c) **16.** (d) **17.** (b) **18.** (b) **19.** (a) **20.** (a)

Chapter 2: HyperText Transfer Protocol (HTTP)

1. (c) **2.** (d) **3.** (b) **4.** (c) **5.** (b) **6.** (a) **7.** (c) **8.** (a) **9.** (c) **10.** (b) **11.** (b) **12.** (c) **13.** (b) **14.** (c) **15.** (d) **16.** (c) **17.** (d) **18.** (c) **19.** (c) **20.** (d)

Chapter 3: Java Network Programming

1. (d) **2.** (c) **3.** (d) **4.** (a) **5.** (d) **6.** (d) **7.** (b) **8.** (c) **9.** (a) **10.** (d) **11.** (b) **12.** (a) **13.** (c) **14.** (a) **15.** (c) **16.** (b) **17.** (a) **18.** (b) **19.** (b) **20.** (d)

Chapter 4: HyperText Markup Language (HTML)

1. (c) **2.** (b) **3.** (a) **4.** (b) **5.** (d) **6.** (c) **7.** (b) **8.** (d) **9.** (a) **10.** (c) **11.** (a) **12.** (d) **13.** (b) **14.** (c) **15.** (b) **16.** (d) **17.** (c) **18.** (c) **19.** (a) **20.** (b)

Chapter 5: Cascading Style Sheet (CCS)

1. (a) **2.** (d) **3.** (c) **4.** (c) **5.** (d) **6.** (b) **7.** (b) **8.** (d) **9.** (b) **10.** (a) **11.** (d) **12.** (c) **13.** (c) **14.** (b) **15.** (a) **16.** (b) **17.** (d) **18.** (a) **19.** (c) **20.** (d)

Chapter 6: eXtensible Markup Language (XML)

1. (d) **2.** (b) **3.** (c) **4.** (a) **5.** (d) **6.** (a) **7.** (d) **8.** (c) **9.** (c) **10.** (a) **11.** (a) **12.** (b) **13.** (a) **14.** (c) **15.** (a) **16.** (b) **17.** (c) **18.** (b) **19.** (d) **20.** (d)

Chapter 7: XML DTD

1. (c) **2.** (c) **3.** (c) **4.** (c) **5.** (b) **6.** (d) **7.** (a) **8.** (b) **9.** (d) **10.** (c) **11.** (b) **12.** (c) **13.** (c) **14.** (c) **15.** (d) **16.** (d) **17.** (b) **18.** (c) **19.** (a) **20.** (b) **21.** (b) **22.** (b) **23.** (c) **24.** (b) **25.** (d) **26.** (a)

Chapter 8: W3C XML Schema

1. (c) **2.** (c) **3.** (b) **4.** (d) **5.** (c) **6.** (b) **7.** (a) **8.** (c) **9.** (d) **10.** (b) **11.** (c) **12.** (b) **13.** (b) **14.** (a) **15.** (c) **16.** (a) **17.** (b) **18.** (d) **19.** (c) **20.** (b)

Chapter 9: Parsing XML

1. (c) **2.** (b) **3.** (a) **4.** (a) **5.** (c) **6.** (d) **7.** (c) **8.** (b) **9.** (d) **10.** (c) **11.** (b) **12.** (c) **13.** (d) **14.** (a) **15.** (b) **16.** (c) **17.** (c) **18.** (a) **19.** (b) **20.** (b)

Chapter 10: XPath

1. (b) **2.** (a) **3.** (c) **4.** (c) **5.** (d) **6.** (a) **7.** (c) **8.** (d) **9.** (c) **10.** (c) **11.** (b) **12.** (b) **13.** (b) **14.** (d) **15.** (b) **16.** (d) **17.** (d) **18.** (a) **19.** (b) **20.** (c)

Chapter 11: XML Transformation

1. (c) **2.** (a) **3.** (d) **4.** (a) **5.** (b) **6.** (c) **7.** (d) **8.** (d) **9.** (c) **10.** (b) **11.** (d) **12.** (a) **13.** (d) **14.** (c) **15.** (b) **16.** (b) **17.** (a) **18.** (c) **19.** (d) **20.** (d) **21.** (b)

Chapter 12: Other XML Technologies

1. (a) **2.** (b) **3.** (b) **4.** (d) **5.** (a) **6.** (d) **7.** (a) **8.** (b) **9.** (c) **10.** (d) **11.** (d) **12.** (b) **13.** (d) **14.** (b) **15.** (c) **16.** (a) **17.** (b) **18.** (c) **19.** (c) **20.** (a)

Chapter 13: JavaScript

1. (b) **2.** (d) **3.** (c) **4.** (b) **5.** (a) **6.** (b) **7.** (a) **8.** (c) **9.** (a) **10.** (a) **11.** (c) **12.** (b) **13.** (b) **14.** (a) **15.** (d) **16.** (c) **17.** (c) **18.** (a) **19.** (d) **20.** (d) **21.** (c) **22.** (b) **23.** (c) **24.** (c) **25.** (b) **26.** (c) **27.** (c) **28.** (d) **29.** (c) **30.** (b) **31.** (a) **32.** (c)

Chapter 14: JavaScript and HTML DOM

1. (b) **2.** (b) **3.** (d) **4.** (a) **5.** (b) **6.** (c) **7.** (a) **8.** (d) **9.** (c) **10.** (c) **11.** (b) **12.** (b) **13.** (a) **14.** (d) **15.** (a) **16.** (b) **17.** (b) **18.** (b) **19.** (d) **20.** (d) **21.** (c) **22.** (a) **23.** (c) **24.** (a)

Chapter 15: Advanced JavaScript and HTML Forms

1. (d) **2.** (b) **3.** (c) **4.** (b) **5.** (d) **6.** (a) **7.** (c) **8.** (b) **9.** (d) **10.** (b) **11.** (a) **12.** (d) **13.** (c) **14.** (d) **15.** (c) **16.** (b) **17.** (d) **18.** (a) **19.** (b) **20.** (b)

Chapter 16: JavaScript Regular Expression

1. (a) **2.** (c) **3.** (b) **4.** (a) **5.** (a) **6.** (a) **7.** (d) **8.** (d) **9.** (b) **10.** (d) **11.** (d) **12.** (b) **13.** (c) **14.** (a) **15.** (b) **16.** (d) **17.** (b) **18.** (b) **19.** (a) **20.** (c)

Chapter 17: AJAX

1. (b) **2.** (c) **3.** (d) **4.** (a) **5.** (d) **6.** (c) **7.** (b) **8.** (d) **9.** (a) **10.** (d) **11.** (a) **12.** (c) **13.** (d) **14.** (d) **15.** (b) **16.** (c) **17.** (d) **18.** (d) **19.** (d) **20.** (a)

Chapter 18: Applets

1. (c) **2.** (c) **3.** (b) **4.** (d) **5.** (a) **6.** (c) **7.** (a) **8.** (d) **9.** (c) **10.** (a) **11.** (b) **12.** (d) **13.** (a) **14.** (d) **15.** (c) **16.** (a) **17.** (c) **18.** (d) **19.** (c) **20.** (a)

Chapter 19: Common Gateway Interface (CGI)

1. (a) **2.** (d) **3.** (b) **4.** (c) **5.** (d) **6.** (a) **7.** (b) **8.** (a) **9.** (d) **10.** (a) **11.** (a) **12.** (d) **13.** (c) **14.** (b) **15.** (c) **16.** (b) **17.** (d) **18.** (a) **19.** (c) **20.** (a)

Chapter 20: Servlet

1. (c) **2.** (d) **3.** (a) **4.** (b) **5.** (b) **6.** (d) **7.** (b) **8.** (a) **9.** (c) **10.** (d) **11.** (c) **12.** (a) **13.** (b) **14.** (a) **15.** (c) **16.** (b) **17.** (a) **18.** (b) **19.** (a) **20.** (d) **21.** (b)

Chapter 21: Java Server Pages (JSP)

1. (b) **2.** (d) **3.** (c) **4.** (d) **5.** (a) **6.** (d) **7.** (c) **8.** (c) **9.** (b) **10.** (b) **11.** (d) **12.** (a) **13.** (d) **14.** (b) **15.** (c) **16.** (c) **17.** (b) **18.** (a) **19.** (d) **20.** (d) **21.** (c) **22.** (b) **23.** (a) **24.** (b) **25.** (a) **26.** (c) **27.** (c) **28.** (a) **29.** (b) **30.** (b) **31.** (c) **32.** (a) **33.** (b) **34.** (a) **35.** (a) **36.** (d) **37.** (d) **38.** (b)

Chapter 22: Introduction to J2EE

1. (b) **2.** (c) **3.** (d) **4.** (a) **5.** (d) **6.** (d) **7.** (d) **8.** (d) **9.** (b) **10.** (b) **11.** (b) **12.** (c) **13.** (a) **14.** (d) **15.** (d) **16.** (b) **17.** (d) **18.** (c) **19.** (a) **20.** (d)

Index